readings in
mass communi-
cation

fourth
edition

readings in
mass
communi-
cation

Michael Emery
California State University, Northridge

Ted Curtis Smythe
California State University, Fullerton

cation
concepts
and issues
in the mass media

wcb
Wm. C. Brown Company Publishers
Dubuque, Iowa

wcb
Wm. C. Brown, **Chairman of the Board**

Book Team

Thomas W. Gornick, **Editor**
Elizabeth Munger, **Production Editor**
Marla A. Schafer, **Designer**
Mary Jo Wentz, **Design Layout Assistant**

Wm. C. Brown Company Publishers, College Division

Lawrence C. Cremer, **President**
Raymond C. Deveaux, **Vice President/Product Development**
David Wm. Smith, **Assistant Vice President/National Sales Manager**
Matt Coghlan, **National Marketing Manager**
David A. Corona, **Director of Production Development and Design**
William A. Moss, **Production Editorial Manager**
Marilyn A. Phelps, **Manager of Design**

Consulting Editor

Curtis D. MacDougall, **Northwestern University**

Contents

Contents Cross-referenced
by Medium and Message

*Title listed under more than one category

Cable Television

Radio

Movies

Photography

Magazines

Books

Preface

This book of readings is now in its fourth edition. A glance at the contents of the different editions suggests that there has been great change in media life in the United States in the last decade. However, recognizable themes do run through all four editions, blurred though they may be sometimes by the rush of new technology, by major complaints about media performance, by landmark government-media disputes, and by the insistent demands of women and minorities for places in the media world.

It does seem that nothing of substance changes in journalism, only the cast of characters and the events. When the first edition was being prepared in the summer of 1971, the Pentagon Papers case and *The Selling of the Pentagon* controversy were breaking. The second edition came out during the Watergate investigations. The third carried additional expressions of alarm about possible future dangers to the First Amendment. And this edition continues along the same line, with articles about tough new secrecy rules and the rights of broadcasters. It is clear that our First Amendment rights always will be open to interpretation and should not be taken for granted, no matter who occupies the presidency, statehouse, or mayor's office.

In the area of press-bar relations, the first edition did not emphasize the concern about "free press-fair trial" problems that had been debated for years, but instead concentrated on the rising issue of "access" to the media. We led off with those articles, and subsequent editions continued that approach. It appears now that the courtroom problems of "gag orders" and confidentiality of sources will be with us for years to come. This edition gives all of these issues equal billing.

A new section in this edition focuses on the effects of mass communication in our society. This section opens the volume with five articles new to our collection. The placement indicates our judgment of how important it is that we know more about how the barrage of news, advertising messages, and entertainment of all types affects us psychologically, spiritually, and perhaps even physically.

The section on media criticism and ethical standards has been not merely continued from the previous edition, it has been strengthened. Two new articles have been added. The fact that all the articles about technology are new must demonstrate that the machines are constantly delivering new miracles. But a check of previous editions shows that the worries about their use—such as in international communication—remain the same. In the international area we've retained two basic pieces but have added some illustrative material to help the reader better appreciate the mindboggling speed of the computers.

This volume has been streamlined as well as updated. Sections called "Relevance of Reporting Practices" and "Obscenity, Violence and Drugs" in the previous edition have been eliminated and material on these topics inserted into other sections. Several articles have been completely rewritten or edited to incorporate the latest data. An increased number of articles were prepared especially for this book. They include those on the black press, the status of women, Latinos and the media, agenda-setting, media monopoly, court control of news, electronic information machines, and the fragile First Amendment. Some of this information has not been published previously. This edition thereby takes on an added dimension.

The basic format of the book remains the same, however, divided into three parts: "Changing Concepts of the Function and Role of the Mass Media," "Revolution in the Mass Media" and "Multiplying Media Debates." In many cases we have presented new ideas with the understanding that other sides of a situation are part of what we call "conventional wisdom"—meaning that the arguments are well known and could be further explained in the classroom. Besides a conventional Contents which lists the sequence of presentation—Part title, section title, section subtitle, and article title—another Contents, cross-referenced by medium and message, is presented. We assume that instructors will assign articles to supplement basic lecture information, and perhaps in an entirely different order than presented in either table of contents. To assist the more curious, we have provided a brief bibliography after each article. An index includes the basic terms and people's names.

We are always limited by space considerations when selecting articles. Some pieces have been edited for timeliness and clarity, but few substantial changes were necessary. We do not necessarily agree with the opinions expressed by an author, and in some cases we strongly disagree. But we feel these writers and critics deserve the attention of those learning about the media in our challenging times. In that spirit, we take full responsibility for the selections and welcome suggestions for further improvement of the contents.

Michael Emery
Ted Curtis Smythe

Introductory Bibliography

Two standard bibliographic sources for every student of mass communications are *The Literature of Journalism* (1959), compiled by Warren C. Price, and *An Annotated Journalism Bibliography: 1958–1968* (1970), compiled by Price and Calder M. Pickett. Both are published by the University of Minnesota Press. Dr. Pickett enlarged and updated the latter volume substantially following Dr. Price's death. These bibliographies offer basic, comprehensive annotations of most of the books dealing with American mass communications published through 1968. Students may start here and then seek information about contemporary books and articles from other sources.

Books

For an up-to-date, thorough analysis of recent *books* on mass communications, students should consult regularly the book review sections of *Journalism Quarterly* and *Journal of Broadcasting*. The School of Communications, University of Illinois, publishes in mimeograph form an annotated list of mass communications books, which may be available in some schools and departments of journalism and communication. Another outstanding source of information on and criticism of books in the mass communications field is Christopher H. Sterling's extensively annotated "Mass Media Booknotes," published monthly at Temple University.

Articles

For *articles* on mass communications, the standard bibliographic sources should be supplemented by *Communication Abstracts, Business Periodicals Index, International Index,* and *Topicator* (which indexes only advertising, public relations, and broadcasting publications). Students should also consult the back pages of *Journalism Quarterly, Columbia Journalism Review,* and *Journal of Marketing.* All three periodicals list and categorize current articles on mass communications. Using these sources, students can quickly find up-to-date material on nearly any mass communications topic that is receiving attention in the nation's periodicals.

Many specialized indexes are available also. A few are mentioned in the bibliography listings following individual articles in this book.

Most of the materials listed in the bibliographies in this edition are books that deal with mass media subjects. However, some subjects have not yet been covered—or covered well—in a book. In such cases, we have listed magazine articles. Since pertinent new articles and books are always being published, the listing here can never be complete. For this reason, we suggest that students establish the habit of regularly reading some of the periodicals in the field. That is the best way to keep abreast of media issues. The following paragraphs identify and annotate many of these periodicals.

Journalism Reviews

For a general overview of what is happening in mass communications, students should consult *Columbia Journalism Review,* the top magazine in the field of media criticism, *Quill,* and *Washington Journalism Review.* Some twenty journalism reviews have been established in the past decade, but at least eight have ceased publication or drastically reduced their publishing schedule. Students should consult one of the journalism reviews relevant to their community, state, or area, if one is available.

Trade Periodicals

Excellent sources of industry statistics, news, and information about media practices are: *Editor & Publisher,* a weekly newsmagazine for publishers; *Publishers' Auxiliary,* a publication for suburban and weekly newspaper publishers; *Broadcasting,* a weekly newsmagazine on radio, television, and cable; *Variety,* a weekly news tabloid about broadcasting and film; *Advertising Age,* a weekly tabloid on the advertising industry; and *Folio,* a monthly magazine for the magazine industry.

Professional Periodicals

In addition to these news publications, students should regularly read *The Bulletin* of the American Society of Newspaper Editors, a monthly magazine on issues as viewed by editors of the metropolitan press; *Grassroots Editor,* a bimonthly dealing with issues of press responsibility, law, and practice, primarily from the small newspaper point of view; *Nieman Reports,* a quarterly that publishes comments about press practices and press freedom by former Nieman Fellows; *Freedom of Information Center Reports* (FoI), a biweekly dealing with issues of freedom of information and surveys of current issues in mass media; *FoI Digest,* a bimonthly bulletin summarizing FoI news developments around the United States; *Public Relations Journal,* a monthly magazine concerning that field; *AV Guide — The Learning Media Magazine* and *Media & Methods,* both dealing with application of media to teaching; and *Film in Review,* a magazine issued by the National Board of Review of Motion Pictures.

Scholarly Journals

Scholarly publications are another source that students should become acquainted with. They offer—usually—much greater depth and insight on media issues, past and present. These publications seldom are able to keep abreast of the issues in the field. The articles are usually the result of research conducted over a period of time. Included in this group are *Journalism Quarterly* and *Journal of Communication,* both of which encompass the entire field of mass media experience; *Journal of Broadcasting; Public Telecommunication Review; Index on Censorship,* which covers free press problems around the world; *Gazette* (in English) which deals primarily with European media subjects, often historical; *European Broadcasting Review,* Sec. B, which thoroughly covers the radio and television field in Europe from an administrative, program, and legal point of view; *Public Opinion Quarterly,* often useful for studies on the effects of mass media; *American Film,* magazine of the American Film Institute; *Film Quarterly,* which offers serious comment on the art of film; and *Television Quarterly, Public Relations Quarterly,* and *Public Relations Review,* which carry thoughtful articles on their respective fields. *Journalism History,* a quarterly, deals with both print and broadcast topics.

In a category by itself is *The Mass Media: Aspen Institute Guide to Communication Industry Trends,* 1978, compiled by Christopher H. Sterling and Timothy R. Haight. This outstanding book provides historical and contemporary statistics on all the mass media, from advertising to television. It is organized by important categories, from audiences to ownership. The serious student is advised (to paraphrase a well known commercial message): "Don't study in the field without it." The appendix in this edition presents current statistics on mass media in the United States

readings in
mass communi-
cation

Changing Concepts of the Function and Role of the Mass Media

If the amount of comment about the mass media in American society is any measure of their power, persuasiveness, and impact, then they are very powerful indeed. For probably never in the history of the American experience have so many critics written and said so much about the mass media: newspapers, magazines, broadcasting, film, advertising, and public relations. While this commentary may not represent a large *percentage* of the vast outpouring of those same media, the *total* amount is enough to demonstrate that, whatever else Americans may be concerned about, they are greatly concerned about the roles, functions, and performance of their mass media.

A large number of issues must be considered. This section—indeed, the entire book—barely scratches the surface of those stimulating and abrasive media-social issues that both contribute to and reflect the tensions and conflicts in our society. Nevertheless, wherever we have scratched, nuggets of information, insight, and inspiration have been revealed.

One area of concern that has received extraordinary attention during the past two decades is the "effects of mass communications" in American society. The readings in this book show that there is some disagreement over those effects and their meaning. Some effects seem to be indirect; others appear to be very direct in their impact upon certain observers. Some appear to be disfunctional; others appear to provide society with benefits that would not be available were not the media so pervasive.

In examining the readings, the student should be aware that "censorship by social science" is a real possibility. The vast majority of Americans now seem to be unwilling to censor sex or violence on television. Yet, should social scientists "prove" that such programming is harmful to individuals and society—much as the Surgeon General's report "proved" that cigarette smoking was linked with cancer—then pressures to reduce or stop such forms of programming will surely increase. Whether or not this is desirable is a question each student should confront and seek to answer. The readings provide one step toward an informed opinion.

Another area of current concern developed during the late sixties and seventies out of the social activism on behalf of the disenfranchised segments of our society—the racial, ethnic, religious, and sexual minorities and the poor. One goal of this activism was to secure a voice in or access to the mass media and to the established agencies of mass communications in the U.S. In some cases there was great success; in others the movement was rebuffed by both the agencies of communication and the government, including the Supreme Court.

In *Miami Herald v. Tornillo,* 1974, mentioned in the readings of this section, the Supreme Court seemingly wiped out all efforts to redefine the First Amendment so as to require that newspapers, in particular, open their pages to diverse voices, to political opponents, or to whoever wishes to use those pages to express personal or group viewpoints. But, as our readings indicate. the access concept still lives. Writers are now suggesting ways of getting around the Supreme Court's decision, largely because they feel the need is still there. They argue that access to the mass media must be available to more groups than now use them.

Others have sought to harness the press through internal and/or unofficial methods which do not require rewriting or reinterpreting the Constitution. News councils, national and local, have been established; journalism reviews edited by reporters from the staffs of local newspapers have been issued (many of which have failed); and systematic criticism by informed observers has been published. The press itself has undertaken serious self-analysis. Numerous "ombudsmen" on metropolitan newspapers now represent the reader in newspaper editorial and management decisions. Several newspapers have assigned reporters to cover media-related topics, much as they cover medicine or sports or politics. Most of those reporters had had great freedom in dealing with national and even local issues. The "ethical" practices of mass media personnel will continue to receive attention from critics and colleagues alike.

One of the more serious problems in contemporary reporting is the protection of sources of information. Investigative reporting virtually requires anonymity of sources, or so reporters feel. The tenuous ties which have bound bench, bar, and police to the press have been stretched to the breaking point largely because of the vigor with which investigative reporters have pursued their craft. As our readings indicate, the concern is very real on all sides; but not all newsmen agree about the proper way to attack or solve the problem.

Another tactic in the bench-press confrontation has been resurrected of late in the form of "gag laws," the court-imposed restraints on reporting "prejudicial information" in pre-trial and trial situations. Despite much discussion, and despite the development of "guidelines" during the past decade, the problem of judicial restraint of the press is unresolved. In fact, it is growing worse. According to an editorial in the *Los Angeles Times,* prompted by increasingly restrictive decisions by the judiciary, "We have reached a strange point in this country. The publicity generated not by the press but by the nature of monstrous crimes is used as an excuse by the courts to impose censorship on the public. Under the rationale used by the federal court in Atlanta [which ordered a new trial for the man who abducted the former editor of the *Atlanta Constitution,* Reg Murphy], all information about the Watergate conspiracy could have been suppressed once the Watergate burglars, the most petty actors in the sordid drama, were arrested and charged. The implications of this kind of judicial tyranny by the courts need to be thoroughly understood by the public."

Effects of the Mass Media

The Messages Behind the News

Herbert J. Gans

A sociologist weighs the news and finds that it is neither neutral nor impartial in surveying American society.

Journalism is, like sociology, an empirical discipline. Like other empirical disciplines, the news does not limit itself to reality judgments; it also contains values, or preference statements. This in turn makes it possible to suggest that there is, underlying the news, a picture of nation and society as it ought to be.

The values in the news are rarely explicit and must be found between the lines—in which actors and activities are reported or ignored, and in how they are described. Because journalists do not, in most instances, deliberately insert values into the news, these values must be inferred.

I shall employ a narrow definition of values, examining only preference statements about nation and society, and major national or societal issues. I also distinguish between two types of values, which I call topical and enduring, and I will analyze only the latter. Enduring values are values which can be found in many different types of news stories over a long period of time; often, they affect what events become news and even help define the news.

The list that follows is limited to the enduring values I have found in the news over the last two decades, although all are probably of far more venerable vintage; obviously, it includes those which this inferrer, bringing his own values to the task, has found most visible and important. The methods by which I identified the values were impressionistic; the values really emerged from continual scrutiny of the news. Some came from the ways actors and activities are described, the tones in which stories are written, told, or filmed, and the connotations that accrue to commonly used verbs, nouns, and adjectives, especially if neutral terms are available but not used. When years ago the news reported that Stokely Carmichael has "turned up" somewhere, while the president had, on the same day, "arrived" somewhere else, or when another story pointed out that a city was "plagued by labor problems," the appropriate values were not difficult to discern, if only because neutral terms were available but were not used. However, sometimes neutral terms are simply not available. The news could have called the young men who refused to serve in the Vietnam War draft evaders, dodgers, or resisters, but it rarely used the last term.

The enduring values I want to discuss can be grouped into eight clusters: ethnocentrism, altruistic democracy, responsible capitalism, small-town pastoralism, individualism, moderatism, order, and national leadership.

Herbert J. Gans, of the Center for Policy Research and of Columbia University, both in New York City, has studied mass media in the United States from a sociological perspective. This article was first published in *Columbia Journalism Review,* January/February 1979. It is part of chapter 2 in his book *Deciding What's News: A Study of CBS Evening News, NBC Nightly News, Newsweek and Time,* Pantheon Books, copyright 1979. It is reprinted with permission.

Ethnocentrism

Like the news of other countries, American news values its own nation above all others, even though it sometimes disparages blatant patriotism. This ethnocentrism is most explicit in foreign news, which judges other countries by the extent to which they live up to or imitate American practices and values, but it also underlies domestic news. While the news contains many stories that are critical of domestic conditions, they are almost always treated as deviant cases, with the implication that American ideals, at least, remain viable. The Watergate scandals were usually ascribed to a small group of power-hungry politicians, and beyond that, to the "imperial presidency"—but with the afterthought, particularly following Nixon's resignation, that nothing was fundamentally wrong with American democracy even if reforms were needed.

The clearest expression of ethnocentrism, in all countries, appears in war news. While reporting the Vietnam War, the news media described the North Vietnamese and the National Liberation Front as "the enemy," as if they were the enemy of the news media. Similarly, weekly casualty stories reported the number of Americans killed, wounded, or missing, and the number of South Vietnamese killed; but the casualties on the other side were impersonally described as "the Communist death toll" or the "body count."

Again, as in war reporting everywhere, atrocities, in this case by Americans, did not often get into the news, and then only toward the end of the war. Seymour Hersh, the reporter credited with exposing the Mylai massacre, had considerable difficulty selling the story until the evidence was incontrovertible. The end of the war was typically headlined as "the fall of South Vietnam," with scarcely a recognition that, by other values, it could also be considered a liberation, or, neutrally, a change in governments.

Altruistic Democracy

While foreign news suggests quite explicitly that democracy is superior to dictatorship, and the more so if it follows American forms, domestic news is more specific, indicating how American democracy should perform by its frequent attention to deviations from an unstated ideal, evident in stories about corruption, conflict, protest, and bureaucratic malfunctioning. That ideal may be labeled altruistic democracy because, above all, the news implies that politics should be based on the public interest and service.

Although the news has little patience for losers, it insists that both winners and losers should be scrupulously honest, efficient, and dedicated to acting in the public interest. Financial corruption is always news, as is nepotism, patronage appointments, logrolling, and "deals" in general. Decisions based, or thought to be based, on either self-interest or partisan concerns thus continue to be news whenever they occur, even though they long ago ceased to be novel.

Politicians, politics, and democracy are also expected to be meritocratic; the regular activities of political machines are regularly exposed, and "machine" itself is a pejorative term. Although the news therefore regards civil-service officials more highly than "political appointees," the former are held to a very high standard of efficiency and performance; as a result, any deviant bureaucratic behavior becomes newsworthy. "Waste" is always an evil; the mass of paperwork created by bureaucracy is a frequent story, and the additional paperwork generated by attempts to reduce the amount of paperwork is a humorous item that has appeared in the news regularly.

The news keeps track of the violations of official norms, but it does so selectively. Over the years, the news has been perhaps most concerned with freedom of the press and related civil liberties; even recurring local violations, school boards that censor libraries, say, have often become national news. Violations of the civil liberties of radicals, of due process, habeas corpus, and other constitutional protections, particularly for criminals, are less newsworthy. Another official norm observed by the news is racial integration. Because citizens are expected to live up to these norms altruistically and because the norms are viewed as expressions of the public interest, the violations of the legal and political rights of blacks in the South were news even before supporters of the civil-rights movement began to demonstrate.

While—and perhaps because—the news consistently reports political and legal failures to achieve altruistic and official democracy, it concerns itself much less with the economic barriers that obstruct the realization of the ideal. Of course, the news is aware of candidates who are millionaires or who obtain substantial amounts of corporate or union campaign money, but it is less conscious of the relationship between poverty and powerlessness, or of the difficulty that Americans of median income have in gaining political access.

The relative inattention to economic obstacles to democracy stems from the assumption that the polity and the economy are separate and independent of each other. Under ideal conditions, one is not supposed to affect or interfere with the other, although, typically, government intervention in the economy is more newsworthy and serious than private industry's intervention in government. Accordingly, the news rarely notes the extent of public subsidy of private industry, and it continues to describe firms and institutions which are completely or partly subsidized by government funds as private—for example, Lockheed, many charities, and most privately run universities.

Responsible Capitalism

The underlying posture of the news toward the economy resembles that taken toward the polity: an optimistic faith that, in the good society, businessmen and women will compete with each other in order to create increased prosperity for all, but that they will refrain from unreasonable profits and gross exploitation of workers or customers. While monopoly is clearly evil, there is little explicit or implicit criticism of the oligopolistic nature of much of today's economy. Unions and consumer organizations are accepted as countervailing pressures on business (the former less so than the latter), and strikes are frequently judged negatively, especially if they inconvenience "the public," contribute to inflation, or involve violence.

Economic growth is always a positive phenomenon, unless it brings about inflation or environmental pollution, leads to the destruction of a historical landmark, or puts craftsmen or craftswomen out of work. In the past, when anchormen gave the stock market report, even the most detached ones looked cheerful when the market had had a good day, assuming this to be of universal benefit to the nation.

Like politicians, business officials are expected to be honest and efficient; but while corruption and bureaucratic misbehavior are as undesirable in business as in government, they are nevertheless tolerated to a somewhat greater extent in the former. For example, the January 2, 1978, issue of *Time* included a three-page critique of government bureaucracy, entitled "Rage Over Rising Regulation: To Autocratic Bureaucrats, Nothing Succeeds Like Excess"; but a business-section story reporting that General Motors had sent refunds to the purchasers of Oldsmobiles equipped with Chevrolet engines was only one column long and was headed "End of the Great Engine Flap."

It is now accepted that the government must help the poor, but only the deserving poor, for "welfare cheaters" are a continuing menace and are more newsworthy than people, other than the very rich, who cheat on their taxes. Public welfare agencies are kept under closer scrutiny than others, so that although the news reported on the "welfare mess" in the 1960s, it did not describe equivalent situations in other government agencies in the same way. There was, for example, no "defense mess," and what is "waste" in H.E.W. programs is "cost overruns" in Pentagon programs.

Small-Town Pastoralism

The rural and anti-industrial values which Thomas Jefferson is usually thought to have invented can also be found in the news, which favors small towns (agricultural or market) over other types of settlements. At one time, this preference was complemented by a celebration of the large city and of the vitality of its business and entertainment districts; but the end of this period can be dated almost exactly by *Life's* special issue on the cities, which appeared in December 1965.

For the last ten years cities have been in the news almost entirely as problematic, with the major emphasis on racial conflict, crime, and fiscal insolvency. Suburbs are not often newsworthy, despite the fact that a near majority of Americans now live in them, and they, too, have generally received a bad press. During the 1950s and 1960s, suburbs were viewed as breeding grounds of homogeneity, boredom, adultery, and other evils; since then, they have come into the news because they are suffering increasingly from "urban" problems, particularly crime, or because they keep out racial minorities.

The small town continues to reign supreme, not only in Charles Kuralt's "On the Road" reports for CBS News, but also in television and magazine stories about "the good life" in America. Stories about city neighborhoods judge them by their ability to retain the cohesiveness, friendliness, and slow pace ascribed to small towns, and during the period of journalistic interest in ethnicity, to the ethnic enclaves of the past.

Needless to say, the pastoral values underlying the news are romantic; they visualize rural and market towns as they were imagined to have existed in the past.

Small-town pastoralism is, at the same time, a specification of two more general values: the desirability both of nature and of smallness per se. The news dealt with the conflict between the preservation of nature and the activities of developers long before the environment and ecology became political issues; and, more often than not, the news took at least an implicit stand against the developers. The postwar developers of suburbia were seen as despoiling the land in their rapacious search for profits; that they were concurrently providing houses for people was rarely noted.

The virtue of smallness comes through most clearly in stories that deal with the faults of bigness, for in the news, big government, big labor, and big business rarely have virtues. Bigness is feared, among other things, as impersonal and inhuman. In the news as well as in architecture, the ideal social organization should reflect a "human scale." The fear of bigness also reflects a fear of control, of privacy and individual freedom being ground under by organizations too large to notice, much less to value, the individual. As such, bigness is a major threat to individualism.

Individualism

It is no accident that many of the characters in Kuralt's pastoral features are "rugged individualists," for one of the most important enduring news values is the preservation of the freedom of the individual against the encroachments of nation and society. The good society of the news is populated by individuals who participate in it, but on their own terms, acting in the public interest, but as they define it.

The ideal individual struggles successfully against adversity and overcomes more powerful forces. The news looks for people who act heroically during disasters, and it pays attention to people who conquer nature without hurting it: explorers, mountain climbers, astronauts, and scientists. "Self-made" men and women remain attractive, as do people who overcome poverty or bureaucracy.

The news often contains stories about new technology that endangers the individual—notably the computer, which is viewed anthropomorphically, either as a robot that will deprive human beings of control over their own lives or as a machine endowed with human failings, which is therefore less of a threat. In any case, there is always room for a gleeful story about computers that break down. The news has, however, always paid attention to the dangers of new technology: when television sets were first mass-produced, they were viewed as dehumanizing because they robbed people of the art of conversation; similar fears were expressed at the time of the institution of digit-dialing in telephones.

Conversely, the news celebrates old technology and mourns its passing, partly because it is tied to an era when life was thought to have been simpler, partly because it is viewed as being under individual control.

Moderatism

The idealization of the individual could result in praise for the rebel and the deviant, but this possibility is neutralized by an enduring value that discourages excess or extremism. Individualism that violates the law, the dominant mores, and enduring values is suspect; equally important, what is valued in individuals is discouraged in groups. Thus, groups that exhibit what is seen as extreme behavior are criticized in the news through pejorative adjectives or a satirical tone.

For example, the news treats atheists as extremists and uses the same approach, if more gingerly, with religious fanatics. People who consume conspicuously are criticized, but so are people such as hippies, who turn their backs entirely on consumer goods. The news is scornful both of the overly academic scholar and the oversimplifying popularizer: it is kind neither to highbrows nor to lowbrows, to users of jargon or users of slang.

The same value applies to politics. Political ideologists are suspect, but so are completely unprincipled politicians. The totally self-seeking are thought to be consumed by excessive ambition, but the complete do-gooders are not believed. Political candidates who talk only about issues may be described as dull; those who avoid issues entirely evoke doubts about their fitness for office. Poor speakers are thought to be unelectable, while demagogues are taken to be dangerous. Those who regularly follow party lines are viewed as hacks, and those who never do are called mavericks or loners—although these terms are pejorative only for the politically unsuccessful; the effective loner becomes a hero.

Order

The frequent appearance of stories about disorder suggests that order is an important value in the news, but order is a meaningless term unless one specifies what order and whose order is being valued. Social disorder is generally defined as disorder in the public areas of the society. A protest march in which three people die would be headline national news, whereas a family murder that claimed three victims would be a local story. Disorders in affluent areas or elite institutions are more likely to be reported than their occurrence elsewhere. In the 1960s, the looting of a handful of stores on New York's Fifth Avenue received as much attention as a much larger looting spree taking place in a ghetto area that same day. Peaceful demonstrations on college campuses, especially elite ones, are usually more newsworthy than those in factories or prisons. But the major public area is the seat of government; thus, a trouble-free demonstration in front of a city hall or a police station is news, whereas that in front of a store is not.

Still, the most important criterion of worthiness is the target of the demonstration. The anti-war demonstrations of the past decade were covered as disorder stories because they were aimed at presidents. Likewise, the 1978 coal strike did not become a magazine cover story until it involved the president.

Beneath the concern for political order lies another, perhaps even deeper concern for social cohesion, which reflects fears that not only the official rules of the political order but also the informal rules of the social order are in danger of being disobeyed. Hippies and college dropouts of the 1960s were newsworthy in part because they rejected the so-called Protestant work ethic; even now, drug use by the young, and its consequences, is in the news more than alcohol use because it signifies a rejection of traditional methods of seeking oblivion or mind expansion. Indeed, the news evaluates the young almost entirely in terms of the adult rules they are in the process of rejecting.

Moral disorder stories are, in the end, cued to much the same concern for social cohesion, particularly those stories which report violations of the mores rather than the laws. Such stories are based on the premise that the activities of public officials, public agencies, and corporations should derive from the same moral and ethical values that are supposed to apply to personal, familial, and friendship relations. Even if every political reporter knows that politicians cannot operate with the same ideal of honesty as friends, the failure of politicians to do so continues to be news. In the last analysis, the values underlying social and moral disorder news are the same, although the two types of news differ in subject and object: social disorder news monitors the respect of citizens for authority, while moral disorder stories evaluate whether authority figures respect the rules of the citizenry.

With some oversimplification, it would be fair to say that the news supports the social order of public, business and professional, upper-middle-class, middle-aged, and white-male sectors of society. Because the news emphasizes people over groups, it pays less attention to the institutionalized social order, except as reflected in its leaders; but obviously the news is also generally supportive of governments and their agencies, private enterprise, the prestigious professions, and a variety of other national institutions, including the quality universities. But here, too, always with a proviso: obedience to the relevant enduring values.

Nevertheless, the news is not subservient to powerful individuals or groups, for it measures their behavior against a set of values that is assumed to transcend them. Moral disorder stories can bid the elites to relinquish, or at least hide, their moral deficiencies. To be sure, the values invoked in moral disorder stories are themselves often set by and shared by these elites. The president's policies are not often viewed from the perspectives of, or judged by, the values of low-income and moderate-income citizens; corporate officials are even less rarely judged by the values of employees or customers; or university presidents, by the values of students or campus janitors. Instead, the values in the news derive largely from reformers and reform movements, which are themselves elites. Still, the news is not simply a compliant supporter of elites, or the establishment, or the ruling class; rather, it views nation and society through its own set of values and with its own conception of the good social order.

If the news values moral and social order, it also suggests how to maintain them, **Leadership** primarily through the availability of morally and otherwise competent leadership. The news focuses on leaders; and, with some exceptions, public agencies and private organizations are represented by their leaders. In the past, magazine cover stories often reported national topics or issues in relation to an individual who played an instrumental or symbolic leadership role in them. When necessary, the news even helps to create leaders; in the 1960s, radical and black organizations functioning on the basis of participatory democracy sometimes complained that journalists would pick out one spokesperson on whom they would lavish most of their attention, thereby making a leader out of him or her.

Although several practical considerations encourage the news media to emphasize leaders, the news is also based on a theory of society that would argue, were it made explicit, that the social process, above all others, is shaped by leaders—people who, either because of their political or managerial skills, or personal attributes which inspire others, move into positions of authority and make things happen. A lengthy 1974 *Time* cover story that surveyed existing definitions of leadership concluded that most "emphasize honesty, candor, and vision, combined with sheer physical stamina and courage"; to which the magazine added that "courage without brains was [not] sufficient." A leader must also be strong and able to control subordinates; their moral failings and inefficiencies are a sign of weak leadership.

The foremost leader in America is the president, who is viewed as the ultimate protector of order. He is the final backstop for domestic tranquility and the principal guardian of national security, his absence from the White House due to resignation or death evoking fears of an enemy attack or possible panic by a now leaderless populace. Through his own behavior and the concern he shows for the behavior of others, the president also becomes the nation's moral leader. He sets an example that might be followed by others: should he permit or condone corruption among his associates or appointees, he is suspected of moral disorder. Finally, he is the person who states and represents the national values and he is the agent of the national will.

News Values and Ideology

If the news includes values, it also contains ideology. That ideology, however, is an aggregate of only partly thought-out values which is neither entirely consistent nor well integrated; and since it changes somewhat over time, it is also flexible on some issues. I call this aggregate of values and the reality judgments associated with it para-ideology, partly to distinguish it from the deliberate, integrated, and more doctrinaire set of values usually defined as ideology; it is ideology nevertheless.

The para-ideology can itself be placed on the conventional spectrum, but not easily, since journalists are not much interested in ideology or aware that they, too, promulgate ideology. As a result, individual stories and journalists can span various parts of the spectrum, although their values rarely coincide with those on the far right or the far left. Even the news media as a whole, and the news, analyzed over time, are not easily classified.

In its advocacy of altruistic and official democracy, the news defends a mixture of liberal and conservative values, but its conception of responsible capitalism comes closest to what I would call right-leaning liberalism. On the other hand, in its respect for tradition and its nostalgia for pastoralism and rugged individualism, the news is unabashedly conservative, as it is also both in its defense of the social order and its faith in leadership. If the news has to be pigeonholed ideologically, it is right-liberal or left-conservative.

In reality, the news is not so much conservative or liberal as it is reformist; indeed, the enduring values are very much like the values of the Progressive movement of the early twentieth century. The resemblance is often uncanny, as in the common advocacy of honest, meritocratic, and anti-bureaucratic government, and in the shared antipathy to political machines and demagogues, particularly of populist bent. Altruistic democracy is, in other words, close to the Progressive ideal of government. The notion of responsible capitalism is also to be found in Progressivism, as is the dislike of bigness, the preference for craftsmanship over technology, the defense of nature, and the celebration of anti-urban pastoral society. Journalistic para-ideology and Progressivism are further akin in their mutual support of individualism, their uneasiness about collective solutions, other than at the grassroots level, and their opposition to socialism. Moreover, the preservation of an upper-class and upper-middle-class social order, like the need for morally and otherwise competent national leadership, has its equivalents in Progressive thought.

The Progressive movement is long dead, but many of its basic values and its reformist impulses have persisted. The news is reformist and its being so helps explain why it is not easily fitted into the conventional ideological spectrum. Of course, Progressive thought can be placed on the spectrum, although historians have not yet agreed whether the movement was liberal, conservative, or both. In any case, the news may be marching to a somewhat different drummer; and when journalists are unwilling to describe themselves as liberal or conservative, and prefer to see themselves as independents, they may be sensing, if not with complete awareness, that they are, as a profession, Progressive reformers.

The Agenda-Setting Role of Mass Communication   2

Chaim Eyal
Jim Winter
Maxwell McCombs

Chaim Eyal and Jim Winter are in the doctoral program at Syracuse University. Dr. Maxwell McCombs has written extensively on the "agenda-setting function" of the mass media. He is a professor in the S. I. Newhouse School of Public Communications, Syracuse University. Their article was written especially for this edition of *Readings in Mass Communication: Concepts and Issues in the Mass Media.*

Are the media responsible for public perceptions of reality, the "pictures in our heads"?

Over the years the conventional view of mass media influence has fluctuated between the belief that they have a marked influence on our daily lives and the belief that they exert minimal impact. Early research into mass media effects revolved around a *hypodermic needle* model—a view that the media directly inject the public with attitudes which subsequently affect their behavior. This notion arose out of the perceived effects of wartime propaganda. It led to the establishment of an Institute for Propaganda Analysis at Columbia University in the late 1930s.

However, when political scientists and psychologists attempted to document this dramatic media impact in the 40s and 50s, they failed. Studies conducted during election campaigns, for example, found that individuals' attitudes were largely predetermined by their political party, religious affiliation, and socio-economic status. Those studies concluded that media messages are selectively absorbed and organized within existing patterns of attitudes. These findings led to a reversal of the hypodermic needle notion of media effects and the advancement, instead, of a *law of minimal consequences,* which holds that media influences are subordinated to other social influences.

This early communications research focused on attitude change rather than knowledge and awareness. The notion of minimal mass media effects on public opinion largely arose because researchers were looking for media-generated attitude change rather than media influence on the prior stages of awareness and knowledge.

If, as the early sociologist Robert Park suggested, the function of news is to create an *awareness* of issues rather than *knowledge* or *attitudes* about issues, then it is important to look for media effects on public awareness. This approach to the mass media/public opinion relationship has been labeled the *agenda-setting* function of mass communication. It is an attempt to validate empirically Walter Lippmann's assertion more than a half century ago that the media are responsible for public perceptions of reality, the "pictures in our heads."

Therefore, studies of the agenda-setting role of mass communication examine an early stage in the formation of public opinion: the stage at which issues emerge. These studies focus on the development of public awareness and subsequent learning about issues.

The mass media are our primary sources of information about public issues, but of course they do not faithfully reflect all of reality. Selection is inherent in reporting the day's news. What the mass media choose to report significantly influences *what* individuals learn about and respond to.

The agenda-setting idea hypothesizes that issues prominently displayed and frequently emphasized in the mass media will be regarded as important by the media consumers. In other words, the priorities that the media assign to issues are learned by the audiences. This is more than simple awareness. Media priorities become, to a certain extent, public priorities.

Media Agendas

The agenda of each newspaper, television network, and magazine is made up of the information that each selects for presentation to its audience. Any news outlet reflects in various ways its order of priorities and the relative importance it places on the items. In a newspaper, for example, issues considered important are likely to be emphasized by placement, headline size, and amount of coverage. Page one typically presents the top items on each day's agenda. Important issues stand a good chance of becoming manifest in other ways as well: editorial comments, discussion by columnists, and letters to the editor.

In television, similarly, a network's agenda is expressed by the topics selected to be broadcast and by the pattern of coverage. A televised issue may be regarded as important if it is featured frequently and prominently, if it takes a relatively large amount of broadcast time, if it is enriched with visual and graphic elements, and so on.

Television and newspapers are the media most often used in studies of agenda-setting, for they are the dominant news channels. In early agenda-setting inquiries, no attempt was made to differentiate between the role or influence of the two. More recently, however, it has become clear that television and newspapers perform separate agenda-setting roles, and, in fact, do not merely replicate each other. For example, in their book about the 1972 presidential election, Donald Shaw and Maxwell McCombs suggest that, in general, television appears to exert a lesser agenda-setting influence than do newspapers. At the initial stages of issue-emergence, the newspaper agenda has more impact on public concern. But, as time passes, and as topics in the news become established as important, the match between the television agenda and audience concerns becomes stronger. In other words, newspapers seem to function as initiators, while television networks spotlight the issues that have already gained prominence in the press and in the minds of the public.

Thus, both newspapers and television play important roles in agenda-setting. Their influence is at work at different times, operating in different styles, and with different technologies. Because of these differences, the two media play separate and distinct roles in agenda-setting rather than merely competing with or reinforcing each other.

Obviously, today's news agenda is not immediately and wholly reflected in tomorrow's agenda of concerns among the public. Agenda-setting involves a learning process that typically stretches across a considerable span of time. In contrast to the hypodermic needle model of mass communication, which implied immediate influence, the agenda-setting model implies long-term, cumulative mass media effects. While some issues may move quickly from the media agenda to the public agenda, the average lag is some two to four months. Since public awareness and knowledge about public issues involves incidental learning more than a formal educational process, such a long period of time is not surprising.

Of course, various sources of information influence the shape of the agenda distributed by each news outlet to its audience. News and information flowing through mass communication channels pass a number of *gatekeepers* before reaching the audience. The news editor of the local newspaper or local broadcasting station is simply the last in a sequence of gatekeepers who monitor the news channels, each deciding which items will pass, which will be cut, and which will be deleted. There is far more news available each day than there is capacity to transmit it.

The wire service is an especially important gatekeeper or agenda-setter. Reanalysis of the classic Mr. Gates studies shows a significant correlation between the agenda of news provided by the wire services and the smaller agenda of items finally selected by Mr. Gates for publication. The categories of news emphasized by the wire services tend to become the categories of news emphasized by local news media.

Another example of how an agenda of one news medium, or particular outlet, may influence that of others is provided by journalist Les Brown. In his book on the television industry he described the New York *Times's* two-fold influence on network journalism: first as a model of standards and news judgment; then as an evaluator of the performance of the television networks. Brown suggested that favorable recognition from the *Times* for a news effort is a sign of high achievement within the industry.

Audience Agenda   While it is a straightforward application of the agenda-setting concept to analyze its operation within the news media themselves, it has more frequently been applied to the influence of the news media on audience agendas. The term "audience agenda" refers to people's perceptions of what are the most important issues of the day. Obviously, the first phase is simple awareness of a public issue. But, as has been previously noted, the idea of an agenda-setting role of mass communication goes beyond simple awareness of issues. It involves some perception among members of the public of the relative importance or priority of each issue on the public agenda. Of course, the heart of the agenda-setting idea is the assumption that public perceptions about these issues have been significantly influenced by coverage of them in the news media.

While ascertaining each news medium's agenda is relatively straightforward, ascertaining the audience agenda is a bit more complex. There are several ways of considering and measuring the audience agenda. Public opinion manifests itself in a variety of ways.

In his classic book *Public Opinion*, Walter Lippmann's concern was with media influence on the public's view of reality: how the media help us determine what is important in the world out there. Sociologist Robert Park, on the other hand, was more concerned with how the media influence our everyday conversations and discussions. Both of these notions are represented in empirical examinations of the audience agenda.

One approach, in the Lippmann tradition, asks what issues are of *personal concern* to the individual. Public opinion (or the agenda of issues on which opinions are expressed) is the sum of individual beliefs and perceptions. This is the traditional route taken by the Gallup poll and many other public opinion polls.

Another approach, more along the lines of Park's idea, examines which issues are discussed among friends and acquaintances—what people talk about. Emphasis is on the *public* aspect of public opinion, in contrast to the Lippmann tradition, which is more psychological in its emphasis on individual cognitions and *opinions*. Studies have shown that these are related, but different, aspects of the audience agenda. What people personally regard as important has some relationship to what they talk about with other people, but the two are far from synonymous. Furthermore, there is some evidence that the conversational agenda changes rather rapidly from week to week while the agenda of personal issues is more stable across time.

A third kind of expression of public opinion can be called the perceived community agenda—that is, what issues does each individual think are important to others in the community at large? This is each individual's perception of public opinion in the entire community. A study conducted during the 1976 presidential election campaign found that when respondents were asked about the perceived community agenda, the most frequent response was "taxes." When they were asked about the most important issue for them personally, the most frequent response was "inflation."

It is thus apparent that the audience agenda depends on which questions are asked and from whose viewpoint: individuals' perceptions of themselves; their perceptions of their friends; or their view of the community at large. There are many varieties of public opinion.

The original agenda-setting research conducted in Chapel Hill, N.C. during the 1968 presidential campaign found a strong correlation between what undecided voters *personally thought* were the key campaign issues and the actual news *content* of the media.

The Evidence

This relationship between press coverage and the audience agenda was considerably elaborated and extended by the 1972 presidential election study of Shaw and McCombs. They followed a panel of Charlotte, N.C. voters from early summer to election day. This study demonstrated that the newspaper had strong agenda-setting effects during the months of the campaign. The study also began the exploration of new domains. It examined political advertising in the media. And it investigated how personal characteristics of voters, such as need for orientation and frequency of talking with others, may enhance or limit the agenda-setting influence of the press.

These relationships have been tested in several nonelection settings. One study reviewed public opinion trends across the entire decade of the 1960s. In addition to comparing the press and public agenda on issues like Vietnam, campus unrest, and drugs, this study also examined actual statistics such as the number of troops in Vietnam. A substantial positive relationship was found between the press coverage and public concerns during the 1960s. But when press content and public opinion were compared to the "real life" data, the relationship was much weaker. With Vietnam, for example, both media coverage and public opinion actually peaked some two years before the maximum number of American troops were in the field.

Another nonelection study, conducted in Toledo, Ohio, compared media influence on local versus national issues. People were found to be more dependent on the media for information about distant national issues than about local issues. At the national level, network television exerted greater influence than did the newspaper on people's perceptions of the most important issues of the day, while at the local level the newspaper was by far the major agenda-setter. The authors of the study suggested that the superior influence of television here in contrast to the contrary effects found in the 1972 presidential election study by Shaw and McCombs was because of a key difference in social setting of the two studies.

Variations in the amount and kinds of media effects found by different studies are also due to different approaches. For example, the time lag between the media agenda and the audience agenda; which audience and media agenda are measured; and how the two are matched. Despite the differing approaches, the majority of studies have confirmed agenda-setting effects.

In sum, there are two major aspects of agenda-setting. The first involves the flow of news and information among the various mass media themselves. This aspect of agenda-setting is concerned with how one news medium's pattern of coverage influences the pattern of coverage in another. Of course, this aspect of agenda-setting could be extended to examination of how specific news sources, in turn, influence the agenda of the news media.

But the bulk of the empirical research to date on agenda-setting has examined a second aspect of agenda-setting: the influence of the news media and their agenda of topics on the audience's agenda, their perceptions of what are the most important topics and issues of the day.

While most of these studies have focused on public issues, the idea that mass communication media have an agenda-setting role can extend into the political arena. With the help of ample media exposure, newcomers to the national political scene, such as Jimmy Carter in 1976, can defeat an incumbent president with several decades of national political exposure.

To return to our original point about the influence of mass communication, while the media may not be able to tell us what to think, they can be quite successful in telling us both what and whom to think about.

Bibliography

The following books and articles deal with the agenda-setting issues raised in this article: Les Brown, *Television: The Business Behind the Box* (Harcourt Brace Jovanovich, 1971); G. Ray Funkhouser, "The Issues of the Sixties: An Exploratory Study in the Dynamics of Public Opinion," *Public Opinion Quarterly* (Spring 1973), pp. 62–75; Walter Lippmann, *Public Opinion* (Macmillan, 1922); Maxwell E. McCombs, "A Comparison of Intra-Personal and Inter-Personal Agendas of Public Issues," a paper prepared for the Annual Convention of the International Communication Association, New Orleans, April 1974; Maxwell E. McCombs and Donald L. Shaw, "The Agenda-Setting Function of the Mass Media," *Public Opinion Quarterly* (Summer 1972), pp. 176–87, and "Structuring the 'Unseen Environment,' " *Journal of Communication* (Spring 1976), pp. 18–22; Phillip Palmgreen and Peter Clarke, "Agenda-Setting with Local and National Issues," *Communication Research* (October 1977), pp. 435–52; Robert E. Park, *The City* (University of Chicago Press, 1925); Donald L. Shaw and Maxwell E. McCombs, *The Emergence of American Political Issues: The Agenda Setting Function of the Press* (West Publishing Co., 1977); Paul B. Snider, "Mr. Gates Revisited: A 1966 Version of the 1949 Case Study," *Journalism Quarterly* (Autumn 1967), pp. 419–27; David Manning White, "The 'Gatekeeper,' A Case Study in the Selection of News," *Journalism Quarterly* (Fall 1950), pp. 383–90.

Television as New Religion

George Gerbner
Kathleen Connolly

3

Perhaps the most widely held misconception about television is that it is a medium among other media. Television is perceived by many as a medium that differs from other forms of mass media only in form. The conclusion that results is that television has the same effect on people as do print, movies, theater, and radio; that television can be analyzed in the same fashion; and that its portrayal of reality is analogous to the representations found in print, on stage, and the movie screens, and over the air waves.

The truth of the matter is that the special characteristics of television set it apart from other mass media in a way that makes comparison shaky at best. In order to understand the role that television plays in the lives of viewers, it is necessary to understand how radically different television is from all other media.

1. Television consumes more time and more attention of more people than all other media and leisure activities combined. In the average American home, the television set is on for six and one-quarter hours a day.
2. Television requires no mobility. Unlike movies or the theater, you do not have to go out to watch television. It is there in the home, available at any time.
3. Television does not require literacy. Unlike print, it provides information about the world to the poorly educated and the illiterate. In fact, for those who do not read (by choice or inability), television is a major source of information, much of which comes from what is called entertainment.
4. Unlike most other mass media, television is "free" (supported by a privately imposed tax on all goods). Unlike radio, which many see as the media form closest to television, television both shows *and* tells.
5. All media are symbol systems. This is as true of television as of any other mass media. However, as a symbol system, television is unique in all of history. There is little age-grading of the symbolic materials that socialize members into the community. Television tells its stories to people of all age groups all at the same time. Television presents its message to a heterogeneous audience. People of all ages, races, ethnic groups, economic groups, etc., see the same message, and, most importantly, unlike books, movies, etc., most people use television *nonselectively*.

George Gerbner is professor and dean at the Annenberg School of Communications, University of Pennsylvania. He has published extensively in the area of communications. Kathleen Connolly is an assistant editor at Paulist Press.
Reprinted with permission from *New Catholic World*, March–April 1978.

This means that minority groups have their image formed by the dominant interests of the larger culture. Television presents a total world of meaning whose relationship to the state is not unlike that of the Church in an earlier time.

There are many implications that flow from the above differences. Television must be judged as a total system and not by isolating one component of television fare from all others. The uniqueness of television in the world of mass media means that we cannot study its effects in the same way as we do other media. We cannot presume that what is portrayed on television will have the same effects on viewers as would similar portrayals in other media. This is particularly true of violence, the incidence of which on television has been a topic of concern and debate over the last ten years.

In 1967, the Eisenhower Violence Commission was established to study violence in the United States. This same year marked the beginning of studies in violence on television by the communications research team at the Annenberg School of Communications of the University of Pennsylvania. In the intervening ten years, much has been written and discussed in the area of violence in general and television violence in particular. Take a moment to test your own knowledge in this area by answering the following true-false statements.

1. The goal of violence is to hurt or kill.   T   F
2. All violence is basically alike.   T   F
3. Violence on television is like violence in movies or books.   T   F
4. Violence on television reflects a violent world.   T   F
5. The main danger of television violence is that it makes children (and perhaps other viewers) more aggressive and violent.   T   F
6. Scientists have no evidence so far that television viewing alone has any significant and systematic effect on behavior.   T   F

These statements all *sound* correct, but are false. Let us examine why these statements are erroneous.

1. The goal of violence is to hurt or kill. Violence actually has two objectives, which we might call immediate and ultimate. The immediate goal of violence is *fear*. In order to be effective, violence need not hurt or kill. It is only necessary that violence generate a fear of pain or death in its victim. The ultimate goal of violence is the *power* to control behavior of others. Having generated fear of pain or death in the victim, violence moves toward its ultimate goal of power. If fear is created, the aggressor has then gained the power to make the victim do something that he or she would not ordinarily do. This is true of all forms of violence, from muggings to war. Only in a relatively few pathological cases is violence itself the goal or purpose of a violent act.
2. All violence is basically alike. The presentation of a violent scene carries a message with it. A violent act might be committed to thwart injustice

or brutality, or to perpetrate them. In each case, the message of the act will be vastly different. The outcry against television violence is not directed at acts of violence which, by helping people to distinguish just and unjust uses of power, serve a legitimate, dramatic purpose. Rather, the area of concern is violence that cultivates fear and prejudice, or the inhuman and unjust use of power.

3. Violence on television is like violence in books and movies. As we have noted above, television is different from all other mass media. The ubiquitous nature of television means that television violence will have different effects from violence that is read, seen, or heard selectively.

4. Violence on television reflects a violent world. Television distorts the violence found in reality. Highway and industrial accidents are the leading causes of violent death and injury in this country. One would never know that from watching television. Violence on television portrays how power works in society and who can get away with what.

5. The main danger of television violence is that it makes children (and perhaps other viewers) more aggressive and violent. The real effect of television violence is the result of the selective and stereotypical portrayals of power and people in society. Television shows us who are the victims and who are the aggressors. It demonstrates who has power and who will have to acquiesce to that power. Television violence achieves the immediate goal of violence, the generation of fear. This fear, and the power that can be achieved because of it, are the main dangers of television violence to all viewers, children and adults alike.

6. Scientists have no evidence so far that television alone has any significant and systematic effect on behavior. As we will show below, there is evidence regarding the effect of television viewing on the way people deal with reality. The evidence shows that heavy television viewing creates an exaggerated sense of danger, mistrust, and vulnerability.

What is the actual incidence of violence on television? What groups are most likely to be victims of television violence, and which are most likely to be aggressors? The Violence Index, one component of the Violence Profile, is a composite of measures of the prevalence, rate, and characterizations involved in violent action. The Violence Index, based on an analysis of a fall 1976 sample of prime time, late evening and weekend daytime network television dramatic programming, will enable us to see graphically how violence is portrayed on television.[1] This analysis focused on clear-cut and unambiguous physical expression of overt violence in any context.

In an overall summary of the incidence of violence, we find that 74.9% of all characters were involved in some violent action, and that 89.1% of all programs contained some violence. The saturation of programs with violence, indicated by the rate of violent episodes, was 6.2 per play and 9.5 per hour. These figures all represent increases in the figures for 1975.

1. Gerbner, George and Larry Gross, Michael F. Heey, Marilyn Jackson-Beeck, Suzanne Jeffries-Fox, and Nancy Signorelli, "TV Violence Profile No. 8: The Highlights," *Journal of Communication,* Spring 1977.

A closer look at the specifics of television violence is found in the Violence-Victim Ratio. These Ratios are obtained by dividing the more numerous of the two roles by the less numerous within each group. A plus sign indicates that there are more aggressors or killers than victims or killed, and a minus sign indicates that there are more victims or killed than aggressors or killers.

Since 1969 when this measure was developed, the overall Violence-Victim Ratio is −1.21, meaning that for every aggressor there were 1.21 victims. While the overall victimization ratio for men is −1.20, for women it is higher: −1.32. This means that female viewers are more likely to see a female victimized than a male. This leads to serious questions about the effect of television viewing on a woman's sense of her own safety.

Are there particular groups which have a high rate of victimization? A look at the following summary[2] will show which groups in the television population have high victimization rates. Minus signs indicate more victims than aggressors or killers.

2. Ibid.

Group	Violence-Victim Ratio
"Bad" characters (both sexes)	−1.02
"Good" characters (both sexes)	−1.28
Non-whites (both sexes)	−1.40
Unmarried women	−1.50
Children	−1.73
Lower class women	−2.25
Non-white women	−2.50
Old women	−3.00

It is interesting to note that while the overall Violence-Victim Ratio has declined from −1.25 in 1975 to −1.06 in 1976, the relative power positions of groups has remained the same. Television makes a very strong statement about who in society can expect to be the victims of violence, and what groups may be expected to exert that power. Of further interest to us here is the *context* in which violent action occurs. On television, violence rarely stems from close personal relationships. Yet according to the National Commission on the Causes and Prevention of Violence, statistics compiled in 1969 show that only 16% of actual homicides occur between strangers, while 64% involved family members or friends.[3]

Research thus far has shown us that television has a very definite lesson to teach about the perpetrators and victims of violence. In a much broader sense, television teaches a lesson about the social constructs of our world. Television is a medium of socialization of most people into standardized roles and behavior. Its function is, in short, enculturation. Television viewers are exposed daily to a value system acted out within the framework of "entertainment." People can and do learn values from television: what roles people play (and are expected to play) in our society, what types of behavior are socially acceptable, what characteristics are prized in our society. We need only examine the casting of television programming to see the roles and behavior patterns offered as standard fare.[4]

Three out of every four leads are males. These males tend to be American, middle- and upper-class and in the prime of life. Only one in three of these male leads has ever been or is intending to be married. Women, on the other hand, represent a romantic or family interest. Their roles almost always carry some suggestion of sex. Two out of three female leads are married or expect to be married. Nearly half of them come from the sexually eligible young adult population, as compared to one-fifth of the males. Women are disproportionately represented among the very young and the very old. Children, adolescents, and old people account for less than fifteen per cent of the total fictional population. In the total population of the television world, men outnumber women four to one.

In terms of employment, five in ten characters can be clearly identified as gainfully employed. Three of these five hold what we would call managerial or

3. Gerbner, George and Larry Gross, "Living with Television: The Violence Profile," *Journal of Communication,* Spring 1976.

4. Ibid.

professional positions. One-fifth of all characters specialize in violence as either law breakers or law enforcers.

The logical conclusion of our examination of the "world" constructed by television is that it enforces and maintains conventional beliefs, conceptions, and behaviors. The small percentage of very young and very old people who comprise television's world reinforces America's infatuation with youth and the "prime of life." Women's roles support the traditional stereotypes of women prevalent in society. Only recently have shows begun to move away from a particular set of economic (middle- and upper-middle-class) and cultural (white American) presuppositions.

With regard to violence in particular, TV violence is a dramatic demonstration of power which communicates much about social norms and relationships, about goals and means, about winners and losers, about the risks of life and the price for transgression of society's rules. Violence-laden drama shows who gets away with what, when, why, how, and against whom. A major worry about television violence is that it will teach aggressive people new means of being aggressive against others. Without minimizing this concern, an even more critical result of television violence may be what it teaches people about being *victims*. It is to this effect of television's influence that we must now turn our attention.

These results of television viewing have been studied in a research project called Cultural Indicators, a periodic study of television programs and conceptions of social reality that viewing cultivates. Before going on to the actual results, it is important to note the two steps in this particular research.[5]

1. The first method of research is the periodic analysis of large and representative aggregates of television output (rather than individual segments) as the system of messages to which total communities are exposed. The purpose of message system analysis is to establish the composition and structure of the symbolic world. Dramatic programs are studied with regard to geography, demography, thematic and action structure, time and space dimensions, personality profiles, occupations, and fate.

2. The second step is cultivation analysis; determining what, if anything, viewers absorb from living in the world of television. The findings of message system analysis are turned into questions about social reality, each of which has a "television answer," which is like the way things appear in the world of television, and another, different answer which is biased in the opposite direction, closer to the way things are in the observable world. For example, approximately 1% of the population are employed as law enforcement officials. The percentage of the television population employed in this field is greater. The margin of heavy viewers over light viewers giving the television answer within and across groups is the "cultivation differential" indicating conceptions about social reality that viewing tends to cultivate.

5. Ibid.

One can object that light and heavy viewers are different prior to—and aside from—television. The present research, as well as other studies, indicates that heavy viewing is part of a complex syndrome that includes lower education, lower mobility, higher anxieties, and other class-, age-, and sex-related characteristics. Television viewing helps to cultivate elements of that syndrome, but it also makes a separate and independent contribution to the "biasing" of conceptions of social reality within most age, sex, educational, and other groupings, including those most presumably "immune" to its effects.

The extent of television "bias" is best indicated by studying the breakdown of figures for those giving the "television answer" mentioned above.[6] While both college education and regular newspaper reading seem to reduce the percentage of "television answers," heavy viewing boosts it within both groups. This seems to be the general pattern of TV's ability to cultivate its own reality. Furthermore, television conditions the view of the world of those who grew up with television. All the figures show that the "under 30" respondents exhibit consistently higher levels of "television answers," despite the fact that they tend to be better educated than "over 30" respondents.

Let us look at two of the questions used in the survey and examine how light viewers compared with heavy viewers. The "television answer" corresponds to the world portrayed by TV, while the "alternative" is slanted more in the direction of reality.

1. What proportion of people are employed in law enforcement?
   Television answer: 5%
   Alternative: 1%

Heavy viewers (those watching an average of four hours a day or more) were always more likely to give the television answer, even among those viewers who are college educated or read newspapers regularly. Television thus cultivates an exaggerated idea of how many people are law enforcement agents. Of more serious concern is the possibility that TV also creates an exaggerated idea of the *need* for such officials. This is reflected in the answers to the following question.

2. What is your own chance of being involved in violence in any given week?
   Television Answer: 1 in 10
   Alternative: 1 in 100

Again, heavy viewers were always more likely to give the television answer. This may help to explain why recent studies have shown that respondents' estimates of danger in their own neighborhoods had little to do with crime statistics or even their own experience. Symbolic violence may cultivate exaggerated assumptions about the extent of threat and danger in the world and lead to demands for protection.

The net result of this research indicates that the effect of symbolic violence is very different than we might at first assume. A heightened sense of risk and

6. Ibid.

insecurity (different for groups of varying power) is more likely to increase acquiescence to and dependence upon established authority, and to legitimize its use of force, than it is to threaten the social order through occasional imitations of criminal violence.

This general trend seems to be true of other aspects of social reality. TV appears to cultivate assumptions that fit its socially functional myths—myths regarding age, sexual stereotyping, cultural backgrounds, who in society is powerful, and who acquiesces to that power. These myths form a value system that is presented almost twenty-four hours a day, every day, in millions of homes across the country. Television may indeed be the established religion of the industrial order.

Bibliography   Consult the bibliography that follows the article by George Comstock, "The Impact of Television on American Institutions," number 4 in this book.

4 The Impact of Television on American Institutions
George Comstock

George Comstock has written extensively on the effects of mass media in American society. His latest book, with several other scholars in the field, is *Television and Human Behavior,* Columbia University Press, 1979. He is a professor in the S. I. Newhouse School of Public Communications, Syracuse University. Reprinted with the permission of the *Journal of Communication.*

1. Based on data from (79), with the assumption of an average broadcast day of 18 hours for commercial stations and 12 hours for public and educational stations.

2. Data from (65) and Nielsen data published elsewhere. Audience size data represent viewing for each average minute of the time segment or program.

A synthesis and interpretation of research bearing on family life and socialization, religion, laws and norms, leisure time, public security, and politics.

About 700 television stations operated as privately-owned profit-seeking ventures annually broadcast 4 million hours of programming. In addition, about 250 "public" and educational stations supported by contributions and subsidies annually broadcast an additional 1.4 million hours.[1]

Almost every American home has one or more television sets, and 70 percent have color sets. The set in the average television household is on almost seven hours each day. On a typical evening between 8 and 9 P.M., the audience is 98 million persons, about half the population of the country. Such spectacular presentations as the championship game that concludes the professional football season, Super Bowl, and the eight-part dramatization of the black odyssey, Alex Haley's *Roots,* draw audiences of 75–80 million.[2]

The impact of this phenomenon on American institutions and the American public has engaged the attention of social critics, journalists, politicians, social and behavioral scientists, and citizens for the past 25 years. I will review television's influence on several major institutions:

Family life and the socialization of children

Church and religion

Enforcement of laws and norms

Mass media and leisure

Public security

Politics and public affairs

American television is shaped by the exigencies of competition to attract viewers. Despite the public prominence of news and public affairs programming, it is primarily an entertainment medium. The broadcasting system is the creation of federal regulation in terms of its structure. However, programming is largely free of government influence. Public television, although increasing the diversity of programming available, is a minor element.

Television's presence in the American home has brought many changes to family life and the rearing of children, including new patterns of interaction, alteration of activities, and vicarious socialization.

The large number of hours that the set is on each day in the average household makes it the framework within which human interaction occurs. Sets of data that permit comparison of present with pre-television behavior in the home are few. It appears that television has reduced time spent in conversation (67, 76). This gives support to the speculation that it reduces interaction among family members. Whether the point of reduction is trivial conversation, the exchange of opinions, play with children, the display of affection, the exchange of confidences, or some other dimension of interpersonal communication is moot. The same data also support the speculation that viewing increases the privatization of experience. The unfolding sound and images of television to some degree separate the viewer from others.

Almost half of American households have two or more television sets. With multiple sets, viewing alone increases and joint viewing by family members decreases (17). In addition, the composition of social viewing changes. Joint viewing by husbands and wives increases. Viewing by children with adults not present increases. The consequence is to further the separateness of adult and child experience.

Parents typically do not much influence or monitor their children's viewing (17, 57). Nevertheless, there are numerous instances when family members must decide on what to view. A fairly consistent composite of the dynamics of this decision-making emerges (17, 58, 81). Disagreement is fairly frequent (about half of the time of adult couples and for both parents and children, about three-fourths of the time for mothers and children). When the choice is not mutual, children prevail almost as frequently as adults. This supports the speculation that in the family television often has the status of the "children's medium" for which, by dint of interest and attention, the young have become the acknowledged resident experts.

The most obvious effect of television is the introduction of a variety of images, statements, and portrayals into the home.

This has led some to argue that television is a source of vicarious socialization that competes with parents, teachers, and other acknowledged agents of socialization in providing models for emulation and information that influence individual beliefs, values, and expectations (4). The evidence on behalf of the proposition that television is to some degree an agent of socialization is convincing. What is uncertain is the degree of its influence, and whether on balance that influence is positive or negative.

One strand in this evidence is the amount that children view and the content itself. Children typically are heavy viewers, and most of their viewing is of general audience or "adult" programming; the average of children of elementary school age is 27 hours per week. Television presents the viewer with a world that often is at variance with the one he/she inhabits. This is particularly so for children, whose experiences and knowledge are limited. Thus, what television conveys often has no corrective in actual experience. One long-term trend has been increasing liberality in the treatment of sexual relations, personal problems and crises, and various kinds of deviant—in the sociological sense of departing from the norm—behavior. The effect has been to remove parents' control over what information is introduced into the home. Thus, television by its very nature has the potential to supplement as well as to reinforce other agents of socialization.

A second strand consists of studies of the information derived from television by children. Children learn from television the names and specialties of pop entertainers (72). They have been found to perceive occupations with which they are personally unfamiliar as they are portrayed on the television they view, while perceptions of occupations with which they have actual experience are not so similar to the television portrayal (32). Television was the major source of children's knowledge about the Vietnam war, and much more important as an information source than parents or teachers (80). Black youths are much more likely to report that they obtain ideas for dating from television than are whites (46). Blacks and children from families of lower socioeconomic status more frequently report that they use television as a source for learning (47). The common element to these findings is the reliance on television for information not available in the child's own environment.

The third strand is made up of several dozen laboratory-type experiments that demonstrate that children of nursery school age can acquire new ways of behaving from television (5). The observation of the performance of an act by a person in real life or in a film or television portrayal increases the likelihood that children subsequently will themselves behave in a similar manner (6). Even if the children do not spontaneously perform the act, they can do so upon request, indicating that observation of behavior can alter capability of subsequent performance (3). The implication of these experiments is that television can alter the repertoire of possible behavior on which children will draw in a future situation.

The fourth strand consists of another several dozen laboratory-type experiments that demonstrate that the level or intensity of performance of an act by youth of college age can be increased by exposure to television portrayals. In some of these experiments, performance apparently has been augmented by lowering inhibitions or otherwise facilitating behavior (9, 10). Aspects of portrayals found to augment subsequent behavior include the depiction of the kind of behavior in question as justified (13), the characterization of the portrayal as real rather than fictional (40), and the making of a particular kind of behavior more relevant through the inclusion in the portrayal of stimuli or clues similar to those encountered in the real-life measurement situation (11, 12, 41). In other experiments, the physiological excitation or arousal instigated by the portrayal augmented subsequent behavior (77, 78). Types of portrayal found capable of augmenting subsequent behavior include erotic and violent sequences (84), humor (77), and an ambiguous, unresolved climax to a drama in which the hero engages in intense physical combat (85). The implication of these experiments is that television may alter the behavior that real-life experience negatively or positively reinforces, thereby contributing indirectly to the future pattern of behavior.

Most of the laboratory-type experiments that make up these final two strands are concerned with the effects of televised portrayals, and particularly violent portrayals, of aggression.

Their relevance for real-life aggression is limited in that the time frame is unrealistically brief and the viewing experience differs markedly from that occurring in the home (48, 83). However, they gain credence by the finding of a positive correlation in several surveys between previous violence viewing and real-life aggression by adolescents against peers not explainable by the preference of typically aggressive youths for violent entertainment (20). This convergence of experimental findings where causal inference is permissible with survey evidence reflecting the real world devoid of experimental artifact makes causation the most plausible interpretation (20, 27, 54, 75). The implication of this evidence on television violence is that television has somewhat increased the likelihood of aggressive behavior on the part of young viewers. What is less clear is the degree to which it contributes to truly harmful antisocial aggression or criminal acts or heightens the level of aggressive interaction among the adults young viewers eventually become (29).

The broader implication of the two experimental strands is that there are a number of psychological processes by which television may influence subsequent behavior. There is no reason to think that effects would be limited to aggression, although such attributes of aggression as being discrete, physical, and employable in a wide range of contexts may make it particularly subject to influence. This broader implication is supported by several experiments demonstrating that other kinds of behavior are open to alteration by their portrayal on television (18, 19, 71). There is also some evidence suggesting that television violence may desensitize young viewers to real-life violence. In one experiment, children who viewed a violent portrayal were subsequently slower to signal for adult help when children whose play they had been asked to supervise became destructive (35). Possible mechanisms are an increase in the perceived normativeness of violence, a decrease in the importance assigned the real-life violence, or a diminution in emotional responsiveness and quickness of action. The former two interpretations gain some support from the finding that a belief that one learns from television, that portrayals reflect reality, and identification with violent characters are positively correlated with adolescent aggressiveness (62); the latter is given some credibility by an experiment in which children who were heavy television viewers were less physiologically aroused by violent portrayals (24). The major implication of any desensitization is that the level of interventive helpfulness in cases of human endangerment may be reduced.

In sum, television appears to function in America as an agent of socialization.

It captures children's attention for long periods, and presents them with information and portrayals not duplicated or readily testable in their real-life environment. It is turned to by children for information not available to them in real life. It provides models of behavior children may emulate. It can alter the level of intensity of behavior, and such alterations may shape the future pattern of behavior through the positive or negative reinforcement children receive. Viewing of violence increases the likelihood of aggressive behavior on the part of the young, but the larger implication is that television may influence other classes of behavior.

The socializing influence of television, however, is subject to severe modification by other agents. Although television was found to be the principal source of children's knowledge about Vietnam, opinions about the war were found to be primarily influenced by parents, and the viewing of television news was found to be increased by parental interest in the war (80). Parental support for aggression as a means of problem solving has been found to have greater influence on attitudes favorable to the use of aggression than the viewing of television violence (34). When parents de-emphasize aggression for problem-solving, the correlation between the viewing of violent television and aggressive behavior is sharply reduced (20, 62). The implication is that, to some and possibly to a great degree, the socializing prowess of television depends on the lack of intervention by nonvicarious agents, such as teachers and parents.

The relationship between the institutions of mass communication and religion has received almost no attention from social and behavioral scientists.

Gerbner (42) has pointed out that religion, education, and mass media are all systems by which the public is acculturated, or introduced to the norms, conventions, and taboos of society. What sets religion and mass media apart is their continuing, repetitious presence throughout life.

One might expect that the great quantity of time consumed by television would infringe on time spent in religious practice. The scant evidence available is that it does not (67). A more obvious effect is the broadcasting of religious services, most of which rely upon ecclesiastics with exceptional forensic skill and visible show biz flair. No audience figures for religious programming are available. However, the Sunday morning audience when many of these religious broadcasts occur averaged 13 million adults.[3] This underestimates the number of individuals viewing particular programs, because it is the average per minute and viewers tune out to be replaced by new viewers. This is a sizable audience, although small compared to the 70 million viewing during early prime time. Much of this Sunday viewing appears to be solitary, for the average adult audience per viewing household is 1.04 compared to 1.51 for that prime-time hour. It is almost equally male and female, contrary to the 25 percent more females than males in the prime-time hour, and surprisingly it is not noticeably older. Whether this is a fair picture of the audience for religious television is uncertain, because it may be distorted by the other programming in the same time period. What we are equally uncertain about is the meaning to be attached to the phenomenon of religious television.

It has been suggested that television in the United States can be looked upon as an institution that has assumed some of the functions of a dominant religion, and thus might be thought of as the successor to conventional religion (44). This is an intriguing perspective. The television industry, of course, represents a concentration of economic power, as historically does religion, but economic power is common to many institutions. Where television particularly resembles religion is that the basis of this power is the acceptance of its communications by the intended audience. Television also would appear to resemble religion in the communication of values and interpretation of the world. Television does not do so explicitly as does religion, except in religious and other exhortatory programming, but implicitly. For example, it has been argued with great plausibility that television drama as a whole presents a text on the attributes associated with success, power, and dominance, or their absence, through its violence and through the high frequency with which persons fall victim to the hostile and dangerous nature of the world (45). Similarly, the attributes of figures chosen to appear as entertainers, newscasters, or the subjects of interviews in a favorable context are implicitly identified as the equipment of prominence and success. Television inherently presents winners, and winners represent values.

3. Data from (65). Audience size data for Sunday morning represents viewing for each average minute between 7 A.M. and 1 P.M., and for the early primetime hour, averaging viewing per minute between 8 and 9 P.M. Monday through Sunday.

The connection does not end with the common dissemination of values. Television also allocates status and bestows approval through inclusion in its glance. Television does not only make certain entertainers and news personnel national figures. By so doing, it also establishes a mechanism for the giving or withholding of status. Television's preeminent figures function much like priests in guiding those who attend to them to people and things fit for their scrutiny. Television, in this respect, has become an arbiter of acceptability. In this context, it is amusing to note that when CBS radio newsman Charles Kuralt criticized ABC's Barbara Walters for the sentimental and circumspect interview with President and Mrs. Carter shortly before the inauguration, he characterized Ms. Walters as the female "pope" of television giving benediction to the new secular leader.

One of the continuing concerns of all societies is the enforcement of laws and norms.

What constitutes a violation of law or deviation from norms varies from society to society, but each has a set of boundaries beyond which behavior is punished or leads to special treatment. The purpose is to resist change and disruption and maintain social relations in their current manifestation. Many questions have been raised about the contribution of television to such enforcement in the United States.

The issue that has drawn the most attention has been the possible contribution of violent television entertainment to delinquency, crime, and other seriously harmful antisocial acts. I have argued that the evidence supports the proposition that the viewing of television violence increases the likelihood of subsequent aggressiveness on the part of the young. The evidence does not equally strongly support the proposition that violence viewing increases violations of the law and seriously harmful antisocial acts (29).

I do not concur with those writers (50, 74) who argue that there is little or no empirical evidence on behalf of the proposition that violence viewing contributes to seriously harmful antisocial acts. Admittedly, there are no data in which anything approaching a direct link occurs. However, this fact must be interpreted in the context of the opportunity for such a link to appear, and that context is one of no opportunity at all. The sole study focusing on the issue, a field experiment by Milgram and Shotland (64), found no evidence of a link but this negative finding is not very persuasive because the rate of antisocial behavior required in this instance for statistical significance is far in excess of that necessary for significant social impact (28).

Several writers have argued that television is a powerful reinforcer of the *status quo* (21, 22, 45). The ostensible mechanisms are the effects of its portrayals on public expectations and perceptions. Television portrayals, particularly violent drama, are said to assign roles of authority, power, success, failure, dependence, and vulnerability in a manner that matches the real-life social hierarchy, thereby strengthening that hierarchy by increasing its acknowledgment among the public and by failing to provide positive images for members of social categories occupying a subservient position. Content analyses of television drama support the contention that portrayals reflect normative status (26, 43, 45, 49, 51, 55, 73). The finding of a correlation between amount of television viewing and perception of the real world as more closely resembling the demographics of television drama than actuality (45) is consistent with the contention that portrayals affect the understanding of reality. That the amount of viewing is correlated with a belief in greater risk of falling victim to violent crime (45) further supports the argument that television reinforces the *status quo* because such belief is likely to encourage support for stricter laws and more vigorous suppression of any behavior construable as deviant. However, the proposition that television reinforces the *status quo* inevitably must remain speculative; as Gerbner and Gross (45) observe, the proposition is so wholistic that it is somewhat like asking about the effects of Christianity or Confucianism.

It has also been argued that television contributes to a homogenization of norms.

One of the attributes of a television society is an historically unprecedented sharing of the same experience. The only comparable sharing prior to television are religious and patriotic rites. Although amount of viewing and attitudes toward television do vary by social strata, with viewing and favorability of attitude inversely related to education, viewing is sufficiently similar for television to be considered a national experience (17, 31). The results, because of the normative nature of television's portrayals, are said to reduce tolerance of deviation from norms (14), and because of their emphasis on middle-class values, to assimilate blue-collar and presumably other groups to a middle-class perspective (15). The findings that black youths are more likely to look to television as a guide to dating norms (56), that socioeconomic differences in family activities were reduced slightly by the introduction of television in England (8), and that persons of lower socioeconomic status and minority group membership are more likely to consider television as a source for learning (17, 47) give support to these views.

The issues raised by these arguments about television's contribution to the *status quo,* homogenization, and assimilation of various segments of the population to middle class values revolve around the heterogeneity of society. The first holds that television strengthens the current social hierarchy; the second holds that television reduces differences among strata; and the third holds that changes in the values of a particular segment are the means of that reduction. Since social distinctions are rooted in education, income, occupation, and ethnic and family background, attributes not eradicated by the adoption of values or common sources of diversion, it is quite possible that all three are occurring simultaneously and that the latter two reflect not a diminution of the hierarchy but an increased acceptance of the outward norms and values on which it is based.

If these arguments are valid, television smoothes the social hierarchy without disrupting it. Disruption would be confined to television's possible contribution to seriously harmful antisocial acts. Ironically, like television's alleged enhancement of fears of violent crime, any such disruption may augment the laws and agencies concerned with the control and suppression of deviance by strengthening public support in their behalf. Any degree of desensitization that reduces the assistance customarily offered endangered persons would have a similar effect by increasing feelings of personal risk. Nevertheless, it would be a mistake to think of television as not contributing to change. Homogenization and assimilation themselves represent change.

Television has revolutionized the leisure environment of Americans by not only affecting their allocation of time, but the options for the disposal of time.

For an understanding of the impact of television on daily life in America, I am particularly indebted to an extraordinary UNESCO study of the way time is spent in modern society. Diaries of time allocation were obtained from large samples of 15 industrialized cities in the United States, Western Europe, and Latin America (69, 76). The resulting data, in conjunction with data from other studies, provide striking evidence on the impact of television on American life.

Television has increased the time Americans spend on the mass media by 40 percent. Three-fourths of the time spent on the mass media is devoted to television. A third of leisure is devoted to viewing as the primary activity. Television ranks third behind sleep and work as a consumer of time. The incursion of television on time is a major social effect, and gives support to the arguments about its effects on the public's values and perceptions, particularly to the propositions that television has a homogenizing and, for certain segments of the public, an assimilative influence.

Data from studies of the adoption of television in the United States (16, 25) and comparisons in the UNESCO study between set owners and non-owners in societies where ownership has not reached the saturation of the United States, indicate that the time spent on television represents reductions in time spent sleeping, at social gatherings away from home, radio listening, magazine and book reading, movie going, conversing, on household tasks, and on other leisure. Unaffected, apparently, was time devoted to newspaper reading.

The steadily upward trend since the 1950s of hours of television use by households with television (31) suggests that this impact on time allocation has progressively increased over the past two decades. The impact also has not been equal among social strata and population segments. The extensive viewing typical of all strata groups makes television a national medium, but there are noteworthy differences. The impact has been greatest on those of lower socioeconomic status, blacks, women, and the elderly, because they view more (16, 17, 31, 47, 69). This certainly has been true over the past two decades, and remains so despite a long-term trend toward convergence in amount of viewing between those of higher and lower socioeconomic status where the principal individual attribute inversely related to viewing is education (31).

The relationship between blacks and television is remarkable. Blacks typically not only view more than whites, but the inverse relationship between education and both viewing and favorable attitudes toward television that holds for whites is, depending on the measure, either not present or sharply reduced (17). Since the introduction of television, blacks have become more strongly oriented towards it as a source of political news than whites (59).

Television is primarily approached as a medium rather than as a supplier of specific programs.

People almost never include the desire to see a particular program when asked about their reasons for viewing, although about three-fourths will affirm that the desire to see a particular program was a motive when the question is phrased that way. About a third acknowledge that what they view is determined by the channel that happens to be on or what someone else is watching (68). The concept of viewing for a particular program is not predominant.

Television severely reduced the audience for movies (16). Equally important, it has probably contributed to the increasing violence and explicit and frank treatment of sexual themes in theater films. Television also appears to have brought about the demise of such mass audience periodicals as the *Saturday Evening Post, Collier's, Life,* and *Look* by providing advertisers with an ostensibly superior means of reaching consumers. The sale of comic books decreased from about 600 to 300 million between the early 1950s and 1970. Book publishing, fiction, poetry, and drama declined in the same period from 22 to 13 percent of all commercially published titles for sale in retail outlets, although the absolute number of such titles increased. Television converted radio from a national to a local medium.

Television has also reshaped other media by the opportunities it offers for informing the public about media availability and for the more extensive distribution of media products. Potential promotion of books on talk and discussion shows has become a factor in the selection of what will be published. Similarly, the likely sale of television rights has become a factor in estimating the potential profits to be derived from movies and novels.

Television has also altered leisure options outside of the media. It in effect demolished minor league baseball (attendance fell from 42 to 10 million during the two decades ending in 1970) through its attractiveness as home entertainment and its presentation of major league baseball and other sports (16). At the same time, it has undoubtedly increased attendance at various kinds of sporting and cultural events where it increased public knowledge and interest. For example, Belson (7) concluded from his data that television led to a 47 percent increase in horse racing and horse jumping attendance and an 18 percent increase in major soccer match attendance.

One of the apparent phenomena of modern life is the tendency of terrorist acts and outbreaks of violence of a particular kind to occur in a series.

It would be silly to hold television responsible apart from other mass media—newspapers, radio, and news magazines. Nevertheless, it is possible that in certain instances television may have a particularly strong role in any such effect.

The dynamics by which television might play a particularly prominent role are quite complex. Television coverage may encourage similar acts because the initial coverage appears to insure subsequent attention by the medium. Its often vivid camera portrayals may supply an image of concreteness, realism and actuality around which the typically more detailed accounts of print media may be organized and assigned meaning by potential perpetrators. The apparent contribution of the *Doomsday Flight* drama to a subsequent increase in airline bomb threats gives some credence to this view.

Television coverage may also influence the way events unfold. Television coverage occasionally is a condition for safe treatment of hostages or the conduct of negotiations. The access to public attention implied by television may distort the decisionmaking and behavior of those involved. The concept of all the world as a stage is heightened by television coverage.

"The whole world is watching!" This phrase implies another way in which television may shape rather than report events. Television coverage itself may be the goal in a particular instance. It is a standard tactic for disaffected groups to seek public sympathy through publicity or the provoking of violent reprisals in which they appear to be innocent parties. Thus, television exposure may be the calculated outcome rather than the concomitant of organized displays of dissatisfaction and unrest.

It is a myth of the mass media that events determine news. News, in fact, is manufactured by journalists through the selection of what to present and the treatment given. This is validated in the finding that amount of violence on newspaper front pages and in television newscasts are uncorrelated (23), documented in the case of public events where television will convey an impression unlike that gained by those actually in attendance (52), and is made quite clear from the close examination of the operation of news organizations (1, 2, 38, 39, 82).

It is widely agreed that television has reshaped American politics through its effects on the behavior of politicians and on the conduct of political campaigns (53, 68). Among the effects are the devising of campaign strategy to maximize favorable exposure on television, the heightened importance of communications and advertising experts in the mapping of campaigns, the organization of nominating conventions to present the public with a favorable impression of party and candidates, and the devotion of major portions of campaign budgets to television.

Television certainly provides a notable proportion of the public's exposure to events, issues, and public figures, and in conjunction with other mass media probably has some influence on the public's agenda of who and what is important, although the evidence in behalf of this agenda-setting function is somewhat stronger for newspapers than for television (30, 60, 61).

The biases of television as a medium probably diminish possible effects on voter choice (66). Television news emphasizes events and image-related activities that provide good film or live coverage, such as parades, and handshaking and the consumption of ethnic foods by candidates. Political knowledge among voters has been found not to be increased by exposure to television news (56, 66).

This attribute of the medium probably has two outcomes. When image is crucial to a decision, television has more potential for influence, and because of the event-and-image bias of television news, paid political advertising has the potential to influence by providing information about the stands of candidates not conveyed in the news. Paid political spots in this context would appear to have a particularly strong potential because they reach viewers unexpectedly, many of whom might avoid news or other campaign-related broadcasts. However, the opportunity for impact appears to be confined to a modest segment of the voting population, for in a mid-American sample in the 1972 election those who appeared to have been influenced by commercials were limited to about one out of 10 who were younger, educationally non-mobile, low in socioeconomic status, politically ignorant, high in exposure to media campaign coverage, and oriented toward television rather than newspapers for political information (63).

Expenditures on political advertising increased 600 percent, six times the rate of inflation, between 1954 and 1970 (70).

The potential for influence may be increasing. Television presumably has greater opportunity to influence voters who consider themselves undecided or not aligned with any party, and there is some evidence that the proportion of such voters is increasing (33, 36).

One study of the Carter-Ford election suggests that such television coverage may play a crucial role in voter decision-making through its effect on candidate image, although not necessarily on favoring one candidate over another. In analysis of data from 3,042 adults in western Pennsylvania cities collected in September and early October, Lucas and Adams (56) demonstrate that decided, leaning, and undecided voters were very much alike in previous political participation, political knowledge, and media exposure, but that the reaching of a decision was positively correlated with interpersonal communication about the campaign and exposure to network news. Television's specialty of shaping the image of candidates held by voters may play a crucial role in the electoral process whether or not the outcome is affected.

The public's evaluation of television is predominantly favorable. The single most disliked aspect of television is its commercials. Almost three-fourths of the American public believes there are too many commercials. However, the same proportion believes that commercials are a "fair price" to pay for the medium

(17). Again, the discrepancy between what the public wants from television and what it delivers is insufficient to affect popularity significantly.

About half the adult public over the past two decades has believed that children may be exposed to portrayals that in some way are undesirable (17). Almost a third consistently have believed that violence falls in this category. There has also been increasing concern over morality, with the percent objecting to "bad language," sexual suggestiveness, portrayals of alcohol consumption, smoking, and narcotics use, and introduction to adult topics rising from five percent or less in 1960 to about ten percent in 1970. The concern on the part of some over the competition from television in the socialization of children is reflected in the increase in the attempt by parents to prevent the viewing of certain programs as their children reach the late elementary school years (17) when the portrayals of general audience programming become relevant as a model for future behavior.

The past years have seen a remarkable series of steps against television violence, including the joint agreement by the networks and the stations belonging to the National Association of Broadcasters to reduce television violence in early evening hours. This was in response to pressure from the Federal Communications Commission and the Congress, active opposition by the American Medical Association and the national Parent-Teachers Association, and the efforts of many major advertisers to dissociate themselves from violent programming (30).

Television advertising has also been the focus of attacks by groups concerned over the medium's influence on children (30). The grounds have included the alleged encouragement of narcotic, alcohol, and over-the-counter drug use, the purveying of nutritionally-deficient breakfast cereals and other foods, the tempting of children to play with dangerous household substances and tools, and the doubtful ethicality of directing advertising at children who may be too young to distinguish a self-interested sales pitch from authoritative advice and counsel. Advertising appears to be susceptible to government regulation because it is generally believed not to enjoy the protection of the First Amendment, and the Federal Trade Commission over the years has become increasingly active in devising rules and imposing fines to protect viewers from supposedly deceptive and misleading advertising (37).

Where these various trends converge is in the heightened acceptance of the proposition that broadcasting content is a legitimate subject for public and governmental concern and action.

References

1. Altheide, D. L. *Creating Reality: How TV News Distorts Events.* Beverly Hills, Cal.: Sage Publications, 1976.
2. Bailey, G. A. and L. W. Lichty. "Rough Justice on a Saigon Street: A Gatekeeper Study of NBC's Tet Execution Film." *Journalism Quarterly* 49, 1972, pp. 221–229 *passim.*
3. Bandura, A. "Influence of Models' Reinforcement Contingencies on the Acquisition of Imitative Responses." *Journal of Personality and Social Psychology* 1, 1965, pp. 589–595.
4. Bandura, A. "Social-learning Theory of Identificatory Processes." In D. A. Goslin (Ed.) *Handbook of Socialization Theory and Research.* Chicago: Rand McNally, 1969, pp. 213–262.

5. Bandura, A. *Aggression: A Social Learning Analysis.* Englewood Cliffs, N.J.: Prentice-Hall, 1973.
6. Bandura, A., D. Ross, and S. A. Ross. "Imitation of Film-mediated Aggressive Models." *Journal of Abnormal and Social Psychology* 66, 1963, pp. 3–11.
7. Belson, W. A. "Effects of Television on the Interests and Initiative of Adult Viewers in Greater London." *British Journal of Psychology* 50, 1959, pp. 145–158.
8. Belson, W. A. "The Effects of Television upon Family Life." *Discovery* 21(10), 1960, pp. 426–430.
9. Berkowitz, L. "Violence in the Mass Media." In *Aggression: A Social Psychological Analysis.* New York: McGraw-Hill, 1962, pp. 229–255.
10. Berkowitz, L. "Words and Symbols as Stimuli to Aggressive Responses." In J. F. Knutson (Ed.) *Control of Aggression: Implications from Basic Research.* Chicago, Ill.: Aldine-Atherton, 1973, pp. 113–143.
11. Berkowitz, L. and R. G. Geen. "Film Violence and the Cue Properties of Available Targets." *Journal of Personality and Social Psychology* 3, 1966, pp. 525–530.
12. Berkowitz, L. and R. G. Geen. "Stimulus Qualities of the Target of Aggression: A Further Study." *Journal of Personality and Social Psychology* 5, 1967, pp. 364–368.
13. Berkowitz, L. and E. Rawlings. "Effects of Film Violence on Inhibitions Against Subsequent Aggression." *Journal of Abnormal and Social Psychology* 66, 1963, pp. 405–412.
14. Bogart, L. "American Television: A Brief Survey of Research Findings." *Journal of Social Issues* 18(2), 1962, pp. 36–42.
15. Bogart, L. "The Mass Media and the Blue-collar Worker." In A. Shostak and W. Gomberg (Eds.) *Blue-collar World: Studies of the American Worker.* Englewood Cliffs, N.J.: Prentice-Hall, 1965, pp. 416–428.
16. Bogart, L. *The Age of Television* (3rd ed.) New York: Frederick Ungar, 1972.
17. Bower, R. T. *Television and the Public.* New York: Holt, Rinehart and Winston, 1973.
18. Bryan, J. H. "Model Affect and Children's Imitative Altruism." *Child Development* 42, 1971, pp. 2061–2065.
19. Bryan, J. H. and N. H. Walbek. "The Impact of Words and Deeds Concerning Altruism Upon Children." *Child Development* 41, 1970, pp. 747–757.
20. Chaffee, S. H. "Television and Adolescent Aggressiveness." In G. A. Comstock and E. A. Rubinstein (Eds.) *Television and Social Behavior,* Vol. 3: *Television and Adolescent Aggressiveness.* Washington, D.C.: U.S. Government Printing Office, 1972, pp. 1–34.
21. Clark, C. C. "Television and Social Controls: Some Observations on the Portrayal of Ethnic Minorities." *Television Quarterly* 8, 1969, pp. 18–22.
22. Clark, C. C. "Race, Identification, and Television Violence." In G. A. Comstock, E. A. Rubinstein, and J. P. Murray (Eds.) *Television and Social Behavior,* Vol. 5: *Television's Effects: Further Explorations.* Washington, D.C.: U.S. Government Printing Office, 1972, pp. 120–184.
23. Clark, D. G. and W. B. Blankenburg. "Trends in Violent Contact in Selected Mass Media." In G. A. Comstock and E. A. Rubinstein (Eds.) *Television and Social Behavior,* Vol. 1: *Media Content and Control.* Washington, D.C.: U.S. Government Printing Office, 1972, pp. 188–243.
24. Cline, V. B., R. G. Croft, and S. Courrier. "Desensitization of Children to Television Violence." *Journal of Personality and Social Psychology* 27, 1972, pp. 360–365.
25. Coffin, T. E. "Television's Impact on Society." *American Psychologist* 10, 1955, pp. 630–641.
26. Comstock, G. A. "New Research on Media Content and Control." In G. A. Comstock and E. A. Rubinstein (Eds.) *Television and Social Behavior,* Vol. 1: *Media Content and Control.* Washington, D.C.: U.S. Government Printing Office, 1972, pp. 1–27.
27. Comstock, G. A. *Television Violence: Where the Surgeon General's Study Leads.* Santa Monica, Cal.: Rand Corporation, 1972, P–1831.
28. Comstock, G. A. *Milgram's Scotch Verdict on TV—A Retrial.* Santa Monica, Cal.; Rand Corporation, 1974, P—5248.
29. Comstock, G. A. *The Evidence on Television Violence.* Santa Monica, Cal.: Rand Corporation, 1976, P—5730.
30. Comstock, G. A. *The Role of Social and Behavioral Science in Policymaking for Television.* Santa Monica, Cal.: Rand Corporation, 1977, P–5788.
31. Comstock, G. A., S. Chaffee, N. Katzman, M. McCombs, and D. Roberts. *Television and Human Behavior.* New York: Columbia University Press, in press.
32. DeFleur, M. L. and L. B. DeFleur. "The Relative Contribution of Television as a Learning Source for Children's Occupational Knowledge." *American Sociological Review* 32, 1967, pp. 777–789.

33. DeVries, W. and L. Tarrance Jr. *The Ticket-splitter: A New Force in American Politics.* Grand Rapids, Mich.: Eerdmans Publishing, 1972.
34. Dominick, J. R. and B. S. Greenburg. "Attitudes Toward Violence: The Interaction of Television, Exposure, Family Attitudes, and Social Class." In G. A. Comstock and E. A. Rubinstein (Eds.) *Television and Social Behavior,* Vol. 3: *Television and Adolescent Aggressiveness.* Washington, D.C.: U.S. Government Printing Office, 1972, pp. 314–335.
35. Drabman, R. S. and M. H. Thomas. "Does Media Violence Increase Children's Toleration of Real-life Aggression?" *Developmental Psychology* 10, 1974, pp. 418–421.
36. Dreyer, E. C. "Media Use and Electoral Choices: Some Political Consequences of Information Exposure." *Public Opinion Quarterly* 35, 1971, pp. 544–553.
37. Emery, W. B. *Broadcasting and Government: Responsibilities and Regulations.* East Lansing: Michigan State University Press, 1971.
38. Epstein, E. J. *News from Nowhere: Television and the News.* New York: Random House, 1973.
39. Epstein, E. J. "The Values of Newsmen." *Television Quarterly* 10, 1973, pp. 9–33.
40. Feshbach, S. "Reality and Fantasy in Filmed Violence." In J. P. Murray, E. A. Rubinstein, and G. A. Comstock (Eds.) *Television and Social Behavior,* Vol. 2: *Television and Social Learning.* Washington, D.C.: U.S. Government Printing Office, 1972, pp. 318–345.
41. Geen, R. G. and L. Berkowitz. "Some Conditions Facilitating the Occurrence of Aggression After the Observation of Violence." *Journal of Personality* 35, 1967, pp. 666–676.
42. Gerbner, G. "An Institutional Approach to Mass Communications Research." In L. Thayer (Ed.) *Communication: Theory and Research.* Springfield, Ill.: Charles C. Thomas, 1967, pp. 429–451.
43. Gerbner, G. "Violence in Television Drama: Trends and Symbolic Functions." In G. A. Comstock and E. A. Rubinstein (Eds.) *Television and Social Behavior,* Vol. 1.: *Media Content and Control.* Washington, D.C.: U.S. Government Printing Office, 1972, pp. 28–187.
44. Gerbner, G. Unpublished address in symposium entitled, "Do we really know anything about the long-range impact of television?" Presented at the meeting of the American Association of Public Opinion Research, Asheville, North Carolina, May 1976.
45. Gerbner, G. and L. Gross. "Living with Television: The Violence Profile." *Journal of Communication* 262), 1976, pp. 173–199.
46. Gerson, W. M. "Mass Media Socialization Behavior: Negro-white Differences." *Social Forces* 45, 1966, pp. 40–50.
47. Greenburg, B. S. and B. Dervin. *Use of the Mass Media by the Urban Poor.* New York: Praeger, 1970.
48. Hartley, R. L. *The Impact of Viewing "Aggression": Studies and Problems of Extrapolation.* New York: Columbia Broadcasting System. Office of Social Research, 1964.
49. Head, S. W. "Content Analysis of Television Drama Programs." *Quarterly of Film, Radio and Television* 9, 1954, pp. 175–194.
50. Kaplan, R. M. and R. D. Singer. "Psychological Effects of Televised Violence: A Review and Methodological Critique." *Journal of Social Issues,* in press.
51. Katzman, N. I. "Television Soap Operas: What's Been Going on Anyway?" *Public Opinion Quarterly* 36, 1972, pp. 200–212.
52. Lang, K. and G. E. Lang. "The Unique Perspective of Television and its Effects: A Pilot Study." *American Sociological Review* 18, 1953, pp. 3–12.
53. Lang, K. and G. E. Lang. *Politics and Television.* Chicago: Quadrangle Books, 1968.
54. Liebert, R. M., J. M. Neale, and E. S. Davidson. *The Early Window: Effects of Television on Youth and Children.* Elmsford, N.Y.: Pergamon Press, 1973.
55. Long, M. L. and R. J. Simon. "The Roles and Statuses of Women on Children and Family TV Programs." *Journalism Quarterly* 51, 1974, pp. 107–110.
56. Lucas, W. A. and W. C. Adams. "The Undecided Voter and Political Communication in the 1976 Presidential Election." Paper presented at the meeting of the Southwestern Political Science Association, Dallas, April 1, 1977. (Rand P–5833, April 1977).
57. Lyle, J. "Television in Daily Life: Patterns of Use." In E. A. Rubinstein, G. A. Comstock, and J. P. Murray (Eds.) *Television and Social Behavior,* Vol. 4: *Television in Day-to-day Life: Patterns of Use.* Washington, D.C.: U.S. Government Printing Office, 1972, pp. 1–32.
58. Lyle, J. and H. R. Hoffman. "Children's Use of Television and Other Media." In E. A. Rubinstein, G. A. Comstock, and J. P. Murray (Eds.) *Television and Social Behavior,* Vol. 4: *Television in Day-to-day Life: Patterns of Use.* Washington, D.C.: U.S. Government Printing Office, 1972, pp. 129–256.

59. McCombs, M. E. "Negro Use of Television and Newspapers for Political Information, 1952–1964." *Journal of Broadcasting* 12, 1968, pp. 216–266.
60. McCombs, M. E. and D. L. Shaw. "The Agenda-setting Function of Mass Media." *Public Opinion Quarterly* 36, 1972, pp. 176–187.
61. McCombs, M. E. and D. L. Shaw. "A Progress Report on Agenda-setting Research." Paper presented at the meeting of the Association for Education in Journalism, San Diego, August 1974.
62. McLeod, J. M., C. K. Atkin, and S. H. Chaffee. "Adolescents, Parents, and Television Use: Self-report and Other-report Measures from the Wisconsin Sample." In G. A. Comstock and E. A. Rubinstein (Eds.) *Television and Social Behavior,* Vol. 3: *Television and Adolescent Aggressiveness.* Washington, D.C.: U.S. Government Printing Office, 1972, pp. 239–313.
63. Mendelsohn, H. and G. J. O'Keefe. *The People Choose a President.* New York: Praeger, 1976.
64. Milgram, S. and R. L. Shotland. *Television and Antisocial Behavior: Field Experiments.* New York: Academic Press, 1973.
65. *Nielsen Television Index. National Audience Demographics Report November 1976.* Northbrook, Ill.: A. C. Nielsen Company, 1976.
66. Patterson, T. E. and R. D. McClure. *Picture Politics.* New York: G. P. Putnam, 1976.
67. Robinson, J. P. "Television's Impact on Everyday Life: Some Cross-national Evidence." In E. A. Robinson, G. A. Comstock, and J. P. Murray (Eds.) *Television and Social Behavior,* Vol. 4: *Television in Day-to-day Life: Patterns of Use.* Washington, D.C.: U.S. Government Printing Office, 1972, pp. 410–431.
68. Robinson, J. P. "Toward Defining the Functions of Television." In E. A. Robinson, G. A. Comstock, and J. P. Murray (Eds.) *Television and Social Behavior,* Vol. 4: *Television in Day-to-day Life: Patterns of Use.* Washington, D.C.: U.S. Government Printing Office, 1972, pp. 568–603.
69. Robinson, J. P. and P. E. Converse. "The Impact of Television on Mass Media Usages: A Cross-national Comparison." In A. Szalai (Ed.) *The Use of Time: Daily Activities of Urban and Suburban Populations in Twelve Countries.* The Hague: Mouton and Co., 1972, pp. 197–212.
70. Rothschild, M. L. "The Effects of Political Advertising on the Voting Behavior of a Low Involvement Electorate." Doctoral dissertation, Stanford University, 1975.
71. Rubinstein, E. A., R. M. Liebert, J. M. Neale, and R. W. Poulos. *Assessing Television's Influence on Children's Prosocial Behavior.* Stony Brook, N.Y.: Brookdale International Institute, 1974. (Occasional paper 74–11.)
72. Schramm, W., J. Lyle, and E. B. Parker. *Television in the Lives of Our Children.* Stanford, Cal.: Stanford University Press, 1961.
73. Seggar, J. F. and P. Wheeler, "World of Work on TV: Ethnic and Sex Representation in TV Drama." *Journal of Broadcasting* 17, 1973, pp. 201–214.
74. Singer, J. L. "The Influence of Violence Portrayed in Television or Motion Pictures upon Overt Aggressive Behavior." In J. L. Singer (Ed.) *The Control of Aggression and Violence: Cognitive and Physiological Factors.* New York: Academic Press, 1971, pp. 19–60.
75. Surgeon General's Scientific Advisory Committee on Television and Social Behavior. *Television and Growing Up: The Impact of Televised Violence.* Report to the Surgeon General, United States Public Health Service. Washington, D.C.: U.S. Government Printing Office, 1972.
76. Szalai, A. (Ed.) *The Use of Time: Daily Activities of Urban and Suburban Populations in Twelve Countries.* The Hague: Mouton and Co., 1972.
77. Tannenbaum, P. H. "Studies in Film- and Television-mediated Arousal and Aggression: A Progress Report." In G. A. Comstock, E. A. Rubinstein, and J. P. Murray (Eds.) *Television and Social Behavior,* Vol. 5: *Television's Effects: Further Explorations.* Washington, D.C.: U.S. Government Printing Office, 1972, pp. 309–350.
78. Tannenbaum, P. H. and D. Zillmann. "Emotional Arousal in the Facilitation of Aggression Through Communication." In L. Berkowitz (Ed.) *Advances in Experimental Social Psychology,* Vol. 8. New York: Academic Press, 1975, pp. 149–192.
79. *Television Factbook 1976.* Washington, D.C.: Television Digest, 1976.
80. Tolley, H., Jr. *Children and War: Political Socialization to International Conflict.* New York: Teachers College Press, Columbia University, 1973.
81. Wand, B. "Television Viewing and Family Choice Differences." *Public Opinion Quarterly* 32, 1968, pp. 84–94.
82. Warner, M. "Organizational Context and Control of Policy in the Television Newsroom: A Participant Observation Study." *British Journal of Sociology* 22, 1971, pp. 283–294.

83. Weiss, W. "Effects of the Mass Media of Communication." In G. Lindzey and E. Aronson (Ed.) *The Handbook of Social Psychology,* Vol. 5: *Applied Social Psychology* (2nd ed.) Reading, Ma.: Addison-Wesley, 1969, pp. 77–195.
84. Zillmann, D. "Excitation Transfer in Communication-mediated Aggressive Behavior." *Journal of Experimental Social Psychology* 7, 1971, pp. 419–434.
85. Zillmann, D., R. C. Johnson, and J. Hanrahan. "Pacifying Effect of Happy Ending of Communications Involving Aggression." *Psychological Reports* 32, 1973, pp. 967–970.

5 A Mellow Appraisal of Media Monopoly Mania
Gerald C. Stone

One day this year the towering statue in the Jefferson Memorial shrinks magically to lifesize proportions and former U.S. President Thomas Jefferson walks through the colonial archways onto the well manicured lawns of the nation's Capitol grounds.

Each step of his short stroll causes him to pause with amazement as he encounters new marvels: the tourists with their Instamatics; the passing taxicabs; women in shorts and halter tops; the shiny, white-marbled buildings of the Capitol complex itself.

"How long has it been?" he wonders. "Only about 150 years. Why, in my day we still wore the same styles of clothes our great-grandparents wore. Where are the horses?"

On a park bench he finds a discarded issue of the Washington *Post.* "What manner of picture book is this?" he puzzles.

Emboldened, he halts a passing ice cream vendor. "Sir," he inquires, "what news of the Continent?"

But his words are drowned by a thunderous roar in the sky, and Thomas Jefferson stands immobile, gaping at a Concorde en route from Dulles Airport.

Yes, even a man of uncommon vision would be awed by the progress he might see between the first quarter of the 19th century and the last quarter of the 20th. And consider that this Thomas Jefferson hasn't yet heard about space exploration, or had a chance to watch television.

The scenario serves a purpose if only to tweek the noses of those who lament how deplorable Thomas Jefferson would find this or that American institution if he were alive today with a tally sheet. It's probable Jefferson would be too busy jotting notes to keep score.

Since he is here, let's ask him about the present-day problem of the concentration of mass media in the hands of a few industrial giants: the media monopoly issue.

Gerald C. Stone is chairman, Department of Journalism, Memphis State University, and Editor of *Newspaper Research Journal.* He has conducted several studies dealing with the newspaper field. His article was written especially for this edition of *Readings in Mass Communication.*

"What do you think, Mr. Jefferson," we might ask, "about the majority of the nation's 1,765 daily newspapers being held by only some 170 chain owners?"

Jefferson pauses to consider the figures and responds, "In my day, the few daily newspapers we had were owned by only two political parties—the one in power and the one seeking power."

"But," we insist, "what do you think of the country's information media being owned by a couple dozen huge industrial conglomerates? Why, one even makes ladies stockings!"

Jefferson doesn't bother to pause. "Would you be more comfortable being told of the day's events through the eyes of several businesses or through the eyes of a single government?"

Now it's our turn to reflect.

Although we might like the businesses better, neither choice seems pleasant. Admittedly, we've reached the meat of the issue, but fortunately we really aren't being forced to make a choice between having our image of reality shaped by either government or big business. American media don't face imminent threat of government regulation of subject matter, but there is a move underway from both media critics and government to limit the concentration of media ownership. In light of our First Amendment guarantee that government shall make no law abridging the freedom of the press, why have we arrived at this crossroad about media monopoly? To deal with that question, we must trace two intertwined philosophies on which this country has operated for 200 years: the libertarian press theory, and capitalism.

Briefly, the media are supposed to be independent, singly-held enterprises whose editorial policy is established by the owner. Assuming that all owners will hold differing ideas on the important issues of the day, each should have total freedom of expression regarding editorial (nonadvertising) content. An educated and concerned public will then select the media voices it chooses to hear and, in the long run, will be able to discern the truth in a free marketplace of conflicting ideas. The theory does not prohibit two or more like-thinking owners from merging their enterprises to produce a single voice. The trouble comes, however, when the marketplace of ideas is reduced to only one booming voice. In the classic libertarian view, such dominance is prevented by relying on economics: if the public ceases to attend to a particular publication, it loses its audience. The only other explanation for single dominance is offered by the American philosophy of capitalism.

Very simply put, capitalism relies on the superiority of a product in a free market unfettered by government regulation. It is almost a rephrasing of the libertarian press theory on a grandiose scale. By capitalism's tenets, if a product is superior or is marketed in a superior manner, it will succeed while its competitors fail. The difficulty arises when there is anything other than a free marketplace. When this happens, the government is forced to intercede to prevent a closed market.

Ignoring the present-day inconsistencies in both of these traditional American philosophies, we can look at where they have led the nation's media today with respect to usurpation of governmental power and the electoral process; media content that affects public policy, social issues, or corporate finances; and, lastly, the concentration of ownership and the "evil" national media plot to put all ideas under the huge umbrella of U.S. Media, Inc.

Usurpation of Government Power and Elections

No one today doubts that media are more politically influential than ever before in history. Even if they can't tell us what to think (and research shows that their persuasive powers are limited), they do set our agendas of what is important or current. This ability to arrange our frame of reference is, so far as most government leaders are concerned, tantamount to control.

The late Walter Lippmann spoke of this power at a global level after World War I when he said the images in our heads of the hidden environment (he was writing about the countries of Europe) are provided us by the mass media. With the rapid pace of modern society and the need for instant communication, the hidden environment is anything that occurs outside the place we have been today—and we must rely on the mass media to show-tell us what important events occurred. This information lag is greatly narrowed by the mass communication media, and their ability to deliver information makes the messenger seem more powerful than a king.

But are the media really more powerful than the government? Can they make law or determine the outcome of an election? Today they can do neither; which is surprising, because as recently as 50 years ago—when the majority of media were individually owned—they could usually do both. In the murky past of most daily newspapers was a time when their owners virtually controlled local government. Readers clipped editorial pages and actually took them into the voting booth on election day. There was a time when *Nation, Newsweek, Time, Life, Saturday Evening Post,* and a number of other respected magazines were purchased partly for their editorial pages, which charted a political course and had earned a following among the opinion leaders across the country. These times—as with many of the big magazines themselves—are past.

Television today may be considered the prime political socializer. The medium does possess almost the same agenda-setting capacity of daily newspapers. But television is a poor medium for raising the public's consciousness on difficult-to-explain topics, including energy, inflation, taxes, education—almost anything that really matters. Between the Federal Communication Commission's equal time rule for elections and the fairness doctrine for social issues, the broadcast media really have little power to determine outcomes.

Even Watergate—which has been hailed as explicit proof that the media control government—falls far short of an example that the media control either public policy or elections. It took two full years from the discovery of the Watergate break-in to the Nixon resignation; one full year from when the media coalesced on the issue until it was resolved. This surely is an example of long-term agenda-setting rather than of "control" in any sense of the word.

If we view the media as communication conduits between events and the public, rather than independent and action-initiating institutions, we may deal with the question of usurpation. We may remember what happened in Jefferson's time when an important trial was scheduled in Philadelphia: the folks who wanted to see it just went over to the courthouse. Compare that simplicity with the crowds that waited in line two days prior to the Patty Hearst trial in San Francisco. Had it not been for the mass communications media, our knowledge of the Hearst trial would have been only by word of mouth or official proclamation. As society has developed, the mass media have evolved into their present position, not of authority, but as the major transmission lines for public interest issues.

Even if the media are only conduits, they both wittingly and unwittingly have an impact on the American audience. Whether their intention is direct, through editorials and through advertising, or indirect, by their decisions of what constitutes news on a given day or over a period of time, most agree that the media influence public policy, social issues, and the flow of corporate goods and services. For the sake of expediency, we may concede that the media do succeed—over time—in altering the course of society, but we should question whether they are more successful today than in the past.

Effects of Media Content

There was a time in our history when the First Amendment freedom of the press was regarded as sacrosanct. The mass media have been credited with such social developments as labor unions, public education, and social security. The examples of newspapers and magazines exposing corruption in the judicial system, political regimes, and law enforcement are too numerous to cite. Much of this success was dependent on the belief that a strong and free press, acting as a watchdog on the excesses of those holding power, was precisely what the framers of the Constitution had in mind. But there are also hundreds of instances of media managers having used their publications for ideological or even corporate gains.

The ideological uses are primarily in the realm of politics. Media owners have consistently supported their cronies for office and have even used their outlets to seek political office themselves. But if these are abuses today, they've been abuses since the First Amendment was passed—and it was passed to insure that the media would have a free hand in supporting favored political candidates and issues. Since the beginning, newspaper publishers have denied space to personally disagreeable ideas and to those supporting such ideas, while insuring that their favorites received good coverage, prominent advertising space, and editorial endorsements. Newspaper space is one of the last strongholds where media owners are still afforded their First Amendment rights.

The same is true for corporate gains. Rarely does a story appear about the lawsuit resulting from a shopper's slipping on a banana peel left on the floor of a supermarket, or a case resulting from an elevator crash in a major department store. Not until the very recent consumer movement have the media begun to adversely cover products that might be advertised.

On a macro scale, the mass media almost categorically ignore news that might adversely affect their businesses, but they give inappropriate attention to those events which might help their businesses. Exceptions do occur, but most media owners promote legislation that will result in higher profits for them, and have always done so. The First Amendment was designed to guarantee their right to do this by giving them total discretion over the content of their publications.

Today, however, through statute and ordinance, a significant portion of the freedom media owners had been granted has slipped away. No longer do the mass media have absolute control over their advertising: the Federal Trade Commission intercedes in a host of actual and potential excesses by both the broadcast and print media. Censorship laws, which fluctuate, have recently taken a turn toward tighter control. And in both these instances the public may applaud the content limitations as necessary and timely restraints. Certainly there has been wide public acclaim for the recent attempts to restrain sex and violence on television.

Changes have come about precisely because of the concentration in media ownership and the subsequent decrease in the number of media voices available. Dozens of court cases and agency regulations have tightened the screws on what may be broadcast or printed, using "lack of competition" as a rationale for overriding the First Amendment.

Some efforts have resulted in limiting media content because of the lack of competition. (1) The *equal time* rule was designed to give balance in the air time political candidates receive. It has approached that goal but also has resulted in much less media exposure for all political candidates. (2) The *fairness doctrine* was designed to keep both sides of social issues before the public. It has forced some gains in this area, but it also has resulted in less willingness by broadcasters to air any social commentary. (3) *Family viewing time* was designed to push the more adult television fare to later viewing hours. It has put the more violent shows in post-9 P.M. slots but has left the earlier evening viewing more mindless than ever and has exchanged the more explicit violence for sexual innuendo, which had never before been part of TV's usual sitcom fare. (4) *Limitation of network offerings* in the early evenings was designed to encourage local stations to produce public affairs programming. It has made some inroads in this direction, but has done more to promote game shows, "I Love Lucy" reruns, and locally produced "Bowling for Dollars." These examples deal only with the broadcast media, but the concentration of ownership in the print media may also lead to content limitations for them.

Consider the following:

In 1977 the manager of Pantax Corporation sent two stories to his editors of a string of small daily newspapers. Reportedly, he instructed that both stories (one suggesting that President Carter condoned free love by his White House staff, the other alleging that Rosalynn Carter was being groomed to replace Walter Mondale as vice president) be published on page one of his newspapers. Only one editor refused to follow the instructions, and he no longer works for Pantax.

Although such orders from above are rare by media barons today, the public outrage over this kind of content manipulation might make the next instance grounds for laws prohibiting such excesses in all of the nation's print media.

The figures don't lie. There has been a steadily accelerating trend since 1910 toward concentration of ownership among U.S. media. The number of newspaper chains had proliferated until the 1970s, then ebbed only because the larger chains were gobbling up the smaller chains. Today's figures show that 170 chains own 1,277 newspapers, accounting for about 32 million in total circulation. Chains own 62 percent of all dailies and control more than 53 percent of total daily circulation. In radio, more than 375 firms own two or more AM stations, and 32 percent of all AM stations fall in this category. Some 415 television stations are in groups, and 58 percent of all TV stations are in combination ownership even though the FCC has a seven-station limit per owner.

Concentration and the Evil "U.S. Media, Inc."

There is no doubt, then, that the mass media are becoming concentrated in the hands of fewer and fewer owners. The recent history of the entire field shows that this concentration is a continuing and accelerating phenomenon. No one who values freedom according to its definition in America can view these figures without some degree of concern and probably a great deal of alarm. The trend seems fixed and the result predictable under the present systems that promote media concentration.

But it is necessary to keep our perspective about the matter and avoid the pitfall of viewing media concentration as some evil plot on a huge scale: a premeditated attempt by a few media barons to control the national means of communication. Evidence leads to the conclusion that media concentration is not necessarily linked with control of editorial content. Many of the larger chains insist on local control of the content of their media while centralizing the management and record-keeping end of their properties. As a holding company uses resources from a centrally located pool, the media baron can use leverage provided by the size of his enterprise to create efficiencies that need not impinge on the public's information flow. The baron can use a central computer for payroll and corporate record-keeping; can purchase a paper mill to assure a cheap source of supply for all his newspapers; can secure syndicated materials for all his outlets; can move personnel from one publication to another or even from print to broadcast media; can sponsor a reporter or editor retraining workshop for all such employees; can divert funds from a secure television station to help bolster a troubled newspaper; or can lease satellite transmissions to provide faster news flow to all his outlets. None of these efficiencies should cause public concern.

On the other hand, a host of efficiencies also exist that would anger the public, such as the Pantax example; or folding one paper to reduce competition for a more profitable paper nearby; or sharing editorials between newspapers and broadcast stations in the same local market; or contracting for only liberal or conservative columnists and commentators; or doubling advertising rates as soon as monopoly control of a market area is gained. In all, though, even the excesses have tended to be purely monetary, and there have been many instances of increased service to the public derived primarily from the media baron's streamlining of an existing journalistic disaster.

There seems to be no evidence of a power grab in all of this ownership concentration; no political, social, or ideological motive that compels a media owner to add to his empire as there was in the days of Hearst, Pulitzer, and Scripps. The only advantage is greater profit, and the only driving force is greed, flamed by existing laws which make media concentration inevitable. Still, the motive makes little difference if the end is that one or a few media barons are able to control the country's mass media. Also, today's lust for profit might easily shift to a craving for power once the concentration is complete. But if we recognize the current practices as reflecting capitalistic enterprise we can evaluate the situation through calm logic rather than irrational panic. And that seems the proper place to begin an analysis of exactly what has caused the concentration predicament and what may be done—without seriously thwarting the First Amendment guarantees—to either check or reverse it.

Some Classic Recommendations

Since the problem of media concentration has been festering for more than twenty years, it is not surprising that several suggestions have already been offered on how to halt the trend. We may look at a few of the more prominent and consider their merit.

1. Phil Jacklin, a California philosophy professor and chairman of the Committee for Open Media of Santa Clara Valley, American Civil Liberties Union, has suggested a media access rule he calls "tithing," like the practice of giving ten percent of one's income to a church annually. Jacklin recommends that the media be forced (or, preferably, should volunteer) to give ten percent of their space or time—their content—to public issue representatives. Rather than limiting media concentration by interfering with private ownership in the capitalistic system, tithing can preserve the public's access to communication by setting aside a tenth part of the available space in all media for discussion or presentation of ideas. The media would not choose the format and spokespersons; instead, they would offer up a tenth share of their content with no strings attached. This would guarantee an open forum for controversial opinions or views from people not normally included in our highly concentrated media. [Ed.: See article 8 by Jacklin for his views.]

   The suggestion has some philosophical merit, provided that the media would not be forced to give up a tenth of their space or time, which would obviously be an infringement of the First Amendment. If voluntary, such a practice might preserve enough space for the free flow of ideas, thereby skirting the main argument against concentration of media ownership. But beyond the difficulty of assuring that this noble gesture is made without force, there could be a morass of sticky prob-

Is being smallest bad?

Not necessarily.

Just as being the biggest is not necessarily bad, either.

The *Little Falls Daily Transcript*, "serving the heart of Minnesota since 1892," is proving both points these days.

The *Daily Transcript's* 3,802 reader families make it the smallest member of the Gannett Group, which is the biggest numerically and geographically in the United States with 78* dailies in 30 states and two U.S. territories.

Since joining Gannett, *Daily Transcript* news staffers have had a new opportunity—the opportunity to make their newspaper an even more important part of the daily life in Little Falls.

The news staffers listened to the people of Little Falls, tapped the resources of Gannett and went to work putting more Little Falls in the *Daily Transcript*.

More local news made headlines. More local photographs on Page One. More social news from local readers instead of syndicated columns from someplace else.

The *Daily Transcript* also had the resources of Gannett, resources it didn't have before. Gannett News Service coverage from Washington and across the country. Recruiting and training activities. An idea exchange with newspaper professionals at 77 other newspapers. New photo equipment. And the marketing and technical expertise of one of America's most successful businesses.

By becoming part of Gannett, the *Little Falls Daily Transcript* did not become big, just better. That is because Gannett has gotten big by doing the little things well. At Gannett, the size of the newspaper is not what counts. Nor the size of its ownership. Only the size of its commitment to its readers.

Gannett demonstrates this commitment daily in distinctive local newspapers from Little Falls, Minn., to Honolulu, Hawaii, from Burlington, Vt., to Boise, Idaho, from Fort Myers, Fla., to Fort Collins, Colo., from Reno, Nev., to Rochester, N.Y., and from the Virgin Islands in the Atlantic to Guam in the Pacific.

Since Gannett went public in 1967, its commitment has produced gains for readers, advertisers, employees and shareholders: 44 consecutive quarters of comparative earnings gains; annual revenues up from $184 million to more than a half billion; annual earnings per share up from 58 cents to $2.60; dividends up from 22 cents to $1.40; more than 2,500 professional awards.

In Gannett's case, the smallest and the biggest come together to make better newspapers.

To learn more about the exciting rewards and responsibilities of America's newspapers, write for a free copy of "Newspapers: Your Freedom Wrapper," care of Director of Information, Dept. WS Gannett Co., Inc., Rochester, New York 14604.

*Gannett has announced an agreement to merge with Combined Communications Corporation, a Phoenix-based diversified media company with seven television stations, 13 radio stations, two newspapers and outdoor advertising facilities in 11 U.S. states and in major Canadian cities.

lems in implementing the tithe concept. Who would insure that the space or time would be prominent enough for good public dissemination? Wouldn't the broadcast media continue their present practice of public service messages at 2 A.M. and merely expand around this time frame to achieve the tenth share? Might we expect the print media to bury its tenth somewhere in the classifieds or a specially stapled insert in magazines? And this problem is small compared with the question of who is to decide which spokespersons will be allowed to participate and in what format. How will the libel laws be changed in the tithe zone? Who will edit the copy or the video tape, for if the content isn't presented in a professional manner, what audience will attend to it?

We may accept the philosophical portion of the solution that Jacklin is offering but must reject the idea of tithing on the grounds of its total impracticality.

2. Media critic Ben Bagdikian has written extensively on the media monopoly situation and has offered a number of suggestions to impede the concentration of media ownership. Two points may be evaluated here, and a third will be dealt with shortly.

Bagdikian suggests that each paper using the second-class mailing privilege of the U.S. Post Office be required to file at the local post office a listing of holders of the paper. Further, the list should contain the percentage of ownership held by each along with all their other significant financial holdings. This is the same disclosure requirement made of publicly held corporations by the Securities Exchange Commission. The idea, according to the author, is to let local citizens know who controls their monopoly media and what the related financial interests of the owners might be.

The suggestion is at best a stop-gap measure. It will not be a major impediment to any media baron intent on acquiring another holding. At worst, the suggestion enters the realm of further government regulation and does so in a way that should cause some legitimate concern to press freedom. Why should the privately held media be forced to disclose ownership when this regulation is not applied to any other nonpublic corporation? Bagdikian counters that media provide information, and that makes them different from other businesses. Granted. But we should still be skeptical of any government regulation that addresses itself only to media. And in this case the potential effectiveness of this measure is so limited that the precedent which might be set doesn't seem worth the little good that might be gained.

Bagdikian's second suggestion—and the one which has caused great debate in the profession—is that the news staff elect editors, get a representative delegate on the corporate board of directors, and have access to the committee that allocates the annual news budget, all with the consent of the media owner. He points to *LeMonde*, a quality

European paper, as proof that staff-elected editors don't lead to mediocre newspapers.

This highly controversial Bagdikian suggestion for news staff autonomy includes pitfalls the author foresees also, including newsroom politicking and the possibility newsroom democracy will bring no public benefits. There are real problems with this tactic that make both editors and reporters uneasy about newsroom decision-making under an election procedure, about professionalism, and about formalizing an adversary relationship between news people and management. There has been no clamor to jump on the newsroom election bandwagon. Further, should the public entrust its mass communication to a handful of media barons and be satisfied that its best interest is being preserved because the editorial staff has input to management of the newsroom? This doesn't seem a satisfactory guarantee.

But, more importantly, the same criticism can be made of staff control as was made of the tithing principle: both require the media owner's consent therefore are equally likely to come about; neither will occur.

3. Kevin Phillips, lawyer, publisher, author, and syndicated columnist, sees the solution in straightforward legal steps. He makes a case in *Harper's* (July 1977) for speedy government intervention into media ownership concentration via the antitrust laws. (Actually, Phillips suggests a dozen other possible government interventions so contrary to the First Amendment that the reader almost breathes a sigh of relief when the antitrust action is finally offered as an easy out.) Phillips is not too concerned with how the government might break up media conglomerates. The move might begin with regulations against owning more than one type of medium in the same town; being allowed only one medium outlet in a locality; putting a ceiling on the total number of media outlets that can be owned anywhere by one corporation; allowing media ownership only by those who already own media (hence divorcing the stocking and toy magnates from their coupling with the nation's media); or any other divestiture the Justice Department sees fit to require.

Of course, this plan of action is the very thing the media must be shielded against, at least if past experience is any teacher. The majority of antitrust-type actions against the media have taken the form of retribution by government for indiscretions of specific content or continued antagonism; they have not been applied broadly or impartially. Still, any antitrust action on a national plane and designed only to decrease the concentration of media ownership would set a dangerous precedent and would certainly result in interference in media content and the flow of information as it has evolved to date.

The Phillips suggestion may be the plan of choice—the one the government decides to use—but it seems unnecessarily drastic. Other measures would be almost as effective as antitrust legislation and much less government-intrusive.

4. The final method suggested for limiting the concentration of media ownership approaches the problem almost entirely from a tax standpoint. Bagdikian mentions the Internal Revenue Code's promotion of conglomerates by allowing a media owner to set aside profits made on one enterprise if these funds will be used to purchase related enterprises. The benefits of the law are immense. Instead of paying corporate taxes on the profit, the media owner could purchase a paper mill to supply his newspaper's printing stock at a low price; a fleet of trucks; an electronic manufacturing firm to build typesetters for his paper; related media such as a chain of weekly newspapers or radio and television stations (although with local monopoly limitations). The owner could also create a feature syndicate; begin a cable television operation; buy a book or magazine publishing business. In all, the media baron could increase his holdings and the federal tax laws would act as the springboard.

The tax laws even encourage media concentration by allowing an owner to depreciate his new properties. Thus, the owner doesn't pay taxes on current profits that are reinvested and he gains a write-off against future profits by depreciating newly acquired businesses.

The interplay of these two tax incentives has been the primary cause of the present state of media concentration. Purchasing a new media outlet is worth more to a new buyer than keeping the property is worth to the seller.

Finally, a compounding tax consideration is the law which requires those who are left property to pay inheritance taxes within six months of the time the property coming into their possession is appraised (either at the time of death or one year later). It works this way. The family of a publisher receives a $10 million daily newspaper and must pay an inheritance tax on the full appraised value of the property. To raise the capital to pay the tax may require either selling off portions of the property, mortgaging it, or some other drastic measure to raise cash quickly. Any step taken will cause the property to be dangerously strapped for operating capital after the taxes are paid. Faced with the choice of possibly putting the paper into bankruptcy or accepting an offer from a media baron of $15 million for the property, only a very confident inheritor would gamble against the future earnings of the paper. The roster of small dailies now held by chains indicates that most inheritors take the cash, pay their taxes, and live comfortably on the remaining millions.

Now it should be mentioned that each of these tax considerations applies equally to all other businesses, and each has contributed its share to the growth of America's huge industrial conglomerates.

Congressman Morris Udall (D-Ariz.), an activist in the effort to curb media monopoly, has proposed legislation to unknot the tax tangle that has so well promoted the interests of media barons at the expense of individually owned media outlets. Of course, Udall has also proposed that a commission be established to examine ways to break up the media conglomerates by using antitrust legislation.

At this time, with so much of the damage already done, it is doubtful a solution exists that will *reverse* the media concentration trend without abridging the First Amendment (at least to those who accept the First Amendment literally). Nothing short of government intervention will reduce the present state of monopoly control of the nation's media.

Is There a Solution That Preserves Press Freedom?

The question then becomes: Is it worthwhile merely to halt the concentration of ownership, on the assumption that it can be accomplished without direct government intervention? Yes. All but the most dedicated capitalist should agree that media concentration has gone far enough; that halting its continued spread is a necessity. Granted that keeping media monopoly at its present state is at least a worthwhile starting point, it should be clear that the series of suggestions offered in point 4 above is the most efficient approach. We should look to the tax laws—the primary cause of the problem—for the solution.

One specific suggestion has been made in the tax law area: extend the inheritance payment over a period of up to fifteen years. Although suggested as a special dispensation to the media, offered in the spirit of halting ownership concentration, it is a concession that could also be applied to all other inheritance situations without seriously affecting the long-term tax proceeds collected by the federal government. Alteration in the other two areas—depreciating new properties and investing profits in related businesses—would cause havoc in American industry.

If we make the argument that no government legislation should be aimed specifically at the mass media (which isn't also applied to the rest of the nation's businesses), then we assure the continued concentration of media ownership. If we agree that certain government regulations must be applied only to the nation's media, then we might as well shrug our shoulders and opt for the *reduction* of media ownership concentration via antitrust legislation.

The matter resolves itself to a damned-if-we-do, damned-if-we-don't proposition that leads to a compromise of principles for a very practical reason: the alternative to compromise is the application of antitrust laws aimed specifically at the mass media industry. Therefore, although it is difficult for First Amendment absolutists to accept, the compromise must be the fifteen-year inheritance proposal, to apply to all U.S. businesses, and changes in the two other tax provisions, to apply only to the mass media industry. Perhaps the guidelines should be on the order of the following three suggestions.

1. Limit the application of incentives to invest profits in related businesses by prohibiting purchase of other media outlets. This rule would preserve the media owner's right to buy a paper mill or trucking fleet but would discourage attempts to purchase another paper, broadcast station, book publishing firm, or magazine. The rule would not forbid the practice, it would only make it less lucrative.

2. Alter the depreciation rule applied to new media purchases by those already owning media. A graduated plan might serve the purpose by accelerating the percentage of depreciation that could be taken in succeeding years (as is generally the case today), but a ceiling would be placed on the first five or ten years of ownership which could be raised in later years. This change would make a new media outlet a less attractive immediate investment for current media owners than it now is. Again, the rule would not make new media purchases impossible, just less profitable on a short-term basis. In tandem, the two measures would make the continued concentration of media ownership much less likely than under the present system.

3. Offer some type of tax savings incentive to present media barons who decide to divest themselves of a media outlet. It might be in the form of an outright tax write-off or other tax savings bonus. This third alteration could produce *reduction* in media ownership concentration by incentive rather than mandate.

In all, the measures seek to prevent future media ownership concentration through the same channels which have been responsible for the present monopoly situation. They are not restrictive rules but simple economic incentive plans which should result in a reversal of today's media ownership trends. If the philosophy is acceptable, the details can be easily and practicably established. This is a rather straightforward, workable plan.

Are the measures satisfactory? Not really, because they do apply government regulations specifically to the media, regulations which are not being applied in an across-the-board manner to nonmedia businesses. This unsavory aspect is mitigated somewhat by the voluntary decisions left to media owners and by the purely economic approach to the media conglomerate situation. If the suggested solution is not totally satisfactory, it is a practical approach to achieving the desired end.

What would Jefferson say about this abridgment of the First Amendment press freedom?

Well, Jefferson understood business and taxes as they existed in his society. Although he might be somewhat concerned about the present media ownership situation, he would certainly be more alarmed at the antitrust legislation the government has been proposing to curb it. He would surely be appalled at the way the federal government has grown to dominate all other institutions with its centralized powers, and he might not wish the same problems on the nation's mass media.

After all, from his banks-of-the-Potomac Memorial, Jefferson keeps a watchful eye on the nation's capitol, not on the Washington *Post*.

Times Mirror Company

1977 Fortune 500 rank: 219
1977 total sales: $1.14 billion

Principal Operations

Newspapers (6): *Los Angeles Times; Newsday, Dallas Times Herald* (Tex.); *Orange Coast Daily Pilot* (Costa Mesa, Calif.); *Advocate* (Stamford, Conn.); *Time* (Greenwich, Conn.). L.A. Times-Washington Post News Service (joint).

Magazine and Book Publishing: New American Library; Signet, Signet Classics, Mentor, Meridian paperbacks; Abrams art books; Matthew Bender law books; Year Book medical books; C.V. Mosby medical, dental, and nursing books and journals; *Outdoor Life; Popular Science; Golf; Ski; The Sporting News; Ski Business; How to; The Sporting Goods Dealer.*

Television: KDFW-TV, Dallas, Tex.; KTBC-TV, Austin, Tex.; WSYR-TV, Syracuse, N.Y.; WYSE-TV, Elmira, N.Y.; WAPI-TV, Birmingham, Ala.; WTPA-TV, Harrisburg, Pa.; KTVI-TV, St. Louis, Mo. Also owns CATV systems.

Other: Owns two newsprint mills, 10 wood products mills, and 329,000 acres of timberland; information services; cable communications; directory printing; Graphic Controls Corp.

Gannett

1977 Fortune 500 rank: 368
1978 total sales: $672.5 million (estimate)

Principal Operations

Newspapers (78): *Pacific Daily News* (Agana, Guam); *Sunday News, Enquirer and News* (Battle Creek, Mich.); *Bellingham Herald, Sunday Herald* (Bellingham, Wash.); *Evening Press, Sun-Bulletin, Sunday Press* (Binghamton, N.Y.); *Burlington Free Press* (Burlington, Vt.); *Courier-Post* (Camden, N.J.); *Public Opinion* (Chambersburg, Pa.); *Gazette* (Chillicothe, O.); *"Today"* (Cocoa, Fla.); *Commercial-News* (Danville, Ill.); *Star-Gazette, Sunday Telegram* (Elmira, N.Y.); *El Paso Times* (El Paso, Tex.); *Fort Myers News Press* (Fort Myers, Fla.); *Tribune* (Freemont, Neb.); *News-Messenger* (Fremont, O.); *Coloradoan* (Fort Collins, Colo.); *Honolulu Star-Bulletin, Star-Bulletin & Advertiser* (Honolulu, Hawaii); *Herald Dispatch, Huntington Advertiser, Herald Advertiser* (Huntington, W. Va.); *Press-Citizen* (Iowa City, Iowa); *Ithaca Journal* (Ithaca, N.Y.); *Journal and Courier* (Lafayette, Ind.); *State Journal* (Lansing, Mich.); *Daily Transcript* (Little Falls, Minn.); *Times* (Mamaroneck, N.Y.); *Marietta Times* (Marietta, O.); *Chronicle Tribune* (Marion, Ind.); *News-Star, World* (Monroe, La.); *Argus* (Mount Vernon, N.Y.); *Phoenix & Times Democrat* (Muskogee, Okla.); *Nashville Banner* (Nashville, Tenn.); *Valley News Dispatch* (New Kensington-Tarentum, Pa.); *Standard-Star* (New Rochelle, N.Y.); *Niagara Gazette* (Niagara Falls, N.Y.); *Journal-News* (Nyack, Rockland, N.Y.); *Daily Olympian, Herald* (Olympia, Wash.); *Citizen Register* (Ossining, N.Y.); *Pensacola Journal, Pensacola News, Pensacola News-Journal* (Pensacola, Fla.); *News-Herald* (Port Clinton, O.); *Times Herald* (Port Huron, Mich.); *Daily Item* (Port Chester, N.Y.); *Journal* (Poughkeepsie, N.Y.); *Evening Gazette, State Journal* (Reno, Nev.); *Palladium-Item* (Richmond, Ind.); *Times-Union, Democrat & Chronicle* (Rochester, N.Y.); *Morning Star, Register-Republic* (Rockford, Ill.); *Capital Journal, Oregon Statesman* (Salem, Ore.); *Californian* (Salinas, Calif.); *Sun-Telegram* (San Bernardino, Calif.); *New Mexican* (Santa Fe, N.M.); *Times* (Shreveport, La.); *Argus-Leader* (Sioux Falls, S.D.); *Leader & Press, News, Sunday News & Leader* (Springfield, Mo.); *Daily Times* (St. Cloud, Minn.); *Record* (Stockton, Calif.); *Daily News* (Tarrytown, N.Y.); *Daily Citizen* (Tucson, Ariz.); *Observer Dispatch, Press* (Utica, N.Y.); *Times-Delta* (Visalia, Calif.); *Reporter-Dispatch* (White Plains, N.Y.); *News-Journal* (Wilmington, Del.); *Herald-Statesman* (Yonkers, N.Y.); *Review Press-Reporter* (Bronxville, N.Y.); *Suburban Newspaper Group* (10 weeklies) (Cherry Hill, N.J.); *Fairpress* (Fairfield, Conn.); *Times* (Melbourne, Fla.); *Butler County News,*

(Felienople, Pa.); *North Hills News Record* (Pittsburgh, Pa.); *Commercial News* (Saratoga Springs, N.Y.); *Taos News* (Taos, N.M.); *Star Advocate* (Titusville, Fla.).

Broadcasting: WBRJ (radio; Marietta, Ohio); WHEC-TV (Rochester, N.Y.); WKFI (radio; Wilmington, Ohio).

Other:Louis Harris & Associates and Louis Harris International.

Pending: Gannett has agreed to merge with Combined Communications Corp. subject to FCC and tax rulings. CCC owns newspapers, including the *Cincinnati Enquirer* and the *Oakland Tribune* (Oakland, Calif.), 7 television stations, 12 radio stations, a television commercial and documentary film-production system, outdoor advertising systems, and a supermarket merchandising system.

Time, Inc.

1977 Fortune 500 rank: 198
1978 total sales: $1.6 billion (estimate)

Principal Operations

Publishing: *Time, Fortune, Sports Illustrated, Money,* and *People* magazines (35% of total sales); Time-Life Books; Little, Brown & Co.; Book-of-the-Month Club; New York Graphic Society (Alva Museum Replicas); minority interests in publishers in Germany, France, Spain, Mexico, and Japan.

Films and Broadcasting: Time-Life Films; TV production and distribution, multimedia, TV books; Home Box Office; Manhattan Cable TV; American Television & Communications; WOTV (Grand Rapids, Mich.).

Newspapers: *Pioneer Press,* Inc., 17 weekly newspapers in suburban Chicago.

Selling Areas-Marketing, Inc. (distributing marketing information).

Printing Developments, Inc. (printing equipment).

Other: Temple-Eastex, Inc. (pulp and paperboard, packaging, building materials, timberland); Inland Container; AFCO Industries, Inc. (interior wall products); Woodward, Inc. (bedroom furniture); Lumberman's Investment Corp.; Sabine Investment Co.

C B S

1977 Fortune 500 rank: 91
1978 total sales; $3.25 billion (estimate)

Principal Operations

Broadcasting: owns five TV stations (New York, Los Angeles, Philadelphia, Chicago, St. Louis); seven AM radio stations and seven FM radio stations (42% of total sales); has Canadian CATV investments.

Records: Columbia, Epic, and Portrait labels (27% of total); Columbia Group record and tapes club, musical instruments (e.g., Steinway pianos, Leslie speakers, Rogers drums and organs); 67 Pacific Stereo retail stores; Creative Playthings (toys); Gabriel Industries (toys); Wonder Products (toys) (16% of total).

Publishing: Holt, Rinehart & Winston; Fawcett Publications (mass-market paperback); Popular Library (mass-market paperback); W.B. Saunders (professional book publisher); NEISA (Latin American and Spanish books) (14% of total).

Magazines: *Field and Stream; Road and Track; Cycle World; World Tennis; Sea; PV4; Popular Gardening Indoors; Astrology Your Daily Horoscope; Astrology Today; Your Prophecy; Psychic World; Popular Crosswords; Popular Word Games; Special Crossword Book of the Month; New Crosswords; Giant Word Games; The National Observer Book of Crosswords; Popular Sports: Baseball; Popular Sports: Grand Slam; Popular Sports: Kick-Off; Popular Sports: Touchdown; Popular Sports: Basketball; Mechanix Illustrated; Woman's Day.*

Knight-Ridder

1977 Fortune 500 rank: 293
1977 total sales: 751.7 million

Principal Operations

Newspapers (34): *Aberdeen American News* (N.D.); *Akron Beacon Journal* (Ohio); *Boca Raton News* (La.); *Boulder Daily Camera* (Colo.); *Bradenton Herald* (Fla.); *Charlotte Observer* (N.C.); *Charlotte News* (N.C.); *Columbus Enquirer, Ledger* (Ga.); *Detroit Free Press* (Mich.); *Duluth News-Tribune, Herald* (Minn.); *Gary Post-Tribune* (Ind.); *Grand Forks Herald* (N.D.); *Journal of Commerce* (N.Y.C.); *Lexington Herald, Leader* (Ky.); *Long Beach Independent, Press-Telegram* (Calif.); *Macon Telegraph, News* (Ga.); *Miami Herald* (Fla.); *Pasadena Star-News* (Calif.); *Philadelphia Inquirer, Daily News* (Pa.); *St. Paul Pioneer Press, Dispatch* (Minn.); *San Jose Mercury, News* (Calif.); *Seattle Times* (Wash.); *Tallahassee Democrat* (Fla.); *Walla Walla Union-Bulletin* (Wash.); *Wichita Eagle, Beacon* (Kan.); *Arcadia*

Tribune (Calif.); *Temple City Times* (Calif.); *Monrovia Journal* (Calif.); *Duartean* (Calif.); *Buena Park News* (Calif.); *La Mirada Lamplighter* (Calif.); *Huntington Beach Independent* (Calif.); *Anaheim-Fullerton Independent* (Calif.); *Orange County Evening News* (Calif.); *Broward Times* (Fla.); *Coral Gables Times and Guide* (Fla.); *Florida Keys Keynoter* (Fla.); *North Dade Journal* (Fla.); *Union Recorder* (Ga.).

Television: Poole Broadcasting Co.: WPRI-TV (Providence, R.I.), WJRT-TV (Flint, Mich.), WTEN-TV (Albany, N.Y.), WCDC-TV (Adams, Mass.).

Other: Commercial Terminals of Detroit, Inc. (Mich.); Commodity News Services, Inc. (Kansas City, Mo.); Knight-Ridder Newspaper Sales, Inc. (New York); Knight News Services, Inc. (Detroit, Mich.); The Observer Transportation Co. (Charlotte, N.C.); Portage Newspaper Supply Co. (Akron, O.); Twin Cities Newspaper Services, Inc. (St. Paul, Minn.).

The New York Times Company

1977 Fortune 500 rank: 385
1977 total sales: $511 million

Principal Operations

Newspapers (11 dailies): *New York Times* (N.Y.C.); *International Herald Tribune* (one-third owner) (Paris); *Gainesville Sun* (Fla.); *Lakeland Ledger* (Fla.); *Ocala Star Banner* (Fla.); *Leesburg Daily Commercial* (Fla.); *Palatka Daily News* (Fla.); *Lake City Reporter* (Fla.); *Fernandina Beach News-Leader* (Fla.); *Sebring News* (Fla.); *Avon Park Sun* (Fla.); *Marco Island Eagle* (Fla.); *Lexington Dispatch* (N.C.); *Hendersonville Times-News* (N.C.); *Wilmington Star-News* (N.C.).

Magazines: *Family Circle; Australian Family Circle; Golf Digest; Golf World; Tennis; Us.*

Broadcasting: WREG-TV (Memphis, Tenn.); WQXR-AM/FM (New York City); Educational video publishing systems.

Books: Quadrangle/NYT Book Co.; Arno Press, Inc.; Cambridge Book Co.

R C A

1977 Fortune 500 rank: 30
1978 total sales: $6.6 billion (estimate)

Principal Operations

Electronics: consumer products and services (25% of total sales); commercial products and services (13% of total).

Broadcasting (19% of total): NBC, which owns one TV station each in Chicago, Los Angeles, Cleveland, New York City, Washington, D.C., and one AM and one FM station in Chicago, New York, San Francisco, and Washington, D.C.

Publishing (5% of total): Random House; Alfred A. Knopf; Pantheon; Ballantine Books; Vintage; Modern Library.

Other (38% of total): Banquet Foods; Coronet (carpets); Oriel Foods (United Kingdom); vehicle renting and related services (e.g., Hertz); government business.

Gulf & Western

1977 Fortune 500 rank: 59
1978 total sales: $4.31 billion (estimate)

Principal Operations

Manufacturing (25% of total sales).

Leisure time: Paramount Pictures (motion picture production and distribution, TV exhibition and series production), which owns Oxford Films (distribution of nontheatrical films); Magicam, Inc. (rents camera systems); Future General Corp. (research, special effects services). Cinema International (49% interest), which owns four theaters in London, one in Amsterdam, two in Egypt, 17 in Brazil, 10 in other South American countries, 19 in South Africa.
Famous Players Ltd. (51% interest), which owns or operates about 300 theaters in Canada, one in Paris, and owns 50% of a French company operating 35 theaters in France.
Sega Enterprises, Inc. (coin-operated amusement games).
Madison Square Garden (sports), which owns Washington Diplomats soccer team (19% of total).

Publishing: Simon & Schuster, including Fireside and Touchstone paperbacks, and mass-market paperbacks from Pocket Books, Washington Square Press, Archway.

Other: natural resources (zinc and cement); apparel products (apparel, hosiery, shoes); paper and building products; auto replacement parts; financial services (consumer and commercial financing, life insurance, casualty insurance); consumer and agricultural products (sugar, Minute Maid [citrus], livestock, Consolidated Cigar, Schrafft Candy Co.).

The Washington Post Company

1977 Fortune 500 rank: 435
1977 total sales: $436.1 million

Principal Operations

Newspapers (5): *Washington Post* (D.C.); *Trenton Times* and *Sunday Times-Advertiser* (N.J.); *Everett Daily Herald* (Wash.); *International Herald Tribune* (30% participant) (Paris); Washington Post Writers Group (syndication and book publishing); L.A.

Times-Washington Post News Service (50% interest).

Magazines: *Newsweek.*

Books: Newsweek Books.

Broadcasting: WJXT-TV (Jacksonville, Fla.); WPLG-TV (Miami, Fla.); WFSB-TV (Hartford, Conn.); WWJ-TV (Detroit, Mich.).

Other: Robinson Terminal Warehouse Corp. (newsprint storage); Bowater Marsey Paper Co., Ltd. (49% interest, Canada); newsprint mill under development.

Bibliography

Although the theme of media ownership concentration is one of the most widely discussed mass communication issues today, an excellent understanding of the major issues involved can be gained through a few recent articles. Ben Bagdikian's more current presentations of the issue can be found in "Newspaper mergers—the final phase" in the March-April edition of *Columbia Journalism Review;* "The Media Monopolies" in *The Progressive* of June 1978; and in "Space Is Money" in the Winter 1978 edition of *feed/back* magazine. Different approaches to the topic are available through Stephen R. Barnett's, "Merger, Monopoly & A Free Press," in the January 15, 1973 edition of *The Nation;* Walter Pincus's "Is Bigness a Curse? Media Monopolies" in the January 26, 1974 edition of *The New Republic;* Kevin Phillip's "Busting the Media Trusts" in the July 1977 edition of *Harper's;* and a two-part series by the staff of *Media Decisions* magazine, September and October 1978, entitled "Is big better?"

6 The Impact of Photographs
Nancy Stevens

Nancy Stevens is a New York based freelancer who writes for the *French Photo,* the *Village Voice* and *Camera 35.* Her article is used with the permission of *News Photographer,* the official publication of the National Press Photographers Association Inc. It appeared in the October, 1975 issue. Photographs by Stanley Forman are used with permission of the *Boston Herald American.* The article points out how even the black and white photographs which appear in the newspaper can have an important impact upon those who see the pictures. This is one of the issues she raises. The other issue, which is one of taste or ethics, is explored in the section called criticism of the Mass Media, articles 12, 13, and 14.

The photographs made by Boston *Herald American* staff photographer Stanley Forman of a firefighter's attempt to rescue a young woman and a two-year-old child, the subsequent collapse of the fire escape, and the young woman's plunge to her death have raised many troubling questions and aroused angry responses from newpaper readers. Forman's photographs, of what he had expected to be an ordinary rescue scene, were picked up by AP and UPI wire services. Within hours, they appeared on front pages of newspapers from the *Herald American's* competitor, the Boston *Globe,* to the morning editions in Tokyo. According to Boston *Herald American* managing editor, Sam Bornstein, his office has received about 250 tear sheets from foreign and domestic papers.

The actual pictures have been heralded as a photojournalist's once-in-a-lifetime achievement.

But for most people who viewed the photographs in their local newspaper, the experience evoked feelings more often associated with a nightmare.

Reader reaction was violent and outspoken against the publication of Forman's photos. Hal Buell, AP executive Newsphoto Editor, conducted a survey of national reader reaction and editorial response. Those readers who agreed that pictures should have been published cited considerations of public safety, need for reform, and the need to be realistic. One reader of the Costa Mesa (California) *Daily Pilot,* wrote in favor of editor Tom Keevil's decision to pick up the AP photos. "Everyman lives and dies. Maybe we will all have better social awareness."

Nora Ephron, in her media column in the November issue of *Esquire* magazine, responded to the taboo of publishing photographs depicting death. "Death happens to be one of life's main events," declared Ephron. "And it is irresponsible—and more than that, inaccurate—for newspapers to fail to show it . . . ."

Voices raised against publication were strident in their condemnation of their local editors' judgment. Newspapers were criticized for "cheap journalism," voyeurism, irresponsibility, poor taste, and invasion of privacy. One irate reader of the *Seattle Times* cancelled his subscription. Another wrote, "You're giving our kids a nightmare."

For many editors the most important question was one of censorship. Marshall L. Stone, the managing editor of the *Bangor (Maine) News,* wrote "If it were a mistake to run them, it would likewise have been a mistake not to run them. Those are the horns of the editor's dilemma."

Lenora Williamson, in a column in *Editor and Publisher* (August 30, 1975), quoted Buell as he explained an editorial decision to publish the photographs. "You're cursed if you do, and cursed for manipulating the news if you don't."

However, there is another side to the impact of the photographs on the public. In the Boston area there were signs of immediate reforms instigated by the fire photos. Two weeks after the fire, the Boston *Herald American* ran an article about the city's new safety drive. Mayor Kevin H. White announced the addition of 100 building, fire, and housing inspectors. Previously, seven city employees had routinely inspected emergency escape exits. Furthermore, Housing and Building Commissioner Francis W. Gens announced a new regulation requiring periodic private certification for all apartment and mercantile buildings, lodging houses, and places of public assembly.

A fire in Boston is not news in California, but the photographs will serve a purpose. Forman has received requests from fire departments across the country for copies of his photos for study purposes to improve fire fighting techniques. Copies have also been requested to call attention to the ongoing campaign to improve safety conditions.

"The only newsworthy thing about the pictures," concluded Nora Ephron in *Esquire,* "is that they were taken. They deserve to be printed because they are great pictures, breathtaking pictures of something that happened. That they disturb readers is exactly as it should be: that's why photojournalism is often more powerful than written journalism."

Boston Herald American—Wednesday, July 23, 1975—Page 1

Exclusive Photos

Rescue at Hand and Then a Fall

Victims Wait As Firefighter Reaches for Ladder.
Exclusive Photo Sequence by Stanley Forman
Copyright 1975 by The Boston Herald American

Dramatic Rescue Attempt Begins.

Photographer's Story of Pictures

"I made all kinds of pictures because I thought it would be a good rescue shot over the ladder . . . never dreamed it would be anything else."

Photographer Stanley Forman was talking about taking today's dramatic pictures of a fire escape collapse.

"I kept having to move around because of the light situation. The sky was bright and they were in deep shadow. I wouldn't have had any detail."

"I was making pictures with a motor drive and lit, the fire-fighter was reaching up and, I don't know, everything started failing.

"I followed the girl down taking pictures . . . I made three or four frames.   FORMAN

"I realized what was going on and I completely turned around, because I didn't want to see her hit.

"I just knew in my mind, it wasn't going to add to anything. She fell behind a picket fence. I wouldn't have seen it anyway."

Forman, a native of Revere, will complete his sixth year on the staff of The Hearst Newspapers in Boston in November.

Fire Escape Collapses Under Victims   Woman and Child Plunge as Firefighter Dangles.   They Plummet to Ground.

Access to the Mass Media

Who Will Take Care of the "Damrons" of the World?

7

Roy M. Fisher

The magnificent building that houses the Miami *Herald* stretches for more than a city block aside the shallow waters of Biscayne Bay. It rises at the land side of MacArthur Causeway, an architectural bulwark separating the work-a-day world of the Miami residents from the pleasureland of Miami Beach, on the yonder side of the bay.

The *Herald* building rivals the resort hotels in size and opulence. It is of brown brick, glass, and stone and is properly called the Miami *Herald* and the Miami *News* building, for it houses both newspapers, The first is the powerful flag paper of the nation's most vigorous newspaper group, founded in the thirties by Editor John S. Knight. The second is the once financially anemic *News,* a sort of kissing cousin of the *Herald*. The *News* is owned by the Cox newspaper chain, but depends upon the *Herald* for its business management, advertising sales, printing, and distribution. While this agreement came into being before Congress got around specifically to legalize joint operating arrangements, the result was consistent with the purposes of the Newspaper Preservation Act of 1970. Miami remains one of the decreasing number of cities to have more than one newspaper voice. Editorially, at least, the papers are competitive.

The *Herald,* nonetheless, dominates Miami and most of South Florida. And while Jack Knight, an unpretentious man, would not build his newspaper's plant in the style of a gothic cathedral—as did the late Col. Robert R. McCormick of the Chicago *Tribune*—the *Herald* building on Biscayne Bay obviously bespeaks more than simply, "This is a newspaper plant."

Its proportions are monumental. Dominating the west facade which overlooks the city is a gigantic portico mounted on eight granite columns, each four stories tall. Even the biggest Cadillac limousine appears underscaled alongside those massive columns. No one can drive up to the building of the Miami *Herald* without an awesome feeling that he is about to enter a Very Important Place; that if, indeed, this be the free press that defends the freedom of America, this freedom rests in very strong hands.

The visitor who pulled up under that portico at a few minutes before 11:30 a.m. on September 27, 1972, drove up not in a Cadillac limousine, but in a little black and white Pontiac Firebird. He was a short dapper fellow wearing modishly long hair and a sharply tailored suit. He glanced up at the towering portico, gestured with his head to his attorney who climbed out of the Firebird after him, and strode through the huge glass doorway. He passed around the escalator that angles up through the four-story lobby, and together the two men walked to an

Roy M. Fisher is dean of the School of Journalism of the University of Missouri and is a former editor of the *Chicago Daily News.* Reprinted with the author's permission, this article appeared in *The Trial of the First Amendment,* a monograph published by the Freedom of Information Center, Columbia, Mo., 1975.

elevator used mainly by *Herald* employees. The visitor punched the fifth floor button that would take him and his attorney to the offices of the editor of the Miami *Herald,* Don Shoemaker.

The visitor that morning was Pat Tornillo, Jr., whose name has since become an important part of our constitutional history: the case of *Tornillo v. The Miami Herald.* Pat is the peppery little labor boss of the 8,000 Dade County classroom teachers. His perennial battle for collective bargaining rights for teachers, which led to an illegal strike, had made Tornillo, over the years, a sort of minor public enemy in the eyes of Editor Shoemaker. Now Tornillo was running for the State Legislature, and the *Herald* had blasted him and his candidacy editorially. The primary election was only four days away.

Politicians in Miami routinely go to the *Herald* building before elections, hat in hand, to seek the newspaper's endorsement of their candidacy. For the more timid ones, the thought of advancing through that portico and up that elevator is enough to keep them awake at night.

Even Tornillo says he felt "that certain awe" on that morning as he rose to the fifth floor editorial rooms. "It wasn't as though I were a stranger there, myself," he said later, bragging a little "Why, I guess I'd been at the *Herald* building 50 or 60 times before. Once I even had lunch with Don Shoemaker, himself, in the executive dining room. Some of the *Herald* guys are my personal friends, after hours."

As Pat Tornillo and his attorney, Tobby (for Tobias) Simon, reached the editorial offices they were met not by Shoemaker, who was busy, but by one of his editorial writers, Frederic Sherman. "Hi, Pat. What can we do for you?" Sherman called.

"I want you to print my reply to that editorial you clouted me with last week," Pat said. "Here's my reply: same number of words, same length. I'd like it on the same page, just as the law says."

As Tornillo recalls the conversation, Sherman looked at Tornillo in disbelief. "You gotta be kidding."

"No, I'm not kidding. I'm demanding my right under the law. Here Toby, read Fred the law."

Tornillo's attorney read a 60-year-old Florida statute that provides that any political candidate depicted unfavorably by a newspaper must be permitted a right to reply. A criminal statute, its violation could result in an editor's imprisonment and, a few months earlier, had been used to that end briefly in Daytona, Florida, against another editor.

"You're threatening us," Sherman said.

"No, we're not threatening, we're just telling you that we're going to court if you don't follow that law."

The Miami *Herald* took it as a threat, although some thought it was more grandstand politics by Tornillo, who needed publicity to fire up his faltering campaign. The *Herald* rejected Tornillo's reply.

Thus was laid the basis for *Tornillo v. The Miami Herald,* an exceptional challenge to the traditional interpretation of the First Amendment to the United

States Constitution, which permits the American people to speak freely, worship as they please, and publish without legal inhibition. Before the *Tornillo* case was concluded, the First Amendment itself would stand trial.

We will follow the fascinating path of this battle to the highest court in the land—and beyond into the legislative halls and American homes, where, ultimately, our freedoms are written. But first we should explore more fully the reasons why editor Shoemaker, by refusing Tornillo's demand, triggered the case on its way.

The Miami *Herald* had long before established a reputation as a fair, honest, and independent reporter of news. It had opened its columns countless times to views in sharp conflict with those of the editor. It had, in fact, on many occasions published previous statements and letters from this same Pat Tornillo. James Dance, associate editor who sometimes marked Tornillo's letters for the typesetters, estimates that eight of every ten Tornillo contributions were published by the *Herald* without hesitation. "Why," said Dance, "Pat's publishing record in our paper was probably better than my own!" To which Tornillo replied, "I don't doubt that—and Jim is a better writer than I am, too."

This particular demand, however, coming as it did from an active candidate for public office, fell afoul of one of the *Herald's* traditional policies: that during a political campaign the *Herald* would not permit candidates to preempt editorial space normally reserved for reader comments. The rationale of editor Shoemaker was that during such times the *Herald* devotes many columns of space to reporting the candidates and their various campaigns. Thus satisfactory avenues are available to candidates without using the letters-to-the-editor columns.

But obviously Shoemaker gave special consideration to this particular Tornillo request. Before making up his mind, he asked the advice of Dan Paul, the *Herald's* attorney. Paul told him that the old right-of-reply statute was obviously invalid. And, furthermore Paul said he considered Tornillo's demand, in itself, a challenge to the intent of the First Amendment: that an editor make his editorial judgments without coercion.

So Shoemaker rejected the Tornillo demand, muttering that, "No one shoots his way into the Miami *Herald*." Tornillo, good as his word, beat it to the Circuit Court of Dade County, where he asked Judge Francis J. Christie to order the *Herald* to print his reply and to pay him damages. In an emergency hearing, Judge Christie held that the old statute was an unconstitutional restraint upon freedom of the press. On Tuesday, Tornillo was defeated at the polls, in spite of the endorsement by the "other" newspaper, the Miami *News*.

Undismayed, Tornillo appealed to the Florida Supreme Court, where, in a decision that surprised even Toby Simon, the court ruled 6 to 1 in favor of Tornillo. The *Herald* took the battle on to Washington, where Chief Justice Warren E. Burger led the Supreme Court of the United States in a unanimous decision supporting the Miami *Herald*.

On its way up the judicial escalator, *Tornillo v. The Miami Herald* picked up a lot of extra riders. Almost all of the major news organizations, including the National Association of Broadcasters, joined as friends of the court on behalf of the *Herald*. On the other hand, some politicians, including Senator John McClellan (D.-Ark.) and President Richard M. Nixon sided publicly with Tornillo's cause. A number of state legislatures prepared to enact right-of-reply laws similar to Florida's.

Then one morning in April 1974, the Supreme Court called for oral arguments in *Tornillo v. The Miami Herald,* now, because the *Herald* had brought the appeal, renamed *The Miami Herald v. Tornillo.* After questioning of Dan Paul, the *Herald's* Miami attorney, the court turned its eyes on Professor Jerome Barron, an outspoken civil liberties lawyer, a former dean of the Syracuse University School of Law, now a professor at George Washington University, and Tornillo's joint counsel, with Toby Simon.

Before we can understand the position in which Professor Barron found himself at that moment, we should know something of his own philosophical views of the First Amendment.

For some years, Barron had been among those who had deplored the increasing centralization of the mass media in the United States. Newspaper mergers, the growth of newspaper chain operations, and the common ownership of newspaper and broadcasting companies, he pointed out, gave a few corporations massive influence on the media. A combination of economic problems, tax law, and new technology had made this so.

As newspaper production costs increased and advertisers diverted more of their advertising dollars to broadcasting, many metropolitan newspapers fell on hard times. In city after city, competing newspapers merged, partly (as in Miami) or totally (as was more common). The result: another city with only one newspaper voice. In the 20 years between 1945 and 1965, the number of American cities having more than one metropolitan newspaper fell from 117 to 65. Today, newspaper monopoly exists in 19 of every 20 cities.

While the number of newspapers in metropolitan cities declined, the number of newspaper owners declined even more sharply as newspaper chain operations boomed. Tax laws offered tempting benefits to local publishers who would sell their properties to the big operators. Thus, by 1973 two of every three newspaper copies printed in the United States each day were printed by chain owners.

The advent of television did little to preserve the declining diversity. Three networks that dominate television news deliver identical programs to all of their owned or affiliated stations. Furthermore, owners of television stations often are the same people who own radio stations or newspapers. More than half of the television stations and 80 percent of the radio stations, FCC records show, are owned by companies that also own one or more other media outlets, either broadcast or print.

To preserve diversity of news and opinion amidst this increasing standardization, Barron had advanced the idea that that each newspaper should be required by law to open its columns to stories and opinions adverse to its own. This, he said, would make each newspaper a true community forum, accessible to any person and any idea regardless of the views of the publisher. Barron contended that in fact this is what the Founding Fathers had in mind when they wrote the First Amendment. Picking up a phrase from a previous Supreme Court case, he said this right of access would encourage "open and robust debate on public issues." Thus Barron argued that it is no longer enough to guarantee press freedom just "to those who are rich enough or lucky enough to own a printing press." Every man should be assured access to the press. If so, surely the Florida statute of right-to-reply was consistent with that objective.

Now here he was in the highest court of the land, faced with the need to convince the justices that they should reinterpret one of our nation's basic documents. He had considered carefully the difficulty of this task before permitting himself to be persuaded by Tornillo and Simon to join them in the case. At worst, he had decided, he would be able to project his new doctrine to a large and sensitive audience. So, as the court finished with its questions to Dan Paul and looked now at him, Professor Barron realized that his historic moment was at hand. He had been greatly encouraged by his unexpected victory at Tallahassee. He was bolstered also by what he had construed as being a growing disillusionment by the public in the mass media. Certainly he could count some benefit from the obvious anti-press attitude of members of the Nixon administration, whose appointees now dominated the thinking of the Court. But Professor Barron's hopes were quickly dashed.

In a series of rapid-fire questions by the justices, he began to sense the existence of a seemingly unlikely alignment of court conservatives and court liberals—both hostile to his thesis. Conservatives Rehnquist, Blackmun and Chief Justice Burger, and a liberal, Marshall, began to chip away at Barron's stated philosophy of the First Amendment freedom.

Rehnquist, President Nixon's last appointee, fired an early question at the professor. To Barron's contention that the First Amendment was operating only to guarantee freedom to the owners of the media—not to the public—Rehnquist wanted to know whether he was suggesting that the First Amendment intended that one man could commandeer another man's printing press for his own use. Rehnquist's was a traditional, conservative question based upon a simple statement of property right. (It's my ball; I can play with it as I like.)

Then Chief Justice Burger took a whack: "What if Tornillo announced that on next Friday night he was going to hold a public meeting and take care of the Miami *Herald,* and the Miami *Herald* informed him that it wanted one of its editors present to answer Tornillo from the platform at that meeting. Would the newspaper have that right?"

Professor Barron replied that that statute wouldn't apply to that situation.

Then Marshall, the liberal, took the floor: "The Florida statute covers only candidates for public office, is that right?"

Barron: "I guess so; it only covers candidates."

The Justice: "Then we must presume that the press can attack to destruction in Florida anyone excepting a candidate, is that right?" To which a puzzled Jerome Barron replied, "Sadly, that's true."

"So," said Marshall, "anyone could silence the press by simply becoming a candidate!"

Justice Brennan took a small part in the dialogue, Stewart was seen to nod in agreement from time to time, and Powell and Douglas kept their own counsel. But any doubt about which way the wind was blowing must have vanished when Rehnquist added this rhetorical question:

"Mr. Barron, isn't the First Amendment there for only one reason, this is to protect the people from the government? The government is the entity that the First Amendment is there to protect you from. It wasn't intended to protect one citizen from the speech of another citizen, was it, Mr. Barron?"

Barron gamely battled for his thesis, but, even before his final argument was completed, one justice walked out of the room. And Barron himself gave up his argument with five minutes still available on the clock. He still held hope that he might have won over a majority of the court, but it was an idle hope.

It was no surprise to most people when the opinion came down, three months later. By a vote of nine to zero, the United States court overturned a one-to-six finding of the Florida court: the Florida right-to-reply statute was an unconstitutional infringement upon the First Amendment.

Chief Justice Burger wrote the court's opinion himself. While there was little doubt as to his destination, the chief justice explored a number of paths. Obviously, the concentration of the press in so few hands bothered him, as well as Professor Barron. The chief justice said:

"The result of these vast changes has been to place in a few hands the power to inform the American people and shape public opinion. . . . The abuses of bias and manipulative reportage are, likewise, said to be the result of the vast accumulations of unreviewable power in the modern media empires. In effect, it is claimed, the public has lost any ability to respond or to contribute in a meaningful way to the debate on issues. . . .

"The obvious solution . . . would be to have additional newspapers. But the same economic factors which have caused the disappearance of vast numbers of metropolitan newspapers have made entry into the marketplace of ideas . . . almost impossible."

Thus Justice Burger tended to support Professor Barron's description of the problem, but not his proposed solution. He saw no difference between a law that would force an editor to publish a given story and a law that would prohibit the editor from publishing a given story. He stated very simply that, "The clear implication has been that any such compulsion to publish . . . is unconstitutional."

Elaborating further, Justice Burger wrote:

"The choice of material to go into a newspaper . . . and treatment of public issues and public officials—whether fair or unfair—constitutes the exercise of editorial control and judgment. It has yet to be demonstrated how governmental regulation of this crucial process can be exercised consistent with the First Amendment guarantee of a free press. . . ."

The court's opinion was a clear, if perhaps visceral and simplistic, enunciation of the traditional view of press freedom. It laid to rest the movement in other states for Florida-style access laws and shushed the clamor in Washington for a federal statute of similar intent. In that respect, we all owe a debt to Pat Tornillo for bringing his confrontation, and to editor Don Shoemaker for defying a bad law and refusing to let Tornillo shoot his way into print.

The case confirmed the judgment of Malcolm Johnson, editor of the Tallahassee *Democrat,* who said, "Motherhood is a noble concept, but under compulsion it is a product of rape and begets illegitimacy."

While the Supreme Court of the United States snuffed out a grassroots movement for laws that would infringe upon a newspaper's editorial judgments, its opinion leaves untreated a certain social sickness that expressed itself at this particular time in the *Tornillo* case, but will break out again on another day in another state with an entirely different set of symptoms.

Many persons will agree that the American people suffer from a gnawing anxiety that the press—and the other communications media as well—have grown too big for their britches, that the economic concentration of media control has reduced the average citizen's access.

The public senses—even though it may not articulate its feelings well—that our civilization has, indeed, entered into a new age. That just as we passed through the stone age, the bronze age, the iron age, and the space age, we now stand on the threshold, and are about to enter, the "communications age." . . . That the man who controls the world from this time on will not necessarily be the man who commands the biggest armies or holds the biggest bomb, but rather the man whose finger is closest to the mechanism that turns on the radio and television stations and controls the starting and the stopping of our newspaper presses. . . That wars will no longer be won or lost by the capture of a man's land or even his body, but by the capture of his mind. . . And that this will go to him who controls the media.

While we can hail the simple logic of the Burger opinion, we may get a more ominous view of the threat to press freedom today from the Florida decision, where six of seven justices held for Tornillo. Theirs was bad law, no doubt, but it may still have been good politics. And the Florida justices, who sit in their Neo-Greek whitewashed courthouse in Tallahassee, are, after all, politicians first and Supreme Court justices later. They must be elected in a partisan campaign, and they must keep their political fences mended if they are to be reelected after six years. They sit in the eye of a political hurricane and have learned to read the political skies with care.

When this writer interviewed the Florida justices in their chambers, he found they had accepted their federal rebuff calmly. They believe time is on their side, that if they have misread the law as it stands today, they have not misread the political realities which ultimately determine all laws. Furthermore, the justices had more immediate problems distracting them at the moment.

The Florida Supreme Court, which often has had occasion to defend its honor, was now virtually fighting for its life. Three of the seven justices faced possible impeachment, another's capacity to serve was impaired by alcoholism, and a fifth was being asked to justify the court's unusual intervention in a parole board matter on behalf of a robber who had good connections in the crime underworld. This sorry state of affairs had resulted from a number of challenges of the court's integrity and competency. The Judicial Qualifications Commission had recommended that two justices be removed for accepting improper help from a utilities lawyer in the preparation of a decision favorable to the utility (a court-appointed panel later settled for reprimands only). The commission similarly denounced a third justice for failing to exclude himself from a deliberation which involved lawyers with whom he was engaged in real estate transactions. Further undermining the court's credibility at the moment was the discovery of a notation written on a court document that indicated a strong personal bias against the Miami *Herald,* although the justice whose initials appear under the notation denied this was so.

This bad situation does not mean that the court is without any wisdom. To the contrary, this same court upheld the toughest open meetings law in the land, and was duly hailed by the press and public spirited groups for its position. The Florida meetings law, incidentally, guarantees the public (and the press) access to all meetings of public bodies, regardless of the subjects to be discussed. In Florida, two members of a local school board who happen to meet on a street corner cannot legally mention board business without first notifying the public of their intent.

The man who wrote the bold opinion upholding this open meetings law is Justice James C. Adkins, Jr., who claims with good reason that he has fought fiercely to protect the rights of the press.

"I have no animosity toward newspapers," he told us. "I wrote the first opinion construing our Sunshine Law. I believe in the right of the press to be present at every meeting so that we can have a real marketplace of ideas any time any public body meets."

A little later, however, Justice Adkins talked about some things that make him uneasy about the press today:

"Twenty-five years ago the editor of a newspaper was a leader in his community. He more or less formulated the ideas of that community. If you had a community project, you went to him and you got the support of the newspaper, because he was so closely attuned to the problem. He was looked upon with a great deal of respect, and people usually followed the newspaper. Today people look at the newspaper as being managed by someone outside their own community. When these editors of outside chains come into communities—especially smaller communities—they are accepted socially, you understand, but insofar as their thoughts and views are concerned, the public doesn't have the confidence in them that they had in those days when the editor was more accepted as one of them. As a result I think the newspapers have lost a great deal of their community influence."

So when Justice Adkins explains how he feels about newspapers, he says, in effect, that they have become sort of outside intruders, not really as "attuned" or as much a part of the "in" communities as before. Now there is no law requiring that an editor be "attuned" to a community, and Justice Adkins did not use such a reason for casting his vote against the Miami *Herald*. As he explained later, Justice Adkins sided with Tornillo on the grounds that Tornillo was a candidate running for public office. It has long been established that the government can regulate free speech as part of the election process. For example, the justice pointed out, the government can prevent anyone from making a campaign speech or handing out handbills within 100 feet of the polls. This is a restriction on free speech and free press, but it is legal. So, why can't the government also require certain standards of fairness elsewhere during a campaign? What's the magic about 100 feet? he asks.

One can wonder, after talking with the Florida justices, how much of their legal thinking had been influenced by their personal opinion that the press has grown away from the people it serves. This wonderment becomes even stronger when one learns that the Florida court became greatly preoccupied during its hearing of the *Tornillo* case with another case, legally quite disassociated. This unreported chapter leads one to believe that the Florida court—essentially Populist in spirit—decided as it did partly because it had the fortune, or misfortune, to have sitting with it on the *Tornillo* case a substitute, Justice J. S. Rawls, who was summoned from the state appellate bench to take the place of a Supreme Court judge who was unable to be present for this case. In the opinion of some persons most familiar with the Tornillo case, including Tornillo's lawyer Toby Simon, Justice Rawls swung the court to his view.

Imagine if you can the scene in that Florida Supreme Court Building that day when the *Tornillo* case was called up on the docket. The seven judges—six elected judges of the Supreme Court and one six-foot, 235-pound substitute called up from his lower court bench—were seated in their leather chairs behind one long bench. Before them sat labor boss Tornillo, his lawyers, and those who represented the powerful interests of the Knight Newspapers and the Miami *Herald*, plus friends of the court, associated by counsel, and a few spectators.

Dan Paul, the *Herald's* attorney, was stating the opening arguments on behalf of the *Herald* when he was interrupted by an unfamiliar voice from the far end of the bench:

"Mr. Paul, what is the *Herald* doing about the Damrons of this world?"

Mr. Paul, perhaps not hearing the remark, continued, but was interrupted again. "The Damrons, what about the rights of the Damrons of this world?"

The voice this time was identified as that of Justice Rawls, the substitute judge. While Paul searched for an answer, Toby Simon sat bewildered. Then Simon jotted down a note on a scrap of paper and handed it to the bailiff. The bailiff slowly walked to the end of the bench, proceeded behind six other justices to Rawls' chair. He handed Judge Rawls the note. Rawls scribbled an answer, and the bailiff proceeded slowly back to Simon's table. He opened the answer and showed it to Barron, who now recognized the citation: "*Leonard Damron, appellant,* v. *the Ocala Star-Banner.*" From that point on, in the opinion of some informed lawyers, the Florida court may have been talking about Tornillo that day but was thinking more about Leonard Damron. It became preoccupied by what it considered to be a judicial injustice to Damron, who in 1966 was mayor of the Florida town of Crystal River, population 1,423.

Leonard Damron was running for the office of county assessor when, two weeks before the election, a story about a federal perjury charge against his brother, James, appeared in the regional newspaper, the Ocala *Star-Banner.* Because of a "mental aberration," the rewriteman who transcribed the story from the court reporter mistakenly substituted the mayor's name for that of his brother, James. The story appeared under a three-column headline on page one. Although the *Star-Banner* printed two corrections prior to the election, the mayor lost and blamed the *Star-Banner* for his defeat.

The mayor sued for libel. He won by directed verdict in the trial court, which awarded him $22,000 in damages. The *Star-Banner* immediately appealed to the Florida District Court of Appeals. There, as fate would have it, sat Justice J. S. Rawls, now the substitute judge in *Tornillo.*

The Rawls court upheld a finding of libel against the *Star-Banner* assessing compensatory damages for its gross negligence in reporting. The *Star-Banner* appealed to the U.S. Supreme Court, which overturned Justice Rawls' court with a curt citation of *New York Times v. Sullivan.* As you know, *New York Times v. Sullivan* made libel against a political figure dependent upon proven malice. In effect, the U.S. Supreme Court spanked Justice Rawls on the presumption that he should have read the Sullivan case more carefully.

Justice Rawls had been smarting ever since. In *Tornillo* he was to get his retribution. And hence his question, "What are you doing for the Damrons of this world?" the innocent people who are wronged by careless or negligent or hurried or just simply wrong reporting. If the editor of the *Star-Banner* had run over Damron in a street because of careless driving, he would have been liable. What's the difference if the instrument of negligence is a printing press instead, Justice Rawls wanted to know.

If a public figure is to remain immune from libel, the Florida Supreme Court reasoned, is not a legal right of reply at least an acceptable alternative? So it upheld the 1913 Florida law, which, incidently, had been introduced by a legislator who was himself a newspaperman and signed into law by a Florida governor, who was himself a newspaper publisher.

By such ironies history is made.

Justice Rawls and his one-time associates on the Florida Supreme Court are not at all persuaded that the Supreme Court spoke the final wisdom in the *Tornillo* case.

Justice Joseph A. Boyd makes that clear. Boyd (the "Herald's man," according to another justice) is the "one" in the Florida Court's six to one decision. He alone, of all the court, voted against Tornillo, holding that, indeed, the Florida 1913 statute infringed upon the First Amendment.

"The whole bill of rights I consider a sacred document," Justice Boyd said when we talked with him. "But under the law it is no more sacred than any other part of our constitution. I remember what happened to the 18th Amendment, that was extremely popular among some people when it was adopted. But the 21st Amendment cancelled the 18th Amendment because the people finally decided that there was not a proper respect being shown for the 18th Amendment.

"That can happen to the First Amendment, too, whenever the people feel that there is not a proper respect being shown to it. So, in a way, it doesn't matter too much what I said—or what even the Supreme Court of the U.S. said in *Tornillo*. It's the attitude of the people of the United States that finally counts.

"My very firm hope is that the *Tornillo v. The Miami Herald* will be construed by the media as a greater opportunity for them to write what needs to be written. But to do so in such a way that they will not alienate a number of Americans."

Which brings us to the concluding chapter of our narrative.

What lies ahead? If Justice Boyd's fears are well founded—that the American people are, indeed, capable of repealing the First Amendment—how much *time* do we have, in what *form* will our new restrictions likely appear, and what steps can we take to forestall such a tragic and decisive action in the history of freedom?

Perhaps we have less time than we think.

Clay T. Whitehead, former head of the White House Office of Telecommunications Policy, has observed that even now, "the courts are building precedents that will lead to do-goodism regulation of the print media." He predicts that the First Amendment will be re-interpreted to apply some sort of so-called "fairness doctrine" to newspapers, similar to that already imposed on the broadcasting industry.

If this should come to pass, the courts would embrace the basic philosophy propounded by Professor Barron. In the *Tornillo* case, such a doctrine would no doubt have required Editor Shoemaker to print Pat Tornillo's reply, regardless of the editor's judgment as to its accuracy or its worth. Chief Justice Burger's opinion would collapse.

Richard M. Schmidt, Jr., general counsel to the American Society of Newspaper Editors, believes that the present Supreme Court has already reined back on press freedom.

On the same day the court returned its findings in *Tornillo*, it also handed down a decision in the case of *Gertz v. Robert Welch, Inc.* The two opinions were connected in no way but a happenstance of the calendar, but they spoke to the same general issue. And they took essentially opposite sides. Whereas the court ruled clearly *for* editorial freedom in *Tornillo*, it ruled *against* editorial freedom in *Gertz*.

The decision in *Gertz,* a case brought by Chicago attorney Elmer Gertz against a John Birch Society publication, reinterpreted the laws of libel in such a way as to make it easier for private citizens to establish proof of a newspaper's wrong-doing. By further revising the libel laws, the court seriously inhibits newspaper behavior in the future.

Thus we see emerging two thrusts that would seek to counter the growing power of the media. One would modify the First Amendment to permit the courts, or some other agency, to enforce standards of performance, presumably those considered by that agency to be in the public interest. This would be a simple extension of the regulatory philosophy already controlling broadcasting. It is the kind of action Whitehead has in mind when he predicts that the courts will reinterpret the First Amendment to include some sort of "fairness doctrine" for the press. This is what Justice Boyd warns against, and it is perhaps what Professor Barron believes would make newspapers the kind of "public forums" he envisions.

Of the two thrusts against media power, this has been the most frequently discussed and, upon examination, appears as the most radical departure from our First Amendment concept of a free and independent press. Such a move, in effect, says the Founding Fathers were wrong when they made government powerless to preempt the editor's decisions. To paraphrase Malcolm Johnson, we would have legalized editorial rape, so long as the rapist carried the imprimatur of government.

The second thrust against growing media power would work within the First Amendment, seeking to dismantle the financial concentration of the media and thus to restore local ownership and control. This would mean busting up the group operations, eliminating cross-ownerships, and restricting the role of the conglomerates. Its wrecking tools would be the anti-trust laws—from which newspapers are now given special exemptions—and tax reforms that would remove the present enticement for independents to sell to group owners. The first legislation to bring such a dismantling was introduced to Congress in 1970 by Senator Thomas J. McIntyre (D-N.H.). It was short-lived, but would have prohibited any newspaper and television cross-ownership in the same market. It also would have restricted the number of daily newspapers owned by any group to five.

Opponents of this approach point out that dismantling of big business flies in the face of economic winds. The very essence of capitalism is the use of capital to increase capital. That's how the big publishing and big broadcasting companies grew to what they are today. To attempt to reverse this trend is to attempt an unnatural economic act. Is it possible, or even desirable? If it could be done, what would be the fate of the independent companies so created? Would they survive as economic units against the ever-increasing need for larger capital to meet increased production and creative costs? Or would these independents ultimately become economic wards of the government, thereby ending the concept of freedom embodied in the First Amendment?

Chief Justice Burger's tortuous opinion agonized about the state of the media today. But within the confines of existing law and the First Amendment, the Chief Justice had no better alternative to suggest. In this regard, his opinion perhaps reflects a cautious wisdom which is likely to be overlooked.

If we are seriously to consider reshaping our media, we have little enough time in which to judge their merit against likely alternatives. For all their faults, America's corporate press and broadcast media contribute in many ways to the strength of our society. They provide American people with the most complete and balanced news report available anywhere. They report government more thoroughly and monitor it more effectively. The media serve their respective publics, more solicitous of public concerns and more knowing of public habits than any other mass communication system in the world.

The fact that our media are run as business enterprises—and not as instruments of political action—shapes their basic character. Typically of business enterprises, they are beholden ultimately to their customers. Unlike the press and broadcast systems of most of the world—and of earlier times—the American media do not answer to any political party or candidate.

As corporate journalism supplants personal and party journalism, the publisher himself becomes not so much the entrepreneur as the manager appointed by a board of directors, which is answerable, in turn, to the stockholders. Ultimately, the corporate communications enterprise flourishes to the extent that it retains the respect of the public and is able to satisfy the needs of its customers. The rise of the professional manager in the publisher's office coincides with the rise of the professional editor in the newsroom. Each exists to serve the customer.

With all the faults described by Chief Justice Burger and Justice Adkins, such a system embodies powerful safeguards for our society. A whole new editorial ethic has developed to support this new professionalism. So all-pervasive is this ethic that it is a rare publisher who would buck its code to bias a news report even for his own or his corporate interests. To make such an attempt would trigger a newsroom explosion and a public outcry. Thus the corporate media possess controls inherent in their nature. Such controls lie beyond the reach of anyone who would bend them to his personal ambition, governments included. That is good.

Surely editor Shoemaker would agree with that, and so also would Justice Rawls and his colleagues of the Florida Supreme Court, and Chief Justice Burger, and Professor Barron—and even Pat Tornillo.

Bibliography

Consult the bibliography which follows the Jacklin essay for books and articles on access to the press. Students should familiarize themselves with the entire publication from which the Fisher piece has been reprinted. See *The Trial of the First Amendment*, Freedom of Information Center monograph, 1975, and the article by Paul A. Freund, "The Legal Framework of the Tornillo Case." Opinions of the U.S. Supreme Court and of the Florida Supreme Court are reprinted in the monograph.

8   A New Fairness Doctrine: Access to the Media

Phil Jacklin

Phil Jacklin is chairman of the Committee for Open Media of the Santa Clara Valley (Calif.) chapter of the American Civil Liberties Union. He teaches philosophy at San Jose State University. Reprinted with permission from the May/June 1975 issue of *The Center Magazine,* a publication of the Center for the Study of Democratic Institutions, Santa Barbara, California.

Government regulation of broadcasting is under attack. This is nothing new. Like all industries, the broadcast industry resists regulation. Unfortunately, only the industry point of view is heard and good people are persuaded by it. Thus, in the . . . [magazine] *Civil Liberties,* Nat Hentoff argues against the Federal Communication Commission's fairness doctrine. He understands the fairness doctrine in the conventional way as the obligation imposed on broadcasters to balance their presentation of controversial issues. More generally, the broadcaster faces an obligation to present programming in the public interest; this general obligation is particularized by the fairness doctrine which requires the broadcaster to balance discussion of controversial issues *and* to cover and present issues of public importance.

The standard argument against regulation of broadcast programming goes as follows:

> There is an asymmetry in the regulation of radio and television on the one hand and the print media on the other. We have government regulation of radio and television under the fairness doctrine; but the First Amendment is understood to prohibit government regulation of newspapers under any comparable fairness doctrine.

> There is no longer a justification for this asymmetry. The rationale of the fairness doctrine (and of all regulation of broadcast content) is the scarcity of usable broadcast frequencies. But there are now far fewer daily newspapers than there are radio and television stations (1,749 to 7,458). Few cities (five per cent) have competitive daily newspapers, but most are served by several television stations and plenty of radio.

> Therefore, in order to be consistent, we should defend freedom of the electric press and oppose the fairness doctrine.

Hentoff does not affirm this conclusion. He offers it for discussion. As he says, it is "new ground" for him. His argument is all too familiar to those who read *Broadcasting* magazine and follow industry attempts to expropriate the First Amendment. On the strength of it, Senator William Proxmire has recently filed a bill to end regulation of broadcast programming.

The two premises of the above argument are correct. There is an asymmetry and there is no basis for it. Still, the conclusion of the argument is a *non sequitur.* We need not achieve consistency by changing broadcast law and giving up the fairness doctrine. We can also achieve it by extending the fairness doctrine from broadcasting to the print media. We can do this using the media-scarcity rationale as in broadcasting. If daily newspapers are more scarce than broadcast frequencies, it does not follow that frequencies are not scarce. There is scarcity when demand exceeds supply; in the media case there is scarcity when more people want access to the public than can have it.

We have a choice. Should we extend the fairness doctrine to newspapers which have no competitors and risk further government involvement? Or should we adopt the same laissez-faire policy for broadcasting that is traditional in the print media? I submit that there is a third and better alternative. If we believe in an open society and political equality, if we want to avoid the domination of mass communications by a few big corporations, then we must regulate any preponderant message-source in any medium. But, there is available to us a regulatory strategy which is fundamentally different from that involved in the fairness doctrine as presently understood and is wholly consistent with the First Amendment. We can choose to regulate access rather than content, to insure fairness about who is heard rather than fairness in what is said.

When, if ever, is there a need (justification or rationale) for government regulation of media? If there is media scarcity, does that justify regulation? Is there a way to regulate media without abridging freedom of the press? Answers to these questions are suggested by a model well known to political economy. Consider the following principles—all applicable to the problems of media law:

That a free (unregulated) and competititve marketplace is preferable to a government-regulated or planned economy.

That when there exists an economic monopoly or a concentration of economic power, the government must regulate that power to prevent abuses and protect the public interest. As Adam Smith explained, laissez-faire or the absence of regulation is desirable only in a condition of natural competition. When merchants must compete for their customers, the competition insures that people will be well served. But when economic power is monopolized or concentrated in a few hands, then competition ends and the government must protect the public interest. This takes us to a third and less familiar principle.

That, in the absence of natural competition, it is better to regulate so as to guarantee a competitive marketplace by limiting the extent to which power can be concentrated (e.g., to establish antitrust laws) than to attempt to regulate the behavior of monopoly powers (e.g., by setting production quotas and standards of quality, and administering prices and wages).

I take the traditional view that democracy absolutely requires the kind of communications generated in a competitive marketplace of ideas.

The problem is that in a society of millions dependent on the technology of mass communications, most messages that reach any substantial number of people are transmitted by means of a very limited number of media. In general, the scarcity of access to substantial audiences exists, not because there is a physical scarcity of communication channels, but for economic and sociological reasons. There is no shortage of "channels" in the print media, no shortage of presses or paper; but most dailies enjoy absolute monopolies. And, although there are weekly papers and periodicals, the publisher of the daily newspaper controls eighty per cent of all print communications on local and state issues.

In most big cities, there are at the present time fifteen to twenty usable television frequencies (VHF and UHF)—the same number as will be provided in a standard cable system. But the three network-associated stations control the programming viewed by eighty-five per cent of the total television audience. (Cable television and future technology will not solve our problem.)

Each of the channels with a substantial audience—print or broadcast—is wholly controlled by a single large message-source. Thus, in a typical city, control of mass conmunications is concentrated in the hands of a single daily newspaper and three television stations, with the addition in some places of an all-news radio station. The power of a message-source is a function both of the number of messages produced (as counted roughly by measuring the space and time they fill) and of the number of people actually reached by those messages.

It is at this point that the battle is joined by the newspaper and broadcasting industries, which argue thus: "Suppose, as is claimed, that media regulation *is* necessary when a concentration of the power to communicate reduces competition in a marketplace of ideas. There is indeed a limited number of important communicators, but there has been no showing at all that these communicators have abused their powers or refrained from a competition of ideas. The press is doing its job. Our Watergate experience proves that the system works. It is unnecessary and foolish to run the risk of government regulation of communications."

What, then, is the performance of the media? What, if anything, is left out? National media coverage is issue-oriented and admirable in that way. But "Presidential television" and dominance of the media generally led us in the late nineteen-sixties to the brink of disaster and over. Denied regular television exposure, neither congressional leaders nor the opposition party could check Presidential power. The Chief Executive dominates national attention. He is the only one with enough continuity of access to exercise national leadership. On state issues, and especially on local issues, there is virtually no one with the access appropriate to leadership except perhaps the press itself.

What ideas are left out? Ask those moved by a conception of the public interest, those who would seek access to their brothers and sisters in the media marketplace of ideas. Ask elected officials, consumer advocates, reformers, ecologists, socialists, the would-be vocal poor, church people, feminists, *et al.*

On both the national and local levels, the restraints on the competition of ideas are most apparent in the absence of day-to-day political competition. Political competition is the competition of leaders and their programs for public support as expressed in the formation of public opinion. No one except the President has long-term visibility or the concomitant ability to engage in the long-term communications essential to leadership.

Why? Part of the answer lies in the fact that the most powerful media are commercial and business-oriented. There is competition, but it is a competition for the advertiser's dollar and not a competition of ideas. We ignore this because we have been taught to identify the media with the press and to understand the press on the old model of precommercial, crusading journalism. In the good old days, the newspaper publisher wrote and edited his own stories and even ran the press himself. He was a political activist, a Sentinel, an Observer vigilant in behalf of his subscribers, an Advocate with the courage to set himself and his paper against the powerful few. Things have changed. The publisher's source of revenues has shifted from subscribers to advertisers and this has changed the newspaper business in two ways. Advertisers are more interested in circulation than in editorial policy. As a result, in almost every city the largest daily has slowly achieved a monopoly position, not because of the superiority of its editorial policy but because it is the first choice of advertisers. Second, the shift of revenues has changed editorial policy. It has shifted the editor's attention from the problems of the many to the ambitions of a few. As a monopoly message-source on local issues, the paper becomes, in a technical sense, propaganda. On one hand there is the propaganda of boosterism and Chamber of Commerce public relations (e.g., in San Jose, a new sports arena before new schools, airport expansion before noise abatement). On the other hand, with respect to the problems of ordinary people, and especially the poor, there is silence, the propaganda of the *status quo*. Most big city dailies do not by themselves sustain a marketplace of ideas on local issues.

What, then, is added by the multiplicity of broadcasters? Broadcasters are typically large corporations, not crusading journalists, not people at all. Corporate broadcasters program so as to generate the largest possible audiences. Then they rent these audiences to advertisers at the rate of four dollars per thousand per minute. The lawyers and public-relations men who represent them try to identify the electronic medium with the electronic press. But does the corporation have a First Amendment right to program exclusively for profit? (The fairness doctrine prohibits it.) In fact, only about five per cent of the electronic medium is occupied with the traditional journalistic function—news, documentaries, and public affairs—the rest is electronic theater. Audience-profit maximization leaves very little place for authentic journalism. Television journalists go unprotected while the First Amendment is interpreted as the right of the broadcasting corporation to edit in order to maximize profits, and even to make the local news a form of entertainment, to make of the news itself just another format for stories of sex and violence. What these corporations seek is not freedom for journalism but freedom from journalism. (They have succeeded very well. In point of fact, the FCC's fairness obligation to cover issues has been enforced in only one case.)

There is nothing wrong with an electronic circus as long as the medium also delivers the kind of communications required for democracy. We owe very much to the journalism of the last five years. Still, even the best journalism is no substitute for free speech. There is a profound reason why this is so. Journalists are supposed to be objective and non-partisan. They themselves are not supposed to participate in the competition of ideas, or to lead people to action. The press sustains a competition of ideas only to the extent that it provides access to spokesmen who are not themselves journalists.

The question then arises: How can a journalist decide in a disinterested way what issues and spokesmen to present? There is no solution to this problem. Indeed, the question is unintelligible. Message-choice, like all choice, presupposes the chooser's interests and needs. Journalists usually avoid the problem by reporting new events relative to something that is already in the news. But in a mass society, the news is identical with what is reported; and what has not been reported is not yet news.

How, then, can the journalist decide what *new* issues and spokesmen should gain access to the public? He can decide only because he does have values and interests; hopefully only by making a judgment about what people want and need to know. Authentic journalism is public-interest journalism. But when businessmen-publishers and corporations do the hiring and the firing, there is no guarantee that we will have authentic journalism. Spiro Agnew's concern was not misplaced: "A small group of men decide what forty to fifty million Americans will learn of the day's events. . . . We would never trust such power in the hands of an elected government; it is time we questioned it in the hands of a small and unelected elite."

There is another consideration here which is decisive all by itself. Even if there were a competition of ideas between five or ten powerful sources that would not be good enough for democracy. As society is democratic to the extent that all its citizens have an equal opportunity to influence the decision-making process. Clearly, communication is essential to this process—just as essential as voting itself. (Imagine a society of one thousand in which everyone votes, and all are free to say what they please, but only five people have the technology and power to reach *all* the others. Each of the other 995, except at overwhelming expense, can communicate only with a small circle of friends. Suppose the "five" are wealthy businessmen.)

The media must be regulated, not only to insure a competition of ideas, but so that all citizens have an equal opportunity to influence and shape this competition. "Fine, but is democracy possible in a society of two hundred million people?" Representative democracy is possible. As voters, we are represented in city hall, at the state capitol, and in the Congress by people who, to some extent at least, vote on our behalf and answer to us. These people are supported at public expense and use public facilities. All right, we need to establish parallel institutions which give us representation in public debate, i.e., representation in the media market place.

There are many possibilities. Our elected representatives and their ballot opponents and/or prospective opponents—leaders all—might be provided free media time and space on a regular basis. But we should not limit representation in the media marketplace to elected officials and party leaders. There are other ways in which spokesmen representative of whole groups can be identified. Formally organized nonprofit groups like the Sierra Club and the Methodist Church can select spokesmen, and membership rolls will demonstrate that these spokesmen are representatives. Small, informally organized groups of the type characteristic of much citizen activity could achieve short-term access by demonstrating by petition that a substantial number of people supported their efforts (as in the access-by-petition procedure in Holland). A plan for a system of representative access recognizing these four kinds of access has been drawn up by the Committee for Open Media. The details establish the feasibility of the general proposal. The FCC could establish some such system of access in broadcasting under its present authority, or Congress could do it. But what about the monopolistic daily newspapers?

It is useful to imagine what a new Communications Act would be like if we sought to develop a new strategy for media regulation oriented to regulation of access. We could regulate monopolistic or dominant message-sources in order to protect a competition of ideas in which all have some opportunity to participate or be represented. We could create a system of representative access of the sort sketched above or, alternatively, a new Communications Act might have the four following provisions:

The One-tenth Concentration Rule.   Any dominant message-source (one which controls over one-tenth of the messages reaching any population of over one hundred thousand) in any medium—be it print or broadcast— shall recognize an affirmative obligation to provide access to the public.

The Tithe in the Public Interest.   Each dominant message-source shall make available ten per cent of all message capacity (time and/or space) for citizen access. Message capacity shall be defined in terms of time and space and also audience-availability to that time and space. Since in broadcasting there is a fundamental difference between the function of full-length programs and spot messages, ten per cent of each would be made available. (Perhaps there should also be a tithe or tax of ten per cent on all profits to pay for production of citizen messages.)

The Allocation of Access by Lot.   Access to time and space shall be allocated by lot among registered citizens. Every registered voter is, in virtue of this act, a registered communicator.

The Access-Contribution Mechanism.   It shall be permissible for individuals to make access-contributions to designated representative persons or groups. It will be permissible for the citizen to designate a representative person or group to use his or her access spot. Individual organizations will be permitted and encouraged to solicit contributions of access time and space.

The access-contribution mechanism makes possible effective grass-roots support for various organizations at low cost (in time and money) and may lead to individual identification with the groups supported. It is a communications institution which generates community and community organization.

Access designations will, in effect, be votes—expressions of concerns and priorities—with respect to what is communicated. Everyone will participate in message-selection. Communication will reflect the needs, values, and priorities of all citizens.

The great advantage of the access approach is that it provides a strategy for media regulation which is in the spirit of the First Amendment and wholly consistent with it. The decisive difference between the regulatory strategy of the old law and the proposed new law is the distinction between the regulation of message content and the regulation of access. Or, to put the difference another way, it is the difference between the prohibition of certain message-content and the prohibition of monopolization of access by any message-source or group of sources.

The First Amendment prohibits government censorship; it prohibits laws regulating message content. But regulation of access does not entail regulation of content. Whatever source gains access is free to express any message whatever in the sole discretion of that source. While it is arguable that total denial of access is a form of censorship, surely it is not censorship to tell someone who talks all the time to stop talking for a bit so that others may speak. In contrast, the present law requires a regulation of content (broadcast programming). It requires "government censorship" in order to protect "the public interest" and especially to prevent an imbalance of programming that is not "fair" to some points of view. The tension between the Communications Act of 1934 and the First Amendment generates a choice between finding a way to regulate program content which does not risk government control of mass communications, and not regulating broadcast programming out of respect for the First Amendment. Given the preferences and power of the broadcast industry, the government has usually opted for no regulation. The fairness doctrine is rarely enforced. Unfortunately laissez-faire—*de jure* or *de facto*—is morally unacceptable in any context in which power is concentrated.

This returns us to the three principles of political economy and the general theory of regulation. Consider the third principle once more: that, in the absence of natural competition, it is better to limit the size and power of large entities, so as to protect competition, than it is to regulate the behavior of these powers. Thus, it is better for the government to use antitrust laws to force, say, Standard Oil to divest than for the government to mandate production quotas, set product standards, and administer prices. Surely, in such a sensitive field as communication, it is better to regulate access than to rely on government paternalism in the regulation of message-content. As always, free speech in a marketplace of ideas is our best hope.

Bibliography

Much of the material discussed by Jacklin also is included in David M. Hunsaker, *The Print Media and Equal Time,* Freedom of Information Center, Opinion Report No. 0016 (April 1975), but Hunsaker proposes a "Model Right of Access Statute" which would give political candidates for office access to the press. Arguments supporting the broader issue of access to the print media have been covered thoroughly in Jerome A. Barron, *Freedom of the Press for Whom? The Rise of Access to Mass Media* (Indiana University Press), 1973. This book was published before the Supreme Court's decision in *Miami Herald v. Tornillo,* 1974. The book still is useful for background. It should be supplemented by Benno C. Schmidt, Jr., *Freedom of the Press Versus Public Access* (Praeger Special Studies Edition, 1975). See also the bibliographies that appear in the bi-monthly *FoI Digest,* published by the Freedom of Information Center at the University of Missouri. These bibliographies include articles on mass media legal issues which have appeared in general periodicals as well as in the legal journals. An excellent article summarizing many of the issues covered in this section of the book is Ben H. Bagdikian, "First Amendment Revisionism," *Columbia Journalism Review* (May/June 1974), pp. 39–46. Recent books to consult include Theodore J. Schneyer and Frank Lloyd, *The Public-Interest Media Reform Movement: A Look at the Mandate and a New Agenda* (Aspen Institute, 1977) and a fascinating report of three studies of access: one on the U.S., another on Canada, and the third dealing with European models of access. It is Frances J. Berrigan, ed., *Access: Some Western Models of Community Media* (Unesco, 1977).

   One of the reasons there is such concern for access to the media is that ownerships of newpapers and newpaper/broadcast facilities constitute a monopoly situation in many cities in the U.S. Consult article 5, by Gerald C. Stone, for up-to-date information on this issue. See also Peter Dreier and Steve Weinberg, "Interlocking Directorates,"*Columbia Journalism Review* (November/December 1979), pp. 51–55, 58–68, which shows that "most of the 290 directors of the 25 largest newspaper companies are tied to institutions the papers cover."

Rights of Access and Reply

Clifton Daniel

9

So far as I am concerned, we can begin with a stipulation. I am perfectly prepared to concede that there is a problem of access to the press in this country. However, the dimensions of the problem have been greatly exaggerated, and the proposed legal remedies are either improper or impractical.

   My contention is that the remedies should be left largely to the press itself and to the reading public, and that adequate remedies are available.

   About the dimensions of the problem: I suppose there *are* some publishers and editors who capriciously and arbitrarily refuse to print material with which they disagree. But I don't know them.

   In an adjudication made two years ago, the British Press Council, which is the official British forum for complaints against the press, had this to say: "We are finding more and more than even quite large localities cannot support more than one newspaper. We are satisfied, however, that most editors of such newspapers are now accepting it as a duty to see, as far as possible, that events and views of interest to all shades of opinion are impartially reported while reserving the editorial right to come down on one side or the other."

   Exactly the same thing could be said—and truthfully said—about the press in this country. More than thirty years ago, Eugene Meyer, who had quarreled with the New Deal, resigned from the Federal Reserve Board, and bought the Washington *Post,* set out deliberately to find a New Deal columnist for his newspaper. He thought his readers were entitled to get the New Deal point of view as well as his own.

Clifton Daniel, associate editor of the *New York Times,* was a member of a six-man panel before the Section on Individual Rights and Responsibilities, 1969 American Bar Association Convention. The text was reprinted in the December 1969 *Seminar Quarterly* and is used with Mr. Daniel's permission.

Mr. Daniel's comments are directed toward proposals which were being advanced (in 1969) by Professor Jerome Barron and others regarding access to the press by minorities and politicians, Daniel's arguments stand today in rebuttal to the preceding article, number 8, by Phil Jacklin.

Hundreds of American publishers and editors take the same attitude today. They go out of their way to find columnists and commentators who are opposed to their own editorial policies.

New ideas are not being suppressed. On the contrary, a hurricane of dissent is blowing through the world. It is shaking the foundations of all our institutions. Can anyone here doubt the truth of that statement?

When and where has it ever before been possible for a man like the Rev. Ralph D. Abernathy to reach an audience of millions by simply painting a few signs, assembling 150 poor people, and appearing before the television cameras at the gates of Cape Kennedy?

The great guru of the right of access, Prof. Jerome Barron of the George Washington Law School speaks of insuring "access to the mass media for unorthodox ideas."

I thought until I got into this argument that the main complaint against the press was that we were giving too much access to the unorthodox—hippies, draft-card burners, student rioters, black militants, and the people who make dirty movies and write dirty books. At least, that's the message I get from the mail that comes across my desk.

In spite of the mail, I still concede that there is a problem of access to the press. But its dimensions are not great and the solutions proposed are not practical.

Advocates of the right of access blandly ignore the problems and techniques of editing a newspaper. Prof. Barron speaks of the press as having "an obligation to provide space on a non-discriminatory basis for representative groups in the community."

Note the key words: Space. Non-discriminatory. Representative groups.

First: Space! How much space?

The New York *Times* received 37,719 letters to the editor in 1968. At least 85 to 90 per cent of these letters, in the words of our slogan, were "fit to print." However, we were able to accommodate only six per cent. If we had printed them all—all 18 million words of them—they would have filled up at least 135 complete weekday issues of the New York *Times*. Yet, every letter-writer probably felt that he had some right of access to our columns.

Some letter-writers and readers have been aggressively trying to enforce that presumed right. For many months the adherents of an artistic movement called Aesthetic Realism have been petitioning and picketing the New York *Times,* demanding reviews for books and paintings produced by members of the movement. Criticism, incidentally, would be meaningless if critics were required to give space to artistic endeavors they consider unworthy of it.

Art galleries in New York plead for reviews. They contend that it is impossible to succeed in business without a critical notice in the *Times*. That is probably true. But no one, surely, is entitled to a free ad in the newspapers. No artist has a *right* to a clientele. He has to earn his audience by the forcefulness of his art, the persuasiveness of his talent. How much more cogently does this apply to political ideas!

Non-discriminatory! Discrimination is the very essence of the editing process. You must discriminate or drown.

Every day of the year the New York *Times* receives an average of a million and a quarter to a million and a half words of news material. At best, we can print only a tenth of it. A highly skilled, high-speed process of selection is involved—a massive act of discrimination, if you like—discrimination between the relevant and the irrelevant, the important and the unimportant.

When I was preparing these remarks, I suggested to my secretary that she buy a bushel basket, and fill it with press releases, petitions, pamphlets, telegrams, letters and manuscripts. I wanted to empty the basket here on this platform just to show you how many scoundrels, scroungers and screwballs, in addition to respectable citizens and worthy causes, are seeking access to the columns of our newspaper.

Actually, 168 bushels of wastepaper, most of it rejected news, are collected and thrown away every day in the editorial departments of the New York *Times*. Do you imagine that the courts have the time to sort it all out? Do they have the time and, indeed, do they have the wisdom? Even if judges do have the time to do my job as well as their own, I think Ben Bagdikian, the leading critic of the American press, is right when he says that "judges make bad newspaper editors."

Representative groups! What constitutes a representative group? Who is to decide? I would say that representative groups already have access to the press. It's the unrepresentative ones we have to worry about.

I am not prepared to argue that it's easy for anybody with a cause or a grievance to get space in the newspapers. Indeed, it isn't easy. In my opinion, it shouldn't be. When you begin editing by statute or court order, your newspaper will no longer be a newspaper. It will be "little more than a bulletin board," as Mr. Jencks has said, [Richard W. Jencks, then President, Columbia Broadcasting system Broadcast Group] "—a bulletin board for the expression of hateful or immature views."

Nowhere in the literature on access to the press do I find any conspicuous mention of the hate groups. Does this newfangled interpretation of freedom of the press mean that an editor would be obliged to give space to ideas that are hateful to him? Must he give space to advertisements that are offensive to his particular readers? Must a Jewish editor be forced to publish anti-Semitism? Must a Negro editor give space to the Ku Klux Klan?

Prof. Barron, it seems to me, looks at these problems in a very simplistic way, and defines them in parochial terms. All but the most localized media have national connections of some sort: They broadcast network television programs. They buy syndicated columnists. They subscribe to the services of the great national news agencies. An idea that originates in New York is, within a matter of minutes, reverberating in California.

In determining who is to have access to the press, who would decide how widely an idea should be disseminated? Must it be broadcast in prime time on the national networks? Must it be distributed by the Associated Press and United Press to all their clients? And must all the clients be required to publish or broadcast it? Just asking these questions shows how impractical it is to enforce access to the press by law or judicial fiat.

It is impractical in another sense. In contested cases, it might take a year or more to gain access to the press for a given idea or item of news. And if there is anything deader than yesterday's news, it's news a year old.

Not only is it impractical to edit newspapers by statute and judicial interpretation, but it would, in my view, be improper—that is to say, unconstitutional.

My position on that point is a very simple one: Freedom of the press, as defined by the First Amendment, means freedom of the press. It doesn't mean freedom *if,* or freedom *but.* It means freedom *period.* Prof. Barron's proposition, however exhaustively elaborated, cannot disguise the fact that it involves regulation of the press—freedom *but.*

I cannot guess what the makers of our Constitution would have said about television, but I have a pretty good idea of what they meant by freedom of the printed word, and they certainly did not mean that it should be controlled, regulated, restricted or dictated by government officials, legislators or judges. Indeed, the makers of the Constitution meant exactly the opposite—that officialdom, constituted authority, should keep its hands off the press, that it should not tell newspapers what to print or what not to print.

To repeat: My proposition does not mean that there is no need for greater access to the press. It simply means that legislators and judges should not be—indeed cannot be—the ones to decide how much access there should be. Editors should decide, under the pressure of public and official opinion, constantly and conscientiously exercised.

There are effective devices that the newspapers and their readers could employ. Mr. Bagdikian mentions some of them in the *Columbia Journalism Review:*

1. Start a new journalistic form: an occasional full page of ideas from the most thoughtful experts on specific public problems.
2. Devote a full page a day to letter-to-the-editor.
3. Appoint a fulltime ombudsman on the paper or broadcasting station to track down complaints about the organization's judgment and performance.
4. Organize a local press council of community representatives to sit down every month with the publisher.

Press councils have already been tried in several small cities. They work well. A press council for New York City—or perhaps a media council, taking in broadcasters as well as newspapers and magazines—is under consideration by the Twentieth Century Fund. In September, 1969 the Board of Directors of the American Society of Newspaper Editors went to London to make a study of the British Press Council. [See articles 15 and 16 in this book for information on press councils.]

There are also other ways, as Mr. Bagdikian says, "of keeping the press a relevant institution close to the lives of its constituents."

One way is hiring reporters from minority groups, as the newspapers are now doing. Not only is opportunity given to the minorities, but also they bring into the city room the special attitudes of their communities.

In New York the communities themselves, with outside help, are bringing their problems to the attention of the press. Community representatives have been meeting with newspaper editors and broadcasting executives under the auspices of the Urban Reporting Project. A news service is being organized by the Project to provide continuous reporting from the neglected neighborhoods to the communications media.

In one of the neighborhoods—Harlem—a new community newspaper, the *Manhattan Tribune,* has been established to train Negro and Puerto Rican journalists.

I am aware that not everybody with a cause can afford a newspaper to promote it. It is not as difficult, however, to launch a new newspaper as some people would have you believe.

In 1896 a small-town publisher, Adolph S. Ochs, came to New York from Chattanooga, Tenn., borrowed $75,000, bought the moribund New York *Times,* and converted it into an enterprise that is now worth $400 million on the American Stock Exchange.

They say nobody will ever be able to do that again. But I wonder.

Fourteen years ago, Norman Mailer, the novelist, and Edwin Fancher put up $5,000 apiece to start an offbeat, neighborhood weekly in Greenwich Village. Altogether, only $70,000—less than Adolph Ochs needed to gain control of the New York *Times*—had to be invested in the *Village Voice* before it turned a profit. Its circulation is now more than 127,000—greater than the circulation of 95 per cent of United States dailies. Its annual profit is considerably more than the capital that was required to launch it.

From the beginning, the *Village Voice* has been a forum for those unorthodox opinions that are said to be seeking access to the press.

It was the *Village Voice* that blazed the trail for the underground press. While you may think that the underground press is scatological and scurrilous, its existence is nevertheless welcome proof that our press is indeed free, and that the First Amendment does not have to be reinterpreted, rewritten or wrenched out of context to give expression to unorthodox ideas.

I had not intended in these remarks to discuss the right of reply. But I think I should respond to Commissioner Cox, [FCC Commissioner Kenneth A. Cox] who says that Congress could constitutionally apply equal time and right-of-reply obligations to newspapers.

I don't agree with him. The First Amendment very plainly says—it couldn't be plainer—that Congress shall make *no law*—*no* law—abridging freedom of the press.

However, the right of reply does not provide as much of a problem for newspapers as enforced access to the press. Indeed, the right of reply is widely recognized and accepted. In practice, most newspapers recognize a prior-to-publication right of reply when dealing with controversial matters.

On the New York *Times*, we have a standing rule that anyone who is accused or criticized in a controversial or adversary situation should be given an opportunity to comment before publication. The rule is sometimes overlooked in the haste of going to press. It is often not possible to obtain comment from all interested parties, but the principle is there and the effort is required. More importantly, the same is true of the news agencies which serve practically every daily paper and broadcasting station in the United States.

The right of reply after publication is also widely accepted. However, I would caution against creating an absolute right of reply or trying to enshrine such a right in law. Newspapers, it seems to me, *must* have the right to refuse to publish a reply, provided they are willing to accept the consequences of doing so—a suit for damages, for example.

Bibliography

Clifton Daniel's argument that the First Amendment protects the print media against access efforts was reaffirmed in *Miami Herald v. Tornillo, 1974.* Several law articles have been written on this case. A good, general survey is found in Note, "Reaffirming the Freedom of the Press: Another Look at *Miami Herald Publishing Co. v. Tornillo*," *Michigan Law Review* (November 1974), pp. 186–214. Daniel's point that newspapers already are opening their pages to non-staff members is treated in David Shaw, "Newspapers Offer Forum to Outsiders," Los Angeles *Times* (October 13, 1975)., pp. I–1 ff. The Shaw study deals with the Op-Ed pages (pages opposite the editorial page) of metropolitan newspapers, treating in depth the New York *Times* and the Los Angeles *Times.*

10 What Can We Do About Television?

Nicholas Johnson

Nicholas Johnson, former FCC Commissioner, is the author of *How to Talk Back to Your Television Set.* This article appeared in *Saturday Review,* July 11, 1970, and is reprinted with the permissions of Mr. Johnson and of *Saturday Review,* copyright 1970. Mr. Johnson now is publisher of *access,* biweekly magazine of the National Citizens Committee for Broadcasting, located in Washington, D.C.

Television is more than just another great public resource—like air and water—ruined by private greed and public inattention. It is the greatest communications mechanism ever designed and operated by man. It pumps into the human brain an unending stream of information, opinion, moral values, and esthetic taste. It cannot be a neutral influence. Every minute of television programing—commercials, entertainment, news—teaches us something.

Most Americans tell pollsters that television constitutes their principal source of information. Many of our senior citizens are tied to their television sets for intellectual stimulation. And children now spend more time learning from television than from church and school combined. By the time they enter first grade they will have received more hours of instruction from television networks than they will later receive from college professors while earning a bachelor's degree. Whether they like it or not, the television networks are playing the roles of teacher, preacher, parent, public official, doctor, psychiatrist, family counselor, and friend for tens of millions of Americans each day of their lives.

TV programming can be creative, educational, uplifting, and refreshing without being tedious. But the current television product that drains away lifetimes of leisure energy is none of these. It leaves its addicts waterlogged. Only rarely does it contribute anything meaningful to their lives. No wonder so many Americans express to me a deep-seated hostility toward television. Too many realize, perhaps unconsciously but certainly with utter disgust, that television is itself a drug, constantly offering the allure of a satisfying fulfillment for otherwise empty and meaningless lives that it seldom, if ever, delivers.

Well, what do we do about it? Here are a few suggestions:

STEP ONE: *Turn on.* I don't mean rush to your sets and turn the on-knob. What I do mean is that we had all better "turn on" to television—wake up to the fact that it is no longer intellectually smart to ignore it. Everything we do, or are, or worry about is affected by television. How and when issues are resolved in this country—the Indochina War, air pollution, race relations—depend as much as anything else on how (and whether) they're treated by the television networks in "entertainment" as well as news and public affairs programing.

Dr. S. I. Hayakawa has said that man is no more conscious of communication than a fish would be conscious of the waters of the sea. The analogy is apt. A tidal wave of television programing has covered our land during the past twenty years. The vast majority of Americans have begun to breathe through gills. Yet, we have scarcely noticed the change, let alone wondered what it is doing to us. A few examples may start us thinking.

The entire medical profession, as well as the federal government, had little impact upon cigarette consumption in this country until a single young man, John Banzhaf, convinced the Federal Communications Commission that its Fairness Doctrine required TV and radio stations to broadcast $100-million worth of "antismoking commercials." Cigarette consumption has now declined for one of the few times in history.

What the American people think about government and politics in general—as well as a favorite candidate in particular—is almost exclusively influenced by television. The candidates and their advertising agencies, which invest 75 per cent or more of their campaign funds in broadcast time, believe this: to the tune of $58-million in 1968.

There's been a lot of talk recently about malnutrition in America. Yet, people could let their television sets run for twenty-four hours a day and never discover that diets of starch and soda pop can be fatal.

If people lack rudimentary information about jobs, community services for the poor, alcoholism, and so forth, it is because occasional tidbits of information of this kind in soap operas, game shows, commercials, and primetime series are either inaccurate or missing.

In short, whatever your job or interests may be, the odds are very good that you could multiply your effectiveness tremendously by "turning on" to the impact of television on your activities and on our society as a whole—an impact that exceeds that of any other existing institution.

STEP TWO: *Tune in.* There are people all over the country with something vitally important to say: the people who knew "cyclamates" were dangerous decades ago, the people who warned us against the Vietnam War in the early Sixties, the people who sounded the alarm against industrial pollution when the word "smog" hadn't been invented. Why didn't we hear their warnings over the broadcast media?

In part it is the media's fault, the product of "corporate censorship." But in large part it's the fault of the very people with something to say who never stopped to consider how they might best say it. They simply haven't "tuned in" to television.

Obviously, I'm not suggesting you run out and buy up the nearest network. What I am suggesting is that we stop thinking that television programing somehow materializes out of thin air, or that it's manufactured by hidden forces or anonymous men. It is not. There is a new generation coming along that is substantially less frightened by a 16mm camera than by a pencil. You may be a part of it. Even those of us who are not, however, had better tune in to television ourselves.

Here is an example of someone who *did.* The summer of 1969, CBS aired an hour-long show on Japan, assisted in large part by former Ambassador Edwin Reischauer. No one, including Ambassador Reischauer and CBS, would claim the show perfectly packaged all that Americans want or need to know about our 100 million neighbors across the Pacific. But many who watched felt it was one of the finest bits of educational entertainment about Japan ever offered to the American people by a commercial network.

Ambassador Reischauer has spent his lifetime studying Japan, yet his was not an easy assignment. An hour is not very long for a man who is used to writing books and teaching forty-five-hour semester courses, and there were those who wanted to turn the show into an hour-long geisha party. He could have refused to do the show at all, or walked away from the project when it seemed to be getting out of control. But he didn't. And as a result, the nation, the CBS network, and Mr. Reischauer all benefited. (And the show was honored by an Emmy award.)

There are other Ed Reischauers in this country: men who don't know much about "television," but who know more than anyone else about a subject that is important and potentially entertaining. If these men can team their knowledge with the professional television talent of others (and a network's financial commitment), they can make a television program happen. Not only ought they to accept such assignments when asked, I would urge them to come forward and volunteer their assistance to the networks and their local station managers or to the local cable television system. Of course, these offers won't always, or even often, be accepted—for many reasons. But sooner or later the dialogue has to begin.

There are many ways you can contribute to a television program without knowing anything about lighting or electronics. Broadcasters in many large communities (especially those with universities) are cashing in on local expertise for quick background when an important news story breaks, occasional on-camera interviews, suggestions for news items or entire shows, participation as panel members or even hosts, writers for programs, citizen advisory committees, and so forth. Everyone benefits. The broadcaster puts out higher-quality programing, the community builds greater citizen involvement and identification, and the television audience profits.

Whoever you are, whatever you're doing, ask yourself this simple question: What do I know or what do I have to know or might find interesting? If you're a Department of Health, Education and Welfare official charged with communicating vital information about malnutrition to the poor, you might be better off putting your information into the plot-line of a daytime television soap opera than spending a lifetime writing pamphlets. If you're a law enforcement officer, you might do better by talking to the writers and producers of *Dragnet, I Spy,* or *Mission: Impossible* than by making slide presentations.

STEP THREE: *Drop out.* The next step is to throw away most of what you've learned about communication. Don't make the mistake of writing "TV essays"—sitting in front of a camera reading, or saying, what might otherwise have been expressed in print. "Talking heads" make for poor television communication, as educational and commercial television professionals are discovering. Intellectuals and other thinking creative people first have to "drop out" of the traditional modes of communicating thoughts, and learn to swim through the new medium of television.

Marshall McLuhan has made much of this clear. If the print medium is linear, television is not. McLuhan's message is as simple as one in a Chinese fortune cookie: "One picture worth thousand words"—particularly when the picture is in color and motion, is accompanied by sound (words and music), and is not tied to an orderly time sequence.

Mason Williams, multitalented onetime writer for the Smothers Brothers, is one of the few to see this new dimension in communication. He describes one of his techniques as "verbal snapshots"—short bursts of thought, or poetry, or sound that penetrate the mind in an instant, then linger. Here are some that happen to be about television itself: "I am qualified to criticize television because I have two eyes and a mind, which is one more eye and one more mind than television has." "Television doesn't have a job; it just goofs off all day." "Television is doing to your mind what industry is doing to the land. Some people already think like New York City looks." No one "snapshot" gives the whole picture. But read in rapid succession, they leave a vivid and highly distinctive after-image.

Others have dropped out of the older communications techniques and have adapted to the new media. Those students who are seen on television—sitting in, protesting, assembling—are developing a new medium of communication: the demonstration. Denied traditional access to the network news shows and panel discussions, students in this country now communicate with the American people via loud, "news-worthy," media-attractive aggregations of sound and color and people. Demonstrations are happenings, and the news media—like moths to a flame—run to cover them. Yippie Abbie Hoffman sees this clearer than most.

> So what the hell are we doing, you ask? We are dynamiting brain cells. We are putting people through changes. . . . We are theater in the streets: total and committed. We aim to involve people and use. . . . any weapon (prop) we can find. All is relevant, only "the play's the thing." . . . The media is the message. Use it! No fund raising, no full-page ads in *The New York Times,* no press releases. Just do your thing; the press eats it up. Media is free. *Make news.*

Dr. Martin Luther King told us very much the same thing. "Lacking sufficient access to television, publications, and broad forums, Negroes have had to write their most persuasive essays with the blunt pen of marching ranks."

Mason Williams, Abbie Hoffman, Dr. Martin Luther King, and many others have set the stage for the new communicators, the new media experts. All dropped out of the traditional communications bag of speeches, round-table discussions, panels, symposia, and filmed essays. And they reached the people.

STEP FOUR: *Make the legal scene.* Shakspeare's Henry VI threatened: "The first thing we do, let's kill all the lawyers." Good advice in the fifteenth century perhaps. But bad advice today. We need lawyers. And they can help you improve television.

Examples are legion. The United Church of Christ successfully fought *two* legal appeals to the United States Court of Appeals for the District of Columbia, one establishing the right of local citizens groups to participate in FCC proceedings, and one revoking the license of WLBT-TV in Jackson, Mississippi, for systematic segregationist practices. In Media, Pennsylvania, nineteen local organizations hired a Washington lawyer to protest radio station WXUR's alleged policy of broadcasting primarily right-wing political programing. In Los Angeles, a group of local businessmen challenged the license of KHJ-TV, and the FCC's hearing examiner awarded them the channel. [Editor's Note: The challenge was rebuffed by the Commission.] There are dozens of other examples of the imaginative use of rusty old legal remedies to improve the contribution of television to our national life.

For all their drawbacks, lawyers understand what I call "the law of effective reform"; that is, to get reform from legal institutions (Congress, courts, agencies), one must assert, first, the factual basis for the grievance; second, the specific legal principle involved (Constitutional provision, statute, regulation, judicial or agency decision); and third, the precise remedy sought (legislation, fine, license revocation). Turn on a lawyer, and you'll turn on an awful lot of legal energy, talent, and skill. You will be astonished at just how much legal power you actually have over a seemingly intractable Establishment.

STEP FIVE: *Try do-it-yourself justice.* Find out what you can do without a lawyer. You ought to know, for example, that every three years *all* the radio and television station licenses come up for renewal in your state. You ought to know when that date is. It is an "election day" of sorts, and you have a right and obligation to "vote." Not surprisingly, many individuals have never even been told there's an election. [Editor's note: The renewal schedule is given below in this article.]

Learn something about the grand design of communications in this country. For example, no one "owns" a radio or television station in the sense that you can own a home or the corner drugstore. It's more like leasing public land to graze sheep, or obtaining a contract to build a stretch of highway for the state. Congress has provided that the airwaves are public property. The user must be licensed, and, in the case of commercial broadcasters, that license term is for three years. There is no "right" to have the license renewed. It is renewed only if past performance, and promises of future performance, are found by the FCC to serve "the public interest." In making this finding, the views of local individuals and groups are, of course, given great weight. In extreme cases, license revocation or license renewal contest proceedings may be instituted by local groups.

You should understand the basic policy underlying the Communications Act of 1934, which set up the FCC and gave it its regulatory powers. "Spectrum space" (radio and television frequencies) in this country is limited. It must be shared by taxicabs, police cars, the Defense Department, and other business users. In many ways it would be more efficient to have a small number of extremely high-powered stations blanket the country, leaving the remaining spectrum space for other users. But Congress felt in 1934 that it was essential for the new technology of radio to serve needs, tastes, and interests at the local level—to provide community identification, cohesion, and outlets for local talent and expression. For this reason, roughly 95 per cent of the most valuable spectrum space has been handed out to some 7,500 radio and television stations in communities throughout the country. Unfortunately, the theory is not working. Most programing consists of nationally distributed records, movies, newswire copy, commercials, and network shows. Most stations broadcast very little in the way of locally oriented community service. It's up to you to make them change.

You have only to exercise your imagination to improve the programing service of your local station. Student groups, civic luncheon clubs, unions, PTAs, the League of Women Voters, and so forth are in an ideal position to accomplish change. They can contact national organizations, write for literature, and generally inform themselves of their broadcasting rights. Members can monitor what is now broadcast and draw up statements of programing standards, indicating

The controversial "family hour" plan whereby shows depicting much sex and violence would be kept off the air until small children supposedly were in bed brought cries of "censorship" from television artists. But other critics said it was not stopping the flow of offensive materials. Still others suggested that while the networks should be more responsible, each family was responsible for its own hours of watching television. The courts decided against the NAB Code application, but many stations followed the practice voluntarily. In their own sensuous way, so did the networks.

Television's Family Viewing Concept... A Big Step Forward!

We believe in Freedom of Expression…
Freedom without responsibility
destroys itself.

Broadcasters are increasingly demonstrating their responsibility through their adoption of the Family Viewing concept of the NAB Code.

The family is the most important organization in our society. There is a crucial need for television programs that—
  —effectively communicate the moral standards and vital ideals so essential in
   a wholesome society.
  —help strengthen the family and the home.

WE ENDORSE THE NAB CODE **FAMILY VIEWING** CONCEPT AND SUPPORT ALL THOSE WHO ARE CONCERNED AND ACTIVE IN ITS IMPLEMENTATION.

> "Television is a gift from God....
> and God will hold those who utilize this
> divine instrument accountable to Him."
> —Philo T. Farnsworth
> Leading Inventor of Television

Bonneville International Corporation

The Bonneville Group

KIRO AM·TV Seattle, Washington	KSL AM·FM·TV Salt Lake City, Utah
KSEA·FM Seattle, Washington	KMBZ/KMBR Kansas City, Missouri
WRFM New York, New York	KBIG/KBRT Los Angeles/Avalon, Calif.
WCLR Skokie/Chicago, Illinois	Bonneville Broadcast Consultants, Tenafly, N.J.

what they would like to see with as much specificity as possible. They can set up Citizens Television Advisory Councils to issue reports on broadcaster's performance. They can send delegations to visit with local managers and owners. They can, when negotiation fails, take whatever legal steps are necessary with the FCC. They can complain to sponsors, networks, and local television stations when they find commercials excessively loud or obnoxious. If you think this is dreamy, pie-in-the-sky thinking, look what local groups did in 1969.

Up for Renewal?

All licenses within a given state expire on the same date. Stations must file for license renewal with the FCC ninety days *prior* to the expiration date. Petitions to deny a station's license renewal application must be filed between ninety and thirty days prior to the expiration date. Forthcoming expiration dates* of stations located in the following states include:

- Iowa and Missouri: February 1, 1980, and 1983.
- Minnesota, North Dakota, South Dakota, Montana, and Colorado: April 1, 1980, and 1983.
- Kansas, Oklahoma, and Nebraska: June 1, 1980, and 1983.
- Texas: August 1, 1980, and 1983.
- Wyoming, Nevada, Arizona, Utah, New Mexico, and Idaho: October 1, 1980, and 1983
- California: December 1, 1980, and 1983.
- Washington, Oregon, Alaska, Guam, and Hawaii: February 1, 1981, and 1984.
- Connecticut, Maine, Massachusetts, New Hampshire, Rhode Island, and Vermont: April 1, 1981, and 1984.
- New Jersey and New York: June 1, 1981, and 1984.
- Delaware and Pennsylvania: August 1, 1981, and 1984.
- Maryland, the District of Columbia, Virginia, and West Virginia: October 1, 1981, and 1984.
- North Carolina and South Carolina: December 1, 1981, and 1984.
- Florida, Puerto Rico, and the Virgin Islands: February 1, 1982, and 1985.
- Alabama and Georgia: April 1, 1982, and 1985.
- Arkansas, Louisiana, and Mississippi: June 1, 1982, and 1985.
- Tennessee, Kentucky, and Indiana: August 1, 1982, and 1985.
- Ohio and Michigan: October 1, 1982, and 1985.
- Illinois and Wisconsin: December 1, 1982, and 1985.

*Dates subject to change.

Texarkana was given national attention [in 1969] when a large magazine reported that the city's population of rats was virtually taking over the city. Of lesser notoriety, but perhaps of greater long-run significance, was an agreement hammered out between a citizens group and KTAL-TV, the local television station. In January 1969, the Texarkana Junior Chamber of Commerce and twelve local unincorporated associations—with the assistance of the Office of Communications of the United Church of Christ—filed complaints with the FCC, and alleged that KTAL-TV had failed to survey the needs of its community, had systematically refused to serve the tastes, needs, and desires of Texarkana's 26 per cent Negro population, and had maintained no color origination equipment in its Texarkana studio (although it had such equipment in the wealthier community of Shreveport, Louisiana). But they didn't stop there. Armed with the threat of a license renewal hearing, they went directly to the station's management and hammered out *an agreement* in which the station promised it would make a number of reforms, or forfeit its license. Among other provisions, KTAL-TV promised to recruit and train a staff broadly representative of all minority groups in the community, employ a minimum of two full-time Negro reporters; set up a toll-free telephone line for news and public service announcements and inquiries, present discussion programs of controversial issues, including both black and white participants, publicize the rights of the poor to obtain needed services; regularly televise announcements of the public's rights and periodically consult with all substantial groups in the community regarding their programing tastes and needs.

The seeds of citizen participation sown in Texarkana have since come to fruition elsewhere. Just recently five citizens groups negotiated agreements with twenty-two stations in Atlanta, Georgia, and similar attempts have been made in Shreveport, Louisiana; Sandersville, Georgia; Mobile, Alabama; and Jackson, Mississippi.

In Washington, D.C.,. . . a group of students under the supervision of the Institute for Policy Studies undertook a massive systematic review of the license applications of all television stations in the area of Washington, D.C., Virginia, West Virginia, and Maryland. They used a number of "performance charts" by which they evaluated and ranked the stations in amounts of news broadcast, news employees hired, commercials, public service announcements, and other factors. The result was a book that may become a working model for the comparative evaluation of television stations' performances.[1] Citizens groups all over the country can easily follow their example.

I have felt for some time that it would be useful to have detailed reviews and periodic reports about the implications of specific television commercials and entertainment shows by groups of professional psychiatrists, child psychologists, educators, doctors, ministers, social scientists, and so forth. They could pick a show in the evening—any show—and discuss its esthetic quality, its accuracy, and its potential national impact upon moral values, constructive opinion, mental

1. IPS, *Television Today: The End of Communication and the Death of Community,* $10 from the Institute for Policy Studies, 1540 New Hampshire Avenue, N.W., Washington, D.C.

health, and so forth. It would be especially exciting if this critical analysis could be shown on television. Such professional comment would be bound to have *some* impact upon the networks' performance. (The 1969 *Violence Commission Report* did.) It would be a high service indeed to our nation, with rewards as well for the professional groups and individuals involved—including the broadcasting industry. It is not without precedent. The BBC formerly aired a critique of evening shows following prime-time entertainment. It would be refreshing to have a television producer's sense of status and satisfaction depend more upon the enthusiasm of the critics and audience than upon the number of cans of "feminine deodorant spray" he can sell.

These examples are only the beginning. Television could become our most exciting medium if the creative people in this country would use a fraction of their talent to figure out ways of improving it.

STEP SIX: *Get high (with a little help from your friends).* Have you ever made a film, or produced a TV documentary, or written a radio script? That's a real high. But if you're like me, you'll need help—lots of it—from your friends. If you've got something to say, find someone who's expert in communication: high school or college filmmakers, drama students, off-time TV reporters, or local CATV outlets with program origination equipment. Bring the thinkers in the community together with the media creators. CBS did it with Ed Reischauer and its one-hour special on Japan. You can do it too. Get others interested in television.[2]

STEP SEVEN: *Expand your media mind.* Everyone can work for policies that increase the number of radio and television outlets, and provide individuals with access to existing outlets to express their talent or point of view. Those outlets are already numerous. There are now nearly ten times as many radio and television stations as there were thirty-five years ago. There are many more AM radio stations, including the "daytime only" stations. There is the new FM radio service. There is VHF television. And, since Congress passed the all-channel receiver law in 1962, UHF television (channels 14–83) has come alive. There are educational radio and television stations all over the country. There are "listener-supported" community radio stations (such as the Pacifica stations in New York, Los Angeles, Houston, and Berkeley). This increase in outlets has necessarily broadened the diversity of programing. However, since the system is virtually all "commercial" broadcasting, this diversity too often means simply that there are now five stations to play the "top forty" records in your city instead of two. In the past couple years, however, educational broadcasting has gained in strength with the Public Broadcasting Corporation (potentially America's answer to the BBC). Owners of groups of profitable television stations (such as Westinghouse and Metromedia) have begun syndicating more shows—some of which subsequently get picked up by the networks.

Cable television (CATV) offers a potentially unlimited number of channels. (The present over-the-air system is physically limited to from five to ten television

2. A free pamphlet, "Clearing the Air," has been published by Media Ithaca Department of Sociology, Cornell University, Ithaca, New York 14850. It explains how average citizens can obtain free air time over radio, television, and CATV.

stations even in the largest communities.) Twelve-channel cable systems are quite common, twenty-channel systems are being installed, and more channels will undoubtedly come in the future. Your telephone, for example, is a "100-million-channel receiver" in that it can call, or be called by, any one of 100 million other instruments in this country.

Cable television offers greater diversity among commercial television programs—at the moment, mostly movies, sports, and reruns—but it can also offer another advantage: public access. The FCC has indicated that cable systems should be encouraged and perhaps ultimately required to offer channels for lease to any person willing to pay the going rate. In the *Red Lion* case, the Supreme Court upheld the FCC's fairness doctrine and, noting the monopolistic position most broadcasters hold, suggested that "free speech" rights belong principally to the audience and those who wish to use the station, not the station owner. This concept—which might raise administrative problems for single stations—is easily adaptable to cable television.

If someone wants to place a show on a single over-the-air broadcast station, some other (generally more profitable) program must be canceled. A cable system, by contrast, can theoretically carry an unlimited number of programs at the same time. We therefore have the opportunity to require cable systems to carry whatever programs are offered on a leased-channel basis (sustained either by advertising or by subscription fee). Time might even be made available free to organizations, young film-makers, and others who could not afford the leasing fee and do not advertise or profit from their programing. Now is the time to guarantee such rights for your community. City councils all across the nation are in the process of drafting the terms for cable television franchises. If your community is at present considering a cable television ordinance, it is your opportunity to work for free and commoncarrier "citizens' access" to the cables that will one day connect your home with the rest of the world.

Television is here to stay. It's the single most significant force in our society. It is now long past time that the professional and intellectual community—indeed, anyone who reads magazines and cares where this country is going—turn on to television.

Bibliography   Consult Nicholas Johnson's *How to Talk Back to Your Television Set*. See also *Public Access/Public Interest,* Notebook No. 11 (Spring 1975), The Network Project. Following the publication of this notebook, The Network Project ceased to produce its Notebook series on electronic communication issues. These typescript publications have been useful attempts to inform people about major issues, including such problems as satellite communications, cable television, public television and other major electronic organizations or industries. For a list of publications and cassette tapes, write The Network Project, 101 Earl Hall, Columbia University, N.Y. 10027. Consult also *access,* the magazine which Johnson helped found. A good, brief summary of the development of access agreements, which Johnson has pushed and which Jencks, in our next selection, attacks, is Ronald Garay, "Access: Evolution of the Citizen Agreement," *Journal of Broadcasting* (Winter 1978), 95–106.

Broadcast Regulation by Contract: Some Observations on "Community Control" of Broadcasting

11

Richard Jencks

As America enters the second year of the decade of the Seventies, its most characteristic protest movement is no longer the Civil Rights Movement—or the Peace Movement—or the revolt of youth.

Instead, it is that combination of causes which has been summarized by the awkward word "consumerism.". . .

The consumerism movement is in many ways typically American. It is reformist in its objectives, populist in its rhetoric, intensely pragmatic in its methods.

On issues ranging from the ecological impact of pesticides to the urgent need for automobile safety, and from thermal pollution to the SST, consumerism is persuading the public to demand of government that it reorder its priorities, and that it pay less attention to conventional notions of progress.

In all of these activities the aim of consumerism was to induce government action, whether by the executive branch, by the Congress, or by regulatory agencies.

In broadcasting, consumerism has stimulated regulatory action in a number of areas, of which one of the most notable was in connection with the broadcast advertising of cigarettes.

Consumerism is responsible for another development in the broadcast field in which its role is quite different—in which it seeks not so much to encourage regulatory action as to *substitute* for government regulation a novel kind of private regulation.

That development is a trend toward regulation of broadcasting through contracts entered into by broadcast licensees with private groups—contracts entered into in consideration of the settlement of license challenges. This form of regulation has been called the "community control" of broadcasting. It begins with the monitoring and surveillance of a broadcast station by the group. It ends with the group's use of the license renewal process in such a way as to achieve a greater or lesser degree of change in—and in some cases continuing supervision of—a broadcast station's policies, personnel and programming. . . .

A strategy was developed in which a community group would, prior to the deadline for a station's renewal application, make demands for changes in a station's policies. If a station granted these demands they would be embodied in a contract and embodied, as well, in the station's renewal application. If a station refused to grant these demands the group would file a petition to deny renewal of the station's license. Such a petition, if alleging significant failures by the

Richard W. Jencks, now President, CBS Broadcast Group, delivered these remarks on "Broadcast Regulation by Private Contract: Some Observations on 'Community Control' of Broadcasting" at the 1971 Broadcasting Industry Symposium, Washington, D.C. This edited version is used with his permission.

licensee to perform his obligations, can be expected to bring about a full-scale FCC hearing. As a result, there is obviously a powerful incentive in these situations, even for the best of stations, to try to avoid a lengthy, costly and burdensome hearing by attempting to reach an agreement with such a group. . . .

Probably the most fundamental demand made in recent license challenges is that a large percentage of the station's weekly schedule be programmed with material defined as "relevant" to the particular community group—usually an ethnic group—making the demand. . . . The demands I am referring to here go far beyond even what the most responsive broadcast stations have done in the way of local public service programming or what the FCC has expected of them. In one recent case it amounted to a demand that more than 40 percent of a station's total programming schedule must be programmed with material defined as "relevant" to the minority group. . . .

Philosophically, this kind of demand raises a basic question as to the purpose of a mass medium in a democratic society. Should the broadcast medium be used as a way of binding its audience together through programming which cuts across racial and cultural lines? Or should it be used as a means of communicating separately with differentiated segments of its audience?. . . .

It seems possible that there is a strong thread of racial separatism in the demand for relevance. Like the demand of some black college students for segregated dormitories, it may be regarded in large part as a demand for segregated programming. . . .

Connected with the notion of relevance is the interesting idea that programming done as part of a requirement of "relevance" must be an accurate reflection of the "life-style" of the particular minority community.

The director of a national organization whose purpose is to encourage license challenges by local groups recently spelled out what he meant by the idea of the truthful portrayal of a life-style. On his arrival in Dayton, Ohio, to organize license challenges by local groups there *Variety* described his views as follows: "If one third of Dayton's population is black, then one third of radio and TV programming should be beamed to the black community. And this should be produced, directed and presented by blacks." Referring to "Julia," the NBC situation comedy, he was then quoted by *Variety* as saying: "How many black women really live like 'Julia'? I'd like to see her get pregnant—with no husband. That would be a real life situation."

Now, I think that was meant seriously and it is worth taking seriously. . . .

Considerations like these go directly to the heart of what a mass medium is, and how it should be used. We live in an era in which the mass media have been dying off one by one. Theatrical motion pictures are no longer a mass medium and less and less a popular art form. They now reach relatively small and diverse social groups—not infrequently, I might add, with strong depictions of social realism. They no longer reach the population at large. Magazines, once our most potent mass medium, are almost extinct as such. There are plenty of magazines to be sure, but almost all serve narrow audiences. . . . Central city newspapers, as suburbanization continues, find their ability to reach megalopolitan areas steadily decreasing. . . .

Television can be said to be the only remaining mass medium which is capable of reaching most of the people most of the time. Is it important to preserve television as a mass medium? I think so. I think so particularly when I consider the racial problem in this country.

For the importance of television as a mass medium has not been in what has been communicated *to* minorities as such—or what has been communicated *between* minority group leaders and their followers—but in what has been communicated *about* minorities *to the general public.* . . .

Such communication occurs when programs are produced for dissemination to a mass audience for the purpose of *uniting* that audience in the knowledge of a problem, or in the exposure to an experience, not for the purpose of fragmenting that audience by aiming only at what is deemed "relevant" by leaders of a single minority group. . . .

I referred earlier to the excoriation by some black leaders of NBC's "Julia," the first situation comedy to star a black woman. The question may well be asked whether the shift for the better in white American attitudes about black people is not more likely to have been caused by programs like "Julia"—and by the startling increase in the number of black faces on other television entertainment programs which began in the mid-60s—as it is to any other single cause.

No one should doubt that racial attitudes *have* changed, even though much remains to be done. A Gallup poll, published last May, asked white parents in the South whether they would object to sending their children to school where any Negroes were enrolled. In 1963, in answer to the same question, *six* out of every *ten* white parents in the South had told Gallup pollers that they would object to sending their children to schools where any Negroes were enrolled. In 1970, seven years later, according to Gallup, only *one* parent in *six* offered such an objection. Other recent public opinion polls show similar gains in white attitudes toward blacks.

These advances in the direction of an integrated society were made possible in part, I suggest, by a mass medium which, with all its faults, increasingly *depicted* an integrated society. . . . Americans who in their daily lives seldom or rarely deal on terms of social intimacy with black people have been seeing them on the television screen night after night for some years now. . . .

If audience fragmentation to meet the special requirements of minority groups would destroy television as a *local* mass medium it would, by the same token, of course, make impossible the continuance of network television as a *national* mass medium. Again, some might welcome this. Some think it might happen anyway. John Tebbel, writing recently in *The Saturday Review,* observed: "There is no reason to suppose that network television is immune to the forces that are gradually breaking up other national media." He does not, however, celebrate that possibility. "It is seldom realized," writes Tebbel, "how much network television binds the nation together. . . . To fragment television coverage into local interests might better serve the communities, as the egalitarians fashionably argue, but it would hardly serve the national interest which in the end is everyone's interest."

I have discussed what seems to me to be the basic objective in community group demands upon the media—the fragmentation of programming to serve what are perceived as ethnically relevant interests.

The *means* used by the community groups may have an important impact on the nature of American broadcast regulation, and in particular upon the FCC. Commissioner Johnson often has provocative insights and this instance is no exception. He has praised the idea of regulation by community groups and has called upon his colleagues on the Commission to, in his words, "set a powerful precedent to encourage local public interest groups to fight as 'private attorney generals' in forcing stations to do what the FCC is unable or unwilling to do: improve licensee performance." [Ed.: See article 10.]

This puts the question quite precisely. *Should* private groups be encouraged to do what official law enforcement bodies are "unable or unwilling to do"? In particular, should they police a licensee by means of exploiting the power of that very regulatory agency which is said to be "unable or unwilling" to do so?

It would seem that to ask the question is to answer it. Despite the trend of vigilantism in the Old West, it is not a theory of law enforcement which has found many supporters in recent times.

In the first place, private enforcement is unequal. Although Commissioner Johnson may refer to the role of these groups as that of "private attorney generals," they do not act as a *public* attorney general has to act; the demands they make on a television or radio station are rarely if ever concerned with any constituents other than their own.

In the second place, private law enforcement is hard to control. Whenever law enforcement depends on the action of private groups, the question of private power is apt to become all too important. A medium which can be coerced by threat of license contest into making such concessions to black or Spanish-speaking groups can as readily be coerced by a coalition of white ethnic groups. More so, in fact, since in most American cities there is, and will continue to be for some time, a white majority. To expect a situation to exist for long in which tiny minority groups can coerce stations into providing special treatment, and not to expect the majority to seek the same power over the station, is to expect, in Jefferson's famous phrase, "what never was and never will be."

Clearly there is at the heart of this matter a broad question of public policy—namely, whether public control of licensee conduct should be supplemented by any form of private control. It is plain that the encouragement of "private attorney generals" will result to some degree in the evasion of the legal and constitutional restraints which have been placed upon the regulation of broadcasting in this country. . . .

For a weak broadcaster, if not a strong one, will doubtless be found agreeable to entering into a contract under which he will be required to do many things which the Commission itself either *cannot do, does not wish to do* or *has not yet decided to do. . . .*

All this might be questionable enough if community group leaders were clearly representative, under some democratically controlled process, of the individuals for whom they speak. However public spirited or *bona fide* their leadership, . . . this is rarely the case. The groups making these challenges are loosely organized and tiny in membership. Not infrequently, the active members of a group seeking to contract with stations in a city of several million number scarcely more than a few dozen.

So far the effectiveness of community group strategy has rested upon the paradoxical willingness of the Commission to tacitly support these groups and their objectives. . . . Many of those who believe that the Commission is a "do-nothing" agency may not be concerned with where regulation by private contract is likely to lead. Others may feel that to weaken duly constituted regulatory authority by condoning such private action is, in the long run, to make the performance of broadcast stations subject to undue local community pressures. These pressures may not always be exerted in socially desirable ways.

Not long ago the Commission held that it was wrong for a broadcast licensee to settle claims made against it by a community group by the payment of a sum of money to the group even for the group's legal expenses. The Commission felt that this would open the way to possibility of abuse, to the detriment of the public interest. But nonmonetary considerations which flow from the station to a community group can be just as detrimental. Suppose, for example, a weak or unwise station were to give a community group special opportunities to influence the coverage of news. Is such a concession less damaging to the public interest than the payment of money?. . . . I mentioned early in this talk that the consumerism movement, at its best, is in many ways fully within the American tradition. . . . But it must be added that the movement is also typically American in its excesses. It is sometimes puritanical, usually self-righteous and often, in its concern with ends, careless about means.

The American system of broadcasting, while not perfect, has made real contributions to the public good and social unity. It has done this through the interaction of private licensees, in their role as trustees of the public interest, on the one hand, and the authority of government through an independent nonpartisan regulatory agency. Heretofore in this country when we have spoken about the community, we have generally meant the community as a whole, acting through democratic and representative processes.

I suggest that those who are interested in the quality of life in this country— as it pertains to the preservation of a vigorous and independent broadcast press— should wish to see that private community groups do not supplant the role either of the broadcaster or of the Commission.

Bibliography

Richard Jencks' complaint regarding challenges to station renewals expresses a view shared by many professional broadcasters. Since this is clearly a regulatory issue, publications that deal with license renewals are valuable. Don R. LeDuc, editor, "Issues in Broadcast Regulation," *Broadcast Monographs*, No. 1 (1974) is an excellent source of information on this and related issues. Richard E. Wiley, former chairman of the FCC, has expressed his views regarding challenges in a speech delivered to the Florida Association of Broadcasters. It has been reprinted in Ted C. Smythe and George A. Mastroianni, eds., *Issues in Broadcasting: Radio, Television, Cable* (Mayfield Publishing Company, 1975). Two solid, recent books on broadcast regulation are Barry Cole and Mal Oettinger, *Reluctant Regulators: The FCC and the Broadcast Audience* (Addison-Wesley, 1978), and Erwin G. Krasnow and Lawrence D. Longley, *The Politics of Broadcast Regulation,* revised edition (St. Martin's Press, 1978). Both are necessary reading for the student who intends to master the field.

Criticism of the Mass Media

Let's Come Out Front
So Maybe We Have Some
Conflicts of Interest

Cassandra Tate

12

The large color photograph of the late A. L. (Bud) Alford which has decorated the Lewiston Morning Tribune newsroom for more than a decade was moved recently from the north wall to the south.

The relocation was not undertaken lightly, the Tribune being an institution with a particular reverence for tradition, thanks in part to Alford, its publisher for 22 years.

Alford was a staunch member of the swivelchair school of journalism. He used to go off on expense-paid cruises on Navy ships and then come back and write unabashed and lengthy feature stories about the virtues of the Navy and its ships. As a member of various civic boards and commissions, etc., he would either tell a reporter what to write about a group's meeting or write the report himself. He was considered a very public-spirited citizen.

Times change. Yesterday's public spirit is today's conflict of interest.

"Our standards have changed," says Ladd Hamilton, the Tribune's day managing editor. "We're a lot cleaner than we used to be. We don't go on the junkets we went on. We don't accept the freebies we used to. When the circus came to town, some guy would always come in and pass out 50 tickets. We're not accepting those types of gifts anymore. People aren't offering them anymore, either.

"Those cruises Bud Alford used to go on—that wasn't right. That was the Navy buying a whole bunch of cheap publicity. But it was accepted in those days."

The times have changed to the point that the current publisher, A. L. (Butch) Alford Jr., who took over after his father's death in 1968, offers to make a complete personal financial statement available to anyone who wants to see it. Alford is even more active in civic affairs than his father, but he no longer writes reports on any of the groups he is affiliated with. He meticulously avoids any contact with the newsroom over his more controversial activities. And he still worries that he is open to conflict-of-interest charges.

This story itself is a further gauge of changes since Bud Alford's day.

"It's the first time in my association with the paper that we've thought to look at ourselves," says Alford Jr. "This is a healthy thing. I hope as a result of this editorial coverage of ourselves we can see the weaknesses in our own process."

Early in 1978 the Los Angeles *Times* ran David Shaw's extensive article on conflict of interest among journalists: "Journalists—to March or Just Observe?" Copies were distributed to other newspapers across the country; some reprinted. The Lewiston *Morning Tribune* (Idaho) assigned Cassandra Tate to localize the story, to "examine potential conflicts of interest right in the paper's own back yard." This article is the result. It is a remarkable document because it probably is the most thorough such examination a newspaper has ever published about itself.

What Is a Conflict?

There are about as many definitions of what constitutes conflict of interest for today's journalists as there are journalists.

At one end of the spectrum in the Tribune's newsroom is the young reporter who argues that any type of community involvement, from joining the Jaycees to serving on a beautification committee, poses a potential conflict. At the other end is an old pro who thinks a political reporter can get involved in party politics with no loss of credibility.

Should the journalist exercise the rights and responsibilities of citizenship by participating in civic and political affairs? Or should he/she remain above the fray, a neutral observer? There is danger of conflict in the first course, the potential for social isolation and sterility in the second.

As far as Alford is concerned, the answer is "responsible participation," with the journalist disqualifying himself from covering subjects in which he has a direct personal or financial interest.

"There is an undetermined but definite loss of credibility when people from the newspaper become newsworthy," he says, "but there's a very real gain. Newspaper types must involve themselves in civic responsibilities just the same as lawyers, morticians and Indian chiefs. I caution to point out that journalists must maintain their own vigil for potential self-conflict, but so too should the lawyer, mortician and Indian chief.

"I feel uneasy that there is potential conflict of interest with myself and several other people at the Tribune. But I think responsible participation—as opposed to absolutely no participation in civic affairs—is in the best interests of both the community, the Tribune and the individual."

Alford is president of the Idaho Board of Education and a director of the Lewiston Roundup Association (the city's rodeo, a major civic event), the Lewis-Clark Boys Club, the Nez Perce National Historical Park Advisory Committee and the Twin County United Way. He is a member of the St. Joseph's Hospital Lay Advisory Board and the Bonneville Power Regional Advisory Council, a trustee of the Potlatch Corp. Foundation for Higher Education and a director of the Idaho First National Bank. He represents the Board of Education as a director of the University of Idaho Foundation. He is active in the Lewiston Chamber of Commerce.

Alford's sources of income are his Tribune salary, dividends from the Tribune Publishing Co.; salary and dividends from Hahn Supply, Inc., which he operates in partnership with his brother, Charles; Hahn Investments, another partnership with his brother; dividends and director's fee from Idaho First National, and dividends from investments in three mutual funds.

Copies of his complete income tax return are filed with the Tribune newsroom secretary and may be examined by anyone.

The question then arises: Can a newspaper fairly report and freely comment on the activities of a public body headed by its publisher?

"The biggest cross that Butch has is the Board of Education," says Hamilton, "but I think we've worked that out fairly well. He just doesn't see anything anybody's writing about the state board. Normally, if he's in the office, he sees the edits before they go on the hook. Except those. He's never seen any of those."

Reporter Kevin Roche, who covers the board regularly, says the boss's presence does affect what he writes, but only because of his own sense of propriety. "If I get his name in there too often, I guess I think of readers receiving that as being an effort to enhance Alford's position on the board," he says. "So I have to make a conscious effort to err on the side of using him perhaps less than I normally would. While it is a generally enlightened board, he's a better speaker, a better advocate for a particular position. It would be easy to use too much of what he says. If I weren't working for him, I would use him more.

"This isn't at all on his direction, incidentally—he doesn't tell me what to do or what not to do."

Alford says his involvement with the Board of Education has serious potential for the appearance of conflict—which can damage a newspaper's credibility as much as or even more than actual conflict.

"Many, hopefully not most, people are going to see a conflict there," he says. "When my explanation of complete separation is given, heads will nod, but I'm sure there will be those who think it's a lot of crap."

Alford does occasionally, through assignments given to the managing editors, tell reporters what to do with less controversial subjects.

But there is room for conflict in even the generally innocuous things that most people would regard as "worthwhile." The United Way, for instance, competes with other groups for charity dollars. People can get caught with their hands in the cookie jars of any organization. Could the Tribune cover any such squabble or scandal with its credibility intact in view of the publisher's involvement? It could be a problem and it would be awkward, Alford concedes.

The Publisher's Projects

The publisher's interest in a particular civic project, too, can affect the paper's coverage of that project.

A case in point is the Valley Racquet Club. Two years ago, the club undertook to cover the tennis courts at Lewis-Clark State College. Alford, a member of the club, frequently asked for stories promoting the project. The opponents' point of view—that the covering was ecologically unsound, an ugly intrusion onto the campus and unneeded in the "banana belt" Lewis-Clark Valley—was not given equal coverage.

"I suppose we did overplay the covered tennis courts," Hamilton says. "As I recall those days, the assignments were coming down from Butch's office. I'd get a reminder note to check on the progress of the tennis courts—the same kind of note I'd get on anything he was aware of. This happened to be a thing he was aware of."

There is general agreement among the staff that the Tribune consistently overplays another of Alford's interests: the Roundup. But he is given little personal credit, or blame, for that.

Hamilton says the Roundup is overplayed because "it's a tradition here to overplay it."

Reporter Roche, voicing the majority view, says, "I've heard that Roundup week is the biggest retail sales week in Lewiston and Clarkston. Even if he wasn't on the board, it's an important event."

That's a majority view, but it's not unanimous. Speaking for the loyal opposition is reporter Gary S. Sharpe.

"I don't know how many times I've been confronted by a person [involved with Roundup and who is] aware of Butch's membership on [its] board who says, 'I think Butch would like to see this in the paper.' Any time there's a directors' meeting, we have to report it. Some of those meetings have minimum news value. We have a tight news hole all the time, and people probably would get along just as well without knowing that 16 of the 21 Roundup board members were present at a meeting at the Grizzly Bear.

"About the only negative thing that's ever written about the Roundup is how many cowboys get injured."

Nevertheless, says reporter Thomas W. Campbell, "We are a little dinky town of 31,000. If we start putting on these high-falutin' airs, we'll be in a lot of trouble. I detest the Lewiston Roundup, but a lot of people like it. It is our duty to write about what people like."

Two Schools of Thought

The young Sharpe and the veteran Campbell are members of opposing schools of thought on the journalist as participant.

"I've gone to great lengths to stay out of things I write about," says Sharpe. "I think reporters should at all times give the appearance of being neutral. When do you know that a group is going to become embroiled in some sort of controversy? When it does, who will write about it?

"The people at the Tribune would take every step to make sure it was balanced and fair, and usually the things that people are involved in are non-controversial—everyone agrees we have a sick downtown. United Way does things everyone benefits from—but you never know when it'll come back to haunt you."

Sharpe's only community involvement is serving as a high school basketball referee.

"All my outside activities are confined to things that don't appear to offer any conflict of interest," he says.

"Especially now, we have a real conflict-of-interest-oriented society because we as journalists have made people more aware of conflicts of interest. Why should we tolerate them among ourselves when we won't tolerate them among people we report on?

Campbell is chairman of the Lewiston Historic Preservation Commission, a member of the Civic Theater board of directors and a Democratic precinct committeeman. He's been told he can't continue to write about politics if he holds on to the precinct post, and he's not happy about that.

"They're saying I won't give a fair interview to the Republicans because I'm a Democratic precinct committeeman. I'm saying that doesn't make a damn bit of difference! Let your conscience be your guide."

Campbell thinks reporters should be encouraged to participate in community affairs. Limiting such activities denies reporters outlets for their interests and cheats the community out of needed expertise, he says.

"I'd be uncomfortable in something that would involve the way the Tribune would handle a story. For example, being involved in a sewer committee when a sewer bond election was going on and writing stories about the election. But historical preservation? For God's sake, everybody's in favor of that!"

The Tribune's general policy concerning staff members who are active in a particular group is to assign someone else to stories involving that group. But that is not always practical on a paper with only seven full-time reporters in the home office.

Covering Yourself

"It puts us in a real bind," says Hamilton. "We have a small staff."

Campbell recently wrote a story reporting on actions taken by the Historic Preservation Commission of which he is chairman. It was a clear-cut case of conflict of interest as far as Hamilton is concerned.

"I'm sure Tommy's fair, that he would never twist a story, but you're still covering yourself," he says. "You can't divorce yourself. You can be the most devout adherent to the principles of good journalism and still unconsciously blur the distinctions between yourself as a reporter and yourself as a participant."

Among other Tribune staffers who are active in community affairs are part-time writer Diane Pettit, a member of the Nez Perce County Planning and Zoning Commission, and business writer Sylvia Harrell, chairman of the Lewiston Planning & Zoning Commission. Neither writes stories about those groups.

Harrell has served on various city planning commissions since 1964.

"If someone would really point out to me a case for conflict with the planning and zoning board, I probably would withdraw," she says. "I would hate to. I enjoy that work. Am I serving two masters? I don't think so, but I wonder if there may be some question about it in the community. Reporters are second-class citizens in some ways. Some of us have fought against this and asserted our rights by accepting appointments to boards and commissions. In general, I think reporters should have the full rights and responsibilities of citizenship, but exercise those rights with considerable caution."

Generally, the younger members of the Tribune's staff are less involved in community affairs than the veterans.

"I think reporters should abstain from participation," says Roche, a member of the new guard. "Even if that reporter isn't covering that board, there likely will be a colleague who will have to report on those activities, and would therefore be less objective covering it."

But News Editor James Kresse, who is young and uninvolved, thinks participation, overall, is positive. "It gives the impression that the people who work for the paper are truly interested in the community's welfare," he says.

Sylvia Harrell's beat as the Tribune's business writer includes the Potlatch Corp., the area's largest industry and biggest polluter and, consequently, frequent news-maker.

Reporters, Editors and Friends

Her husband works for Potlatch.

It's a "decidedly uncomfortable" situation, she says.

Journalists, it's been said, should be friendly, but never friends. They make friends anyway, and they get married, and a conflict of interest can lurk behind every such personal association.

"I try to play it as I consider it ethically, as far as Potlatch is concerned and as far as friends are concerned," says Harrell. "I try to stay aloof.

"A reporter is by the very nature of the profession a lonely person, and he or she has got to accept that as part of a career. I can remember once when R.B. Rivers of Rivers Navigation Co. called me angrily about some story I had written and said, 'Sylvia, I thought you were my friend.' I said flatly, 'Dick, reporters aren't anybody's friends.' "

But most reporters and editors do have friends and causes and biases. And all for the best, insists Perry Swisher, the Tribune's night managing editor.

"I do not like cloistered, celibate people writing stories about people who are neither cloistered nor celibate," he says. "This town's too small. A metropolitan area is a different story, but that kind of divorcement is monastic here."

It gets to be a problem when the reporter's friends happen to be his news sources.

"People who have plowed the same furrow for too long can become advocates for people who live along those furrows," says Swisher. "You guard against that coziness in the way you handle assignments. You keep the beat and the civic activities separate.

"In any organization, perhaps 20 percent of the people are activists. Not everybody is that committed to something. Sure, those who are have influence on how something is covered. But what harm is done if a couple of people on the paper are active in the Civic Theater, friendly with Civic Theater people, and that results in better coverage of the Civic Theater?"

Swisher does as many civic pushups as almost anyone on the staff. He is chairman of the Governor's Blue Ribbon Committee on Taxation and a member of the Idaho Manpower Board and the Idaho Advisory Committee to the U.S. Commission on Civil Rights and adviser to the Lewiston Downtown Beautification and Public Safety Building committees. He served two terms in the Idaho House and one in the Senate, two of the three as a Republican, the last as a Democrat. "You shouldn't shut the newspaper off from the heartbeat of the community," he says.

Executive Editor James E. Shelledy agrees.

"I have found that truly sterile reporters are devoid of emotion, feeling, understanding and a sense of fairness. Every good reporter's got friendships. A reporter without friends, I don't want. Above all, you should attempt to be fair with your friends and your enemies.

"You can't say reporters can't know and be friends with people. I think that's more dangerous than apparent conflicts. You have to be part of the community; otherwise, you're just a journalistic android."

Editorial Page Editor Bill Hall's association with Idaho Sen. Frank Church is **Crossing Over**
the most controversial of any potential conflicts of interest involving Tribune
staff members.

Hall served as Church's press secretary for 16 months, returning to the
paper about two years ago. He is often accused of still being on Church's team.

The argument for "crossing over" is that the experience of working inside
government provides insights well worth the risk of any potential taint. But the
reporter who does so can end up with a permanent credibility problem.

Alford believes that Hall did the right thing anyway. "It has chipped away
at his credibility," he says, "but that's to be expected. It's part of the liability.
But I think he is a better editor and writer for having served in a presidential
campaign than for not having served. He is best prepared for his job by going
away and getting some hands-on experience."

Hamilton doesn't think Hall did the right thing. "It was not pristine pure
for him to go to work for a candidate and then come back. He feels inhibited
when he writes about Church. He feels this inhibition because he's an honorable
person and he's sensitive. But it still impairs his value to the newspaper."

Hall, however, says he doesn't think he's lost much credibility or gained
much insight. He regrets the continuity he lost by being absent from Idaho
politics for 16 months. He has no regrets about his "crossovers."

"There will always be people who might read my motives instead of answering my arguments, and I'm just going to have to live with that the rest of my
days," Hall says. "But I don't think the rank-and-file reader cares or remembers
that I worked for Frank Church two years ago. I'm either right or wrong; it
doesn't matter if I worked for Frank Church or the Yellowstone Park Co.

"I was in agreement with Church about 80 to 90 percent of the time before
I worked for him, and I'm about 80 to 90 percent in agreement with him now.
It comes as no shock to the readers of the Tribune that I'm opinionated on the
subject of Frank Church, or on any other subject. My bias is what I'm paid for
as an editorial writer.

"I still, with Frank Church or anyone else, call it as I see it. The readers
are going to have to judge. It's all out there in black and white."

News Editor Kresse disapproves of crossovers in general, but makes an
exception for editorial writers like Hall, "because it's his job to have opinions—
I don't think people think he has much objectivity about Church, but then again,
he's not supposed to be objective."

Shelledy, who was the campaign coordinator for Democrat Bud Davis' 1972
bid for James McClure's seat in the Senate, says it boils down to a matter of
individual professional ethics.

"If you're an honest journalist, you can be an honest public official or an
honest press secretary and come back and be an honest journalist again. You
can't be both simultaneously, but you can be both consecutively. When it's all
said and done, a good reporter is a good reporter."

These are confusing times.

It was easy enough when a conflict of interest was a clear-cut matter of, say, a financial writer who buys stock in some obscure company and then writes a glowing story about the company which causes the stock to rise.

It gets difficult when it gets subtle. Should a reporter put bumper stickers on his car? Be married to a bureaucrat? Be friends with a county commissioner? Cover the education beat if he has a child in school? Should an editor write reports for a legislative committee when he edits copy involving the legislature?

"There might not be, really, anything that's absolutely pure," says Hamilton. "But you can't be a hermit. You can't say that because you're a newspaperman you have to be a monk and stay in a cell all day. You have to live a relatively normal life and be involved in the community.

"At the same time, you've got to be clear-eyed, and write on the basis of what you see, not what you belong to or where your money might be."

Bibliography

Books dealing with some of the ethical problems in news and opinion include John Hulteng's *The Messenger's Motives: Ethical Problems of the News Media* (Prentice-Hall, 1976). See also Robert Cirino, *Don't Blame the People: How the News Media Use Bias, Distortion and Censorship to Manipulate Public Opinion* (Random House, 1971): Curtis D. MacDougall, *News Pictures Fit to Print . . . Or Are They?* (Journalistic Service, 1971); Alfred Balk and James Boylan, eds., *Our Troubled Press: Ten Years of the Columbia Journalism Review* (Little, Brown, 1971); Hillier Krieghbaum, *Pressures on the Press* (Thomas Y. Crowell, 1972); Laura Longley Babb, ed., *Of the press, by the press, for the press (And others, too)* (The Washington Post, 1974), and Richard Pollak, ed., *Stop the Presses, I Want to Get Off! Tales of the news business from the pages of [more] magazine* (Random House, 1975); George Seldes, *Even the Gods Can't Change History: The Facts Speak for Themselves* (Lyle Stuart, Inc., 1976); John M. Phelan, *Mediaworld: Programming for the Public* (Seabury Press, 1977); David Shaw, *Journalism Today: A Changing Press for a Changing America* (Harper & Row, 1977); Bruce M. Swain, *Reporters' Ethics* (Iowa State University Press, 1978); Bernard Rubin, ed., *Questioning Media Ethics* (Praeger Special Studies, 1978). These books, which are listed in chronological order, contain large numbers of examples of ethical problems in American journalism, print and electronic.

13 Ethics and Journalism
John C. Merrill

John C. Merrill is professor in the School of Journalism, University of Missouri. He is the author of several books in the field of mass media criticism and evaluation. His latest is *Ethics and the Press,* Hastings House, 1975, edited with Ralph D. Barney. This selection is reprinted with permission of Dr. Merrill and is taken from *The Imperative of Freedom,* Hastings House, 1974. This edited version also appears in *Ethics and the Press.*

When we enter the area of journalistic ethics, we pass into a swampland of philosophical speculation where eerie mists of judgment hang low over a boggy terrain. In spite of the unsure footing and poor visibility, there is no reason not to make the journey. In fact, it is a journey well worth taking for it brings the matter of morality to the individual person; it forces the journalist, among others, to consider his basic principles, his values, his obligations to himself and to others. It forces him to decide for himself how he will live, how he will conduct his journalistic affairs, how he will think of himself and of others, how he will think, act and react to the people and issues surrounding him.

Ethics has to do with duty—duty to self and/or duty to others. It is primarily individual or personal even when it relates to obligations and duties to others. The quality of human life has to do with both solitude and sociability. We do right or wrong by ourselves in that part of our lives lived inwardly or introvertedly and also in that part of our lives where we are reacting and responding to other persons. This duality of individual and social morality is implicit in the very concept of ethics. The journalist, for example, is not simply writing for the consumption of others; he is writing as *self*-expression, and he puts himself and his very being into his journalism. What he communicates is in a very real way what he himself *is*. He pleases or displeases himself—not just those in his audience. What he does to live up to some standard within him not only affects the activities and beliefs of others, but in a very real way, the very essence of his own life.

A concern for ethics is important. The journalist who has this concern obviously cares about good or right actions; such a concern indicates an attitude which embraces both freedom and personal responsibility. It indicates also that the journalist desires to discover norms for action that will serve him as guiding principles or specific directives in achieving the kind of life which he thinks most meaningful and satisfying. Ethical concern is important also for it forces the journalist to commitment, to thoughtful decision among alternatives. It leads him to seek the *summum bonum,* the highest good in journalism, thereby heightening his authenticity as a person and journalist.

What characterizes most journalists today is a lack of commitment and consistency, a lack of a coherent life plan. Before any journalist chooses any particular ethics, he must decide whether or not to be ethical: this is the first and most important choice facing him. However, it may well be, as Sartre and other Existentialists have believed, that "not to choose is already to have chosen"; that the "refusal to choose the ethical is inevitably a choice for the nonethical." There is a tendency today to identify as "ethics" any personal decision to act; anything I want to do, I do—therefore, it is ethical for me to do it. Hazel Barnes points out that this is exactly parallel to what has happened to "religion." She says that "an age which is willing to apply the term 'religion' to communism, aesthetic awe, devotion to one's fellow man, and allegiance to impartial demands of pure science has no difficulty in labeling any guiding motif or choice a personal ethics." If one accepts this position, he is really saying that nobody is really nonreligious or nonethical; all meaning will have been drained from the concepts "religious" and "ethical" if nobody can be non-religious or non-ethical.

Ethics is that branch of philosophy that helps journalists determine what is right to do in their journalism; it is very much a normative science of conduct, with conduct considered primarily as self-determined, voluntary conduct. Ethics has to do with "self-legislation" and "self-enforcement"; although it is, of course, related to *law,* it is of a different nature. Although law quite often stems from the ethical values of a society at a certain time (i.e., law is often reflective of ethics), law is something that is socially determined and socially enforced. Ethics, on the other hand, is personally determined and personally enforced—or should be. Ethics should provide the journalist certain basic principles or standards by which he can judge actions to be right or wrong, good or bad, responsible or irresponsible.

It has always been difficult to discuss ethics; law is much easier, for what is legal is a matter of law. What is ethical transcends law, for many actions are legal, but not ethical. And there are no "ethical codebooks" to consult in order to settle ethical disputes. Ethics is primarily personal; law is primarily social. Even though the area of journalistic ethics is swampy and firm footing is difficult, as was mentioned earlier, there are solid spots which the person may use in his trek across the difficult landscape of life.

First of all, it is well to establish that ethics deals with *voluntary* actions. If a journalist has no control over his decisions or his actions, then there is no need to talk of ethics. What are voluntary actions? Those which a journalist could have done differently had he wished. Sometimes journalists, like others, try to excuse their wrong actions by saying that these actions were not personally chosen but *assigned* to them—or otherwise forced on them—by editors or other superiors. Such coercion may indeed occur in some situations (such as a dictatorial press system) where the consequences to the journalist going against an order may be dire. But for an American journalist not to be able to "will" his journalistic actions—at least at the present time—is unthinkable; if he says that he is not so able and that he "has to" do this—or—that, he is only exhibiting his ethical weakness and inauthenticity.

The journalist who is concerned with ethics—with the quality of his actions—is, of course, one who wishes to be virtuous. Just what a virtuous person is, however, is somewhat circular and gets us back to the question: What is a moral or ethical person? However, the nature of virtue is not really so relative or vague if we have any respect for the great thinkers of history; there has been considerable commonality of meaning among philosophers generally, even though "virtue" has been conceptualized in terms containing considerable semantic noise.

The "Virtuous" Journalist

The virtuous journalist is one who has respect for, and tries to live by, the cardinal virtues which Plato discusses in *The Republic*. First is *wisdom,* which gives "direction" to the moral life and is the rational, intellectual base for any system of ethics. Wisdom is part natural and part acquired, combining knowledge and native abilities; it largely comes from maturing, from life experiences, from contemplation, reading, conversing and study. Second, there is *courage,* which keeps one constantly pursuing his goal, the goal which wisdom has helped him set for himself. Courage is needed to help the journalist resist the many temptations which would lead him away from the path which wisdom shows.

The third virtue is *temperance,* the virtue that demands reasonable moderation or a blending of the domination of reason with other tendencies of human nature. It is this virtue, giving harmony and proportion to moral life, which helps us avoid fanaticism in pursuit of any goal. And, last, there is *justice,* distinguished from the other cardinal virtues in that it refers more specifically to man's social relations. Justice involves considering a man's "deservingness"; each man must be considered, but this does not mean that each man has to be treated like every other—for example, justice would not require that every person elected to a city, state or national office receive equal attention on television or the same amount of space in a newspaper. Equal treatment simply does not satisfy deservingness—does not imply "just" coverage.

One sign of virtue in journalism may well be a deep loyalty to truth. At least the pursuit of truth by the journalist surely takes wisdom, courage, temperance and justice. John Whale, an editorial writer for the *Sunday Times* of London, contends that at the base of journalistic ethics is an allegiance to truth. It is the authenticity of the information contained in the story that is the journalist's chief ethical concern, according to Whale. What methods should a journalist use in trying to get at this "truth"? Whale answers: *Only those methods which the journalist would be willing to publish as part of the story.* This is one reason why Whale and many others (including me) are opposed to the passage of "shield laws." What is far more important than keeping a source's name secret, he maintains, is whether what he said is true. It is hard to verify truth if the source's name is hidden from the public. This allegiance to truth, not to some person (source) who reveals information, is what is important. Too often those who reveal information and elicit the journalist's promise not to identify them have motives other than a desire to let the truth come out. Virtue in journalism, believes Whale, has to do with getting as much truth as possible into the story—and, of course, the source of the information is *part* of the "truth" of the story.

The desire to search out and present the truth does, indeed, seem to be one of the moral foundations of libertarian journalism. Most journalists think of truth as they do of objectivity—as temporary, splintered and incomplete. Accuracy, fairness, balance, comprehensiveness are generally related to objectivity by the journalist—and, therefore, have to do with truth.

Naturally, the main problem with such truth is that it must be considered in context with editorial determinism. *What* truth—or what parts of what truth—will a journalistic medium choose to present? "All the news that's fit to print," replies *The New York Times,* proclaiming to all that certain matters (even if *truthful* or contributing to the truth) which are not considered "fit" will not be printed. Therefore, *The Times* is explicitly saying what all journalists believe and practice: truth is what journalists consider fit to call truth, just as news is what they decide is news—nothing more and nothing less.

Moral philosophers have at least given us a wide variety of alternative standards for determining virtuous actions. In general, these ethical standards boil down to two main ones: *teleological* theories and *deontological* theories. The first consider the moral rightness or wrongness of an action as the good that is produced. The second, on the other hand, hold that something other than (but sometimes, perhaps, in addition to) consequences determine which actions are morally right or good.

Teleological Theories

Teleologists look at the consequences of an act; they consider consequences and only consequences as determining the moral rightness or wrongness of actions. Teleologists differ among themselves only as to whose good it is that one ought to try to promote. Egoists, for example, hold that one should always do what will promote his own greatest good; this view was held by Epicurus, Hobbes, and Nietzsche, among others. Utilitarians—or ethical socialists—take the position that an act or rule of action is right or good if and only if it is, or probably is, conducive to the greatest possible balance of good over evil everywhere. Some utilitarians (e.g., Jeremy Bentham and J. S. Mill) have been hedonists in their view of good being connected with the greatest happiness (pleasure) to the greatest number.

Ethical egoism, one of the teleological theories, holds that it is the duty of the individual to seek his own good. This stance has a great deal to say for itself; for if we regard the moral end as perfection, it is likely that we can do very little to achieve the perfection of anybody other than ourselves. A man may influence to some degree the activities of others, but he can *control* only his own activities. This is somewhat related to Kant's "duty ethics" whereby man is urged to seek his own perfection by being obligated to a rationally accepted principle or maxim. Self-perfection is the goal of a moral life.

The universal or social ethics of utilitarianism, on the other hand, holds that every person should seek the good of his group, community, nation—or world—as a whole. It claims, in a way, to combine the true elements of egoism and altruism—as the good of the group or community will include, of course, the agent's own good. Its appeal is that it sets no narrow limits on the range of moral obligations. One form of utilitarianism, the extreme *altruistic* stance, emphasizes the seeking of good of other individuals with no regard for the agent's own good; this is the stance of self-sacrifice, with the emphasis being entirely on *others*.

The social (utilitarian) ethical theory enthrones others—the group, collective or society generally—and sees the good as that which benefits the life of the group or the society. This is usually the ethics of collective altruism, and has been expressed generally in terms of the utilitarian principle that good conduct is that which results in the greatest good to the greatest number. There are two practical problems with this theory: (1) the problem of determining what is really good for most people, and (2) the problem posed by equating "good" with majority opinion or action. The journalist, for instance, in deciding whether or not to present a story, has no sound way of knowing which action will result in the greatest good to the greatest number of people. He can only guess—and hope. The second problem above leads the journalist to a kind of "give them what they want" ethical stance, abdicating personal commitment (and personal reason) for the social determinism of "vote-morality."

Deontological Theories

These theories are quite different from the teleological ones just discussed for they hold that something other than consequences determine which actions are morally right. Some deontologists say the important thing is the motive of the agent; Kant, for example, contends that an action is justified if the intentions of the doer are good, regardless of the consequences that might ensue from the action. A deontologist believes that producing the greatest possible happiness to the greatest possible number has nothing (or may have nothing) to do with the morality of the action. He also believes that personal satisfaction or gain is irrelevant to ethical action. He sees an action being right or obligatory simply because of some fact about it or because of its own nature.

Probably the best example of a deontologist is Immanuel Kant, and his basic principle or rule—the Categorical Imperative—lies at the base of his ethical system: "Act only on that maxim which you can at the same time will to be a universal law." Kant is here offering this "imperative" as the necessary principle for determining what more specific and concrete ethical rules we should adopt to guide our behavior. He is saying, in effect, that a person is acting ethically only if he is—or would be—willing to have everyone act on his maxim. Or, said another way, a person is acting ethically if he would be willing to see his rule applied by everyone who is in a similar situation.

If we ask "Which actions are right" we are really asking for some way to identify right actions. Utilitarians (teleologists) would reply: Those which maximize utility or which do the greatest service for the greatest number, or something like that. Kant and other deontologists would claim that those actions are right which pass the test of some personal and rationally accepted imperative. For Kant, for example, virtue has nothing to do with pleasure or with any other "consequences."

If consequences and states such as happiness are not important in determining ethical actions, then what is relevant must be something to do with basic maxims or principles. For the deontologists what is important is the principle from which the action has been performed; and the test applied to the maxim must be something independent of consequence. The Categorical Imperative is not really a specific maxim from which one acts—rather it is a principle or general rule which will allow a journalist (or anyone else) to test all maxims from which he acts. It is a kind of "super-maxim" which serves to guide thinking about specific rules to be applied in specific cases. If a journalist accepts the Categorical Imperative, then it is unnecessary for him to carry around in his head (or on a printed Code or Creed) specific rules or guidelines to follow. These he formulates on the basis of his "super-maxim" as the various occasions arise. If these guidelines for each case pass the test of the Categorical Imperative, then his action based on that "super-maxim" is ethically sound, and the journalist may be considered virtuous.

Although Kant's philosophy has profoundly influenced Western thought, it is obvious that at least among modern intellectuals his strict and absolutist "duty ethics" has lost considerable appeal and force. A kind of relativism or situationism is in ascendency, an ethics which has a great appeal to those who like to think of themselves as "rational." This new situationism is a kind of synthesis emerging from the clash of ethical legalism, on one hand, and ethical antinomianism on the other. It will be discussed in the following section.

THE SAN FRANCISCO

BAY
GUARDIAN

.66. THE LARGEST CIRCULATION ALTERNATIVE NEWSPAPER WEST OF THE HUDSON. MAY 3 THROUGH MAY 16, 1975. VOL. 9 NO. 14.

C.I.A. DIARY

EXCERPTS FROM THE CIA-SUPPRESSED BOOK:
THE INCREDIBLE STORY OF PHILIP AGEE, EX-DIRTY TRICKS
OPERATIVE IN LATIN AMERICA. PAGE 17

BOOK SUPPLEMENT: INSIDE THE FICTION COLLECTIVE. THE RISE OF
WEST COAST PUBLISHING. THE FALL OF STRAIGHT ARROW BOOKS.

THE SENSITIV
OF BUDDY HA
Page 23

MorE

THE MEDIA MAGAZINE

OCTOBER 1976

GOVER
BRO
HAS HE O
IN HIS FIRS

CH
FLI
AVE UP

January 17, 1977 / $1.00

ewsw

Local Programs Dec. 6-12

TV
GUIDE

DOES
AMERICA
WANT

25¢
4

FAMILY
VIEWING
TIME?

**RESULTS OF
TV GUIDE'S
NATIONWIDE POLL**

HE **DAILY**
plash

PRESS

New Yorker cover drawing by Saxon; © 1972, The New Yorker Magazine, Inc.

THE REPUBLICAN FUNERAL· BY KARL HES

ROLLING STONE

How
Carter
Plays
The
Press:
Who'll
Win?

BY KEN
AULETTA

And:

John Simon
On Women

THE
DOUBL
EDGE
HELIX
A Biomedica
Detective Stor
y Michael Roger

KISS
Gotham Glitte

THE
Quill

OR JOURNALISTS NOVEMBER 1975 SEVENTY-FIVE CENTS

TIME

THE PRESS:
FAIR OR FOUL

E PRESIDE

OF THE

DE:
ycoon's
g Story!

ORD
AKES
CITY

Murdoch Bags
New York Post

Battles for Mags

Gotham Agog!

The ethics of "law," of "duty" and "absolute obligation" is a little strong for most thinkers. So this *legalistic* stance in ethical thinking has been confronted by its opposite: what has been called *antinomianism*. The rebel against Kantianism and other legalistic ethics has accepted what might actually be considered by some as a "nonethics"—a completely open kind of morality which is against any rules. The antinomian has, in effect, tossed out all basic principles, precepts, codes, standards and laws which might guide his conduct. Just as the legalist tends toward absolutist or universal ethics, the antinomian tends toward anarchy or nihilism in ethics. He is against standards; he thinks he needs no *a priori* guidelines, directions or moral rules. He is satisfied to "play it by ear," making ethical judgments and decisions intuitively, spontaneously, emotionally, and often irrationally. He is a kind of Existentialist—or very closely related—in that he has great faith that personal, existential instincts will give the ethical direction needed.

The antinomian in journalism is usually found in the free-wheeling ranks of rebellious journalism where an anti-Establishment stance is considered healthy. The antinomian journalist affronts mainstream journalism, making his ethical decisions as he goes—almost subconsciously—about his daily activities. His ethical (or nonethical) system might be called "whim ethics," and his confrontation with mainstream journalism is not very potent or successful because it is weakened considerably by a lack of rational force.

From the clash of these two ethical "extremes"—legalism and antinomianism—a kind of synthesis has developed which has a potent impact on ethical thinking. It is usually known as *situation ethics*. Although it is related to code or legalistic ethics more closely than it is to antinomian ethics in most of its characteristics, it does synthesize certain strains of both orientations. Like code ethics, it is basically rational, and like antinomian ethics it is relativistic and is not tied securely to absolute principles. Situation ethics begins with traditional legalistic ethics but is willing to deviate from these basic principles when rationality and the situation call for it.

The journalistic situationist may well be the one who believes that he should tell the truth *as a basic principle,* or that he should not generally distort his story, but who will, after due consideration of the situation in which he finds himself, conclude that it is all right to distort *this particular story,* or even to lie. Do the circumstances in this case warrant a departure from basic—generally held—moral guidelines: this is the rational question which always confronts the situationist. He is one, then, who takes special situations into consideration in making his ethical decisions; he is a relativist to be sure, but a rational relativist, one who *thinks* before breaking a basic ethical rule.

One who subscribes to what may be called "Machiavellian ethics" is one type of situationist. Maurice Cranston has pointed out that Machiavelli believed that persons (statesmen, at least) should not allow their relationships with other states always to be governed by the same ethical scruples that govern their dealings with private persons. His ethics, however, were really absolutist, says

Cranston; he accepted one true morality, but he believed the ruler should sometimes disregard it. As Machiavelli says in *The Prince,* the ruler "should not depart from what is morally right if he can observe it, but should know how to adopt what is bad when he is obliged to." Machiavelli does not contend that the bad is anything other than bad; he only contends that bad things are to be done only sparingly—and then only in a concealed manner, if possible.

Journalists like to point out Machiavellianism in others (especially in government officials), but they themselves very often operate under this variant of situation ethics. They usually contend they believe in absolutes (such as giving their audiences all the pertinent facts or not changing or distorting quotes from a source), yet they depart from these principles when they think that "in this special case" it is reasonable to do so. They normally talk about their belief in "letting the people know" but they determine innumerable exceptions to this principle—times when they will not (because of the circumstances of the special situation) let the people know. And, of course, they are not very interested in letting the people know that they are not knowing.

The press is much more interested, of course, in pointing out Machiavellian situationism in government officials. This is natural and it is very healthy for the press to do this, for certainly our government is filled with myriads of Machiavellian functionaries busy justifying to themselves (and sometimes to others) their departure from basic moral principles. It is interesting to note how closely members of the Nixon Administration—especially some of his closest "advisors"—followed Machiavellian situationism in rationalizing the many unethical practices connected with the Watergate Affair which got world-wide airing in 1973. Not only did these officials seem to know that what they had done was wrong or unethical, but they felt that it would be best if they kept these things secret. Certainly they were not inclined to reveal them until the press and the Congress (and the courts) forced their disclosure.

Very little has been written about journalistic ethics beyond certain repetitious phrases appearing in "codes" and "creeds" designed largely for framing and hanging as wall trappings. Perhaps one reason for this is that most editors, publishers, news directors and other journalists simply write the whole subject of ethics off as "relative," giving little or no importance to absolute or universal journalistic principles. A newspaper friend put it succinctly recently when he said that he looked at ethics as "just the individual journalist's way of doing things." Certainly a free journalist has the right to consider ethics in this way, but such a relativistic concept relegates ethics to a kind of "nothingness limbo" where anything any journalist does can be considered ethical. Or, said another way, what one journalist does can be considered just as ethical as what any other journalist does.

If we throw out absolute theories of ethics (exemplified by Kant), then a discussion of morality becomes merely a discussion of preferences, arbitrary choices, detached judgments—none of which establishes obligation. The statement "this was the right journalistic decision" means no more than "I liked this decision"—just as one might say "I liked the view of the ocean." One form of relativism in ethics contends that a journalistic practice in Context A may be quite good—ethical—while if practiced in Context B it might be bad or unethical. In other words, it would be all right to submit to government censorship without objection in the Soviet Union but not all right to submit to government censorship in the United States. Or, taking this further, it would be all right to submit to censorship in the United States "under certain conditions" but wrong to do this under other conditions. Circumstances dictate the ethics; contexts determine "rightness" or "wrongness," say the relativists.

Often I have heard, for instance, that in Mexico journalists often accept bribes to supplement their meagre incomes; I am also informed that many journalists also work for a newspaper part-time and for some politician as a sort of private "press agent"—therefore having a conflict of interest. And, I am told, that this is all right in Mexico—maybe not in the United States—but quite "acceptable" (therefore ethical?) in Mexico where the conditions are different. The relativist's position here is: If it's good in a particular society, it's good, and if it's bad, it's bad—there is really no objective or universal principle. Also I hear from Soviet journalists that close party-government control of what goes into the press and over the air-waves is quite "ethical" in the Soviet Union; it is not only "all right" that this happens—it is actually the best situation, the most moral.

The situationist positions mentioned above can be considered a part of "subjectivist" ethics for what one does in a certain situation is determined *subjectively* by the individual at the time when an ethical decision is demanded. The temper of the times has thrust the subjectivist into a dominant moral position— at least from the point of being in the majority. And for many persons today if the majority believe something ethical, then it is ethical. These are the days of the subjectivist—the relativist and situationist. These are the days when it is considered unenlightened to make a value judgment, to take a stand, to feel a sense of "duty" or have a commitment. These are the days of the person who believes one opinion is as good as another and that one man's moral standards are as good as his neighbor's. These are the days of the "we-are-probably-both-right" school of thinking, the days of the tolerant men—the "adapters"—who feel no impulse to speak out loudly and clearly on moral standards.

Although the relativistic position is indeed intriguing due to its aura of individualism . . . I must reject it. In fact, at the risk of making a value judgment, I will even say that it is not really an ethical position at all; rather it is a "non-ethics" or an "anti-ethics." When the matter of ethics is watered down to subjectivism, to situations or contexts, it loses all meaning as ethics. If every case is different, if every situation demands a different standard, if there are no absolutes in ethics, then we should scrap the whole subject of moral philosophy and simply be satisfied that each person run his life by his whims or "considerations" which may change from situation to situation. . . .

Books dealing specifically with John Merrill's topic include his own *The Imperative of Freedom* (Hastings House, Publishers, 1974), from which this was reprinted, and his edited volume, with Ralph D. Barney, *Ethics and the Press* (Hastings House, Publishers, 1975). See also Richard L. Johannesen, *Ethics in Human Communication* (C. E. Merrill, 1975); and Lee Thayer, ed., *Communication: Ethical and Moral Issues* (Gordon and Breach, 1973). An article by John M. Harrison, "Media, Men and Morality." *The Review of Politics* (April 1974), pp. 250–264, cites several examples of media performance that Harrison feels violate "a loosely defined set of standards of fairness, decency and honor in human relationships—not a monolithic dogma, but a generally accepted body of principles [p. 256]." See also the bibliography for article 12, by Tate.

Bibliography

Journalism and Criticism: The Case of an Undeveloped Profession

James W. Carey

14

It is a truism, albeit a contentious one, that in the United States there is no tradition of sustained, systematic, and intellectually sound criticism of the press. The press is certainly one of our most important institutions but in serious attention it ranks slightly ahead of soccer and slightly behind baseball. The press is attacked and often vilified, but it is not subject to sustained critical analysis— not in public, and rarely within universities or the press itself.

The task of this paper is to demonstrate that a tradition of press criticism does not exist in the United States, that a critical tradition is indispensable to the operation of democratic institutions, and that journalism criticism, properly conceived, is the criticism of language. . . .

Let us begin from this simple observation, contained implicitly at least, in everything that has been previously said: democracy is not only a form of politics; it is a form of community. As perhaps our greatest theorist on these matters, John Dewey, argued, democracy is a form of associated life, of conjoint communicated experience. But he also argued, in *The Public and Its Problems,* that today all individuals find their interests and concerns conditioned by large impersonal organizations and consequently the possibility of community as well as ethical fulfillment is seriously compromised. Dewey insisted upon communication and public debate as the instrument of realizing society as a process of association, as a community. This process of criticism, of debate, became in his thought the means by which human experience can be expanded and tied together not only in the domain of politics but in all the domains of our experience.

One of the domains of experience shared by members of modern society is that experience of the media of communication, the newspapers particularly. And this is a domain about which there is little debate of significance out in the brightly lit arena where the public lives.

James W. Carey is dean of the College of Communications at the University of Illinois, Urbana. He has written extensively in the field of mass media criticism. This article appeared first in *The Review of Politics* (April 1974) and has been edited rather severely because of space limitations. Students wishing to see the full development of Dr. Carey's arguments should turn to the original publication. Reprinted with permission of *The Review of Politics.*

Let us now assume that all areas of experience, all institutions of modern society, must be subjected to criticism. This criticism must be based upon precise observation, clear procedure, unemotional language, subject to the cooperative correction of others, and occurring in the public forum where all affected by the institution can at least observe and comment on the critical process. Moreover, it must clarify our experience of the institution and scrutinize the values upon which the institution is based. The only things sacred in this process are the rules and procedures by which it is done and the manners necessary to make this a continuing process.

If we assume that the newspaper press is the most general forum in which this process can operate, let us look at an omnibus newspaper like the *New York Times*. In its pages, particularly the Sunday edition, one finds information, analysis, criticism of every contemporary institution. It treats art, architecture, literature, education, politics, business, religion, finance, film, and so forth. We need not discuss how well it treats these several institutions it covers. The record is, of course, quite uneven. But that aside, the fact remains that one institution is curiously exempt from analysis and criticism—the press itself. The *Times* does, of course, deal with books and devotes a daily and Sunday column to television. Aside from the quality and relevance of this, the *Times* is virtually silent about the newspaper: itself in particular, the medium in general. A rise in the wholesale price of newsprint will be reported, but that, we all know, is merely to signal an impending rise in the price of the newspaper itself. The newspaper does not, perhaps it cannot, turn upon itself the factual scrutiny, the critical acumen, the descriptive language, that it regularly devotes to other institutions. And one of the things readers are curious about, one of the things that is an important fact of their experience, one of the things they must understand if they are to critically know anything, is something critical about the newspaper itself.

There are a number of responses to this argument that must be anticipated. The first argument heard from many editors, namely, that "we are criticized all the time, that criticism of the press is abundant," simply will not wash. The critical literature in all the fields about which newspapers report, from art through education, to government and science, is enormous and often of quite high quality. For every first-class work of journalistic criticism there are a hundred exemplary works of literary criticism. There is, simply, no important critical literature concerning journalism and while the newspaper fosters such literature in every other field, it does not foster it in its own domain.

It is often argued that criticism of the press is found in the newspaper because the press reports the statements of its critics and in turn press professionals respond. But this is wholly inadequate. First, it is altogether too sporadic and undisciplined. . . . Moreover, it is usually opinions undisciplined on both sides by fact or substantial analysis, a kind of shouting match that usually talks by the point in question.

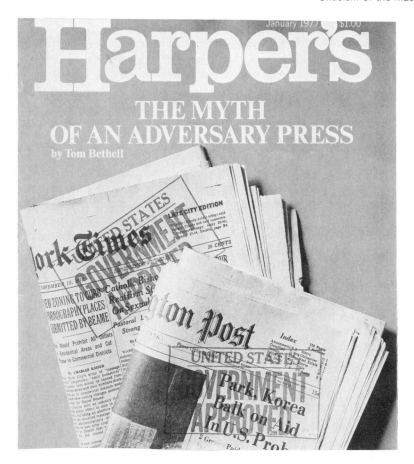

In making such responses the press often violates every standard of journalism. Journalists generally agree that dispassionate language and analysis, where affect is tightly controlled and information is maximized, are the appropriate mode of reasoned public discourse. But any criticism of the press or threat is treated as a matter of high drama. It calls forth new versions of Armageddon and the most stereotyped, bloated language imaginable. Norman Isaacs in the *Columbia Journalism Review:*

> The date was June 29, 1972—and while the countdown to 1984 stood at eleven years and six months, one had to reflect that George Orwell was, after all, author, not infallible seer. The Supreme Court of the United States, by five to four vote, ruled that the power of a grand jury took precedence over the heretofore presumed protection of the first amendment.

The problem here is in Mr. Isaacs' facts and tone. How can something be right—the sly inclusion of presumed almost saves it—that has never been recognized in common, constitutional or legislative law? Moreover, the lead violates every standard of argument known to journalism. He is talking about an important problem, but he brings to it deceptive high church rhetoric. . . . Rarely does the press respond in the language [it] expects from others, and all too often banners of constitutional rights and the people's right to know are used to paper over real difficulties.

Let me anticipate two more responses to the argument that the press is perhaps the least criticized of our important institutions. Editors often point to attempts on the part of some newspapers to create columns about the press or to create a new role within the newspaper, that of ombudsman. I applaud both of these gestures, look upon them as promising, and wish to say nothing that would discourage them. . . . Neither of these practices is completely sufficient. . . . [Both suffer] from the same ailment of being within the newspaper, internal to it rather than outside of it. . . While [they] enlarge the critical compass, [they do] not create a sufficiently diverse forum for the critical examination of the newspaper. . . .

A final defense against criticism is usually expressed as the belief that the public does not, and probably cannot, understand newspapers, and that independent critics, because they are not journalists, are not qualified to criticize the press. This is argument by mystification. When a university president rejects criticism directed against him and his institution because journalists are not academics and cannot hope to understand the university, the press quite properly points out that every institution attempts to protect itself by hiding behind special mysteries of the craft, mysteries decipherable only by the initiated and that the mystery behind the mystery is that there is no mystery at all. Newspapers defend themselves against outside criticism in the same terms they properly reject when offered by the institutions they cover. . . .

I sometimes feel, and I do not wish to be overly argumentative here, that the press has been corrupted by its own influence. Since World War II we have witnessed a decline in the independent influence of character-forming, culture-bearing agencies such as religion, the family, the ethnic group and neighborhood. The Commission on Freedom of the Press recognized this, perhaps even encouraged it, and argued that the press itself would have to become an authoritative source of values, would have to, along with the schools, enter the vacuum left by the decline of older agencies of culture and character. The press has happily stepped into this vacuum not only for the profit it brings but also for the influence it yields. Journalists, particularly those drawn in from the arts and the "new journalists," have also sensed the new avenue to power and fame through the press. But as the press has become more important, as it has become more professional, as it has become the spokesman for the community, it has also become more remote from community life. And whenever there is remoteness of an institution, a critical community grows to mediate between that institution and the community itself.

The emergence of a critical community should not be resisted by the press: it should be encouraged. . . . The criticism of the press in America, as sporadic, as inadequate, as ill-intended as it often is, is a tribute to the importance of the press in American life, an importance felt not only by government officials but by the community generally. The proper response is not a retreat behind slogans and defensive postures but the encouragement of an active and critical tradition and an important body of professional critics. . . .

But how does a newspaper connect with its community? The most generally accepted method of connection is through the roles of the representative and spectator. Here the newspaper is the eyes and ears of the audience; it goes where the reader cannot go, so that the newspaper is representing the audience at city hall because the audience as an assembled community, a public, cannot be present. It is in this vein that the newspaper takes itself to be representing the public, or more fashionably these days, the people. . . .

In fact, I think it is not a system of representation at all. The reporter at city hall less represents his audience than he represents his profession in both its commercial and literary aspects. . . . The newspaper becomes effectively responsible to itself: to its own professional standards and to its own commercial needs. In the process it loses contact with its audience [which], like the spectator at the construction of a new building grotesquely marring a community, [is] asked to bow to the standards of the professionals constructing the building when those standards are not even explained let alone defended.

A second and more desirable method of connection is through criticism; that is, through the creation of an ongoing process of judgment that sets standards for the production, distribution and consumption of journalism, and in which the community participates in significant ways. There are, at the moment, three modes of criticism: two of them are inadequate and it is to the third I wish to pay major attention.

The first form of criticism is what we might call criticism by standards of public or social responsibility. This is the form of criticism that we have largely talked about up to this point. It involves the discussion of freedom, rights and objectivity. As a critical process it largely involves various government officials and members of the press who have, at this point, largely succeeded in talking by one another and the public. The weakness of this situation has led to the recommendation for national and local press councils to be the vehicle of assessment of social responsibility.

Are such institutions the answer? I think not. In the United States national press councils are likely to be presided over by blue-ribbon panels though run by a professional staff. That is, the blue-ribbon panel is selected so as to represent the community under the theory that the press itself does not and cannot adequately represent the public interest. This interest also cannot be represented by government. . . . The operation of these councils is likely to be invested in the hands of professional staffs and the blue-ribbon panel is likely to be remote from their everyday operation. . . . In the United States press councils are likely to become one more bureaucracy.

What about local press councils? Perhaps they will work, but I am not sanguine for the reasons announced above. The people who are expected to participate in the details and time-consuming work of such councils—participation absolutely necessary if they are not to become bureaucratized—are already riddled by overparticipation. This crisis in participation has already defeated some of the best elements of the public and does not augur well for local councils.

A second critical tradition to connect the public with the media is that proposed by the social scientists and might be called scientistic criticism. Here the standards for judging the press are not abstract rights, or codes of press performances or press council evaluations of responsibility—all things on which social scientists are rather quiet—but standards derived from scientific studies of the impact of the media upon audiences. The prototype here is the national commissions on violence and pornography where the fitness, rightness, and suitability of the material are judged not by intrinsic merit or abstract rights but by the effect the material has on audience attitudes and behavior. This standard of criticism is simply wrongheaded. Its disastrous results already can be seen in the report of the Commission on Obscenity and Pornography, for the social scientific standards are in a general way destructive of culture. The questions permit no consideration of the quality, truth, or reasonableness of material, and it is obvious that any criticism of the press cannot merely test audience reactions—this would enshrine public opinion into an even more unbearable niche than it now occupies—but must work toward autonomous standards in which the audience participates but which does not allow the mere criterion of audience appetite to dictate the cultural terms of journalism.

A third tradition of criticism can be termed cultural criticism and defined, first of all, by what it excludes. Cultural criticism is not debate over abstract shibboleths such as the people's right to know, problems of access, protection of reporters' sources or standards of press performance derived from abstract canons. As much as these items may occasionally enter the critical tradition, they do not constitute such a tradition in any significant measure. By cultural criticism I mean an ongoing process of exchange, of debate between the press and its audience and, in particular, those among the audience most qualified by reason of motive and capacity to enter the critical arena. But what is the substance of this criticism, toward what is it directed? Earlier on I argued that a democratic tradition of criticism required at least three things: a set of procedures for indicating how we observe what we observe, a language relatively neutral in terms of affect or emotional coloring, and a forum in which an active response can be made to the procedures of observation and the language of description. In addition I indicated certain habits of mind were necessary: a desire to take account of contrary findings, to correct errors and revise postulates. These are the terms and manners of press criticism at the highest level of development and also the form and character of criticism that are in the shortest supply.

I am arguing that press criticism is essentially the criticism of language: it is a vital response on the part of the public to the language the press uses to describe events and to the events that accepted standards of journalistic language allow to be described. It is fully analogous to literary criticism or criticism of any cultural object: an assessment of the adequacy of the methods men use to observe the world, the language they use to describe the world, and the kind of world that such methods and language imply is in existence. It requires therefore close public attention to the methods, procedures and techniques of journalistic investigation and the language of journalistic reporting. Moreover, this scrutiny must occur before the same audience that every day consumes the end product of these procedures and language. This is the basic critical act in journalism, or so I take it, but I take it also to be the case that little criticism of this kind is in existence and that which is in existence—found largely in the reviews—rarely reaches the public.

It is a remarkable fact that each year most of us read more words by a reporter such as Homer Bigart of the *New York Times* than we do of Plato and yet today 2500 years after Plato wrote there is more critical work published on Plato every year than there is on Bigart. In fact, there is nothing published on Bigart, here used as an archetypal reporter, yet what he writes provides the critical diet for a major segment of the national "elite" community. I myself have read more words by James Reston than perhaps [by] any other human, living or dead, yet I have never seen this work "reviewed" or criticized except when a few pieces are collected in book form and then the review is inevitably by a comrade in the press. It is an anomalous fact that all of us consume more words by journalists than any other group and yet our largest and perhaps most important literary diet is never given close critical scrutiny in any systematic way. In universities we critically review the work of men in every field, devoting thousands of hours to the perceptions, methods and style of obscure 18th-century Romantic poets, yet never consider that journalists, who daily inform our lives, require, for their good and ours, at least the same critical attention. In journalism schools, preoccupied as they are with teaching the givens of the craft plus the academic asides in press history and law, critical attention is rarely given to journalistic procedure or writing or the major figures whose work exemplifies the strengths and limitations of journalism practice. Moreover, unlike other professions, journalists rarely gather to critically review one another's work, to expose its weaknesses, errors of commission and omission, and its failure to live up to professional let alone public standards. Let me make the judgment general: journalists, of all groups who expose their work to the public, are less critically examined by professional critics, the public or their colleagues. At journalistic gatherings professionals do not critique one another's work: they give one another awards.

Why should this be true? There are a number of reasons deriving from the nature of journalism but a fundamental reason is that journalism is rarely thought of as a literary act, parallel with the novel, the essay and the scientific report. However, journalism is, before it is a business, an institution or a set of rights, a body of literature. Like all literature journalism is a creative and imaginative work, a symbolic strategy; journalism sizes up situations, names their elements and names them in a way that contains an attitude toward them. Journalism provides what Kenneth Burke calls strategies for situations—"strategies for selecting enemies and allies, for socializing losses, for warding off evil eye, for purification, propitiation and desanctification, consolation, and vengeance, admonition and exhortation, implicit commands or instructions of one sort or another." Journalism provides audiences with models for action and feeling, with ways to size up situations. It shares these qualities with all literary acts and therefore like all literary acts must be kept under constant critical examination for the manner, method and purpose whereby it carries out these actions.

Journalism is not only literary art; it is industrial art. The inverted pyramid, the 5 W's lead, and associated techniques are as much a product of industrialization as tin cans. The methods, procedures and canons of journalism were developed not only to satisfy the demands of the profession but to meet the needs of industry to turn out a mass-produced commodity. These canons are enshrined in the profession as rules of news selection, judgment, and writing. Yet they are more than mere rules of communication. They are, like the methods of the novelists, determiners of what can be written and in what way. In this sense the techniques of journalism define what is considered to be real: what can be written about and how it can be understood. From the standpoint of the audience the techniques of journalism determine what the audience can think—the range of what is taken to be real on a given day. If something happens that cannot be packaged by the industrial formula, then, in a fundamental sense, it has not happened, it cannot be brought to the attention of the audience. If something happens that is only rendered in distorted fashion by the canons of journalism, then it is rendered in such distorted fashion, often without correction.

Now I am overstating the case to give a deliberate emphasis. We do not think of the conventions of journalistic investigation and reporting as stylistic strategies which not only report the world but bring a certain kind of world into existence. These canons, as I think I could demonstrate if space allowed, were derived from 19th century utilitarianism and today reflect a basically utilitarian-scientific-capitalistic orientation toward events. The conventions of journalism implicitly dissect events from a particular point of view. It is a point of view that emphasizes, as one would expect from utilitarianism, the role of personalities or actors in the creation of events and ties the definition of news to timeliness. What these conventions lack, to engage in a little criticism of my own, are precisely those elements of news which constitute the basic information on which popular rule rests: historical background and continuity, the motives and purposes of political actors, and the impact of technology, demographic change and other impersonal forces which contribute so much to the shape of contemporary events.

We must, in short, devote continuous critical attention to the methods and conventions of journalism for these methods and conventions order the world we live in into a comprehensible or baffling whole. Many of the conventions in which journalism is rooted—the inverted pryamid style, the obsessive reliance on the interview as a method of observation—are products of the 19th century and their contemporary existence implies a silent conspiracy between journalists and audiences to keep the doors of the house locked tight even though all the windows have blown out. What we lamely call the conventions of journalism were developed for another time and place. They were designed to report an orderly world of politics, international alignments, class structure and culture. Such conventions reflected and enhanced this order and fleshed out with incidental information an already settled mode of life. Human interest, entertainment, trivia, political events could be rendered in a straightforward 5 W's manner for they occurred within a setting of secure meanings and structures. Today the structure is not set and the meanings are not firm. Politics, culture, classes, generations, and international alignments are not at all orderly, yet we still filter them through conventional glasses which reduce them to type, which exorcise the realities of the world through conventional stylistics and conventional names. Indeed, this is what is meant by the now occasionally heard epithet that "communications is a menace."

Let me give three examples of the way in which journalism as a stylistic strategy renders a disservice to its audience. The examples are not new or unusual; in fact, they are well known. The first case is the reporting on Viet Nam. Allow me an extended quote from an essay I wrote in 1967:

> How does one render the reality that is Viet Nam in intelligible terms? The question is not merely rhetorical, for increasingly the ability of the American people to order and enhance their existence depends on their ability to know what really is going on. But we have this great arrogance about "communications." We treat problems of understanding as exercises in message transmittal. So here we sit shrouded in plastic, film, magnetic tape, photographs and lines of type thinking that two minutes of film or four column inches of canned type adequately render what is happening in Viet Nam or for that matter anywhere else. In point of fact, the conventions of broadcast and newspaper journalism are just about completely inadequate to "tell" this story. I am not merely caviling about turning the war into an elaborate accounting exercise of hills, tonnage and dead (after all, that is the only measure of hope and progress one has in such a war). But why is this after all a war of accounting exercises? What are the political realities that underscore the day to day events? They are known—dimly of course—and can be found in the pages of more esoteric journals of opinion and in a half hour conversation with a war correspondent when he is not talking through an inverted pyramid. But this is not a war that affects elites alone nor is it a time when we can all spend after hours with exhausted correspondents. What is sinful is that

what is known about the war, and, what is the same thing, the stylistics that can render this knowledge rarely make their way to the television screen or the newspapers. There the conventions of the craft reduce what is a hurly-burly, disorganized, fluid, non-rectilinear war into something that is straight, balanced, and moving in rectilinear ways. The conventions not only report the war but they endow it, *pari passu,* with an order and logic—an order and logic which simply mask the underlying realities. Consequently, for opponents and advocates of the war, as well as those betwixt and between, the war haunts consciousness like a personal neurosis rather than a reality to be understood.

. . . Viet Nam might have been a story but it is not like one of those we read in our youth.

Second, American journalism is still absurdly tied to events and personalities. American journalists are, in general, at a loss for what to do on the days when there isn't any news breaking. We have not learned how to report to the underlife of the country, how to get at the subterranean and frequently glacial movements that provide the meaningful substructure which determines the eruption of events and the emergence of personalities that we now call news. We still do not know how to bring to life the significance of the invisible: a slow shift in Black migration patterns out of the South, the relation between grain sales to the Soviet Union and grain elevators failing in small Illinois towns, the significance of the reduction of the birthrate and the strains created by radically unequal age cohorts, the relatively rapid embourgeoisment of Blacks—all these "events" which, because they are not tied to personalities or timeliness, escape daily journalism yet constitute the crucial stories determining the American future.

A third example I draw from a colleague, Howard Ziff. The conventions of journalism have led to an increased distance between "the Press and the pace and detail of everyday life." The ordinary events of everyday lives—things which in their meaning and consequence are far from ordinary and insignificant for the audience—have no place in daily journalism. We lack the techniques of investigation and the methods of writing to tell what it feels like to be a Black, or a Pole, or a woman—or, God forbid, a journalist or professor today. This mainstream of overwhelming significant ordinary life—what a literary critic would call the "felt quality" of life—is a main connection between the newspaper and its audience, yet we do not know how to report it well. As a result the newspaper reports a world which increasingly does not connect with the life of its audience in the most fundamental sense that the audience experiences life.

The basic critical act in journalism is public scrutiny of the methods by which journalists define and get what we call news and the conventions by which they deliver it to the public. This criticism must not only be sustained and systematic, as with literary criticism, but it must also occur in the pages of the newspaper itself, in front of the audience that regularly consumes, uses or digests what is presented. Who should do it? In a certain sense, everyone. I have suggested that the newspaper itself must bring this critical community into existence.

It must search out and find within its public those laymen that can and are interested in making a critical response to what they see and read daily. Hopefully such people will come from all strata of the public and represent its major segments. But such a community will not come into existence if the press passively awaits its appearance. The press must recognize that it has a stake in the creation of a critical community and then use its resources to foster it. For it is only through criticism that news and the newspaper can meet the standard set out for it by Robert Park: "The function of news is to orient man and society in an actual world. Insofar as it succeeds it tends to preserve the sanity of the individual and the permanence of society."

Bibliography

James Carey's article suggests the need for a type of media criticism that has not been practiced widely or well in the U.S. Two individuals stand out in their consistent pattern of media criticism, of a type suggested by Carey. One is Ben Bagdikian, national correspondent of *Columbia Journalism Review*. The other is Edward Jay Epstein. Both have written extensively, both books and articles. Bagdikian's *The Effete Conspiracy and Other Crimes by the Press* (Harper & Row, 1972), reprints 15 of his articles and short reports. They are well worth reading. Epstein seems, in many ways, to be one of the more perceptive critics today. His range of analysis is exhibited in *Between Fact and Fiction: The Problem of Journalism* (Vintage Books, October 1975), which reprints many of his articles, most of which have appeared in *The New Yorker* and *Commentary*. His "Journalism and Truth," *Commentary* (April 1974), pp. 36–40, is a very careful analysis of the limitations of present methods of gathering and presenting news. It is reprinted as the lead article in *Between Fact and Fiction*. For a survey of media criticism, see Lee Brown, *The Reluctant Reformation: On Criticizing the Press in America* (David McKay Co., Inc., 1974). For a different approach to media criticism, see Loren Ghiglione, *Evaluating the Press: The New England Daily Newspaper Survey*, copyright 1973 by Ghiglione, and William Rivers, *et al., A Region's Press* (University of California, Institute of Governmental Studies, 1971), which analyzes the newspapers of the San Francisco Bay region. Several writers discuss the role of educators in actively assessing media performance in Herbert Strentz, *et al., The Critical Factor: Criticism of the News Media in Journalism Education,* Journalism Monograph No. 32 (University of Minnesota School of Journalism, 1974). See especially the chapter "Criticism of the Media, With the Media," David L. Anderson and Loren Ghiglione. For an interesting, critical view of American journalistic practices under First Amendment protection, see Leopold Tyrmand, "The Media Shangri-La," *The American Scholar* (Winter 1975/76), pp. 752–775.

The role of journalism reviews is discussed briefly in Carey's article. For further information consult Marty Coren, "The Perils of Publishing Journalism Reviews," *Columbia Journalism Review* (November/December 1972), which was reprinted in the second edition of this book. Coren outlines the difficulties in producing journalism reviews; events occurring since the publication of our second edition bear out his pessimistic conclusions. The *Chicago Journalism Review,* one of the standard bearers in the field, folded in 1975; *The Unsatisfied Man* (Denver) collapsed in 1974. The loss of *CJR* was a particular blow because of the importance of Chicago as a media center. One of the trends in this field, aside from the tendency toward smaller numbers, is the movement toward journalism reviews produced by or in conjunction with departments of journalism. This has been particularly noticeable on the West Coast where the *Review of Southern California Journalism,* published by the campus chapter of the Society of Professional journalists, Sigma Delta Chi at California State University, Long Beach, started the trend. Unfortunately, it also died, in 1976. Following its inception, the department of journalism at San Francisco State University established *feed/back,* the School of Communications at the University of Washington established *NW Review,* and the Department of Journalism, University of Arizona, established *The Pretentious Idea.* The issues of "reporter power" and media ombudsmen have been deemphasized somewhat in recent years. Reporting on the national and world-wide condition of reporter power is Harry L. Connor, *Democracy in the Newsroom,* Freedom of Information Center, Report No. 328 (October 1974). For a brief discussion of the role of the ombudsman, see John Maxwell Hamilton, "Ombudsman for the Press," *The Nation* (March 16, 1974), pp. 335–338. The magazine entitled [more] folded in 1978; a new review, *WJR: Washington Journalism Review,* a bi-monthly established in 1978, was having financial difficulties, despite excellent coverage of Washington, D.C. media and national media.

15 Statements and Case Studies on Media Ethics

National News Council
Society of Professional Journalists,
Sigma Delta Chi

**"Statement on
General Ethics"
by National News
Council[1]**

The issue of "full disclosure of association" by syndicated columnists has escalated strongly since the National News Council held that the National Conference of Editorial Writers was quite correct in objecting to Victor Lasky and the North American Newspaper Alliance not making clear to editors being serviced with the column that he had received a $20,000 fee from the Committee to Re-Elect the President.

Although no new formal complaints have as yet been filed, the National News Council has figured in editorial comment and in tart correspondence in three other cases.

Two of the episodes have focused on columns written by Tom Braden (Los Angeles Times Syndicate) and William Buckley (Washington Star-News Syndicate), both defending Vice President-designate Nelson Rockefeller in the matter of gifts, loans and other payments made by him, or in his behalf. The third has been a controversy prompted by a letter from the president of the National Conference of Editorial Writers to Publishers-Hall Syndicate over a trip made to the Peoples Republic of China by columnist Ann Landers as a delegate of the American Medical Association.

In a column defending Mr. Rockefeller's gifts, Mr. Braden failed to state that he had sought and received a $100,000 loan from the former New York Governor. Mr. Braden's friendship with Mr. Rockefeller was of long standing, the loan was repaid with interest and the record on the transaction is clear and clean.

The Des Moines Register & Tribune made the essential point that while the column appeared to be the viewpoint of a disinterested observer, it was "instead, the sentiments (of) a man who was himself a beneficiary of Rockefeller's generosity."

The issue was identical in the episode of Mr. Buckley's column, which devoted itself to commentary about the book written by Victor Lasky about Arthur Goldberg and financed by Laurance Rockefeller to assist his brother's campaign. Mr. Buckley was not aware of all the nuances when he wrote his column, but certainly he was cognizant of the fact that the publisher of the book, Arlington House, is a subsidiary of Starr Broadcasting, Inc., of which he (Mr. Buckley) is chairman. In his column, however, Mr. Buckley saw fit only to describe Arlington House as a conservatively oriented publishing firm and that the editor "happens to be a good friend of mine."

1. This "Statement on General Ethics" was approved by the National News Council on December 10, 1974, at a meeting of the Council in Boston, Mass. Prepared by Norman F. Isaacs, Council Adviser, the statement was presented to the Council by the Council's Freedom of the Press Committee.

After the matter had been publicized, Mr. Buckley acknowledged the point candidly and said in one of his regular columns that on any such future issues, he would notify editors of any possible conflicts.

The dispute surrounding Ms. Landers' trip to China was different in that it raised the issue of financing of a trip by an outside organization as well as whether ample disclosure had been made. Both Ms. Landers and the syndicate insist that the disclosure was clear. Some editorial writers hold that it was not. That the confusion exists at all indicates some lack of clarity. More important in this issue is the financing. Where do news organizations draw the line on journalists serving as delegates for outside organizations? It is obviously a matter deserving far more thought and consideration than American news organizations have seen fit to give it.

The year 1974 has been one of breakthrough in the long battle waged within journalism for higher ethical standards. The National News Council has played a vital part in this growing movement, if it is not indeed the fulcrum of the central drive for a more responsible journalism. Hence the Council cannot but approve the spirit which has brought a determined "patrolling of the precincts" by various national news organizations, including the American Society of Newspaper Editors, the Associated Press Managing Editors Association, the Society of Professional Journalists/Sigma Delta Chi, the National Conference of Editorial Writers, and those organizations representing photographers and business and food writers.

Many editors hold that the national syndicates have been remiss in not imposing and maintaining strong standards. The syndicates have a rational defense in that they are primarily service agencies selling and distributing the work of independent producers. However, the News Council is impelled to remind both the independent writers and artists and the syndicates that awkwardness for them is certain to grow unless there comes a general recognition that all communicators are under the obvious obligation to live under the same standards they demand of those who hold public office.

It is the Council's view that every journalist should either refrain from commenting upon matters in which he or she has a familial or financial interest or make those interests so clear there can be no misunderstanding.

Twenty-seven years ago, the Commission on Freedom of the Press issued its report on mass communication. In that report was this brief passage:

> "Freedom of the press can only continue as an accountable freedom. Its
> moral right will be conditioned on its acceptance of this accountability. Its legal
> right will stand unchallenged as its moral duty is performed."

The National News Council subscribes to that concept. It is the Council's considered view that American journalism faces the immediate responsibility of moving with all the means at its command to accept the principle of full accountability in ALL of its functions.

NNC Case Study I:
Complaint No. 46
Accuracy in Media
against Jack
Anderson (Filed
September 7, 1974)

Nature of Complaint   Accuracy in Media complained of Jack Anderson column (United Features Syndicate) published in *New York Post* on August 3, 1974, and in many other newspapers on or about that date.

The column asserted that "students at the International Police Academy, a school run by the State Department to train foreign policemen, have developed some chilling views about torture tactics." In support of this statement it quoted from papers written by five students at the Academy—two from South Vietnam, one from Nepal, one from Colombia and one from Zaire. AIM asserted that the quotations were taken out of context, and misrepresented the attitudes of the students in question on the subject of torture. Mr. Anderson and his associate, Joseph C. Spear, denied this.

Members of the Council staff visited Washington and examined the five papers in full and in detail. They found that the quotations by Anderson did in fact misrepresent the attitudes of the students toward torture as set forth in their papers. In addition, they found that all five papers were written in the years 1965–1967, a fact not mentioned in the Anderson column (which gave the impression that they were reasonably contemporary).

Response of News Organization   In a letter dated December 30, 1974, Mr. Anderson insisted that the statements in his column were supported by sources whose identity he could not reveal, and suggested that members of the Council staff "spend a couple of months talking to Amnesty International and the National Council of Churches," as well as with Sen. James Abourezk and unnamed members of his staff—all of whom, it was suggested, would support Anderson's charges.

Conclusion of the Council   If such support as was alleged by Mr. Anderson exists, it is up to him, not this Council, to develop and publish it. AIM's complaint alleged simply that the five quotations set forth and relied on in the original Anderson column misrepresented the views of the writers; and the complaint is quite correct.

2. Since adoption of the above conclusion, the Council has learned that the title to the article, as prepared by Mr. Anderson's syndicate, was "U.S. Trained Foreign Cops Prefer to Stick To Torture." The title "The Torture Graduates" was placed on the column by the *New York Post*. The Council's conclusion is accordingly amended to reflect these facts. Approved by the full Council at its April 8, 1975 meeting.

Nor can Mr. Anderson escape responsibility for the misrepresentations by pointing to the second sentence of his column, which stated, "After a lengthy investigation, we found no evidence that the academy actually advocates third-degree methods." In the first place, exculpating the academy itself does not excuse leaving a false implication with respect to the views of the five named students. In the second place, the sentence was simply inconsistent with the general thrust of the column, which Mr. Anderson's own syndicate titled "The Torture Graduates."

In the circumstances, we believe the complaint is justified.

Concurring, *Cooney, Dilliard, Fuld, McKay, Otwell* and *Rusher.*

Dated   February 4, 1975.[2]

Nature of Complaint   John Haydon, former governor of American Samoa, complained that an NBC-TV "Weekend" program was inaccurate and "designed deliberately to malign the Samoan people, the administration of the territory, the Department of Interior."

The program was telecast on NBC-TV on October 19, 1974. The particular segment complained about was approximately twelve minutes in length. In his complaint, the complainant pointed out that the NBC crew spent several weeks in American Samoa filming material.

The complainant submitted his own lengthy analysis of the "Weekend" transcript, concluding with the statement:

> The film is viciously slanted and untrue. Its consistent and deliberate use of erroneous material makes it appear obvious that the producer and NBC came to American Samoa to make a film that would be controversial and would serve to give their new "Weekend" series a good kickoff. . . .

Response of News Organization   The Council held a public hearing on February 3, 1975, at which expert testimony was taken from Dr. Margaret Mead and Mr. M. G. Bales, a retired official with the Department of Interior's Office of Territorial Affairs.

NBC News responded to the Council's inquiry and to the invitation to participate in the public hearing with the following statement:

> NBC will not have a representative at the hearing. As Mr. Richard Wald stated in his letter of November 14, 1974 to Mr. William B. Arthur, NBC News is interested in maintaining standards of fairness and objectivity; but NBC News does not believe that any purpose is served by debating comments such as those made by Mr. Haydon except before the Federal Communications Commission, to which NBC, as a licensee, is accountable.
>
> NBC has cooperated with the Council in providing transcripts of the "Weekend" program involved in the Haydon complaint and in arranging for a viewing of a tape of the program.

In view of NBC's refusal to participate in the Council's investigation, the staff consulted with additional experts. These included:

> John M. Flanigan, an educator in the school system of American Samoa for six and a half years.
>
> Robert F. Williams, a television teacher in American Samoa who served also as Director of Education for a period during his stay of six years in American Samoa.
>
> Lyle M. Nelson, an educator, presently Chairman of the Department of Communication at Stanford University, who has been associated with the Samoan educational system for almost ten years.
>
> Judge Joseph W. Goss, an administrative judge who served in American Samoa with the High Court during the administration of Governor Haydon.

NNC Case Study II: Complaint No. 47 Haydon against NBC-TV (Filed November 11, 1974)

William Wohlfeld, who served as Special Assistant to Governor Haydon during his first year in American Samoa and who acquired particular familiarity with American Samoa while employed in the Department of Interior's Office of Territorial Affairs, the Department of State, the Bureau of the Budget, and various fiscal policy and management offices.

John R. Dial, who served as comptroller in American Samoa for two and one-half years, eight months under Governor Aspinall and the remainder under Governor Haydon.

Carl Mussen, who served as the Treasurer of American Samoa for six years, the first year under Governor Aspinall and the remainder under Governor Haydon.

Melvin Ember, Professor of Anthropology at Hunter College and Executive Officer of the Ph.D program in Anthropology at the Graduate School and University Center of the City University of New York.

Dan Klugherz, producer of the 1967 television documentary entitled "American Samoa: Paradise Lost?"

A. P. Lutale, the present Washington delegate-at-large from American Samoa.

In addition, the Council examined a study of instructional television in American Samoa by Wilbur Schramm of the Institute of Communication Research, Stanford University; reports of various hearings before the Subcommittee on Territorial and Insular Affairs of the House of Representatives; and newspaper articles which appeared in *The New York Times* and the *Los Angeles Times*.

Conclusion of the Council   The Council first viewed the television program complained of, then received the oral testimony of two witnesses: the distinguished and well known anthropologist, Dr. Margaret Mead, and Mr. M. G. Bales, a government official who served in American Samoa under Governor Rex Lee, and thereafter in the Department of Interior until his retirement in 1973, visiting Samoa about twice a year. The staff also interviewed a number of other experts who offered additional views on various points. It is upon the Council's evaluation of this extensive record that this opinion is based.

In Mobil against ABC, the Council held that a television producer is not required, in producing a documentary, to meet the test of absolute fairness. Under the principles of free speech, the Council believes he is entitled to very considerable latitude in determining which facts he will stress and which he will play down or totally ignore. The result may not—indeed, probably will not—be altogether "fair," balanced or dispassionate, but the disadvantages of what is often described as robust journalism are surely preferable to any attempt— certainly by this Council—to suggest a standard that is probably unattainable in any case. We must, and do, have confidence that a free interplay of biased views is likelier to produce effective guidance than a determined effort to compel adherence to a highly hypothetical "objectivity."

But while great latitude must be accorded to television producers in the case of any given documentary, that is not to say that there is not, or ought not to be, a limit to the degree of distortion and misrepresentation that a producer can indulge in. We believe that the NBC documentary on Samoa clearly exceeds that limit.

One of the most egregious single instances of misrepresentation in the documentary is its comparison of American Samoa with (formerly British) Western Samoa. The latter has ten times the area, and is capable (as American Samoa is not, and may never be) of sustaining itself economically. Political and economic solutions perfectly suited to Western Samoa are simply not applicable to American Samoa, according to expert after expert, and the documentary's clear implication to the contrary is seriously misleading.

But it is not the comparability (or otherwise) of Western Samoa, or any other single assertion in the documentary, that has led us to our conclusion. It is the over-all effect of a series of distortions and misrepresentations in the production, writing and editing, effectively contradicted by impressive witnesses in whom the Council has confidence.

We do not find or imply that Governor Haydon's administration of Samoa, or the entire American presence there, has been beneficial—or otherwise. There are clearly various opinions on both questions. Nor do we pass on Governor Haydon's charge that misrepresentations and distortions were deliberate: that is unclear, and its determination is in any case, unnecessary. But we do find, on the basis of the detailed testimony of Dr. Mead and Mr. Bales, that the aforesaid distortions and misrepresentations go well beyond any that could be justified under the rubric of robust journalism, and to that extent we find the complaint warranted.

Concurring, *Cooney, Dilliard, Fuld, Ghiglione, Height, Ivins, Otwell, Renick, Rusher* and *Straus.*

Abstentions *Brady.*

Dated April 8, 1975.

In the Public Interest (The National News Council, Inc., 1975) is a report by the NNC containing a summary of all of the Council's decisions from 1973–1975 as well as numerous special studies and reports. Appendix A lists all complaints and conclusions. See *A Free and Responsive Press: The Twentieth Century Fund Task Force Report for a National News Council*, 1972, for the rationale behind the establishment of the NNC. This report also contains studies of the Minnesota and Hawaii state news councils as well as a summary of local press councils in the U.S. A more complete report of local press council experiments in America can be found in William Rivers, *et al., Backtalk: Press Councils in America* (Canfield, 1972). A recent account can be found in Robert Koenig, *Community Press Councils—II.* Freedom of Information Center, Report No. 331 (November 1974). While the news council or press council concept has met with general acceptance in the U.S. (in November 1975 the Society of Professional Journalists, Sigma Delta Chi, passed a resolution supporting the concept of a National News Council without endorsing all of its specific procedures or the actions), many people, professionals and scholars, have argued against it. The *New York Times* has refused to cooperate in any way. The most articulate criticism has been that of Ralph L. Lowenstein of the School of Journalism, University of Missouri. Lowenstein, in two Opinion papers issued by the Freedom of Information Center, has attacked the council concept (in *The Case Against a Press*

Bibliography

Council, 008 [December 1969]) and the council's performance (in *National News Council Appraised,* 0015 [December 1974]). For the council's rebuttal to his second report, see *NNC Appraises An Appraisal,* 0017 [May 1975]). The reports of the NNC now appear regularly in a special section of *Columbia Journalism Review.*

Code of Ethics of the Society of Professional Journalists, Sigma Delta Chi

The Society of Professional Journalists, Sigma Delta Chi, believes the duty of journalists is to serve the truth.

We believe the agencies of mass communication are carriers of public discussion and information, acting on their Constitutional mandate and freedom to learn and report the facts.

We believe in public enlightenment as the forerunner of justice, and in our Constitutional role to seek the truth as part of the public's right to know the truth.

We believe those responsibilities carry obligations that require journalists to perform with intelligence, objectivity, accuracy and fairness.

To these ends, we declare acceptance of the standards of practice here set forth:

Responsibility. The public's right to know of events of public importance and interest is the overriding mission of the mass media. The purpose of distributing news and enlightened opinion is to serve the general welfare. Journalists who use their professional status as representatives of the public for selfish or other unworthy motives violate a high trust.

Freedom of the press. Freedom of the press is to be guarded as an inalienable right of people in a free society. It carries with it the freedom and the responsibility to discuss, question and challenge actions and utterances of our government and of our public and private institutions. Journalists uphold the right to speak unpopular opinions and the privilege to agree with the majority.

Ethics. Journalists must be free of obligation to any interest other than the public's right to know the truth.

1. Gifts, favors, free travel, special treatment or privileges can compromise the integrity of journalists and their employers. Nothing of value should be accepted.

2. Secondary employment, political involvement, holding public office and service in community organizations should be avoided if it compromises the integrity of journalists and their employers. Journalists and their employers should conduct their personal lives in a manner which protects them from conflict of interest, real or apparent. Their responsibilities to the public are paramount. That is the nature of their profession.

3. So-called news communications from private sources should not be published or broadcast without substantiation of their claims to news value.

4. Journalists will seek news that serves the public interest, despite the obstacles. They will make constant efforts to assure that the public's business is conducted in public and that public records are open to public inspection.

5. Journalists acknowledge the newsman's ethic of protecting confidential sources of information.

Accuracy and objectivity.   Good faith with the public is the foundation of all worthy journalism.

1. Truth is our ultimate goal.

2. Objectivity in reporting the news is another goal, which serves as the mark of an experienced professional. It is a standard of performance toward which we strive. We honor those who achieve it.

3. There is no excuse for inaccuracies or lack of thoroughness.

4. Newspaper headlines should be fully warranted by the contents of the articles they accompany. Photographs and telecasts should give an accurate picture of an event and not highlight a minor incident out of context.

5. Sound practice makes clear distinction between news reports and expressions of opinion. News reports should be free of opinion or bias and represent all sides of an issue.

6. Partisanship in editorial comment which knowingly departs from the truth violates the spirit of American journalism.

7. Journalists recognize their responsibility for offering informed analysis, comment and editorial opinion on public events and issues. They accept the obligation to present such material by individuals whose competence, experience and judgment qualify them for it.

8. Special articles or presentations devoted to advocacy or the writer's own conclusions and interpretations should be labeled as such.

Fair play.   Journalists at all times will show respect for the dignity, privacy, rights and well-being of people encountered in the course of gathering and presenting the news.

1. The news media should not communicate unofficial charges affecting reputation or moral character without giving the accused a chance to reply.

2. The news media must guard against invading a person's right to privacy.

3. The media should not pander to morbid curiosity about details of vice and crime.

4. It is the duty of news media to make prompt and complete correction of their errors.

5. Journalists should be accountable to the public for their reports and the public should be encouraged to voice its grievances against the media. Open dialogue with our readers, viewers and listeners should be fostered.

Pledge.   Journalists should actively censure and try to prevent violations of these standards, and they should encourage their observance by all newspeople. Adherence to this code of ethics is intended to preserve the bond of mutual trust and respect between American journalists and the American people.

16 Press Councils: An Evaluation
Claude-Jean Bertrand

Press Councils are now to be found all the world over, from Israel to Australia, from Finland to Portugal. With the exception of France, all industrialized democracies have some kind of Press Council, or are working on one, like Belgium or Luxembourg. Yet most non-newspeople do not know what a Press Council is, and have never heard of any. One reason is that the institution is new.

The first was created by the Swedes in 1916, but Press Councils have only multiplied since the early 1960's. Over half of them date from the 1970's, and the last three were started in 1976. Another reason is that little publicity has been given to the developing phenomenon by the mass media, be they privately- or State-owned. This lack of enthusiasm on the part of press barons may be due to their awareness that Press Councils are a symptom of a very slow trend towards control of the mass media by producers and consumers, i.e. by journalists and public. And they could become a major element in a flexible system insuring that the press is both free and socially responsible. That double hypothesis undergirds the present evaluation.

The first Press Councils to include lay people, and thus not to be glorified disciplinary commissions, were those of Turkey and South Korea—yet those few persons who *have* heard of a Press Council, know the one in Great Britain. The British Press Council was established by the national organizations of publishers, editors and journalists. It now consists of 20 representatives of those associations, of 10 co-opted members of the public, and of a retired judge as chairman. The Council does little except adjudicate complaints made against the print media. Its only means of retribution is publication of its decisions by the press.

Because of its relative success and of its visibility, the British PC has been an inspiration to many promoters and reformers of PC's over the world. It is, however, impossible to turn a description of it into *the* definition of a PC for the simple reason that a majority of existing councils would not fit in. Democrats in all countries have felt the need for an institution that would make their mass media more socially responsible while no less free, but in every nation local conditions and needs were, and are, bound to shape a different institution.

To cover every one of them, one would have to define a Press Council as a group of persons whose concern for the quality of mass media performance prompts them to use their moral influence, and little else, to improve it. Such a definition is so vague as to be useless. Press Councils cannot be apprehended precisely unless they are distributed into categories. As a preliminary to that, four points should be stressed.

Claude-Jean Bertrand, a French media scholar who has specialized in American Studies, originally published this article in the Winter 1977 issue of *Gazette*, the international journal for mass communication studies.

The first is that the mass media make up the larger part of the nervous system of a modern nation. Hence the well-being of the social body is predicated on their functioning properly. Hence, also, the media have given unprecedented power to every member of the social body. A Press Council is a means of using public opinion to pressure the media into serving 'the interest, convenience and necessity'[1] of the people. Consequently, a PC is unimaginable in any kind of dictatorship, be it white, red or polka-dot; and it is unworkable in an under-developed nation.

The second point is that the press is a public service, a fourth branch of government and an industry rolled into one. This alone accounts for most of its problems in the present day since it implies a conflictual association of four protagonists. On the one hand, the *citizens,* who have the right of information (i.e. to inform and to be informed), and the *journalists,* who possess the talent and training to obtain and convey the information. And on the other hand, the *owners* of the equipment with which the information is gathered and distributed, and the elected or appointed *managers of the nation.*

Through apathy, ignorance or narrow-mindedness, the public can jeopardize press freedom, just as the journalists can through incompetence or dishonesty. Neither group, however, can be considered a positive menace. For at least four centuries, the major threat to freedom of information has come from power-hungry political rulers. It is thus unthinkable for a PC to include agents of the government. A second major threat to the freedom of information appeared less than a century ago when the press became big business: the threat is that of profit-hungry media-owners. They too ought to be kept out of a PC. Alas, to be efficient, a council needs money and power. As neither can come from the State, the council in most cases depends on the Press Lords for funds and for access to its only source of strength, public opinion.

The third point to be made is that ideally a PC should use all possible means to improve the press. It should, among other goals, concern itself with the own-ership-structure of the mass media and with the nation's communication policies. It should ceaselessly study the evolution of the media and report on it to the public. It should serve as a permanent forum for the discussion of issues relative to mass communication. At the present time, however, a PC can usually only afford to pursue one or both of the following aims: try and help the press in its fight against the traditional enemy of its freedom, the government and its bureau-cracy; and try to make the press answerable to the public. The first objective is easy to attain. The PC has merely to warn public opinion against abuses of power by the State. In fact, that purpose is often served by older and more powerful organizations. The second objective is more elusive. Two obvious ways of reaching it are either to wait for the public to complain and then denounce abuses of power by the press; or to take the initiative, which, except for the most blatant violations of ethics, implies monitoring the press.

The fourth and last point to be made before attempting a classification of PC's, is that the media world is vast and diversified. The action of a PC can

1. Such are the terms used by the *Radio Act* of 1927 and the *Broadcasting Act* of 1934 to define the social obligations of radio (and later television) in the USA.

consequently have a larger or smaller scope depending on the area and the particular media it covers. The area covered can be anything from a small town to a continent like the US or a multinational community like the English-speaking Caribbean. The media covered can range from a single local weekly to a nation's entire printed and broadcast press.

With those considerations in mind, it is possible to distinguish between three major types of Press Councils:

A. The pseudo-Press Councils. These self-styled PC's include representatives of government, official in Sri Lanka, undercover in the Philippines. In extreme cases, all members are appointed by the government, as in Indonesia, and presided over by the Minister of Information. All such councils can be dismissed as mere instruments to muzzle the press.

B. The semi-Press Councils. These can achieve some, but only a few, of the purposes of a PC, because they do not include any lay members, except maybe the independent chairman that nearly all PC's have. At best, these PC's have been set up jointly by publishers and journalists, as in Austria. More often they represent only one group, the publishers in Denmark, the journalists in Switzerland.

Within this category, one meets with three models, the German, the Japanese and the Italian. The German *Presserat* was copied from the original British version of a PC, that of 1953. Publishers and newspeople took action to deter Federal regulation and have gone on doing just that. The *Presserat* deals with governments as representative of the industry, and it gives little attention to the ethics of the profession quite to the grievances of the public. The Japanese *Newspaper Contents Evaluation Chamber* is a bureau within the *Nihon Shinbun Kyokai,* the association of newspaper publishers. The seven veteran newsmen who man it monitor the press and report violations of its Canons of Journalism. The NSK then applies pressure on editors and publishers. The Italian *Ordine dei Giornalisti* gathers all newspeople in the country. To enter the Order and the profession, one must pass an entrance examination organized by the Order. Violations of the Code of Ethics are dealt with by regional councils, but these cases can appeal to the national council before exclusion becomes effective.

C. The true Press Councils. All involve laymen and professionals in varying proportions. The professionals are usually representatives of their associations, but they are not in the American *National News Council.* Owners usually participate, but they do not in the Dutch *Raad voor de Journalistiek.* True PC's come in three sizes, national, regional and local. In fact, such regions as Minnesota and Québec are larger than nations like the Netherlands or Israel, and their PC's are basically similar. Local PC's are very different. Not simply because they are only to be found in North America (and, with one exception, in the USA), but because they are neither lobbying agencies nor unofficial courts. They aim principally at providing direct contact between the local media and the local citizens. Hence they are usually composed only of laypeople who meet regularly with media executives to provide them with feedback and to discuss particular grievances.

Whatever they should or could do, regional and national PC's for lack of imagination and courage, and mainly for lack of funds and recognition, have all focussed on watching the media by proxy, in other words, on hearing the complaints of media consumers and giving them access to the press. Most have formed both a Freedom of Information Committee and a Committee on Ethics, but the latter is always the more active, or at least the more visible. And it functions everywhere on approximately the same pattern.

To most PC's anyone can complain, whether or not he/she has been personally hurt by the press. All complaints are screened by a special committee (Québec) or an ombudsman (Sweden) or a legal adviser (Israel). If they prove serious, the plaintiff is asked to try and settle the difference with the newspaper or broadcasting station. If that proves impossible, the PC accepts to consider the complaint, provided (most often) the plaintiff waives his right to pursue the matter before a regular court. Then an investigation takes place. The ensuing report is presented to the Council which usually holds hearings, and then makes its decision public. If it is unfavorable to the defendant, the latter is morally obliged to publish it. No appeal is allowed. At regular intervals, the PC brings out reports which provide a body of case law to supplement the Code of Ethics that a majority of PC's have adopted.

To set up a PC is no easy task, but once established it proves to be a hardy creature. If one sets aside local PC's which could be considered temporary by nature, and if one sets aside the PC's that were started in underdeveloped nations, all of which, except one, are now inoperative, no Press Council has ever died and in 1976 all reported that their influence had increased since their inauguration. A PC certainly meets many obstacles on its way to existence, but it possesses such advantages over other means of making the press socially responsible as always justify its survival.

The first and most serious obstacle which promoters encounter is psychological. A Press Council is a new idea, and as such it is disturbing. Quite naturally, professionals tend to interpret it in the light of past experience: to them it looks like some sly means to introduce government regulation. Media-owners hate it, with good reason, as a limitation to their privileges. Newspeople, accustomed as they are to criticizing others and not being criticized, resent having their work publicly evaluated by arrogant colleagues and incompetent strangers. Both employers and employees band up to protest that there is no use for a PC since the press does a good job. And that if it did not, a PC would be powerless to help: good papers do not need a council and bad papers do not care. If the consumer is displeased with the product, he/she may complain to the producer or cease to purchase the product or even go to court. What a PC does is to focus attention on the few failings of the press and to intimidate the better media into blandness.

As far as the public is concerned, the reaction is just as negative. The extreme-right and extreme-left do not trust self-regulation. Conservatives cling to the 18th century idea that free enterprise is a cure-all, while socialists find it hard to believe that a PC is more than a public-relations ploy to escape regulation. Detached observers doubt that a Press Council can influence Big Government, Big Business and Big Labour, considering its composition and the weapons at its disposal. Lastly there are lawyers who object to the parody of justice meted out by PC's. As for the citizen-in-the-street, he/she does not know about PC's and couldn't care less.

The resistance is such that few PC's have been set up without direct or indirect pressure from a government or from a legislature, even in the U.S. Usually the initiative has come from journalists. Once the owners decide they had better cooperate, two problems inevitably appear: one is setting the proportion of owners and journalists in the council, the other is deciding whether or not to admit lay people and, if so, how many and who. The more owners sit on the council, the more immediately powerful it is and the less credible. The more non-professionals sit on the council, the more credible it is and the less cooperative the press people become. How are the lay members to be selected? If they are eminent citizens chosen at random, as in Great Britain, the PC may adopt an elitist attitude. If they are to be delegates of social groups, chosen or not by organizations like labour unions, churches or political parties, the PC will be unmanageably large or will become the prey of special interests.

Once its members have been selected, the PC must decide on a policy. If it concentrates on defending the press, it will never obtain popular support, as is the case in Germany. If, on the contrary, it concentrates on attacking the press, it will lose press support and die, as it did in Turkey. Whatever policy the PC decides upon, it must have the means to implement it, i.e. money. The State should not be appealed to (though it is in Finland). Journalists cannot afford to finance a PC. Foundations are rare outside the U.S. And, of course, media-owners dislike paying for getting shot at. Once financing is more or less (usually less) provided for, the PC must acquire visibility and moral authority. In the best of circumstances, this takes years of effort, to educate the public, and of diplomacy, not to alienate the professionals.

In recent years, PC's have multiplied so much as to become a fixture in parliamentary democracies. The cause lies in the coincidence of four factors: the increasing importance of mass communications, the increasing commercialization of the media, the increasing dissatisfaction of the public with their performance, and the increasing tendency of governments to use that dissatisfaction as a pretext to regulate the media. However, PC's are not the only instrument that can be used to make a free press responsible. A quick look at some alternatives will bring out the advantages that PC's have over them.

The most obvious alternative is legislation, and it should not be dismissed out of hand with, for Americans, a reference to the First Amendment. In all democracies, even in the U.S., laws passed by a regularly elected parliament and enforced by independent courts, actually protect the press against abuse by its controllers or by outsiders. The trouble with laws is that they are subject to self-serving interpretation by whoever holds power.

The least dangerous instrument, on the contrary, is criticism, both internal and external. Peer-group pressure, ethics committees of professional organizations, readership surveys, letters-to-the-editor, accuracy forms sent to people mentioned in the news, ombudsmen, media criticism columns, journalism reviews, consumer groups, congressional reports, books and university courses provide a steady flow of criticism in the USA, and they could too elsewhere. No owner or practitioner can remain indifferent to it. The trouble is that the pressure exerted is either too general and thus weak, or too localized and thus uninfluential.

The most efficient instrument is research and education, as provided mainly by the universities. Technological and sociological research can define what is being done to inform the public, what can be done and what should be done. Education can train journalists to do their job better and make them more aware of their responsibilities to the public. The trouble here is that such a strategy produces no immediate results.

The most utopian, and maybe the most attractive, means of reform would be gradually to change the structures of the mass media along the lines suggested by British sociologist Raymond Williams. The technical equipment would pass under public ownership (not State ownership) and would be managed by boards of eminent citizens, as is now more or less the case for commercial television in Great Britain. Just as companies of actors are entrusted with a theatre, teams of journalists could use the facilities long enough to determine if they had something to say that a minimum public wanted to listen to. The obstacles to such a solution are too obvious to need elaboration.

Now, what advantages does a Press Council offer that has made so many countries decide that they needed one? Some are implied in the definition of a PC. It is democratic and yet not conditioned by a particular type of democracy or press regime. The Finnish PC covers both privately-owned newspapers and State-owned broadcasting. If all the media were publicly-owned, the need for a PC would be just as great as it is now in the U.S. where all are privately-owned. A PC is a permanent and independent body which brings together and represents capitalists, who own the power to inform; producers, who have the competence to inform; and consumers, who possess the right of information. As it is endowed with no restraining powers, its efficiency depends entirely upon the cooperation of the protagonists. The PC can adapt to various environments and to all levels of the social structure, provided only that there exists a minimum degree of economic, political and journalistic development. Lastly, a PC is multi-functional. As a master of ethics, it works not in the abstract but from experience, and it does not teach in ponderous volumes but in the columns of the daily press. As an unofficial court, it provides simple, inexpensive, competent, fast and flexible service. As a protector of freedom, it can wield the great and safe power that derives from independence and public respect.

All such qualities show in the blueprint of a true Press Council. But a PC is no longer a project. Some have been at work for a generation, and experience has proved how vain was much of the criticism that greeted their appearance. The existence of a PC never leads a government to limit the freedom of the press, on the contrary, a PC is not powerless before government. In Korea and Germany, a PC has blocked the passage or the enforcement of restrictive laws. In Britain and in Hawaii, the PC has contributed to the passage of laws favourable to the press. A PC is not powerless before the media industry. From its inception, some of the media always cooperate with it. And all others are so sensitive to bad publicity that they finally join in and start heeding its guidelines. There develops what has been called 'a conformism of quality'. A PC is not anti-media. Not even the lay people within it manifest such a bias. In fact the council proves most complaints to be groundless and preserves the honorable press from being tainted by the abuses of the few. A PC does not intimidate the media. It steers clear of the opinions they express, and, as regards news, it differentiates better than would a court between libellous and justified accusations, between sensational and investigative reporting. It thus encourages vigorous journalism.

To end the list, it may be added that Press Councils are not static institutions. Not only does their influence grow but they improve on the way. For instance, the Dutch PC is getting ready to include media-owners and thus increase its impact greatly. The Danish PC is preparing to accept lay members. The Minnesota PC has just extended its scope to broadcasting. Since few PC's can hope for the independence of the National News Council, in the US, most seem to be moving towards the Québec model. It improves on the British model in that it covers radio and television, gives equal representation to owners, journalists and laymen, uses its power of initiative and has the strong intention of dealing with concentration of ownership. The second age of PC's may not be far away when local and regional PC's will be established in nations that already have a national one. One can dream of a hierarchy of autonomous councils that would provide surveillance, access, protection and education at all levels, with the irresistible support of a finally awakened public opinion.

Does this mean that a miracle remedy has been developed? Certainly not. Press Councils, as they exist today, cannot solve the fundamental, Catch-22 problem in mass communications. That is to say the paradox that, on the one hand, wherever free enterprise has been suppressed, the freedom of the press has gone with it—and that, on the other hand, the press cannot be truly free and responsible when it is run as an industry primarily aimed at making a fortune. The worst sins of the press are sins of omission, from a television network programming no weekly public affairs show in prime time to a newspaper ignoring an unflattering report on the products of one of its major advertisers. There is not much a PC can do about this. As a matter of principle, because it is not supposed to meddle with the editing or the money-making of a newspaper or broadcasting station. Practically, because it cannot afford to monitor all the media. Or, to put it more candidly: a PC cannot tap its only font of power, public opinion, without permission from media-owners. What owners want is to maintain the status quo at the smallest possible cost. They usually sit on the council and fund it—and they always decide whether or not to publish its decisions. So, what they don't want the PC to do, the PC does not do. Even when, according to its constitution, a PC is supposed to take initiatives, to encourage research or to watch over concentration of ownership, it does not engage in such activities. It concentrates on investigating relatively rare complaints about isolated and relatively benign violations of ethics. The long record of the British Press Councils shows this clearly.

At this early stage in the evolution of Press Councils, then, what evaluation can be made of them? They are signs of a slow revolution and, to a lesser extent, agents in its progress. A new regime is being introduced in which freedom of the press is no longer the right of the rare individuals who own a press—but a right of all citizens. In no sense can this development be described as evolutionary: it *is* revolutionary. A proof of this is the rabid protests and morbid indifference which greeted the first famous manifesto of this democratically subversive movement, the report of the Hutchins Commission on the Freedom of the Press, and also the report of the first British Royal Commission on the Press. Almost 30 years later, for true revolutions are slow, the Press Council of Great Britain and the National News Council in the US have become accepted parts of the media scene. Both give journalists and lay people the actual, if unofficial, right to judge how mediaowners serve the public.

Press Councils may eventually grow into institutions guaranteeing that the control of mass communication is in the hands of the public, and of its agents, the journalists—not in those of Big Government or Big Business, so that the present technological revolution in the media may serve and not hinder a budding social revolution. But even a present-day Press Council, limited as it is, can speed up the process of positive change. Its existence and activities raise the consciousness of newspeople and of enlightened citizens. They are encouraged to use other means to the same end. About 30 Journalism Reviews were launched in the radical late 1960's and early 1970's at the time when local PC's sprouted here and there in the US. In the apathetic mid-1970's, the part of the Journalism Reviews has been taken over by many more media criticism columns in the alternative *and* in the regular press, while many more ombudsmen seem to have taken over the functions of a score of local PC's These days, professional associations and Schools of Journalism seem to have become more sensitive to the needs of the public and less concerned with the requirements of the industry. Press Councils could become the center-pieces of a loose network of non-governmental agencies fighting for press freedom and responsibility. There are straws in the wind: the *Columbia Journalism Review,* which itself is closely linked with the Columbia University Graduate School of Journalism in its March/April 1977 issue, has started publishing the current decisions and actions of the National News Council. One can easily imagine how in Minnesota the PC, the Free Press-Fair Trial Committee, the Joint Media Committee, the Twin Cities Journalism Review, the School of Journalism, the local chapter of the Society of Professional Journalists (Sigma Delta Chi), the Newspaper Guild, the Workers Participation Committee at the Minneapolis *Star* and *Tribune,* and the *Tribune's* ombudsman, might work in cooperation.

The U.S. could be the country where such a pattern of self- and public control may first emerge. One reason is that it needs it most, for the American press is the most unregulated in the world and the most commercialized. The other reason is that the US is the only nation already to possess all the elements needed to build up such a system, even though they are very much underdeveloped. The country is unique in that it has local and regional and national Press Councils; in that its national PC is independent from professional organizations and yet is obtaining recognition by them: in that American media criticism has forced its way from books and quality magazines into the newspaper press; in that a variety of journalistic organizations have developed intense interest in press ethics (e.g., the AP Managing Editors, the American Society of Newspaper Editors, the Society of Professional Journalists, the Association of Educators in Journalism). Lastly the U.S. is unique in the number of Schools of Journalism it has which produce the best trained journalists, and the most abundant and scholarly research in the world.

General List of Press Councils

I. Press councils in operation today (29+)
  A. Press Councils with lay participation (22+)
    1. National Press Councils (11)
      Sweden, founded 1916, remodelled 1969
      Finland, founded 1927, remodelled 1968
      Norway, founded 1928, remodelled 1972
      Netherlands, founded 1948, remodelled 1960
      Great Britain, founded 1953, remodelled 1963
      Israel, founded 1963
      New Zealand, founded 1972
      United States (NNC), founded 1973
      Portugal, founded 1975
      Australia, founded 1976
      West Indies, founded 1976
    2. Regional Press Councils (6)
      USA, Honolulu, founded 1970
      USA, Minnesota, founded 1971
      USA, Delaware, founded 1975
      Canada, Quebec, founded 1971
      Canada, Ontario, founded 1972
      Canada, Alberta, founded 1972
    3. Local Press Councils (5+)
      a. USA: under various names, over 12 PC's functioned between 1967 and 1973. Four
        at least are now in operation:
        Littleton, Colorado, founded 1946, remodelled 1967
        Peoria, Illinois, founded 1970
        Hawaii, Hawaii, founded 1971
        Eagle Valley, Colorado, founded 1976
      b. Canada
        Windsor, Ontario, founded 1970
  B. Press Councils without lay participation (7)
    1. Set up jointly by journalists and media-owners (2)
      West Germany, founded 1956
      Austria, founded 1961, remodelled 1963

    2. Set up by journalists (2)
       Italy, founded 1963
       Switzerland, founded 1972 (1976)
    3. Set up by media-owners (3)
       Japan, founded 1946
       South Africa, founded 1962
       Denmark, founded 1964
II. Press Councils Dissolved or Incapacitated (7)
    Chile, founded 1956, incapacitated 1973
    Turkey, founded 1960, dissolved 1968
    South Korea, founded 1961, incapacitated 1973
    Burma, founded 1962, dissolved 1964
    Pakistan, founded 1965, dissolved 1968
    India, founded 1965, dissolved 1975
    Ghana, founded 1968, dissolved 1970
III. State-controlled 'Press Councils' (5)
    Indonesia, founded 1946, remodelled 1963 and 1966
    Taiwan, founded 1963, remodelled 1974
    Philippines, founded 1965,[2] remodelled 1972, 1973, 1974
    Nepal, founded 1967
    Sri Lanka, founded 1973

Composition	Mode of action *Complaints only*	*Initiatives only*	*Monitoring only*	*Complaints & initiatives*	*Complaints & initiatives & monitoring*
Media-owners	Denmark	∅	Japan	(Philippines)	∅
M-owners & journalists	∅	∅	∅	W. Germany	∅
M-owners & public	∅	∅	∅	∅	∅
M-owners & journ. & public	Ontario	∅	∅	Quebec, etc.	S. Korea
Journalists	Switzerland	∅	∅	∅	∅
Journalists & public	Netherlands	∅	∅	Norway	∅
Public	∅	∅	∅	(local-USA)	∅

Social Responsibility and Press Councils

Bibliography

ASNE, *Ethics 1975,* American Society of Newspaper Editors, Easton (PA), 1975.
Bradley, H. J., *Enquiry on Press Councils,* 1971–1972, Bruxelles, FIJ, 1972 (mimeographed).
Bradley, H. J., *Press Councils of the World,* London, The Press Council, 1974 (mimeographed).
Commission on the Freedom of the Press, *A Free and Responsible Press,* University of Chicago Press, 1947.
Direction des droits de l'homme, *Table ronde sur les Conseils de presse,* Stockholm, 9/26–27/ 1974, Strasbourg, Conseil de l'Europe, 1974 (mimeographed).
Gerald, J. Edward, *The Social Responsibility of the Press,* Minneapolis, University of Minnesota Press, 1963.
Geyer, Francois, *Les Codes déontologiques dans la presse internationale,* FIJ and UNESCO. 1975 (mimeographed).
IPI, *Press Councils and Press Codes,* Zürich, International Press Institute, 1964 and 1967.
Loffler, M., et al., *Les Organismes d'auto-contrôle de la presse à travers le monde,* Munich, C. H. Beck, 1968.
Lowenstein, R. L., 'Press Councils: Idea and Reality', in *Fol Foundation Series,* no. 1. April 1973, Columbia, University of Missouri.
Rampal, Kuldip, *The Concept of the Press Council,* Fol Center Report no. 350, March 1976, Columbia, University of Missouri.

2. Was then a true PC, on the British model.

Richstad, Jim, *Press Councils,* Honolulu, East-West Center, September 1975 (mimeographed).
Rivers, W. I., et al., *Responsibility in Mass Communications,* New York, Harper & Row, rev. ed. 1969.
Sanders, Keith P., 'A Survey of US Daily Newspaper Accountability Systems,' in *ANPA News Research Bulletin,* no. 9, November 1973.
Sarkar, Chanchal, *Press Councils and Their Role,* New-Delhi, Press Institute of India, 1965.
Siebert, F. S., et al., *Four Theories of the Press,* Urbana, University of Illinois Press, 1956.
Vasak, Karel, *Introductory Report to the Stockholm Round Table on Press Councils,* Strasbourg, Conseil de l'Europe, September 1974 (mimeographed).

Particular Press Councils or Type of PC's

Korea
KPEC, *The Function and Working Procedures of the Korean Press Ethics Commission.* Seoul, KPEC, 1965.
Great Britain
Paul, Noel S., 'Why the British Council Works', in *Columbia Journalism Review,* March-April 1972.
Levy, Phillip, *The Press Council: History, Procedures and Cases.* London, St Martin's Press, 1967.
Murray, George, *The Press and the Public: the Story of the British Press Council,* Carbondale, Southern Illinois University Press, 1972.
Press Council, *The Press and the People,* London. The Press Council, yearly publication.
Snider, Paul B., *The British Press Council: A Study of its Role and Performance, 1953–1965,* Iowa City, University of Iowa (unpublished thesis).
India
Adhikari, G., *Press Councils: The Indian Experience,* New Delhi, Press Institute of India, 1965.
Japan
Komatsubara, H., 'The Role of the Nihon Shinbun Kyokai', in *The Japanese Press 1973,* Tokyo, NSK, 1973.
Korea
KPEC, *The Function and Working Procedures of the Korean Press Ethics Commission,* Seoul, KPEC, 1965.
Netherlands
de Meij, J. M., *De vrijheid en verantwoordelijkheid van de pers, een onderzoek naar de betekenis van de Raad voor de Journalistiek in het kader van de informanevrijheid,* University of Utrecht, 1975 (unpublished thesis).
Sweden
Groll, Lennart, *The Press Council and the Press Ombudsman in Sweden,* Strasbourg, Conseil de l'Europe, 1974 (mimeographed).
Turkey
Ipekci, Abdi, *Autocontrôle de la presse turque,* Strasbourg, Counseil de l'Europe, 1974 (mimeographed).
Tiryakioglu, S., 'La Cour d'honneur de la presse turque', in: *Journalisme* no. 22, 1964.
United States
ASNE, 'National Press Council: Threat or Opportunity', in *Proceedings of the ASNE,* 1973.
Balk, Alfred, *A Free and Responsible Press,* New York, Report to the Twentieth Century Fund, 1973.
Landau, Lise, *D'une déontologie de la presse à un concept de responsabilité sociale, aux Etats-Unis,* University of Paris-X, 1975 (unpublished thesis).
NNC, *In the Public Interest,* New York, The National News Council, yearly report.
US-Honolulu
Zelco, Trudi, *Purposes, Functions and Procedures of the Honolulu Community-Media Council,* Honolulu. HCMC, 1970.

US-Minnesota
Gerald, G. E., 'Press Council: How it Works in Minnesota', in *ASNE Bulletin,* March 1972.
US-Local PC's
Atwood, E. L. et al., 'Effects of Community Press Councils', in *Journalism Quarterly,* Summer 1972.
Rivers, W. L. et al., *Back Talk: Press Councils in America,* San Francisco, Canfield Press, 1972.
Starck, K., 'What Community Press Councils Talk About', in *Journalism Quarterly,* Spring 1970.
Waring, H., 'The Press Council in Littleton', in *Grassroots Editor,* March-April 1968.

Legal Restraints

The Federal Shield Law We Need

17

Fred P. Graham
Jack C. Landau

[In June, 1971] the U.S. Supreme Court ruled that the First Amendment does not grant newsmen a privilege to withhold from grand juries either confidential information obtained during legitimate newsgathering activities or the source of that information. In addition to this specific 5 to 4 holding in the *Caldwell-Pappas-Branzburg* cases, Justice Byron R. White implied even broader limitations against the press by repeatedly stating, in one form or another, that reporters have no more rights than "all other citizens":

> We see no reason to hold that these reporters, any more than other citizens, should be excused from furnishing information that may help the grand jury in arriving at its initial determinations. . . . Newsmen have no constitutional right of access to the scenes of crimes or disaster when the general public is excluded, and they may be prohibited from attending or publishing information about trials if such restrictions are necessary to assure a defendant a fair trial before an impartial tribunal.

What is important about these statements is that the issue of press access to public disasters or public trials was extraneous to the *Caldwell* case; and in fact the statements appear to be erroneous as a matter of public record.

1. A great many "other citizens" have privileges not to testify before grand juries. There are more than 300,000 attorneys who may, in all federal and state courts, invoke the attorney-privilege to protect confidential information from clients which might solve a case of heinous murder or treason; about 300,000 physicians who may withhold confidential information about crimes under certain conditions in federal and state courts; and several hundred thousand clergymen who have a recognized privilege, in one form or another, in federal and state courts to protect confidential information obtained from penitents. (The priest-penitent issue, however, is somewhat murky because there has never been a Supreme Court case in that area.)

2. So far as we know, newsmen may not be prohibited from attending public trials. In fact, the only Supreme Court cases on the subject state that newsmen must be admitted and that they may not be held in contempt of court for publishing public trial events.

3. It has never been decided that a representative of the public—in the person of the news media—is not guaranteed some access to public disaster areas. It is true that public officials would have a strong argument against admitting 1 million persons to a disaster area in New York City. But the current concept

Fred P. Graham is a Washington correspondent for CBS News. Jack C. Landau is a Supreme Court reporter for Newhouse Newspapers. Both men are members of the steering committee of the Reporters Committee for Freedom of the Press. Reprinted from *Columbia Journalism Review*, March-April 1972.

is that the public "has a right to know" and that, while the number of visitors may be restricted, to guarantee a flow of information the public is entitled to be represented by a reasonable number of journalists.

The point here is that Justice White felt so strongly about the *Caldwell* case that he interpreted issues against the news media which were not even litigated and made statements of constitutional policy which, consciously or unconsciously, appear to misrepresent existing constitutional law to the detriment of the media. It is therefore imperative for journalists to realize that, while they must continue activity in the courts—meeting every censorship challenge head-on—they must seek a redress of their grievances at the legislative level—an invitation, no matter how gracelessly offered, by Justice White in *Caldwell:*

> Congress has freedom to determine whether a statutory newsman's privilege is necessary and desirable and to fashion standards and rules as narrow or as broad as deemed necessary to address the evil discerned and equally important to refashion those rules as experience . . . may dictate.

Congressmen responded by introducing twenty-eight bills granting various types of newsmen's privileges in the last session and twenty-four bills within the first fortnight of the new session. Hearings were held on some of these bills last fall by a Subcommittee of the House Judiciary Committee chaired by Rep. Robert W. Kastenmeier of Wisconsin. Both Rep. Kastenmeier and Sen. Sam Ervin of North Carolina, who chairs the Constitutional Rights Subcommittee of the Senate Judiciary Committee [continued holding hearings.]. . .

The Kastenmeier hearings were perhaps more educating for the press than for Congress. The news media displayed a disturbing lack of unity (with various organizations supporting different bills); a disheartening public exhibition of intramedia rivalry between a book author representative who accused TV of producing "warmed-over" documentaries, and a broadcasters' representative who declared, "I see the authors didn't mention Clifford Irving" (both comments were edited out of the formally published committee hearings); and a failure to present convincing factual evidence of the necessity for new legislation.

In an effort to consolidate the media position, Davis Taylor, publisher of the Boston *Globe* and chairman of the American Newspaper Publishers Assn., invited major media-oriented organizations to participate in an Ad Hoc Drafting Committee to prepare a bill which could be used as a model. The committee included representatives of the ANPA, the American Society of Newspaper Editors, the Newspaper Guild, the National Assn. of Broadcasters, the Society of Professional Journalists, the American Civil Liberties Union, the Reporters Committee for Freedom of the Press, the New York *Times, Newsweek,* ABC, CBS, and NBC. The ANPA has endorsed the whole bill; many other groups support only various portions of the bill or have not yet taken a formal position. The operative language of the bill is:

Section 2: No person shall be required to disclose in any federal or state proceeding either

1. the source of any published or unpublished information obtained in the gathering, receiving or processing of information for any medium of communication to the public, or

2. any unpublished information obtained or prepared in gathering, receiving, or processing of information for any medium of communication to the public.

Because there are so many bills and they vary so widely, the following discussion will only briefly note particular bills—mainly the ANPA absolute privilege bill introduced in this session and the Joint Media Committee qualified privilege bill, and the Ervin bill (both of which were introduced in the last session). The Ervin bill is the most restrictive of those that appear to have some chance of widespread support.

Problem One: Which members of the "press" should qualify for a federal "shield law" privilege which at least protects the source and content of "confidential" information? (Underground newsmen? Freelance news writers? Lecturers? Researchers? Book authors?)

Pending suggestions: The narrowest commonly used definition is contained in several state shield laws which grant only protection to "newspaper, radio, or television . . . personnel." All of the pending Congressional legislation is considerably more expansive, ranging from bills which protect "persons directly engaged in the gathering of news" to the broadest possible definition of "any person who gathers information for dissemination to the public." This would appear to include even dramatists and novelists.

Comment: This threshold question—of who should receive shield law protection—poses most disturbing moral, political, and legal problems which could easily fragment the media.

Those who argue for the broadest definition—describing researchers and would-be authors as members of the press—present a strong historical and constitutional case that the First Amendment was written against a background, not of multinational communications and great news empires, but of individual letter writers, Committees of Correspondence, and citizen pamphleteers. Justice White, in the *Caldwell* opinion, emphasized the historical validity of a broad definition for members of the press by noting that the "liberty of the press is the right of the lonely pamphleteer who uses carbon paper or a mimeograph machine." The Authors League, in its testimony, stressed that many major political scandals of recent years have been unearthed by individual authors working alone, rather than by investigative reporters for major newspapers, magazines, or TV networks. In effect then, a broad definition—including authors, researchers, and freelances unconnected to any established news organizations—would, in many ways, make the newsman's privilege virtually coordinate with the freedom of the speech protection of the First Amendment and would mean, in practical terms, that any person interested in public affairs could probably claim shield law protection.

Those who argue for a narrower definition favor limiting the privilege to persons connected with recognized news organizations. They argue that the author-researcher definition is so broad as to create the privilege for virtually any person interested in public events. Such a broad definition might invite many fraudulent claims of privilege, perhaps even "sham" newspapers established by members of the Mafia (as Justice White hinted); would alienate Congress and the Courts; and would give opponents of a shield law their most powerful political argument against creating any privilege at all. Furthermore, they argue that while the legendary individual author from time to time does engage in muckraking on a grand scale in the most hallowed traditions of Lincoln Steffens, the great majority of investigative reporting is conducted by employees of established news organizations. It is they who are going to jail and it is they who need the coverage more than any other identifiable group.

Suggested solution: While politics and pragmatism would dictate limiting the privilege to news organization employees, morality and history dictate that the greatest possible number of journalists be covered without attempts to include all purveyors of information and opinion. Therefore we suggest that the bill grant the privilege to "recognized members of the press" and permit the courts to decide who should and should not qualify. The bill should specifically state that the privilege covers the underground and minority press (the true heirs of the eighteenth century pamphleteers), the student press, and at least previously published "legitimate" freelance nonfiction writers.

Case examples: The Justice Department has claimed recently that Thomas L. Miller, a writer for the Liberation News Service and other underground publications, is not a "news reporter" and should not be accorded any of the protections under the Justice Department Subpoena Guidelines for members of the press. The District Attorney for Los Angeles County has claimed that William Farr should not qualify for the newsman's privilege in California because at the time he was asked to disclose his confidential sources he was not regularly employed by any news organization. He obtained the information sought while he was a reporter for the Los Angeles *Herald-Examiner* but then left its employ.

Problem Two: Which proceedings should be covered by a shield law (grand juries, criminal trials, civil trials, legislative investigations, executive agencies)?

Pending suggestions: These range from the narrow coverage in the Ervin bill, which would grant the privilege only before federal grand juries and criminal trials, to the broadest coverage, which would protect a news reporter before any executive, legislative, or judicial body.

Comment: There is general agreement among the press as to which government proceedings should be covered—all of them. If a newsman is protected only from testifying at a criminal trial, his testimony can still be coerced by a legislative body or by an executive agency which has the contempt power, such as state crime investigating commissions. Furthermore, it seems unfair to deny to a criminal defendant confidential information which might help to acquit him but at the same time give the information to a state legislative committee which may have no better purpose than to further some ambitious Congressman's stepladder toward the governorship.

Suggested solution: While politics and pragmatism would dictate limiting the executive, and legislative proceedings.

Case examples: While the current subpoena problem originated with federal grand juries (Earl Caldwell), and with state grand juries (Paul Pappas and Paul Branzburg), the infection is spreading. Joseph Weiler of the Memphis *Commercial Appeal* and Joseph Pennington of radio station WREC were called before a state legislative investigating commission. Dean Jensen, Stuart Wilk, and Miss Gene Cunningham of the Milwaukee *Sentinel* and Alfred Balk of the *Columbia Journalism Review* (in a case involving an article in the *Saturday Evening Post*) were asked to disclose confidential sources during civil hearings before federal district courts. William Farr resisted a [Superior Court] judge's personal investigation into violations of his Manson trial publicity order. Three St. Louis area reporters appeared before a State Ethics Committee which appears to be some kind of executive committee authorized by the state legislature to investigate state judges. Brit Hume of the Jack Anderson column and Denny Walsh of *Life* resisted libel case subpoenas. [In late 1976, four reporters and editors of the *Fresno* (Calif.) *Bee* spent 14 days in jail for defending their source of information.]

Problem Three: What types of information should be protected?

a. Confidential sources of published information (e.g., Earl Caldwell was asked to disclose the confidential source of material published in the New York *Times.* William Farr was asked the confidential source of a Manson trial confession published in the Los Angeles *Herald-Examiner)?*

b. Confidential sources of unpublished information (e.g., TV news reporter Paul Pappas was asked what occurred inside Black Panther headquarters; CBS News was asked the identity of the person in New York who supplied a Black Panther contact in Algiers in connection with a *60 Minutes* story on Eldridge Cleaver)?

c. Unpublished nonconfidential information (e.g., Peter Bridge was asked further details of his nonconfidential interview with a Newark Housing Commission member; CBS News was asked to supply outtakes of nonconfidential interviews in *The Selling of the Pentagon;* the St. Louis *Post-Dispatch* was asked for unpublished photos of a public antiwar demonstration)?

d. Published nonconfidential information (e.g., Radio station WBAI in New York City was asked for tapes of published interviews with unnamed prisoners involved in the Tombs riot; WDEF-TV in Chattanooga was asked for the tapes of a published interview with an unnamed grand juror)?

Pending suggestions: The narrowest commonly accepted protection is contained in several state shield laws which protect only the "source" of "published" information, giving no protection, of course, to the confidential source of background information never published and no protection to the unpublished confidential information itself. All the pending Congressional bills protect both the *source* and the *content* of "confidential" information whether or not the information is published. Interestingly, all the Congressional bills also protect the source and content of "nonconfidential information," which could even protect TV outtakes or a reporter's notes of a Presidential speech ("nonconfidential information").

"Official Secrets" Legislation

Congress has introduced during the past two sessions bills which would reform the Federal Criminal Code—called S.1. Opposition to the latest bill has come from various media groups, particularly over several provisions that would make it a crime to publish certain information or to gather it in certain ways. While this particular law may not pass during the current legislative session, it most likely will be a subject of congressional inquiry in the future. The bill, as outlined at the time of our publication, has two broad categories under which reporters might commit illegal acts. One deals with national security; the other with the theft or receiving of government property that has been stolen. Students should follow closely the progress of the debates on this or on similar bills which might be introduced in future sessions.

While the broadcasters generally support the printed media's desire to protect "confidential" sources and information, the real TV interest in the shield law debates will center on the nonconfidential information problem, from both a practical and philosophical point of view. The classic cases cited by the TV news executives concern the difficulties of television cameramen covering riots, dissident political demonstrations, and student disorders—"nonconfidential" events whose film records could be used by the FBI or local law enforcement to identify participants for criminal prosecution. TV executives and, to a lesser extent, news cameramen recite incidents of stonings by demonstrators, breaking of cameras, and destruction of equipment because demonstrators believed that journalists were collecting evidence for the police. The TV news executives argue that their news operations are not an "investigative arm of the Government" and that their cameramen must be able to represent to hostile demonstrators and to the general public that the only film the FBI will see is the film that is actually shown on the tube. But this raises a logical dilemma: Is a film outtake of a public demonstration to be given the same protection from subpoena as a "confidential" source in the Watergate bugging scandal?

Television also has a practical financial objection to permitting its film to be subpoenaed. It is expensive and time-consuming to run through reel after reel of film, an objection similar to that of newspapers whose morgues have been subpoenaed.

Suggested solutions: It is our suggestion that the shield law privilege might be bifurcated like the attorney-client privilege: There could be an "absolute" privilege to refuse to disclose the source or content of confidential information; there could be a "qualified" privilege to refuse to disclose nonconfidential information—such as outtakes of a public demonstration. The outtakes would be available only if the Government demonstrates an "overriding and compelling need."

This two-level absolute-qualified privilege would be similar to the privileges available to attorneys. Attorneys may refuse to disclose the content of confidential communications from their clients and in some cases even the identity of their clients. However, attorneys have only a limited privilege to refuse to turn over nonconfidential "work product" evidence—such as an interview with a witness to a crime who is now unavailable. There are three advantages to offering to a news reporter or cameraman the absolute-qualified privileges held by attorneys.

First: The press is not asking Congress to create a novel or unique concept by establishing a specially privileged class of citizens. In facts the press is merely saying that confidentiality is as important for the performance of newsgathering as it is for the performance of legal representation; and to deny the press a privilege which Congress has granted to an attorney would be saying that the right of the public, via the press to learn about the Bobby Baker or Watergate scandals is to be accorded less protection than the right of a member of the public, via his lawyer, to be represented in a land transaction or a patent case.

Second: The attorney-client relationship is so well established that a whole new body of law would not have to be developed for the multitude of unanswered questions which naturally arise with establishment of a new and untested right. (How is the privilege asserted? Who has the burden of proving it is properly invoked? etc.)

Third: As of July, there will be in effect new federal rules of evidence which grant new federal confidentiality privileges to the attorney for his client, to the policeman for his informer, to the priest for his penitent, and to the psychiatrist for his patient. With regard to timing, it might be advisable for the press to obtain its privileges in connection with the new federal rules.

Problem Four: Should there be any specific exceptions to the privilege to refuse to reveal confidential and nonconfidential information or sources? (Libel suits? Eyewitness to a murder? Information about a conspiracy to commit treason?)

Pending suggestions: The Congressional bills vary. The Joint Media Committee qualified privilege bill would permit confidential and nonconfidential information to be obtained if "there is a compelling and overriding national interest." The Ervin bill would not protect information which "tend[s] to prove or disprove the commission of a crime." The CBS bill would permit the confidential information to be disclosed "to avoid a substantial injustice." The Pearson bill would force disclosure of confidential information to prevent a "threat to human life." The ANPA absolute privilege bill permits no exceptions.

Comment: Most of the bills would not have protected Earl Caldwell because the grand jury in the *Caldwell* case was allegedly investigating a threat by Eldridge Cleaver to assassinate the President. Once the Congress suggests that newsmen may protect confidential information except for national security or libel or felonies or to prevent injustices, the media will end up with a bill which is full of procedural loopholes, moral dichotomies, and legal inconsistencies.

Furthermore, judges have proved ingenious in discovering ambiguities in statutes in order to force reporters to testify in situations that would boggle the nonlegal mind. Paul Branzburg was ordered to name his source of a drug abuse story despite a state law protecting reporters' sources! The Kentucky courts ruled that he saw the sources making hashish and thus they became "criminals" and not news sources. A California law protects reporters' sources, but a Los Angeles judge waited until William Farr temporarily became an ex-newsman and then ordered him to talk; the California legislature promptly passed a new law protecting former newsmen. The moral is that shield laws should be as broad and tight as words will permit, or judges will find ways to evade the intent of the statutes.

Critics of the unqualified privilege often fall back on a stable of horribles ("what if a kidnaper had your child and a reporter knew where"?) to argue for leeway to compel testimony in extreme situations. But some states have had unqualified laws for years and no such incident has ever occurred. Either a reporter believes that it is his duty to talk or he feels so strongly against disclosing the information that no judge or turnkey could break his silence.

Of all the qualified bills, the Joint Media Committee bill is closest to the absolutist approach. Its exception for the "national interest" would place a heavy burden on the Government or a private litigant—a burden that would appear to be satisfied in those rare situations similar to the Pentagon Papers litigation.

The conceptual difficulties of attempting to cover all confidential and nonconfidential information under the same broad legal standards have persuaded us that the privilege perhaps could be tailored to the major problems of confidential and nonconfidential information rather than attempting to make a series of subjective evaluations for certain types of crimes or proceedings. Libel presents an unusual situation; in other testamentary confidentiality situations such as the attorney-client privilege, if the client refuses to waive the privilege then he is subject to an automatic default judgment as the penalty for invoking the right.

Suggested solutions: Attorneys, clergymen, and psychiatrists cannot be forced to violate the confidences of their clients, penitents, and patients, even upon a showing of an investigation into espionage or murder. In fact, how many attorneys know that their own clients or other persons are guilty of heinous crimes but are protected by the attorney-client privilege? It seems grotesque to accuse a news person of being an unpatriotic citizen because he has a privilege to refuse to disclose confidential information of a serious crime, when attorneys (50 percent of the Congress are lawyers), physicians, and clergymen are considered upstanding citizens if they invoke their privileges to refuse to divulge the same criminal information to a grand jury or a trial. Therefore it is suggested that any exemptions for confidential information be drawn as narrowly as possible and that there be a heavy burden of proof for forced disclosure of nonconfidential information.

Problem Five: Should the shield bill apply only to newsmen involved in federal legislative, executive, and judicial proceedings? Or should the bill cover newsmen involved in attempts by state government agencies to obtain confidential sources and information?

Pending solutions: All of the Congressional bills apply to federal proceedings. The ANPA bill would cover both federal and state proceedings.

Comment: No single issue divided the ANPA Ad Hoc Drafting Committee more than the question of federal-state coverage. While lawyers all agree that Congress can cover federal proceedings there is serious disagreement—both on constitutional and political grounds—as to whether the press should aggressively push for state protection in the federal bill.

If statistics were the only issue, then the media would all agree that Congress should cover state proceedings because the subpoena problem is much more serious now in the states and counties than in federal jurisdictions. Ever since Atty. Gen. John N. Mitchell promulgated his Justice Department Subpoena Guidelines in July, 1970, the Justice Department, which had issued a large number of subpoenas to the press in the prior eighteen months, has issued only thirteen subpoenas. The celebrated cases today are mostly state cases: William Farr, Peter Bridge, Harry Thornton, David Lightman, James Mitchell, Joseph Weiler, Joseph Pennington.

Furthermore, there are only eighteen state shield laws in effect and they offer varying degrees of coverage. A federal-state law would fill the void in the remaining thirty-two states, thus eliminating the necessity of new legislation in these states and of corrective legislation in most of the existing states whose laws offer less protection than the ANPA bill. A subcommittee of the Conference of Commissioners on Uniform State Law is now working on a model reporters' privilege law. But even if the commissioners eventually approve a model statute, it might be years before any substantial number of state legislatures adopt it.

Then there is the potential legal impact of the *Farr* decision in the California courts. They held that the state legislature has no power under the state constitution to pass a shield law which invades the inherent constitutional power of the state courts to protect their own integrity by forcing news reporters to disclsoe confidential information. What this means potentially is that California and perhaps other states must pass a state constitutional amendment—rather than a shield law—to give complete protection to news reporters involved in many types of contempt proceedings.

There are, however, serious constitutional and political problems with a federal-state shield law. Constitutionally, the ANPA bill attempts to give Congress two different methods to intervene in state court and legislative proceedings. First: It notes that news is in commerce and therefore the ANPA bill uses Congress's power to control "interstate commerce." Second: It notes that, under the Fourteenth Amendment, Congress has the power to pass legislation protecting rights guaranteed in the First Amendment. While Congress has used its power to protect federally guaranteed rights by passing the Civil Rights Acts of 1965 and 1968, Congress has never attempted to pass legislation implementing the Bill of Rights.

Suggested solution: The federal government is only one of fifty-one jurisdictions. In fact, when one remembers that the Farr-Bridge-Thornton cases were processed in the county courts, there are the federal government; fifty states; and some 3,000 county court jurisdictions. Under the Justice Department guidelines, there is a lessening danger from the federal government. Therefore, we consider it absolutely essential that, despite the political difficulties of this position, the shield law protects every news reporter in the nation—not just those who, by happenstance, are involved in federal proceedings.

Assuming that the media can agree on which bill they want, can the press persuade Congress to pass the legislation? Three years ago, the newspaper publishers succeeded in obtaining passage of the Newspaper Preservation Act with its exemption from the antitrust laws, over the public opposition of the then antitrust chief, Richard McLaren. Two years ago, the broadcasters, within forty-eight hours, were able to muster enough support to protect CBS president Frank Stanton from being held in contempt of Congress, over the objections of Rep. Harley Staggers, who was attempting to obtain nonconfidential outtakes of *The Selling of the Pentagon.* The conclusion is quite simple: What the media owners want from Congress, the media owners get from Congress. The only question that remains is whether the First Amendment is of as much concern to the media owners as was exemption from the antitrust laws.

Editor's note: When New York *Times* reporter Myron A. Farber was jailed for refusing to reveal his notes to a judge in a murder trial, he became but the most recent—as we go to press—of a long line of reporters who have been jailed or fined because they have refused to divulge their sources or to produce their notes. The shield law is designed to apply to both situations. What set the Farber case apart from earlier press-judiciary conflicts was that the defense subpoenaed Farber's notes in an effort to bolster its contention that Farber was the "architect" of the prosecution's case against Dr. Mario Jascalevich. The judge ordered Farber to turn over the notes for *in camera* review; that is, so the judge could determine whether the notes were relevant to the defense contention. Farber refused. He was jailed; the *Times* was fined; the decision had been upheld by the New Jersey Supreme Court, and the U.S. Supreme Court refused to review the case. Dr. Jascalevich was found innocent. This case, in conjunction with recent Supreme Court decisions such as the *Stanford Daily* case, which permits police access to newspaper office files with only the issuance of a search warrant, has caused many journalists to cry out against the perceived trend. A few critics have claimed that the press is over-reacting. Certainly the ground rules of reporting seem to be threatened or even "chilled" by recent decisions. It is useful to note that Farber was jailed in a state (N.J.) which has a shield law. In fact, the judiciary has had little difficulty in deciding that the Sixth Amendment to the Constitution takes precedence over statute law, which is a point raised by John S. Knight in the next article.

To keep abreast of on-going changes, consult regularly both *News Media and the Law,* which is mentioned below, and *Media Law Reporter,* published by

The Bureau of National Affairs, Inc. *The Reporter* is very expensive and will be available only in specialized collections. It provides a weekly service as well as an annual bound volume. Its great strength is that it provides media law decisions down to the state appeals courts.

Bibliography

The Graham and Landau article is one of the more comprehensive treatments of the concept of the need for a shield law. David Gordon, *Newsman's Privilege and the Law.* Freedom of Information Foundation, Series No. 4 (August 1974) is a useful treatment of the subject. It can be up-dated, even as the Graham and Landau article can be up-dated, by referring to the continuing series of Freedom of Information reports published by The Society of Professional Journalists, Sigma Delta Chi. The *1976 Report of the Advancement of Freedom of Information Committee* of the SPJ/SDX summarizes current developments and includes a useful state-by-state compilation of cases related to freedom of information and shield laws. There also is a chapter on the electronic media. A useful bibliography is Lisa Epstein, *Newsman's Privilege: An Annotated Bibliography 1967–1973* (Law Library, California State Library, 1973). This 19-page booklet contains over 100 annotations, primarily from legal journals. In addition, The Reporters Committee, suite 1112, 1750 Penn Ave., NW, Wash., D.C., 20006, distributes its bi-monthly *Press Censorship Newsletter* (a thick booklet detailing all relevant First Amendment and FOI cases), now entitled the *News Media and the Law.*

A related issue, and one where there is increasing tension between the press and the judiciary, is that of Free Press and Fair Trial. An excellent basic work is Donald M. Gillmor, *Free Press and Free Trial* (Public Affairs Press, 1966). Marlan Nelson has compiled a 576-item—*Free Press-Fair Trial: An Annotated Bibliography* (Utah State University Department of Journalism, 1971), which includes citations through 1969. More current publications include Deby K. Samuels, *Judges and Trial News Challenges,* Freedom of Information Center, Report No. 317 (December 1973) and the several articles in *Nieman Reports* (Winter 1974). The *Nieman Reports* articles deal with the problems that have arisen between the mass media and the law over trials, secrecy of grand jury information, and use of stolen documents. This entire issue is well worth consulting for deeply disturbing insights into the problems. See also Benno C. Schmidt, Jr. "A New Wave of Gag Orders," *Columbia Journalism Review* (November/December 1975), pp. 33–34.

Another area of increasing concern is the still ill-defined concept of "privacy." A good summary will be found in E. Jeremy Hutton, *The Constitutional Right of Privacy: Supreme Court Decisions and Congressional Action in Brief,* Library of Congress, Congressional Research Service, 1974. *The Privacy Act of 1974,* Freedom of Information Center, Report No. 342 (September 1975) was written by James T. O'Reilly. He outlines the provisions of the act and suggests that it will have a major impact on both the government's gathering of information and its dissemination of that information, including dissemination to the press. A special report on "Government, Business and the People's Right to Know" appeared in *Media Law Reports* (February 14, 1978). It dealt with the ineffectiveness of the Freedom of Information Act.

Shield Law for Newsmen: Safeguard or a Trap?

18

John S. Knight

John S. Knight was editorial chairman, Knight Newspapers, Inc., at the time of writing this editorial. He won a Pulitzer Prize for editorial writing in 1968. This editorial was published in March 1973 and is reprinted with the permission of the author.

Can a reporter be compelled by government to reveal the identity of confidential sources of information or the content of unpublished information?

Most newspaper editors and the television networks say "No," since Article I of the Bill of Rights specifically states: "Congress shall make no law . . . abridging the freedom . . . of speech, or of the press."

Yet the Supreme Court decided last June by a 5-4 vote in the Caldwell case that the sources of a reporter's information are not and cannot be held confidential.

The Caldwell decision has given rise to any number of state and local judicial actions which have held reporters in contempt of court for refusing to disclose confidential information to grand juries. Several newsmen have been jailed, and the subpoena process is currently being applied against the *Washington Post* in the Watergate case.

Members of the Fourth Estate, well aware of the Nixon administration's hostility toward the press, are pressing Congress to enact a shield law which will protect the reporter's position of confidentiality. Some 18 state legislatures have already passed laws which provide some form of protection. Similar bills have been before the Congress since 1929, but as Sen. Sam J. Ervin Jr. says, "To write legislation balancing the two great public interests of a free press and the seeking of justice is no easy task."

Sen. Ervin, an authority on constitutional law who has been attempting to draft legislation to protect the free flow of information, finds it a bothersome assignment indeed.

On the one hand, Ervin declaims, "there is society's interest in being informed—in learning of crime, corruption or mismanagement. On the other, we have the pursuit of truth in the courtroom. It is the duty of every man to give testimony. The Sixth Amendment specifically gives a criminal defendant the right to confront the witness against him, and to have compulsory process for obtaining witnesses in his favor."

Yet we find in a separate concurring opinion by Supreme Court Justice Lewis Powell a statement that the court may not in the future turn deaf ears upon newsmen if the government can be shown to have harassed the newsmen, or has otherwise not acted in good faith in the conduct of its investigation or inquiry.

But Justice Byron R. White, writing for the majority, stated: "Until now, the only testimonial privilege for unofficial witnesses that is rooted in the federal Constitution is the Fifth Amendment privilege against compelled self-incrimination. We are asked to create another by interpreting the First Amendment to grant newsmen a testimonial privilege that other citizens do not enjoy. This we decline to do."

The net effect of the court's decision in the Caldwell case was to leave it to the Congress to determine the desirability and the necessity for statutory protection for newsmen. And that is where we are now.

For one, I confess to some ambivalence on this question. Can Sen. Ervin draft a law which, as he says, "will accommodate both the interest of society in law enforcement, and the interest of society in preserving a free flow of information to the public?"

Or, will the enactment of any law—qualified or unqualified—invite Congress to tamper with the law as it serves its pleasure in the future? Vermont Royster

"*...COPY BOY...!*"

of the *Wall Street Journal* sees "booby-traps" in this procedure, since "for what one Congress can give, another can take away, and once it is conceded that Congress can legislate about the press, no man can know where it might end."

The mood of the press is quite understandable. For here we have the Nixon administration's palace guard—a grim and humorless lot—in a posture of open hostility to the press and attempting to hinder the free flow in information with every device available to them.

We also have the courts, "traditionally unhappy" as Sen. Ervin says, "about evidentiary privileges which limit judicial access to information, and by and large refusing to recognize a common-law right of reporters not to identify sources or to disclose confidential information."

So the key question remains: Will the press and the public interest best be served by a congressional shield law holding confidentiality to be inviolate—a law which as Royster points out could be changed and diluted by a future Congress?

Or had we better stick with the First Amendment, under which a free press has survived for nearly 200 years without any law to make newsmen a class apart? Why not stand with the courageous history of the press, and continue to wage battle against all attempts at censorship by the courts and intimidation by a hostile administration?

Sen. Ervin now thinks he has devised a third-draft bill which "strikes a reasonable balance between necessary, if at times, competing objectives." Yet what Congress gives, Congress can take away. Neither the senator nor the proponents of any protective law for journalists address themselves to this crucial point.

The more I study this question, the more I am persuaded that, since the First Amendment has nurtured the freest press of any nation, reporters, editors and publishers should not petition Congress but rather continue to contest all erosions of press or public freedom and be prepared to defend their convictions at any cost.

Our precious freedoms of speech and publication are guaranteed by the Bill of Rights which has served us well throughout our history. Freedom is not something that can be assured by transitory legislation, worthy as the intent may be.

When Congress is involved, there lies the risk—as Royster has said—that it might start legislating about the freedom of the press even in the guise of protecting it. This could be a dangerous precedent.

I readily concede that what I have written above represents a modification of what I had previously believed, and that it is open to challenge from my journalistic colleagues who hold a contrary view.

Before the press potentates pursue too enthusiastically the case for a shield law, they would be well advised to ask themselves whether the remedy they propose will ultimately sustain or destroy press freedom.

19 Big-Time Pressures, Small-Town Press
Robert J. Boyle

Robert J. Boyle is editor of the Pottstown (Pa.) *Mercury*. This column appeared on the Op-Ed page of the *New York Times*, March 24, 1973. Copyright 1973 by the New York Times Company. Reprinted by permission.

Pottstown, Pa.—The bee stings in Washington and the pain is felt in Pottstown, too. The Government clamps Les Whitten, Jack Anderson's aide, in jail for eight hours, and the clanking jail door is heard round the world. Pottstown Council holds a secret meeting, and when it's uncovered, the news about it is confined to

Pottstown. Censorship, government controls and secrecy aren't limited to people like Anderson. The small-town newsman is also feeling the sting.

Certainly, officials in Washington aren't telling officials in Pottstown not to cooperate with the press. But when the Government hides things from the national press, and when Government officials make snide remarks against the press, small-town politicians feel that they, too, should follow the leader and they institute roadblocks to limit freedom.

The label a politician or an official wears doesn't matter. Pottstown is a swing community in a solid Republican county. But both Democrats and Republicans alike have started attacking the press.

Small-town police departments suddenly are setting themselves up as censors. They become "unavailable" when the press calls them. Justices of the peace are starting to determine what cases to give to the press and what cases to hold back.

One Pottstown justice of the peace tried to stop a *Mercury* reporter from using a pencil and notebook at a hearing because they were "recording devices." Use of a recording device is banned in justices of the peace courts. It took a ruling from the county solicitor before the reporter could use his pencil and notebook again.

School boards have been using the "executive sessions" ploy more and more. The public and press are barred from executive sessions. Board members decide at these sessions what course of action to follow, and then simply approve the action at a regular meeting.

The simple news story, too, is getting more difficult to come by. Recently there was a small fire in the Army officers' club of Valley Forge General Hospital. Damage amounted to $750. The *Mercury* tried to get an item on the fire and the story would have amounted to a paragraph or two.

But the Army refused to give any information until the "news release cleared the channels."

In Pottstown, a community of 28,000 some 35 miles from Philadelphia, the council meetings always have been open and above board. But late last year, council held a secret meeting. It wasn't advertised, the press wasn't alerted, and those who attended were told to keep it secret. The action taken at the meeting affected the entire community.

The council voted, in secret, to get rid of the police chief, Dick Tracy. As God is my judge, that's his name. A group from council, including the Mayor, was selected to secretly tell the chief to look elsewhere for a job. He was told it would be in his best interest to keep the decision secret.

"Keep your mouth shut and we'll make it seem as if it is your choice to leave," he was told. "Open it and it'll make it rougher for you to get another job."

He kept his mouth shut.

But one of the participants of the secret meeting discussed it at a local bar. He was overheard and the newspaper, *The Mercury,* was tipped.

Chief Tracy was confronted with the story and confirmed that he was told to leave. He eventually did. He wasn't a bad cop. With a name like that he couldn't be. But he was ousted because he refused to play small-town politics. He refused to fix parking tickets, he refused to let old-time politicians run the department and he was strict. He got the axe because he wouldn't play ball.

The Mercury headlined the story of the secret meeting. And the community was disturbed for several weeks. Later *The Mercury* investigated and revealed conflict-of-interest possibilities on some council proposals.

In nearby Collegeville, a community of 5,000, the newspaper there, *The Independent,* was creating a stir in a nine-part exposé on the Pennsylvania state prison at Graterford. *The Independent* doesn't make much of a splash statewide but ripples from it reached the state capital at Harrisburg. The word went out that no one from the state prison was to talk to *The Independent* publisher, John Stewart. Because he uncovered and published some sordid facts about Graterford he was put on the "no comment" list.

If you multiply the troubles *The Mercury* and *The Independent* are having in their small areas by the number of smaller papers across the country then you must recognize the press is being hamstrung nationally and on all levels.

Remarks by the Vice-President and the President may be targeted at papers such as *The Washington Star.*

But they are also hurting the smaller papers. By design or not, those officials in Washington who are anti-Anderson, anti-*The Times,* anti-*The Post,* are also anti-*The Mercury* and *The Independent.* They're antipress. Antifreedom.

20 Court Control of "News" after *Nebraska*
Ted Curtis Smythe

Ted Curtis Smythe is co-editor of this volume and of *Issues in Broadcasting,* Mayfield Publishing, 1975, and Professor of Communications, California State University, Fullerton.

The long-simmering controversy between proponents of the First and Sixth Amendments to the Constitution came to a boil during 1975 when judges in Lincoln County, Nebraska imposed restrictive orders ("gag" orders in newspaper parlance) on what the press could report about a brutal murder that had occurred in the community of Sutherland. The unanimous 9-0 Supreme Court decision affirming press rights created press freedom history.

While the issues decided by the Court are of primary interest and importance to us, it is necessary first to provide a little background to the case.

Six members of the Henry Kellie family were murdered in their home on the night of October 18, 1975. Police issued a description of the suspect, 29-year-old Erwin Charles Simants, a neighbor of the Kellies. Simants was arrested and arraigned the next morning.

County Judge Ronald Ruff held a preliminary hearing to determine whether there was cause to hold Simants for trial (this hearing performs the same function as a grand jury in some states). At that hearing he restricted the press from reporting testimony given in the hearing and required that the Nebraska bar-press voluntary guidelines be mandatory.

Lawyers for Nebraska news media appealed to Judge Hugh Stuart of the district court to set aside the restraining order. Although Judge Stuart had earlier counseled Judge Ruff not to impose such an order, he now terminated Judge Ruff's order and imposed his own. His order was more selective than was Judge Ruff's order but it still restricted the press from reporting Simant's confession, the results of the pathologist's report (which had revealed the sexual basis for the assault as well as necrophilia), the identity of the victims who had been sexually assaulted, and the description of those crimes. He also required that the voluntary bar-press guidelines be mandatory. He then prohibited the Nebraska press from reporting the details of the "gag" order itself.

This order was appealed to the Nebraska Supreme Court. Because the Court delayed in acting on the appeal, the appellants sought help from Justice Harry Blackmun of the U.S. Supreme Court. Under a provision which permits a single Supreme Court Justice to intervene when he feels that legal remedies have been exhausted at the local level and that an emergency exists (Justice Blackmun argued, "delay itself is a final decision" in these cases) he set aside certain provisions of the order, although "he declined 'at least on application for a stay and at this distance, [to] impose a prohibition upon the Nebraska courts from placing any restrictions at all upon what the media may report prior to trial.' "

The Nebraska Supreme Court finally issued its *per curiam* opinion (that is, it reflects the opinion of the whole court and is not identified with one justice) on December 2, 1975. It modified the District Court's order in an effort to balance the defendant's right to a fair trial against the Nebraska media's "interest in reporting pretrial events." The order "prohibited reporting of only three matters: (a) the existence and nature of any confessions or admissions made by the defendant to law enforcement officers, (b) any confessions or admissions made to any third parties, except members of the press, and (c) other facts 'strongly implicative' of the accused."

The U.S. Supreme Court granted *certiorari* (a review of the case) in order to address the important issues raised in the District Court's order and the modification of it by the Nebraska Supreme Court. By the time the U.S. Supreme Court acted to decide the issue, Simants was convicted of murder and sentenced to death. His appeal was pending when the U.S. Supreme Court issued its decision.

The Court endorsed the right of the press to report pretrial matters without restriction by the judiciary. Chief Justice Warren Burger, writing the opinion, was joined by four other justices, two of whom wrote concurring opinions. Justice

William Brennan wrote a separate concurring opinion in which he was joined by two other justices. Justice Paul Stevens also wrote a brief concurring opinion.

In his opinion, Chief Justice Burger reviewed the historical conflict between the First and Sixth Amendments and recounted numerous Court decisions that had dealt specifically with the issue. He reaffirmed previous Court solutions to the problem—solutions that do not require prior restraint of the press.

He concluded that not only were there other avenues open to the trial judge but, given the circumstances, "it is far from clear that [even] prior restraint on publication would have protected Simants' rights."

What were those other "avenues"? One would be to change the site of the trial (change of venue) to someplace "less exposed to the intense publicity" in the county. (One reason the judge had not done so is that Nebraska law permits a change only to adjacent counties, and those counties had been exposed to the same pretrial publicity. The Supreme Court held that Nebraska law had to give way in this case—that fair trial was constitutionally more important.)

Other avenues suggested by Justice Burger would be to postpone "the trial to allow public attention to subside;" to use "searching questions of prospective jurors," and to use "emphatic and clear instructions on the sworn duty of each juror to decide the issues only on evidence presented in open court." The Chief Justice even suggested sequestering the jury after it was chosen as a partial remedy because insulating the jurors "enhances the likelihood of dissipating the impact of pretrial publicity and of emphasizing the elements of the jurors' oaths."

The suggestion was made in passing that the "trial courts in appropriate cases [could] limit what the contending lawyers, the police and witnesses may say to anyone." While the Chief Justice did not deal with this issue, Justice Brennan in his concurring opinion suggested that this was a viable alternative to prior restraint of the press. He wrote: "As officers of the Court, court personnel and attorneys have a fiduciary responsibility not to engage in public debate that will redound to the detriment of the accused or that will obstruct the fair administration of justice. It is very doubtful that the court would not have the power to control release of information by these individuals in appropriate cases . . . ."

Does this mean that Chief Justice Burger and the entire Court support the press-promoted concept that prior restraint can never be imposed in free press/fair trial cases?

No.

Several times in his opinion, the Chief Justice argued against a blanket statement on prior restraint. He wrote that since the "authors of the Bill of Rights did not undertake to assign priorities as between First Amendment and Sixth Amendment rights . . . it is not for us to rewrite the Constitution by undertaking what they declined."

He concluded by reaffirming "that the guarantees of freedom of expression are not an absolute prohibition [to prior restraint] under all circumstances, but

the barriers to prior restraint remain high and the presumption against its use continues intact."

The concurring opinions issued by other justices of the Court tended to go further, suggesting there may not be any situation in respect to free press/fair trial conflicts where prior restraint would be acceptable. Justice Brennan staked out such a position: ". . . the press may be arrogant, tyrannical, abusive, and sensationalist, just as it may be incisive, probing, and informative. But at least in the context of prior restraints on publication, the decision of what, when and how to publish is for editors, not judges." Justices Potter Stewart and Thurgood

Marshall concurred with him. Justices Byron White and Paul Stevens also indicated they were leaning in that direction.

The use of "gag" rules would now appear to be unconstitutional under all but extraordinary circumstances, and even then only after the trial judge had used other means of relief before restraining publication.

Since the press now has greater freedom than ever before in reporting criminal trials, another problem is raised—what is the proper ethical response of the news media?

Chief Justice Burger hinted at this problem when he wrote that "it is not asking too much to suggest that those who exercise First Amendment rights in newspapers or broadcasting enterprises direct some effort to protect the right of an accused to a fair trial by unbiased jurors." Many editors and reporters have made such efforts by seeking to accommodate "on a voluntary basis, the correlative constitutional rights of free speech and free press with the right of an accused to a fair trial." The Nebraska Bar-Press Guidelines from which this quotation is taken was the result of such an accommodation.

In the summer of 1979 attempts at accommodation were shattered. The U.S. Supreme Court handed down its decision in *The Gannett Co., Inc. v. DePasquale* case on July 2. The *DePasquale* decision held that *pre-trial* suppression-of-evidence hearings in a murder case could be closed to the press upon the request of the defendant if certain conditions were met. Justice Stewart's majority opinion has been criticized, however, because it is a "loosely drafted, sweeping denial of the public's right of access to the criminal justice process." The result has been confusion and opportunism in the lower courts. Within two months at least ten trials were closed by judges who cited the *DePasquale* ruling. This "rush to judgment" by the judiciary sparked a remarkable series of public comments on the decision from four Supreme Court justices, something that is extremely rare.

The National News Council (NNC), at its meeting in September 1979, supported efforts by press and bar to find ways of communicating with each other in order to avoid "conflicts and adversary relationships injurious to both groups in discharging their indispensable duties to the American people." According to the NNC, one of the results growing out of the Nebraska case was a tendency on the part of the press in many states "to shy away from such collaborative efforts [because] the Nebraska Supreme Court [had] turned the voluntary fair trial/free press guidelines in that state into legal mandates devoid of any flexibility." It was hoped by the NNC that new canons issued by the House of Delegates of the American Bar Association would provide the needed flexibility.

As we go to press, the Supreme Court has accepted for review *Richmond Newspapers v. Virginia*. Students should follow the outcome of this case as it is reported in the law journals or mass media magazines, especially *Quill* and *Columbia Journalism Review*. For a report of the NNC position, see "Statement on Closing Courtrooms," *Columbia Journalism Review* (November/December 1979), p. 108. An excellent, balanced overview of the perceived conflict between the Supreme Court and the press is Robert Friedman, "The Freedom of the Press Under Siege," *New Times* (December 11, 1978), pp. 34–35, 39–42, 47–50. It is symbolic that Friedman, former editor of [*more*], the media review that died in June 1978, had this article published in the last issue of *New Times* before it died. Both magazines had contributed useful commentaries on mass media in our society.

Dirty Business in Court

21

Harriet F. Pilpel
Marjorie T. Parsons

No government has ever succeeded in finding a balanced policy of combatting unhealthy sexual propaganda without injuring legitimate freedom or provoking other or equally grave disorders. —Jacques Leclerq, Catholic University of Louvain

It is one of the odder paradoxes of the Victorian era that while motherhood was enshrined, sex, which must have had something to do with that hallowed state, developed a bad name and came increasingly to be equated with obscenity. In the early years of this republic, laws reflected concern with such social warts as blasphemy and public drunkenness, but obscenity was not viewed as a major problem. By 1873, however, obscenity was perceived as a full-fledged issue in the United States, and the federal Comstock Act was passed to cope with it, followed by a train of "little Comstock Acts" in the states. Nonetheless, as time went on, the courts and various administrative agencies tended to recognize that the sweeping sexual prohibitions of the Comstock laws violated constitutional guarantees. By 1957 the United States Supreme Court in *Roth v. U.S.* and other cases appeared to permit a wide latitude of expression. Then, on June 21, 1973, by a narrow 5 to 4 majority, the Court handed down a series of rulings with grave implications for First Amendment freedoms.

While some commentators expressed cautious optimism that the new holdings might not prove too damaging, it soon became apparent that Justice Brennan, in his dissenting opinion, had all too accurately diagnosed them as "nothing less than a rejection of First Amendment premises . . . and an invitation to widespread suppression." As the effects of the rulings became evident, the optimists reasoned that the manifest confusion might generate its own remedy: the Court would amend or clarify or reverse itself in its decisions on pending cases.

Harriet Pilpel is an author-lawyer who specializes in First Amendment freedoms and sex and the law. She also chaired the ACLU Communications Media Committee. Marjorie Parsons is coordinator for the National Ad Hoc Committee Against Censorship. She was for many years executive story editor for MGM; in recent years she has been a free-lance writer and editor. This piece appeared in *The Civil Liberties Review*, Vol. 1, No. 4 (Fall 1974)© 1974 American Civil Liberties Union and is used with permission of that publication.

The long-awaited decisions last June in the *Carnal Knowledge (Jenkins v. Georgia)* and *Hamling v. U.S.* cases did little to encourage that hope.

What is the background of the 1973–1974 Supreme Court obscenity decisions? What follows from them? How should they be approached? Most significantly, what can be done about them?

The First Amendment to the U.S. Constitution prohibits government from passing any law abridging freedom of speech and press. For many years, two Supreme Court Justices, William O. Douglas and Hugo Black, steadfastly maintained that the Constitution means exactly what it says: no abridgement of expression. Nevertheless, for decades the majority of the Court has held that "obscenity is not protected by the First Amendment," though a precise definition of what it is has eluded the court and led to a tangle of confusing rulings. Justice Potter Stewart said at one point: "I may not be able to define it, but I certainly know it when I see it." So, it seems, does everyone else. But what is "known" to be obscene varies erratically with the viewer. A Girl Scout pamphlet is "obscene" in the state of Washington; *The Dictionary of American Slang* in Florida; *Soul on Ice* in Connecticut; *Spoon River Anthology* in Illinois; *Slaughterhouse-Five* in North Dakota; *Catcher in the Rye* in half the states of the union.

The 1966 *Memoirs v. Massachusetts* decision attempted to pin down the eely concept of obscenity. For a work to be judged obscene, it had to pass all three parts of the Court's new test: 1) the "dominant theme" of the material "taken as a whole" had to appeal to "prurient interest in sex" and 2) it had to be "patently offensive to the average person, applying contemporary community standards" and 3) it had to be "utterly without redeeming social value." In the earlier *Roth* decision, the Court had carefully noted that "sex and obscenity are not synonymous. . . . Sex, a great and mysterious motive force in human life, has indisputably been a subject of absorbing interest to mankind through the ages; it is one of the vital problems of human interest and public concern."

Certain refinements of the general test evolved at various times in response to specific situations. For example, the Court made it clear that if material was beamed directly at children, a somewhat different test would apply. Moreover, the question of whether particular material is obscene could be affected by the context of its presentation. The Court took a dim view of "thrusting" explicitly sexual material on unwilling adults in public places, and of "pandering" or promoting material in an offensive manner. Two federal postal statutes were passed, one requiring the sender of "sexually oriented material" to identify it as such on the wrapper. The other provided that people not wishing to receive material they regard as obscene need only register at the post office their refusal to accept mail from a named sender and such mail would not be delivered to them.

On the surface the obscenity issue appeared to be taking on more rational dimensions. Obscenity actions were still being brought (sometimes aimed more at politically or socially dissident ideas than at over-explicitness about sex), but on the whole they did not succeed. Beneath the surface, however, a well organized anti-obscenity ferment was working. The "traffic in obscenity and pornography"

In a cover article surveying contemporary American attitudes toward and laws on pornography, *Time's* editors expressed concern about the relationship between print and film pornography and prostitution, massage parlors, and criminal elements.

was found to be of such "national concern" that Congress funded a commission in 1967 to study "the causal relationships between such materials and anti-social behavior" and to recommend appropriate means to deal with the problem. The president appointed nineteen distinguished members (one, Kenneth Keating, subsequently resigned to become Ambassador to India) to the Commission on Obscenity and Pornography, and they embarked on an intensive two-year study of the subject. Since there were little or no hard data to support a causal connection between pornography and crime, 70-odd carefully designed scientific studies were undertaken to determine what, if any, the connection might be.

The conclusion, the commission reported in 1970, was that none existed. On the contrary, empirical evidence clearly indicated that pornography appeared to act as a safety valve to ease tensions that might otherwise erupt into criminal activity. Offenders imprisoned for sex-related crimes, for example, reported they had a more restrictive upbringing and significantly less early exposure to pornography than their peers who did not become entangled with the law. The profile of the typical user of pornography revealed a middle-aged male, white, middle class, married, very likely to have gone to college and with a 25% chance of having attended graduate school.

Almost every adult American is exposed to some pornography at some time, but it is estimated that only about 2% become more-or-less steady consumers of it. In one study married couples volunteered to view explicitly sexual films over a considerable period of time. They showed little change in their sexual behavior patterns beyond increased ease between husband and wife in talking about sex; they did, however, develop growing and finally overpowering boredom with the films. Yet 56% of Americans apparently feel that pornography causes "moral breakdown," although only 1% thought they personally could be in any way affected by it. It is noteworthy that their concern is not for themselves but for others who, they fear, are more vulnerable.

As a result of these and other studies, two-thirds of the commission recommended repeal of all laws restricting the access of consenting adults to any material of their choice. President Nixon ridiculed and the Congress disowned the report. On the other side, concerned groups formed an Ad Hoc Committee to urge that the report be given a fair hearing and judged on its merits.

Then in June 1973, a Supreme Court majority consisting of Nixon's four appointees (Chief Justice Warren Burger and Justices William Rehnquist, Harry Blackmun, and Lewis Powell), joined by Justice Byron White, handed down a number of decisions that the dissenting justices and many others regarded as a major threat to First Amendment freedoms. One immediate result was that more than 150 anti-pornography bills were introduced in 38 of the 44 state legislatures in regular session during 1973-1974. New laws, by no means all of them bad and many much less restrictive than the Court said was permissible, were passed in fourteen states; action may still be taken in others. Much of the trouble deriving from the 1973 holdings has originated in the rash of city, county, and other local ordinances, some so restrictive they would ban the portrayal of an infant's bare bottom. (What, asked one plaintive librarian, was she to do about *Your New Baby*, a popular illustrated book on the care of newborns.)

Many specific problems stemmed from the 1973 holdings. Thus, while to many it had seemed clear that the "community standards" part of the tripartite obscenity test established by the Court in 1966 referred to national standards, the majority opinions in 1973 declared that national standards were not intended, and observed that the standards of Maine and Mississippi (states) and those of

New York and Las Vegas (cities) need not necessarily be the same. It is not surprising, therefore, that a hodge-podge of laws were adopted, defining the community as the state, "the county or lesser subdivision" (Florida), the "local community" (Iowa and Virginia), or "the community from which a jury is drawn" (Alabama). Whether material is considered obscene could depend, in border towns, on which side of the street it is distributed.

Under the June 1973 decisions the "social value" part of the test changed; the question was no longer whether a work was "utterly without redeeming social value" but whether it lacked "serious literary, artistic, political, or scientific value." Apparently if religious, educational, and just plain entertainment values count at all, they have to be smuggled in under one of the four approved categories. In *Miller v. California* the Court said that to determine whether a work is obscene, the "trier of fact," that is, usually a jury made up of "average persons," applying "contemporary community standards," would have only to "find that the work, taken as a whole, appeals to prurient interest." This might make some sense if a 1969 nationwide Gallup poll had not found that 58% of the adult sample, presumably made up of average persons, had never read a book from cover to cover. In any event, the 1973 holdings have led a number of communities to deny their citizens the right to enjoy a wide range of obviously non-obscene works: *The Grapes of Wrath* by John Steinbeck, *Go Ask Alice*, Anonymous (Christopher Award 1972, Maxi Award 1973), *In the Night Kitchen* by Maurice Sendak (winner of six "Best Children's Book of 1970" awards including the Hans Christian Andersen Medal), *The Learning Tree* by Gordon Parks (Spingarn Medal 1973), *Playboy* magazine, and the 1973 Motion Picture Academy Award nominee, *Carnal Knowledge*.

Jenkins v. Georgia, one of the two cases on which the Supreme Court ruled on June 24, 1974, involved *Carnal Knowledge*; the Court unanimously decided that the film was not obscene. It had been hoped, in the face of the legislative and judicial chaos that followed the 1973 holdings, that perhaps one or more of the majority justices would be moved to join Justice Douglas in his minority opinion that all expression is protected by the First Amendment; or with the Brennan-Marshall-Stewart position that the government has no right to dictate to consenting adults what they may choose to look at or listen to in private. Instead, the same five-justice majority that produced the 1973 opinions reaffirmed its earlier stance with some emendations that rendered the whole obscenity problem even more obscure.

On the positive side, *Jenkins* does seem to narrow the range of what may be judged obscene. The Court reiterated the *Miller* rule that what is intended to be prohibited is "representations or descriptions of ultimate sexual acts, normal or perverted, actual or simulated," and "representations or descriptions of masturbation, excretory functions, and the lewd exhibition of the genitals." But it observed that "Nudity alone does not render material obscene." The fact that the Court unanimously regarded *Carnal Knowledge* as not obscene would be more reassuring if on the same day the Court had not also decreed that defendants in obscenity cases have no right to introduce as a defense "comparable materials" that have been judged non-obscene.

However, the Court pointed out in the 1974 decisions that "juries do not have unbridled discretion in determining what is 'patently offensive.' " Normally a jury's decision on the *facts* of a case are not subject to judicial review; only errors of procedure of convictions based on laws thought to be in violation of the Constitution are. The Supreme Court stated in 1973 that obscenity is a matter of fact to be determined by a jury; the Georgia Supreme Court, in upholding the lower Georgia court's decision, had gone along with this view. Once again enmeshed in the nettlesome question of what obscenity is, the Supreme Court in 1974 decided it is not so much a matter of simple, or even complex, fact as a "legal term of art" (*Hamling*). "Obscenity," then, concerns an evaluation so basically unreliable that jury verdicts on it must be subject to judicial review to ensure that they square with what the Court had in mind in *Miller* and related cases. "It would be wholly at odds with *Miller*," the Court stated, "to uphold an obscenity conviction based on a defendant's depiction of a woman with a bare midriff, even though a properly charged jury unanimously agreed on the verdict."

This may legitimate bikinis and perhaps *Your New Baby*; but it does not, in the minority opinion of Justices Brennan, Stewart, Marshall, and Douglas, "extricate the Court from the mire of case-by-case determinations of obscenity." Nor does it "diminish the chill on protected expression that derives from the uncertainty of the underlying standard." As long as the *Miller* formula prevails, "one cannot say with certainty that material is obscene until at least five members of this Court, applying inevitably obscure standards, have pronounced it so."

As for community standards, the Court not only failed to rescue them from the limbo of *Miller*, but drew community boundaries even more amorphously. Jurors need not rely on the standards of a "hypothetical statewide community," much less a national community, but may be guided by their understanding of the standards of "the community from which they come." And it is even "proper to ask them to apply community standards without specifying what 'community' "!

Hamling v. U.S., decided the same day as the *Carnal Knowledge* case, was, like the 1973 majority opinions a 5 to 4 determination. Again the majority addressed itself to "community standards." The parties appealing the lower courts' rulings were convicted of mailing sexually explicit material to advertise their illustrated edition of *The Report of The Commission on Obscenity and Pornography*. The jury was unable to reach agreement on whether or not the book was obscene, but it did decide that the advertising brochure, also illustrated, was. Much of the argument in the case (tried prior to *Miller*) concerned the admissibility of evidence indicating that by the standards of southern California, where the case was heard, the material was not obscene. A university student, under the direction of her journalism professor, had polled a random sample of 718 residents of San Diego County, a substantial majority of whom expressed the view that "the material should be generally available to the public." The presiding judge refused to admit the poll in evidence, solely on the ground that it reflected local standards rather than the standards of "the nation as a whole," which he understood earlier Supreme Court decisions to mandate.

The Supreme Court majority in *Hamling*, though it stated that the publishers should have whatever benefits *Miller* afforded them on this score, declared that the failure to admit local standards, and the judge's instruction that the jury must consider only the sensibilities of the nation as a whole, would not have "materially affected the deliberations of the jury." The minority opinion differed rather vehemently: " . . . in addition to the palpable absurdity of the Court's surmises that the introduction of the San Diego study could not have affected the jury's deliberations . . . the Court's assertions that the jury could not have ruled differently if instructed to apply local, not national, standards evinces a claim to omniscience hardly mortal." The minority opinion recalled that the *Miller* rationale for supporting local rather than national standards was precisely that it *would* permit a local community to apply a more permissive test to materials it found acceptable, regardless of what the rest of the nation thought.

If the "local standards" of *Miller* provided cold comfort for those in the case found guilty of promoting an obscene publication, the *Hamling* gloss offered no greater solace. They argued that since the postal statute under which they were convicted was a federal law, yet subject to widely varying local interpretation, the law should be declared void because it is too vague. The majority opinion dismissed this argument summarily, seeing no inconsistency or constitutional impediment. Not so the minority: "Under today's 'local' standards construction . . . the guilt or innocence of distributors of identical material mailed from the same locale can now turn on the dicey course of transit or place of delivery of the materials. . . . National distributors choosing to send their products in interstate travels will be forced to cope with community standards of every hamlet through which their goods may wander. Because these variegated standards are impossible to discern, national distributors, fearful of risking the expense and difficulty of defending against prosecution in any one of several remote communities, must inevitably be led to debilitating self-censorship that abridges First Amendment rights of the people.

Another disappointing aspect of the 1974 decisions concerns the question of the need for prior civil proceedings to determine whether a work is legally obscene before criminal actions may legitimately be brought against those who purvey or present that work. Without this safeguard, the situation is analogous to a road where the speed limit varies capriciously from five to 55 miles an hour, with no speeds posted, though drivers on the highway are held criminally liable if they violate limits they have no way of knowing until they are arrested. The 1973 Supreme Court majority opinion in *Paris Adult Theater I v. Slayton* seemed to bear in the direction of prior civil proceedings; it was hoped that in the *Hamling* and *Jenkins* decisions, the Court would advance further in that direction. Instead it by-passed the issue, merely echoing the 1959 ruling in *Smith v. California* which held: "It is constitutionally sufficient that the prosecution show that a defendant had knowledge of the contents of the materials he distributes, and that he knew the character and nature of the materials." In effect, where even the sophisticated intellects of the Supreme Court justices cannot reach agreement, a teacher, bookseller, or librarian who looks at a work must decide in advance whether or not it is obscene, risking criminal prosecution if the guess is held to be wrong.

On balance, it would seem that *Jenkins* and *Hamling* leave the First Amendment in greater disarray in 1974 than even *Miller* portended in 1973. The Supreme Court has made it clear that a woman's bare midriff is not obscene, but we can be sure of very little else. What may be judged obscene is apparently subject to the standards of communities which have no ascertainable boundaries and in fact need not even be *any* specific community. Criminal actions may constitutionally be pursued against librarians, booksellers, film exhibitors, museums and gallery staffs, and many others without any prior notice that what they are presenting may be considered offensive under whatever "community standards" turn out to be. A producer of materials distributed nationally may be liable to prosecution at any or all points en route as well as at the points of origin and destination. Everyone engaged in the transmission of ideas is charged with the responsibility of not merely outguessing the Supreme Court, but of correctly divining what thousands of communities, by their own idiosyncratic lights, may decide is obscene.

The picture, however, is not wholly discouraging. The Court's rulings caused many legislatures to reexamine their obscenity laws, and several of them decided to remove some of the more restrictive facets despite the Court's decisions. South Dakota, West Virginia, and Iowa repealed their adult obscenity statutes and substituted laws regulating only materials for minors. Vermont, which only had a minors statute, added a mandatory prior civil proceedings provision. North Carolina retained the pre-1973 *Memoirs* test and added mandatory prior civil proceedings. A highly threatening bill was defeated in Pennsylvania and another was significantly diluted in New York. On the negative side, Nebraska passed a most repressive bill. In Oregon, which had a perfectly workable minors-only and public display statute, a "bad" bill was pressured through the legislature, but determined opponents managed to gather enough signatures to force a referendum. The voters will decide in November (after this article goes to press) whether to retain the old law or adopt the new one. In many other states, legislatures have been marking time to see how the Court's 1974 decisions might affect proposed legislation, much of it very repressive. Legislative action may now, of course, be expected.

At no time in recent years has the right to read, see, and hear been under more serious challenge than it is today, not only for young people but for their elders. The real target in many "anti-obscenity" actions is not obscenity at all, but unpopular, dissident, irreverent, or satirical expression unsettling to current complacencies. The crux of the problem, as Justice Douglas has observed, is that censorship "casts too wide a net," suppressing ideas that clearly deserve protection, and often destroying innocent people in the process.

Trying to legislate morality can prove a tricky business; our earlier noble experiment, Prohibition, should alert us to some of the traps into which we may be stumbling. At best it is an exercise in futility, since it is doubtful that any culture has ever succeeded in wiping out pornography. At worst it imperils the very basis of the society it purports to protect, the freedom of expression that Justice Cardozo called "the matrix, the indispensable condition of nearly all our other freedoms."

Bibliography

For a better understanding of the issues raised here, besides checking basic texts used in mass communication law classes, the student might consult Victor B. Cline, editor, *Where Do You Draw the Line? An Exploration into Media Violence, Pornography and Censorship*, Brigham Young University Press, 1974, several articles debating the issue of complete freedom and regulated freedom in some areas. Also see Ray C. Rist, ed., *The Pornography Controversy*, Transaction Books, 1975. Contains 14 articles on pornography, tending toward the pro-freedom view.

Also important is a piece by Paul Bender, "The Supreme Court's Decision on Obscenity," which appeared in the previous edition of this reader and originally was published in the *Los Angeles Times*. Bender was general counsel for the national Commission on Obscenity and Pornography (1968-70) and is a professor of law at the Pennsylvania Law School. A special issue of *Public Interest* (Winter, 1971) offered four responses to Walter Bernes' "Pornography vs. Democracy: The Case for Censorship." Other journals, and law reviews, have carried similar articles. One of interest was Leonard Berkowitz' "Sex and Violence: We Can't Have It Both Ways," found in *Psychology Today* (Dec. 1971). Regarding the content of films, excellent background could be gained by reading the *Wisconsin Law Review* (1970) article "Self-Censorship of the Movie Industry: An Historical Perspective on Law and Social Change"—a 47-page treatment discussing movie ratings and the response of the film industry to law and public policy.

Revolution in the Mass Media

Whether changes in the mass media are a reflection of social change or of technological change is an oft-debated subject in academic circles. Certainly we can choose a middle position and suggest that some changes are the result of new social mores and/or values while others appear to be the result of new technology. The decline in movie theater attendance and in the number of films produced during the sixties, for example, is best explained as a result of the widespread dissemination of television, which was a relatively new technology. On the other hand, many changes in the content or themes of the movies during the same period are perhaps reflections of our changing mores which permitted—indeed encouraged—the new content. A case can also be made for the interaction of technological and social change. Our selections in this part of the book tend to reflect one or the other of these views, usually without trying to establish a cause and effect relationship.

It is easily demonstrated that the established or commercial mass media are adapting to the new technology in many ways, just as they are adapting to social pressures from minority groups as well as from women. Change has taken place; improvement has been made, and those who historically have been excluded from the media have been heard. There still are obvious needs for further improvement, but on balance what has occurred has been encouraging.

The auxiliaries to the mass media—advertising and public relations—also have been influenced by changes in society. Our selections describe just a few of the areas where further change is needed and/or can be expected.

Finally, in this part, we confront the problem of American mass media and their effect on international and national communication. Great resistance to American media and programming has arisen in some areas of the world in recent years. Canada is only one example of a country trying to protect its own communications industry by restricting the movement of American mass media in that country through tax laws and other regulations. If mass communication is important to a nation's well being, we should expect more reaction on the part of other nations in the years ahead.

Students who wish to explore these and other issues more fully should use the bibliographies which accompany the individual articles. No collection of readings can include all issues or even all important articles. Research in the bibliographies is absolutely necessary for a comprehensive view of the issues that confront the mass media and society in America during a period of rapid technological, social, and international change.

New Technology

The Newspaper of the Next Decade

Jon G. Udell

22

A Newspaper Reader of the late 1980s is likely to find that his or her daily newspaper looks very much like that of today. The paper on which it is printed *may* be somewhat lighter and manufactured, at least in part, from materials other than costly wood pulp; pages may be slightly narrower, and typography less crowded and more attractive. Technology is the driving force which will make newspaper changes possible. However, more sophisticated management techniques and better-trained employees also will play an essential role in the free newspaper's future.

So-called experts have predicted the demise of newspapers as we know them since the 1930s; yet the "traditional" newspaper continues to be the nation's largest communication medium in news and editorial content, employment, advertising and sales revenue. On the other hand, the technology necessary to "replace" newspapers as we know them is already decades old. Newspapers have been printed in the home on a small printer controlled by electronic impulses. But traditional newspaper production and distribution methods prevail because the cost of an in-home printer, its maintenance, transmission fees and paper continue to substantially exceed the costs of more traditional methods.

In the 1950s and 1960s television became a major new medium of news and entertainment in the communications business. Newspaper publishers were stimulated to spur development of technology for newspapers.[1] The resulting revolution in newspaper technology has laid the groundwork for substantial further benefits for the future.

Newspapers of the next decade probably will be printed by the same processes available today, but on lighter-weight presses and with more and improved printing-plate options. The shift to offset printing will continue, particularly among small and medium-sized newspapers. Hot metal type-setting machines will be totally replaced by photocomposition and cold type. Laser scanners and laser plate-engravers likely will become an economic alternative to the camera platemaking process.[2] Press plates will be plastic or light-weight metal.

Another printing option, now in development, could eliminate press plates altogether. This process uses computer-controlled ink jets to "spray" the ink onto newsprint. It could lead to a fast, flexible newspaper-printing process that would allow a change of editions without stopping the plateless printing machine.

Application of electronic text-processing, automated typesetting and photosensitive platemaking technologies should improve productivity by at least 10 to 15 percent more.[3]

The Technological Horizon

Jon G. Udell is on the faculty of the School of Commerce, University of Wisconsin. He has been an industry consultant for several years. This article is from chapter 10 of his recent industry study, *The Economics of the American Newspaper* by Jon G. Udell and Contributing Authors, copyright 1978 by American Newspaper Publishers Association Foundation. Reprinted by permission of Hastings House, Publishers, New York 10016.

1. For a discussion of this historical development, see Chapter 6 in Udell, *The Economics of the American Newspaper.*

2. Arthur D. Little, *Threats and Opportunities Within the Newsprint—Newspaper Industry*, Cambridge, Mass., October 1974, Part I, p. 17.

3. *Ibid.*, p. 18.

Computers will play an expanded role, especially in composition and makeup of a newspaper; the entire content of many newspapers may be processed electronically.

On-line display terminals for advertising will simplify the most complex part of newspaper composition, and the computer may provide for complete, electronic full-page assembly. But, the cost of hardware and supporting programs to handle full-page composition may continue to be greater than the cost of the paste-up activity it would replace in most newspapers.

With computers, video-display terminals and other electronic devices, editors will be able to revise copy to meet readers' needs with greater speed and efficiency. While it is possible to install a completely integrated computerized system, minicomputer installations are more likely. Such installations cost less and minimize transition problems.

During the last ten years, small and medium-sized newspapers changed production techniques more than big-city dailies. Large metropolitan newspapers will change the most in the next decade.

Metropolitan newspapers of the late 1980s may have more than one plant. New microwave transmitting technology is enabling newspapers to transmit page images for printing at satellite plants. Such a plant needs no composition facilities, only an offset press. Eventually, newspapers in our largest cities each may have three or four satellite presses located strategically throughout their distribution areas. Satellite pressrooms may be used to print other newspapers as well. A suburban paper, for example, could publish without building its own press facility, and a metropolitan paper could make greater use of its pressroom capacity. Big papers could start their own suburban shoppers.

Advancing technology will do more than change composition and printing presses. It will enhance newspapers' economic viability through increased efficiency. Production personnel will enjoy more sophisticated jobs with less drudgery and better working conditions. Advertisers will have greater flexibility in using the newspaper medium for delivery of their messages. Perhaps most significant, readers may find newspaper content better oriented to their individual needs and desires. Computers and satellite press locations will make it economically feasible to produce special editions catering to specific urban or suburban locations. While special sections or editions will add to newspaper costs and circulation and advertising rates, newspapers will have greater value to readers and advertisers.

These exciting developments are already occurring. *The Minneapolis Star and Tribune* has installed the first full-page pagination system, and will be among the first newspapers in the world without a composing room.[4] *The Wall Street Journal* transmits its entire Florida edition from Massachusetts to Florida via domestic satellite, making it possible to run the entire Florida plant with just 19 people.[5] The ANPA Research Institute is spearheading the perfection of low cost microwave receivers that can fit on the roof of a newspaper plant to receive information from a satellite instead of telephone lines. This could lead to a nationwide satellite microwave communications network for newspapers, bypass-

4. Robert G. Marbut, "Newspaper Technology: Today and Tomorrow," Congress of the International Federation of Newspaper Publishers, Bologna, Italy, June 1, 1976.

5. *Ibid.*

ing traditional telephone cables and towers. Not only would such a system offer economic advantages, it would provide a nationwide system for instantaneous transmission of advertising and editorial messages.

While the promise is great, a caveat is in order. Advancing technology, in and of itself, does not guarantee new efficiency, better newspapers or improved profit. Technology must be wisely managed to be beneficial. Newspaper management must analyze carefully its needs, evaluate advances in light of those needs and train appropriate personnel to use the new tools which are adopted. Without a cautious and carefully managed approach, new technology can bring confusion and dissention between management and employes, increase costs and destroy customer and employe goodwill. *Advanced technology is merely a tool which must be selected and used wisely.*

Converting a newspaper from old systems and processes to all the latest available technology in a new plant challenges even the best managers. Many employes must develop entirely new skills; some skills become totally obsolete. Training and personnel problems usually are horrendous. Before employes iron out bugs in new equipment and processes, printing errors, delayed press runs and a poor-quality product often cause customer dissatisfaction and conflicts within the newspaper family. Technological advances constitute progress only when well managed.

The Physical Product

In the last 20 years newspapers have gone through several format changes, largely dictated by periodic shortages and skyrocketing prices of newsprint. Faced with a need to conserve paper, publishers moved toward narrower pages and rediscovered readability formulas showing that somewhat longer lines are easier to read. This led many papers to a six-column page or one of its many variations.

Many advertising sizing problems already have been ameliorated through standards which enable advertisers to produce their materials in a minimum number of variations. Technology—such as computer composition—will make it possible in the future for advertisers and editors to arrange their material in almost any format desired, and space communications could enable newspapers to swiftly receive both advertising and news via satellite-signal direct to the newspaper plant.

Newsprint conservation will continue as prices rise and shortages occur because of surges in demand, delays in mill capacity expansion and occasional mill or railroad strikes. For publishers, however, emphasis will be on efficient newsprint use. Newsprint consumption will continue to increase, as waste reductions are outweighed by newspaper growth and increased paper consumption for specialized editions or sections to serve diverse reader desires. Research efforts will focus on finding new newsprint-production technology so that new, lightweight newsprint machines may ultimately be located nearer both newspapers and new fiber-crop pulp sources.

The 1980s will be a transition period from essentially one edition for all readers to the twenty-first century basic edition supplemented by specialized

The miracles of electronic editing, computerized delivery systems, and other innovations have eliminated much of the extra toil common to publishing, but reporters will always be there, ready to send important news around the world in minutes, and even seconds in the event of a "flash." The interpretation and analysis can come later.

```
▼
▼
QUEUE aa ...... TIME IS 05:22▼
▼
ITEMS IN PROCESS▼
▼
aa180 court... o. 0383 05:26▼
▼
ITEMS ON QUEUE▼
▼
aa181 europe-. o. 0418 05:34▼
aa177 opec.... o. 0290 05:40▼
aa213 talks-.. o. 0300 05:46▼
aa201 bufalino o. 0306 05:52▼
aa165 interest o. 0225 05:56▼
aa199 cuba.... om 0273 06:01▼
aa200 abortion o. 0243 06:06▼
aa204 tomcat.. o. 0363 06:13▼
aa207 freedom. o. 0139 06:16▼
aa208 Marchi.. o. 0181 06:20▼
aa210 defense. o. 0471 06:29▼
aa214 ervin... o. 0281 06:35▼
aa215 rescue.. o. 0221 06:39▼
aa221 boycott. o. 0531 06:49▼
aa225 turkey-. m. 0299 06:55▼
```

sections or editions for various major segments of the population. Electronic composition and satellite printing will make product differentiation practical—to the benefit of readers, advertisers and publishers alike. A news story or an advertisement with general interest will continue to appear in the basic paper. Those of special interest to certain readers only will appear in specialized sections or editions which go to those readers.

In the next decade new technology will make the newspaper a more sophisticated and widely used advertising medium. Technology will make it easier for a newspaper to adopt the "marketing concept" in selling advertising. Advertising personnel will be better able to coordinate with other divisions to group advertising with related news and special features. Some newspapers will be able to offer their full circulation to those advertisers wanting to reach the entire public, and "split" runs for those seeking to reach only identifiable segments of a newspaper's audience, such as readers in a specific geographic area. Computer text-processing, with ads sorted and formatted by a computer, will make it possible to accept and typeset advertisements within an hour of press time. This will allow a newspaper to offer its advertisers more timely changes in their advertising keyed to the weather or unexpected news events.

Advertising and Competition

Thousands of small retailers today do not use metropolitan newspaper advertising because the involved circulation extends far beyond their trading areas. To the extent that newspaper specialization occurs, it will provide new marketing opportunities for these retailers. They will be able to place their advertisements in the edition of the daily newspaper which primarily reaches their potential customers. Similarly, readers will appreciate receiving more local shopping information. Specialization represents substantial potential for newspaper advertising growth in the years ahead.

The same techniques also will be applied to classified advertising. For many years virtually all classified advertising has been "full run" in all copies or editions of a daily newspaper because it was too expensive to pull out small ads and "remake" pages. Computer technology will make it possible to offer classified advertising on the same split-run basis. This will be particularly useful to small retailers and service shops and will increase classified advertising's readership and value. While the advertising rate per copy distributed will be higher for split than full runs, the rate per potential customer reached will be considerably lower.

The newspaper will continue to be the major medium for classified advertising. The broadcast media simply cannot serve this market because of a lack of time. Also, the typical classified advertiser cannot afford broadcast rates.

The electronic media's only real opportunity to reach specialized segments of the population is through cable systems. However, glowing predictions for the cable have not and are not likely to materialize during the next decade. The cost of cable systems has increased greatly and cable operators are restricted by federal, state and local regulations and must pay exorbitant charges to some municipalities for the right to operate. Cable restrictions may be loosened, but cable will remain largely a supplement to television. Even if successful, cable television is unlikely to attract a large volume of advertising because the large number of stations and proliferation of television channels would fragment the viewing audience, tending to make newspapers more attractive for general audience advertising.

Also boosting newspaper advertising are expanding state and federal rulings concerning television advertising and sales techniques. Already the federal government prohibits cigarette advertising on radio and television, and requires certain factual information in advertisements for some products and services. Additional restrictions promise to make it increasingly difficult for some advertisers to prepare broadcast sales messages. If certain facts are legally required in an advertisement, an advertiser will need to purchase additional broadcast time or reduce the promotional content of the advertising message. Frequently, only printed media offer enough space to economically present a full story in a single advertisement while meeting government requirements.

Television's share of advertising revenues appears to be stabilizing; it is no longer rising at a rapid pace. Newspapers should, therefore, enjoy a greater growth rate. Their competitive position may also be enhanced by economic advantages. As pointed out in a study by Arthur D. Little, "The newspaper industry in the next 10 years will deal successfully with inflationary forces and improve its cost performance and competitive position relative to competing advertising media (TV and magazines)."[6] Because of productivity increases and better managerial controls made possible by emerging technology, newspaper ad rates are expected to remain low enough to capture a larger share of the advertising dollar.

However, the competition for advertising dollars will continue to be intense and television will continue to push the expansion of local spot advertising. Because of the rising diversity of life styles, the media are becoming increasingly fragmented. For example, the tennis buff is more likely to purchase a tennis magazine than mass appeal magazines such as *Life* and *Look*, which have now disappeared from the marketplace.

The trend toward fragmentation will have a mixed impact on community newspapers. While fragmentation tends to adversely affect general interest media, the community newspaper has survived because of its wide range of content which includes something for almost every interest group. Therefore, it continues to be one of the few media reaching many specialized interest groups *and* a wide general audience. This capability should favor the growth of newspaper advertising.

It is in the arena of news-editorial competition that a newspaper of the next decade will face one of its stiffest challenges. Based on public opinion polls—with the same questions used year after year—newspapers have declined in public esteem, both as a prime source of news and as a believable medium.

News-Editorial Competition

Ironically, adoption of new production technology has sometimes impacted reader confidence. Many newspapers installed new composition equipment before all the bugs had been ironed out, and produced a plethora of typographical errors. New computerized composition and makeup systems, properly programmed, will produce fewer typographical errors.

Measured by most opinion polls, public trust in the accuracy of news reporting in all media is too low for editors' tastes. Many newspapers have been attacking the "credibility" problem through a variety of techniques. Several papers have appointed ombudsmen to hear and act on reader complaints. Many publish columns or feature articles explaining problems of news coverage, and many more regularly run corrections of errors in news stories. Future editorial success of newspapers will depend in great measure on newspaper efforts to improve accuracy, to communicate with readers, to inspire confidence in the accuracy of news columns and to convey a sense of fairness and even friendliness on every page.

The news content of large newspapers probably will be of more interest to readers in the future because of specialized sections for neighborhoods or "interest profiles." However, readers will recognize inaccuracies even more readily than today because they are likely to be even more knowledgeable about topics which interest them.

6. Arthur D. Little, *Threats and Opportunities Within the Newsprint-Newspaper Industry*, Part III, December 1974.

In competition with other media, a newspaper should have an advantage in reader appeal. Its basic edition will cover international, national and local news of interest to the general reader. Specialized editions and sections will fill out news packages for readers in various interest groups.

Like newspaper advertising, newspaper editorial content is not subject to broadcasting's time limits. This is an enormous competitive advantage, particularly since a newspaper of the future will need to be increasingly tailored to comprehensively meet the needs of diverse readership groups. Displays of factual text and competing opinions are possible on a television screen, but not in any comprehensive way during the foreseeable future.

In much of its content the newspaper will be a medium of explanation. It will have moderated the historic emphasis of being first with spot news, recognizing that broadcast media have an inherent time advantage. But, investigative "scoops" will continue to be a newspaper's preserve. And, a newspaper has sufficient space to explain the background and details of an event, relate it to other events or pending developments and present commentaries from a wide variety of knowledgeable persons.

At the same time, the newspaper of the future will have an improved capacity to report news quickly. Portable remote terminals have been developed which allow a reporter to prepare copy in the field on the keyboard of a device which rapidly can transmit copy directly to a newsroom computer by telephone. This advance, coupled with rapid composition and typesetting systems, will permit a story which breaks near press time to be published almost as rapidly as it is broadcast, but in far more detail. Some day the remote terminal will also handle still pictures.

The future editor's control of a newspaper's content and appearance probably will be firmer than today. Because of computerized data banks of information and of travelling reporters equipped to transmit stories directly to the newsroom, editors will have a wider selection of stories from which to choose. In addition, editorial affiliations may develop within newspaper groups or among independents which will provide whole sections, pages or inserts on a timely basis which are shared via satellite or microwave transmission in much the same way that wire service material is shared today.

Looking to the twenty-first century, newspapers will be marketing a wide variety of information which they now discard. This will take several different forms. Each day a newspaper receives many times as much information as it can publish. In the future, news from wire services will be digitally encoded in computers, ready for manipulation into packages of data useful to special interest groups such as sports enthusiasts, business people and homemakers. Such packages could take the form of local specialized publications issued weekly or more frequently.

Distribution

Of all the elements of newspaper operations, distribution presents the most nagging problems. No other industry creates and delivers such a complex product on a daily basis, or even tries to deliver such a modestly-priced item on such a rigid time schedule. In most cases home delivery is no more expensive to a reader than buying a single copy at a newsstand. Furthermore, final delivery usually still depends on a boy or girl. This delivery system has been a great success and is unlikely to be discarded during the next decade. However, major changes will be well underway by that time.

New ideas for newspaper distribution are being tried. The newspaper "mail" room already is partially automated, but more automation will come, particularly for insertion of special sections and preprinted advertising supplements into the basic paper.

New ideas for truck routing from the plant to distribution points are being tried, including the use of large trucks where a major traffic artery makes it feasible. This involves trucking to a distribution center from which many smaller trucks can depart without getting into midtown traffic. New types of energy-efficient trucks will be developed and used.

A newspaper with satellite printing plants around the rim of the core city will have fewer distribution problems at least from plant to distribution center. But juvenile carriers dislike early morning delivery and periodic collecting at night. More adults will be carriers. Also, most newspapers will use computers to bill all subscribers for direct payment, relieving carriers of the collecting chore.

Unfortunately, even a modern distribution system may not always help newspapers reach urban apartment dwellers and persons in high-crime, central-city areas. Security measures in some apartment complexes make it difficult for carriers to gain admittance. Despite the current economic disadvantages of in-home printers, some metropolitan newspapers eventually may utilize them—or even video cassettes—for reaching subscribers in locations where the carrier system is not feasible.

Newsprint Supply

Future U.S. newspaper growth depends upon adequate newsprint supply. Historically, periodic shortages have limited newspaper expansion. For example, in 1973 strikes in Canada greatly reduced the flow of paper to the United States. After the strikes, supply expanded but at a substantially higher price.

However, newspapers do have a major resource advantage—they utilize a renewable and recyclable resource—fiber pulp—which in the future may include both wood pulp and pulp from other, faster growing plants. In addition, newsprint weight can be reduced further to conserve the pulp resource. By the late 1980s most U.S. newspapers may be using 28-pound newsprint as opposed to 30-pound in 1975 and 32-pound in 1965. Today, European newspapers rapidly are adapting to newsprint equivalent to a 27.7-pound weight.

Most U.S. newspapers are currently unable to economically use the 27.7-pound newsprint because over 60 percent of U.S. paper supply comes from Canada, and U.S. tariffs are charged on newsprint with less than a 28.5-pound basis weight. This legal barrier to economic use of lighter weight newsprint probably will be repealed in the next decade, particularly if paper manufacturing technology improves the quality of lighter newsprint.

Meanwhile, improved forest management will ensure that trees used for paper-making are harvested only in replaceable quantities. And new technology may make non-wood-fiber newsprint economical.

A newsprint mill which will use sugar cane stalks (bagasse) for pulp is under construction in South America. The American Newspaper Publishers Association Research Institute is studying newsprint made of "kenaf" a farm product which can be grown in most areas of North America. Also, used newsprint is and will be recycled. While most recycled newsprint today is used for paperboard or other products such as insulation, an increasing proportion is being de-inked and used again to make newsprint.

Economics

The major economic problem for newspapers during the next decade is inflation. The cost of labor and materials will continue to rise, forcing up advertising and circulation rates. However, emerging technology and improved management methods will help slow the rise of production costs. Productivity gains will occur primarily in pre-press production operations as a result of improved information-handling and typesetting systems. More efficient press operations, page formats and careful control will save newsprint. The latest information on street sales and subscriptions will be used to set press runs and reduce "overruns."

As a result of increased efficiency, newspaper costs and prices *may* not rise as fast as those of competitive industries. However, large newspapers will not achieve a competitive advantage without increasing distribution efficiency. That efficiency may depend on advancing data transmission technology and satellite printing operations. Newspapers will continue to enjoy a rapid growth of pre-printed advertising inserts by being able to deliver the inserts more cheaply than bulk-rate mail or other delivery systems.

Newspaper Employes

As a place to work, the newspaper is likely to become even more attractive than it is today. The hot-metal production facility of the past has been described as a combination of a dungeon and a blacksmith shop, with the added discomforts of ink mists and loud noise. Conditions will be greatly improved during the next ten years.

New technology already has eliminated much drudgery in the production process. Future advances will bring about a more efficient, quiet, safer operation from preparation of news and advertising copy to final printing. In the old days newspaper production employes had to wear work clothes and wash up before going home. By the late 1980s many production workers will dress more like today's doctors and business executives.

News and advertising employes will find their work highly integrated with the production process. Original news and advertising copy will flow—without re-keyboarding—through editing, proofreading, page assembly and printing, with other employes controlling the process with computers and video display terminals.

Editors will have greater control of a newspaper's content and appearance. They will have a wider selection of national and regional material from which to choose. More photographs will be transmitted, and they will be of improved quality. Better national telecommunications facilities and satellite communications systems around the world will support an expanded data transmission system, perhaps at lower costs than today.

A new category of employes will emerge, probably managed by the editorial department. They will be responsible for computer and electronic systems.

Most newspapers will have more traveling reporters, each equipped with a remote terminal for transmission of news stories. Locally, the reporter will continue to be the eyes and ears of the newspaper. A reporter will be dispatched, as now, by an editor. He or she will gather the news, but will not necessarily have to return to the main plant to prepare his story. The typical reporter may use an on-line portable typewriter. With software support it will be possible for the reporter to backspace and strike out as he or she types, and read the story in its final form as it is filed in the data base. Where computer support is not available, a reporter's typewriter will "output" to a cassette. The cassette story then will be read into the data base without sophisticated computer support.

During the next decade there will be a greater emphasis on technical and managerial expertise in all newspaper departments. A smaller percentage of the workforce will be production workers, but they will be better paid than today. Coordination will be essential, with news and advertising personnel required to understand and participate more in the production process than they do today. There will be substantial use of the "marketing" or "total newspaper" concept. The importance of marketing will rise as newspapers adjust to the increasingly dynamic society.

The growth and prosperity of a newspaper is highly correlated with the economics of the community it serves. Therefore, the greatest threat to newspapers and to the free press of the future is possible stagnation of the U.S. economy or the communities which many newspapers serve. Inflation continues to be an "economic cancer" which destroys healthy economic cells in the economic system it ravages. Fortunately, some progress has been made in the battle against inflation.

A Long-term Economic Threat

From the turn of the century until the 1960s, methods of producing the American newspaper remained virtually unchanged. However, few industries have greeted massive technological change as enthusiastically as today's newspapers. As a result, the newspaper of the next decade should easily survive all competitive challenges from other media.

Conclusion

More important, newspapers will perform their constitutional, public-service role more effectively than ever before. Readers will find their familiar-appearing newspapers to be even better and more useful sources of news and advertising information.

As publishers and editors acknowledge their own weaknesses and take steps to correct them, the public will gain further confidence in the press as a source of objective information. With this continued public acceptance free newspapers will play their indispensible role in a free society—during the next decade, and for so long as a free society thrives.

Bibliography

Jon Udell's projections regarding the American newspaper in the 1980s should be supplemented with the following material, which also deals with the impact of technology on the American newspaper and other media. Dineh Maghdam, *Computers in Newspaper Publishing: User-Oriented Systems* (Marcel Dekker, Inc., 1978), is an excellent example of the practical type of book which concentrates on how-to-use the computer in newspaper publishing. A more theoretical approach is found in Glen O. Robinson, editor, *Communications for Tomorrow: Policy Perspectives for the 1980s* (Praeger Special Studies, 1978), which includes Marc U. Porat's essay "Communication Policy in an Information Society," an excellent overview of the role of communications, and Bruce Owen's essay "The Role of Print in an Electronic Society" on the future of the print media. Both are found in the Robinson volume. There are several magazines which deal with the production side of printing and newspapers. These should be consulted for case studies on the application of technology to the field. See, among many, *Graphic Monthly, WEB,* and *Inland Printer*.

23 Information Without Limit Electronically
Kenneth Edwards

Five hundred top-level newspaper executives watched a showing of slides and heard an explanation about electronic information delivery to home television sets during a convention in 1977. Afterward, when the speaker asked for questions, there were none! Those executives were too shocked to speak because they had just seen "the electronic newspaper" as it is operating now in England. They knew it would happen "someday," but they thought it was still far in the future.

That was in the fall of 1977. As this book goes to press, *teletext*—which those newspapermen had viewed—is still a little-known wonder in the United States, even to people in communications.

You can experience it easily in London. Simply check into the Portman Hotel, a popular place with businessmen visiting London. You can have a full day of business activities, shopping, or sightseeing and know full well that you will miss out on nothing important because you have teletext monitoring the world for you that day. When you return to your hotel after a day on the town and start preparing for evening activities, you can dial for the latest information on the television set in your room.

You dial a three-digit number on your teletext keypad for the latest news flashes or for an index of information. Brilliant six-color "print" displays flash the latest headlines. Those include page numbers you can dial on your screen about any headline that interests you.

If you want scores of the afternoon ball games in England, you dial sports scores and get up-to-the-minute results.

Kenneth Edwards is a member of the journalism faculty at the University of Alabama. A professional journalist for many years before entering teaching, Edwards has written and lectured extensively on electronic news dissemination. He prepared this article especially for this book.

If you want stock market information, you dial the financial index for a general picture of market conditions. And if you want to check on a particular stock, you dial another number to learn how your investment fared that day.

All this—and much more—is instantly available on the TV screen in your hotel room, when you want to know it, and it is constantly updated.

But that isn't all.

Let's say you plan to leave tomorrow for New York and you want to check the airline schedules. You dial the phone-connected Prestel service for airline schedules, which are then flashed on your television screen. And if you want information about New York, you can dial and read page after page about hotels, restaurants, and entertainments in New York. This comes by courtesy of *The New York Times*, an information supplier for the Prestel market trials going on now in London.

But there's still more.

With plans now complete for leaving, you think of going out tonight. So you dial "Going Out" on Prestel and quickly sort out the entertainment you want, in the area you choose, at the price you want to pay, offering programs and menus you choose while still in your hotel room.

In a matter of minutes, teletext has given you the latest news, market changes, sports scores, airline schedules, New York information—and helped you plan the evening's adventure. You have had instant gratification for your needs and wishes because you get information you need, exactly when you want it, right where you are. It is computer display technology, common enough in some business or newspaper offices, reaching new levels of sophisticated usage in delivering a better life for every kind of person.

When those newspaper executives I mentioned earlier first saw the demonstration, they could see marked similarities between British teletext and operations they had seen on video display terminals (VDTs) in American newsrooms.

In newsrooms today you see a reporter write a story that appears on a small electronic screen, looking much like a home TV screen. Then the reporter sends that story along its way for paste-up, plating, and printing.

The English reporter may write a similar story on a similar screen, but then something different happens if he is using one of the new British teletext systems. He presses a button and his words are instantly readable in electronic print on teletext sets all over Great Britain! No waiting for printing and delivery at all!

The British writer bypasses both printing and delivery. His video display unit is matched by similar VDTs in the shape of color TV sets in the homes of his readers. They can instantly read his story. The new teletext technology has changed, seemingly like magic, the picture tube in a living room into an information screen.

"Teletext" is the generic name for three British systems of electronic information delivery—Ceefax, Oracle, and Prestel, originally known as Viewdata. Teletext is electronic "print" that is readable with a maximum of 24 lines on a glass screen.

BBC news on Ceefax.
Note the directions for
further information.

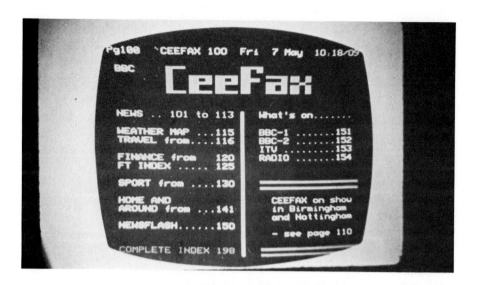

Ceefax—"see facts"—is owned by the British government and the British Broadcasting Company, or BBC. It carries no advertising. Oracle is owned by the Independent Television Authority, expects to earn a profit, and carries advertising. Oracle is short for "Optional Reception of Announcements by Coded Line Electronics." Prestel—"press tell"—is owned and operated by the British Post Office and transmits information on TV sets over telephone lines.

Ceefax and Oracle make use of two TV lines at the top of a home TV screen which are not seen on a properly working TV set. Both Ceefax and Oracle transmissions are continuous and may be received and read by anyone who has a TV receiver equipped with a decoder.

A "page" of teletext information consists of 24 rows of 40 upper and lower case characters which may be displayed in seven colors. Headlines take space, of course, and in actual practice, the average page is 80 to 100 words long.

In operation, the desired page is selected from an index or from memory by the viewer, who chooses page numbers from a small keying mechanism about the size of a pocket calculator. When the page is dialed by the operator, the decoder on the TV set catches the desired page from a continuous data stream so that the operator can view it for as long a time as desired. When finished, the operator presses buttons similar to those on a touch telephone and captures another subject or another story. The viewer sees only pages he wants to read and these pop onto the screen immediately.

To understand the possible impact of teletext upon American mass media, we must also understand the kinds of breadth of information available on teletext.

Recently a research project of the American Newspaper Publishers Association revealed that a great majority of Americans want newspapers to provide them *much more* consumer information. Not just more, but *MUCH MORE*.

Teletext could make available to every American just about every published bit of consumer information there is. In a matter of seconds, the viewer could select and see whatever kind of information is wanted.

Whatever one's interest—autos, television, new appliances, roofing repairs, nutrition, cooking recipes, calorie counting, education courses, road condition, airline schedules, and "whatever"—absolutely *"whatever"*—it could be called up in seconds on one's own home information screen.

That is the astonishing information capability of teletext.

Ceefax and Oracle offer their viewers choices of about 100 different topics within the present 800-page format.

General topics, most of them with numerous subtopics, include headlines, news, people in the news, features, and prospective news indexed for the news section. The sports section includes headlines, news stories, sports, and racing results. One editor has said he thinks newspapers will have to change sports emphasis away from reporting results and develop more background stories because any teletext viewer can call up every sports result immediately—just as soon as the game is over!

Weather and travel subjects include weather maps and forecasting maps, plus information about road travel, rail travel and sea travel. Also included is information about delays, road repairs, detours, and other facts of special interest to travelers.

The entertainment section shows pages of TV programming, film programs and reviews, music and book reviews, information about the theater, and questions and answers from viewers.

Consumerism is important with information about food prices, food availability, farm prices, recipes, science news, police news, and special information on education, farming, and gardening.

Finance news includes headlines, the *Financial Times* index, news of industries, news of companies, a market report, stock price report, exchange rates, and information relating to international as well as national finance.

Other features of the teletext system include "printed" news bulletins to overprint the conventional TV picture, six-color graphic display of maps and charts, and a "reveal" button for "hidden answers" in educational use or for puzzles or games seen on the screen. (The screen displays a question; you try to answer; and then you press the "reveal" button to see the correct answer appear underneath the question.)

One of the earliest firms to use teletext as a sales attraction was the Portman Hotel, which leased 100 sets in 1977 and placed them in its larger hotel rooms. The hotel management said the expense is highly justified. Businessmen, particularly, find teletext transmissions fascinating, interesting—and extremely valuable. The Portman decided to add Prestel because of the favorable reaction to Ceefax.

Prestel, formerly called Viewdata, is a different system from Ceefax and Oracle. Developed by the British Post Office, Prestel displays "print" in the same way as Ceefax and Oracle on a TV screen, but that is the only real similarity. Prestel connects on the TV set from the telephone and is a part of a two-way communication system the post office supplies. Its stored information is unlimited, for all practical purposes. Any home with both TV and telephone can be connected to the system in Great Britain. The phone company makes a small charge for service comparable to a local phone call charge.

Prestel, being two-way, offers viewers the opportunity of asking for any information in the post office memory bank. This could include all the information in an encyclopedia. But for the market trials in England, about 100,000 pages of information will be available.

Topics in Prestel being offered during the market trial are also varied. They include news, sports, radio and TV, going out (for entertainment) holidays and travel, tourist guide, education (including college of the air), jokes, quizzes and games, home and family help, advertising, cars and motoring, houses and insurance, jobs and careers, facts and figures, and other information. There are numerous subheads for each general subject.

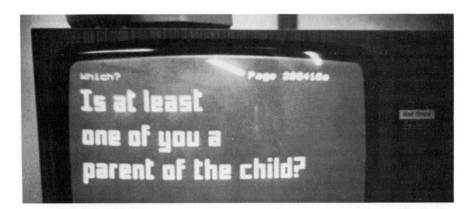

Prestel series offer information on particular topics—in this case, how to adopt a child. Note how the viewer is requested to respond to questions on the video screen.

If you were job-hunting in London, you could dial in "jobs and careers" on your television set and get information about the kinds of jobs available. If you were looking for a job in advertising, public relations, or as an editor, Prestel would tell you if any such jobs are open and give you the names of firms that might be interested in hiring you!

To operate Prestel, the viewer chooses a general subject, then a division of the subject, then a subdivision of that division and continues for up to ten steps to get the exact information desired. In each step, the viewer makes a choice from an index to the next branch of the selection tree. Only five or six steps are needed to offer a precise choice from 25,000 subtopics, but all ten steps can be performed by the viewer in less than one minute.

Prestel offers patrons quick access to many kinds of information that require great effort or cause nasty frustrations for people trying to find them.

Let's examine a question of this kind: "Can we adopt a child?"

The viewer's question is answered by a question testing his eligibility.

The viewer dials one or zero in answer to each question as it appears on the screen. As long as the answers are satisfactory, Prestel offers question after question until the viewer knows whether he can adopt a child or not. In a couple of minutes, the viewer can get the answers to serious, complicated questions that might require days of effort to satisfy through conventional means and bureaucratic run-around.

Prestel information providers come from many different parts of industry and government. They include Reuters, Westminster Press, and *Financial Times* as well as consumer organizations, the Tourist Board, the Commodities Exchange, and many others, including *The New York Times* and Harte-Hanks Communications of San Antonio, Texas.

There is also a fourth British system, which operates a lot closer to home. Reuters News Agency is offering its IDR teletext out of New York in conjunction with American cable systems.

Reuters offers two News-view systems, one including financial and sports news, and the other offering general news. The general news channel includes a daily horoscope, Hollywood chit-chat, a sports quiz, pet care, consumer stories, and many other topics, including seasonal news such as ski slope conditions and resort weather. The Reuters information is available on demand to viewers who have their sets equipped with retrieval terminals which call up information from an index similar to those on Ceefax and Oracle. Some financial firms in the New York area have had the financial-sports system since 1977.

Teletext ceased to be regarded as "experimental" with final government approval in Great Britain in 1977. But even before that, some astute observers in the communications industry were aware that they had a new competitor.

John Beverley, managing director for a chain of 67 newspapers, told me in 1977: "We had better stop thinking of the 'electronic newspaper' as something in the future. It has been a reality now for more than two years and we had better start thinking of the home TV set as something much more important than just an entertainment medium. It has become an information screen, instead."

Five years earlier, in 1972, the BBC announced development of its Ceefax system and invited others in the television industry to join in perfecting it.

The BBC, Independent Broadcasting Authority (now called ITV), and British Radio Equipment Manufacturers' Association (BREMA) announced agreement upon a unified standard for teletext equipment specifications in March 1974.

But even before teletext specifications gained official approval, Texas Instruments of Dallas, Tex., in its Bedford factory in England, had spent a half million dollars to develop decoders to fit into television sets. These decoders were necessary to intercept the teletext signals.

Experiments continued in England, and several equipment exhibitions and colloquia exhibited and sparked discussions about teletext through 1975 and 1976 before the British government announced its full approval for the systems in November 1976. British manufacturers still held off, however, awaiting the full report of Lord Annan's Committee on the Future of Broadcasting. And when that report was favorable in early 1977, British companies, too, put aside their apprehension about the future of teletext (and the British economy) to try to catch up with Texas Instruments.

In the summer of 1977, competitive versions of teletext receivers with British trade names began appearing at trade fairs and in the important High Street radio and TV shops in London. This was the result of agreement upon manufacturing specifications followed by official government approval of the systems.

In England, 75 percent of television viewers rent rather than buy their sets. Radio Rentals, with 70 percent of the rental business, began in October to exhibit teletext units in each of its numerous rental and repair shops. The company said thousands of its customers exchanged their old sets, costing $9 a month, for teletext sets renting for about $15.

By the end of 1977, the first year of operation, estimates of the numbers in operation ranged from 30,000 to 50,000. An independent consulting firm earlier had forecast that 4 million sets would be in use in England by the end of 1982 and 7.5 million by 1985.

Texas Instruments and other companies interested in the American mass market look upon installation of teletext sets as the first step in an industry goal of placing a full-scale computer in every home in the United States.

American communications industries, most of them, depend upon advertising to provide revenue which makes these industries profitable. What, then, are the advertising potentials for the wired Prestel system, which most worries British publishers, and for the broadcast ITV stations, which accept advertising?

Christopher Lorenz, a writer for the *Financial Times*, has predicted, "Our lifeline, classified advertising, may change radically."

Martin Hedges, writer for a British advertising trade journal has said that regional newspapers alone stand to lose $44 million in revenue yearly if Oracle (ITV) succeeds.

The Newspaper Society, which represents the local press, made a strong presentation to the Annan Commission asking that teletext development be delayed for five years. The Commission report said the society "believed rapid development of teletext would be crippling in its financial consequences for the newspaper industry."

The Society, in a letter to this writer, observed ruefully that "the Commission did not pay a great deal of attention to what we suggested. . . . The Society has not given up hope and will continue making representations to the Government [seeking delay]."

The chief operating executive of the Westminster Press, John Beverley, told me in 1977 that he believed the wired Prestel system would become a serious threat to classified advertising revenues in his organization's 12 daily and 55 weekly newspapers. But a year later, after seeing firsthand the complicated input system being used by Prestel, Beverley said he is no longer so concerned. He had the proper perspective, however, in realizing that the input system could become less complicated as development progresses.

Beverley did not think that either broadcast or wired systems would put his newspapers out of business, but "they will make us consider some pretty drastic changes," he said.

Geoffrey Hughes, ITV's Oracle editor, declared that the company would not have invested huge sums of money for the present extremely small advertising revenue if it had not expected to make money from advertising in four or five years.

British broadcast Ceefax is presently only a small side-line to conventional television. It uses only two of the 625 lines that form the British television picture.

You don't have to be an electronics expert to realize that total capacity of Ceefax would be up to 300 times greater if the other 623 lines of transmission were teletext instead of television picture.

Development in Britain was slowed by two very serious conditions—the high cost of decoders and the depressed British economy. (Per capita income is less than half the U.S. figure.) But most British publishers see neither of these as deterrents to development in America. John Beverley said, "The American propensity for eagerly accepting new ideas will be a positive factor. Your people buy gadgets like we buy bread, but teletext is no gadget," he added. "It is a tool for instant dissemination of any information people want to know about."

Like all new electronic inventions, teletext decoders were very expensive at first, costing $500 for the decoder. The first British color TV sets with decoders cost about $2,000, but the price is much less already—about $1,000.

Texas Instruments sells decoders for about $100 now, and one FCC Commissioner, Robert E. Lee, has predicted that mass-produced decoders will cost only twenty dollars in a very few years. The public will demand the product, and low cost will surely follow.

The future of teletext in America is linked directly to the problem of finding some way to pay its way—to earn a profit for somebody who provides the service. It would be foolish to assume that nobody is going to do that.

Teletext is a British development, but it is also rapidly becoming international. Visitors from eighty foreign countries have visited the London studios of Ceefax.

The Ceefax chief editor said, "The most exciting new development is the international aspect. Australia is moving very, very fast; and pretty deep studies or trials are reported from Sweden, Denmark, and Holland."

The German Newspaper Proprietors Assn. and German broadcasting organizations have been disputing the right to transmit teletext in Germany for two years. A similar battle, newspapers vs. television, erupted in Australia with some Australian newspaper writers saying the new systems might ruin the newspaper industry.

Switzerland is deep into studies of Ceefax. Swiss journalists compiled Ceefax pages which were flown to Zurich daily for a Radio-TV exhibition despite the air traffic controller strikes in September 1977.

There is no question that teletext will become international, with multilanguage transmission over much of western Europe. Some of its enthusiasts believe it offers new opportunities for international cooperation through vastly improved communication. They see it as a medium promoting understanding and peace.

Pilot operations are operating now in at least six countries, and this expansion trend will continue.

American network broadcast executives, particularly at CBS, have shown great interest. Many important CBS executives have visited both Ceefax at BBC and the new American teletext operation in Salt Lake City.

You have read of the misgivings of British and American newspaper executives about the possible impact of teletext upon their publications. Some of the same concern was exhibited by TV network newmen after they saw some teletext slides at the national convention of Radio-Television News Directors in September 1978.

One young writer for an American network said he could see grave problems facing network news television when much greater volume of news available on teletext becomes available to the public.

I think Lord Lew Griade, head of the British Independent Television network, shares that feeling. He has been widely quoted as saying, "I need teletext like I need a hole in my head!" He said he has long tried to figure out ways to keep people from going to the bathroom when the commercials come on.

Of course, it was his main competitor, BBC, which developed the teletext system that enables TV viewers to switch to news, market reports, and sports scores while commercials are showing on conventional TV channels. (That may not do much for cultural advancement, but it might reduce British water bills.)

Many people have said that they can't understand how the British got so far ahead of the United States in this development. But we should remember that British engineers were also far ahead of us in the development of radar and jet aircraft engines. So it isn't the first time the British have beaten us in scientific development.

It is in commercial application of scientific inventions that the English have been slower than Americans. And my best-informed British publisher friends say that those are the very same reasons why commercial teletext will develop much faster in the United States after it gets started here. I think the only thing that might prevent this growth is the Federal Communications Commission and its ownership regulations.

BBC's Colin McIntyre says, "Americans have shown more interest in teletext than anybody else except possibly the Australians."

Many American publishers as well as television executives have shown interest. Many newspaper executives have visited the Ceefax Studios. They represented some of the most prestigious newspaper organizations in the United States.

Robert Marbut, chief executive and president of Harte-Hanks Newspapers, announced in March 1977 that his company was deeply involved in the Prestel market trials in England. "We will purchase 10 percent of the 100,000 frames in the database and will be an information provider," he said. "We hope to test several ideas, including a new system for accessing information in a sort of Dewey Decimal System for classifying electronically stored and microfiche information."

A Philadelphia common carrier in microwave broadcasting, Micro TV, began broadcasting a limited teletext service to businesses last year. It began as a supplement to its regular common carrier service, which includes "Home Box Office," to cable systems in the area. This is really business teletext on a "pay TV" basis, which Bill Gross, company president, calls "American Ceefax." His company has offered both transmitting and receiving equipment for sale.

Prestel opened a New York sales and promotion office last year intending to establish a connection with an American company to market Prestel in the United States. It has already been licensed to operate in Germany.

I began this article by telling about the shock that swept through a convention of 500 American newspaper executives when I first showed them slides and described the British developments. They recovered from their shock, however, when they learned of four limitations of teletext that do not apply to newspapers. While much of their hopefulness was based upon those limitations, it is now certain that those particular limitations have since been corrected. Let me describe those changes and new developments for you.

First, there was originally a limitation of about 350 to 400 words on the length of a teletext story. New software at BBC has eliminated that. If the story requires 100 pages, you could watch it that long. But if you wanted to cut it off at any point, you can do so exactly as you leave an American newspaper story. You just dial in another story that interests you.

Second, there is the limit to the amount of broadcast information, initially about 800 pages. This can be transmitted with maximum delay of 25 seconds in call-up time on two lines of the TV screen. British systems have approval for sending data on four or six lines, but there is actually no real limit to the amount of information that can be transmitted on two lines. More information simply increases the call-up time between articles.

The French Antiope system, still experimental, broadcasts on the entire TV broadcast spectrum during times when the station is not broadcasting conventional television programs. The broadcast possibilities in delivering hundreds of times as much information through this system are mind-boggling.

The only real limitation lies in the quality of TV receivers. Home television sets of the present are designed to receive pictures rather than the binary signals of teletext. You can appreciate information delivery potentials more easily when you consider that more than 50 kilobits of data are transmitted each second during every American manned space flight. And that is the equivalent of about one complete set of the *Encyclopaedia Britannica every minute.*

The third limitation was in the difference between American and British television screens. But Texas Instruments and KSL-TV in Salt Lake City, working closely together, developed a modification of both British transmitters and decoders in about six months. KSL-TV has been transmitting teletext signals, along with conventional television, much like British Ceefax, since June 1978.

Several American television manufacturers have shown interest in placing teletext decoders in their color TV sets. Many have sent executives to visit Salt Lake.

And if you can get KSL-TV on either your TV antenna or cable system, you can buy a decoder from Texas Instruments for about $125 to start receiving Salt Lake teletext in your home. Any TV repairman can quickly install the decoder in any high quality color TV set. It seems likely that other TV stations, in addition to KSL-TV, will deliver teletext transmission before the end of 1979.

Fourth, and probably most important—in the minds of newspaper publishers, at least—is belief that most readers like to hold printed information in their hands. Readers save clippings. Some like to take coupons to stores to save money. Newspapers have made coupons a big promotional tool. But paper printouts will be no problem for teletext operations. The BBC, ITT, and at least one other British company have working models of small printout machines to operate with TV sets. BBC's new model, with very sharp printing, will allow the viewer to press a button and get an instant paper printout of printed information on the accompanying television screen. I heard mass production cost estimates of $80 for the hard copy attachment.

These developments are startling. But I still don't believe they signal the death of the newspaper industry. Newspapers have survived other doomsday predictions that came with the advent of shoppers, radio news, television advertising and news, and mass distribution of circulars by direct mail.

I think newspapers of the future may have to become more controversial and specialize more in human interest, depth stories, background articles, and investigation. But I believe the best newspapers, at least, will survive even though widespread availability of comprehensive teletext broadcasts would certainly cut into newspaper circulation, perhaps deeply in some areas.

Network television news as we know it now would need to depend even more on its show-business attributes to survive. And some special interest magazines will find teletext satisfying in greater volume the same special interests that have created their present subscription markets.

Display advertising has presented one of the more optimistic viewpoints for British publishers in their appraisal of future competition between teletext and newspapers. This optimism stems from British belief that all advertising is "an intrusion" upon the desire for information by a reader or viewer.

This belief is partly because British newspapers have not developed the huge volume of advertising found in American and Canadian newspapers. Even the large British stores like Selfridge's and Harrod's don't advertise very much. So the homemaker in England is not accustomed to looking for those big ads from K-Mart, Penneys, Sears, Macy's, or other large department stores represented in American newspapers.

For that reason British broadcasters and newspaper executives overlook the fact that American women—and men, too—are conditioned to look for advertising as well as news.

A recent American Newspaper Publishers Association (ANPA) survey revealed 34 kinds of newspaper information which people would like to see increased in newspapers. "Ads of interest" ranked third highest on this list. Two-thirds of the respondents, both old and young, wanted *more* newspaper advertising. Why? Because advertising provides keys to the quality of life, and that pursuit of happiness to which Malcolm Muggeridge has said we "Americans are nationally dedicated." There is ample research reason to think American viewers would call up advertising pages if they are classified by commodities and as easy to find as the indexed news articles.

British publishers are particularly apprehensive about the adaptability of teletext to classified advertising. They foresee teletext making serious inroads into classified revenue, because the viewer can immediately eliminate from his sight and consideration everything being advertised except products he is interested in buying.

Teletext can do the same thing for display advertising. It can be classified for men's wear, women's wear, meat, new cars, vegetables, kitchenware, golf clubs, garden tools, and again—*whatever*. And with capital requirements only a fraction of the huge sums necessary for the printing equipment for newspapers or magazines, it seems certain that advertising capability will be developed. Teletext ads can be produced for a fraction of their cost in the printed media. In England, ITV's Oracle is working on this adaptation now.

Some American publishers see teletext as a medium to help them achieve the "tailored newspaper," which would present supplemental information to satisfy special interests.

But nobody in his right mind would try to forecast all the forms the new medium will take. Any thinking person must accept the idea that teletext, already here, will some day become another medium of communication alongside radio, television, magazines, mailings, newspapers, and shoppers. The newspaper industry would be most likely to use teletext wisely for its own interest if it is not restricted from doing so. Newspapers have a great recent record for using electronic developments in their printing operations. But definite restrictions against newspapers acquiring television channels now exist in the United States. Current regulations of the Federal Communications Commission, affirmed by the U.S. Supreme Court in June 1978, prohibits newspaper owners from acquiring broadcast media in the same market. These regulations would have to be revised before newspapers could participate fully in teletext development. There is no reason to think this drastic change of FCC policy is going to occur at any time soon. Newspapers cannot broadcast in their own home cities at the present time.

Television licensing and broadcasting restrictions have already been the cause of conflicts between the newspaper and the television industries in Germany, Australia, and Great Britain. The newspaper industry contends that teletext is a printed medium, while television people say that teletext is broadcasting. Each industry is trying to exclude the other from competition.

Right now, then, TV and cable have the inside track. Anybody not in the broadcasting business must get a license through the FCC to begin broadcasting teletext signals in the United States. Those licenses are difficult to acquire.

American television manufacturers are deeply interested. They ought to be, because teletext development would make all present American TV sets obsolete. Replacing them would increase profits for manufacturers.

Ten of eleven American TV manufacturers were represented at a teletext seminar and show sponsored by KSL-TV and Texas Instruments at the Salt Lake City studios in August 1978. All representatives said they were impressed, but most expressed concern about federal regulation of the industry.

Those restrictions are seen by some authorities as strengthening the probability that cable TV might be in the forefront of American teletext development. But to do that, the CATV industry would have to shake off the developmental inertia characteristic of its recent past.

The FCC has acted favorably upon a request to allow use of one line of the vertical blanking interval of TV pictures for captioning for deaf persons seeing TV pictures. This would allow the broadcaster to transmit captions in teletext along with the picture. This is exactly the way teletext began operation in Britain—as an aid to deaf persons in understanding television.

There is a fundamental difference between government involvement in Great Britain and in the United States. In Britain, the government takes the initiative in pushing new developments; but in the United States, private capital must do that.

Wallace E. Johnson, chief of the broadcast bureau of the FCC, stated in a letter to this writer on April 7, 1978: "It is highly unlikely that the Commission would, on its own initiative, undertake embarking on a rule-making proceeding (involving teletext). We are inclined to await the filing of a formal petition requesting initiation of such a proceeding, since without a petition, and the showing which must be made in support of the requested action, we have little to go on to indicate the degree of interest, the potential viability, the extent of need and the public interest considerations pertaining to such a service." In other words, nothing much will be done outside the television industry to develop teletext until somebody files an application for a teletext facility and secures a license from the FCC. Some say it will never happen. Others point out that there are now television channels available in many markets.

We know there are entrepreneurs who are considering the possibilities. When one of them decides that the profit potential is worth the gamble, the first application will be made. Meanwhile, others who are interested will wait for someone else—like Texas Instruments in England—to go ahead with development. To estimate the time schedule is obviously impossible now. Five years? Ten years? Nobody knows.

When I write or talk about teletext, I always get two reactions—and mail from as far away as the Philippine Islands last time.

Some people ask how they can "get in on the ground floor" of this new industry. I'm not sure of the best way, so I don't answer that question.

Others ask me if there is any *limit* to the amount or kind of information that can be delivered electronically to home TV screens. I *do* have an answer for that. This answer engineers agree upon.

I asked this question of four teletext engineers—one with BBC, another with the large British manufacturer Mullard, another with Texas Instruments in Dallas, and the fourth with KSL-TV in Salt Lake. All said essentially the same thing: The *capacity* of technology for delivering information electronically has *no* real limits. It is restricted *only* by the desires of the public and by the *imagination* of people responsible for providing information.

So imagination is the *only* limitation. That doesn't leave very much that technology cannot deliver, does it?

Bibliography

To supplement Kenneth Edwards's essay, consult recent issues of *EBU Review* (published by the European Broadcasting Union) and *InterMedia* (published by the International Broadcast Institute). Both cover the technical developments in broadcast or electronic transmission of information and news in Great Britain, Europe, Japan, and the United States. They will provide details on current developments—if any—of the systems mentioned by Edwards.

Perils and Prospects Over the Electronic Horizon

Broadcasting

24

There is a revolution going on in communications—a technological revolution that is changing both the game and the names. Boundaries that in the past have separated telephones and computers and newspapers and cable television and broadcasting are blurring. The telephone companies are finding their long-held monopolies invaded by computer businesses. Closer to home, cable television finds the only thing separating it from AT&T in the broadband communications business is an FCC rule barring telephone ownership of cable.

Broadcasters, while not in immediate danger, face perhaps the most confusing future of all. Until now, the home television set has been virtually the property of commercial broadcasters, but today businesses that only a few years ago were not even remotely interested in electronic communications are coveting that cathode ray tube (CRT) and developing means of providing a great variety of services that could both compete with and complement the broadcaster's programming—businesses such as banks, the Postal Service, newspapers and retail stores, not to mention the computer makers.

William J. Donnelly, vice-president of Young & Rubicam, gives one reading of what is in television's crystal ball. "The current TV set will become the modular display device for a whole host of electronic information and entertainment resources." He has predicted that the typical American consumer will soon be receiving 36 channels of cable television with one or more pay channels—"perhaps one supported in part by advertising."

What Mr. Donnelly and others have called the "home video environment" will be fed by several devices: a video cassette machine "with everything from the son's bar mitzvah to the daughter's wedding to a program recorded from one of the networks or local stations"; a video disk "bringing in the Audubon Bird Guide and Elton John in concert"; programable video games providing "casino-type enjoyment" as well as the ability to balance a checkbook.

"Conceivably," Mr. Donnelly said, "there will be an AT&T wire also attached to that television set and further attached to a transaction telephone. Finally, there may well be another wire belonging to the post office to provide facsimile copies of the mail or supplied by a computer company with a service such as [the British] Viewdata [Prestel]."

The revolution is no longer going on, as one futurist suggested, in the minds of "flaky academics." Rather, it is proceeding on the shelves of the radio and television departments of the nation's retail stores and in the board rooms of some of the nation's largest and wealthiest corporations.

Perhaps more than any other single technological advance, the advent of inexpensive computers with capacities far exceeding advanced computing systems of a decade ago has led to a redefinition of electronic communications. Many of the recent advances in communications—satellites, digital television, "interactive" or two-way cable and the like—have been made possible by the new computer technology.

Digital electronics, microprocessing, integrated circuitry and the other attendant wonders of the wizards in the research and development centers of the principal electronics manufacturers are, in not so narrow a sense, a part of the computer explosion that has been occurring since the early 1960s and promises to continue for at least another 10 years. If the mention of computers brings to mind visions of room-size grey boxes with whirling rolls of electromagnetic tapes attended and watched over by hordes of humorless men and women in white coats, then the electronics revolution has passed by yet another who should know better.

Consider that one consumer electronics firm is now mass-marketing an $800 computer package for the home that can do just about all that a top-of-the-line commercial IBM unit of the early sixties could, that it is already possible in many cities across the country to carry on any number of personal business transactions by punching pre-arranged codes of numbers on modern telephones, that it takes only a relatively inexpensive unit to unite the home cathode ray tube to a telephone system that already is used to tie together virtually every home, office and computer terminal in the country.

What does it all mean for broadcasters? For now, that seems to depend on which fortune teller you talk with. A moderate's assessment comes from Anne Branscomb, a lawyer and a communications consultant, who said it may not mean a whole lot more than that there are opportunities for broadcasters to use their spectrum in new ways—and, by extension, from her remarks, to make money.

But there is also the far less moderate view of Irving Kahn, chairman and president of Broadband Communications Inc. and a new pioneer in the field of fiber optics, who seemed to compare broadcasters to ostriches with their heads buried in the sand. "Rather than setting the pace for new communications developments which can shape the future of this industry, [broadcasting] concentrates instead on such lofty decisions as how well the color is projected for the set of the 6 p.m. news."

The question, according to Mr. Kahn, is whether it will be broadcasters who "call the shots" on how new technology is used in this industry "or whether you will allow its form and impact to be determined by others in adjacent industries, whose mouths water at the very prospect."

The local television station, which already receives the bulk of its programming from outside sources such as the networks, independent producers and syndicators, could find itself in the unenviable position in the not-too-distant future of being by-passed by those suppliers as they try to get their products to the home viewer—even without the implementation of some of the more technologically and politically difficult plans such as direct-to-home program delivery via satellite.

As the suppliers are presented with alternative means of delivering their programs—satellite networks, video cassettes, video disks, pay television channels and the like—they could find the local station becoming less and less attractive as a means of distribution. Satellite networking, for example, which allows a supplier to deliver a program to hundreds of localities at the same distribution cost as one or two is, perhaps, the most obvious and immediately practical alternative delivery system.

Paul I. Bortz, deputy assistant secretary for the National Telecommunications and Information Administration, suggested, for example, that broadcasters who maintain an outdated anti-cable position could find themselves locked out of the home of the future. The broadcaster, Mr. Bortz said, "could view a cable system as an opportunity" and make arrangements to lease two or more channels from the local system. In doing so, the broadcaster could expand his opportunities in the very field he knows best—local delivery. "What broadcasters had in the fifties and sixties," Mr. Bortz said, "was a distribution system. That's no longer unique."

Mr. Donnelly concurs, "We believe that the business of providing mass entertainment in an advertiser-supported manner to consumers will always exist," he said, "Those who are providing that service today will, in one form or another, be providing that service in the future." If there should develop a wired nation—and Mr. Donnelly thinks there will be—broadcasters should "get rid of your transmitters and lease channels on cable systems or . . . sell programming through the satellite to cable systems."

Thomas Bolger, executive vice-president of WMTV (TV) Madison, Wis., and television board chairman of the National Association of Broadcasters, said that he sees the problem as a set of new business opportunities for broadcasters. He has already dreamt up a few solutions of his own. Why shouldn't the broadcaster use his current work force and expertise to branch out into ancillary businesses, he wondered. And a few of those he suggested: (1) A station could sell syndicated shows that it doesn't plan to run and whose licenses haven't yet expired to the local cable television system—if it could get the syndicator's permission (he hasn't been able to); (2) it could lease channels on the local cable system and program them itself. "We may even sell spots in it because we've got a marketing department in places"; (3) "Another thing we've got in place is a news department . . . Why not program a cable channel with 24 hours of news?"

But wouldn't some of these proposals amount to the station competing with itself? "I'd rather do it myself than have someone else do it," Mr. Bolger answered.

Not that cable's situation is really that different, however. Mr. Bortz said both services have been "defined by their technology." That is, the basic difference between the broadcaster and the cable operator has in the past been a technological one—the broadcaster distributes over the air while the cable operator delivers his product via a wire. What the home viewers see, however, is not that different.

Even cable, Mr. Bortz said, is a "1950s technology"—an analog, a continual transmission system as opposed to the pulsed signals of digital transmissions, that is considerably less sophisticated than the systems of delivery being developed or already in use by common carriers. He called Warner Communications Inc.'s two-way Qube cable system in Columbus, Ohio—the most advanced in this country—"interesting" but nothing AT&T, for example, could not do with its present telephone system. "An analog system is just not all that impressive."

And that suggested another question—the role of the telephone company in the video environment of the future. AT&T, Mr. Bortz said, "should participate in providing a broad range of services." He said the terminal market "should be totally deregulated"—but only with the assurance of "full and fair competition." Translated, that means Mr. Bortz believes the telephone companies should be allowed to run video lines into homes and sell the equipment necessary to receive the new services.

But Mr. Bortz draws the line at programing. Bell, he said, may be allowed to get into the cable business, but it "should do so as a common carrier" and not as a programer.

Cable operators, of course, have long held that the telephone companies are a far greater threat to their business than broadcasters. The likelihood that they may have to compete head-on with AT&T, the world's largest utility, is not one they look on with pleasure. Like broadcasters, the cable operators may have to broaden their horizons and adopt some of the newer services if they wish to maintain a strong stance in the new communications mix.

A. Michael Noll, an AT&T residential marketing supervisor, said that Bell's interest in the home market does not take in computers right now: "We're not in the computer business." But Bell is exploring new markets, such as for its Picturephone service. Right now, for instance, Bell offers a "Picturephone meeting service" that allows people to converse and to see each other from public rooms that AT&T has established in various cities. That does not have anything directly to do with home television, but as the House of Representatives Communications Subcommittee's staff engineer, Chuck Jackson, pointed out—Picturephones and two-way cable are practically the same thing.

AT&T is experimenting with fiber optics, too, which, if the rules permitted, could place the telephone company squarely in the broadband video business.

There are other players. The modern newspaper, for instance, is already being written, edited and typeset electronically. A reporter composes his story on a CRT at his desk, pushes a button to send it to an editor, who pushes another button and sends it to the composing room. Technologically, there is nothing to stop that story from being distributed via the telephone system or a local cable system to any home or office that may subscribe to the "paper"—a word, by the way, that could cease describing the news journal of the future.

Another partner in the new communications world will be information companies that also will be competing with the entertainment program suppliers for home television screen time. One, for example, is Digital Broadcasting Corp. of McLean, Va., which plans to have a prototype computer time-sharing project available for the Washington area sometime this spring. William F. VonMeister, president of the young company, said the new service—Compucom, a combination of the words computer and communication—will take advantage of the "tremendously underutilized resource" of spectrum space available on the subcarrier frequencies of television channels.

(Another DBC project introduced last year was an addressable message service that uses FM subcarriers. According to Mr. VonMeister, the present subcarrier capacity on FM would allow for transmissions at the rate of one million words a second across the United States.)

Using subcarrier space leased from local television stations, DBC plans to offer home terminals that, using the home screen, will tie the user to a large central computer. Among the initial services being offered are classified advertising, daily news and features, a dining-out guide, games, personal business and finance, social and fashion news and personal calendar and notebook. The monthly charge is expected to be less than $20.

Local stations, Mr. VonMeister said, could offer a similar service, leasing home terminals to users themselves rather than waiting for the telephone company, a cable system or, for that matter, DBC to move into an area. Cable, he said, "has the capacity to bring enormous amounts of data in" but "have been extremely backward in taking advantage of this."

But the telephone companies and other huge industrial firms have not been so backward. AT&T, he said, would "love" to be into the cable and data processing fields. IBM, Xerox, GT&E and other firms have been moving into the hybrid world of computers and communications, however, and at least one of them—Xerox—has a plan for a communications system that would do away with any reliance on AT&T for most business communications. The proposed Xerox Telecommunications Network (Xten) is a planned web of satellites, earth stations and microwave towers that would handle the voice, data, video, facsimile (print-outs of digitally delivered information) and teleconferencing (two-way video) requirements of most business in a community. Estimates as to the cost of constructing the proposed network have ranged as high as half a billion dollars.

Mr. VonMeister called the Xten system "most interesting because it uses radio" as a means of connecting business throughout the country. It is not, however, a broadcast service. Rather, Xten is planned as a point-to-point system "in direct competition with Bell." And although it is a satellite network, "the neat thing about Xerox is you don't have to have earth stations in every parking lot." That should bring down construction costs considerably as well as make it far easier to expand as needs dictate.

Xten is designed with the business user in mind, as are AT&T's proposed Advanced Communications System (ACS), Satellite Business Systems (a joint project of IBM, Aetna Life & Casualty and Comsat) and Telenet, a packet-switching network that GT&E announced that it intends to acquire.

The SBS plan also envisions a series of satellite networks to connect businesses. Bob Evans, vice-president for engineering, programing and technology at IBM, said IBM's interest in entering the communications field was to find cheaper and more efficient ways than the telephone lines to connect rapidly multiplying numbers of computer terminals. He emphasized that SBS's only aim is to serve business users—large corporations, government and other operations with a need to send information between offices spread over a broad geographical area—and not home users. Mr. Evans would not comment on computer terminals for the home, but as far as their communications uses go, he said IBM isn't making any plans. For years, people talking about uses for home digital communications have been covering the same ground—"shopping, education, fun and games and paying your bills," Mr. Evans said. And surely "everybody would like to get into the homes if they could find a business proposition." But IBM doesn't see one that would work. "That's not our present business," Mr. Evans said.

Portia Isaacson, with Electronic Data Systems Corp. in Dallas and president of the Computer Retailers' Association, is convinced on the other hand that there is ample opportunity today for programers to move into the home computer field. In a recent article in *Datamation*, a computer industry trade journal, Dr. Isaacson wrote that the home computer is a potential advertising medium as well. "Advertising," she said, "can be handled much the same as newspapers by forcing it into articles. Buy and sell advertisements can be paid for by the person placing the ad. Subscriptions can be implemented through encryption (encoding) of the data being transmitted and selling of monthly encoding keys that need only be typed into the receiving computer."

Mr. VonMeister sees the advertising possibilities going well beyond that. He suggested that the Sears, Roebuck catalogue could be delivered (with pictures) electronically to homes. The "book" could be updated constantly as prices and availability of products change. He also pointed out that such a regular feature could highlight the specials and sales itself rather than relying on the advertising that is now done through newspapers and local stations.

And local automotive dealerships, for example, could sponsor an automotive magazine-type channel offering consumer tips and repair information while, on another channel, local theaters and restaurants are offering an evening-out guide. As Mr. VonMeister put it, the possibilities are "limited only by your imagination."

But as Mr. Noll, also points out, the future success or failure of the home computer also depends on how the people in the home react to it. And trying to predict that is more than a little difficult in the absence of home computer experience. Ask people how they would feel about having a computer in their home allowing them to dial up a data base and have information displayed on their TV screen, Mr. Noll says, and the response is usually "Gee, I don't know."

Sharon Taylor of the New York Times Information Bank, a data service that is already being used by over 800 firms, also spoke of the "acceptance factor" of home viewers. She said that her firm is interested in the home market, but "we don't know when or where or how."

But then look at what happened to the calculator. That's the analogy home computer advocates invariably get around to. The first Hewlett-Packard calculator, which could do no more than add, subtract, multiply and divide, cost $800—a product not within the price range or the imagination of most consumers. But dramatic improvements in the technology, making it both smaller and cheaper, have turned that piece of electronic gadgetry almost into a household item. Why not the home computer, too?

The prospect of digital electronics in the home has been talked about, of course, for many years. But the difference now, says Mr. Jackson, is that those doing the talking are not those aforementioned "flaky academics. They're the people who want to get rich."

That observation is partly borne out in Mr. Donnelly's discussion. He talks about a new world of television so far beyond the current networks, independents and public stations that he has to give it a new name—the "video environment." But the most striking thing about his vision is that he says it is foreseeable. "We at Young & Rubicam," he told an NAB executive seminar held last September in Reston, Va., "believe that environment will be here many many years before most of us in this room retire."

For examples of the kinds of programs one might expect to find in the future home "video environment," many look to the teletext services now in use in Europe—especially Great Britain, where the Independent Broadcasting Authority's Oracle and the BBC's Ceefax are already offering a broad range of services to home viewers. KSL-TV, Salt Lake City, a Bonneville International station, is experimenting with a teletext system, and other American broadcasters—most notably CBS, Inc.—are anxious to introduce systems here.

The British Post Office is also in the business with its Prestel, a system using a telephone link allowing users to tie into a vast data base stored in central computers and have various "pages" of information appear on television sets. And the United States Postal Service is now undertaking an examination of the possibilities of some sort of electronic mail service.

All of these services will compete with entertainment for screen time in the video environment, a home center that futurists envision including a computer keyboard, a video cassette recorder, a television set, a cable, a telephone interface and a facsimile printer producing hard-copy versions of virtually anything that appears on the television screen.

The home video center would also allow for the implementation of a communication function that is attracting considerable attention in the financial world—electronic funds transfer. Dale E. Reistad, chairman of the board of Payments Systems Inc., New York, a wholly owned subsidiary of the American Express Co., is looking at the home center as a place where consumers may pay bills, transfer money from one account to another, conduct most of their banking business and other forms of money management. Much of what PSI wants to do, he said, "conceivably" could be handled by two-way cable systems, such as Qube, today.

He called the DBC project "very exciting." Mr. Reistad pointed out that a home center could cost as much as $5,000 today, but, as technology progresses through the next decade, the same hardware could go for a more easily affordable $500 by 1990. Sooner or later, he said, PSI is convinced that home electronic funds transfer systems are "going to make some kind of economic sense."

And what, if any is the role of the local broadcast stations in this electronic wonderland of the future? Will they be participants or will they watch as their present monopoly on the home screen is whittled away by the competing services? Are today's local stations tomorrow's dinosaurs? "Not if they wise up, they won't be," Mr. VonMeister said. By that, he said, he means that station owners must open themselves to "service diversity," and look for new ways to use the facilities and frequencies they now have.

In the regulatory world of the future envisioned by Mr. Bortz, competition will rule—"a lot more competition" than any of the various players are used to today. Broadcasters, cable operators, common carriers, and information companies will be competing for the home viewer's attention, with "mixes of technology" quite unlike that of the seventies and early eighties.

For the broadcasters, that means, he said, that only the "quick" will survive, those who are aware of the changes taking place in their industry and who capitalize on them. "The slow among them are not going to be much of a factor," Mr. Bortz said.

But Dan Lacy, senior vice-president and executive assistant to the president of McGraw-Hill, thinks the new uses for the TV set won't do much to disturb conventional broadcasting. He holds to the theory that the other two-way uses of the TV screen, the video newspaper idea, for instance, will just be the "fringes" of television use.

There may be 30 channels of programing in most homes, but trying to figure out what to put on them "boggles the mind," he said. "We fill the seven channels available on UHF in New York now only by repeat programs and a stock of Hollywood films." For the future, "the acute problem is having enough worthwhile material to fill the channels," Mr. Lacy said.

No, there won't be a dramatic change in the kind of mass-appeal network entertainment that dominates now, Mr. Lacy concludes. Furthermore, he thinks that the increased level of advertising he foresees will also insure the health of the local TV station.

McGraw-Hill is apparently willing to put its money behind that projection. "There's no question that we'd like to expand our holdings in TV stations," he says.

Irving Kahn, on the other hand, is one who subscribes to the theory that broadcasters had better look for ways to branch out. His proposal is that they should "test the waters" of new technology by installing some fiber optics—"not because I'm after your business . . . but rather because it represents a relatively simple yet extremely meaningful move forward into the new world of high technology."

To connect the TV or radio studio with the transmitter would improve the signal at minimal cost for many stations, he said. And more importantly, "this kind of installation would give the broadcaster a first-hand, hands-on experience with this whole new technology of fiber optics.

Others would argue Mr. Kahn's contention that fiber optics will play a major role in the home communications world of the future. And he is vague about how experience with fiber optics would open "a brand new portal" to a new realm of communications services. But he expresses what seems to be a gut feeling that by using some of the new technologies "[you can] enhance your signal, enlarge your sphere of influence, pinpoint your specialized audiences, interconnect with other media, and, in general, become the truly local servant within your community, to whom the public turns for all of its major communications needs."

Broadcasters have already passed up one opportunity, Mr. Kahn feels, in cable television, where they could have made use of the available leased channels to spread their programing talents.

And broadcasters may be falling behind newspapers, over whom they already have a clear advantage in audience and advertisers, he said. While broadcasters are "basking in that advantage," he said, the newspaper business is making "exciting headway in its use of computers and microprocessors and all of the magical new technological components which could enable it to better segment its markets, better key its specialized audiences, better offer a specific demographically defined readership to its advertisers, better extend its deadlines and react to newsbreaks with more immediacy, and so on—all to your detriment."

Taking his argument to the limit, Mr. Kahn feels broadcasters share with their cable television cousins the scary prospect of being swallowed up one day by the telephone company, "a foe who can, through sheer size and political power, squash the future opportunities for both industries."

There are of course regulatory barriers to keep AT&T from becoming the monopoly purveyor of entertainment and information into the home that Mr. Kahn fears. But his point is not lost about future competition for the TV screen from major competitors of sizable weight. "Please remember," he said, "that the TV receiver is an indiscriminately hungry animal; it little cares who feeds it."

Bibliography

For a rather theoretical perspective on what changes to expect in broadcasting in the next decade, consult Glen O. Robinson, editor, *Communications for Tomorrow: Policy Perspectives for the 1980s* (Praeger Special Studies, 1978), especially Walter Baer's essay "Telecommunications Technology in the 1980s," and William A. Lucas's essay "Telecommunications Technologies and Services." For a technical view of the future, see James Martin, *Future Developments in Telecommunications* (Prentice-Hall, 1977), a severely revised version of an earlier study by the same author. For a more general approach to the same material, see James Martin, *The Wired Society* (Prentice-Hall, 1978).

Two magazines must be consulted regularly for their on-going coverage of the technological change in broadcasting. *Broadcasting* magazine, from which our selection is taken, regularly assesses change in technology, in addition to providing news reports on the field. *BM/E* (Broadcast Management/Engineering) provides the most consistent on-going analysis of the new technology, oftentimes using case studies to show what is being done. A good example of this kind of coverage is found in the January 1979 issue, which is devoted to developments in ENG (Electronic News Gathering). *BM/E* contains more technical data than *Broadcasting*. They supplement each other very well. For a general survey of trade journals in the broadcasting field and an assessment of their political impact, see Barry Cole and Mel Oettinger, "Covering the Politics of Broadcasting," *Columbia Journalism Review* (November-December 1977), 58-63.

Change in the Traditional Media

The Intellectual In Videoland

Douglass Cater

25

On a hot summer night in 1968 I was sitting in my Washington home, watching TV coverage of the disastrous Democratic convention in Chicago. Suddenly, all hell broke loose where the Wisconsin delegation was seated. TV cameras quickly zoomed in, of course, and reporters rushed to the area with walkie-talkies.

The whole nationwide TV audience thus knew in an instant what the uproar was all about. But Speaker Carl Albert, who was presiding over the convention, didn't have a clue, and he was the one who had to decide what to do about it. There, in microcosm, one saw how our leadership can be hustled by the formidable communications system of television.

No doubt about it, television is a looming presence in American life, even though most of us hardly know what to make of the medium. It arrived so swiftly and so totally: in January 1949 only 2.3 percent of American homes had the box with the cathode-ray tube. Five years later television had penetrated more than half of our homes. Today, 97 percent of them have one or more sets—a distribution roughly matching that of indoor plumbing. With American TV approaching its quarter-century anniversary as a household phenomenon, one might think we would by now have devoted serious attention to the effects of this medium on our culture, our society, our lives. Certainly, we might expect at this point to be trying to anticipate the consequences of the even more enveloping telecommunications environment that lies ahead. Yet, as the prescient Mr. Marconi predicted a long time ago, telecommunications has become part of the "almost unnoticed working equipment of civilization."

Why unnoticed? What has prevented thinking people from applying their critical faculties to this medium, which reaches greater masses than do all the other mass media combined (the number of sets in U.S. homes is nearly double the total daily circulation of newspapers)? Why haven't more of our talented scholars been attracted to the study of this new environment? Why do the media themselves devote so little attention to serious television analysis and criticism? Why have our foundations provided only very limited resources for the study of communications, which is as fundamental to society as education, health, and the physical environment?

I would suggest three reasons for these failures. In the first place, scientific evidence suggests that thinking people—at least those over 25—are left-brained in development. That is, they rely mainly on the left hemisphere, which controls sequential, analytical tasks based on the use of propositional thought. But TV, we are informed, appeals mainly to the *right* hemisphere of the brain, which controls appositional—that is, non-sequential, non-analytic—thought.

Douglass Cater was formerly director of the Aspen Institute's Program on Communications and Society. He is now a Fellow of the Institute. This article is reprinted with permission from *Saturday Review*, May 31, 1975. Copyright *Saturday Review* 1975.

Scientists and theologians alike have pondered how the two halves of the brain relate—whether they ignore, inhibit, cooperate, or compete with each other, or simply take turns at the control center. Whole cultures seem to show a preference for one or the other mode of thought, and thinking people of the Western world up until now have plighted their troth with propositional thought. After five centuries of slowly acquired sophistication in distinguishing the truth from the trickery transmitted by Mr. Gutenberg's invention, we now find ourselves having to master the nonlinear logic created by a steady bombardment of sights and sounds on our senses. The thinking person is therefore apt to be somewhat bewildered by the telly and to regard it in the same way that a backsliding prohibitionist regards hard liquor—as something to be indulged in with a sense of guilt.

According to *Television and the Public,* Robert T. Bower's analysis of viewing habits, the "educated viewer" has learned to live with ambivalence: although he may be scornful of commercial TV fare, "he watches the set (by his own admission) as much as others during the evening and weekend hours; . . . even when he had a clear choice between an information program and some standard entertainment fare, he was just as apt as others to choose the latter."

The peculiar structure of the American television industry is a second reason why the thinking person refuses to think seriously about the medium. The broadcast industry is based on a marketplace unlike any other in our private enterprise economy. Broadcasting offers its product "free" to the consumer and depends on advertising to supply, by the latest count, gross annual revenues of $4.5 billion. As a result, commercial TV's prime allegiance is to the merchant, not to the viewer. To attract the advertising dollar, the programmer seeks to capture the dominant portion of the viewers and to hold them unblinking for the longest period of time. Everything else is subordinated to this dogged pursuit of mankind in the mass. A program attracting many millions of viewers is deemed a failure and discarded if it happens to be scheduled opposite a program attracting even more millions.

Within this iron regime of dollars and ratings, a few ghettos of do-goodism exist. Network news and documentaries, as well as occasional dramas of exceptional quality, reveal an upward striving in television (some cynics dismiss this as tithing to the federal regulators). But these programs fare poorly in the competition for television's most precious commodity—time. A former network news chief has remarked of TV management, "They don't mind how much money and talent we devote to producing documentaries so long as we don't ask for prime-time evening hours to show them." Even the daylight hours have to be tightly rationed when the real-life marathon melodramas of Washington start competing with the soap operas of Hollywood.

Thinking people do not know how to cope with a system whose economic laws, they are led to believe, are immutable. Any suggestions they may have for the betterment of TV are characterized as naive, elitist, and offensive to the First Amendment. The proper posture is to sit back and be thankful when broadcast officialdom chooses to violate its own laws and reveal fleetingly what a fantastic instrument of communication television can be.

A third reason why thinking people have difficulty coming to grips with television is that they have yet to develop satisfactory ways to gauge the effects of this environmental phenomenon. Consider, as an example, the Surgeon General's inquiry into the effect of televised violence on the behavior of children. Conducted over a period of three years, at a cost of $1.8 million, and based on 23 separate laboratory and field studies, this probe was the most far-reaching to date into the social consequences of television. In its final report, the Surgeon General's committee could acknowledge only "preliminary and tentative" evidence of a causal relationship between TV violence and aggression in children.

As members of an industry dedicated to the proposition that 30-second commercials can change a viewer's buying behavior, producers would be foolish to ignore this warning about the not-so-subliminal effects of its program content. But these studies, mostly gauging immediate response to brief TV exposure, could not adequately measure the impact of the total phenomenon—the experience of the child who spends as many as six hours a day, year in and year out, before the set. This cumulative effect is what makes watching television different from reading books or going to the movies.

How to measure the longer-term, less flamboyant effects of the environment created by television? In 1938 E. B. White witnessed a TV demonstration and wrote, "A door closing, heard over the air, a face contorted, seen in a panel of light, these will emerge as the real and the true. And when we bang the door of our own cell or look into another's face, the impression will be of mere artifice."

Now, a third of a century later, comes Tony Schwartz to carry the speculation further in his book *The Responsive Chord*. Mr. Schwartz's insights have peculiar power, because he created the ill-famed political commercial for the 1964 campaign, which showed a child innocently picking daisy petals, one after another, as a countdown for a hydrogen bomb blast. Though there was no mention of the Presidential candidate at whom the message was aimed, the effect of the commercial was so unnerving that its sponsors withdrew it after a single showing. Schwartz appears to know whereof he theorizes.

Gutenberg man, he writes, lived by a communication system requiring the laborious coding of thought into words and then the equally laborious decoding by the receiver—similar to the loading, shipping, and unloading of a railway freight car. Electronic man dispenses with this by communicating experience without the need of symbolic transformations. What the viewer's brain gets is a mosaic of myriad dots of light and vibrations of sound that are stored and recalled at high speed. Amid this electronic bombardment, Schwartz speculates, a barrier has been crossed akin to the supersonic sound barrier—or, in his image, the 90-mile-an-hour barrier beyond which a motorcycle racer must turn *in to* rather than *out with* a skid: " . . . In communicating at electronic speed, we no longer direct information into an audience but try to evoke stored information out of it in a patterned way."

The function of the electronic communicator, according to Schwartz, "is to achieve a state of resonance with the person receiving visual and auditory stimuli." The Gutenberg communicator—for the past 500 years patiently transmitting experience line by line, usually left to right, down the printed page—is no longer relevant. TV man has become conditioned to a total communication environment, to constant stimuli which he shares with everyone else in society and to which he is conditioned to respond instantly. Schwartz believes that the totality and instantaneousness of television, more than its program content, contributes to violence in society.

His premises lead him to the shattering conclusion that "truth is a print ethic, not a standard for ethical behavior in electronic communication." We must now be concerned not with Gutenberg-based concepts of truth, but with the *effects* of electronic communication: "A whole new set of questions must be asked, and a whole new theory of communications must be formulated."

Without going all the way with Schwartz, we clearly need to examine the effects of TV more diligently. What, for example, is television doing to the institutions and forms and rituals of our democracy? Politicians are still struggling to learn the grammar of TV communication and to master its body English, which is so different from that of the stump speech. TV has markedly influenced the winnowing process by which some politicians are sorted out as prospects for higher office from those who are not. TV has contributed to the abbreviation of the political dialogue and even changed the ground rules by which candidates map their campaign itineraries.

TV has encouraged the now widespread illusion that by using the medium we can create a Greek marketplace of direct democracy. When citizens can see and hear what they believe to be the actuality, why should they rely on inter-mediating institutions to make the decisions for them? When political leaders can directly reach their constituents without the help of a political party, why should they not opt for "the people's" mandate rather than "the party's"? Recent Presidents and Presidential candidates have been notably affected by this line of reasoning. It exposes an ancient vulnerability of our Republic, in which too much political lip service is paid to the notion that public opinion should rule everything.

How can democracy be strengthened within the environment of television? Why, in an age of abundant communication, has there been a continuing decline in voter participation? Prof. Michael Robinson, a political scientist, has cited surveys indicating that heavy TV viewers are more apt than light viewers to be turned off by politics. He speculates that the more dependent someone becomes on TV as his principal source of information, the more likely he is to feel that he cannot understand or affect the political process. TV, unlike newspapers, reaches many who are not interested in public affairs, and these "inadvertent" audiences, in Robinson's view, are frequently confused and alienated by what they see. Such a proposition runs directly counter to the usual reformist instinct to prescribe more programming to overcome voter apathy. Professor Robinson's speculations need to be probed more deeply.

What will be the future? George Orwell had a vision of a time—now less than a decade away—when the communications environment would be employed for the enslavement, rather than the enlightenment, of mankind. Orwell called his system "Big Brother." For the present, anyway, we can conceive of a less ominous communications future with MOTHER, which is the acronym for "Multiple Output Telecommunication Home End Resources."

What will be the technical characteristics of MOTHER? First, she will offer infinitely more channels—via microwave, satellite, cable, laser beam—than the present broadcast spectrum provides. There will also be greater capacity crammed within each channel—more information "bits" per gigahertz—so that one can simultaneously watch a program and receive a newspaper printout on the same channel.

A life-sized MOTHER, the images on her screens giving the illusion of three-dimensionality, will be able to *narrowcast* to neighborhoods or other focused constituencies. MOTHER will be "interactive," permitting us to talk back to our television set by means of a digital device on the console. Recording and replay equipment, which is already being marketed, will liberate us from the tyranny of the broadcast schedule, and computer hookup and stop-frame control will bring the Library of Congress and other Gutenberg treasures into our living room.

Finally, via the satellite, MOTHER will offer worldwide programming in what the communications experts artfully call "real time" (even if real time means that Muhammad Ali must fight at 4:00 A.M. in Zaire in order to suit the prime-time needs of New Yorkers). Although MOTHER will be able to beam broadcasts from the People's Republic of China directly to a household in the United States and vice versa, she may face political barriers.

Until recently, prophets foresaw that the cable and other technological advances would transform television from a wholesale to a retail enterprise, directly offering the consumer a genuine diversity of choice. The "television of abundance" would bring not just greater variety of programs but also new concepts of programming—continuing education, health delivery, community services. Television would become a participatory instrument of communication rather than a one-way flow.

Today, these visions are not so bright. Some critics now glumly predict that the new technology will suffer the fate of the supersonic transport. Others expect that the technology will be developed, but that it will serve strictly commercial, rather than social, purposes. Computer may be talking to computer by cable and satellite, but householders will still watch "I Love Lucy" on their TV sets.

My own expectation is that the next decade or two will radically alter America's communications. The important issue is whether the change will be for better or for worse. If it is to be for better, we must give more critical attention to TV than we have given in the past. Too much critical time has been wasted worrying about the worst of television. More attention should be paid to the best, not simply laudatory attention but a systematic examination of style and technique and message. Criticism should also extend its reach beyond the intellectual elite into elementary and secondary schools, where children can be stimulated to think about the medium that so dominates their waking hours. We must endeavor to raise the viewer's capacity to distinguish truth from sophistry or at least their awareness, in Tony Schwartz's vocabulary, of the "resonance" being evoked from them.

We should have more widespread analysis and debate on the potential for new media and for new forms within the media. Could an electronic box office for pay programming repeal the iron laws governing "free" commercial television? How do we move beyond the limits of present broadcasting toward broader social purposes for television? In an era when lifelong learning has become essential for the prevention of human obsolescence, television surely has a role to play. And television might regularly deliver some types of health service now that the doctor is seldom making house calls. Health and education are gargantuan national enterprises which cost upward of $200 billion annually. Yet only paltry sums are being invested for research and demonstration to develop TV's capacity to enrich and extend these vital fields of social service.

Finally, we must move beyond our preoccupation with the production and transmission processes in media communication. An equally important question is, What gets through? The editors of *Scientific American* report that man's visual system has more than a million channels, capable of transmitting instantly 10 million bits of information to the brain. Yet the brain has the capacity for receiving only 27 bits of information per second. These are the raw statistics of communication within the human anatomy. They lead Sir John Eccles, the Nobel Prize-winning physiologist, to believe that the most important frontier of brain research involves the study of inhibition—our capacity to censor stimuli in order to prevent overload. Sir John makes the comparison: "It's like sculpture. What you cut away from the block of stone produces the statue."

Our journalists, both on TV and in print, pledge fealty to the proposition that society thrives by the communication of great gobs of unvarnished truth. Our law courts make us swear to tell "the truth, the whole truth, and nothing but the truth." Yet we only dimly understand how, in an all-enveloping informational environment, man chisels his little statues of perceived reality. As we approach a time when communication threatens to fission like the atom, we need to delve more deeply into these mysteries.

Looking far ahead, Robert Jastrow, director of the Goddard Institute of Space Studies, foresees a fifth communications revolution even more radical than the previous four revolutions of speech, writing, printing, and radio. "In the long term," Jastrow predicts, "the new satellites will provide a nervous system for mankind, knitting the members of our species into a global society." He compares this breakthrough with that change in the history of life several billion years ago when multicellular animals evolved out of more primitive organisms.

Before such an awesome prospect, thinking people may feel overwhelmed. Or else, we can screw up our courage, ask the fundamental questions, and make the critical choices necessary for the shaping of our destiny.

Bibliography

Cater's reflections on television's potential include many of the concerns that professionals and scholars have discussed for years. Three highly useful books that cover in one respect or another many of the points raised by Cater are Charles S. Steinberg, editor, *Broadcasting: The Critical Challenges* (Hastings House, 1974); Robert H. Stanley, editor, *The Broadcast Industry: An Examination of Major Issues* (Hastings House, 1975); and Ted C. Smythe and George A. Mastroianni, editors, *Issues in Broadcasting: Radio, Television and Cable* (Mayfield, 1975). Two general, contemporary examinations of television are Martin Mayer, *About Television* (Harper & Row, 1972), and Les Brown, *Television: The Business Behind the Box* (Harcourt Brace Jovanovich, 1971). A well thought-out criticism of television is Harry J. Skornia, *Television and Society: An Inquest and Agenda for Improvement* (McGraw-Hill, 1965). The Skornia book, although written in the sixties, still offers a worthwhile, comprehensive program for changing television in order to make it a more positive force in improving society. Rather severe criticism of television can be found in Rose K. Goldsen, *The Show and Tell Machine: How Television Works and Works You Over* (Dial Press, 1978), and Jerry Mander, *Four Arguments for the Elimination of Television* (Wm. Morrow, 1978). A more positive approach is found in Robert R. Smith, *Beyond the Wasteland: The Criticism of Broadcasting* (Speech Communication Association, 1976).

26 Strong Shift in TV's Role: From Escape Toward Reality

Robert T. Bower/Broadcasting

In the public mind American television has ceased to be primarily an entertainment center and has become a major force in journalism as well.

This change occurred in a decade when, paradoxically, viewers were losing some of their enthusiasm for television but nevertheless were watching it more—and enjoying it more—than when the decade began.

These are among many findings made public [in 1973] from 1970 research that duplicated—and thus permitted direct comparisons with—major elements of the 1960 surveys that formed the basis of the late Dr. Gary Steiner's landmark volume, "The People Look at Television" (*Broadcasting,* Feb. 18, 1963, et seq.).

Other major findings and conclusions from the 1970 study:

• Viewers in 1970 found TV less "satisfying," "relaxing," "exciting," "important" and generally less "wonderful" than had those in 1960 (possibly, the report suggests, because some of the newness had worn off), but the change was not from "praise" to "condemnation"—more nearly it was "from summa to magna cum laude." (Table 2.)

• Better-educated viewers in 1970, as in 1960, held TV in lower esteem than did other viewers, but they watched as much—and essentially the same things—as everybody else.

• In 1970 as in 1960 viewers showed a high degree of acceptance of commercials. At most, viewer attitude has become only slightly more negative. "The average viewer still overwhelmingly accepts the frequent and long interruptions by commercials as 'a fair price to pay.'" (Table 4.)

• Most adults in both surveys felt children are better off with television than they would be without it, but the percentage has increased from 70% to 76%. College-educated parents now give TV the heaviest vote on this score (81%, up from 68% 10 years earlier), and grade-school-educated parents the lowest (68%, down from 75%).

• Educational benefits remain the biggest advantage adults see in television for children, but by a much bigger percentage in 1970 than in 1960 (80% versus 65%), and entertainment has replaced the baby-sitting function as the second greatest advantage. (Table 6).

• "Seeing things they shouldn't" is still the top-rated disadvantage of TV for children in adults' minds, but there have been some changes since 1960 in what those things are. "Violence" is still number one, but sex, seminudity, vulgarity, smoking, drinking and drugs have increased as causes of concern. (Table 7).

This *Broadcasting* magazine article is a condensation of Robert T. Bower's book *Television and the Public.* Dr. Bower has been director of the Bureau of Social Science Research in Washington, D.C. since 1950. Copyright 1973, Broadcasting Publications, Inc., publishers of *Broadcasting,* newsweekly of broadcasting and allied arts, *Broadcasting Yearbook,* and *Broadcasting Cable Sourcebook* (annual). Reprinted by permission.

Table 1.

"Now, I would like to get your opinions about how radio, newspapers, television, and magazines compare. Generally speaking, which of these would you say...?"

In percentages

Which of the media:	Television 1960	Television 1970	Magazines 1960	Magazines 1970	Newspapers 1960	Newspapers 1970	Radio 1960	Radio 1970	None/NA 1960	None/NA 1970
Is the most entertaining?	68	72	9	5	13	9	9	14	1	0
Gives the most complete news coverage?	19	41	3	4	59	39	18	14	1	2
Presents things most intelligently?	27	38	27	18	33	28	8	9	5	8
Is the most educational?	32	46	31	20	31	26	3	4	3	5
Brings you the latest news most quickly?	36	54	0	0	5	6	57	39	2	1
Does the most for the public?	34	48	3	2	44	28	11	13	8	10
Seems to be getting worse all the time?	24	41	17	18	10	14	14	5	35	22
Presents the fairest, most unbiased news?	29	33	9	9	31	23	22	19	9	16
Is the least important to you?	15	13	49	53	7	9	15	20	7	5
Creates the most interest in new things going on?	56	61	18	16	18	14	4	5	4	5
Does the least for the public?	13	10	47	50	5	7	12	13	23	20
Seems to be getting better all the time?	49	38	11	8	11	11	10	15	19	28
Gives you the clearest understanding of the candidates and issues in national elections?	42	59	10	8	36	21	5	3	7	9

1960 base: 100 percent = 2427
1970 base: 100 percent = 1900

Table 2.

"Here are some opposites. Please read each pair quickly and put a check some place between them, wherever you think it belongs, to describe television. Just your offhand impression."

Television is generally: Proportion of 1960-1970 samples choosing each of six scale positions.

	(1) 1960	(1) 1970	(2) 1960	(2) 1970	(3) 1960	(3) 1970	(4) 1960	(4) 1970	(5) 1960	(5) 1970	(6) 1960	(6) 1970	
Relaxing	43	33	21	23	19	27	9	11	3	4	4	3	Upsetting
Interesting	42	31	21	23	19	24	9	13	4	5	4	3	Uninteresting
For me	41	27	16	20	19	24	10	15	6	8	8	6	Not for me
Important	39	30	17	19	21	24	10	15	7	7	6	6	Unimportant
Informative	39	35	25	27	20	23	8	9	5	3	3	3	Not informative
Lots of fun	32	22	20	20	25	31	12	16	5	6	6	5	Not much fun
Exciting	30	19	18	17	29	35	13	17	5	7	4	6	Dull
Wonderful	28	19	16	15	33	36	16	22	4	6	3	3	Terrible
Imaginative	26	19	21	20	28	33	14	15	6	7	5	6	No imagination
In good taste	24	18	21	19	31	33	19	19	6	7	4	4	In bad taste
Generally excellent	22	15	19	18	32	36	18	21	5	6	4	4	Generally bad
Lots of variety	35	28	16	20	19	21	12	14	10	9	8	8	All the same
On everyone's mind	33	21	22	18	24	29	15	20	4	7	3	5	Nobody cares much
Getting better	25	16	19	15	24	23	16	21	8	11	9	15	Getting worse
Keeps changing	23	22	17	18	22	24	18	20	10	9	9	8	Stays the same
Serious	8	7	8	8	31	35	29	33	12	10	12	7	Playful
Too "highbrow"	4	3	3	4	29	28	42	43	11	12	9	11	Too "simple minded"

1960 Base: 100 percent = 2427
1970 Base: 100 percent = 1900
(Excluding NA's which vary from item to item)

Table 3.

Proportion of each group taking most extreme position on two scales.

	Superians Percent who check extreme positive positions				Vilifiers Percent who check extreme negative positions				Base: 100% =	
	"Wonderful"		"For me"		"Terrible"		"Not for me"			
	1960	1970	1960	1970	1960	1970	1960	1970	1960	1970
Sex:										
Male . . .	27	17	40	24	3	4	7	7	1177	900
Female . . .	28	20	41	31	3	2	9	6	1246	982
Education:										
Grade school . .	44	33	54	43	3	3	9	7	627	367
High school . .	26	19	42	28	3	3	7	6	1214	1030
College . . .	12	7	20	15	3	2	11	8	516	490
Age:										
18-19	32	17	44	25	0	2	6	7	84	182
20-29	19	17	33	29	3	1	8	6	473	331
30-39	23	18	39	24	2	3	7	6	544	356
40-49	27	13	38	23	2	3	7	9	463	378
50-59	34	21	44	27	4	2	10	5	400	311
60+	36	24	50	33	4	5	10	6	440	419

• Parents are "a bit stricter" than they were about controlling their children's viewing (43% say they have "definite rules" as against 41% in 1960). But better-educated parents, the biggest group in approving of TV for children, are much more inclined to have rules (46%) than grade-school-educated parents (25%), who are most fearful about TV for children. In general, however, "there are about as many parents who look to the children for help in deciding what they (parents) are going to watch as there are parents who try to decide about their children's viewing."

The 1970 study was financed by a grant by CBS, which also underwrote the 1960 study, to the Bureau of Social Science Research, a Washington-based independent nonprofit organization. Based on a national probability sample, some 1,900 adults (aged 18 and over) were interviewed by the Roper Organization, New York, in late winter and early spring of 1970—exactly 10 years after interviewing was done in the 1960 study. In addition there was a separate special study in Minneapolis-St. Paul, where, in cooperation with the American Research Bureau, the researchers were able to measure what viewers said against what they actually watched, corresponding to a similar special study in New York as part of the 1960 work (see boxed summary below in this article).

The report is by Robert T. Bower, director of the Bureau of Social Science Research, who emphasizes in his preface that CBS had no control over any aspect of the study or report. It is being published as a 205-page book titled "Television and the Public" by CBS's Holt, Rinehart & Winston subsidiary, which will offer it later at $7.95 a copy, but for the present CBS is distributing it widely to editors, educators and other opinion leaders.

The report ranges over many areas covered in the 1960 study, but the rising role of television as a journalistic force in the public's perception of the medium represents one of the most striking changes of the decade.

It is demonstrated in many ways. In 1960, for example, television had been voted best mass medium in only one of four specified news categories: giving the clearest understanding of candidates and issues in national elections. But by 1970, Dr. Bower reports, "we find television surging ahead of newspapers as the news medium that 'gives the most complete news coverage', overtaking radio in bringing 'the latest news most quickly', edging out newspapers in 'presenting the fairest, most unbiased news' and increasing its lead" in the one area where it was ahead in 1960, national political coverage. (Table 5.)

Dr. Bower notes that these findings parallel the results of studies conducted—also by a Roper Organization—for the Television Information Office since 1959. (He also notes at another point that when an Apollo 13 moon-flight emergency occurred during interviewing in Minneapolis-St. Paul, where 52% had rated TV the fastest news medium, 58% got their first word of the emergency from radio, as against 40% from TV. However, he says, TV regained its position as predominant source of information in the remaining four days of the flight.)

As another evidence of the public's growing perception of TV's news role Dr. Bower recalls that viewers and critics in 1960 were talking primarily about entertainment and cultural values, but in 1970 had shifted their focus to news functions, objectivity, concentration of control and effects of news coverage on audience behavior. And even in the area of TV and children, he notes, much of the violence parents object to their children's seeing is violence that is reported in the news.

He cites Vice-President Spiro Agnew's celebrated Nov. 13, 1969, attack on network news specifically. That was just three months before interviewing was done for the 1970 study—and still TV was voted the fairest and most unbiased medium.

The study looked for bias in a number of directions. In one, 53% of the conservatives, an equal percentage of liberals and a few more middle-of-the-roaders (56%) said they thought newscasters in general "give it straight," while 30% of the conservatives, 26% of the liberals and 25% of the middle-roaders thought newscasters tend to color the news. Republicans were more suspicious (32%) than Democrats (22%). In the total sample, viewers divided about equally as to whether the newscasters they individually watch most are liberal (14%) or conservative (13%); more consider them middle-roaders (36%) and even more can't tell (38%). But overwhelmingly they feel their favorite newscasters give the news straight (78%) rather than let their personal opinions color it (6%).

Dr. Bower offers this summary: "It appears that a sizable proportion (about one-fourth) of the public feels that television news is generally biased in its presentation. A much smaller group of hardcore critics think even their own favorite newscaster colors the news. But the vast majority of people either accept the objectivity of television newscasting in general or find a specific newscaster to watch who is felt to be objective in his reporting. . . . If the public at large were the judge, the medium would probably be exonerated [of bias charges] or at worst be given a suspended sentence."

Table 4.

"Here are some statements about commercials. I'd like you to read each statement and mark whether you generally agree or disagree with each statement."

Percent who agree that:	1960 total	1970 total	1970 occupation of head of household	
			White collar	Blue collar
Commercials are a fair price to pay for the entertainment you get.	75	70	69	71
Most commercials are too long	63	65	67	65
I find some commercials very helpful in keeping me informed	58	54	50	57
Some commercials are so good that they are more entertaining than the program	43	54	56	52
I would prefer TV without commercials	43	48	49	47
Commercials are generally in poor taste and very annoying	40	43	42	43
I frequently find myself welcoming a commercial break	36	35	31	38
I'd rather pay a small amount yearly to have TV without commercials	24	30	30	29
There are just too many commercials	(Not included in 1960)	70	71	70
Having special commercial breaks during a program is better than having the same number of commercials at the beginning and end	(Not included in 1960)	39	35	42
Base: 100 percent =	(2427)	(1900)	(674)	(873)

Table 5.

"Now, I would like to get your opinions about how radio, newspapers, television and magazines compare. Generally speaking, which of these would you say. . ."

		Percent	
		1960	1970
"Gives the most complete news coverage?"	Television	19	41
	Magazines	3	4
	Newspapers	59	39
	Radio	18	14
	None or don't know	1	2
"Brings you the latest news most quickly?"	Television	36	54
	Magazines	0	0
	Newspapers	5	6
	Radio	57	39
	None or don't know	2	1
"Gives the fairest, most unbiased news?"	Television	29	33
	Magazines	9	9
	Newspapers	31	23
	Radio	22	19
	None or don't know	9	16
"Gives the clearest understanding of candidates and issues in national elections?"	Television	42	59
	Magazines	16	8
	Newspapers	36	21
	Radio	5	3
	None or don't know	1	9

1960 Base: 100 percent = 2427 (minus NA's which vary from item to item)
1970 Base: 100 percent = 1900 (minus NA's which vary from item to item)

Table 6.

"What do you think are some of the main advantages of television for children?"

The advantages of TV for children by respondent's general attitude (pro or con) toward television for children *

Percent who mention:	1960						1970			
	Parents		Others		1960 Total	1970 Total	Parents		Others	
	Pros	Cons	Pros	Cons			Pros	Cons	Pros	Cons
Education	74	49	72	45	65	80	85	69	85	62
Baby-sitting	34	21	31	13	28	16	17	13	18	9
Entertainment	21	15	23	8	19	22	27	20	21	17
Programs good generally	4	17	6	16	8	2	2	2	2	2
Stimulates socializing	2	—	1	—	1	2	3	—	2	2
Adult supervision necessary	4	2	10	4	6	2	2	1	2	1
Other, general	1	4	1	4	2	4	3	6	2	6
Base: 100% =	(858)	(292)	(781)	(419)	(2350)	(1592)	(589)	(159)	(607)	(237)

*Multiple response item: percentages do not necessarily add up to 100 percent.

Table 7.

"What do you think are some of the main disadvantages of television for children?"

Disadvantages of television for children by parental status and general attitude (pro and con) toward television for children. *

Percent who mention:	1960						1970			
	Parents		Others		1960 Total	1970 Total	Parents		Others	
	Pros	Cons	Pros	Cons			Pros	Cons	Pros	Cons
See things they shouldn't:	46	55	48	64	51	52	48	55	50	64
Violence, horror	26	32	28	40	30	30	27	32	30	35
Crime, gangsters	7	8	11	13	10	8	6	10	9	12
Sex, suggestiveness, vulgarity	4	7	4	6	5	11	10	12	11	13
Smoking, drinking, dope	2	2	2	3	2	5	4	5	6	7
Adult themes	2	3	1	3	2	9	6	11	10	12
Harmful or sinful products advertised	1	1	1	—	1	1	1	—	1	1
Wrong values or moral codes	3	5	2	5	3	8	8	11	8	9
Other, general	7	11	8	9	8	2	3	5	2	5
Keeps them from doing things they should	34	51	31	41	36	30	29	40	26	34
Programs bad, general	10	9	8	13	10	2	2	6	2	3
Other, program content	3	9	2	6	4	6	7	10	5	6
Physical harm	3	7	4	8	5	5	3	4	5	7
Advertising too effective	2	3	1	—	1	2	3	3	2	3
Other	2	3	1	3	2	5	6	5	5	3
Base: 100 percent =	(858)	(292)	(781)	(419)	(2350)	(1583)	(586)	(157)	(604)	(236)

*Multiple response item: percentages do not necessarily add up to 100 percent.

The study also undertook to learn which news medium people think puts most emphasis on "good things" and which puts most on "bad things"—and found that TV was voted number one on both counts. Dr. Bower suggests a possible explanation: "that for a large group of viewers television is simply so dominant a medium in bringing all the news, any sort of news, they see it as emphasizing all things—both the good and the bad—without any sense of contradiction. Yes, it emphasizes the good things; yes, it emphasizes the bad things; it emphasizes everything."

The study found 57% rated TV's performance in presenting 1968 presidential election campaign issues and candidates as good (44%) or excellent (13%); 32% wanted more political programs in the 1972 campaign while 15% wanted fewer, and 43% said TV played a "fairly important" (30%) or "very important" (13%) part in helping them decide whom they wanted to win in 1968. He doesn't think that last finding should be construed to mean TV caused large numbers to bolt their parties but, rather, that it reflects "a sense of increased familiarity with the candidates and, most likely, a reinforcement of pre-existing tendencies."

At another point Dr. Bower says: "The indications are that television does not tend to favor one faction over another in such a way as to suggest a partisan political influence during a campaign, or even to discriminate among the social groups of which the population is composed. To an amazing degree, the perceived effects of television's political coverage are spread evenly among the public."

In summary, he says: "The high assessment of television in its journalistic role that has been shown in this chapter certainly represents a general public endorsement, all the more resounding since it occurs at a time when TV news is under attack.

"Clearly, this part of television's content has largely been exempted from the trend toward a lower public esteem for the medium as a whole. But the vote is by no means unanimous. TV news presentation is not free of the suspicion of bias that the American public accords to all the mass media; and while the improvements in the technology of rapid worldwide coverage of daily events may be roundly applauded, there are those who would prefer less emphasis on the unpleasant and disturbing national conflicts."

These presumably would be older viewers, for in another section the study found age to be the great differentiator of views about social strife such as riots, street protests, race problems and campus unrest. "The young applaud what the old condemn in what would seem to be expressions about the world at large, attributed to television only as the bearer of bad tidings," Dr. Bower observes.

Age also figured in one of the major changes found in viewing patterns in 1970. Ten years earlier, the heaviest viewing had been found among teenagers; in 1970, teenagers watched less than any of the other age groups. They also were the only age group that failed to watch more in 1970 than their counterparts did in 1960. In itself the decline was not considered large—from 26.25 median hours per week in 1960 to 25.33 in 1970—but in a broader context, Dr. Bower suggests, it could be huge.

The 1970 dip might be a transitory one, he says, with the teenagers increasing their viewing as they grow older, as viewers who were 28 or 29 in 1970 watched more than those 18 or 19 in 1960. "But," Dr. Bower cautions, "if it happens to be a way of life that will endure as the generation ages," the uptrend of TV viewing is threatened.

Among other changes found in 1970:

• Where 1960 viewers preferred regular series to specials (49% to 32%), 1970's preferred specials (44%) to series (36%).

• Despite a somewhat declining esteem for TV as a whole, viewers found more specific programs to applaud. On average, the proportion of all programs rated "extremely enjoyable" rose from 44% in 1960 to 50% in 1970. In addition, or perhaps as a factor in that increase, Dr. Bower reports that 70% of the viewers said they thought there were more "different kinds of programs" in 1970, giving them a broader range to choose from.

As for changes in television itself, reaction was overwhelmingly favorable (55% had only favorable things to say, as opposed to 16% who were solely unfavorable, with the rest neutral, balanced or in the no-answer category).

Generally they felt neutral about 10-year changes in sports programs and movies, were critical on such morality questions as sex, nudity and vulgarity (10%) and on violence (4%), which they often linked with news, and were favorable toward changes perceived in general entertainment (19%), technical advances such as color and increased numbers of stations (23%) and, most of all, changes in news and information (33%).

What They Said and What They Saw

The Bureau of Social Science Research's special study in Minneapolis-St. Paul, made in conjunction with its national study, confirmed again what many already knew: Viewers don't always watch what they say they want to see on television.

With the cooperation of the American Research Bureau, the researchers interviewed some Minnesotans who had previously kept ARB diaries, and then compared what they said with what they had watched. One conclusion: "The people who say they usually watch television to learn something do watch news and information programing more than others, but only a little bit more. Those who feel there is not enough 'food for thought' on television watch as many entertainment shows as the rest of the viewers. Those who want television stations to concentrate on information programs spend only slightly more time watching such programs than those who want the 'best entertainment', despite the fact that a great deal of informative fare is available in the Minneapolis-St. Paul area for those who could just switch the dial to another channel."

The researchers also rated respondents on a "culture scale" and examined their viewing in that context; the "high-culture" people, it turned out, "watched television somewhat less than those who scored lower; when they did watch, their viewing was distributed among program types in almost precisely the same way as the low-culture scorers, hardly a hair's breadth between them except in the news [higher viewing] and sports [lower] categories."

"Live coverage of national events, educational television, more channels, television by satellite and longer news programs are all viewed as changes for the better by 70% or more of the sample," Dr. Bower writes. "At the other end, talk shows, fewer westerns and live coverage of civil disruptions *are* approved by only about a third."

Noting that coverage of space shots and other national events ranked at the top of changes rated for the better, while coverage of riots and protests ranked at the bottom, Dr. Bower assumes that in these cases "people are responding to the message at least as much as to the medium, probably it is the space effort people like and the riots they dislike."

Dr. Bower also cautions that it should not be assumed that "the American television audience has changed in 10 years from a population of entertainment fans to a population of news hawks." Entertainment, he notes, still dominates TV fare and commands most of the viewer's time.

"But," he continues, "there is apparently a general shift in people's perception of what television is and what it means to them, and the new focus on the news and information content of television has undoubtedly altered people's views about various other aspects of the medium's role—from how it affects the 12-year-old to whether it is a benign or malevolent force in society." More than that, he concludes, "the journalistic emphasis may have introduced important new criteria by which TV will be judged in the future."

Bibliography

This summary by *Broadcasting* magazine of Dr. Bower's report should be supplemented first of all by turning to the full report, published as *Television and the Public* (Holt, Rinehart & Winston, 1973). For a comparative look at television of a decade earlier, see Gary A. Steiner, *The People Look at Television* (Alfred A. Knopf, 1963). Background readings on the development of the broadcast industry can be found in several books. A few of the better choices are Sydney W. Head, *Broadcasting in America: A Survey of Television and Radio,* 3rd ed. (Houghton-Mifflin, 1976), which contains a valuable bibliography on the field; Giraud Chester et al., *Television and Radio,* 5th ed. (Prentice-Hall, 1978), which contains studio production information in addition to its survey of broadcasting; Eugene S. Foster, *Understanding Broadcasting* (Addison-Wesley, 1978); and Harrison E. Summers et al., *Broadcasting and the Public,* revised edition (Wadsworth Publishing Co., 1978), which contains highly useful information on historical and contemporary programming. Good historical background can be found in Lawrence W. Lichty and Malachi C. Topping, compilers, *A Source Book on the History of Radio and Television* (Hastings House, 1975), and Erik Barnouw, *A History of Broadcasting in the United States,* the standard history on the subject, a three-volume study issued by Oxford University Press in 1966, 1968, and 1970. An excellent one-volume history of broadcasting is Christopher H. Sterling and John M. Kittross, *Stay Tuned: A Concise History of American Broadcasting* (Wadsworth Publishing Co., 1978). Barnouw also has a short study on television, entitled *Tube of Plenty: The Evolution of American Television* (Oxford University Press, 1975).

Investigative Reporting: Is It Getting Too Sexy?

27

Timothy Ingram

"I think it's going to get incredible," says Melvin Mencher of the Columbia School of Journalism, who was teaching seminars on investigative reporting when it was still considered a grubby trade. "Every little paper in the country and every reporter on a beat is going to want a scalp." As journalism schools, including his own, bulge with would-be Woodwards and Bernsteins, and reporters on every paper in the country try to nail a prominent hide to the wall, "investigative reporting" has become the profession's most popular—and most worrisome—gimmick.

"Ninety percent of these smaller newspapers have no tradition of this kind of digging, no editors with experience in it," Mencher says. "A lot of poor devils in public office are going to catch hell for simple mistakes. When the movie comes out, I guess it's going to get worse."

"The movie," of course, is the Robert Redford All-Star version of the Watergate case; the apprehension is that it may exaggerate the set of double standards under which many people publicly denounce political dirty tricks while glamorizing the dirty tricks of journalists who pressure middle-aged bookkeepers for information or filch private telephone or credit records. [Ed. note: It didn't.]

According to Ben Bagdikian, a former *Washington Post* national editor and ombudsman, this trenchcoat psychology could easily lead to frivolous exposes and shoddy reportorial practices. The added pressure to unearth the "big stories," Bagdikian says, will make it almost impossible for reporters to resist pursuing the "easy fish," the scandal stories where information is obtained by dubious means.

"Editors want to look like investigative editors—but on the cheap," explains Bagdikian. "They tell a good reporter to come up with a story in two days. . . . It usually results in stories based on half-information and bad sources."

Even the tabloids are boasting of their tough muckraking approach. The *National Star,* "America's Lively Family Newspaper," recently headlined "Two New Shocks in the Kennedy Saga" under the credit, "by Star Investigating Team." The transition from kidnappings and mutilated babies to the political inside story has been made.

No newspaper has calculated the promotional value of "investigation" more closely than the Detroit *Free Press,* whose day-to-day coverage is mediocre but which pulls out all the stops on 10 or 12 investigative stories each year. The stories are designed to win Pulitzers, and often do. Even when they do not, they give the *Free Press* a national reputation out of all proportion to its daily performance.

Timothy Ingram is a contributing editor of *The Washington Monthly.* Reprinted with permission from *The Washington Monthly* (April 1975). Copyright by The Washington Monthly Co., 1028 Connecticut Ave., N.W., Washington, D.C. 20036.

Clearly, we are in the midst of an investigative craze—a craze that has obvious potential for good, even as it presents a less obvious danger of harm to both the profession of journalism and the public at large. It is with these dangers that this article is concerned. We see five that concern us the most.

Seducing the Source

The first hazard of investigative reporting concerns the actual means used to collect the facts. There are many methods of investigation, some of which are clearly improper. Others, however, are well within the commonly accepted rules of this rough game. A journalist may pretend, for example, to know all about X in order to seduce his subject into confirming his information; this confirmation, in turn, may reveal bits about fact Y, the checking of which may lead for the first time to Z. Generally the reporter approaches his source indirectly: "We have enough to run with now, but in the interests of accuracy I'd like your version of what happened." A variant is to convince the source that you have heard an incredibly shocking tale about him but are uncertain whether to print it. In his anguish, he is bound to spill his side of the story.

Sometimes these calls will be timed to catch people off guard: phoning the subject at home in the evening after he has a chance to unwind from the day, and perhaps is loosened by a sip of Scotch; or at 6 A.M. in hopes of catching him half-asleep.

Perhaps the most accomplished telephone technician is Seymour Hersh, now of *The New York Times,* who unearthed the My Lai massacre, and since has been generally regarded as the best investigative reporter in the country. Hersh's technique is to wear down reluctant sources through tenacious pursuit by phone—often badgering, terrorizing, insulting. "I don't know of anyone other than Don Rickles who can be as disgustingly insulting, yet have the right touch for getting someone to respond," says a former colleague. Hersh makes one phone call after another, trading on fine bits of information, and then milking more with sarcastic bursts of "Ah-h, come *awwn.*" Those who have experienced the Hersh treatment are usually either amazed by it, or appalled. "What's with this guy?" one subject said afterwards. "I tell him honestly I don't know anything, and he's yelling and screaming at me and going into tantrums."

James Angleton, who resigned from the CIA last December the day after a Hersh story charged him with being the overseer of a "massive, illegal" domestic intelligence operation against antiwar activists, had one term for Hersh: "son-of-a-bitch." Angleton said Hersh had awakened him one morning at seven to interrogate him about a story in that day's *Washington Post.* Angleton told a *Post* reporter, "I find Hersh's prose offensive to the ear. And his speech . . . I won't go into how I find that."

Free Enterprise

Angleton, not unexpectedly, considers such calls improper. It should be remembered, though, that the subjects of Hersh's aggressive, often vulgar, approach are public servants. While they do have a right to privacy and a good night's sleep, they must be prepared to answer questions about their official conduct, even when the questions come in unorthodox forms. And, when dealing with a man like Hersh, the officials have fair warning that he represents the *Times* and is looking for information he can publish. At the opposite extreme is the reporter who hides his connection with a newspaper, and obtains a story under false pretenses. The distinction—between the Seymour Hersh who announces he is a reporter and the journalist who masquerades as a cop, a waiter, or whatever, in order to trick his source—is significant, although the ethical guidelines are not always easily drawn.

Al Lewis, *The Washington Post's* veteran police reporter, for example, was the only newsman inside the Democratic headquarters at the Watergate on the morning the five burglars were arrested. Wearing white socks and looking very much the cop, Lewis simply accompanied the acting police chief past the 50 reporters and cameramen cordoned off from the Watergate complex by the police. Once inside, Lewis took off his jacket, sat down at a desk, and occasionally pecked at a typewriter. He looked for all the world as if he was supposed to be working there. With a phone at his desk, he was able to provide the *Post* with a description of the office floor plan, details about the surgical gloves and lock-picks and jimmies used, and the name of the security guard who foiled the break-in. Lewis sees nothing deceitful in his actions—all he was doing was remaining anonymous. He never *told* anyone he was a policeman, and presumably had anyone asked, he would have disclosed his true identity.

A similar case occurred in the spring of 1969, when Richard Helms, then-director of the CIA, was scheduled to speak at a dinner meeting of the Business Council, an organization of some 150 top businessmen at the Homestead in Hot Springs, Virginia.

Helms' speech was officially off-the-record and closed to the press; moreover, Helms would not be briefing the press on his remarks afterwards. This caused some grumbling among the reporters at hand, but individually they began to make their own arrangements to have friends in the audience fill them in later. As followers of last summer's impeachment hearings have learned, such second-hand accounts are not always the most accurate.

Jim Srodes, then with UPI, was in Hot Springs for his honeymoon. When he learned about the speech he went into the hall outside the dining room and twisted doorknobs until he found himself in the hotel kitchen. Helms' voice was booming through the room; a loudspeaker had been set up so that waiters would know when the speech was over and they could go in and clear off the tables. Srodes simply stood there and started taking notes.

Was this ethical? Most reporters would agree his actions showed more enterprise than deceit. The speech, as it happened, was a diatribe about the horrors of communism. Helms made a number of policy assertions which would normally be considered beyond his purview, referring to the "morally bankrupt Kremlin leaders" and the futility of disarmament talks. Russia and its satellites, in Helms' terms were "the bear and its pack of wolves."

Aggressive reporting forced the exposure of such events as the "grain scandal," but later some media critics worried that Watergate-style reporting was leading to excesses, including invasion of privacy. *New Times,* which prided itself on its investigative reporting, folded in 1978 while new fluff magazines such as *People* and *Us* found a ready market.

Once he had the story, however, Srodes' troubles had only begun. UPI refused to use it. When Srodes called in his exclusive, he says, the UPI night editor told him the story would hurt UPI's world-wide relations with the CIA and its ability to get other stories. The story finally ran, Srodes is convinced, only because a *Washington Post* reporter to whom he told his tale that night had the *Post* make a client request to UPI for the story—the gun-to-the-head for the wire services, where a client paper in effect says we know you have the story and we want it.

At a certain point, however, the reporter crosses the line that separates enterprise from deceit. Harry Rosenfeld, then the *Washington Post's* metropolitan editor, says that shortly after Howard Hunt became a suspect in the Watergate break-in, Rosenfeld could have obtained Hunt's telephone records through impersonation. The usual method of doing so is to call the phone company's business office and, posing as the person being investigated, claim that you don't recall making certain long-distance calls charged to you. You then request the business office to double-check the numbers and dates of the calls and report them back to you. (A similar pose is used with credit companies to "re-confirm" a loan, or with airlines to check a passenger's flight travel.) Rosenfeld says that *Post* executive editor Ben Bradlee vetoed the subterfuge.

Not all journalists are so moral. There was Harry Romanoff of the now-defunct *Chicago American,* a police reporter who, without leaving his desk, would assume a dozen different disguises in his pursuit of a hot lead. Harry's colleagues referred to him as "the Heifetz of the telephone." He would work a phone 12 hours a day, masquerading as sheriff, governor, sympathetic stranger, or whatever character fit the occasion. After the 1966 mass murder of eight Chicago student nurses, he managed to get the gory details of the deaths from a policeman after introducing himself as the Cook County coroner, and to interview the mother of the suspect, Richard Speck, by pretending to be her son's attorney.

Few reporters use trickery as freely as Romanoff, but many have been tempted. What is wrong with this practice is not just its dishonesty—although that is no insignificant point. As James Polk of *The Washington Star,* who won a Pulitzer last year for his reporting on campaign spending, puts it: "The ethical question is clear. If reporters are dedicated to openness in government and openness in subjects they cover, then they can't use covert methods themselves."

There is, moreover, a practical problem—false premises can result in false information. A reporter conceals his identity in order to hear things the source would not intentionally tell the press. But he may also hear things the source would not tell the press because they are untrue: the source may be lying to impress a stranger; the information may be wrong, or couched in terms that are misunderstood; the person may be careless in what he says because he doesn't think he is speaking for the record.

The ethical rationale for misrepresentation, then, is that an individual has a right to keep his thoughts private and to know whom he's talking to. The practical rationale is that the reporter may get stuck with bad information.

The *Star's* Polk explains: "I think it's more effective to identify myself as a reporter for a Washington paper because, frankly, it carries a little more clout. Most persons you start asking questions of want to explain what they do, and why. They're leery of really getting a rap in the press and think if they turn the reporter off by being uncooperative they've got more chance of getting rapped—which is possibly true. So, if, instead of asking them to *defend* what they've done, you ask their help in *explaining* what they know about something so you can sort it out in your own mind—why, then you get results."

Private Sins

If the first hazard of investigative reporting lies in the way the facts are collected, the second is in their use: is a reporter justified in publishing damaging material about people or institutions, even if the facts are true? In the aftermath of the Wilbur Mills [and Wayne Hays] episodes, we seem certain to be treated to a "new candor" in the coverage of public officials. This would be fine if it meant a less deferential treatment of their public activities. But the apparent effect has been open season for comment on the *private* lives of public figures. Whatever sins against the Republic John Mitchell may finally be called to account for, it is hard to imagine how the public interest is served by seeing the pilfered records of his checking account, which *New York* magazine published last year to prove that he had been short-changing Martha in their divorce proceedings. This is what we're calling "investigative reporting" these days, and such examples show that, when deciding whether to publish or remain silent, reporters and editors are not asking the most basic question: *Is it significant?* The same press which has a duty to fearlessly publish information about the performance of public officials also has a duty not to needlessly defame them.

The distinction doesn't seem clear to many reporters. On a recent television talk show, a respected political writer said, "I dread the first time I spend a day with a politician and find out he's a fag. It'll hurt me, but I'll write it." If the politician's sexual taste affected the way he performed his job—*if,* like Hadrian, he abused public office for the satisfaction of private desire—then, it seems to me, the story should be written.

Raking Muck

A third abuse in investigative reporting is when reporters start working with the institutions of public power they're covering, so that, in effect, they help create stories they will later report.

To give a classic Washington illustration, reporters who cover congressional hearings often chafe with frustration when listening to mushy questioning which leaves major gaps in testimony or whole areas of inquiry unexplored. Although officially they are only observers, some reporters will feed questions and leads to the committee. During the Senate Watergate proceedings, reporters phoned committee staffers after hours with tips or to swap information; some actually sent notes to the senators' table. More traditional reporters, wary of the appearance of collusion, would list the unanswered questions from the day's proceeding in their stories, thereby sending their message to the committee.

The reporters were not asking the committee for special favors; they were acting as any outside citizen might, to provide information. This kind of cooperation between reporters and public officials is not wrong, but there is another that has far more frightening implications. It is best illustrated by an investigation that took place in upstate New York four years ago.

Ray Hill is a hard-drinking Canadian, a bulldog of a reporter. He looks like a cross between TV's "Cannon" and Brendan Behan. His approach is that of prosecutor. He credits his investigations into suburban corruption with 23 convictions and one acquittal. Once his targets have been sent up the river, he takes pride in ensuring they remain there and are not paroled early through political dealings.

In the summer of 1970 the *Buffalo Evening News* assigned Ray Hill and Dan Perry to the city of Lakawanna, just south of Buffalo, with instructions to "shake the trees and see what falls." Perry, then 25, had been a leader in a young-turk revolt in the city room, and assignment to Lakawanna was a convenient way to direct his fire outside of town. Also, for the conservative Buffalo paper, writing about Lakawanna was like writing about California: it was politically safe.

Lakawanna, with its giant steel mills and rust-covered rooftops, is a polyglot community of working class Irish, Poles, Italians, blacks, and Arabs. The town is a muckraker's utopia, where palms are crossed and pockets filled at every political level. Finding corruption, says Hill, is "like tracking a bleeding elephant through fresh-fallen snow."

Within a year, as a result of articles by Hill and Perry a special grand jury had indicted nine members and officers of the Lakawanna school board; six were finally convicted. They were found guilty of accepting bribes, approving phony vouchers for non-existent school equipment, and shaking down local contractors. The series won a first place from the New York Publishers Association and was a finalist in the Associated Press Managing Editors awards.

Hill and Perry's first stories were based on solid evidence, such as the canceled checks and vouchers showing that the school board had kept a dead man on the payroll for four years and had paid out $2,645 for a tractor that was never supplied. They were followed by articles about mismanagement, bidding irregularities, thefts, and skimmings.

But like *The Washington Post's* coverage of Watergate, after the grand jury was empaneled to look into the charges generated by the paper, the direction and momentum of the reporting changed. In an attempt to keep the momentum going, the reporters kept grinding out pieces, just to show that the story was still alive. Often they resorted to artificial exposés by the most dubious techniques.

The following tactics evolved:

Feeding the Mills. Hill fed recalcitrant sources straight to the District Attorney's investigators. "We would tell them, 'Interview X. He won't speak to us; but he'll be able to tell you this and this. We know because we have two others in our backpocket who can verify it. If he tells you something else, he's lying to you.' That's how we fortified our investigation all along."

Laundering Rumors. "We'd pick up a rumor," says Perry, "such as a Mafia-owned construction company having received a special contract with the board. Then we'd call the D.A., give him the tip, and ask, 'Are you going to look into it?' He'd say, 'Yes,' so we'd run a story the next day, 'Grand jury investigating charges that. . . .' We used the D.A. and the grand jury as a springboard to get our stories printed."

Quid Pro Quo. Hill would turn information over to the D.A. only in return for other information. "Do you want to play ball with me? I want to know what information you're presenting to the grand jury—and I don't want the opposition paper to know." Hill would plea-bargain with a source in return for turning over evidence on higher-ups. His activities went further than bargaining for information. He eventually negotiated legal immunity with the prosecutor for a key source. For example, Hill and Perry located a local contractor who told them he had been approached in a contract bidding shakedown, but he was hesitant to be more specific. "When we talked to the guy," Hill explains, "we told him, 'We can't get you immunity for murder, but if you want immunity for this specific testimony, we won't mention your name in the story and we will go to the D.A. for you.' " Hill then persuaded the prosecutor to guarantee the man's immunity in return for testifying before the grand jury. Then he ran the contractor's story.

"What happens frequently," says James Doyle, the press aide for the Watergate Special Prosecutor's office, "is that reporters call up and say, 'Listen, I want to tell you such-and-such; and the next day you read 'The Watergate special prosecution force *is aware of*. . . .' Okay. He tricked me. But if that guy calls back, I tell him, 'Hey, shove it buddy; I know your number, and I don't even want to talk to you.' "

New York Times reporter David Burnham had interviewed Frank Serpico and Inspector Paul Delise in February 1970 and had written Serpico's story of corruption within the New York City police. According to Peter Maas's biography of Serpico, by late April the story had not appeared. Then Burnham met Mayor Lindsay's press secretary at a cocktail party and let slip that the *Times* had a story involving police corruption in the works, and that it was dynamite. Two days later—to blunt the expected *Times* story, Mayor Lindsay announced that a committee was being formed to look into allegations of police corruption. The *Times* editors at last had an obvious, undeniable hook for the story and Serpico's charges were headlined the next day: "Graft Paid to Police Here Said to Run into Millions."

If the *Times'* editors were confident in the story, there was no reason at all for them to have waited for the newspeg—nor should they wait on similar investigative stories. If its editors are satisfied that the story is strong, the paper should be willing to put its own name behind the story instead of waiting to quote the grand jury. On the other hand, if the case is *not* complete, then the grand jury newspeg is a fraud—and, unfortunately, a most common form of fraud. It reflects again the ineradicable journalistic belief that "responsibility" consists of diligent quoting of official sources. Real "responsibility" means putting the paper's imprimatur on the line as a guarantee that the stories it publishes are accurate—and that the paper will take the consequences if they are not.

The fourth abuse of investigative reporting is the boldest of all—"buying" infor-   **Paying the Piper**
mation. The great danger of buying is that journalists may end up staging the news they have paid for. In the mid-sixties CBS is said to have bid more than $30,000 for exclusive film rights to a planned "rebel army" invasion of Haiti. The network apparently had second thoughts when it realized that instead of buying coverage of an invasion it might be subsidizing one.

Most reporters say they would hesitate to pay for news, and would consider the purchased information tainted. In eight years of listening to newsmen at American Press Institute seminars, the API's Malcom Mallette says that "only a few have ever related situations where they've paid. There's more chance of error, that they'll get caught with inaccurate information." Informants who talk to the press may have many ulterior motives: revenge, ego, ambition to destroy an opponent, public conscience, liking the reporter—but no motive is so suspect as the mercenary one.

One of the most controversial of these arrangements was *Life's* purchase in 1959 of the astronauts' "personal stories." Aside from the question of whether government employees should be allowed to profit from recounting publicly-financed experiences, there was a more basic objection. Since *Life* had a vested interest in the success of NASA's space program, the magazine would not be likely to encourage dogged and objective reporting and analysis of the space effort.

Life's purchase of the astronauts' stories had a more profound effect, which helped shape the public reaction to its later investigative efforts, such as the story of Supreme Court Justice Abe Fortas. It was openly speculated that *Life* had kept several Justice Department employees on the payroll to get the information.

Denny Walsh, who joined *Life's* investigative unit very shortly after its inception in 1967, insists that money was never passed to informants. "The Fortas story," says Walsh, "it was a disgruntled bureaucrat, a guy who saw something happening he didn't like. Simple as that." But Walsh also says that because of *Life's* reputation of paying for the astronaut story and other "exclusives," every potential informant wanted a hand-out. "Not government people, but others approaching us every day in every way—letter, telephone, in person—with stories and a request for compensation." Walsh swears, "I'll never work anyplace else where every guy crossing the threshold holds his hand out. That was the case with *Life,* in spades."

Because of its many pitfalls, the purchase of information—even more than the other investigative tactics—should be a last resort, the journalistic equivalent of an act of war. As one illustration of the circumstances that *might* justify it, consider this case:

Jack Nelson, the Washington bureau chief of the *Los Angeles Times,* once paid a Mississippi detective $1,000 for police files on two local informants. The story Nelson broke was a complicated one: it involved the FBI, which had paid two Klu Klux Klansmen to set a trap for two other Klansmen, so that this latter pair could be caught in the act of bombing a home. While the Klansmen were attempting to place a bomb in the garage of a prominent Jewish businessman, the police attacked with guns ablaze, killing one of the Klansmen outright and wounding the other. There was evidence that the police never intended to take either Klansman alive. In his story, Nelson questioned an arrangement in which the FBI, in effect, hired murderers and *agents provocateurs*.

The detective had told Nelson about the incident and what the police files contained, and suggested that Nelson give him "credit" for the documents. Nelson says, "I think I could've gotten it for $250." But it was a hell of a story, Nelson says, and the man risked his skin to get the files. "I don't regret paying, not a bit." Nelson says he did not feel uncomfortable because he was not buying the man's word which might be altered or influenced by the money; rather, the detective was leading Nelson to documents which Nelson could independently verify with the FBI and other sources. Nelson viewed it as a finder's fee.

The Other Side of the Coin

The responsibility we advocate on the part of the investigative press should be accompanied by a burden of responsibility on the part of those whom it investigates and who take it to court. A recent $5-million suit against the worthy but impecunious *Texas Observer* is a reminder of the potential disaster a libel suit represents for all but the richest publishers. Even if the *Observer* wins the suit, the legal fees could easily drive it into bankruptcy. This is a publisher's worst nightmare—that a well-heeled and determined plaintiff will destroy him even when he is telling the truth, simply by appealing to court after court until the publisher runs out of money. This moment will come sooner than later for many of the more interesting and provocative periodicals for whom fiscal fragility is a chronic condition.

A solution would be for our federal and state legislatures to enact a statute providing that a plaintiff pay the defendant's legal fees in any case where the plaintiff is found not to have had a reasonable ground for asserting that he had been defamed. Or, in a reform that would strike fear into the hearts of litigants who are frivolous or vindictive at the same time that it would embolden those who are in the right, the law could provide that in every case all legal costs would be paid by the loser.

Many laymen think this is the way it is for now. It is not. Only in a tiny minority of cases are the winning side's fees paid by the losers.

Malicious Intent

The fifth and by far the greatest danger in investigative reporting is lack of fidelity to the facts. Developments in the law of libel during the 1960s tended to give some reporters the feeling that they could get away with less than the truth. The Supreme Court said in the famous case of *New York Times v. Sullivan,* "The constitutional guarantees require, we think, a federal rule that prohibits a public official from recovering damages for a defamatory statement relating to his official conduct unless he proves that the statement was made with 'actual malice'—that is, with knowledge it was false or with reckless disregard of whether it was false or not."

When reporters think they can safely go to the borderline of recklessness, there is a danger some will cross the line. A recent case illustrates that danger:

James Sprouse was the state Democratic candidate for governor of West Virginia in 1968, running a tight race against then-Congressman Arch Moore, now the governor. Ten days before the November balloting, the Charleston *Daily Mail* unveiled its explosive headlines: "Pendleton Realty Bonanza by Jim Sprouse Disclosed; Cleanup of Nearly $500,000 In View." A second set of banners appeared the next day, reporting on a news conference called by Moore: "Moore Asks Federal Probe Into Sprouse's Pendleton Land Grab; Dummy Firm Seen Proving Corruption." An accompanying editorial, comparing Sprouse's candidacy to "asking the horses to clean their own barn," asked: "More of the Shabby Same or Some Cleansing Change."

Arch Moore was quoted as saying that the "land grab" was achieved with a "dummy corporation set up in the dark of night." The stories implied that Sprouse and his real estate partners had relied on inside information that the U.S. Forest Service would purchase most of the recently acquired property for a recreation area, and balloon the value of Sprouse's remaining sector. One fact was repeated four times in the articles—that the land company had been set up one month before plans for the federal recreation project were announced.

The story had been brought to the *Daily Mail's* political writer, Robert Mellace, by Arch Moore's campaign manager and press aide, and Mellace said he relied on their investigative talents. Before the story was published, a copy was delivered to Moore's campaign aides, who distributed it to all daily and weekly papers for simultaneous publication throughout the state.

The reporter never interviewed Sprouse or any of the owners, or the real estate agent handling the deal. Instead, accompanied by the Moore PR man, Mellace went to see the property, and placed an appraisal value of $1,000 an acre on an estimated 400 acres remaining in the plot. He arrived at that figure by asking a local motel owner his estimate, as well as a stranger he met in a grocery store while buying a Coke. A land staff officer at the Forest Service who had surveyed and appraised the Sprouse property reportedly showed Mellace land charts indicating that there were less than 100 acres in the parcel, worth no more than $50,000 total; but this was not included in Mellace's story.

Mellace acknowledged in court that the sale was completely legitimate. Mellace said there was never any concealment of the public records listing Sprouse as the land company's president, and admitted he had found nothing to indicate Sprouse and his partners had any inside tip about the Forest Service's plans. As for the $500,000 "bonanza," the remaining property later sold for $34,000, with Sprouse's share less than $14,000.

Sprouse lost the election by less than 10,000 votes. A jury awarded Sprouse $750,000. The State Supreme Court upheld the verdict but reduced the amount to $250,000.

Gossip, when checked out, plays an important role in all phases of news, not just investigative reporting. Some publications, of course, feature nothing but gossip.

[With a *Daily Mail* appeal], it is possible that the Supreme Court [would] find that Mellace's behavior did not meet the *Sullivan* test of recklessness. It is also possible that the Supreme Court will revise the test by making it negligence instead of recklessness. In other words, the test would become: Did the reporter exercise the care of a reasonably prudent man in carrying out the investigation that produced the story and did he have reasonable grounds for the allegations in his story, even if the allegations turn out to be untrue and defamatory? Whether the courts move towards this test or not—in the view of many libel lawyers, it, rather than recklessness, has been the test most consistently implied by the concepts of "abuse of privilege" and "actual malice"—it certainly should be the minimum test that each reporter and his editors bring to the decision of whether to publish a possibly defamatory story.

I believe there are two rules of thumb which reporters should employ in developing a story. The first is the rule of full disclosure. If the contents of a closed-door speech are so significant that a reporter must disguise himself to gain entry, or if a secret report involves such a crucial issue that the reporter is willing to steal a copy, then he and the paper should be willing to disclose the means by which they obtained it. Then the public will have the necessary data to decide for itself whether the reporter's calculation of ends and means was correct.

Rules of Thumb

The second rule of thumb is the natural companion of the first: the reporter must be willing to accept responsibility for his actions. Careless defamation should be recognized throughout the world of journalism as a firing offense. Too many reporters now think of themselves as virtuous Davids who can do no wrong bringing down overbearing Goliaths. They could turn the coming wave of investigative reporting into a nightmare.

Bibliography

Timothy Ingram's article expresses a concern about the quality of contemporary investigative journalism, a concern shared by many others in the profession. See the special section in *The Bulletin of the American Society of Newspaper Editors* (September 1975), Stephen Hartgen, "There's More Here Than Meets a Dragon's Eye," *The Quill* (April 1975), pp. 12–15, and an earlier article by Rudy Maxa, "Dealing in Sweet Secrets: News Leaks as a Way of Doing Business," *The Quill* (September 1974), pp. 18–21. Two excellent articles dealing with the methods and results of investigative reporting are Seymour M. Hersh, "The Story Everyone Ignored," *Columbia Journalism Review* (Winter 1969–70), pp. 55–58, which discusses the exposure and publicizing of the My Lai atrocities, and Barry Lando, "The Herbert Affair," *The Atlantic* (May 1973), pp. 73–81, which discusses Lando's efforts as Washington producer of CBS' *Sixty Minutes* to unravel Col. Anthony Herbert's charges of military war crimes in Vietnam. Read together they reveal a temptation which confronts all journalists, print or electronic; that is, the tendency to accept stories at face value if they fit the reporter's preconceptions. More recent items dealing with investigative journalism are Michael F. Wendland, *The Arizona Project: How a Team of Investigative Reporters Got Revenge on Deadline* (Sheed, Andrews & McMeel, 1977), which deals with journalistic efforts to find corruption in Arizona while attempting to find Don Bolles's murderer, and James H. Dygert, *The Investigative Journalist: Folk Heroes of a New Era* (Prentice-Hall, 1976), which offers sketches of many of the investigative journalists on the national scene as well as narrative of how they covered important stories. For a critical report on one journalist's news gathering practices, see an interview by Ken Auletta with Robert Scheer, "Bribe, Seduce, Lie, Steal: Anything to Get the Story?" *More* (March 1977), pp. 14–20.

28 The Joining of Journalists
Warren K. Agee

Warren Agee is a well known journalism educator, on the faculty of the University of Georgia. He is a prolific author of books and articles on media performance and journalism education. This information appeared in a special November 1978 edition of *Quill*, the journal of the Society of Professional Journalists. It is used with the permission of *Quill*.

Traditionally, journalists have not been joiners. To join is to make a commitment; to make a commitment is to compromise one's independence and credibility—or at the very least to *appear* to have done so. Newspeople, the conventional wisdom goes, belong and prefer to belong on the outside.

As far as professional journalism organizations are concerned, however, steadily increasing thousands of American journalists do not subscribe to that notion. So effective have these associations been in recent years in helping to pry open doors and records and so active (if not always successful) in combatting "gag" orders and defending journalists at every turn, that *not* to join in the fray seems to have become the exception, not the rule.

Since World War II, but particularly in the last decade, more than 40 new national journalism associations, centers and action groups have been founded. The ranks of these and older organizations continue to grow. Questionnaires were mailed in August to more than 100 national and regional organizations (yes, there *really* are that many) dedicated wholly or in part to advancing the cause of journalism as defined by The Society of Professional Journalists, Sigma Delta Chi:

"The direction of the editorial policy of, the editing of, the preparation of news and editorial content of newspapers, magazines, press or syndicate services, professional or business publications, radio and television; and the teaching of journalism so defined."

One fact clearly emerged: Almost every journalist in the country either is a member of one or more journalism associations or is represented by the organization for which he or she works. Generally, the managers fulfill institutional membership responsibilities and staff journalists belong to craft organizations. Thousands take part in local organizations not covered in a QUILL survey. The journalism organization story is told on the following pages. Professional journalism organizations have become tough in-fighters.

For three decades they've engaged in fierce slugging matches with all branches of government in most of the 50 states and in Washington. But their persistence and skill have paid off—in opening public meetings, records and courtrooms, and in fending off many actual and potentially repressive government assaults on freedom of the press.

At one time the organizations were known more for their social functions than their legal and public-opinion-marshaling prowess. "A jolly good bunch of fellows" is how a New York Times editor described one organization 20 years ago.

But all that has changed. Scarred by innumerable punches in congressional, executive, legislative, city council, county commissioner and courtroom brawls, the organizations have learned to fight together in the struggle for freedom of information—the proclaimed people's right to know.

Police barge into the Stanford Daily newsroom . . . New York Times reporter Myron Farber is given the choice of jail or disclosure of confidential sources . . . a Nebraska judge restricts coverage of a multiple-murder trial . . . the Senate ponders whether to give the United States the equivalent of the British Official Secrets Act. . . .

In these and countless other cases, a joint media committee springs into action.

It calls in the presidents or freedom of information chairmen of such organizations as The Society of Professional Journalists, Sigma Delta Chi; the American Society of Newspaper Editors; Associated Press Managing Editors Association; National Press Photographers Association; Radio Television News Directors Association; National Press Club; Women in Communications, Inc., and a potent relative newcomer, the Reporters Committee for Freedom of the Press. And powerpacked trade organizations such as the American Newspaper Publishers Association, National Newspaper Association and National Association of Broadcasters, as well.

A course of action is decided upon: lobbying, resolutions, amicus briefs; phone calls and personal appearances (President Ernie Schultz of the Radio Television News Directors Association made three trips to Washington during his term last year). Unremitting pressure and expressions of concern. News stories and editorials. Whatever it takes.

On the international front, a World Press Freedom Committee, directed by George Beebe of the Miami Herald, coordinates 32 free world organizations in such actions as the current effort to kill, delay or soften a UNESCO draft declaration that advocates state control of the media.

In communities and states throughout the United States, journalism groups have banded together to seek passage of sunshine laws, reach free press/fair trial agreements with the American Bar Association, open courtrooms to still photo and TV coverage (broadcasters are now covering trials in 15 states), urge passage of shield laws or strong working agreements with judges and lawyers, combat censorship measures and engage in other such action.

If journalists, indeed, have been essentially non-joiners, then the organized efforts in behalf of a free press should at least partially explain why membership and active participation in professional organizations have reached all-time highs. SPJ,SDX now has almost 300 chapters, many hard at work on freedom of information (FoI) causes; its membership has risen to 35,000. Membership in the Radio Television News Directors Association has leaped to 1,716—a gain of more than 80 percent in four years. And the National Press Photographers Association now claims 3,000 active, 2,000 associate and 1,000 student members.

Much progress has been made. Enactment of the Freedom of Information Act of 1966 and its amendment is another shining example. But disappointment also looms strong. Just ask past president Tom Frawley how he feels about RTNDA's and the National Association of Broadcasters' failure to gain First Amendment guarantees for broadcasting equal to that of print.

Even so, the record of accomplishment by journalism organizations is so stellar that it's difficult to recall the post-World War II years when governmental secrecy was the order of the day.

The struggle, with its year-by-year record of wins and losses, comes to vivid life when one reviews the annual convention proceedings of the American Society of Newspaper Editors, reads the annual FoI committee reports of SPJ,SDX, scans the annual Red Book chronicling the work of the Associated Press Managing Editors and talks with leaders of some of the organizations heavily involved.

The FoI movement received its impetus from the late Harold E. Cross. ASNE persuaded the New York City newspaper attorney and journalism school lecturer to leave near-retirement and pull together all the FoI legal and moral arguments into a book. His historically dynamic volume, "The People's Right to Know" (New York: Columbia University Press, 1953), provided the arguments needed to change repressive laws.

James S. Pope of the Louisville Courier-Journal, ASNE's FoI chairman in 1950–53, recalls that Cross' statement before the House Subcommittee on Governmental Information "accomplished for the fledgling freedom of information movement what the Declaration of Independence did for American freedom from foreign tyranny."

Said Cross: "This is not primarily a newspaper problem. My concern is with the people's right to know—the right of the congressional committee, the individual congressman, the citizen, the taxpayer, the inhabitant, the elector, the student and all others in a self-governing society. And, to put it bluntly but far from least, the right of Harold L. Cross to know."

Rep. John Moss (D-Calif.), chairman of the House subcommittee, spearheaded for many years congressional efforts to reduce secrecy in government.

Throughout most of the 1950s and early 1960s, the annual reports of the Sigma Delta Chi committee headed by V.M. (Red) Newton, then managing editor of the Tampa Tribune and SDX president in 1959–60, made front-page headlines. As chairman, Newton followed Charles Clayton, the Society's first committee head, and Norman Isaacs, now board chairman of the National News Council and a Columbia University lecturer. Isaacs' blistering report in 1951 attacked the fear of the military and "civilians in authority" in the government that "the public may come to know too much."

Sigma Delta Chi, sprung into action by its FoI fireball, Red Newton, and with continuing support along the way by other individuals and press groups, gained much success from the 1950s to the present, in the passage and preservation of open meetings and open records laws (45 states have enacted both). Unlike most other organizations, the Society's structure of local chapters and regional directorships has enabled it to operate more effectively on a grassroots level. In recent years, many chapters of what is now The Society of Professional

Journalists, Sigma Delta Chi, with financial aid from the Society's national coffers, have filed legal suits and taken other action in behalf of press freedom.

"The freedom of information battle has not been won, and the battle will never be finished," Richard Schmidt, legal counsel for the American Society of Newspaper Editors, has declared. But because journalism organizations and their allies—bolstered by a steady influx of combatant-minded new members—know how to fight, the right to report is closer to becoming a matter of course.

This is the decade of ethics and professionalism.

Standards of professional conduct have sprouted after the harsh winters of public distrust of all institutions—including the news media—that buffeted the nation during the Watergate era and which still largely persist.

Out of a Climate of Distrust Comes a Revival of Standards

Sensing the public mood, the Associated Press Managing Editors Association, even before Watergate, began to look at influences on the probity of the press. The report of the APME professional standards committee in 1972 was the first salvo in what turned out to be a barrage of attention to the problem of media ethics.

The APME sent Carol Sutton of the Louisville Courier-Journal to report on the extent of gratuities for the press during three fashion events in New York and Montreal. Two weeks later she returned with a new canvas suitcase full of what her newspaper colleagues termed "loot" and "goodies"—assorted cosmetics, jewelry, tote bags and useless oddities—along with a report of countless other gratuities offered at these events. She returned all the gifts she could and gave others to charity, in line with the Louisville newspapers' long-standing policy against the acceptance of gifts by staff members.

The Detroit News discovered that in 1972 at least $56,000 worth of free gifts and services were offered to its staff members. New York magazine reported on the receipt by news staffers in the city of free tickets to events at Madison Square Garden and the influence of public relations people with the New York Times.

The Public Relations Society of America cooperated in two surveys of its members. PRSA learned that executives of 21 newspapers accepted advertisements on condition that a staff member would write a feature story. Other respondents said they had been asked for special favors by newspaper people.

The model for modern-day codes of ethics is the Canons of Journalism established in 1922 by the American Society of Newspaper Editors. Accuracy, fair play and responsibility are its hallmarks.

The Society of Professional Journalists, Sigma Delta Chi in 1926 adopted the ASNE code as its own. Then, in 1973, SPJ,SDX broke new ground with the introduction of a new code of ethics. Two years later, APME and the National Conference of Editorial Writers adopted codes of their own. Other organizations either did likewise or took closer looks at standards they had previously established. In addition, more than 80 percent of the large newspapers spelled out rules of conduct for their staffs.

The foreword to the code of fair publishing practices adopted in 1955 by the Catholic Press Association points out that, "Like all promises, the code can be as effective as the will and determination of the members of the association make it. . . . But if it is not reaffirmed by practice and conduct it can become only an empty statement, a pledge ignored and a promise forgotten and broken. . . ." Moral law, it added, undergirds all such codes.

The code of the National Press Photographers Association affirms, in part, that, "It is the individual responsibility of every photojournalist at all times to strive for pictures that report truthfully, honestly and objectively." The code ends with the statement: "No code of ethics can prejudge every situation; thus common sense and good judgment are required in applying ethical principles."

The code adopted in 1966 by the Radio Television News Directors Association is regarded as much more stringent than the radio and television codes of the National Association of Broadcasters, which have been criticized as containing "weak, ambiguous, evasive and permissive language."

Enactment of codes has brought legal problems in some instances. In 1975, a National Labor Relations Board judge ruled that the Madison (Wis.) Capital Times committed an unfair labor practice when it imposed an ethics code without first bargaining with its employees. The NLRB later reversed the decision, ruling that newspapers do have the right to adopt ethics codes for reporters and editors without bargaining over their content with labor unions. Freebies, the board declared, were more comparable to improper gifts offered to policemen or politicians than to wages or tips. At least one other such case has been heard.

A study of journalists' opinions about freebies, conducted in 1976 by Keith P. Sanders and Won H. Chang of the University of Missouri School of Journalism, revealed "a strong regard for individual professionalism, a general distaste for freebies, a rejection of freebies as essential and a general support for the SPJ,SDX code of ethics."

The respondents rated highest the statement: "A professional journalist, secure in himself and his understanding of his public trust, will report honestly not because of a code, but because of what he is and believes."

In 1976, the APME's professional standards committee took a look at nearly 50 ethics codes adopted by individual newspapers. "None of the [survey] respondents expressed any negative thoughts about the wisdom of codes of ethics, either written or unwritten," the committee reported. "Most believe they are necessary to set a tone of behavior for all staffers while understanding that not every situation be specifically addressed in a code."

One managing editor expressed a reservation of sorts.

"Our code is rather weak," he wrote, "but it was the only one I could sail past my publisher, who, if given the opportunity, would be the first to accept a gift or trip. The guidelines in the newsroom do little for the newspaper when they are not a part of general company policy and they are disregarded in every other department."

Although some journalists and educators argue that codes are invalid, the fact is that most professional journalism organizations have adopted these codes and expect their members to live up to them. It is clear as more personal introspection comes into practice that only by subscribing to such guidelines will journalists help raise the level of public trust in the media.

Want help to move up in your field of journalism? Ample educational aid is available from dozens of professional and industry organizations, centers, institutes and foundations, The QUILL's survey has found.

The Ways for Advancing One's Education Are Many and Varied . . .

• General news work. The American Press Institute is holding 23 more seminars this year (an estimated 12,000 journalists have attended since 1946). The Washington Journalism Center holds four-day conferences for journalists on critical news issues each year (nearly 1,000 newspeople have participated). Women in Communications, Inc. and the National Federation of Press Women hold seminars providing continuing education credits. The Southern Newspaper Publishers Association sponsors 12 seminars a year. The Ford Foundation offers mid-career fellowships in specialized fields. Numerous other opportunities exist.

• News broadcasting. The Radio Television News Directors Association has a program of assistance for smallmarket news operations, as well as a range of workshops and seminars for all members.

• News photography. The National Press Photographers Association sends what it calls "flying short courses" into your area every year, holds seminars and workshops and lends learning aids.

• Investigative reporting. The Fund for Investigative Journalism offers grants to enable journalists to investigate abuses of authority or the malfunctioning of institutions and systems that harm the public. Investigative Reporters and Editors has a library of investigative stories and tapes, conducts national and regional conferences and publishes widely. The Reporters Committee for Freedom of the Press offers legal help to newspeople who encounter problems. If you're on the West Coast, try the Center for Investigative Reporting. Its methodology file of sources should expedite your work.

• International reporting. The Inter American Press Association provides at least 10 scholarships ($3,500) each year for North and Latin America journalists and students, as well as other awards and consultative help. The research section of the International Press Institute will provide, upon request, information on aspects of its special interests to print and broadcast journalists.

• Media management. The American Newspaper Publishers Association holds 42 conferences a year in this and other fields. The Modern Media Institute offers a two-week management program for young newspaper men and women. Many of the National Newspaper Association and Inland Daily Press Association workshops involve media management. The American Business Press holds seminars. The National Association of Broadcasters sponsors six conferences each fall for management and for managers of the future.

• Science writing. The Council for the Advancement of Science Writing sponsors writers-in-residence programs, trains minority journalists and provides other aids.

• Reporting on women's issues. The Women's Institute for Freedom of the Press is examining new criteria for defining "news" and offering a variety of services.

With such opportunities, and countless more, the spectre of job obsolescence should never haunt newspeople. Almost every organization contacted in The QUILL survey offers a helping hand for continuing education.

Ten to 12 journalists are selected each year for a mid-career sabbatical at Harvard University under Nieman Foundation sponsorship; more than 600 journalists have participated in the 40-year program.

Through year-long work by its standing committees, capped by workshops at an annual conference, the Associated Press Managing Editors Association keeps its members honed professionally.

Many media groups cooperate with journalism schools in providing conferences on almost every aspect of the news. And many, such as Gannett and Harte-Hanks, hold their own employee development programs.

There are more to come: the National Newspaper Publishers Association soon will offer development seminars and sabbaticals for staff members of its black newspapers. And the new Inland Daily Press Foundation plans an extensive program of seminars and workshops geared to editors and reporters of middle-sized newspapers.

Specialized groups such as the Music Critics Association, the Aviation/Space Writers Association and the American Agricultural Editors Association conduct forums and clinics.

. . .and There Is More Enrichment Waiting to Be Had

The number of scholarships and fellowships offered each year by U.S. journalism organizations has increased considerably during the past few years.

Professional associations and allied industry groups covered in The QUILL survey reported grants, available to students and working journalists, totaling more than a half-million dollars.

When grants offered by colleges and universities, the individual news media, foundations and other groups are included, the total financial aid available in 1978 for college students studying journalism or communications exceeds $2 million, The Newspaper Fund's Journalism Scholarship Guide reported.

Many organizations offer financial and other assistance, as well as awards to members and non-members. A parallel seems evident between the age of the organization and the number and value of the awards it bestows.

For example, The Society of Professional Journalists, Sigma Delta Chi, now in its seventh decade of service, recently added the $2,500 Barney Kilgore Award for an outstanding journalism senior, the $5,000 Eugene C. Pulliam Fellowship for Editorial Writers, and First Amendment awards in recognition of individuals and organizations whose efforts strengthen freedom of the press. These join the Society's long-standing distinguished journalistic performance and distinguished teaching awards to professionals and its performance awards and outstanding graduate citations for students.

For the first time, the American Society of Newspaper Editors will offer an award—for excellence in writing—in 1979. The Radio Television News Directors Association will increase, from four to five, the number of its annual $1,000 foundation scholarships for broadcast journalism students.

The National News Council recently instituted Matthew H. Fox Fellowships for first-year law (communications background) students, graduate journalism students, and juniors and seniors, enabling them to serve summer internships with the council.

The Overseas Press Club has begun granting awards of up to $2,000 annually to sons and daughters of foreign correspondents, a program administered by the Association for Education in Journalism.

Other established award programs include:

• The William J. Lookadon scholarship and Joseph Ehrenreich-NPPA awards to students by the National Press Photographers Association, along with its Sprague banquet and numerous contest awards.

• The Robert Eunson award for distinguished service offered by the Associated Press Broadcasters.

• The American Business Press' Neal awards for editorial excellence and Crain award for a distinguished editorial career.

• The $1,000 Heywood Broun award, bestowed by the Newspaper Guild, AFL-CIO,CLC, for an outstanding achievement in the spirit of the Guild's founder and first president.

• The Perley Isaac Reed citation for outstanding service, given to an individual or organization by the American Society of Journalism School Administrators.

• The Clarion, Headliner and distinguished service awards, awards of excellence and the $1,000 Jo Caldwell Meyer research grant, given by Women in Communications, Inc.

• The St. Francis de Sales award—a statuette—and about 50 awards to newspapers and magazines, given by the Catholic Press Association.

• These awards are only a few of the scores of grants and honors.

National awards often are augmented by state and local grants. WICI chapters, for example, bestow more than $30,000 in awards annually. Many of the almost 300 SPJ,SDX chapters conduct awards programs, one of the largest being the $9,000 in scholarship aid given each year by the Fort Worth chapter through its Texas Gridiron Club, Inc.

What does it cost in annual dues to belong to a national or regional journalism organization?

So What Does It Cost to Join Up and What Else Does One Get in Return?

If you cover football, you can join the Football Writers Association of America for only $7.50—the lowest annual dues reported in the QUILL survey.

If you're a cartoonist living in the New York metropolitan area, you'll pay $75 to maintain membership in the National Cartoonists Society; and if you reside elsewhere, only $35.

But if you're a broadcast news manager or staff member at a station where 25 or more newspeople work, you'll pay the stiffest active-member dues of any professional group—$125—to belong to the Radio Television News Directors Association. The smaller the station, the less you pay: $95 if your news staff numbers 5 to 24, $30 if only 1 to 4 persons work there.

Dues for publications and broadcast stations vary widely. If yours is one of the 3,400 stations that automatically are members of the Associated Press Broadcasters, your station has no dues to pay. But if yours is a large newspaper, annual dues could run up to thousands of dollars. The Southern Newspaper Publishers Association reports that its member papers pay 1.2 cents per copy of paid net daily circulation. Dues of the Suburban Newspapers of America, Inc. range from $150 to $1,500.

A number of the professional organizations scale down their dues charges for personal associate and honorary members, but make up for it in charges to associate organizations that profit by being members. The Society of American Travel Writers, for example, bills its 340 members $50 each but nicks its 320 associate members $90.

Without multiplying and adding, an observer can quickly surmise that millions of dollars in dues payments are made annually to journalism organizations. Many groups obtain additional income from member initiation fees, convention exhibits, sales of publications and services, bequests and contributions from foundations and individuals.

What does the member get in return?

Membership development programs, publications, research reports, library services, conventions, exhibits, workshops, clinics, special travel opportunities, insurance benefits, mid-career opportunities, representation in freedom of information and other professional matters, legal and professional advice, participation in fund-raising activities to provide financial aid for beginning journalists and the opportunity for peer recognition, awards and fellowship—in some organizations, a multitude of these and other services.

And it's all tax deductible.

The Organizational Baby Boom Began 40 Years Ago and It's Still With Us

Professional journalism associations are a 20th century phenomenon in America.

Only trade organizations existed before 1908. They were the National Newspaper Association, founded in 1885; the Inland Daily Newspaper Association and American Newspaper Publishers Association, 1887; Southern Newspaper Publishers Association, 1903; American Business Press, 1906.

Newspaper editors, however, fretting over the increasingly heavy business emphasis of newspaper organizations, founded the American Society of Newspaper Editors in 1922 in order to exchange ideas and advance professional ideals. Their banner, the Canons of Journalism, was formulated a year later.

Managing editors of Associated Press member newspapers followed suit in 1933—the same year the Newspaper Guild was organized.

The Depression and World War II slowed the professional journalism movement. In 1946, however, both the National Press Photographers Association and the Radio Television News Directors Association were founded, followed a year later by the National Conference of Editorial Writers.

A burst of zeal in spreading press freedom around the world resulted, during World War II years, in formation of the Inter American Press Association (1942), Inter-American Association of Broadcasters (1946). International Federation of Newspaper Publishers (1948) and International Press Institute (1950).

The organizational rush was on. Since then, more than twice as many national and regional journalism groups have been founded than existed prior to that time.

During its early years, the professional journalism movement was strongly aided by educators in colleges and high schools. Kappa Tau Alpha was organized in 1910 to recognize journalism scholarship and research. In 1912, university professors founded the American Association of Teachers of Journalism, reorganized in 1949 as the Association for Education in Journalism.

Educators in major journalism schools founded the American Association of Schools and Departments of Journalism in 1917. Decades of work with professional and industry groups resulted in the incorporation, in 1946, of the American Council on Education for Journalism, the accrediting agency in journalism and mass communications.

Lending additional support to the movement during its early years were two professional journalism fraternities, Sigma Delta Chi for men and Theta Sigma Phi for women. Founded on separate college campuses in 1909, the two groups soon established professional chapters in major cities.

Organizations for specialized reporters and writers got an early start with the organization in 1908 of the Baseball Writers Association of America, founded to improve the quality of reporting, insure proper facilities for the reporting of baseball games and clarify scoring rules.

Writers of outdoor recreational activities banded together in 1927. Real estate editors organized the following year. An avowed purpose of these and later craft groups—constituting the largest category of any of the organizations—is the promotion of high ethical standards among members.

Foundation support of journalism has increased substantially during the last decade or so, particularly with the formation of numerous organization and media foundations. Among the earliest, the John and Mary R. Markle Foundation (1927) is undergirding numerous media projects. The Frank E. Gannett Foundation (1935) is providing grants to advance journalism education and professionalism. And the Nieman Foundation (1937) continues to send 10 to 12 journalists to Harvard University for study each year.

The predominant trend among organizations during the last decade has been the establishment of numerous centers, institutes and action groups. These groups are providing legal and other aid for investigative journalists, prodding print and broadcast media to improve their accuracy, advancing the cause of female journalists and teachers, helping high school pupils in press freedom causes, bolstering press freedom throughout the world, and providing a mechanism for the airing of complaints against major media organizations.

29 The New Journalism: How It Came to Be
Everette E. Dennis

Everette E. Dennis is on the faculty of the School of Journalism and Mass Communication, University of Minnesota. He is co-author with William L. Rivers of *Other Voices: The New Journalism in America,* 1974, co-editor of *New Strategies for Public Affairs Reporting,* 1976, and editor of *The Magic Writing Machine,* 1971, from which this selection was taken. Permission to reprint was granted by the School of Journalism, University of Oregon.

It was a time when old values were breaking down; new knowledge exploded all around us; people worried about drugs, hippies, and war. We talked of violence, urban disorder, turmoil. New terms like polarization, credibility gap and counter-culture crept into the language. It was during *this* time, somewhere between 1960 and 1970, that the term "new journalism" also began to appear in the popular press. Almost as rapidly as the term became a descriptive link in the vernacular, it was used and misused in so many contexts that its meaning was obscured. First accepted and used by its practitioners, the term found its way into older, more established publications by the mid-Sixties. *Time* called former newsman-turned author Tom Wolfe "the *wunderkind* of the new journalism," while *Editor & Publisher* described Nicholas von Hoffman of the *Washington Post* as an "exponent of the new journalism." And there were others: Lillian Ross, Jimmy Breslin, Norman Mailer, Truman Capote, Gay Talese, and Pete Hamill, all were designated "new journalists" by one medium or another. At the same time a number of different forms of communication, from nonfiction novels to the underground press, were being labeled "new journalism."

By 1970 few terms had wider currency and less uniformity of meaning than new journalism. Yet one wonders whether this curious mix of people, philosophies, forms and publications has any common purpose or meaning. To some the term had a narrow connotation, referring simply to a new form of nonfiction that was using fiction methods. Other critics were just as certain that new journalism was an emerging form of advocacy in newspapers and magazines which previously had urged a kind of clinical objectivity in reporting the news. Soon anything slightly at variance with the most traditional practices of the conventional media was cast into the new journalism category.

While the debate over definition droned on, it began to obscure any real meaning the term "new journalism" ever had. The scope and application of new journalism was not the only point of contention, though. Some critics looked peevishly at the jumble of writers, styles, and publications and suggested that "there is really nothing very new about the new journalism."

And it was true. One could trace every form and application of the new journalism to an antecedent somewhere, sometime. The underground press, for example, was said to be a twentieth century recurrence of the political pamphleteering of the colonial period. "And isn't the alternative press simply muckraking in new dress?" And on it went.

Although much of the criticism of new journalism has concentrated, unproductively I believe, on whether or not it is new, no attempt will be made here to resolve this question. Perhaps we should think of the new journalism as we do the New Deal or the New Frontier. No one argues that using these terms means one believes there was never before a deal or a frontier. So it is with the new journalism.

What began as a descriptive term for a kind of nonfiction magazine article has been mentioned previously. As one who is viewing these journalistic developments I know that a number of dissimilar forms are called "new journalism." This is the reality of the situation. I will not argue with this commonly used and loosely-constructed definition of new journalism, but will look instead at its various forms, outlets, content and practitioners. Much of what is regarded as new journalism can be judged only by the most personal of standards. It is, after all, a creative endeavor of people seeking alternatives to the tedium of conventional media.

Carl Sandberg used to say every generation wants to assert its uniqueness by crying out, "We are the greatest city, the greatest nation, nothing like us ever was." If this is so, one might conclude that every generation will have its own "new journalism" or at least that it will regard its journalistic products as new. Creative journalists have always tried to improve upon existing practices in writing and gathering news. The history of journalism chronicles their efforts. But even when one accepts the notion of each generation having its own new journalism, the decade of the Sixties still stands out as an unusually productive and innovative period.

> Magazines and newspapers, having felt the harsh competitive challenge of the electronic media, realized that the public no longer relied upon them for much entertainment in the form of short stories and longer fiction. As the public demanded something new, the *new nonfiction,* an attempt to enliven the traditional magazine article with descriptive detail and life-like dialog, emerged.
>
> Newsmen who tired of the corporate bigness of metropolitan dailies and their unwillingness to challenge establishment institutions, founded their own papers. We will, they said, offer an *alternative* to traditional journalism, the chain papers and their plastic personnel.
>
> Other newsmen, who stayed with the conventional papers, were arguing against the notions of balanced news, objectivity, and stodgy use of traditional sources of news. They sought and were granted opportunities for open *advocacy* in the news columns.
>
> The alienated young constructed a counter-culture which would reject most of the underlying assumptions of traditional society. Needing communications media that were equally alienated from the straight world, they created the *underground* press which was, as one writer said, "like a tidal wave of sperm rushing into a nunnery."
>
> Still other journalists found the impressionistic newsgathering methods of the media to be crude and unreliable measures. They would apply the scientific method and the tools of survey research to journalism, thus seeking a *precision* before unknown in media practice.

Any look back at the Sixties and the swirl of journalistic activity has the appearance of a confused collage of verbal and visual combatants, seeking change in the *status quo* but not knowing quite what or where in all that was happening; a concern for form, for style often seemed to supersede content. John Corry, who worked with the *New York Times* and *Harper's* during this period, offers this recollection:

> It happened sometime in the early 1960's and although no one can say exactly when, it may have begun in that magic moment when Robert Frost, who always looked marvelous, with silver hair, and deep, deep lines in his face, read a poem at the inauguration of John F. Kennedy, and then went on to tell him afterwards that he ought to be more Irish than Harvard, which was something that sounded a lot better than it actually was. Hardly a man today remembers the poem, which was indifferent, anyway, but nearly everyone remembers Frost, or at least the sight of him at the lectern, which was perhaps the first sign that from then on it would not matter so much what you said, but how you said it.

With similar emphasis on form, Tom Wolfe recalls his first encounter with the new journalism: "The first time I realized there was something new going on in journalism was one day in 1962 when I pick up a copy of *Esquire* and read an article by Gay Talese entitled 'Joe Louis at Fifty.' "[1] Wolfe continues, " 'Joe Louis at Fifty' wasn't like a magazine article at all. It was like a short story. It began with a scene, an intimate confrontation between Louis and his third wife:

> 'Hi, sweetheart!' Joe Louis called to his wife, spotting her waiting for him at the Los Angeles airport.
> She smiled, walked toward him, and was about to stretch up on her toes and kiss him—but suddenly stopped.
> 'Joe,' she snapped, 'where's your tie?'
> 'Aw, sweetie,' Joe Louis said, shrugging. 'I stayed out all night in New York and didn't have time.'
> 'All night!' she cut in. 'When you're out here with me all you do is sleep, sleep, sleep.'
> 'Sweetie,' Joe Louis said with a tired grin, 'I'm an ole man.'
> 'Yes,' she agreed, 'but when you go to New York you try to be young again.'

Says Wolfe, "The story went on like that, scene after scene, building up a picture of an ex-sports hero now fifty years old."

Talese, who gained little recognition until the late Sixties, in the introduction to *Fame and Obscurity* cautions those who deceptively regard the new journalism as fiction:

"It is, or should be, as reliable as the most reliable reportage although it seeks a larger truth than is possible through the mere compilation of verifiable facts, the use of direct quotations, and adherence to the rigid organizational style of the older form."

1. Wolfe's memory betrayed him. The correct citation is Gay Talese, "Joe Louis—The King as a Middle-Aged Man," *Esquire*, June, 1962. Ed.

To Talese the new journalism "allows, demands in fact, a more imaginative approach to reporting, and it permits the writer to inject himself into the narrative if he wishes, as many writers do, or to assume the role of detached observer, as other writers do, including myself."

In the search for a definition of new journalism, Tom Wolfe explains "it is the use by people writing nonfiction of techniques which heretofore had been thought of as confined to the novel or the short story, to create in one form both the kind of objective reality of journalism and the subjective reality that people have always gone to the novel for." Dwight MacDonald, one of Wolfe's severest critics, disagrees, calling the new journalism "parajournalism," which he says, "seems to be journalism—the collection and dissemination of current news—but the appearance is deceptive. It is a bastard form having it both ways, exploiting the factual authority of journalism and the atmospheric license of fiction. Entertainment rather than information is the aim of its producers, and the hope of its consumers."

Dan Wakefield finds middle ground suggesting that writers like Wolfe and Truman Capote have "catapulted the reportorial kind of writing to a level of social interest suitable for cocktail party conversation and little-review comment. . . ." He continues:

> Such reporting is "imaginative" not because the author has distorted the facts, but because he has presented them in a full instead of a naked manner, brought sight, sounds and feel surrounding those facts, and connected them by comparison with other facts of history, society and literature in an artistic manner that does not diminish, but gives greater depth and dimension to the facts.

Each of the other forms of new journalism mentioned previously (alternative, advocacy, underground and precision) have also sparked vigorous criticism, related both to their content and their form. If there is one consistent theme in all the criticism, it is probably the McLuhanistic "form supersedes content." The real innovative contribution of the new journalism has been stylistic. This theme will be expanded later as we examine examples of new journalism.

The theory of causality is of little use in chronicling the development of new journalism. Most of the innovations in form and approach have occurred simultaneously. Some were related to each other; some were not. The new journalism is an apparent trend in American journalism which involves a new form of expression, new writers and media, or an alteration in the patterns of traditional media. It has been suggested that this trend can be traced to the early 1960's and is related to (a) sociocultural change during the last decade, (b) a desire by writers and editors to find an alternative to conventional journalism, and (c) technological innovations such as electronic media, computer hardware and offset lithography.

Rarely has any decade in American history seen such drastic upheaval. Beyond the immediate surface events—rioting, student unrest, assassinations, and war—lies a pervasive youthful alienation from traditional society and the beginnings of a radical rejection of science and technology. Calls for a new humanism were heard. Young people, rejecting the materialistic good life, sought new meaning through introspection, drugs, and religion. The decade witnessed the beginnings of what some would call a counter culture: "a culture so radically disaffiliated from the mainstream assumptions of our society that it scarcely looks to many as a culture at all, but takes on the alarming appearance of a barbaric intrusion."

The new journalism, especially the new nonfiction and the writing of underground editors, seemed to respond to youthful needs. The practitioners of reportage attempted to bring all of the senses to bear in their journalistic product—with special attention to visual imagery. Thus Norman Mailer gave us sight, sound, and inner thoughts as he sloshed through great public events, and issues. It is probably too early to determine how much the social upheaval and its resulting influence on the young affected the organizational and perceptual base that the new journalists would use. Writers like Jimmy Breslin and Studs Terkel would go to the periphery of an event, calling on a spectator instead of a participant to summarize the action. Tom Wolfe thought the automobile and the motorcycle were better organizing principles than war or race relations. Ken Kesey, the central figure in Wolfe's *The Electric Kool-Aid Acid Test,* introduces the reader to the Age of Acid, while a small town in western Kansas is a vehicle with which Truman Capote orchestrates a nonfiction novel about violent crime and its effects.

Journalism would also be influenced by television. Technological change in communications has always meant new functions for existing media. With television bringing electronic entertainment into our homes, we had less need for the *Saturday Evening Post's* short stories. The ratio of fiction to nonfiction in magazines would change as would the nature of the package of the newspaper. The days when newspapers serialized books blended into the distant past. Even the traditional comic strip seems at times to be threatened. Television changed the programming habits of radio, just as it changed magazines and newspapers.

The technological innovation of greatest importance to the new journalism was probably offset printing. It suddenly became possible to produce a newspaper cheaply, without having to invest in typesetting equipment or presses. The rapid reproduction of photo-offset meant that a single printer could produce dozens of small newspapers and that the alternative or underground paper could be produced rapidly at limited cost. Offset also allowed for the inclusion of freehand art work without expensive engravings, thus permitting efforts of psychedelic artists to merge with the underground journalists.

Although "new journalism" is used most often to describe a style of nonfiction writing, the definition has been further expanded to include alternative journalism and advocacy journalism. Although the reiteration of these terms may be following the fads, they do provide some shades of meaning which contribute to an understanding of the richly expansive scope of new journalism.

A Schematic Look at the New Journalism

Form	Medium	Content	Practitioners
The new nonfiction, also called reportage and parajournalism	Newspaper columns; books; magazine articles	Social trends; celebrity pieces; the "little people"; public events	Tom Wolfe, Jimmy Breslin, Gay Talese, Norman Mailer, Truman Capote, others.
Alternative journalism, also called "modern muckraking"	Alternative newspapers; new magazines	Exposes of wrongdoing in establishment organizations; attacks on bigness of institutions	Editor and writers for *San Francisco Bay Guardian, Cervi's Journal, Maine Times, Village Voice.*
Advocacy journalism	Newspaper columns; point-of-view papers; magazines	Social change; politics; public issues	*Jack Newfield, Pete Hamill, Nicholas von Hoffman, others.*
Underground journalism	Underground papers in urban areas, at universities, high schools, military bases	Radical politics; psychedelic art; the drug culture; social services; protest	Editors and writers for LA, New York, and Washington *Free Presses, Berkeley Barb, East Village Other,* many others.
Precision journalism	Newspapers; magazines	Survey research and reporting of social indicators, public concerns	Editors and writers the Knight Newspapers, other newspapers, news magazines.

These descriptive categories are offered more as a tool for analysis than a definite up-to-the-minute classification of the rapidly proliferating output of the new journalists. Through an examination of a few of these new journalistic developments it is hoped that there will be fuller appreciation and awareness of what may be an important trend in the evolution of the mass media.

In the early 1960's it occurred to Truman Capote, who already had a reputation as a writer of fiction, that "reportage is the great unexplored art form." While it was a metier used by very few good writers or craftsmen, Capote reasoned

Reportage

that it would have "a double effect fiction does not have—the fact of it being true, every word of it true, would add a double contribution of strength and impact." Some years after Lillian Ross used a nonfiction reportage form in the *New Yorker,* Capote and other writers had experimented with reportage in magazine articles. *Picture* (1952), a nonfiction novel by Miss Ross, had been hailed as a literary innovation. "It is," one critic said, "the first piece of factual reporting to be written in the form of a novel. Miss Ross' story contains all the raw materials of dramatic fiction: the Hollywood milieu, the great director, the producer, the studio production chief and the performers." Another of the new nonfiction reportage innovators was Gay Talese, whose articles in *Esquire* "adapted the more dramatic and immediate technique of the short story to the magazine article," according to Tom Wolfe. Wolfe says it was Talese's "Joe Louis at Fifty" that first awakened him to the creative potential of reportage.

Some of the best early examples of the new nonfiction, in addition to the writing of Miss Ross and Talese, are articles by Wolfe collected in an anthology with an unlikely title: *The Kandy-Kolored Tangerine Flake Streamline Baby* (1965). Wolfe, like Talese, used scenes, extended dialog, and point of view. A few years later Wolfe described this period of his life as a time when he broke out of the totem format of newspapers. He had worked as a reporter for the *Washington Post* and *New York Herald Tribune* but later found magazines and books a better outlet for his creative energies. Another new journalist, Jimmy Breslin, was able to practice the new journalism in a daily newspaper column. Breslin, whom Wolfe calls "a brawling Irishman who seemed to come from out of nowhere," is a former sportswriter who began using a reportage style in a column he wrote for the *New York Herald Tribune.* Breslin breathed life into an amazing assortment of characters like Fat Thomas (an overweight bookie) and Marvin the Torch (an arsonist with a sense of professionalism). Breslin met many of his characters in bars and demonstrated conclusively that the "little people of the street" (and some not so little) could say eloquent things about their lives and the state of the world. More important, Breslin brought the expectations and intuitions of these people to his readers in vivid, almost poetic style. In doing so, he as much as anyone else added the nonauthority as a source of information to the concept of new journalism.

Truman Capote tried the experimental reportage form on two articles in the *New Yorker* (one on the "Porgy and Bess" tour of Russia and the other on Marlon Brando) before writing his powerful *In Cold Blood* (1966). As Capote describes it: "I realized that perhaps a crime, after all, would be the ideal subject for a massive job of reportage I wanted to do. I would have a wide range of characters, and more importantly, it would be timeless." It took Capote nearly seven years to finish the book which he himself described as "a new art form."

Contributing yet another variation on the new nonfiction theme during the 1960's was Norman Mailer, who like Capote, had already established himself as an important fiction writer. To new journalism reportage Mailer contributed a first-person autobiographical approach. In *Armies of the Night* (1968), an account of a peace march on the Pentagon, Mailer ingeniously got inside his own head and presented the reader with a vivid description of his own perceptions and thoughts, contrasting them with his actions. This was a variation on the approach Talese had used earlier in describing the thoughts of persons featured in his articles and books. He called this description of one's inner secrets "interior monolog."

Examples of nonfiction reportage, in addition to those previously mentioned are: Breslin's *The World of Jimmy Breslin* (1968), Miss Ross' *Reporting* (1964), Talese's *The Kingdom and the Power* (1969), and *Fame and Obscurity* (1970), Wolfe's *Electric Kool-Aid Acid Test* (1969), *The Pump House Gang* (1969), and *Radical Chic and Mau-mauing the Flak Catchers* (1970). Frequent examples of new nonfiction reportage appear in *Esquire, New York* and other magazines.

While Tom Wolfe would like to keep the new journalism pure and free from moralism, political apologies and romantic essays, increasingly the term "new journalism" has been broadened to include the alternative journalists. Most alternative journalists began their careers with a conventional newspaper or magazine but became disillusioned because the metropolitan paper often got too big to be responsive to the individual. Certain industries or politicians become sacred cows, the paper gets comfortable and is spoiled by economic success. At least this was the view of one of the most vigorous of alternative journalists, the late Eugene Cervi of Denver. In describing *Cervi's Rocky Mountain Journal,* he said,

Alternative Journalism

> We are what a newspaper is supposed to be: controversial, disagreeable, disruptive, unpleasant, unfriendly to concentrated power and suspicious of privately-owned utilities that use the power with which I endow them to beat me over the head politically.

Alternative journalism is a return to personal journalism where the editor and/or a small staff act as a watchdog on conventional media, keeping them honest by covering stories they would not have touched. The alternative journalists are in the reform tradition. They do not advocate the elimination of traditional social, political, or economic institutions. In their view the institutions are all right, but those who run them need closer scrutiny.

Little has been written about the contribution of the alternative journalists who have established newspapers, newsletters, and magazines which attempt to provide an alternative to conventional media. "The traditional media simply are not covering the news," says Bruce Brugmann, editor of San Francisco's crusading *Bay Guardian.* Brugmann, a former reporter for the *Milwaukee Journal,* asserts that the kind of material produced by his monthly tabloid is "good, solid investigatory journalism." The *Bay Guardian* has been a gadfly for San Francisco, attacking power companies, railroads, and other establishment interests.

One crusade of long standing is a probe with continuity of the communications empire of the *San Francisco Chronicle,* which Brugmann calls "Superchron." The *Bay Guardian* is a lively tabloid with bold, striking headlines and illustrative drawings which are actually editorial cartoons. *Cervi's Journal,* for years a scrapping one-man operation, is being continued by the late founder's daughter. Cervi, sometimes called the La Guardia of the Rockies, was a volatile, shrill, and colorful man who, while providing news of record to Denver's business community (mortgages, bankruptcies, etc.), fearlessly attacked public and private wrongdoing. *Cervi's Journal* has taken on the police, local government, business, and other interests. Unlike the *Bay Guardian,* which has been in financial trouble almost since its founding, *Cervi's Journal* seems to have found a formula for financial success.

Other publications operating in an alternative-muckraking style are *The Texas Observer* in Austin, *I.F. Stone's Bi-Weekly* in Washington, D.C., [Stone retired and closed his publication] Roldo Bartimole's *Point of View* in Cleveland, and the *Village Voice* in New York City. All of these publications (including the *Village Voice,* which began as an early underground paper in 1955), are read by a middle and upper-middle class audience, although all espouse a decidedly left-of-center position on social and political issues. Brugmann and several of his fellow alternative editors agree that their function is to make the establishment press more responsible. While conveying a sense of faith in the system, the alternative press has little tolerance for abuse or misuse of power.

Also a part of alternative journalism are a little band of iconoclastic trade publications—the journalism reviews. Shortly after the Democratic National Convention of 1968 when newsmen and students were beaten by police in the streets of Chicago, a number of working journalists organized the abrasive *Chicago Journalism Review,* which confines most of its barbs to the performance of the news media in Chicago. Occasionally, other stories are featured, but usually because one of the Chicago dailies or television stations refused to run the story first. The journalism reviews are perhaps the most credible instrument of a growing inclination toward media criticism. The writers and editors of the reviews continue as practicing reporters for traditional media, at times almost daring their bosses to fire them for revealing confidences and telling stories out of school. Other press criticism organs include *The Last Post* in Montreal, the *St. Louis Journalism Review,* and *The Unsatisfied Man: A Review of Colorado Journalism,* published in Denver. [See bibliographical notes to James Carey's article in Chapter 2.]

A talk with the editors of the various alternative press outlets makes one wonder whether they wouldn't secretly like to put themselves out of business. As Brugmann puts it: "In Milwaukee, a *Bay Gurardian* type of publication could never make it because the Milwaukee *Journal* does an adequate job of investigative reporting." Perhaps if the San Francisco media had such a record, the *Bay Guardian* would cease to exist.

The alternative journalist sees himself as an investigative reporter, sifting through each story, reaching an independent conclusion. He does not openly profess a particular point of view, but claims a more neutral ground. The advocacy journalist, on the other hand, writes with an unabashed commitment to a particular viewpoint. He may be a New Left enthusiast, a professed radical, conservative, Women's libber or Jesus freak. The advocacy journalist defines his bias and casts his analysis of the news in that context. Advocacy journalists, usually though not always, suggest a remedy for the social ill they are exposing. This is rarely the case with the alternative journalist who does not see the development of action programs as his function.

Advocacy Journalism

Clayton Kirkpatrick of the *Chicago Tribune* says advocacy journalism is really "the new propaganda." He continues, "Appreciation of the power of information to persuade and convince has been blighted by preoccupation and is a primary influence in the activist movement that started in Europe and is now spreading to the United States. It threatens . . . a revolution in the newsroom." John Corry, writing in *Harper's* says, "the most important thing in advocacy journalism is neither how well you write or how well you report, but what your position in life is. . ." Corry sees advocacy journalists as persons who are not concerned about what they say, but how they say it. The advocacy journalists "write mostly about themselves, although sometimes they write about each other, and about how they all feel about things," Corry says.

Advocacy journalism is simply a reporter expressing his personal view in a story. "Let's face it," says Jack Newfield of the *Village Voice*, "the old journalism was blind to an important part of the truth . . . it had a built-in bias in its presentation: Tom Hayden *alleges*, while John Mitchell *announces*." In the old journalism, Newfield continues, "authority always came first. The burden of proof was always on minorities; individuals never get the emphasis that authorities get." Central to advocacy journalism is involvement. Writers like Newfield, who is an avowed New Leftist, are participants in the events they witness and write about. They debunk traditional journalism's concern about objectivity. "The Five W's, Who Needs Them!" declares an article by Nicholas von Hoffman of the *Washington Post*. Von Hoffman, a community organizer for Saul Alinsky's Industrial Areas Foundation in Chicago before joining the *Chicago Daily News,* has established a reputation as an advocacy journalist who shoots from the hip and calls shots as he sees them, according to *Newsweek*. His coverage of the celebrated 1970 Chicago conspiracy trial likened the courtroom and its participants to a theatrical production. Von Hoffman produces a thrice-weekly column, "Poster," which is syndicated by the *Washington Post-Los Angeles Times* News Service. In his search for advocacy outlets, Von Hoffman has written several books: *Mississippi Notebook* (1964), *The Multiversity* (1966), *We Are The People Our Parents Warned Us Against* (1968), and a collection of his newspaper columns, *Left at the Post* (1970).

Jack Newfield, who writes regularly in *New York* as well as in the *Village Voice,* has produced *A Prophetic Minority* (1966), and *Robert Kennedy: A*

Memoir (1969), said to be the most passionate and penetrating account of the late Senator's life. Another of the advocacy journalists is Pete Hamill of the *New York Post*. Hamill, who seems at times to wear his heart on his sleeve, writes about politics, community problems, and social issues for the *Post* and a variety of magazines ranging from *Life* to *Ladies Home Journal*. He also writes regularly for *New York* where his concern for the unique problems of urban crowding show through in articles like "Brooklyn: A Sane Alternative."

Publications such as *Ramparts* and *Scanlan's* are examples of advocacy journalism. The *Village Voice* seems to fit into both the alternative and advocacy categories as do a number of other publications. Many of the social movements of the recent past and present needed organs of communication to promote their causes. Thus Young Americans For Freedom established what is regarded as a new right publication, *Right-On*. Jesus freaks have a publication with the same name. The Women's Liberation movement has spawned a number of newspapers and magazines. Ecology buffs also have their own publications as do the Black Panthers and other groups too numerous to mention.

The Underground Press

While the literature about underground journalism is growing rapidly—even in such staid publications as *Fortune*—a clarifying definition is rarely offered. Underground journalism has its psycho-social underpinnings in the urban/university counter-culture communities of the 1960's. The underground newspaper is a communications medium for young people who are seeking alternative life styles. Often these persons feel alienated from the message of conventional media. The *Los Angeles Free Press* is regarded as the first underground. Editor Arthur Kunkin explains, "the underground press is do-it-yourself journalism. The basis for the new journalism is a new audience. People are not getting the information they desired from the existing media. The LA *Free Press* is aimed at the young, Blacks, Mexicans and intellectuals." Kunkin says his paper is open to "anyone who can write in a comprehensible manner." He believes the underground press serves as a "mass opposition party." He urges his contributors to "write with passion, show the reader your style, your prejudice." [Kunkin no longer edits the *Free Press*.]

Some critics, however, are not as generous in their descriptions of underground journalism. Dave Sanford, writing in *New Republic* said:

> There is nothing very underground about the underground press. The newspapers are hawked on street corners, sent to subscribers without incident through the U.S. mails, carefully culled and adored by the mass media. About three dozen of them belong to the Underground Press Syndicate, which is something like the AP on a small scale; through this network they spread the word about what is new in disruptive protest, drugs, sex. Their obsessive interest in things that the "straights" are embarrassed or offended by is perhaps what makes them underground. They are a place to find what is unfit to print in the *New York Times*.

Early examples of the underground press were the *East Village Other,* published in Manhattan's East Village, not far from that latter-day Bohemian, the *Village Voice,* the *Chicago Seed, Berkeley Barb, Washington Free Press,* and others. The undergrounds are almost always printed by offset. This "takes the printing out of the hands of the technicians," says editor Kunkin, a former tool and die maker. The undergrounds use a blend of type and free hand art work throughout. They are a kind of collage for the artist-intellectual, some editors believe. The content of the undergrounds ranges from political and artistic concerns (especially an establishment v. the oppressed theme), sexual freedom, drugs, and social services. Much of their external content (that not written by the staff and contributors) comes from the Underground Press Syndicate and Liberation News Service.

In addition to the larger and better known undergrounds, there are underground papers in almost every sizable university community in the country. Most large cities have a number of undergrounds serving hippies and heads in the counter-culture community. Newer additions to the underground are the high school undergrounds and the underground newspapers published on and adjacent to military bases, both in the U.S. and abroad. Some critics foresee the end of the underground press, but the larger undergrounds are now lucrative properties. This, of course, raises another question about how long a paper can stay underground. Can a paper like the *Los Angeles Free Press* with a circulation of 90,000 stay underground? When does an underground paper become a conventional paper? These are among the many unresolved questions about the underground press. The undergrounds have been called the most exciting reading in America. Even David Sanford reluctantly agrees: "at least they try—by saying what can't be said or isn't being said by the staid daily press, by staying on the cutting edge of 'In' for an audience with the shortest of attention spans."

Precision Journalism

Perhaps the persons least likely to be classified as new journalists are the precision journalists, yet they may be more a part of the future than any of their colleagues in the new journalism ranks. Richard Scammon and Ben Wattenberg, authors of *The Real Majority,* a 1970 analysis of the American electorate, declare: "we are really the new journalists." They are concerned with an analysis of people that is as precise as possible. Or, at least as precise as the social survey research method allows. These men try to interpret social indicators and trends in prose that will attract the reader and are doing something quite new in journalism.

A leading practitioner of precision journalism is Philip Meyer, a Washington editor for the Knight Newspapers. Meyer, who has written a book which calls for application of behavioral science methodology in the practice of journalism, conducted a much-praised study of Detroit Negroes after the 1967 riot. Meyer and his survey team interviewed hundreds of citizens of Detroit to probe the reasons behind the disorder. His study, *Return to 12th Street,* was one of the few examples of race relations reporting praised by the Kerner Commission. Meyer is a prolific writer with recent articles in publications ranging from *Public*

Opinion Quarterly to *Esquire*. Whenever possible he uses the methods of survey research, combined with depth interviews to analyze a political or social situation. For example, early in 1970 a series of articles about the Berkeley rebels of 1964 appeared in the *Miami Herald* and other Knight newspapers. An editor's note explained the precisionist's approach:

> What happens to college radicals when they leave the campus? The whole current movement of young activists who want to change American society began just five years ago at the University of California's Berkeley campus. In a landmark survey, Knight newspapers reporters Philip Meyer and Richard Maidenberg located more than 400 of the original Berkeley rebels, and 230 of them completed detailed questionnaires. Of the respondents, 13 were selected for in-depth interviews. The results based on a computer analysis of the responses, are provided in a series beginning with this article.

Says Meyer, "When we cover an election story in Ohio we can have all the usual description—autumn leaves, gentle winds—but in addition we can offer the reader a pretty accurate profile of what his neighbors are thinking." The precision journalists combine the computer with vivid description. Meyer and his colleagues at the Knight Newspapers are also planning field experiments in which they will use the methods of experimental psychology to test public issue hypotheses in local communities. Of the future Meyer says, "We may never see a medical writer who can tie an artery, but a social science writer who can draw a probability sample is not unheard of."

"I like to think," Ben Wattenberg says, "that we are the new journalism—journalism which is not subjective but which is becoming more objective than ever before. We've got the tools now—census, polls, election results—that give us precision, that tell us so much about people. Yet, at precisely the time when these tools become so exact, the damn New Journalists have become so introspective that they're staring at their navels. The difficulty is that when you put tables in you bore people. Yet when I was in the White House, [he worked for L.B.J.] knowing what was going on, reading the new journalists was like reading fairy tales. They wrote political impressionism."

There are an increasing number of precision journalists—some of them are writers and editors who are integrating social science research into stories for news magazines and other mass circulation periodicals. They are, at present, the unsung heroes of the new journalism. Yet, their work is so boldly futuristic that they cannot long remain in the background. The work of precision journalists differs from the traditional coverage of the Gallup or Harris polls in the amount of information offered and the mode of presentation. The precision journalists extract data, add effective prose and attempt to interpret trends and conditions of concern to people.

How It Came to Be

The various forms of new journalism—new nonfiction, alternative, advocacy, reform, underground and precision—all grew up in the 1960's. The reasons for these developments are not easily ascertained in the short run. However, there were coincidental factors—a break away from traditional news format and style; bright, energetic journalists on the scene; established literary figures who wanted to experiment with reportage; urgent social issues and the advancement of technology. But it was more than all this. There was a mood and a spirit which offered a conducive milieu for new journalism.

In the late Fifties and early Sixties those on the management side of the American press were worried. Enrollments in schools of journalism were not increasing at the same rate as other areas of study in colleges and universities. This was only one manifestation of the tired, staid image of the American press. One editor on the speaking circuit in those days used the title, "You Wonder Where The Glamour Went," trading on a toothpaste advertising slogan in an address rebutting the notion that American journalism had lost its glamour. Such a defensive posture says something about the journalism of the day. It was true that youthful enthusiasm for journalism had waned considerably since the time when foreign and war correspondents had assignments any young person would have coveted. The glamour and excitement simply were not there. Journalism was increasingly being viewed as stodgy by many young people. Economic pressures had reduced the number of newspapers in the country. One-newspaper towns, without the lusty competition of another day, were becoming commonplace. Journalism—both print and broadcast—had taken on a corporate image. Personalities of days past gave way to teams of little gray men, and it was a foregone conclusion that starting your own paper was next to impossible. This image may not have represented the reality of the situation, but it was the dismal picture in the minds of college students at the dawn of the Sixties.

To many bright, young writers the form of journalistic writing itself seemed to constrict creativity. The inverted pyramid, which places elements of a news story in a descending order of importance, and the shopworn "five w's and the h" seemed to impose a rigid cast over the substantive issues and events of the day. Many writers, especially those like Wolfe and Breslin, found the traditional approach to journalism impersonal and dehumanizing, at a time when there was little debate in the trade journals about the concept of objectivity, an ideal to which every right-thinking journalist adhered.

The new journalists' assault on objectivity is displaced, press critic Herbert Brucker believes:

> . . .critics of objective news are not as much against objectivity as they make out. What they denounce as objectivity is not objectivity so much as an incrustation of habits and rules of news writing, inherited from the past, that confine the reporter within rigid limits. Within those limits the surface facts of an event may be reported objectively enough. But that part of the iceberg not immediately visible is ruled out, even though to include it might reveal what happened in a more accurate—indeed more objective—perspective.

It is probably too early to assess all of the elements of the Sixties that set the stage for the development of the new journalism. Yet, one might cite as factors the verve and vitality of the early days of the Kennedy Administration, the ascendency of the civil rights movement, the evolution of a counter-culture, the drug scene, the war in Southeast Asia, student unrest, riots, and urban disorder. The media were affected by these events.

Historian Theodore Roszak speaks of the uniqueness of the Sixties in *The Making of a Counter Culture:*

> It strikes me as obvious beyond dispute that the interests of our college-age and adolescent young in the psychology of alienation, oriental mysticism, psychedelic drugs, and communitarian experiments comprise a cultural constellation that radically diverges from values and assumptions that have been in the mainstream of our society at least since the Scientific Revolution of the seventeenth century.

Reporters who covered the turbulence of the Sixties were wont to maintain traditional objectivity or balance, and few claimed to have the necessary detachment. At the same time the dissent abroad in the land pervaded the newsrooms so that by 1969 even reporters for the *Wall Street Journal,* the very center of establishment journalism, would participate in an anti-war march. Today, the traditional news format is under fire. Subjective decision-making at all stages of the reportorial process is evident. As one reporter put it: "Subjective decisions confront reporters and editors at the stage of assignment, data collection, evaluation, writing, and editing." "Who," the reporter asks, "decides what events to cover, which ones to neglect? When does the reporter know he has gathered enough information? What if there are fifteen sides to a story—instead of the two usually acknowledged by the theory of objectivity? Finally, writing and editing are purely subjective acts."

Certainly the turmoil over objectivity has touched conventional media and enhanced the climate for the new journalism. The critics, however, had justifiable concern about some of the practices of new journalists. The work of writers like Breslin involves a good deal of literary license. Some new journalists are simply not as concerned with accuracy and attribution as are their more conservative colleagues. Some say the new journalism is simply undisciplined, opinionated writing. But it is difficult to determine whether the new journalism threatens any semblance of fairness the media has developed in the four decades since the era of jazz journalism, when sensationalism and embellishment were in full force. Many who criticize the new journalism are simply not ready for the diversity now available in the marketplace. Even a writer like Jack Newfield, perhaps the most strident advocacy journalist in America, says many of the new approaches including his own must serve as part of a total continuum of information which would include many of the traditional approaches to news gathering and dissemination.

As others have pointed out, most of the new journalists developed their style after learning the more conventional newspaper style. They are breaking the rules, but they know why. Even the most forceful advocates of the new journalism praise the organizing principles of the old journalism, in much the same way that

The New York Times

CITY EDITION

Metropolitan area weather: Cold
today; clear tonight. Sunny tomorrow.
Temperature range: today 27-40;
yesterday 45-52. Details on page 13.

VOL.CXXIX.... No.44,425   Copyright © 1979 The New York Times   —NEW YORK, SATURDAY, DECEMBER 8, 1979—   30 cents beyond 50-mile zone from New York City. Higher in air delivery cases.   25 CENTS

PRESIDENT REPLACES NUCLEAR UNIT CHIEF IN MOVE FOR SAFETY

HE ACTS ON ACCIDENT REPORT

Outsider to Get Post on Regulatory Commission and Carter Asks More Reactor Licensing

By DAVID BURNHAM
Special to The New York Times

WASHINGTON, Dec. 7 — President
Carter today dismissed Joseph M. Hen-
drie as chairman of the Nuclear Regulatory Commission and announced several
other changes that, he said, would improve the safety of nuclear energy in response to the accident last March at the
Three Mile Island reactor in Pennsylvania.

But the President said the United
States "cannot shut the door on nuclear
energy" and strongly urged the regulatory commission to end its present pause
on the licensing of new reactors as soon
as possible and, "in any event, no later
than six months from today."

Mr. Carter said that the "recent events
in Iran have shown us the clear, stark
dangers that excessive dependence on
imported oil holds for our nation," and
stressed that "We must make every effort to lead this country to energy security."

Oil-Dependence Issue Cited

Mr. Carter added that every domestic
energy source, including nuclear power,
"is critical if we are to free our country
from its overdependence on unstable
sources of high-priced foreign oil."

"We do not have the luxury of abandon-
ing nuclear power or imposing a lengthy
moratorium on its further use," the
President stated.

The President's Commission on the Accident at Three Mile Island asserted in its

Excerpts from statement, page 28.

report Oct. 30 that "fundamental
changes" must occur in the way reactors
were overdependence, operated and regulated if the risks of nuclear power "are to
be kept within tolerable limits."

RHODESIA'S NEW GOVERNOR:
Lord Soames, Winston Churchill's
son-in-law, in London. Page 3.

Firm Nationalist To Follow Lynch As Irish Premier

By R. W. APPLE Jr.
Special to The New York Times

DUBLIN, Dec. 7 — Charles J. Haughey, a 54-year-old symbol of Irish unifica-
tion who nine years ago stood trial on
charges of running guns to the Irish Republican Army, will take office next week
as Prime Minister of the Irish Republic.

Mr. Haughey was elected leader of the
ruling party, Fianna Fail, this morning,
defeating his only rival, George Colley,
by 44 votes to 38. The outgoing Prime
Minister, John Lynch, who supported Mr.
Colley, will submit his formal resignation
on Tuesday morning, and a new and possibly turbulent era in Irish politics will
begin.

UNEMPLOYMENT OFF TO 5.8% FOR MONTH IN SPITE OF LAYOFFS

But Most Job Cuts Aren't Included — New York City Joblessness Climbs to 8.2% From 8%

By PHILIP SHABECOFF
Special to The New York Times

WASHINGTON, Dec. 7 — Unemployment edged down slightly and employment rose last month in the face of layoffs
in the automobile and steel industries and
other signs of sluggishness in the economy, the Labor Department reported
today.

At 5.8 percent, the unemployment rate
in November was two-tenths of a percentage point below the rate of the previous
month. The small dip kept the level of
joblessness at about the same plateau on
which it has been resting for well over a
year.

A small rise in unemployment among
blue-collar workers in the automobile industry and other producers of durable
goods was more than offset by a decline
in the jobless rate among workers in service industries. However, a sharper rise in
layoffs in the auto and steel industries
came later than the Nov. 12-16 period during which the job surveys were conducted, and was not reflected in the report
today.

Female and black workers accounted
for much of the decline in unemployment.

Rate Up in New York City

New York City's unemployment rate,
which is not adjusted, as the national figures are, to reflect seasonal variations in
the economy, rose to 8.2 percent from 8
percent in October. The seasonally adjusted rate for New York State fell to 6.8
from 7.4 percent, and the rate for New
Jersey was 7 percent. [Page 12.]

Nationally, the number of employed
workers rose by 350,000 last month, according to a survey of households used by
the Labor Department's Bureau of Labor
Statistics. Another survey, which measures employment by examining payrolls
of nonfarm establishments, indicated
that employment increased by 220,000.
These and other statistics used in the re-

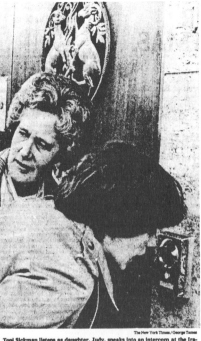

The New York Times / George Tames

Toni Sickman listens as daughter, Judy, speaks into an intercom at the Iranian Embassy in Washington. They were seeking news of Sgt. Virgil Sickman
of the Marines, Mrs. Sickman's son, one of the hostages being held in Iran.

Carter Says He Plans a Trade Ban Against Iran if Hostages Are Tried

By BERNARD GWERTZMAN
Special to The New York Times

WASHINGTON, Dec. 7 — President
Carter said today that the United States | or begin to cause problems for Iran, but
wouldn't lead to bloodshed."

AZERBAIJAN LEADER APPARENTLY BACKS OCCUPIERS IN TABRIZ

SEES AIDES OF IRANIAN REGIME

Shariat-Madari, Pledging Study of Disturbances, Supports Call for Regional Autonomy

By JOHN KIFNER
Special to The New York Times

QUM, Iran, Dec. 7 — Ayatollah Kazem
Shariat-Madari, symbol of the insurgent
Azerbaijani minority, appeared today to
be resisting pressure from the revolutionary authorities to order his followers to
give up the Government buildings and
broadcasting station in Tabriz that they
took over to protest the new Islamic Constitution.

Seated on the edge of a brilliant red
carpet in a small, bare room of his com-
pound in this holy city, the revered,
white-bearded religious figure said after
a morning-long meeting with a delegation
from Ayatollah Ruhollah Khomeini and
the Revolutionary Council that a committee would be named to look into the dis-
turbances.

"In the end, when the committee gives
me the report, I will give you my final answer," Ayatollah Shariat-Madari said,
peering owlishly through his rimmed
spectacles. The row of ranking revolu-
tionaries flanking him, including Ayatollah Khomeini's son, Ahmad, shifted un-
easily on the floor.

He Supports Demands

For the first time today, Ayatollah
Shariat-Madari said he supported the demands for regional autonomy voiced by
the Azerbaijani Turks in the northwest. If
the neighboring Kurds succeeded in their
demands for autonomy, he said, so should
the Azerbaijanis. He stressed, however,
that this did not mean separatism.

"We do not want freedom separate
from Iran," he said.

In Tabriz thousands paraded through
the streets to proclaim their devotion to
Ayatollah Shariat-Madari and to mourn
the killing of a 24-year-old guard at the
Moslem leader's home in Qum during a
demonstration against him two days ago.

Weather

Today—Sunny and mild, high 55 to 60, low 36 to 41. Chance of precipitation is 10 percent. Wednesday —Chance of showers, high 52 to 57. Yesterday—3 p.m. AQI: 65; temperature range: 60-34. Details, Page B2.

The Washington Post

Index	72 Pages 5 Sections		
Amusements	C 9	Financial	D 1
Classified	D 12	Metro	B 1
Comics	E 9	Obituaries	B 6
Crossword	E 11	Sports	E 1
Editorials	A 14	Style	C 1
Fed. Diary	B 2	TV-Radio	C 8

103rd Year   No. 6   © 1979, Washington Post Co.   **TUESDAY, DECEMBER 11, 1979**   Subscription Rates See Box A3   25¢

Chief Rival Of Khomeini Bars Talks

'U.S. Spies' Said To Be Cause of Provincial Unrest

By Stuart Auerbach
Washington Post Foreign Service

TABRIZ, Iran, Dec. 10—Representatives of Iran's ruling Revolutionary Council were rebuffed today in their effort to halt factional fighting between supporters of rival ayatollahs.

In the holy city of Qom, Ayatollah Kazem Shariatmadari, the spiritual leader of this region's Turkish-speaking Azerbaijanis, forbade negotiations with the team and issued a statement supporting his partisans here and accusing the central government of reneging on an agreement reached with him last week.

His rival, revolutionary leader Ayatollah Ruhollah Khomeini, meanwhile put out his statement blaming the troubles in Tabriz on "American spies" and calling on American voters not to reelect President Carter, whom he branded a "traitor."

The Revolutionary Council peace mission, headed by Finance Minister and former foreign minister Abol Hassan Bani-Sadr, was only able to see a Khomeini representative, Ayatollah Mohammed Enghji. Members of Shariatmadari's Moslem People's Republican Party declined to meet with the delegation.

Although the city remained tense

Vance Says Japan Firms Assist Iran

Presses U.S. Case For Joint Policy In London, Paris

By John M. Goshko
Washington Post Foreign Service

PARIS, Dec. 10—Secretary of State Cyrus R. Vance charged today that some Japanese companies are rushing to buy, "at extraordinarily high prices," Iranian oil formerly sold to the United States. He also asserted, according to U.S. officials, that Japanese banks are helping Iran overcome the economic squeeze imposed by the freezing of Iranian assets in American banks.

Vance, seeking the help of major U.S. allies for joint economic pressures on Iran, warned Japan that the U.S. thinks these Japanese actions could harm efforts to free the 50 American hostages in Tehran.

U.S. officials said that at a meeting here tonight Vance told Foreign Minister Subaro Okita that the activities of those Japanese banks and oil companies are "sending ambiguous signals" that might encourage Iranian leaders to ignore international calls for release of the captives.

Vance's reportedly blunt message to Okita came in the course of a fast-paced day that saw the secretary stop

Chicago Tribune

Sunday, December 9, 1979

Final Edition

133d Year—No. 343   © 1979 Chicago Tribune   18 Sections   ☆☆   75¢

Illinois—Wasteland in the making

By John Husar

THERE IS AN environmental crisis in the countryside—one that may be as troublesome as the pollution that degrades life in the cities.

This one is on the farms, in the woods, and along the rivers. And it threatens the most precious resources of man.

Unless checked, it promises to devastate the soil in which we grow our food, the trees that regenerate our air, the

Our farms are losing their topsoil, our lakes and streams are filling with silt, our forests are disappearing, and our wild birds and animals are vanishing. John Husar examines these alarming problems and tells how we are trying to solve them in this article, the first in a five-part series.

wetlands that redeem our waste and purify our waters, the animals in the wild, and the fields, woods, and waters in which we play.

EVERY DAY, EVERY moment, some

of these vital resources disappear. They wash away, dry up, burn. They are dug and plowed or paved. The land is converted relentlessly by "progress" into contrived space, devoid of the life it fostered.

A four-month Tribune study reveals alarming changes in the use of land throughout Illinois. Massive erosion has taken more than a third of the state's precious topsoil. The natural, life-giving character of more than a fourth of the rivers and streams is gone, along with countless forests and natural areas, including farms and meadows. The result is a wholesale decline in wildlife, soil quality, water freshness—actually, the

Continued on page 16, col. 1

Los Angeles Times

Sunday Final

CIRCULATION: 1,057,611 DAILY / 1,344,660 SUNDAY — SUNDAY, DECEMBER 9, 1979 — CC†/654 PAGES/ Copyright 1979 Los Angeles Times / SUNDAY 75c

ARIZONA'S 20%

Private Fire Company—Cutting Cost

By JOAN SWEENEY
Times Staff Writer

SCOTTSDALE, Ariz.—Fire Chief Louis A. Witzeman doesn't just run the fire department, he owns it.

His private Rural/Metro Fire Department Inc. provides fire protection for 2,700 square miles of suburban and rural Arizona, including this affluent Phoenix suburb, and for 20% of this fast-growing state's population.

And Rural/Metro does the job for less money, yet makes a profit despite paying taxes and other fees that public fire departments do not.

How does private enterprise work in an area traditionally the province of local government?

In the case of Rural/Metro, quite well, according to a study by the Institute for Local Self-Government in Berkeley, which compared the performance of Rural/Metro in Scottsdale to that of traditional public fire departments in three other Phoenix suburbs—Tempe, Glendale and Mesa similar in size and income levels

Carter Weighs Trade Embargo Against Iran

Is Consulting Allies on Curbs, Including Food, if Hostages Are Tried

By DON SHANNON
Times Staff Writer

WASHINGTON—President Carter is consulting with U.S. allies on imposing a world trade embargo on Iran if American hostages there are put on trial, it was disclosed Saturday.

The President, who had previously ruled out the use of food as a weapon in securing the release of the hostages, was understood to be ready to include food if necessary. He is maintaining his stand against any military action, however, because of the danger to the captives' lives that a military move would pose.

Carter's views became known after a White House breakfast for radio broadcasters. The ground rules of that background briefing prohibited the direct attribution of the information.

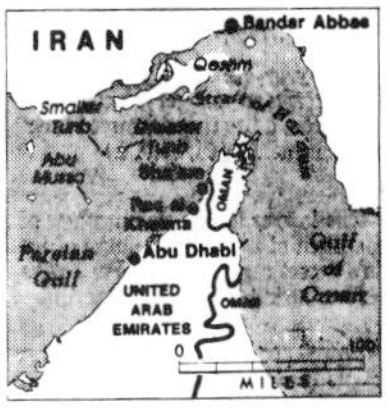

STRAIT OF HORMUZ—Crucial oil conduit for the West.
Times maps

Crisis Underlines Threat to Vital Oil Route From Gulf

By WILLIAM TUOHY

Iran Pledges World Panel on U.S. Crimes

Ex-Court Chief Says New 'Hit List' May Extend to White House

By DON A. SCHANCHE
Times Staff Writer

TEHRAN—Foreign Minister Sadeg Gotbzadeh said Saturday that the government will set up an international tribunal to review "the crimes of the American government" in Iran.

Gotbzadeh, who said he was speaking for the Ayatollah Ruhollah Khomaini, declared that the revolutionary leader has determined that the tribunal will also "display to the people of the world (the) spies" among the hostages held since the U.S. Embassy was seized by student militants Nov. 4.

The foreign minister's announcement came as the Ayatollah Sadeg Khalkhali—who claimed responsibility for the assassination of the shah's nephew, Prince Shahriar Mustafa Shafik, in Paris on Friday, issued a new "hit list" extending to the White

THE WALL STREET JOURNAL.

VOL. LX NO. 40 ★ ★ ★ — MIDWEST EDITION — MONDAY, DECEMBER 10, 1979 — (C) — 30 CENTS

Director Conflicts

Germany's Requiring Of Workers on Boards Causes Many Problems

Firms Say Employe Members Put Their Unions First; But Labor Sees 'Tricks'

Lessons for UAW's Fraser?

By BILL PAUL
Staff Reporter of THE WALL STREET JOURNAL

FRANKFURT—On Oct. 24, directors of AEG-Telefunken, the sickly West German electronics firm, met to work out a plan of reorganization that, it was speculated, would include the firing of up to 20,000 workers, or about a sixth of the work force. But the board decided to make no announcement until its next meeting, in December.

But AEG's workers took matters into their own hands through their representatives who sit on AEG's board. The next day, the labor directors issued a press release saying the board had decided to fire up to 20,000 workers, a decision they opposed.

The other directors, elected by shareholders and reflecting the views of management, replied with their own press release "deploring" the leak and implying that their labor colleagues had broken the oath of secrecy that all German corporate directors sign. The labor directors' response was that when it comes to jobs, their obligation to inform their constituents supersedes any oath of secrecy.

"Difficult to Do Business"

This episode is typical of the conflicts that have arisen since West German industry began complying with a new law that requires substantial labor-union membership on most major companies' boards of directors. The idea of giving workers a say in management, known as co-determination, is having considerable birth problems in Germany and "has made it more difficult to do business," according to Rolf Thuesing of the Confederation of German Employers' Asso-

What's News—

* * *

Business and Finance

THE JOBLESS RATE decline in November, to 5.8% from 6% in October, poses a political dilemma for the election-minded administration and Congress by lessening economic pressures for a tax cut early next year. With most economists predicting a recession, there's a strong incentive to pump up the economy before November voting.

(Story on Page 3)

* * *

A tax cut of $20 billion to $30 billion in January is being sought by the business community to spur productivity and offset inflation. Leaders of the Business Council, which represents large corporations, are to meet Wednesday with White House officials.

(Story on Page 3)

* * *

Consumer credit growth slowed to $2.19 billion in October, the Federal Reserve Board said, the smallest rise since January 1977. September posted a record surge of $4.45 billion.

(Story on Page 3)

* * *

A mild recession is under way, according to the Conference Board's Economic Forum, but it predicted that inflation would slow only slightly in 1980.

(Story on Page 2)

* * *

A synthetic-fuels compromise plan by House Majority Leader James Wright will be taken up by House and Senate conferees. Wright's proposal follows the Senate's plan for a $20 billion program.

(Story on Page 2)

* * *

Use of solar-energy home heating systems that rely on little mechanical help may be spurred by a tax break

World-Wide

THE U.S. PRESSED its allies for support on Iran as the turmoil there deepened.

Secretary of State Vance left for London, Paris, Bonn and Rome to outline U.S. requests for stricter economic cooperation against Iran. Without such support, the Carter administration warns, the U.S. could be impelled to use force to resolve the crisis.

Meanwhile, Iran's foreign minister said he plans to assemble within 10 days an international panel to probe alleged U.S. crimes against Iran. Sadegh Ghotbzadeh also said those among the 50 American hostages in Iran cleared of spying would be freed, but he didn't say when.

For now, the U.S. is only asking allies to make sure that Iran can't evade the effects of the U.S. freeze on its assets and the curtailment of U.S. food shipments to Iran.

The unrest in northwestern Iran worsened, with opponents and supporters of Ayatollah Khomeini battling in the streets in Tabriz. Heavy gunfire erupted near the radio and television station, which Khomeini forces had recaptured. In a broadcast, Khomeini condemned "rebellion against the rule of Islam."

The White House dispatched Attorney General Civiletti to The Hague to present the U.S. case against Iran before the International Court of Justice. Separately, UN Secretary General Waldheim sent a special intermediary to Tehran in a bid to resolve the hostage crisis.

* * *

ZIMBABWE RHODESIA HIT guerrilla bases in Mozambique and Zambia.

Warplanes bombed and strafed guerrilla targets along the Zambezi River in Zambia and pounded a "major terrorist base" in Mozambique, the Salisbury regime said. Ground troops took part in the Mozambique operation. No casualty figures were given.

The latest attacks came as guerrilla leaders in London wrangled over the final details of a cease-fire. The raids apparently were designed to stop any influx of guerrilla forces into Rhodesia in advance of a truce. A guerrilla spokesman called the strikes

Unemployment Rate

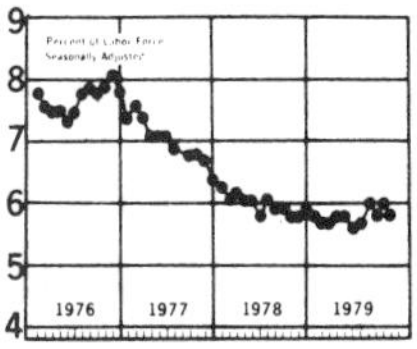

UNEMPLOYMENT in November fell to a seasonally adjusted rate of 5.8% of the labor force from 6% the preceding month, the Labor Department reports. (See story on page 3.)

A Brash Amateur Ruffles the Feathers Of Bird Watchers

* * *

James Vardaman Nears Goal In All-Out Effort to Sight 700 Species in One Year

By URBAN C. LEHNER
Staff Reporter of THE WALL STREET JOURNAL

SAN YGNACIO, Texas—"There it is. I've got it," cries James Vardaman, raising his binoculars.

Perched on a branch several yards ahead is what Mr. Vardaman has journeyed 1,000 miles from Mississippi to hunt down along the Rio Grande River—a rare white-collared seedeater. His guide, John Arvin, an expert on birds of the Rio Grande, quickly confirms the sighting. Mr. Vardaman, dressed in khakis and a baseball cap, has been crawling through the dense brush along the river bank since daybreak. Now he is ecstatic.

"You beautiful bastard!" he hollers, flapping his arms wildly as he proclaims the virtues of the ordinary-looking, three-inch long seedeater.

The 58-year-old bird watcher has reason

The Outlook

Review of Current Trends In Business and Finance

NEW YORK

Two months ago the Federal Reserve System announced strong measures to check inflation and strengthen the dollar. With borrowers and lenders expecting a credit crunch, interest rates soared to new highs. Since then, however, no crunch has materialized and interest rates have been edging downward.

What happened?

To begin with, the Fed on Oct. 6 was aiming partly at psychological results. The system had become deeply concerned by speculation in the commodity and foreign-exchange markets. The speculators were convinced that U.S. inflation would only get worse, and the Fed hoped that strong action would persuade them they were wrong.

The move influenced not only commodity and foreign-exchange traders but ordinary businessmen. The recession that's either beginning or is soon to begin has been the best-advertised slump in history. Many businessmen saw the Fed's move as final confirmation that the recession really was on. As a result they cut inventories and took other steps to batten down for an economic storm.

Neither the traders nor the businessmen paid much attention to Federal Reserve assurances that the system planned no credit crunch. When the Fed in the past had finally decided to clamp down on inflation it had almost always slammed on the brakes, so there was a widespread expectation that it would do so again.

So far it hasn't. As businesses have cut inventories, loan demand to some extent has moderated, but it shows no signs at all of collapsing. The consulting firm of Townsend-Greenspan & Co. suggests that the drop in New York bank business loans in the last two weeks of October "reflected, in large measure, the decision to apply frozen Iranian deposits to a write-off of loans to Iranian borrowers."

As for the money supply, the growth of

Peril in Paradise

Jackson Hole Worries That Developers' Plans Threaten Its Beauty

Community Splits Over How To Manage Local Boom; Elk Herd Is Endangered

What Role for the 'Feds'?

By WILLIAM E. BLUNDELL
Staff Reporter of THE WALL STREET JOURNAL

JACKSON HOLE, Wyo.—Rod Lucas is feeding an orphaned calf. Spread out behind him, an emerald river spilling down between two steep hills, is the rich, green land that his father homesteaded in 1896. To the north, clouds boil around Grand Teton Peak, and a thick bolt of lightning turns twilight into sudden day.

"He's a pest, a real pest," says the 61-year-old rancher as the calf slurps greedily at the bottle. But beneath the Stetson, his face creases in a smile. Rod Lucas and his wife, Joyce, love their work and their 760-acre ranch here, in what has been called the most beautiful valley in America. But they don't know how much longer they can carry on.

The cow business around here has been bad for most of the last 20 years, says Mr. Lucas. Now, more and more houses and people are pressing on the land. Civilization makes ranching more difficult; the calf he feeds was orphaned after a freak accident in which a cyclist hit its mother. To keep going, Mr. Lucas already has subdivided and sold some land to the north. "We didn't want to do it," he says. "I don't want any development around here now or 100 years from now, but we had to."

Too Pretty to Last?

It is a familiar story in this striking place, where the wild, snow-latticed crags of the Teton range give the valley the look of a little Switzerland. Open spaces—including some of the ranches—are being cut up into building lots in an unprecedented wave of

Hemingway hailed the style book of the *Kansas City Star*. They part ways on matters of substance and content, but in the early organizing stages, nothing, they say, is better discipline. The inverted pyramid and the fetish for objectivity may have been too rigid, but these methods do offer something in terms of succinct treatment and synthesis of complex, inter-related facts. Perhaps the ideas and actions of the Seventies are too complex for such simplistic treatment.

The new journalism offers rich detail and what Tom Wolfe calls "saturation reporting." The new journalism in all its forms is a more sophisticated kind of writing aimed at a more highly educated populace than that which gave life and readers to the old journalism. The new journalism is in its earliest stages of development. It has not yet arrived. It is not yet—and may never be—the dominant force in American journalism. Perhaps, like minority parties in American politics, it may suggest opportunities for innovation and thoughtful change. The media will do well to listen to the sounds of the new journalism and the resultant response of the new audience. It may be the stuff that the future is made of.

Bibliography

The new journalism of which Everette E. Dennis has been writing is covered well in his own edited book, *The Magic Writing Machine* (School of Journalism, University of Oregon, 1971), and his co-edited work with William Rivers, *Other Voices: The New Journalism in America* (Canfield, 1974). See also Tom Wolfe and E. W. Johnson, eds., *The New Journalism* (Harper & Row, 1973), and Robert J. Glessing, *The Underground Press in America* (Indiana University Press, 1970). The "precision journalism" mentioned by Dennis receives a full treatment in Philip Meyer, *Precision Journalism: A Reporter's Introduction to Social Science Methods* (Indiana University Press, 1973). Meyer is one of the leading practitioners of social science research techniques in reporting. For an interesting historical background to the new journalism, see the special issue of *Journalism History* (Summer 1974) which contained several articles "Tracing the Roots of the New Journalism." A recent review of what has happened to the underground press, particularly in Boston, is Dan Wakefield, "Up From Underground," *The New York Times Magazine* (Feb. 15, 1976), pp. 14–17+. Don Bonafede's article, which is reprinted in Chapter 8, provides an example of contemporary precision reporting as applied to polls.

30 Magazines: Fighting for a Place in the Market
A. Kent MacDougall

A. Kent MacDougall, a staff writer for the *Los Angeles Times*, is a frequent contributor in the field of media criticism. This article appeared in the April 9, 1978 edition of the *Times* and is used with permission.

When people dream of starting new magazines, they do not dwell on the $30 million that Henry R. Luce and his *Time* Inc. poured into *Sports Illustrated* before it broke even, or the $13 million that Bob Guccione has dropped on *Penthouse's* sickly sister *Viva*, or the fact that most new magazines die in infancy.

They think instead of how *Time* Inc. seems likely to make back on fast-starting *People* magazine more than it lost on *Sports Illustrated*, of how Hugh Hefner started *Playboy* on $7,000 and laid out the first issue on a card table in his modest apartment, of the prestige and the glamor of publishing a glossy magazine.

For more and more would-be magazine moguls, dreams are turning into reality as the nation goes on a new-magazine binge. Several hundred new consumer magazines are expected to start this year, on top of the 488 new titles that *Folio: The Magazine for Magazine Management* counted in 1975–77.

New interests and lifestyles are generating many of the entries. There's *The Runner* for fitness buffs, *Moped Biking* for those who prefer to ride, *Wet* for bathing enthusiasts, *Outside* for outdoors activists, *Games* for puzzle fans, *Blue Boy* for homosexuals, *Inspiration* for the born-again.

Half a dozen new left-of-center magazines are busy analyzing the country's political, economic and social ills. Among them are *Mother Jones* and *Inquiry,* both published in San Francisco, and *Seven Days* and *Politicks & Other Human Interests,* published here in New York.

City magazines continue to proliferate as middle class families move frequently and need basic information on shopping and other matters that used to come from staying put in a particular neighborhood. *Media Decisions,* a business publication for the advertising industry, counted 38 new city and regional magazines in 1976–77.

Oddly enough, television, which helped kill the big general-interest *Saturday Evening Post, Look* and *Life* by siphoning off readers and advertisers, is actually stimulating new magazines. TV soap operas provide the plots that *Soap Opera Digest* and its ilk synopsize. TV entertainers provide grist for the personality mills of *People* and *Us.*

More importantly, television leaves it to magazines to treat minority concerns, special interests and hobbies. Little wonder, then, that American adults are reading 17% more magazines on the average than they did in 1950 before TV became ubiquitous.

Shifting patterns of advertising also favor magazines. With television time in tight supply and ad rates rising rapidly, many advertisers are switching part of their budgets to magazines. Advertisers spent 13.5% more in TV last year than in 1976, but magazine ad spending jumped 21% to score the biggest gain of any medium.

Advertisers like the fact that new magazines commonly target their editorial fare at the affluent, urban and suburban free-spending young adults whom advertisers most want to reach. For instance, *Your Place,* a new bimonthly, goes after men and women in their 20s with such stories as "Living Together: Should You Worry About 'Forever'?"

However, advertisers shun new magazines with controversial contents, such as sex and nudity, and with low circulations. These must rely for most of their revenue on readers who, happily for the new magazines, are paying prices that would have been unthinkable even for established magazines just a couple of years ago. *Heavy Metal,* a new adult comic book, is priced at $1.50 a copy, *Human Nature* at $1.75, *Quest/* 78 at $2, *Mariah* at $2.50, *L'Officiel/USA* at $2.95.

Popular general family magazines like these gave way to the pressures of advertising and specialized publishing. *Life* and *Look* were resurrected in 1978 and 1979, respectively. Both have changed their "editorial" approach completely from what they had been. *Look* folded again in 1979. *Life* continues as a monthly with emphasis on newsstand sales.

Some new magazines with little income from either advertisers or readers nevertheless make it by keeping expenses to a minimum. One old hand at this is Bob Anderson. As a 17-year-old Kansas high school cross-country runner, Anderson started *Distance Running News* on $100. He got runners to contribute articles free and did most of the work himself, hand-stapling, folding and mailing the first 28-page issue to 300 subscribers.

As *Distance Running News* caught on, it grew fatter and slicker, was renamed *Runner's World,* and became the nucleus of a complex of profitable publishing and sporting goods mail order operations that today employs 115 persons in Mountain View, Calif., and racked up revenues of $4.7 million last year.

The 30-year-old Anderson, who still runs 20 miles a week, puts out magazines on biking, soccer, canoeing and cross-country skiing in addition to *Runner's World,* and is starting two more running magazines, *On the Run* and *Marathoner.* Clearly he has caught the tailwind of the nationwide fitness fervor.

Shoestring-to-success stories such as Bob Anderson's are possible because of the relatively low capital requirements of magazine publishing. Unlike daily newspapers, which usually need their own printing facilities, magazines are produced by commercial printers. And printers eager for new business often extend new magazines credit—sometimes more credit than is wise.

R.R. Donnelley & Sons Co., a leading magazine printer, was so eager to fill idle press time when *Working Woman* was started in 1976 that it printed the first four monthly issues on credit before requiring cash in advance for subsequent issues.

The undercapitalized *Working Woman* soon ran out of money and was placed under court protection through Chapter XI of the Federal Bankruptcy Act. A new owner has taken over and Donnelley is continuing to print the magazine. But it expects to get back only a small fraction of the $800,000 it is still owed for the first four issues.

Beside credit from its printer, a new magazine to be sold on newsstands and in stores can usually negotiate an advance payment of part of its expected proceeds from each issue's sale. The advances are made by the national distributor handling distribution of the magazine to local wholesalers and retail store chains.

The most important source of advance payments, however, is the subscriber. Magazines are one of the few businesses that collect from customers before delivering a product or service. The money a subscriber sends in is the magazine's to use, interest-free, any way it likes. New magazines typically use it to pay for more mailings to still more potential subscribers.

The system has potential for abuse. The Magazine Publishers Assn. says it has received complaints from subscribers to a girlie magazine that suspended publication after a single issue and to an opera magazine that delivered no issues at all. The complaints have been referred to legal authorities on suspicion that subscribers were bilked.

More commonly, a new magazine that fails to get off the ground makes refunds, while one that crashes after takeoff gets another magazine to substitute its issues.

Reasons for failure are almost as varied as the magazines that fail. Leading causes include underfinancing, inexpert management, insufficient advertising and public indifference. Conceiving and executing an editorial concept that catches on with both readers and advertisers is so difficult that even old pros who have struck it rich with one or two magazines often fall on their face with subsequent ones.

For example, Hugh Hefner has started four magazines since the instantly successful *Playboy,* but only one of them, *Oui,* is still around. The satirical *Trump* died after a few issues, as did *Show Business Illustrated. VIP,* a monthly for Playboy Club members, also succumbed.

One way to avoid the agony and the uncertainty of creating a new magazine concept is to imitate an already successful one. Nearly every successful magazine has spawned imitators. *People* has its *Us. Cosmopolitan* has its *New Dawn,* whose first cover showed a young woman ripping a copy of *Cosmopolitan* in half.

Playboy has probably been imitated more often than any magazine started since World War II. There is *Penthouse, Hustler, Genesis, Gallery* and several dozen others living and dead. The publishers of some of these have aped Hugh Hefner's ostentatious lifestyle as well.

Playboy's most blatant imitator was *Gallery*. It was the brainchild of Ronald Fenton, a computer-leasing promoter without previous magazine experience who saw quick profits in producing a magazine that looked as much like *Playboy* as the law would allow. He picked the name *Gallery* because it had seven letters ending in "Y," just like *Playboy*.

However, *Gallery* was less than a hit and was soon taken over by its national distributor, Kable News Co., for failing to repay advances against newsstand sales that didn't materialize. Fenton lost his entire $500,000 investment in the magazine and declared personal bankruptcy.

Publishers eager to avoid big losses on new magazines often test-market them before committing themselves to regular publication. The most common method of testing is by mail. A brochure describing the yet-to-be-produced magazine is sent to prospective subscribers offering a "special charter rate." Since the best prospect for any magazine, new or old, is a person who already reads a number of magazines, most of the offers go to subscribers of other magazines. Their names are rented, typically for 3 cents to 5 cents each, from other magazines more than happy to pick up extra income.

Several dozen lists are usually tested to determine which pulls best. Two women who hope to revive *Rags,* an irreverent fashion magazine published in San Francisco in 1970–71, made a test mailing last fall to 200,000 persons on 32 lists. Response ranged from a disappointing 2% on a list of Bloomingdale's department store charge customers to a remarkable 15% on a list of subscribers to *L'Officiel/USA,* the year-old fashion magazine. The women, Mary Peacock and Carol Troy, are using the overall successful test results of 6.7% to try to interest investors in bankrolling *Rags.*

Response rates generally drop markedly after a magazine appears. As one magazine consultant has explained, "It's always been easier to sell the sizzle than the steak, and it's easier to sell a magazine before it exists than after everybody has seen it."

An increasingly popular method of testing a new magazine is to insert a sampler of its editorial contents in an existing magazine. The host magazine gets an editorial feature at little cost, plus revenue from any ads that run with it. The new magazine gets exposure to prospective investors, subscribers and advertisers. *Ms.,* the liberated women's magazine, first appeared as a 44-page insert in a 1971 issue of New York. *Heavy Metal,* the adult comic book, was sampled in *National Lampoon. The Runner* is being previewed in *New Times;* George A. Hirsch, a marathoner, is publisher of both.

New magazines that seek display at supermarket checkout counters are tested to assess the soundness of the multi-million-dollar investment required to buy, place and police the required display racks.

Time Inc. has tested two supermarket magazines in recent years—with significantly different results. *People* was tested in 11 metropolitan markets before starting regular weekly publication four years ago. In cities where it was priced at 35 cents and advertised extensively, it sold a remarkable 86% of copies distributed. Sales in other cities at 50 cents and without promotion were far lower.

Woman, a digest-sized weekly, was tested last fall at 50 cents and 75 cents in 12 cities. Handicapped by blandness and a page size too small for dramatic illustrations, *Woman* failed to grab shoppers. Industry sources say that fewer than 50% of the 164,000 copies distributed were sold. *Time* says only that results were disappointing and are still being evaluated.

Careful evaluation of test results is a wise precaution, given the painful miscalculation that *Us* made. *Us* tested two prototype issues in 11 markets. One featured TV actress Farah Fawcett Majors on the cover and sold particularly well, especially in supermarkets that slipped *Us* into display racks meant for other magazines.

Not realizing that it couldn't duplicate on a national scale what it had accomplished in the 11 test markets with careful preparation, heavy TV promotion and luck, *Us* projected nationwide sales of 750,000 copies per issue and based its advertising rates on that circulation. When actual sales of the first four issues averaged a scant 440,000, *Us* cut its rate base to 500,000 and its ad rates accordingly. Madison Avenue saw it as a sign of weakness.

Magazine men put much of the blame for *Us's* poor sales on its anemic editorial contents. "The problems that *Us* is having getting off the ground are not, I believe, that it attempts to be a copy of *People,*" Good Housekeeping editor John Mack Carter wrote in *Advertising Age.* "The problem is that it is not a very good copy."

Since that wobbly start a year ago, *Us* has brightened editorially and won a place in many homes as light reading during TV commercial breaks. Sales have risen steadily and the rate base has just been raised to 800,000. *Us* seems to be over the hump, though it remains a distant second to *People* in circulation and ad revenue, and doesn't expect its first profitable year until 1980.

"Our biggest single expense is unsold copies we have to eat," complains publisher Porter Bibb. "Each one costs us 25 cents in paper, printing and delivery."

Unsold magazines constitute a long-standing industry-wide problem that has reached plague proportions as new magazines have increased congestion at already overcrowded magazine stands and checkout counters. Industry experts estimate that half of all copies put into national distribution are regurgitated back unsold. This is little wonder considering that the typical magazine stand holds only 100 to 200 titles, while many times that number are in national distribution.

Bestsellers, a magazine for magazine wholesalers and retailers, lists 970 nationally distributed magazines, not counting 300 issued only once or twice a year and several hundred "one shot" special issues and comic book titles.

Good display is crucial because magazines are impulse items. Yet even the payment of a retail display allowance of 10% of the cover price doesn't assure a magazine of full-cover display. Many chains and other major retailers won't accept a new magazine for sale unless it agrees to give them the 10% allowance on top of their standard 20% margin. Yet they routinely fail to give slow sellers the prominent display called for. And there is little the publishers can do about it without hurting themselves more than the retailers.

Even a magazine that wins quick acceptance can find itself buried under returns of unsold copies because of tardy information as to where the magazine is selling briskly and badly. It takes three months after an issue goes off sale for a new magazine to get accurate sales data so that it can make adjustments in the number and destination of copies of subsequent issues it distributes.

"We're setting the print run for the May issue when we have only preliminary results for February," Kent Brownridge, marketing director of *Outside*, complains. *Outside* sold only 38% of distributed copies of its first four issues, but expects adjustments in the print run and distribution pattern to improve that to a respectable 60%.

Cheaply produced "pulp" magazines, which sell few copies by subscription, sometimes can turn a profit on newsstand sales as low as 35%. They do so by keeping costs to a minimum.

Among pulp magazine publishers, Myron Fass is king. Besides dozens of one-shots and annuals, he puts out some 45 monthly, bimonthly and quarterly titles, including *Foxy Story* for lonely ladies, *Popular Pets* for animal lovers, *Punk Rock* for music lovers, *Street Racer* for car buffs, *Shotgun Journal* for sportsmen, *Mobs and Guns* for crime followers and *Space Wars* for science fiction fans.

Fass recently gained notoriety when his *Official UFO* reported that "a fleet of alien invaders" had landed and destroyed the sleepy Mississippi River town of Chester, Ill. Confronted with undeniable evidence that Chester was still standing and residents recalled nothing unusual, Fass boldly followed with "proof positive" that the saucer-borne aliens had indeed looted and burned the town but resurrected it the same night and erased memory of the event from the minds of most Chester citizens.

Fass is equally freewheeling in starting and stopping magazines. He has killed scores and whelped even more. Of his 45 titles, most are less than a year old. And he always has others on the drawing board, among them a satiric magazine to be titled *Moron: For the Intellectual*. Like a racetrack veteran, Fass spreads his bets over many nags and occasionally hits big, as he did last year with a $1.95 one-shot on Elvis Presley that he rushed out after the singer's death and which grossed nearly $1 million.

With their dependence on newsstand sales and their largely blue-collar readership, Fass' pulp magazines stand a class apart from a half dozen new magazines that depend exclusively on advertising income and are distributed free to affluent residents of large cities. Among these are *Avenue* for residents of

Manhattan's chic Eastside, *The Washington Dossier* for the upper crust in the nation's capital and *Chicago's Elite* for well-heeled Chicagoans.

These elitist magazines provide luxury goods advertisers with a medium to reach prime prospects exclusively. This is important because ads for expensive jewelry, Jaguars and estates are only wasted on the middle-class readers of mainstream magazines. Or so Andrew Molchanov, assistant publisher of *Chicago's Elite,* contends. "The middle class are being squeezed to the point where their disposable income for luxuries shrinks a little each year. If you are selling luxury items, you are selling to the upper 3% to 4% of the population."

Molchanov thinks that the year-old *Chicago's Elite's* special focus will spare it the fate of 15 short-lived Chicago magazines that concentrated in recent years on helping middle class residents cope with and enjoy the city. But it hasn't been easy. For one thing, the magazine's original name, *Chicago's Ruling Elite,* had to be shortened after three issues to *Chicago's Elite* because "Ruling" was too candid a reminder of the tie between wealth and power, discomfiting wealthy readers as well as annoying egalitarians.

The survival or failure of magazines such as *Chicago's Elite* that are heavily dependent on advertising is largely in the hands of advertising agencies that make a practice of giving short shrift to most new magazines. Ad agencies don't hesitate to commit their clients' money to new television shows, but they adopt a wait-and-see-if-it-survives stance toward most new magazines.

One reason for this is that TV contracts usually specify that if a new show's ratings fall below estimates, the advertiser will receive make-good spots on other shows. But if a new magazine falls short of its circulation rate base, the advertiser gets only more of the same sorry space.

Equally important, agencies fear the stigma of backing a loser, especially of placing an ad in the last issue of a dying magazine. Although the final issue may become a collector's item, the unwritten rule along Madison Avenue is: Don't get caught in the tomb with the corpse.

Agencies looking for reasons not to buy space in a new magazine often cite the absence of demographic data on readership, the lack of audited circulation figures, and so on. It takes a year for a magazine to become eligible to receive the imprimatur of an Audit Bureau of Circulations audit, but by then it is often too late.

In the interest of getting off to an impressive start, new magazines commonly fatten their first issue with ads sold at special charter rates. *Quest/77* (the digits change with the year) offered any advertiser in its first issue an equal amount of space free in a subsequent issue. That not only helped beef up the first issue but also kept following issues from growing too thin.

New magazines usually suffer a sharp fall-off in advertising after the image-building first issue. For instance, *Us* carried 28 pages of ads in its first issue, only 14 in its second. The drop-off in *New West* was even more dramatic, from 91 pages to 31.

Not surprisingly, it often takes several years for a new magazine to hit on an editorial mix that jells with readers and advertisers. *Playboy* was little more than a girlie magazine until Hefner replaced slutty looking nudes with cheer-leader types and attracted name writers. At New York it took editor Clay Felker several years to develop the consumer service coverage that has been widely copied by city magazines and metropolitan newspapers.

Outside, the slick monthly started last fall by *Rolling Stone,* devoted considerable attention in early issues to environmental concerns. But from now on it will de-emphasize such coverage in favor of more articles on hiking, canoeing and other participant sports for which there is more reader interest and more available advertising, associate publisher D. Claeys Bahrenburg says. "We're in business to make money, not to carry on a cause," he explains.

Viva, the deficit-beset women's magazine started by *Penthouse* publisher Bob Guccione in 1973, featured photographs of nude men for its first three years. But Kathy Keeton, editor and associate publisher, says male nudity "turned off a lot more women than it turned on. It also turned off supermarket chains, newsstand operators and advertisers. It was a terrible mistake."

Correcting the mistake entailed dropping the nudes, stepping up coverage of fashion and beauty, and repositioning *Viva* between *Cosmopolitan* and *Ms.* The new formula seems to be catching on. Advertising jumped sharply last year, circulation is 400,000 and rising, and the magazine may break into the black this year.

Not many publishers would have had the patience, to say nothing of the $13 million, to see *Viva* through its first lean years. Like Henry Luce before him, Guccione epitomizes the determined entrepreneur with faith in his magazines and emotional involvement in their success.

It is by no means certain that Luce's cautious successors at *Time* Inc., now a huge conglomerate with 11,000 stockholders to answer to, would keep faith in a magazine losing 130 million over 10 years, as proprietor Luce did with *Sports Illustrated* until it became profitable in 1964.

Time's present managers have seen *Money* through six straight years of losses, but the magazine has a healthy circulation of 750,000, carried an impressive $8.7 million in advertising last year, and would have shown a profit if it hadn't been charged with a portion of *Time's* heavy corporate overhead.

Despite the advantages their size gives them, many large publishers are sitting on the sidelines watching the new-magazine binge go by. *Time* doesn't look like it is going ahead with *Woman,* though it is considering bringing back *Life* as a monthly. Hearst Corp. (*Good Housekeeping, Cosmopolitan,* etc.) tested a check-out-counter tabloid, *Romance Weekly,* last fall but has shelved plans for it. Triangle Publications, Inc. *(TV Guide, Seventeen)* and Washington Post Co. *(Newsweek)* haven't been heard from, though Conde Nast Publications, Inc. (*Vogue, Glamour,* etc.) has announced plans for its first magazine in 39 years, a "self-discovery" monthly named *Self.*

The pressures under which magazines operate are very real. Chris Welles has explained the market forces at work in the death of *Life* magazine in "Lessons from *Life*," *World* (Feb. 13, 1973). His "The Numbers Magazines Live By," *Columbia Journalism Review* (September/October 1975), pp. 22–27, delves into the conflict between *Time* magazine and W. R. Simmons & Associates Research over the accuracy of Simmons' audience studies. In the process he reveals just how important those "numbers" are to magazine publishers. Background books on the magazine industry include Robert F. Kenyon, editor, *Magazine Profiles* (Medill School of Journalism, Northwestern University, December 1974), a collection of reports categorized by types of magazines; Roland E. Wolseley, *The Changing Magazine* (Hastings House, 1973); James Playsted Wood, *Magazines in the United States*, 3rd ed. (Ronald Press, 1971); Theodore Peterson, *Magazines in the Twentieth Century*, 2nd ed. (University of Illinois Press, 1969). A useful bibliography is John H. Schact, compiler, *A Bibliography for the Study of Magazines* (Institute of Communications Research, University of Illinois, 1972). A slightly different problem is explicated in Dave Noland, "Flying Pussycats," [*more*] (November 1975), pp. 12–13. A former editor of *Air Progress*, Nolan brings special expertise and contacts to his discussion of the influence of advertisers, Beech in particular, on consumer aviation magazines. A review of news magazine journalism can be found in Edwin Diamond, "The Mid-Life Crisis of the Newsweeklies," *New York* (June 7, 1976), pp. 50–54+. R. C. Smith, "The Magazines' Smoking Habit," *Columbia Journalism Review* (January/February 1978), pp. 29–31, suggests that cigarette advertising revenues are causing some leading magazines to avoid comment on the effects of smoking. See also Alan D. Fletcher, "City Magazines Find a Niche in the Media Marketplace, *Journalism Quarterly* (Winter 1977), pp. 740–743, 749, and "City and Regional Magazines and the National Advertiser," *Madison Avenue Magazine* (June 1978), pp. 34–38+, which provides an entirely different perspective, this time from the advertiser's viewpoint.

Bibliography

For Paperback Houses, There's No Business Like Show Tie-In Business

31

Nancy Hardin

Not so long ago the publishing rights for a movie tie-in book could be picked up for the cash equivalent of a song. That is, if the buyer was persistent enough to make his way past the indifference of whoever was handling the sale—usually someone in the publicity department of a film company who felt he had better things to do than shuffle papers for a slow grand or two.

That was then. In the past few years it's become a whole different ballgame. Film and publishing people have finally become aware of how much each can offer the other. And in this era of belt-tightening, film companies no longer turn up their noses at the income they can derive from even a small override on a successful tie-in.

Tie-ins come in several forms, with two common denominators whenever possible: a cover featuring the movie art or star photos, and a publication date timed to coincide with the national release of the film. The traditional type of tie-in consists of merely repackaging the edition which has already come out in softcover—or even hard, with a success like "The Exorcist," for example—to

Nancy Hardin is a former senior editor at Bantam Books and now is vice president and head of the literary department at Ziegler Associates in Los Angeles. She knows from experience both ends of the movie tie-in business. Reprinted from the Feb. 17, 1975 issue of *Publishers Weekly,* published by R.R. Bowker Company, a Xerox company. Copyright © 1975 by Xerox Corporation.

include a tie-in cover and, occasionally, an insert of stills from the film. The other garden-variety type of tie-in consists of a novelization of the screenplay, again with a coordinated cover and stills from the film occasionally included. Least likely to turn up on mass market racks is a third type of movie tie-in, the screenplay itself, containing dialogue and scene settings from the film, minus the more esoteric camera directions but almost always including stills. Some screen-writers feel that their work should only be published in the form in which it was written; and if their names carry enough weight—a William Goldman, say, or a Robert Towne or a Michael Crichton—and the film in question seems assured of success, a publisher may agree to go with the screenplay even though most readers apparently find the form difficult to read, and sales orders can be cut by about two-thirds if even a highly successful film is published as a screenplay. Last, and least in number, since very few films are big enough to warrant such attention, are books written *about* a film—the making of it, its special effects, or whatever. Blockbusters like "Love Story," "The Godfather" and "The Great Gatsby" spawned such books; perhaps the most successful of the genre have been "The Making of 2001" and "William Peter Blatty on the Exorcist: From Novel to Film."

In the days when such deals didn't seem to count for much, an editor who had heard about a film that sounded promising would often have to scramble even to discover who owned the publication rights, much less where he could get hold of a copy of the script, or who was authorized to make a deal and draw up a contract. At best, there was a routine procedure. Someone from the merchandising or publicity department of the studio releasing the film in question would send around a blurry copy of the script, accompanied by what amounted to a form letter with information about the cast and a projected release date. After that, it was pretty much up to the editor to phone in a modest offer. As often as not, the editor in question had no particular expertise (beyond enjoying an occasional movie) in deciding which films to tie-in with; and even the big paperback houses had no one editor who was hired specifically to handle movie tie-ins, as nearly all of them have now (some even have a Los Angeles scout to boot).

Low Pay for Novelizers

Once the editor's offer was accepted, and the studio's lawyers, unused to the byways of publishing contracts, had laboriously been persuaded to return the contract more or less intact, the only further contributions expected from the film company's end were sporadic news of the anticipated release pattern of the film, and eventually—and often belatedly for publishing deadlines—a messenger bearing the film's logo, a few stills, and if you got lucky, a color transparency of the ad campaign. In those days, all the studio hoped to get out of the tie-in was the promotional value of having its film's title and ad campaign displayed in one more place before the public's eye. What went on behind that cover was left entirely to the publisher. This sounds like more of a creative blessing than it was, however, since everything was done so haphazardly on both sides. And the publisher's choice of writers was limited by the fact that the pay usually was a flat fee of between $1500 and $2500, and the novel frequently had to be written within a few weeks in order to be published in time to coincide with the release of the film and in order to make financial sense for the novelizer.

Actually, no matter how early the deal was made, changes in the script, revised release plans, belatedly organized ad campaigns and the like always seemed to wind up making the book a last-minute proposition. When I was handling the movie-tie-ins for Bantam Books I remember once feeling very smug about getting a novelization written and copy-edited months in advance, only to be told that there would be a slight change in casting: the lead would be black, not white. Since the novelizer had gone to some trouble to develop the character he'd originally been presented with, this meant considerable rewriting. Which, grumbling, he did. The film was subsequently made, with said black actor as the lead, and then previewed, whereupon it was discerned by the studio powers-that-be that the audiences were responding badly to the fact that the hero was killed in the end. Another ending was hastily filmed in which the hero was permitted to start a new life in another country. At that point I didn't have the heart—much less the time—to send the galleys to California, where the novelizer happened to live, for yet another rewrite, so that weekend I found myself substituting life for death on the last few pages of the proofs of our book. Small wonder that the book did not turn out to be a fiction masterpiece.

Then there are the times when the film is cancelled after the novelization has already been written. After a few such experiences, the tie-in editor finds himself in the awkward position of trying to explain to the film people that, yes, he wants to make a deal and get started on the book very early in the planning stages—but he'd rather not commit himself before the film becomes a sure thing. This is awkward because as everyone knows, a film is never a sure thing until the cameras start rolling, and sometimes not even then.

Even today, when agents and studios have become much more alert to the potential of tie-ins and prices have escalated in just the past year or so to the point where it's a safe rule of thumb to add at least one and sometimes two zeros to an advance, the publishers and the film people continue to complain about each other—and they're both right. However, new and mutually productive ways and means are being sought—and found—for them to work effectively in tandem.

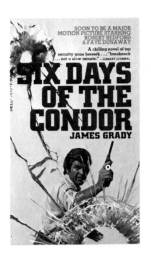

According to Robert Silverstein, a one-time editor at Dell and Bantam who also worked in the film business and now heads his own publishing company, Quicksilver, the change in attitude on everyone's part began with a writer who himself developed material bought for filming into a hugely successful novel, namely Erich Segal, with "Love Story." "Before then, although the screenwriters contractually had first crack at writing the novelization, they invariably turned it down because there wasn't enough money in it," Silverstein says. "But because of the success of this book, the higher figures that reprinters began paying for material in general, and the fact that the independent producers who were increasingly dominating the business wanted total control of the product from

It Started with "Love Story"

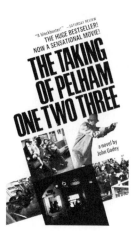

its inception to its release and to that end were retaining rights and approaching publishers directly, tie-ins began to be regarded with new eyes." Around that time, Silverstein himself made a tie-in deal that remains the largest ever for a straight tie-in and he nabbed it right out from under both the studio in question and the publishers who were trying to buy it. As the editors dickered with various executives at United Artists for rights to the screenplay of "Last Tango in Paris," he convinced UA's merchandising executive (who apparently unbeknownst to the other executives autonomously held the rights) that the book should come out as both a novel and a screenplay, and that he was the man to package the property. His deal made, he then held an auction, with a six-figure joint venture floor, and Dell emerged the winner by offering a guaranteed nonreturnable advance in excess of $250,000 against 50% of the publishing profits. At the time there was some flak about the low advance paid UA by Quicksilver, not to mention yelps of outrage from publishers who felt they'd been led down the garden path by the studio, but since UA wound up collecting about $250,000 on its share of the royalties from the publishing proceeds—100 times its original advance, according to Silverstein—and since the incident startled a lot of people on both sides of the fence into seeing potential that had been hitherto overlooked, everyone eventually came out ahead. Including Mr. Silverstein, who went on to package and sell "Deep Throat" to Dell in another successful arrangement.

A Failed Best Seller

"Tango" and "Throat" were published in softcover tie-ins well after the films had been released, whereas "Love Story" appeared—at least to the eye of the public—in the traditional way, as a hardcover best seller first and then as a film with a softcover tie-in featuring a photo of Ali MacGraw and Ryan O'Neal on the cover. It had in fact been written as a screenplay first. This was novelizing at its most gloriously successful, particularly since the book and the film were hits independently and therefore neither could be accused of riding on the coat-tails of the other. Inevitably the approach has had its imitators. Some, such as

Herman Raucher's "Summer of '42," succeeded fairly well; others, like Marc Norman's "Oklahoma Crude," and the recent "Harry and Tonto" by Josh Greenfeld and Paul Mazursky, didn't really make it. In their handling of "Oklahoma Crude," Columbia's Peter Guber and Rosilyn Heller consciously set out to try and repeat the success of "Love Story." It worked up to a point; publishing rights were sold to Dutton, Marc Norman wrote the novel, and Dutton sold the softcover rights to Popular Library for $190,000—roughly five and a half times what the prepublication sale of the softcover rights to "Love Story" had brought, incidentally, and certainly a whole lot more than a straight tie-in sale would have brought. But the attempt to create a best seller prior to and independent of the film failed, and since the film was not a box office hit, the tie-in didn't work either way.

In Los Angeles entertainment lawyer Tom Pollack's opinion, "Crude" was a definite setback to those who had thought "Love Story" would start a new era of partnership between the publishing industry and the motion picture industry. "Although there was a lot of talk about it, if you look at the best seller lists over the past couple of years, you see no indication of it. Softcover publishers are still benefitting a lot more from tie-ins than hardcover publishers," he says. But a few innovative behind-the-scenes deals were made during this period: Doubleday got involved in sponsoring the development of the screenplay for one of its books, "The Parallax View"; Bantam and Paramount cofinanced a book to be written by Fredric Morton on a subject suggested by Peter Bart, then vice-president in charge of production at Paramount, in a deal giving Paramount first crack at the film rights; and Universal initiated "The Bottom Line," a book about a business convention, with author Fletcher Knebel at Doubleday. For the most part, however, tie-ins were handled pretty much as usual, with only an occasional flurry of rumors that film studios were spending thousands of dollars buying up copies of books they owned at key bookstores to get them on best seller lists—rumors that have cropped up repeatedly over the years and are no doubt true in some cases.

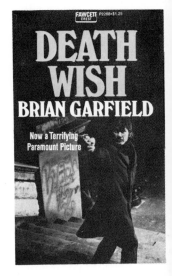

Occasionally there was an attempt to market a novelization a la "Love Story"; in one case, a half-written novelization of the script for Robert Mitchum's upcoming film "Yacuza" was sent around to several hardcover editors but those who saw it passed on it, feeling it would have its best life in softcover. Their decision may have been colored by the fact that as novelizations enter the big time and are presented as hardcover entities unto themselves, they are suffering a certain degree of blacklash, at least from critics. In a recent pan of the hardcover novelization of "Harry and Tonto," *Los Angeles Times* book reviewer Digby Diehl said: "Book critics rarely ever deign to recognize the existence of a 'novelization,' much less go to the trouble of complaining about it." He went on to hypothesize "that neither Greenfeld nor Mazursky had the slightest interest in presenting this story as a book when they began working on the screenplay. The entire conception is cinematic. But somewhere, someone had the not very original idea that a lot of preproduction publicity could be drummed out of a novelization that would eventually help the movie." Another example of this attitude can be found in the *New York Times Book Review* critique of William Goldman's new novel "Marathon Man," which had been warmly received elsewhere. Taking tacit note of the fact that Goldman is a very well-known screenwriter, the reviewer goes beyond judging the book itself to describe his suspicion that "this is one of those cases where the screenplay is father to the novel. Part of the promotional package as it were."

Movie People Out East

From the looks of things, however, reviewers are going to be presented with more and more novels which have evolved from cooperative ventures between publishers and film companies. Movie people seem permanently ensconced at the Sherry-Netherland or the Park Lane, searching for "fresh material" or "first looks" and calling on publishers and agents. One of the first things Twentieth Century-Fox did, for example, with their recently appointed creative affairs executive Ronda Gōmez-Quiñones was to send her off to New York for a three-week round of mingling with the New York literary set. "It was," she says, "mainly to establish contacts." Which is just one indication of the weight being given to having open lines into the world of the written word.

Writers Keep the Rights

Peter Bart, after leaving Paramount to form Bart/Palevsky Productions, kept his lines open and bought, as one of his projects, an outline for a new novel, "Prometheus One," by the authors of "The Glass Inferno," Thomas Scortia and Frank Robinson. Believing that "the novelizing scheme is best used for developing material," Bart hired them to write a first-draft screenplay, with the understanding that they would then write the novel while another writer was brought in to polish the screenplay. The writer's polish was in turn sent to Scortia and Robinson for mulling over in terms of the novel. And the fact that it was Richard Parks at Curtis Brown who sold the outline of the proposed book to Peter Bart illustrates another change in the tie-in business: the increasing tendency of authors and their agents or producers to withhold publication rights from the studio and handle them themselves. According to William Grose, executive editor of Dell, "with only one exception ('Waldo Pepper' by William Goldman), we haven't done a tie-in where the studio controlled the rights for the past few years. On the bigger deals the writer is keeping the rights and writing the novelization himself or at least having a say in who does; either way, he's taking more of an interest, which is good." Grose also points out that since many talented writers are writing for films these days, publishers are looking to them as a good source for material for novels, period. "It could make a lot of sense to buy the novelization rights to just a treatment for a reasonable sum, say $7500, get a novelizer and pay him the same, and wind up with a good softcover original for $15,000 from something that might never see the light of day as a movie. In a sense, we are doing with paperback originals what television is doing with movies-of-the-week—marketing strong topical stories that can be encapsulated in a line or two." He, like other editors, is also buying novelization rights to films or movies-of-the-week well after they've been shown, to publish them not as tie-ins **but** simply as original paperbacks intended to stand on their own.

At Avon Judy Weber notes that "one of the biggest changes in the past year or so is that there are more and more TV tie-ins and people are recognizing the importance of them." Even a one-shot television show with high ratings can sell large quantities of books. Ms. Weber cites "Go Ask Alice," a preexisting book which had 308,000 copies in print in softcover when the television show first aired in January, 1973, six months after its publication and then spiraled to an additional 1,709,000 in the 10 months following it. She also mentioned the after-the-fact novelization of "Sunshine," which came out, novelized by a distinguished writer, Norma Klein, with a first printing of 800,000 more than six months after the show was aired in November of 1973 and is now up to over 1,000,000 copies, a testament to the long-term sales effectiveness that a television special can have on a book tie-in. Bantam's "The Autobiography of Miss Jane Pittman" provides another case in point. Its first printing, in June of 1972, consisted of 160,000 copies; in January of 1973, when the Emmy-winning CBS television special was aired, there were still fewer than 200,000 copies out. But between January and November of 1974, 550,000 copies of the special tie-in edition were printed and shipped, 150,000 of them to coincide with the rerun aired on November 3.

Television has also boosted the book business in that bids from networks and TV producers have of late become competitive with those paid by film companies. And a new market is opening up for certain books that could not carry a feature film but work very well when adapted for television. Film director Ulu Grosbard points out that "it used to be that if a book was dead for films it was just dead. Now, thanks to TV, that's not so."

The tie-in boom is no surprise to Richard Fischoff at Warner Paperback Library. It is his view that people aren't essentially readers any more, that except for famous best-selling or category authors people don't buy by author, and that reading has become a time-killing activity rather than an avocation. This means that people who buy books are likely to be attracted by extra-literary factors such as eye-catching graphics, a photo of a star, a familiar logo—some recognition factor from a non-linear medium that makes the book stand out from the welter of other books on the stands. To Fischoff, tie-ins provide a way to get people back to enjoying reading. "Also prices for tie-ins are going up," he adds, "because of the competitive situation in the softcover industry. Whereas it used to be one or two houses bidding for a property, now half a dozen are going after the same thing. It's no longer a buyer's market. Agents, motion picture companies, publishers, writers, actors and producers—everyone seems to have realized there is pie now and they all want a piece of it." Or, as Patrick O'Connor, editor-in-chief of Popular Library, succinctly puts it, "In the old days, they wanted us . . . desperately. And now, we want them . . . desperately."

In fact, some feel that the market may already be stretched to the breaking point. At Bantam, both editorial director Marc Jaffe and tie-in editor Wendy Broad feel that different criteria have to be used in judging tie-ins and potential

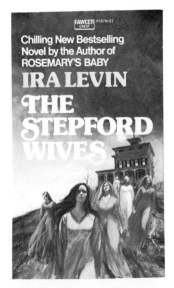

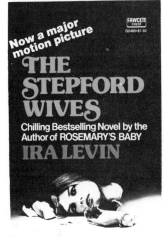

Killing the Golden Goose

best sellers. "We're gambling on the success of a film and that's quite different from gambling on a finished manuscript or an author whose work is proven in the marketplace," says Jaffe. Dell has come up with some pretty whopping advances lately, for "French Connection II" (a reputed $75,000 for a straight novelization), and a couple in which the advances will amount to over six figures if the novelizations come out in hardcover first, "Macho" by Richard Nash and "Ghost Boat" by George Simpson and Neal Burger. But although Grose states categorically that Dell is interested in publishing only the tie-ins they think will be really big, he warns that "if the advances and royalties continue to increase, it'll kill the goose that laid the golden egg. It now costs $25,000 to $45,000 for the tie-in that used to cost from $5000 to $10,000 and obviously not all tie-ins are going to be profitable at those prices."

Other houses take a cooler view of the inflationary spiral in the tie-in business. At New American Library, Robert Haynie says: "Rather than concentrating on novelizations, we've always given a lot of thought to what kind of movie a book will make; and we've been lucky in that books that we've bought reprint rights to have often subsequently become films." He sees no reason to change this approach. And Leona Nevler, publisher of the Fawcett Book Division, concurs: "You can strike it lucky but you can also have a lot of problems with tie-ins. We're primarily interested in books that can stand on their own as books."

Bypassing the Agents

Charles Bloch, Bantam's West Coast editorial representative, feels that a lot depends on whether agents continue to find it worthwhile to make the effort of dealing with publishing rights. Now that it's becoming big business worldwide— "The Sting," for example, has been translated into eight foreign languages—and now that so many factors can be involved (Does Paul Newman get cover approval? How exactly does the Writer's Guild stipulate that the screenwriter's credit should read on the cover? Who handles Charles MacArthur's estate when tying in with a remake of "The Front Page"? And so on . . .), this effort can be considerable. One studio, Universal, has decided to buck the trend to diversification and make dealing with publishers a full-time occupation for Stanley Newman, in a newly created position as vice-president and head of MCA Publishing. "Tie-ins are very complex to publish," he concedes. "But we think it's a big enough business and important enough so that we are pulling in all the rights and dealing [directly with publishers instead of dealing] through agents. Before, when the studios viewed tie-ins as strictly a merchandising and licensing business and not a publishing operation, they just sat back and let the payments come in without trying to make it easier for anybody. The publishers did most of the work. Even the agents were not involved or interested. Then the agents started filling the gap that existed between film companies and publishers. However, what we are doing is offering a single point of communication for publishers with questions about any aspect of publishing or rights. In addition, we are actually creating books which would not otherwise have existed; when, for example, it's not possible to publish the screenplay or the novelization." Two cases in point: NAL's "Earthquake, the Story of a Movie," which is essentially a rack-size variation of a theater program, and "Airport '75," a souvenir 8 x 11-inch magazine published by Award Books with Universal and distributed by Select Magazines, with some copies being sold in the theaters.

Regarding remuneration for such cooperation, Newman feels that "if we contribute to the success of the book, we want to participate in proportion to that success. On the other hand, if our product is not successful and the publisher therefore doesn't benefit, we don't want to be paid. We'll take the same risk as the publisher." What this amounts to is that in the case of a new tie-in edition of a previously published book—with a different title, perhaps, or a star's photo on the cover—Universal will not demand a flat fee for providing the tie-in art but will insist on a graduated royalty of, say, 1% on sales of from 100,000 to 250,000 copies, escalating beyond that up to 3%. Of course, he points out, there are exceptions, such as "Jaws," out recently from Bantam and due in a tie-in edition in June, when the film is released. Where the book can obviously stand on its own, Universal is still willing to tie-in strictly for joint promotional purposes.

Like Fischoff, Newman commented on the importance of the instant recognition factor of a tie-in in selling books, especially in foreign countries. "As the paperback business continues to develop in major non-English markets, tie-in books will be especially valuable. In fact, we are considering withholding world rights, taking less money originally and then selling off the rights country by country as we market our TV series or open our film in each country."

Mel Bloom and Associates' Stuart Miller, a Los Angeles agent who handles a number of screenwriters, comments ruefully, "I'm really surprised it took the studios so long to figure out that there is money to be made in tie-ins. Actually, they probably could make the most money by publishing the tie-ins themselves and then having them distributed by one of the big softcover houses, but the second best way is for them to control the rights and take a percentage. I don't like it, but I can't refute the logic of it. It's sound business on the part of the studio and there's nothing wrong in having a studio, which after all makes an enormous investment in a film, participate in the revenue that accrues from a novelization." He figures the other studios will more than likely follow Universal's lead very shortly. "It would only take one picture that has a tie-in that really works, given that the studio has some significant piece of the profits, to pay for a tie-in operation like Universal's for a year or more, so they'd be foolish not to do it," he reasons.

However, he has a word of caution for the studios. "Studio executives are tuned in to a whole other profit picture and because of their frame of reference and their eagerness to jump into the novelization game, they may be overestimating what the market will bear." He cites as an example a deal he himself just made for one of his screenwriters in which, over and above his fee for writing the screenplay, the writer—but only if the film is made—gets paid an advance in six figures against two-thirds of all publishing revenues, even though someone else

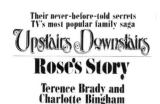

Their never-before-told secrets TV's most popular family saga

Upstairs Downstairs

Rose's Story

Terence Brady and Charlotte Bingham

Their never-before-told secrets TV's most popular family saga

Upstairs Downstairs

Mr. Hudson's Diaries

Michael Hardwick

Overestimating the Market?

will novelize the book. "So if the advance is, say, $100,000, the studio has to make $150,000 from the publishing revenue just to break even and that's tough to do. With numbers like that, even a successful tie-in becomes risky."

So far, the tie-in boom seems to be too new to have affected the Writer's Guild's rules and regulations governing publication rights. In fact, the West Coast branch seems virtually unaware of the situation, and close examination of the Guild's Theatrical and Television Film Basic Agreement, written in prose that is nearly impenetrable to the layman's eye, yields only confusion since the rules it contains bear no resemblance to how such deals are actually handled. As Stuart Miller says, "The Writer's Guild has structured the rules dealing with the selling of a novelization so that not only do they not make any sense, but it would in fact become difficult to make a deal if you followed them." He conjectures that "probably what happened is that somewhere along the line in some contract negotiation between the Writer's Guild and the Producer's Association, someone must have raised the issue of paperback novelizations and in those days the studio didn't care and the Guild clearly didn't understand the mechanics of it, so they just came up with a few guidelines to cover the writer as best they could and let it go at that." There have been no changes in these regulations to keep up with what's happening but it's safe to say that at some point—probably in 1976 during their next contract negotiations—there will have to be.

Tie-Ins for the Schools

Another area where success has not yet bred change is in the tie-ins marketed through the Scholastic and Xerox Education Publications (formerly A.E.P.) book clubs and magazines. According to Michael Hobson, publisher of Scholastic's book club division, "We've been enormously successful with movie and TV tie-ins. They're probably our best-selling titles. The nicest situation for us is when there is a preexisting good book, like 'The Prime of Miss Jean Brodie,' that is made into a movie which enables us to really sell the book, although we've also done a good many novelizations, especially of Disney pictures, and a few screenplays, like our own edition of 'Cabaret,' which we bought from Random House and published with a movie tie-in cover. In other cases, we just buy copies of outside publishers' books to sell through our clubs." These club sales can climb to over a million copies ("The Love Bug" and "Sounder," for example). Strict editorial judgment is exercised as to suitability, for this audience and school use, of such books as "The Godfather" and "The Exorcist" has been considered beyond the pale. Although, according to Barbara McCall, managing editor of the paperback book club program at Xerox, "we sometimes ask a publisher to make an abridgment excising offensive passages, as we did in the case of 'The Glass Inferno.' "

The Scholastic and Xerox magazines run either synopses or adapted and very condensed versions of scripts such as "Jeremy" and "Where the Lilies Bloom," the theory being that not only does this work as a good promotional device for the film but also that children with reading problems seem to like to read these simplified screenplays, so that teachers use them as teaching aids in classrooms. "Up until this year," says Katherine Robinson, editor of *Scope* at Scholastic, "we've had no trouble getting permission to use scripts and we've paid nothing. But now that is beginning to change—although when we were asked to pay, we refused." The only instances in which they are willing to pay to novelize a script is when it is a film that was released some time ago, such as "Cool Hand Luke," and therefore the book has no promotional value for the film.

Creative approaches are being taken to avenues of cooperative promotion these days on many levels. One film—an atypical one, admittedly—has two tie-ins, of sorts, namely, "The Towering Inferno." Just as Warner's and Fox solved the dilemma of having each paid huge sums for different books about the same kind of disaster—Richard Martin Stern's "The Tower" at McKay, and Scortia and Robinson's "The Glass Inferno" at Doubleday—by joining forces and coproducing a screenplay that combined the two narratives, so Warner Paperback Library and Pocket Books, the two softcover houses which bought rights to the books for sizable sums in each case, each have run cover copy lines indicating that the Irwin Allen film is based in part on their book.

Cover Art and
Movie Ads

A less quirky example of intramural cooperation can be seen in the way Max Ehrlich's "The Reincarnation of Peter Proud" is being promoted by the company that made the film, Bing Crosby Productions. Arthur Manson, BCP's executive vice-president in charge of sales and marketing, has been involved from the minute the property was bought for filming, which was after it had been sold by Bantam to Bobbs-Merrill but before it was published. BCP helped design the hardcover book jacket so that it would coordinate with future movie art, put money into the hardcover advertising campaign, placed trade ads for the book in *Variety* and the *Hollywood Reporter* and designed a 30-second television commercial using a clip from the film to advertise the book in eight big cities. Prints of this commercial were also made available to theater exhibitors so that while the book was being launched the commercial was being shown on 500 screens all over the country, with a free book given to each exhibitor who ran it. In addition, Manson attended Bobbs-Merrill's sales conference, then followed up by writing an individual letter to about a thousand key accounts to tell them about the film and offer them a chance to see it free when it opens in their city. (He got a whopping 90% response to this offer, incidentally.) Further, every copy of the first edition of the hardcover contained a coupon which could be sent to Bobbs-Merrill in exchange for a free ticket to the film.

All of this adds up to a lot of cross-pollinating going on, and how fertile it will all prove remains to be seen. But right now; on almost any given day New York editors can be observed digging into the guacamole dip at the Polo Lounge in Beverly Hills, while jarringly tanned producers and creative heads of studios try to catch the waiter's eye at the King Cole Bar in New York as they all hotly pursue the same objective: developing and exploiting material from which they . . . can benefit.

Bibliography

The book industry is a specialized area which seldom receives the serious attention it deserves, outside of specialists in the field. As Nancy Hardin shows in her article, there is great affinity today between the producers of books and the producers of other popular culture media, such as the movies. One of the running debates occurring in the industry is the result of a series of articles by John P. Dessauer, who suggests that book publishers should cut back in production in certain areas because there are just too many books being produced today. Dessauer, contributing editor of *Publishers Weekly,* published his conclusions in August, September, and October of 1974. Three critical responses to Dessauer's thesis appear in *Publisher's Weekly* (Dec. 2, 1974), pp. 42–45, including Dessauer's rebuttal. These articles provide useful information to students interested in current practices in the book publishing field. Dealing with practices and problems in the publishing field are Curtis G. Benjamin, *A Candid Critique of Book Publishing* (R. R. Bowker, 1977), which is the result of fifty years of experience in the industry; *The Business of Publishing: A PW Anthology* (R. R. Bowker, 1976), which includes reprints of appropriate *Publisher's Weekly* articles dealing with the industry; and Benjamin M. Compaigne, *The Book Industry in Transition: An Economic Study of Book Distribution and Marketing* (Knowledge Industries, Inc., 1978), which provides excellent discussion of industry structure, distribution, audience, etc. There are good statistical tables, many of which contain trend data. For historical background on the industry, consult the three-volume *History of Book Publishing in the United States* by John Tebbel: Vol 1, *The Creation of an Industry, 1630–1865* (1972); Vol. II, *The Expansion of an Industry, 1865–1919* (1975), and Vol. III, *The Golden Age Between Two Wars, 1920–1940* (1978). This is the definitive study. A fourth volume is expected to bring the history to the present.

32 Movies: The Problem With G

Georgia Jeffries

In the Motion Picture Association of America's rating system, G stands for "General audience," which is further clarified by the tag, "All ages admitted." One might think, therefore, that a film bearing the G designation would be able to draw the largest possible audience. Is this the case? Curiously, the film industry has become profoundly suspicious of the G ratings applied to its films. Just as suspicious, apparently, is the very audience for which the rating was designed— the underseventeen age-group. It's almost as though, unnoticed, the entire film-going population has emerged into PG status (Parental Guidance suggested).

A year after the Motion Picture Association of America's rating code was introduced in 1968, thirty-two percent of the industry output was rated G, a close second to the thirty-nine percent rated PG. But the following nine years witnessed a steady decline of G movies to a low of thirteen percent in 1977. PG films were again thirty-nine percent of the total product last year, while R (Restricted: under seventeen requires accompanying parent or adult guardian) topped all categories at forty percent. (In 1968 twenty-three percent were rated R.)

In 1968 Paramount Pictures submitted two appeals to the MPAA to reduce a PG rating to a G rating on its multimillion-dollar, all-star musical epic, *Paint*

Georgia Jeffries has her feet in both the journalistic and film worlds. She is a writer, screenwriter, and actress, holding memberships in The Writers' Guild of America and the Screen Actors' Guild. Reprinted with permission from the June 1978 issue of *American Film* magazine, copyright 1978 The American Film Institute, J. F. Kennedy Center, Washington, D.C. 20566.

Your Wagon. Paramount lost, the PG stayed, and the movie did not do memorable business. In other words, the PG rating hindered the film's success.

Ten years later, studios continue to aim for the most marketable rating for their pictures—but now it's very seldom for a G. In fact, *Daily Variety* reported that Twentieth Century-Fox's preliminary cut of *Star Wars* earned a G from the MPAA. But by the time the final cut was submitted, added scenes depicting more explicit "fantasy violence" warranted a PG rating. While the *Daily Variety* story is denied by MPAA president Jack Valenti, and unconfirmed by Fox, it is regarded as a matter of fact by many industry spokesmen. The original G rating for *Star Wars,* it is said, was a perfect example of a G that was undesired—and corrected.

Many producers try to ensure a PG or R rating by the gratuitous addition of "strong" language or nudity or violence. In a risk-taking business one attempts to cover all bets, and a G rating at the box office appears to be more of a gamble than most producers want to take. In this era of "event" moviemaking, the more traditional, conventional G-rated family film cannot compete with the titillating, gimmicky draws of sex and violence. Anything less than "extraordinary," "shocking," "breathtaking," "daringly explicit" can be watched on the home television screen. That is why production and promotion experts must intrigue moviegoers with bigger stars, bigger special effects, and bigger screen sensations than ever before.

People don't simply go to movies any more. They are seduced into seeing them, and few adults can be seduced by a G film. Filmmakers don't see the point of creating a $15 million blockbuster for the G marketplace.

Anyway, in many exhibitors' and moviegoers' minds, G is synonymous with Walt Disney. Let Disney's studio handle the limited market for pet raccoons, lonely little boys, extraterrestrial cats, precocious Pollyannas, and animated dragons. The granddaddy of family films manufactures a popular product with style, grace, and inimitable expertise.

But at the corner of Mickey Mouse Avenue and Dopey Drive in the realm of Disney there is cautious concern about the impact of the G rating. Martin Rabinovitch, director of market planning, theorizes that "the way that the rating system has been used has resulted in some stereotyping of Walt Disney films as kiddie films. They are, in fact, family films for a wide range of ages. . . . Labeling a film has forced the public to be rigid in its response to it. . . . [It's a] problem which we try hard to overcome."

Jerome Courtland, a Disney producer, sees the problem as a serious one that may be worsening: "I've heard eleven year olds say they didn't want to see a G-rated movie, just because it was G and that translated into kid stuff. I think a lot of people have that image, and that type of cultural stereotype has to be overcome by advertising and publicity." He would like to expand the Disney product and move into more substantial dramatic themes that explore the heartbreak as well as the comic adventure of life—still within the environs of a G rating.

However, Disney's slight but visible decline in theatrical revenues from 1975 to 1977 hints that the public may be growing weary of G movies. Domestic gross revenues dropped a total of four percent in the last two years, three percent in 1977 alone.

While Disney is still celebrating an enviable run of box-office successes, notably the critically acclaimed animation *The Rescuers* ($14.5 million in domestic rentals and a projected $28.5 million in foreign rentals), it's the live action feature that appears to be threatened by the G stigma. *Candleshoe,* a suspense comedy starring Helen Hayes and Jodie Foster, was expected to be one of its major commercial successes. Despite the bright, demographic forecast, the December release has not yet lived up to those expectations.

The Disney studio's recent entry into market research for film advertising and promotion sheds some light on why even its secure position at the box office is being reevaluated. Rabinovitch told of inviting teenagers to Disney screening sessions without informing them of the scheduled movie beforehand. Afterward, the majority were enthusiastic about the film but admitted they never would have attended if they had known it was G rated. It is all in the image, and the public is not the only party guilty of responding to an image without first evaluating the substance behind it. "This is not just a culture problem—it is an industry problem. Other filmmakers and film critics almost always stereotype our movies and dismiss them as strictly juvenile fare. We're categorized," concluded Rabinovitch.

Many in Hollywood agree that the G rating has done more harm than good, fostering an unintentional boomerang effect that alienates the public and restricts filmmakers. But it is a stigma that can be confronted and surmounted. The key, as with any film, but crucially so with the G-rated product, is marketing.

Max Youngstein, former vice-president of Paramount Pictures and currently a financial consultant to independent producers, thinks the G-rating obstacle can be overcome if the filmmaker examines three major considerations. First, unless a movie is exclusively oriented to the juvenile market, adult appeal in the theme (i.e., a love story), viewpoint, dramatic conflict, and/or identifiable stars must be built into the film. After production, the marketing approach must be imaginative. Four-walling, regional release, and slow release are alternatives for distribution. Finally, advertising is essential to overcoming the G image, emphasizing the intrinsic adult appeal of the picture.

Youngstein said, "There is a large number of G-rated movies that if handled differently than the established studio route, could be successful. In the past, we had pabulum pictures, but we didn't have any label giving them away. Today, because that label is applied to pabulum part of the time, it automatically stereotypes any movie it designates. The only way it can be overcome is with proper handling."

Some independent producers are already taking advantage of a near void left by the major companies. With innovative marketing techniques, they are reaping large grosses on G-rated movies. One of these successful producers discovered the valuable resources of computer science. Charles Sellier, Jr., president and executive producer of Sunn Classic Pictures in Los Angeles, pioneered cost-control computerization of feature film production.

After serving as president of his own film company, Creative Visual Dynamics in Denver, he came to Sunn in 1974 and took over *The Life and Times of Grizzly Adams*. Sellier then installed his computer systems, a research and testing department, and mapped out advertising strategy for all Sunn releases. He stands behind a four-year track record during which every film has, at least, broken even, and, at best, brought in box-office grosses nearing $20 million. Impressive? Yes. But it doesn't come near to the blockbuster grosses Hollywood has come to expect after such films as *Jaws, Star Wars,* and *Close Encounters of the Third Kind.*

So far Sellier's system works—and he makes it work exclusively for G-rated products such as *The Mysterious Monsters, The Outer Space Connection, In Search of Noah's Ark,* and *Beyond and Back.* His commitment to family films is personal as well as financial: "I'm Mormon—so are most of the people who work at Sunn—and I believe the family is the basic teaching unit of society. That's why we develop film projects that encourage the family to participate. And that's hard to do, because the interests of a thirty-one-year-old father, a twenty-nine-year-old mother, a nine-year-old son, and a five-year-old daughter are diverse. . . . Walt Disney was a creative genius who instinctively knew what I need a computer to tell me. . . . The basis of our test system is to find out what will please each family member and what will draw them into the theater together."

The people Sellier does not please, or make any effort to, are film critics and members of the Hollywood establishment. One exhibitor dismissed Sunn products as "garbage" that nonetheless bring in the public time and time again because of blitzkrieg television advertising campaigns. He noted that exiting patrons often complain about the quality of each film but come back to fill the theater the next time a Sunn release played. Sellier is regarded by many as an exploitative, sensationalistic merchandiser, but what he does, he does well.

Sunn Classic Pictures tests concepts and ideas before they're put into script form, tests again for their market, and finally tests for the appropriate release dates and locations on their distributional four-walling network. With fourteen regional offices nationwide, Sunn is the acknowledged kingpin of four-walling.

Four-walling is a procedure in which a company rents theaters for a flat rate in computer-designated markets, conducts massive television and newspaper promotion and advertising campaigns, and assumes the entire box-office risk. Essentially a boom or bust maneuver, four-walling can break the box-office bank on a film that flies, or it can literally put a company out of business, as happened with American National Enterprises, which brought back the long ignored technique in 1968.

What is behind Sunn's computerized, four-walling modus operandi is control—control of the product, the distribution, and the marketplace. (In an effort to further perfect its distribution system, the company is currently experimenting with feeding satellite-beamed weather forecasts into the computer to avoid premiering a picture during blizzards, rainstorms, and other environmental rampages.) Sellier maintained that "other studios just use computers to write checks and keep track of the grosses, but what we do with computers boggles the mind."

Unsurprisingly, Sellier has been approached by several major studios that want to share the riches of his computer system—for a price, of course. Sellier declined because "if the system can fine tune G-rated films, it can probably tell other filmmakers how many lashes to whip across a girl's back [in an R-rated or X-rated film]."

Sunn's president contended that the G rating has no effect on box-office receipts with his method. But he conceded he doesn't mind if Hollywood continues to espouse that theory, thereby shutting itself out of competition with his market.

Pacific International Enterprises, Inc. (PIE), maker of *The Adventures of the Wilderness Family,* is another four-walling production company. The film, four-walled by its independent producers, opened last year to generally favorable reviews and astounding box-office success domestically and internationally. The film even did unexpected business among the urbane moviegoers of the Big Apple, garnering $2 million in eighty-eight theaters in its first fourteen days. Produced for under $2 million and marketed for $4.5 million annually, it has topped $30 million at the box office and is still climbing in 1978, its second year of release.

The Adventures of the Wilderness Family is an unquestionable commercial success. It is a professionally produced entertainment that while harboring no artistic pretensions, honestly dramatizes a significant yearning of an increasing number of American families. And yet, if it had been up to the Hollywood establishment, this movie would probably never have been made. The script contained none of the supposedly surefire draws—sex, violence, and "provocative" language. (Did a major company miss the boat by not distributing the film?)

PIE has devoted itself exclusively (with one exception, *The Late Great Planet Earth*) to G-rated wilderness sagas. After launching an early series of amateurish 16mm semidocumentaries, it graduated to a more professional product and a wider theatrical feature market with *Vanishing Wilderness* and *The Wonder of It All.*

As production quality improved so did the critical appraisal of its releases. The most recent picture, and first Western, *Across the Great Divide,* impressed the *Los Angeles Times* with its "unsophisticated appeal and thoroughly sophisticated craftsmanship." The movie appeared several weeks straight on *Variety's* list of the fifty top grossing films, along with two other PIE releases, *The Adventures of the Wilderness Family* and *The Late Great Planet Earth.* Clearly second to Sunn in size and ambition, the Oregon company has carved out a more modest but still remarkably successful niche for itself. PIE's next project is a sequel to *The Adventures of the Wilderness Family,* and vice-president Russell Engle sees no change in the future from the family-oriented fare.

Engle said that "admittedly it is very difficult booking extended playing time in theaters that want PG and R movies, although right now we are in our eighth week in twenty Los Angeles theaters with *Across the Great Divide*. But we pioneered the family entertainment film, and we know our markets after playing them for nine years. We know our limitations and our strengths, such as the suburban and rural houses." He added optimistically, "We feel the novelty of sex and violence is starting to wear off among the moviegoing public and that family movies will come back stronger in the next few years."

The wildly successful 1974 release, *Benji,* is another testimony to the family market waiting to be tapped. It is the story of an excessively cute dog's adventures told from its viewpoint! Written, directed, and produced by Joe Camp, the completed film sat on the shelf for months while he tried in vain to get it distributed. Camp said that "the movie was so wholesome that major distributors didn't want to touch it except as a throwaway on Saturday mornings. One major asked us to put in a couple of cusswords so it could be marketed as PG."

Instead, Camp set up a distribution subsidiary to his Mulberry Square Productions, used nonnegotiable contracts to ensure playing time, and refused to book in any but first-run theaters. *Benji* earned $11.5 million in net profits worldwide.

His 1976 G-rated film, *HAWMPS,* a Western based on the first camel cavalry, took in $15 million at the box office. *For the Love of Benji,* also a G, followed in 1977 and brought in $17 million at the domestic box office and netted $6 million before its rerelease this spring.

Bill Lyday, Mulberry's director of advertising and publicity, said, "*Benji* was unique, but weighing story and technical quality, *For the Love of Benji* is a better, more professionally created product. It's not the quality that has hurt us at the box office, it is what has happened to the image of the G film in the last three years. The G is a stigma that turns away more than it draws."

Joe Camp continued, "You see, back in 1974 part of *Benji's* success was timing. So many producers had jumped into hard PG and R films that the public was ready for a film they could enjoy as a family. Today I think the pendulum has started to swing back to more family-type movies, but society has changed, and the rating code has splintered audiences."

Despite this distrust of the G rating on the part of producers and filmmakers, a new group of independent production companies is carefully scanning the commercial potential of a market generally dismissed by the majors. Six Flags, Inc., owner of the world's largest network of theme parks, released its first film, a family comedy called *Barnaby and Me,* starring Sid Caesar, in Texas in April. Its second release, *Not-So-Big,* will open this summer.

According to Andrew Harris, planning and development coordinator, "Disney started with a base in film production and expanded to theme parks. We're doing it the other way around. We feel the Six Flags endorsement in our twenty-two-market area will be equivalent to the Disney endorsement in California and Florida. We're putting all our marketing muscle at the park level behind each picture promotion. We don't feel you can just put a G film out there in the marketplace and support it with television and ad campaigns. The picture will die that way. If you come in with intensive promotion and try to make it an event, then you have a much better chance of succeeding. Public awareness is the key."

Creating consumer awareness is not the lone prerogative of a multimillion-dollar theme park organization. An Atlanta-based production firm called the International Picture Show Company has just launched its first movie, *The Billion Dollar Hobo,* starring Tim Conway, with a successful regional release pattern. Jerry Hopman, a former Disney associate, founded Producers Creative Services, the Los Angeles agency that is handling advertising and marketing for the film. He believes "the advantage of a G film is that you can create promotional tie-ins region by region. You always need a tool. We use a circus approach and make each opening an event."

The Billion Dollar Hobo, like most successful G-rated entertainment, brings in the highest box-office receipts in the South and in the Midwest. It is also that untapped midwestern audience, generally regarded as more traditional than the trend-setting populations on either coast, that another family filmmaker is shooting for.

Bonita Granville Wrather, an Oscar nominee as a child actress and producer of the "Lassie" television series for nineteen years, is bringing back America's most beloved collie to the silver screen—despite the cynical consensus of some industry experts that Lassie will no longer draw today's more sophisticated audiences.

The diminutive woman declared, "I know what Hollywood thinks the public wants, and I know what I have—a stack of amazing research that confirms that a large number of people want to see a wholesome picture. They don't come out to movies more often because the product they want to see isn't being shown. I also know that we're taking a risk, but we have made a total commitment with this project, and that means going with it all the way, even if it means distributing it ourselves."

The Magic of Lassie, a $3.5 million production geared for a fall release, is being entirely financed by the Wrather Corporation. Mrs. Wrather is coproducer, and her husband, Jack, is executive producer. The determined couple has spared no expense in acquiring veterans James Stewart, Alice Faye, and Mickey Rooney to star. Robert and Richard Sherman, whose wide range of previous musical credits include *Mary Poppins,* wrote and scored the picture. Don Chaffey, long associated with a string of Disney hits, including *Pete's Dragon,* is the director. Grammy winner Debby Boone sings the theme song, "When You're Loved." Seemingly, the proper professional ingredients have been added to create an entertaining movie in the family tradition. But many in the industry view that tradition as passé as long as it is marketed with a G rating.

Sidney Ganis, vice-president of advertising and publicity for Warner Bros., said, "In general we prefer to handle PG movies. G says young people's entertainment, and the teenage audiences which compose the majority of moviegoers don't want to see that. Take *Blazing Saddles,* for instance, which was rated R. Demographics showed that kids dominated its audiences. Every time it is rereleased it does landmark matinee business. In this modern world of electronic craziness, the impact of television has created a more sophisticated generation."

Crossed Swords, a Warner Bros. production based on *The Prince and the Pauper,* premiered to a bustling March box office at Radio City Music Hall. The rating, which Ganis conceded they were happy to get, was PG. The company's only two scheduled G releases for the year include *The Sea Gypsies,* the adventures of a widowed father and his daughters on a sailing voyage, and *An Enemy of the People,* based on Henrik Ibsen's classic play, with Steve McQueen.

An Enemy of the People is a highly unusual marketing challenge that has stalled the Warner Bros. advertising and distribution campaigns for months. It is an adult story without sex, harsh language, or violence and with a star in an uncharacteristic role. Is it strictly an art-house market? Or can marketing wizards hit upon a gimmick that will draw the public? Not the least of Warners' problems is the G rating, an MPAA judgment that Ganis confirmed "we are very tentative about."

Nevertheless, not all exhibitors agree with studios and distributors that the bias against G entertainment is warranted. One assistant manager of a southern California theater, Wayne Carpenter, insisted the sophistication of the audience is not what's hurting the G box office. He cited, instead, the quality of the product and the way it is handled.

"A lack of suitable films" was the chief reason Radio City Music Hall was almost forced to close its doors, believes vice-president Patricia Robert. But she puts further blame on the MPAA rating system.

"The introduction of the rating system in 1968 hit us hard because it coincided with a tremendous product shortage. When you put a category on your movie, you also put a category on your audience. Consider a few of the strong, meaningful films we played before the rating system—*Days of Wine and Roses, Cat on a Hot Tin Roof, Some Came Running.* Those were films that drew adults and teenagers as well as families.

"But after the rating system came into effect, because we had an image as a family house, the industry took it for granted that we would only book G and occasional PG films. The industry attitude and the public made us adhere to it. People heard strong language on the streets of New York, but they didn't want to hear it in Radio City Music Hall. The times changed . . . seasonal family occasions like Christmas and Easter were not enough to sustain us during the rest of the year when the families—and those responding to our family image—didn't come in."

Bruce Corwin, president of the Metropolitan Theatres in California, prefers to show PG, "with the exception of Disney." But Roy Evans, a division manager for United Artists Theatre Circuit, Inc., the nation's second largest exhibition chain, rates G movies as second at their box offices (behind PG but ahead of R) and underscored that the rating doesn't have to be a stigma if the film is marketed properly. He added, "I think a lot of producers hide behind the excuse that G movies won't do good business because they personally prefer to make a more sophisticated product."

Seymour Evans, a vice-president of public relations and publicity of G.C.C. Theatres, Inc., the world's largest theater chain, stressed not only is there a shortage of G product but also an equal lack of vision about its marketing. The major distributors might well follow the enterprising marketing techniques of some of the successful independent producers.

Take the case of *Sounder,* for example. Made for a little over a million dollars, the film won large critical acclaim and $11 million in receipts at the box office. Its producer, Robert B. Radnitz, is considered a major force in "quality family entertainment." That is a categorization attributed with respect and admiration, but a categorization he rejects. Until Radnitz's last two releases, *Birch Interval* and *A Hero Ain't Nothin' But a Sandwich,* which won PG ratings, he, along with Disney, had exploited the G market with award-winning films such as *A Dog of Flanders, Island of the Blue Dolphins, And Now Miguel,* and *My Side of the Mountain.*

As the first producer to speak out against the MPAA rating code and still one of its most vocal and unrelenting critics, Radnitz emphasized, "It is true that the negative aspects of a G film can be circumvented in the long run, as with *Sounder . . .* but only with tender loving care. We had to wait a long time until word got out that *Sounder* was a serious film."

While Radnitz was waiting for that word to get out, he personally barnstormed across the country showing the film everyplace he could. Every major city had at least twenty sneak previews, and thousands of "opinion makers" were shown the film. Twentieth Century-Fox, the distributor, held more than three hundred screenings in New York City alone before the movie premiered.

This slow release pattern in selective markets was, the producer said, "a very long and arduous process." But it worked. Today he considers the production of a film strictly "the tip of the iceberg."

Radnitz's emphasis on proper marketing is shared by the other independent family producers at Disney, Sunn, PIE, and Mulberry Square. But other than that, and an equal commitment to avoid gratuitous sex, violence, or language, there is little common ground. The basic difference between a *Sounder* and a *Pete's Dragon* or a *Benji* is content. Radnitz's aim is not just to entertain but to interest an audience with provocative, serious themes. He feels that that aim is hampered by the stereotyped G rating.

As president of the MPAA and initiator of its rating code, Jack Valenti refuted the theory that the G rating itself has had any negative influence on the reduction of G-rated product and a corresponding falloff in box-office returns. Yet he did allow that producers use an easy way to get a PG rating—by throwing in some gratuitous language or violence. "You see, I have a hard time convincing my creative people that the rating will neither help nor hurt a film. Some of the most profoundly significant films could be G films. My personal favorite movie is a G film, *A Man for All Seasons,"* said Valenti.

Actually, the 1966 Academy Award-winning film that Valenti cited was released two years before the rating code's inception. *A Man for All Seasons* carries a retroactive G, and so does every other Hollywood film screened before 1968.

But we are not talking about retroactive ratings. The issue at hand is whether or not the G rating has become obsolete. To place *A Man for All Seasons* in proper perspective, one must ask: If that same historical drama were reshot by a major studio in 1978, would there be an obligatory "goddamn" or a bedroom sequence between Henry VIII and Anne Boleyn added to draw a PG rating and ensure an adult audience?

The irony is that the industry is running out of G-rated products faster than the public is walking away from the theaters that show them. Filmmakers have hyped themselves into believing a limited G market is not a market at all—despite a number of respectable box-office successes that proved creative handling can overcome juvenile stereotyping. If the family film is to survive, it may well have to rid itself of the G-rated anchor around its neck. And until the rating is reevaluated, the public must be reeducated to learn that G can also stand for Grown-up.

Bibliography

The film industry is a truly complex business ranging from the creative element, which borders upon classical art, to the most mundane business problem. The books reflect this diversity. It is suggested here that the serious student consult the following bibliographies for further study possibilities: John C. Gerlach and Lana Gerlach, compilers, *The Critical Index: A Bibliography of Articles on Film in English, 1947–1973* (Teachers College Press, Columbia University, 1974), and Richard Dyer MacCann and Edward S. Perry, compilers, *The New Film Index: A Bibliography of Magazine Articles in English, 1930–1970* (Dutton, 1975). Both books are excellent, comprehensive works that should be used in tandem—one book tends to supplement the other in several respects. For a reasonably current up-date of film books, consult the December issue of *Mass Media Booknotes* each year. *MMB* is issued monthly out of Temple University by Christopher H. Sterling, compiler. For an index of film reviews, consult Stephen E. Bowles, compiler, *Index to Critical Film Reviews 1930–1972* together with *Index to Critical Reviews of Books About Film* (Burt Franklin, 1974), two volumes. Excellent on-going information on the industry, its trends, ups, downs, and general condition can be followed in *Variety,* a weekly trade publication. *Daily Variety* and *Hollywood Reporter* also have some use. An interesting and insightful article on *Variety* can be found in Howard A. Rodman, "Show Biz Bible: Longest-Running Hit on B'Way," *More* (October 1977), pp. 27–32. An excellent magazine covering the industry practices from a working standpoint was *Action,* published by the Directors Guild of America. This hard-hitting, thoroughly candid publication was killed in 1979. For interesting insight into the problems with ratings, see Jack Valenti, "Rating the Movies," *Journal of Communication* (Summer 1976), pp. 62–63, a short discussion of studies which have analyzed public awareness of the rating system and public "rating" of the system, both tables containing data from 1969–1974. For pro and con arguments on the rating system itself, see *The Hollywood Reporter,* 43rd anniversary edition (November 29, 1973), which presents numerous comments, most from people in the film industry.

33   Neovideo: One Step Away

James Monaco

James Monaco has been a prolific writer on mass media subjects. He edited *Media Culture* and *Celebrity,* both published by Delta Books in 1978, and *American Film Now: The People, the Power, the Money* and *Alâin Renais,* both published by Oxford University Press in 1979. This article is reprinted with permission from the November issue of *American Film* magazine, copyright 1978, The American Film Institute, J. F. Kennedy Center, Washington, D.C. 20566.

The monthly program guide to Qube, Warner Communications' innovative two-way cable system that has been in operation in Columbus, Ohio, for almost a year, is a complex document. It is carefully designed, color-coded, twice as large and almost as thick as the *TV Guide* that serves the rest of us. There's a very good reason. *This Month on Qube* must list and describe thirty days of programming available on each of thirty Qube channels; it also has to explain the entertainment services in detail, note special events (town meetings, contests, and surveys), cross-index programs by category, and—perhaps most important—instruct more than twenty thousand subscribers in the intricacies of operating the paperback-sized, eighteen-button Qube console.

Qube is on the front line of the electronic media revolution and thus presents quite a challenge to the ancient medium of print. Print has risen to the occasion. *This Month on Qube* provides a short but thorough course on Qube-style living for the uninitiated. It's more than a little ironic that the cable system must depend on a magazine as the key to its electronic wonders.

This is only one of a number of ironies that confront students of cable television in the late seventies. The world of Qube is so different from standard broadcast television that it deserves to be described as the keystone to a radically new life-style for many Americans. Yet at the same time, a number of knowledgeable observers have suggested that cable television—even in its sophisticated Qube incarnation—may prove to be no more than a transitional medium, a quaint curiosity of late-twentieth-century media culture which will be overwhelmed by even newer technological forms well before it reaches its adolescence.

What are the advantages and restrictions of cable? How are broadcasters meeting its technological challenges? What room is there for the individual entrepreneur? Here is an overview of a subject that daily grows more complex and fascinating.

The Limits of Cable Television

The history of nonprint media has been influenced by two basic forces: technology and economics. Occasionally, politics has played a role, but for the most part, the destinies of television, radio, records, and film have been determined by economics and technology.

Let's take a quick look at the history of cable television. Wired transmission of television sounds and images is extremely costly, a fact whose significance was not lost on the pioneers of the radio-television industry when they chose to broadcast over the air rather than over wire. The model for wired transmission—

the telephone—was there from the beginning, but why invest billions in the arduous task of laying cable when the airwaves reached nearly every home in America—and were free for the asking?

Cable transmission developed only after broadcast television had become established, and then only to serve isolated small towns and rural areas where mountainous terrain blocked the broadcast signal. It wasn't until the mid-sixties, when broadcast television had reached its prime, that a few entrepreneurs began to conceive of cable television as an alternative to the system of networks and local stations.

Selling the concept of cable in major cities already served by network and independent VHF stations (and sometimes by UHF as well) became an exercise in what has come to be known as "blue-sky." Cable advocates promised a media millennium with enough channels for all minority viewpoints and tastes and, eventually, a whole host of electronic services.

Outside of a limited section of Columbus, Ohio, most of us are still waiting for that golden age. The reason? Few companies have the resources to support the enormous capital investment necessary for laying coaxial cable in urban areas. Moreover, the cable industry is still relatively decentralized due to the system of local franchises which has developed.

Nationwide, these conditions will exist for years to come. The saturation figure (the ratio of cable homes to total television homes) now stands at nineteen percent, still far short of the magical thirty percent most experts regard as the critical point in the development of cable as a major competitor to network broadcasting. A number of major cities—Boston, Chicago, Washington, D.C.— have no cable service whatsoever. In New York, San Francisco, and Los Angeles, cable is limited to certain areas. Forecasts of the date when thirty percent saturation will be achieved range from 1981 to 1985. But to achieve either of those goals is going to cost perhaps three to four times the one billion dollars that is estimated to have already been invested in plant construction.

Before that time, the rules of the game may change considerably.

Economically, the value of cable is based on a very simple principle: The coaxial cable can deliver more programming than broadcast television. Although every television set sold in the United States must by law be equipped to receive eighty-two channels over the air, even the prime markets have been limited to no more than seven VHF stations (for various technical reasons), and the seventy-channel UHF band has never reached parity with VHF, since it has never been in the interest of the manufacturing/broadcasting establishment to dilute the economic value of the strictly limited VHF outlets.

The Challenge from Broadcasters

But this need not always be so. People outside broadcasting have been arguing for a reallocation of the technical parameters of the spectrum to permit so-called drop-in stations between markets that are already saturated. More important, Texas Instruments has developed a device, called the TI tuner, which can divide the electromagnetic spectrum so that the number of operative VHF and UHF stations can be increased considerably. Finally, PBS has recently taken the lead in arguing for stricter FCC requirements for UHF tuners. Technical parity for UHF means a great deal to PBS; sixty percent of its member stations are currently relegated to second-class UHF broadcast citizenship. UHF parity would immediately result in the doubling or tripling of competitive signals in any particular market, since the UHF spectrum is vastly underutilized.

Clearly, cable's best bet—its expansive channel capability—may be matched by broadcasting within a very short time.

The cable people know this, and they are already developing second-generation systems. If UHF parity, coupled with TI tuners, will see cable's thirty-channel bet and raise it, then cable can see the broadcaster's eighty-two-channel bid and raise that right off the table—with the thousand-channel capability of fiber optics. The major expense in laying cable in urban areas has to do with conduits, not the wires themselves. Once the rights-of-way are in place, fiber optic "threads" can be added inexpensively. American Television and Communications Corporation (in the process of merging with Time, Inc., owner of Home Box Office and Telemation Program Services, who, between them, control eighty percent of the pay channel market) has announced plans to install a hundred-percent fiber optic link within its San Diego, California, system.

But don't count the broadcasters out of this game. No one has yet argued convincingly that a thousand channels are at all necessary. Also, the air people have two aces in the hole (both of which, by the way, may also prove highly useful for the wire people).

Satellites and Entrepreneurs

The first ace: satellites. The three commercial networks have maintained an iron grip on nationwide television precisely because they control the means of distribution via AT&T coaxial cables. This cozy arrangement began when the Radio Corporation of America was formed by manufacturers General Electric and Westinghouse and longlines operator AT&T. But satellites are not yet subject to this monopoly arrangement. Western Union's pair of Westars can each handle twelve television transmissions; RCA's pair of Satcoms have twice that capacity, for a total of seventy-two channels available to anyone who has the money. A few years ago the price was upwards of $100,000. Now it's less than a third of that and still falling. In the near future it may cost as little as $100 per hour to distribute programs nationwide. Anyone who has a ground station will be able to receive them, and ground station antennas, too, are quickly becoming affordable.

This doesn't exactly mean that reception of satellite signals is within the range of the fanatic television viewer. Direct satellite transmission to homes is still in the future. But it does mean that any number of entrepreneurs can begin to challenge the three major networks. The flamboyant yachtsman Ted Turner, who owns the Atlanta Braves baseball team and WTCG-TV Channel 17, a local station, has already begun to do so. For the last few months, WTCG has broadcast its signal via satellite to 295 cable systems in forty states.

So far, the major networks have refused to take advantage of satellites, preferring to stay with the longlines, which they still consider cost-effective. The real reason may be, however, that they don't want their affiliates to have ground stations at their disposal. The affiliates might be tempted to pick up Ted Turner's signal—or anyone else's—rather than the networks'.

On the other hand, satellite transmission has proved highly useful to both PBS and the cable systems. Satellite transmission is expected to increase the PBS audience in forthcoming months. Meanwhile, cable's rise in the last few years has been due in no small part to Home Box Office and other premium channels. HBO has used the satellites since late in 1975. It rents two transponders (the same program is delayed for the western time zones) and recently received FCC approval for a third. The major link among the four thousand isolated cable system operators, HBO looks to be the first national cable network operation.

The broadcasters' second ace is more theoretical: digital transmission. Like most other commercial electronics systems, television uses a less than precise, analog signal. Digital transmission, used for some telephone connections, would break down a video or audio signal into a figure which could then be expressed binarily, in the universal language of computers.

Digital Transmission and Clarity

There are numerous advantages to digital transmission. Interference—snow, static, and the like—becomes a thing of the past. The signal is either on or off. Time-sharing becomes a possibility: Two signals can be broadcast on the same wavelength. And the bandwidth requirements are greatly reduced, making possible the addition of many more channels without the expansion of the allocated spectrum. (Digital transmission also suggests entirely new methods of picture display that may, in time, lead to a perfectly flat wall screen with a picture dozens of times clearer than present cathode-ray television.)

With digital transmission, broadcasters could offer not only the diversity of programming that cable promises but also the clarity of signal which was the raison d'être for wired transmission. Although digital transmission would require entirely new electronics for television receivers, it may not be as far in the future as it seems. In May, PBS announced a digital system called Digital Audio for Television (DATE) to sharply improve the quality of sound for PBS simulcasts of musical programs. Although the DATE system will be used only to transmit the signal from point of origin to participating stations, PBS has already begun to encourage set manufacturers to build receivers that can accept it directly. If a set can be designed to receive digital audio, why can't digital video be included as well?

By now it must be clear that there are no rules to this contest between the air people and the wire people. What's more, any number can play. Air and wire aren't the only available means of distribution. Books, magazines, and newspapers, for example, are sold in stores and through the mail. Television programming on disc and tape can be circulated the same way. Eventually, all telecasting may have to define itself against permanent records like the tape and disc.

Ma Bell and Beyond

Cable people say that their medium still has one advantage: It can be interactive. That is, it can operate just like the telephone line, whose poles it often shares. Until each of us owns a CB transmitter, broadcasting certainly cannot make this claim.

There's no doubt that two-way cable could provide an enormous number of salable services. Yet if cable operators can provide us with security services, instant call-up of information, and real-time communications, so can Ma Bell. The rewrite of the Communications Act of 1934 now being discussed in Congress includes, as one of its more controversial clauses, permission for AT&T to reenter the television market. If that happens, cable operators might as well recycle their trunk lines as jump ropes. Not even the combined forces of Warner Communications and Time are a match for the Ma Bell monopoly.

As complex as these technologies may seem, we have only skimmed the surface. The permutations are seemingly endless. In England, where systems of video information transmission and retrieval are much further advanced, there are already three systems competing. (One of them, significantly, uses the telephone.) Also, a pilot project has recently begun which uses videotape to replace film in British cinemas. In France, the government has opted for community cable: Movie theaters are connected by two-way wire for meetings of, say, physicians in distant towns.

In the United States, a number of cable operators also transmit FM radio signals as well as television signals, often without even bothering to notify their customers that this service is available. In southern Manhattan, the domain of Manhattan Cable Television, stereo FM sound is available for all HBO presentations. Qube offers five private channels of FM stereo. In communities with limited numbers of broadcast radio stations, such services might prove quite salable. The radio dial could be filled to overflowing at a nominal cost.

Cable's Commercial Future

If all this technological euphoria seems more than a little blue-sky, it is because the language of cable is phrased in the conditional. Technology doesn't determine available services. Economics does. A particular service may seem useful, but it probably won't become available unless someone sees a way to make a profit from it.

In other words, cable can't offer its blue-sky vision of the future until a significant percentage of the nation's homes are wired, while the mass of consumers may not be willing to buy cable if those services don't already exist.

Manhattan Cable turned a profit earlier this year—one of the first major urban cable systems to do so. Attention now shifts at Manhattan, as at many other cable installations, from construction to programming. In the face of a "drop-off" rate of twenty-three percent per year, the aim is to keep subscribers already signed up. In the short run, cable must produce programming and services so irresistible that when a subscriber moves, he will call the cable company at the same time he calls to have his phone and electricity turned on. Cable has to become a utility in order to survive.

The long-term solution is much more obvious. Cable operators won't be able to maintain their commercial-free purity for much longer—nor do they want to. The commercial-free aura was useful in the beginning as a selling tool, but it no longer serves this purpose. Commercials are now beginning to appear on the "normal" cable channels. As with the history of broadcasting, the concept of "leased" channels paves the way.

Manhattan Cable, for example, sells advertising on two of its channels: one devoted to sports, the other programmed with various entertainment packages by the cable operator itself. The company can offer advertisers a "reach" of 350,000 viewers, small when compared to the reach of broadcast stations, but quite competitive, for instance, with magazines the size of *New Times, New York,* or the *Village Voice.* Ad revenues for Manhattan Cable exceeded a quarter of a million dollars last year—not bad, considering the company employs no full-time ad sales people.

Eventually, cable is going to settle into an economic structure not unlike that of magazines. The drop-off problem is directly parallel with magazine renewal efforts. Future income will be derived from a combination of paid advertising and subscription fees, plus "individual copy" sales.

It seems highly likely that the entire television industry will move in this direction. In the late sixties, television advertisers discovered mass demographics. They realized it was smarter to spend $200,000 a minute for an upscale audience than $100,000 a minute for audiences with little disposable income. But despite some demographic differentiation between shows (computer manufacturers spend their money on sports events; dentures and other products used by senior citizens dominate the network news ads), television advertising is still a relatively crude science compared with print advertising.

In the next few years, this should change in conjunction with the rise of cable advertising. In the early eighties, advertisers will be able to buy precisely the audience they require as both broadcast and cable television become highly specialized. Certain shows might even be "published" in separate editions aimed at demographically specific viewerships, just as the few remaining mass magazines—*Time,* for example—print separate editions for high-income zip codes and for certain regions, professions, and life-styles.

Even with only thirty to thirty-six channels to fill, cable's major problem is "software," or programming. There simply isn't enough to go around, nor has the industry developed its own style of production. There's a desperate search on for programming that will be sufficiently different from network shows to attract a paying audience and keep it.

The Programming Shortage

Qube has had some success with local talk shows and consumer services, but most of the innovations have been gimmicky. Qube subscribers voted their choices for Academy Awards last spring and participated in a poll to choose two *US* magazine covers. Qubers gave *Star Wars* the Oscar and chose John Wayne and the Incredible Hulk for the covers. Evidently the children in Qube families dominate the response buttons. None of these choices suggest really upscale demographics among Qube subscribers.

The brightest development in cable programming has been the leased channel. Like the earliest AT&T radio stations, the leased channel presents television as a common carrier, available to all. Unlike public access, it charges for its time, but this simply serves to professionalize production. One of the major successes of Manhattan Cable has been its leased Channel J, which has served up "Midnight Blue," a soft-core talk show recently acquired for Qube, "Greek World," "Emerald City" (a gay show), and, most important, "Telefrance-USA" (something between a show and a programming service), which the French government just bought for $500,000.

HBO and other premium channel services have their programming problems, too. While the Time company has produced its own successful variety programming, movies still dominate the HBO schedule. Time is moving into film production, while HBO may look to miniseries, perhaps in conjunction with Operation Prime Time. This seems like a smart move. Limited series fit very well within the pay television concept. As magazine and newspaper publishers discovered a century ago (and film producers realized very early), there is a significant advantage to hooking the consumer to a continuing story.

Another obvious source of premium programming is Broadway. The most tradition-bound of all entertainment media, legitimate theater has only recently discovered that it pays to advertise. When New York television stations began carrying the "I Love New York" commercial for Broadway last winter, Broadway revenues zoomed a reported forty-seven percent in one week. HBO is very interested in developing the Broadway connection, but no plans are firm yet. An infusion of cash would drastically alter theater economics for the better, and not only for hit shows.

The Brave New World of Neovideo

When you add up the extraordinary number of technological and economic possibilities available to the electronic media industries, Congressman Lionel Van Deerlin's rewrite of the Communications Act of 1934 makes considerable sense. The most controversial portion of the revision is the drastic reduction of federal control of all broadcast and communications industries. Yet, considering the chaotic possibilities of the various technological innovations and economic structures, perhaps it would be wise to permit a period of laissez-faire and then, in ten years or so, to reexamine the patterns created by the electronic communications revolution and adjust them to the public good.

No matter what video wonders await us on the electromagnetic horizon, it's good, too, to remember the lessons of history. Technological innovations have come and gone before. Each time—with film, with television, and now with cable—a new age has been heralded. Each of these products of the wonderful world of science has promised the final realization of the democratic dreams of the Republic—one nation, indivisible, with liberty and justice and media for all. But somehow that annus mirabilis continues to recede into the future like Gatsby's green light. Somehow, each new technical wonder is fitted neatly into

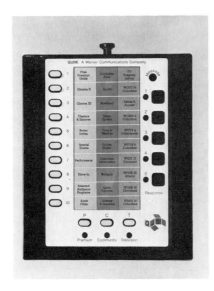

Button box. When Mother Qube desires a reply from the viewer, she asks you to please "touch now." Qube buttons are not to be "pressed"—that word suggests aggressive behavior. Touching is not only easier, it's more intimate, more sensual.

The Qube channels are divided into three categories of ten buttons each. The yellow P channels are nearest to selector buttons. These cost money each time you view a particular program. The green C column provides cable programming not available over the air without a per-program charge. Last is the blue T group—those necessary broadcast stations.

The ten C channels, as of last summer, transmit such local programming as the popular talk show "Columbus Alive," a channel devoted to children's shows, a news ticker, time and weather, "Golden Oldies" featuring series like "The Adventures of Ozzie and Harriet," a consumer information crawl, a religious channel, "Qube Campus," and "Culture and Learning."

The T column provides program listings and an interesting "Extras and Access" channel that supplies network programming local affiliates have chosen not to carry, as well as four Columbus stations and four from other cities.

The viewer's attention is drawn to the P (for Premium) column, with its four movie channels, a "Special Events" channel, a variety channel, and a channel called "Better Living." The Premium column operates only if a key is inserted into the console, providing built-in parental control and selective use of pay programs which might contain sex or violence. The Qube subscriber receives nine P channels; a tenth, carrying soft-core pornographic movies, considerably bowdlerized, must be specifically requested from Qube.

capitalist economics and gives rise to as many problems as it solves. We have no reason to believe we'll be better off with a wired nation than without one.

When the bright age of neovideo finally dawns, perhaps in 1984, we may discover that while most of us are perfectly happy in front of the tube voting yet again for John Wayne, ordering products as fast as they're shown on the screen, and devouring entertainment, information, and culture in mind-boggling quantities, some of us may have revolted, cut the cable umbilicus, escaped the strange rain of microwaves, and retreated to the forest of print, like the book people of *Fahrenheit 451,* wandering in the snow (the cold, white stuff, not the static on the screen).

Bibliography

Cable television has many legal, technical, social and educational issues. A readable background to the development and expectations of the industry is Ralph Lee Smith, *The Wired Nation: The Electronic Communications Highway* (Harper & Row, 1972). Two excellent books dealing with the regulatory problems of cable television are Martin H. Seiden, *Cable Television U.S.A.: An Analysis of Government Policy* (Praeger, 1972), and Don R. LeDuc, *Cable Television and the FCC: A Crisis in Media Control* (Temple University Press, 1973). An interesting position paper is *Broadcasting and Cable Television: Policies for Diversity and Change* (Committee for Economic Development, April 1975). Consult *Broadcasting* magazine for on-going information about cable's development. Qube, the Warner Communications' two-way cable system discussed by James Monaco, is approached from a different direction in Jonathan Black, "Brave New World of Television," *New Times* (July 24, 1978), pp. 41–52, and John Wicklein, "Wired City, U.S.A.: The Charms and Dangers of Two-Way TV," *The Atlantic* (February 1979), pp. 35–47. For experience in two-way cable other than at Columbus, see Mitchell L. Moss, *Two-Way Cable Television: An Evaluation of Community Uses in Reading, Pennsylvania,* a report issued by Alternate Media Center, 144 Bleecker St., New York, N.Y. 10012.

34   Records: The Gorillas Are Coming
Forbes

Reprinted by permission of *Forbes* Magazine from the July 10, 1978 issue.

The new word in the recorded-music industry these days is "gorilla." It stands for a phenomenon of Kong-like scale. Here's the latest example of a gorilla, and the biggest one thus far: One day toward the end of this year, one record album will reach sales of 15 million copies, an achievement unmatched in the 100 years since Edison invented the phonograph. At an average retail price of about $10 (suggested list price for the two-record package, $12.98), the soundtrack from the movie *Saturday Night Fever* will gross $150 million for retailers. For its distributor, the Dutch-German Polygram B.V., revenues from this album will probably exceed $100 million. (Last year the Polygram group did $900 million in sales worldwide.) And for the producer of the album (and the movie), Australian producer Robert Stigwood's RSO Group, pretax earnings from the album alone will come to nearly $50 million.

SNF is a gorilla, a new scale of possibilities for the record business. Though gorillas and even baboons are hard to bring forth, there are more of them all the time. Last year more than 70 record albums "went platinum" (sales of 1 million copies or more, certified by the Recording Industry Association of America). Since 1976 more than 15 have sold 3 million or more. And a half dozen have sold upwards of 6 million, probably the bottom of the gorilla category. They include *Songs In The Key Of Life* by Stevie Wonder, *Come Alive* by Peter Frampton, *Hotel California* by the Eagles, and *Rumours* by Fleetwood Mac. *Rumours,* the number two all-time seller, is still in the top 100 after more than a year on the charts of the industry weeklies that rank sales and has sold over 9 million copies domestically.

Just to put all this in perspective, the smallest of the platinums means upwards of $5 million at retail. Records are where the big money is at in the entertainment business these days.

Like the go-go 1960s on Wall Street, there seems to be no end to the upward trend of the record industry. Its once sharply compartmentalized markets— rock'n'roll, easy listening, jazz and the rest—seem to be merging into the middle of the road. And its once greatest terror—that its audiences would grow old and stop buying records, as their parents did—has all but evaporated, according to a market survey by CBS last year and a bigger one released this year by Warner Communications, Inc. Both studies confirmed what industry insiders have known for years: that record buyers keep buying when they pass their teens. If they keep it up into their 30s, the reasoning goes, why not into their 40s and on into dotage?

A more homogeneous marketplace has emerged, where black rhythm-and-blues, white country-and-western, Tex-Mex, disco, Laurel Canyon, Bakersfield country, heavy metal, rock 'n' roll and every other term—even jazz—that once defined a sound, a style, an ethnic preference, have begun to fuse. More people buy more records, but they buy more of the same kind. With fully refundable returns running as high as 80% for some labels, the risks would still seem to be as great as they ever were. But a gorilla can carry the weight of a lot of losers.

What this means is that either you hit it big or you don't hit it at all, because there are no longer the specialized markets to support a small hit.

The problem is that however lucrative from a purely economic standpoint a multimillion-seller may be, promotion costs can be enormous. And the buildup can take months. That means that marginal producers without big financial resources stand little chance of hitting the top. And even some of the best-heeled companies in the entertainment world—including RCA, ABC, MCA, EMI, United Artists (formerly a Transamerica subsidiary)—have found that money alone won't do the job.

Despite the problems of these companies, the industry itself has never done better. In 1976 records clearly outsold movie tickets. Total retail record sales hit $2.7 billion compared to $2 billion for movie admissions, making music the nation's second biggest entertainment industry, after television. Last year total record sales easily exceeded $3 billion.

Back in 1947, the last "normal" year of the traditional record industry before the advent of long-playing records, stereo and rock 'n' roll, total domestic sales ran to $224 million, mostly in the hands of RCA and CBS. Classical music sales accounted for 25% of the total, compared with only 5% these days (though Vladimir Horowitz' performance of Rachmaninoff's Third Piano Concerto for RCA was No. 102 on the *Billboard* chart last month and climbing fast). Warner, with the biggest share of the record album market in 1977 (over 23%), didn't even exist in 1947. CBS does 19% now, Polygram, 14%. Other significant companies' shares include RCA, 7%, A&M, 7% and Capitol, 7%.

Outsiders may know little more about the industry than occasional scandals involving payola to radio station disc jockeys, cocaine and instant-millionaire star performers studying Oriental philosophy. But people in the business know that it *is* a business and that, these days at least, intelligence, business sense, marketing and market-sensitive commercial taste are the edge that the gorilla owners have had. What's more, the records at the top of the heap, without exception, are the work of skilled veteran performers who have split, come back, changed people and styles, and have known success before.

Lately the business has come to look something like the automobile industry. Three major groups dominate virtually every segment of the domestic market: Warner Communications' Warner Bros., Elektra-Asylum and Atlantic, with many affiliated labels; CBS, with the Epic label, among others; and Polygram, the newest foreign entrant, with a label of its own—Mercury—and two recently acquired partnerships with successful independents, RSO and Casablanca. The big three are getting some 60% of the sales that get on the charts. The rest goes to a swarm of companies, mostly divisions of majors, along with established independents. The biggest of the latter are A&M Records (which got its stake from an unprecedented series of best-sellers in the 1960s by cofounder Herb Alpert and the Tijuana Brass), with sales around $100 million, and Motown Industries (which has been scoring consistently with black acts such as the Supremes, Diana Ross and Smokey Robinson that have been selling to black and white buyers for years), with more than $50 million in record volume.

After 100 years, the record business seems to be passing out of the cottage industry stage. That seems certain to bring further consolidation. United Artists sold its record business to its managers. ABC sold its distribution organization to an independent and will distribute through outside organizations. But the economics of big hits keeps everyone in the industry trying, with Columbia Pictures Industries using the Arista label these days and Bertelsmann, the German publisher that controls Bantam Books, launching its Ariola label in the U.S. in 1975.

While foreign companies like Polygram and EMI (through its subsidiary, Capitol) have moved into the U.S. market, CBS, Warner and RCA have been moving even faster to cash in on the burgeoning overseas record market, which is every bit as large.

The temptation to take a chance in this big crap game is great, maybe even greater than ever. But so, too, are the costs. Consider this: In 1976, 19 labels that distributed through independent warehousing and marketing organizations showed up on one chart of the top 100 singles; last year the number was down to 13. What it means is that the three giants and those independent companies that operate their own distribution outposts have increased their share of the market—to 87% from 81% in about two years.

The companies most likely to succeed are those that have the best hold on the entire marketing chain down to the consumer, starting with their own distribution branches. These units receive the records from pressing plants, warehouse them till they are ordered by big retailers, rack-jobbers and other subdistributors, and handle the promotion activities with radio stations, discotheques and the local press. If you don't have enough business volume to justify the cost of your own distribution system you have alternatives, none of them quite as good.

There are good independent distributors, but they carry the products of more than one company, so there's a lot of competition for the time of promotion people, the collection department and other support services. The advantage of your own system is that there are none of these conflicts of interest. And that is especially important now that the most effective record promotion involves concentrating major effort on a single album to turn it into a gorilla.

Clive Davis, ousted head of CBS Records, who took over as president of Columbia Pictures' Arista Records, says: "With branch distribution, you get a higher price for your product because your first sale isn't at a distributor price. It's at a higher, rack-jobber price. The CBS branch system, when I was there, was expected to make a profit."

But branches work no magic. What happens when you don't have enough business to support your own distribution was demonstrated when ABC finally gave up and sold its branches. In the last three years, ABC's record business lost $64 million pretax on an average annual volume of $160 million.

One of the most immediate effects of having a small market share is that you may not get paid as quickly by wholesalers and retailers as the giants, so your money costs more. David Geffen, a talent manager who created Asylum Records from his client list and then sold it to Warner, puts it succinctly: "Aside from Warner and CBS, everyone else has to increase their market share to get paid. A retailer has got to pay Warner and CBS first. Because if they cut you off for not paying, you lose 45% of your merchandise. But if a retailer is cut off by United Artists, he only loses maybe 5%. So they are the last to get paid."

The biggest money problem stems from the costs of creating and supporting a best-selling record. For years, the industry lived off airplay, the "free" plays of new records on disc jockey shows. In the early days, the process often involved simply giving money to DJs and program directors. If consumers buy what they hear, then it's worth a lot to get a new record on the air. And it still costs a lot. Payola per se may be gone for now. But the cost of sending promotion people around to hand out records and make a pitch, as well as the price of the food, drink, junkets and gifts that are increasingly a part of new record launches, means those who have, get more.

But the industry has also found little public resistance to price hikes. Last year, for example, Warner's decision to raise prices "selectively" from $6.98 for a one-record album to $7.98 eventually became an industry trend. The actual cost of making an LP record disc, including recording, pressing, jacket, advertising and promotion, today comes to about $1.35. These costs have risen about 50 cents per record since the early 1970s; and series of dealer markups raised the wholesale price per record about $1.25 on average. But retail price tags have gone up about $2.

Where has the difference gone? Partly into artists' pockets; they get from 50 cents to $1 per disc sold, depending on how well they sell and negotiate (there are no standard contracts in this industry). And partly to record companies.

Everybody has heard about the big money that goes to kid guitar players, agents, managers and lawyers. And a lot more goes for the expenses of touring, equipment, go-fers and hangers-on of various types. But when a group of four performers plus an arranger takes in even 50 cents apiece on a 1-million record sale, that comes to $500,000 for a few months' work. If the group composes its own material, as many do, it gets still more money from royalties and publishing rights. And if other performers record its songs, it gets another few pennies for each record *that* group sells.

A major record promotion effort can cost up to $1 million for radio spots, even television if the potential volume seems to warrant it. But a lot of acts get most of their sales from appearances. Kiss, an act that features ordinary music, weird costumes, such stage effects as vomiting fake blood and eating fire, is nothing if not visual. The group fills big spaces wherever it goes, which makes money for tour promoters. But Casablanca, its record company, may spend anywhere from $250,000 to $750,000 to back the tour with record promotion as the group moves from arena to arena. Such expenditures pay off for an act like Kiss. But even acts that depend on sound, not sight, can spend several hundred thousand dollars in routine out-of-pocket costs of promotion.

Consumers, for the most part, don't buy labels or companies; they buy performers and sounds. But performers do care about labels and image, especially when they begin to sell well. The relationship between artists and companies is finally determined by bargaining power. The bigger the act, the more likely it is to feel its own power and to make demands on the time, money and people of its recording company. And companies, just as often, attempt to sell their special promotion efforts to prospective artists. Last year, for example, Elektra-Asylum ran ads in the trade press aimed at signing more talent. They were headlined "38 Promotion People, 32 Recording Artists."

The profusion of record labels—not companies—is another aspect of artist relations. Though many of these labels represent tax-shelter companies, others are there because stars want to control everything from the name of their label to the design of the album cover. Ego trips are part of the cost of doing business in an industry that's full of young stars with identity crises.

For the big companies, signing talent—new or established—is an almost routine activity. Nobody wants to depend on a small number of acts. Why? Because the Beatles split and stars like Janis Joplin, Jimi Hendrix, Mama Cass Elliott, Jim Morrison, Otis Redding and countless others overdose on drugs, crash in planes or smash up motorcycles. Still others, looking for hand-holding, move around or try to hold up the company at renewal time. Or they turn cold and stop selling.

So the strong companies send their top executives out to concerts and tiny showcase clubs to hear who is coming along. Even the most business-oriented top managers—Mo Ostin at Warner Bros., Bob Summer at RCA, Clive Davis, even an elder statesman like Atlantic's Ahmet Ertegun—listen to and sign new acts. It is all merchandise, and anybody who has been in the trade for any length of time knows that talent turnover is as much a part of the business as warehouses full of unsold records.

Signing the biggest money deal is another source of friction in the industry. The Rolling Stones wanted a contract bigger than Stevie Wonder got from

Motown. Now Paul McCartney reportedly wants the biggest of all pacts for his Wings group. He is reportedly looking for $20 million from EMI's Capitol. As a superstar, McCartney will probably get what he wants from somebody. But contract figures are almost never divulged, so nobody is ever sure how much anybody gets.

These superdeals usually involve more hyperbole than reality, because whatever figure is leaked, it will almost certainly be somewhat fictional. Typically such contract figures refer to nonreturnable advances payable on delivery of finished recordings. And if an artist misses a delivery date, he usually goes on suspension until he comes up with a record. A $20-million deal for McCartney would be sure to earn back most of the money if he fulfills the contract and brings in the required number of records. Even if he doesn't, the volume the records generate will go a long way toward covering the cost of running the company's marketing apparatus.

For a generation, the U.S. record business was dominated by RCA and CBS, with a few barely perceptible independents like Capitol. The Beatles turned Capitol into a major company during the 1960s, and RCA relied too heavily on the phenomenal sales of Elvis Presley. CBS came late to modern pop music, figuring rock would go away during the days when Mitch Miller, the onetime symphonic oboist, ran the business. But CBS had the money to build a powerful distribution organization and sign a lot of hot acts during a brief period in the 1960s.

These days, RCA has less than 10% of the business, and Warner, which began as the by-product of a moldering movie studio, has parlayed acquisitions and a strong distribution system into a giant with worldwide sales last year of $532 million and an operating profit of $84 million. CBS, with a bigger foreign operation, but with lower profits from its own pressing plants and a major record club, grossed $767 million with $80 million in operating profit.

But anybody who thinks that this financial framework is carved in anything more solid than whipped cream has missed the point. It is true that good management, sound finances and aggressive marketing count for a lot these days. But luck is still a major ingredient of success in selling music to a fickle public.

"It's a taste business," says a veteran record executive. "And when you're hot, you're hot. I think our guys know this. But you never can be sure." Meanwhile, there are at least 1,000 recording studios around the country capable of producing a commercial quality record. And a hit record can still be made with a guitar and a voice. The emergence of stars like Presley and the Beatles changed the shape of the industry profoundly. There's nothing about the daily inventory printouts and the marketing surveys to assure the industry giants that there's not some group of kids making a first record in a converted gas station up in Michigan—around Hamtramck, say—who won't shake the industry to its foundations at least one more time.

Supermogul In The Land Of Opportunity

The executive offices of the Stigwood Group are in the old General Motors Building overlooking New York's Central Park—housed in what was GM's boardroom with walls paneled in mahogany, floors of Italian marble, furnished with antiques like a 15th-century Flemish marquetry chest and similar trinkets.

That's the image RSO Records Chairman Robert Stigwood likes to cultivate: Olympian grandeur. Solid and conservative. Old money.

In a way, Stigwood's magnificent offices are one of his most successful promotions. For while he has money flowing like Niagara, it's far from old. In fact, the 44-year-old expatriate Australian set up shop in the U.S. only in mid-1976 with his partner, Polygram B.V. Records (controlled by the European consortium of Siemens and Philips). Since then he has turned a freewheeling collection of tours and shows (like *Jesus Christ Superstar*), RSO Records (the Bee Gees) and films into—to use the trade vernacular—a gorilla of an organization.

So rapidly has Stigwood grown that, according to RSO Group President Fred Gershon, "Robert's operations will gross around $300 million this year—and that's a very conservative estimate."

Look at what Stigwood's into, and you can see why: films like *Saturday Night Fever* and *Grease,* and music, rock tours and records tied in with them—the Bee Gees *SNF* record album alone has already brought in $100 million in revenues this year.

How do you go up so fast? Stigwood doesn't talk to the press these days. But Fred Gershon put it accurately enough: "Bob Stigwood understood better than anyone else that you could take a musical vehicle and build on it by promoting the music so that it got better known than the play or movie." A pioneer in rock promotion, Stigwood correctly perceived the depth of the changes in the nation's entertainment habits caused by contemporary pop music and its power to drag everything else along with it.

Stigwood started with a smallish company in Britain, where he had such successes as the rock opera *Tommy,* managed groups like the Bee Gees (then far from superstars) and produced *Jesus Christ Superstar.* But his U.K. success was peanuts compared with the vast U.S. entertainment market he saw. The problem was to get the business out from under Britain's taxes. Stigwood had gone public in 1970 but his shares had been down, up briefly, then way down. He made a deal with Polygram to buy all RSO's stock at $1 a share, somewhat above the market price, then set up a new company in the U.S. with Stigwood in command. The deal cost Polygram over $8 million, of which $1.5 million went to Stigwood. Gershon insists, "It was a fair deal with full disclosure. Everyone was satisfied."

In any event, Stigwood and Polygram became partners in RSO America with Stigwood putting up a little cash, ultimately getting control and half the equity in the company. Polygram handles distribution for RSO Records and shares in his other ventures.

Stigwood plunged into the U.S. market with a shrewd and shabby venture. For $500,000 he bought the negative to a quickie Mexican exploitation movie called *Survive,* a knockoff of the *Alive!* adventure saga about cannibalism among survivors of a Chilean plane crash. Stigwood dubbed English dialog, added some stock footage and a new score. Total investment: $800,000. Stigwood and a partner, artist manager Alan Carr, eventually grossed $10 million in six weeks of summertime theater bookings and some inspired promotional blurbs in screaming red letters using this tasty caveat: "Warning! Scenes of cannibalism may be too vivid for certain moviegoers."

But Stigwood's greatest triumph has been high-class by comparison. In 1976 he saw a story in *New York* magazine about a young Brooklyn blue-collar worker who came alive only at the discos on Saturday night. Stigwood decided it would make a good movie. He bought the rights; he put up the first $2.5 million for production (and eventually laid it off to Paramount, who reimbursed him and paid him another $1 million for the distribution rights). Paramount spent additional millions to promote it—in return for a little less than 60% of the profits. Stigwood got his old group, the Bee Gees, to compose and record half a dozen songs, and signed rising John Travolta to star in *Saturday Night Fever*. Virtually all the record revenues go to Stigwood.

Meanwhile, Alan Carr offered Stigwood a half interest in the movie rights to the Broadway musical *Grease*. The film came in cheap, at about $3 million. Now Paramount has mounted a promotional blitz that may cost as much as $3 million. The two-record *Grease* album has already sold 2 million copies, thanks to such stunts as sending "switchblade" combs to disc jockeys.

Stigwood and Carr get along today like cobra and mongoose, but the partnership goes on.

Coming soon is Stigwood's *Sgt. Pepper's Lonely Hearts Club Band,* with Beatles' music but with the Bee Gees starring. It opens next month at Radio City Music Hall for a one-night charity benefit preview that will cost $250,000. In the U.K., Stigwood has the rock opera *Evita,* based on the life of Eva Perón. For that, he's already thrown three "charity" benefits attended by, among others, members of the Royal Family.

And that's the way it goes. The music hypes the movie, the movie hypes the music. Everybody gets rich. Especially Bob Stigwood.

Bibliography

Several books are available on the music industry. One that traces current as well as recent practices is R. Serge Denisoff, *Solid Gold: The Popular Record Industry* (Transactions Books, 1975). The role played by one of the leading innovators in the industry is found in Clive Davis and James Willwerth, *Clive: Inside the Record Business* (Morrow, 1974). Davis was head of Columbia Records from 1965 to 1973. Louis Kraar, "How Phil Walden Turns Rock Into Gold," *Fortune* (September 1975), pp. 106–111 ff., reveals the methods used by Capricorn Records in promoting unknown talent until it becomes successful. Two practical books on the industry are Walter E. Hurst and William Storm Hale, *The Record Industry Book: How to Make Money in the Record Industry,* Vol. I, and *The Music Industry Book: How to Make Money in the Music Industry,* Vol. II, both published by 7 Arts Press, 1971. Students will need to consult both volumes because of the organization of content. A study of the themes of the country music industry is reported in Ann Nietzke, "Country Music . . . Doin' Somebody Wrong," *Human Behavior* (November 1975), pp. 64–69. Her focus is on the woman's role in country music. Also highly useful are Steve Chapple and Reebee Garofalo, *Rock 'n' Roll is Here to Pay* (Nelson-Hall Publishers, 1977) (the sub-title *The History and Politics of the Music Industry* cues the reader as to its content); Tony Palmer, *All You Need is Love: The Story of Popular Music* (Viking Press, 1976), based on the BBC series shown in the United States, and Geoffrey Stokes, *Star-Making Machinery: The Odyssey of an Album* (Bobbs-Merrill Co., 1976), which recounts the making and selling of an album by the singing group Commander Cody and His Lost Planet Airmen.

Media for Minorities / Women

It's Not Too Late to Save the Black Press

Henry G. LaBrie III

35

Since 1827 the black press in America has survived and developed primarily because it provided news that was generally unavailable elsewhere in the mass media. Wedding, birth, and death announcements alone supplied the core of this information monopoly. Add to that religious and social news, dispatches on black sports heroes, and a weekly diet of racial injustice stories and you had the basic contents for a successful black newspaper.

Fortunately, the black press was there to cover news of the early steps of Dr. Martin Luther King; to support the organization of an interracial group (NAACP) to study the discriminatory practices rampant across the land; and to fight for integration of our armed forces. These and so many other events were ignored or covered superficially by our establishment press, and for that reason the black press has become a sort of "history" book for many scholars today.

Unfortunately this lack of competition combined with other factors to cause a vast majority of the black newspapers to overlook traditional journalism standards. The result was a technologically and grammatically poor news product. There were a few exceptions, perhaps the most dramatic being the Norfolk *Journal and Guide* when it was under the direction of the Young family. One press critic referred to the *Journal and Guide* as the *New York Times* of the black press.

Now 153 years old, the black press seems to be assuming a new role in the mass media mix, a quiet less militant role. A telephone survey of publishers and editors conducted between October 1 and December 15, 1978 disclosed a significant decrease not only in the number of black newspapers publishing but also in their total circulation.

As of January 1, 1979, 165 black newspapers were active in the U.S. This number represents four dailies (*Columbus* [Ga.] *Times, Atlanta Daily World,* Brooklyn *New York Daily Challenge,* and the *Chicago Daily Defender*), 155 weeklies, and 6 biweeklies. Compared with a similar survey conducted in January, 1973, when 208 black papers were publishing, this represents a 21 percent loss in membership.

Even more dramatic is the circulation plunge. In January 1973, 202 of the 208 newspapers had a combined circulation of 4,099,511. The present survey lists a total circulation of 2,901,162 with 151 of 165 black papers reporting. The difference over the six-year period, amounting to 1,198,349, represents a 29 percent reduction.

Henry G. LaBrie III has collected statistics on the black press and gathered the thoughts of black editors and publishers for years. He is the author of *The Black Press: A Guide* (Iowa City: Institute for Communication Studies, 1971) and *Perspectives of the Black Press: 1974* (Mercer House Press, 1974). While now teaching and farming in Maine, he remains in touch with the latest trends. He prepared this article especially for this collection of readings.

What is happening to the black newspaper and in what direction is it heading? Will it go the route of our foreign language press, as many journalism scholars have predicted?

"The black press has gone through several enclaves of influence since its beginning but it will continue to grow in future years," claims William O. Walker, publisher of the Cleveland *Call and Post* group. Walker, now in his eighties, and viewed by many as the dean of the black newspaper industry, adds, "The content and context of the black press will improve in years to come and the individual newspapers will become great local influences."

From a journalistic standpoint, Mr. Walker may be a prophet. If the black press does hope to make any difference in the growth and development of this nation in the final decades of the 20th century, it will most certainly occur at the local level. Gone are the days of the nationally circulated *Pittsburgh Courier;* gone are the days of the bold-face headlines atop the *Daily Defender* announcing a lynching in the South.

In light of the dwindling circulations and the death of so many black newspapers, it is not surprising that some wonder if the black press will even remain with us. The prime point to consider here is that the circulation figures of most black newspapers have often been questioned. When the first black press telephone survey was conducted in 1970, no mention was made of whether the circulations were audited. In 1972, the second survey noted that 17 black newspapers were members of the Audit Bureau of Circulations (ABC), and their combined circulations totaled 422,867. Today that group includes 21 newspapers, with an ABC figure of 435,557. While this represents only a three percent increase, it does reflect some expansion of the *core* of the black press.

The other 144 black newspapers remain unaudited. Their circulations might be dropped into three categories. The largest of these groups contains the 20 newspapers that report "controlled circulations." Their combined press runs add up to 942,764. The leaders in this movement are in California, with the Los Angeles *Central News-Wave* group of eight papers heading the list, distributing over 240,000 papers per week. North in San Francisco, the *Metro* group (seven papers and 82,000 copies a week) and the Oakland-based *Post* group (five newspapers and 80,000 copies a week) battle for the runner-up position.

The second largest category includes 64 journals with a combined circulation of 868,741, "publisher's statement paid." Chicago's *Bilalian News,* formerly *Muhammad Speaks,* heads this group with a circulation of 150,000. However, compared with the 1973 survey, the paper has fallen from a circulation of over 600,000. The Flushing *New York Voice* (83,000) and the Baton Rouge (La.) *Community Leader* group (41,400) are two other leaders in this category.

The third unaudited classification is "publisher's statement paid and free distribution," and the 36 newspapers in this cluster account for a combined circulation of 654,100. The Washington, D.C. *Informer* (55,000), the St. Louis *Metro-Sentinel* (36,000), the *Atlanta Voice* (35,000), and the St. Petersburg *Weekly Challenger* (33,000) are the leaders.

It should be noted that many of these 144 newspapers announced that in 1979 they will begin an auditing agreement with Verified Audit of Circulation (VAC) of Los Angeles, California. This would definitely enhance the credibility of their activities and lend a measure of professionalism to the business that has been sorely lacking. One newspaper, the Milwaukee *Community Journal,* founded in 1976, is presently being audited by Certified Audit of Circulation (CAC) of Leonia, New Jersey.

If circulations can stabilize and be substantiated, then the individual papers may have a chance to take a prominent role in their respective communities. Altogether, 24 new listings are included in the present survey, which means that since January 1973, 67 black newspapers have expired. A minority of the newspapers have pre-1950 birthdates. Of the 165 active newspapers, 22 were started in the 1950s, 37 in the 1960s and 39 in the 1970s. Thus, 59 percent of the papers are relatively young.

On the surface, the age difference in the papers may suggest only that more professional training and business acumen should be brought to bear during the early stages of growth of the black newspaper. However, the age difference has prompted another problem, indirectly. Many of the new, younger publishers are anxious to gain large national advertising accounts as well as achieve leadership positions in the national organization. The black press has its own professional organization, National Newspaper Publishers' Association (NNPA), which was founded in 1940 in Chicago.

The NNPA has, over the years, served as a launching pad for the crusading the black press has done to remedy national discriminatory problems. With an office and national executive secretary in Washington, D.C., and up until 1973 a correspondent in the nation's capital, the NNPA has been a catalyst to bring the various factions of the black press together. But NNPA is steered by the "old guard" of the black press. In 1961 Amalgamated Publishers Inc. was founded in New York City to act as national advertising representative for NNPA members. The young publishers and many of the publishers of the smaller black newspapers believe that NNPA and API pay little attention to them. For that reason, Black Media, Inc. was established in New York City in 1976 to represent the young and the small. It is a cleavage the black press can do without, since there are already enough mountains to climb.

John Sengstacke, publisher of the *Chicago Daily Defender* and current president of NNPA, said that the NNPA was bankrupt and efforts were being made to reorganize it. Miss Marjorie Parham, publisher of the *Cincinnati Herald* and treasurer of NNPA, disputed Mr. Sengstacke's statement and reported that the financial situation is bleak but not hopeless.

In the meantime, BMI hailed itself as "The Voice of Black America" representing 104 black newspapers. BMI publishes *Black Monitor* monthly, a kind of *Parade*-looking supplement for black newspapers. Inside the first page a list of 104 members is included: sixteen of the newspapers do not exist, three are what might be called "bar" sheets, and six belong to two controlled-circulation groups.

In contrast to many of the black newspapers, some black magazines enjoy high circulations and advertising revenue. The leading example is *Ebony*, one of publisher John H. Johnson's several enterprises.

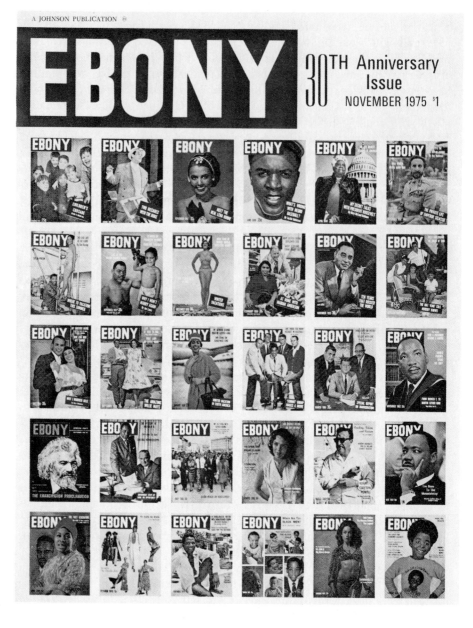

Neither NNPA nor BMI is projecting a positive professional image for the black press. These newspapers desperately need a take-charge, strong organization to make suggestions and provide direction for the future growth and development of the medium.

One of the first steps to be taken would be to urge member papers to hire capable consulting firms to conduct market research studies about the buying habits and informational behavior of the audiences these journals serve. The San Francisco *Sun-Reporter* did just that in 1978, and the resulting report by Behavioral Systems, Inc. claimed that the black newspaper is held in high regard in the black community.

Another goal of the professional organization would be to hold regular workshops on journalistic up-grading of the black press. Short courses on photography, feature writing, editorial writing, and basic reporting would yield big dividends. At present, the conventions held by NNPA and BMI tend to concentrate on the business side of the newspaper: circulation building, distribution methods, increasing advertising lineage. More attention must be paid to the reportorial responsibilities. Here, for example, is a crime story as it appeared in the December 21, 1978 issue of the San Francisco *Sun-Reporter:*

> James Perkins, a 19-year-old City College student, felt more than comfortable in the handsome leather coat he was wearing while waiting for a Muni bus at the intersection of Hayes and Stanyan streets.
>
> The nights have been chilly since the advent of December, and Perkins felt better than some unknown persons who drove up in a car and hailed him in unfriendly tones of voice.
>
> There were three occupants of the auto, described by Perkins as a Fiat, two in the front seat and one in the back.
>
> The driver and the occupant of the front passenger seat not only hailed Perkins, but both of them got out of the car, police said.
>
> One of the two continued his verbal hostility and then suddenly resorted to physical aggression by drawing a switchblade knife, which he placed against Perkins's neck, and ominously he demanded that Perkins "give it up."
>
> Now Perkins, who was only waiting for a bus to take him to wherever he was headed, was rather astonished that someone would walk up to him and put a knife against his neck and demand that he give up something as the unknown did not specify just what he wanted Perkins to give up.
>
> His hesitancy brought more woes to him at the hands of the knife-wielder, who stuck the blade of the knife into Perkins's forearm.
>
> Then the knife-wielder and his assistant relieved Perkins of his warm, comfortable leather coat. Following the robbery both men ran back to the waiting vehicle, which was driven away without a moment's delay.
>
> Perkins, if he was not originally heading for Moffitt Hospital's emergency ward, headed for that institution, where he received medical care for his wounds and related his tale to police.
>
> Perkins's total loss consisted of his leather coat, a Fast Pass for riding the Municipal Railway, and his house keys.

Of greater concern is the staff-building that needs to be done at most black newspapers. According to the January 1973 survey, 2,324 people were employed full time at 195 papers. The current survey discloses that 152 papers are employing 1,880, with the largest numbers claimed by the Baltimore *Afro-American* chain (140), the Los Angeles *Central News-Wave* (80), the *Chicago Daily Defender* (75), and the Oakland *Post* group (75). This short-staffing forces rip-

and-tear-type journalism. Much of the copy in black newspapers today is received in the mail. There is a paucity of good editorial writing, a shortage of critical investigative reporting, and almost a void in follow-through series.

It is almost inconceivable that a staff of only nine turns out the Washington *Informer* each week: circulation 55,000. How do two staffers create enough good copy to attract a paid (publisher's statement) circulation of 12,000 at the *Grand Rapids* (Mich.) *Times?* Is it possible that six people can produce not only the *Minneapolis Spokesman* (paid circulation 13,000) but also the *St. Paul Recorder* (paid circulation 12,000) every week?

Now, more than ever before, the black press will be coming under scrutiny as a news medium. Its audience is more educated and sophisticated than ever before. And the advertiser will be asking for more proof of circulation figures, readership facts, and consumer behavior. If the black newspaper is to survive, it will have to prove its value to both subscribers and businesses.

In his address before the National Press Club on March 17, 1978 (entitled "Don't Order the Coffin Yet . . . The Corpse Is Still Alive"), *Call and Post* publisher William O. Walker warned listeners, "No, don't order the coffin yet. We still have unfinished business to complete. This we will do whatever the odds or obstacles. Through our years of travail and struggle, we have been hurt enough to cry; the question now is are we mad enough to fight."

No one is making funeral plans. But, the diagnosis is serious. Those who are concerned about the survival of the black press wonder if the patient is listening.

Bibliography

In addition to looking up Dr. LaBrie's writings, cited in the note about him at the beginning of this article, the student interested in the history and development of the black press should check Roland F. Wolseley's *The Black Press U.S.A.* (Iowa State University Press, 1971). A special issue of the *Harvard Journal of Afro-American Affairs* was devoted to "The Black Press" in 1971. For the insightful viewpoint of one of the more successful black columnists in the white press, see Carl T. Rowan, *Just Between Us Blacks* (Random House, 1974). Articles include: "John H. Johnson of *Ebony*," *Nation's Business*, April 1974; and William J. Zima, "Directional Quandaries of the Black Press in the United States," *Journalism Quarterly*, Winter 1971; L. F. Palmer, "The Black Press in Transition," *Columbia Journalism Review*, Spring 1970; J. K. Obatala, "Black Journals Reflect Shift from Racialism," in *Readings in Mass Communication*, 3d ed., ed. Michael C. Emery and Ted Curtis Smythe (Brown, 1977). For a general introduction to the problems of minority media, see Sharon Murphy, *Other Voices: Black, Chicano and American Indian Press* (Plfaum-Standard, 1974). See also *Editor and Publisher Year Book*.

The Bleached World of Black TV

36

Pamela Douglas

If a hologram in *THX 1138* had burst the image, screaming, "I'm alive! I'm not a hologram! I'm real! Not a hologram! Alive!" it would have voiced my own outrage during my time as the token black executive at the world's largest film and television company. During that period, one of my spasms of attempting to have blacks portrayed as "real" was to propose a new TV series.

This was the era when "Sanford and Son" had reminded the networks that masses of people would watch blacks on television (as they'd done with "Amos 'n' Andy," despite complaints against it from black groups even then), and Florida was spinning off from "Maude" to "Good Times." So why not use the momentum of success to introduce a show where blacks are intelligent and caring, enlightening for our children (and yours, too) and, yes, also "entertaining"?

With this spirit, I approached a network vice-president at the studio. He leaned over his desk in a this-is-just-between-us pose and said something like, "I'm going to tell you the truth because you work here. Don't waste your time putting blacks in a drama, at least not in a series—on a special, maybe, but not on something that's going into people's houses every week of the year. Give me an updated 'Amos 'n' Andy'; *that* I can sell. Look, don't fool yourself: no one at the networks thinks the audience is laughing *with* the people on those shows. They exist so whites in the audience can relieve their tensions by laughing *at* blacks. I'm doing you a favor by telling you straight."

And he was. The vice-president for another network suggested that I create a starring white role, because blacks are only acceptable in secondary slots. As for the third network, the guy in charge said he was too busy to even listen to the idea but had an assistant relay that the network wasn't interested in any black-oriented subjects at that point. This series of exchanges was typical and would probably have been the same with any vice-presidents at any major studio with anyone proposing that blacks might be alive and real. It has been called by two names that reflect the dimension of the problem: the first is "institutional racism"; the second is "domestic colonialism." Either way, I soon made my exit from the role of hologram.

Years before, white TV analyst Les Brown had assessed the situation in his book *The Bu$ine$$ Behind the Box*. Speaking of broadcast management in the years up to the mid-'60s, he noted: "Negroes were not kept off the air because network managements were consciously racist [they are not consciously anything but businessminded]; they were not used because there seemed to be evidence that they would not *sell*, that is, that they would drive away audience. It was

Pamela Douglas is a freelance writer living in Los Angeles. Her article appeared in the December 1978 issue of *Human Behavior*. It is used with permission.

not their own prejudices they were acting from but rather those they fancied existed within the great TV audience."

Then a money-making formula was found. In the first few months of "The Flip Wilson Show," the network raised the advertising rates four times. Beginning at $46,000 per minute, the rate was up to $65,000 by the second month and two months later had climbed to $80,000 per minute. The secret was simple: the show attracted affluent whites. Perhaps the poor blacks with limited buying power tuned in also, but that was irrelevant to the advertisers. They were satisfied that those who would buy their products were watching and were prepared to back that with millions of dollars a year.

Why did the big white audience flock to this one black entertainer? The *Bu$ine$$ Behind the Box* suggests:

> First because he . . . could conduct a show of his own. Second, because his source of humor was not white society but black, and in that sense it was original for television, other Negroes in the medium having had to pretend the races had a common culture. Third, he was a one-man repertory company, having developed two characters outside his own . . . the Rev. Leroy . . . and Geraldine Jones, both satirical types and so distinctly Negro they had no credible co-ordinates in white society. Fourth, his comedy was not an ethnic argument; rather than sentimentalizing Negro-American culture it seemed to mock it. And fifth, *it did mock it.*
>
> The last may well have been the key. . . . On television, with its vast and heterogeneous audience, the honest kidding of ethnic types becomes something else, tending to validate the stereotype as a true representative of a whole people and in that way contributing to prejudice. . . . Flip Wilson was loved because he substantiated a racist view of blacks.

Regardless of the internal factors in any single show, an observer might reason that if all programming is controlled purely by economics, then the collective buying power of black people should be a heavy enough factor to influence policy. This brings us to the second twist of the trick.

The first twist was that if people don't have enough money to buy what's being sold on TV, they have no right to expect TV to show them anything that might improve their situation, thus helping to perpetuate their inability to buy. The second twist is that regardless of what those people might buy, they're not being counted, anyway.

Quoting Brown once more: "So little valued has been the black man as a consumer of nationally advertised products that he was not properly represented in the Nielsen sample of the American television audience. . . . The Nielsen Company, as well as the other, lesser, rating services, explained that it was difficult to place their hardware in ghetto homes, difficult to get representative families to keep viewing diaries adequately because of the high rate of illiteracy and even a problem in the telephone methods of audience research, because of the shortage of telephone homes in the ghetto."

Of course, those comments date from 1971, and a whole lot has happened since then, hasn't it? Well, hasn't it? I mean, there was "Roots," and, well, there was "Roots" and, oh yes, this season there are such TV-movies as "I Know Why the Caged Bird Sings" and "A Woman Called Moses"; and don't forget all those black faces on all those series such as "The Jeffersons," "Good Times," "What's Happening!" and so forth. They can't be accused of being vehicles for whites to laugh at or demean blacks, can they? Can they? And what about all those black people getting all the jobs at TV stations as a result of pressure from the government? I mean, just about every doggone time we turn on the set, some black face is going to pop up sooner or later, especially as a reporter on the news or, at least, in sports. Blacks must just about be taking over TV, right? Let's look at those assumptions.

Statistics from the Federal Communications Commission (FCC) show that nonwhites (blacks, Latinos, American Indians and Asian-Americans) all together comprise about 11.6 percent of all jobs but represent 49 percent of the laborers and 55 percent—a majority—of the service workers. As for the great oncamera images, especially as reporters and anchorpersons on the news, the record is clear that most of these folks are "holograms": images projected to convey someone else's point of view, because the chances are that they do not write their statements and the decision-making world behind the camera is virtually all white.

But hasn't it been steadily improving? After all, even with the best intentions, doesn't it take time to get people "broken in" to the ways of corporate TV? Well, take a look: from 1971 to 1975, in the category of "officials and managers," black females went from .4 percent to 1 percent, for an increase of .6 percent; and black males went from 1.8 percent to 2.3 percent, for a total increase of .5 percent. In the "professional" category, black females increased 1 percent, but black males actually *decreased* .2 percent. In the "sales workers" category, black male percentages *decreased* .9 percent, and black female percentages showed no gain, being at .6 percent in 1971 and .6 percent in 1975. (All statistics are from the Industry Equal Employment Opportunity Unit, FCC, and appeared in the *Congressional Record* of April 26, 1976.)

According to the Office of Communications of the United Church of Christ, the trend downward accelerated after that. And several observers have noted that the small employment gains made after the urban rebellions of the late '60s have been turned around; so the black presence in real decision-making positions is being pushed back to the level at the time of the rebellions. This point cannot be proven, partly because all the numbers aren't tallied, and partly because some reports are misleading (i.e., people being given "paper promotions" or hired just before the count and fired as soon as the station's license is renewed).

What is clear, however, is an attitude. If monitored and regulated television stations that are legally charged with serving "the public interest" are shaky, then what's going on at the networks (which are not subject to FCC control) or at the major production studios (which exist to make money for their stockholders)?

One aspect of the attitude was reported in *Daily Variety* in October 1976 under the banner headline "Three Majors Shun Hiring Hearings." The article began, "Three major film studios which declined an invitation to report on their hiring practices of minorities face the prospect of being summoned to a U.S. Civil Rights Commission hearing by subpoena." No, there was no subpoena, and the issue seemed to have slunk quietly away—at least as far as the studios were concerned. As for the blacks, Latinos, Indians, and Asians, the response could only be, so what else is new?

Speaking of ownership of TV and radio stations, *Daily Variety* reported, on April 27, 1977, "Discrimination from the investment community, advertisers, ratings services and broadcasters contributes to make it almost impossible for minority groups to succeed in broadcasting and helps point out why less than one-half of 1 percent of all stations are in minority hands."

Finally, back around to network programming, a 181-page report called "Window Dressing on the Set: Women and Minorities in Television" was issued in 1977 by the U.S. Civil Rights Commission, urging Congress to give the FCC authority to regulate employment practices at the networks. The reason wasn't to decrease unemployment rolls, any more than that was my reason for citing the bleak statistics here. Simply, the commission realized that much of the cause for the harmful images beaming into people's minds was a combination of ignorance and arrogance on the part of the white men who run the industry. The report explained: "Programming designed to reach the widest possible audience, coupled with the demands of the ratings race, constrains writers and producers from introducing more realistic and diverse images of women and minorities to the TV screen. Thus, network programmers with one eye on successful old formulas, the other on the inoffensive and with both hands in their pockets are not oriented toward serving the public interest."

Now the stage is set. The context of the industry was needed to make sense of what's going on in black network series. So now we can focus on the shows themselves.

Picture "Sanford and Son" (currently rerunning in off-prime-time syndication): an ignorant old junk dealer has a son in his 30s who still lives at home and whose main occupation seems to be scrapping with his father. Once in a while he might have a date, but the predominant woman is an aunt given to pummeling the men with her handbag while making foolishness out of religion.

Remember "That's My Mama" (now canceled)? A fat mama, whose place is clearly in the kitchen, has a son—yes, here it is again—a grown man in his 30s, still living at home, who makes a few gestures toward being a barber but really has nothing to do in his life worthy of respect.

Try again. "Good Times"—in its original form, it sported a father chronically out of work and a mother not working either. Here the most popular character became a young man, again with nothing much to do in his life, who tickled the public by screaming, *dy-no-mite*! The 12-year-old son was the mouthpiece for "black-conscious thought" and as such was to be laughed at but tolerated, because ideas of pride are understandable in a 12-year-old: after all, a few more years of TV, and he's sure to outgrow them. After John Amos and Esther Rolle (the father and mother) both quit the show in disgust, Dy-no-mite JJ (Jimmie Walker) became the so-called male image in the household, sinking whatever image-building vestiges the program initially attempted under the exploitation of JJ's silliness. Now, with Rolle returning this season, a degree of balance just might reenter. We'll see.

Moving "on up" to "The Jeffersons," at last a black man has a *job*. But, as might be expected, he's a fool, without an iota of concern for his people and devoid of historical or racial context. And again, hostility, bickering, and stupidity characterize the blacks.

A short-lived insult last year was "Baby, I'm Back," based on the premise that a black man who deserted his wife and two children for seven years comes back just before his wife remarries an old stuffed-shirt type out of loneliness. One of the key relationships was the hatred of the woman's mother for her daughter's husband. The husband, meanwhile, has been a shiftless hustler, playing the horses for a living and unable to comprehend what was wrong with walking out on his family. The alternative male image—the wife's new fiancé—was not to be taken seriously, either. Being more of a mummy than a man, he assured the audience one more time that black men aren't really men. As for the women, hysterical and desperate are probably the best descriptions. This is not to indict the actors, who have done their best under the circumstances and are serious performers. The problem is in the scripts, which were written mainly by whites under the dictation of the white producer.

The overwhelming quality of the series was the amount of sheer hatred in it. The problem was not only from such scenes as the mother-in-law beating the man with a baseball bat as he cowers under the table in the presence of his children. The problem was in the texture itself, in the language. The children called one another by such endearments as "toilet-head," and hardly any exchange was free of an insult. Maybe this was some white person's idea of how black families relate. More likely, it's just another example of trying to make money by ridiculing people who do not seem to have the power to fight back.

Do these descriptions sound like your family? No? Well, they don't sound like mine, either. But we should keep in mind that with enough perpetuation of these role models, they could become real.

In 1978, two black dramatic pilots appeared. One, "Kinfolks," was about a black family that moves south and learns to cope with a nonurban lifestyle, the white neighbors, and their own growth. It held out for basic human values, very similar to "The Waltons," and did believe in love. Best of all, it wasn't another comedy, which would have made it the first prime-time black dramatic series. The difference is to the credit of its creator, Melvin Van Peebles, a black writer. Although whites are producing the show, Van Peebles maintained a hand in selecting some black writers for the early scripts, with the hope that at least the show would not make race hatred even worse. But the networks decided not to air the series.

The second, "Harris and Company" (which piloted as "Love Is Not Enough"), stars Bernie Casey as the widowed father of a big family that has plenty of love but not enough money, as they struggle together in Detroit. With black producer Stan Robertson at its head, and a black story editor, it still has a chance to air in 1979. But so far it isn't on the network schedules, either.

The other series are all under exclusive white control, although occasionally a black writer or director might be hired for a segment. This didn't have to be the way. "Good Times," "The Jeffersons" and "What's Happening!" were all created originally by a black man, Eric Monte, who also wrote the feature *Cooley High*. What would have happened if Monte had been given his rightful respect as the series creator is moot by now. What has happened, in fact, is that Monte is suing ABC, CBS, Norman Lear, Tandem Productions, Toy Products, Bernie Weintraub (a big agent), and Fred Silverman (formerly in charge of programming at ABC, now the president of NBC) for $450 million (!) as part of a class-action suit alleging racial discrimination, plagiarism, antitrust violations, fraud, and other crimes. He claims they stole "What's Happening!" and "The Jeffersons" from him and failed to compensate him properly for "Good Times."

At the base of the lawsuit is the issue of black control. Monte wanted to produce his later series and to have a higher level of involvement with the first ones. Currently, network television has not one single black producer. Monte was responsible for ideas that are among the biggest hits in the industry. Yet industry officials call him not qualified to produce his own work. According to Monte, his compensation for "Good Times" is said to be in the range of $150 per show. The likelihood is, however, that he will lose his suit and possibly even be blackballed from the networks. This is not a matter of one individual whose case may or may not have legal merits; it's about seeing clearly why black series are on television, and who they are intended for.

This brings us back to the studio vice-president who warned me, "These shows exist so whites in the audience can relieve their tensions by laughing *at* blacks." If this is, in fact, the way these shows make money for the networks, then, of course, the mind of a conscious black person would be an interference; so, of course, the shows would have to be produced by whites. Their system often goes this way: blacks are invited to submit story ideas (not scripts, just ideas) to a special department, sometimes staffed by a token black who has no real power. This office passes the most useful of these ideas along to the producer, who sometimes buys one (and may "borrow" others, although this can't be proved). After the black is paid minimally for his or her story, it is handed to a white writer—who is the one to get the big credit and the pay. After the white writer has finished, another black person is sometimes brought in to make the script "sound black" by throwing in a few "black" lines or jokes. If this last step isn't taken, the burden falls on the actors to make the script sound plausible, which can go as far as them rewriting on the set, although they would not be paid or credited for this.

Our emphasis has been on series, because that's where the mind is trained, despite the undeniable effect of such specials as "Roots." It's the difference between the influence of one's friends and neighbors and the influence of a one-week trip to Japan. Maybe the sights and sounds of the foreign country intrigued us, and, sure, "we'll never forget it and we'll never be the same after that experience," we tell our friends. But the habits, the patterns of thinking we carry with us day to day are formed more by our friends than by that exotic journey. So it is with the TV people who join our household every week of the year.

Nevertheless, the specials deserve mention as probes into healthier alternatives. Many blacks were disappointed with what they felt was a softening or whitewashing of history (and of Haley's book) in the TV version of *Roots*. And we have noticed that this kind of problem occurs in conjunction with the failure to employ a single black writer in the teleplay of "Roots" or in "Pittman" or in "Minstrel Man" or in others, not to mention always being white-produced. Still, on balance, "Roots" and other specials have done more good than harm and have awakened many people to discovering more of the truth for themselves.

Further, the commercial success and acclaim of "Roots" has caused vice-presidents to think twice before responding as they had in the years before "Roots," that blacks are "only acceptable in secondary slots" or that the public "isn't interested in any black-oriented subjects." So (to requote the U.S. Civil Rights Commission report), "network programmers with one eye on successful old formulas, the other on the inoffensive and with both hands in their pockets" have found it in their self-interest to locate other "Roots"-type projects. A "Roots"-type project is: (1) historical (not something one would have to deal with in "real" life); (2) rural (again, not something most people would deal with in "real" life); (3) a portrayal of blacks as struggling victims; and (4) suggesting that the solutions are to be found within the American system.

This formula has led to a few interesting TV movies scheduled this year. "I Know Why the Caged Bird Sings," based on the autobiography of Maya Angelou, is about a black girl growing up in the rural South in the '30s. Unfortunately, Angelou, who is an accomplished director and screenwriter, did not direct this film and was not permitted to present the wholeness of life as she did in the book. The message of the TV version is that a black little girl in the Deep South in the 1930s could prevail against the hostilities and injustices of the world purely by the strength of her soul. But the autobiography on which the film is based doesn't pretend that. Instead, the book ends with a groping, unsure coming into womanhood, with the birth of Maya's son into a world no less threatening than what the girl had sought to conquer.

The film does have some impact and significance, and at least it is a drama. But when *I Know Why the Caged Bird Sings* was published in 1970, the telling seemed, perhaps, more urgent than it does now. One might wonder whether this and other tales of life in the rural South of the past, especially those featuring children, are becoming convenient ways for the networks to avoid dealing with the realities of contemporary black lives.

Another drama, "A Woman Called Moses," the story of Harriet Tubman and the underground railroad, has a black writer, Lonne Elder III. And on "Roots—Part II," due to air in January, one black writer was, at last, included among all the whites. Maybe it's a sign of hope. Maybe their quality and success will lead the sponsors and the network executives to grow in two ways, by upgrading the black weekly series and by summoning the courage to grapple with black subjects that are contemporary and closer to real challenges of life.

Finally, though, I encourage my black brothers and sisters not to confine their search to the existing structures. Soon satellites, with their capacity for instant global communication, will change the images of people. Since only 10 percent of the world's population is of European origin, the majority of the people of the world are nonwhite. Further, the questions of sharing the world's resources take on different meanings in a global perspective, and thus the relationship of people to one another and to their possessions will have to change. When these changes in consciousness occur, television will not be able to continue in its greedy, hate-filled patterns. Also, as cable television becomes more widespread, with its 80-channel capacity, the preponderance of three network stations will sooner or later be diluted. This is not to say that the situation is going to improve by just waiting for the pie in the sky. But it is to suggest that we are not at the mercy of the three narrow-minded vice-presidents who stopped me cold at the studio.

If we want better shows, we better make them ourselves. Given the roadblocks Eric Monte encountered, I would recommend that blacks had better be trying to gain political and economic control of the systems to deliver them, too.

Bibliography

Two very useful books dealing with blacks in film are Donald Bogle, *Toms, Coons, Mulattoes, Mammies* and *Bucks: An Interpretive History of Blacks in American Films* (Viking Press, 1973) and James P. Murray, *To Find an Image: Black Films from Uncle Tom to Super Fly* (Bobbs-Merrill, 1974). Ann Powers, compiler, *Blacks in American Movies: A Selected Bibliography* (Scarecrow Press, 1974) is a highly useful annotated compilation of books, articles, and indexes. Also see back issues of *Ebony, Black Stars, Now,* and other black publications, including the June 1975 article from *Ebony* published in the previous edition of this reader: Louie Robinson, "Have Blacks Really Made It in Hollywood?" in *Readings in Mass Communication,* 3d ed., ed. Michael C. Emery and Ted Curtis Smythe (Brown, 1977). For another perspective, see "TV Usage Greater Among Non-Whites," from the A. C. Nielsen Company's *The Nielsen Newscast,* 1975, also found in the 3d edition of this book.

For a general background on use of and access to the mass media in the U.S., consult the special issue of *Freedomways* (1974) devoted to the study of "The Black Image in the Mass Media." See especially the bibliography by Ernest Kaiser, which lists books and magazine articles in five categories: general, television, radio, theater, and film. Two recent studies on the image of blacks in television can be found in Churchill Robert, "The Presentation of Blacks in Television Network Newscasts," *Journalism Quarterly,* Spring 1975, pp. 50–55, and James L. Hinton *et al.,* "Tokenism and Improving Imagery of Blacks in TV Drama and Comedy: 1973," *Journal of Broadcasting,* Fall 1974, pp. 423–32. See also Eugenia Collier, "A House of Twisted Mirrors: The Black Reflection in the Media," *Current History,* November 1974, pp. 228–31, and Marilyn Diane Fife, "Black Image in American TV: The First Two Decades," *The Black Scholar,* November 1974, pp. 7–15. Also check the indexes of various research journals. For example, *Journalism Quarterly* has carried a number of articles examining audience perceptions of black newscasters and black entertainers. Also see *Journal of Broadcasting.*

Sexism in the Media World

Barbara Reed

37

Barbara Walters became ABC's "million-dollar baby" and the best-known female media personality in 1976 when she left NBC. "I think the contract was probably the worst thing that ever happened, except that it made me known throughout the world," Walters said. It brought show business to the news business. ABC executives needed to grab rating points, each said to be worth as much as $30 million in advertising revenue, for its evening news program. Walters was supposed to do that by sharing the anchor desk with Harry Reasoner. "When you're in news, you weren't supposed to get paid a lot of money. When Johnny Carson makes $5 million, no one cares; when Merv Griffin makes $3 million and when Mike Douglas makes $2 million, that's okay. It doesn't bother anyone. But someone in news, although news brings in a lot of money, makes a good deal of money, that upset a lot of people, especially my peers," Walters lamented. The $5 million, five-year Walter's contract covers anchoring, "Issues and Answers," radio work, interviewing, and her specials.

Despite the voluminous publicity surrounding her hiring and the softly spoken words among feminists to switch to ABC "for women's sake," the ratings failed to budge. At first some people watched to judge her performance, and Barbara Wa-Wa jokes (from Gilda Radner's "Saturday Night Live" routine) were as widespread as feelings of panic before final exams.

Walters resents her celebrity status, but it is obvious that she has attained the status of people she is interviewing. Criticism ranged from comments on her voice to critiques of her aggressive interviewing techniques. Walters could call on world leaders for interviews and proved to be an asset despite the stable ratings.[1]

Barbara Walters is the most visible woman in the media, and a woman at whom some people point when they want to "prove" how much the status of women in the media has changed. But has it, and if so, to what extent? And what does the future promise for the more than 50 percent of the enrollees in journalism/mass communications programs across the country?

Women have joined the labor force in astonishing numbers in the last thirty years. The Bureau of Labor Statistics in June 1978 estimated the growth to be 123 percent while the female population increased only 52 percent. Women now constitute forty-nine percent of the work force.

Women are not only joining the labor force in record numbers, they are also enrolled in college. The majority of young college students are female: 52 percent of all students under age 22. While the enrollment of men under 22 has remained

Barbara Straus Reed, member of the California State University, Los Angeles journalism faculty, served as chair of the Committee on the Status of Women in Journalism Education of the Association for Education in Journalism. In 1978 she represented the AEJ at a conference of women's groups in Washington, D.C. The result of the meeting was formation of the Coalition for Women in the Humanities and Social Sciences. Ms. Reed wrote this article especially for this edition of *Readings in Mass Communication.*

1. Sally Bedell, "What Made ABC's Harry Reasoner Switch Back to CBS?" *TV Guide,* January 27, 1979, pp. 25 ff.

the same, enrollment of women under 22 rose 35 percent between 1970 and 1976. The strong upward trend in enrollment of women of all ages continues. The increase in enrollment of women aged 22 to 35 between 1970 and 1976 was 103 percent. Women comprise 59 percent of students 33 and older, up from 52 percent in 1975.[2]

This growth is reflected in enrollment figures for journalism too. The 1978 journalism enrollments, nationwide, continued to show more women than men majoring in journalism. Women comprise 53 percent of all journalism students enrolled, or a gain of more than 12 percent in ten years. Moreover, the greatest growth of enrollment of women was in the freshman class, which means that second, third, and senior-level classes will have more women students.[3] And Barbara Walters could serve as one role model for them.

The nature of TV news places emphasis on the anchors; they become "stars" whether or not they want to—superstars who perform rather than report the news. Barbara Walters' role changed after a short time with ABC; the news program was revamped, and she began interviewing exclusively. This failure of Walters could not be interpreted as a failure for newswomen generally. Interviewing happens to be her strength; anchoring is not.

TV news has expanded over the years, from fifteen minutes to a combination local/network show of two hours in some cities, one hour in others. With staff expansions has come a bigger role for women, both on and off camera. A mid-sixties survey found that women held one out of four broadcasting jobs, but nearly all were traffic, continuity, or secretarial positions.[4] Visible network news correspondents and weekend anchors in the seventies include Sylvia Chase, Bettina Gregory, and Catherine Mackin for ABC; Jessica Savitch, Carole Simpson, and Judy Woodruff for NBC; and Margaret Osmer, Marlene Sanders, and Lesley Stahl for CBS. ABC's Ann Compton became the first woman assigned by a network to cover the White House. Pioneering TV woman Pauline Fredericks of NBC opened the doors for them when she staked out serious claims in the traditionally all-male domain of Televisionland. Fredericks encountered many obstacles, and while she and others made it, undoubtedly thousands of equally qualified, motivated, and ambitious women did not.

The stakes are high in TV news. A rating point can be worth up to $1 million a year in a rich market such as Los Angeles. And the prestige of leading, if only by a fraction, is worth many times that amount. Advertising agencies make plans based on the ratings. Can viewers be drawn to women as they have to men? TVQ (a measure of popularity) can be "amazingly high," according to one general manager. Women stand an equal chance of becoming Nielsen sensations. Viewers don't reject them because they are women. Research studies have demonstrated that. Often women anchors first served as weather readers or gave traffic reports, then "showed talent" (initiative) and were promoted to anchor. At first the women were hired as tokens, and the first round of women on TV proved disastrous for some. Sally Quinn exemplified what happened.[5]

2. California Women, a bulletin from the California Commission on the Status of Women, September 1978.

3. Paul V. Peterson, "Enrollment Surges Again, Increases 7% to 70,601," Journalism Educator, January 1979, pp. 3–8.

4. Don C. Smith and Kenneth Harwood, "Women in Broadcasting," Journal of Broadcasting, Fall 1966, pp. 339–355.

5. Sally Quinn, We're Going to Make You a Star, New York: Dell, 1975.

Quinn was hired by the *Washington Post's* Ben Bradlee as party reporter, but in the nation's capital society reporters are political reporters as well. Moreover, the position requires as much knowledge of events as the reporters on the national desk have. Quinn never showed any interest in television and considered herself a journalist. But CBS was "looking for a woman . . . to knock Barbara Walters off the air." (Walters was co-hostess of the morning "Today" show on NBC.) Quinn could not say no to the glamour of TV. In contrast to Walters' title, Quinn was listed as co-anchor of the CBS "Morning News."

The network personnel promoted her as a sexy, blonde bombshell instead of a serious newswoman. Quinn became known as a journalist who uses sex to get her stories. Moreover, she, and other women hastily put before the cameras at that time, was untrained, didn't know which camera to look at, did not understand what a hand-waving stage manager wanted, fumbled with words, and couldn't read the TelePrompTers.

Quinn and others were not given the benefit of talk about how to improve. During her brief encounter with CBS, Quinn was told, "You're a big star now, and people figure if you're a big star you must know what you're doing. Nobody's going to stick his neck out to help you."

It wasn't long before women realized they would have to help themselves and each other. Thus, women's committees were established at many unions and guilds to improve performances and to improve the images of both women and men. Such committees found parallels in professional societies and organizations. AFTRA is an example.

The American Federation of Television and Radio Artists (AFTRA) is a union with more than 35,000 members. These individuals hold a variety of titles. They are reporters, newscasters, announcers, commentators, sportscasters, disc jockeys, singers, dancers, commercial announcers, and actors. Women account for one-third of AFTRA's national membership. The largest category (18,000) is actor, of which 8,300 are women. The "soaps" have the highest percentages of women in all of television programming.[6]

Almost 1,600 people are newscasters; 339 are women. As announcers—a declining profession (because automation keeps eroding the use of live voices)— approximately 500 women are in a field of 3,700. And between 1974 and 1977 three more women became sportscasters, making a total of approximately 11 in a field of just over 200. (See table below.)

Alice Backes, first president of the AFTRA Women's Committee, indicated that a gradual growth of women at the stations has taken place. By March 1977, 15 percent of station on-air AFTRA members in San Francisco, San Diego, and Los Angeles were women. In other markets the ratio is a little higher. Backes reported that in Seattle, as of June 1977, 19 percent of the station personnel were women.

Vernon Stone, Radio-Television News Directors Association research committee chairman and professor of journalism at Southern Illinois University, Carbondale, has charted the growth of women working in TV and radio news.[7]

6. Correspondence with Alice Backes; phone conversation January 1979.

7. Vernon Stone, "Newsrooms Add Many Women, Few Minority Males," *RTNDA Communicator*, January 1979, pp. 1, 12, 13. Also see: Vernon Stone, "More Women Reporting News on the Air," *RTNDA Communicator*, February 1977, pp. 7–10; Vernon Stone and Abigail Jones Nash, "A Survey of Women in Broadcast News," *RTNDA Communicator*, March 1975, pp. 4, 5.

AFTRA Surveys: "Lugubrious Progress"

National Membership:		*1974*	*1977*
	Female	34	38
	Male	66	62
		100%	100%

1974: 95% response rate (26,202 of 27,710)

Announcer		*Newscaster*		*Sportscaster*	
Female	672 (17%)	Female	268 (14%)	Female	8 (3%)
Male	3,372 (83%)	Male	1,648 (86%)	Male	301 (97%)
Total	4,044	Total	1,916	Total	309

1977: 92% response rate (32,752 of 35,735)

Categories: Representing 85.2% of membership in 21 locals (differences appear because category information not available from every local).

Announcer		*Newscaster*		*Sportscaster*	
Female	504 (13.5%)	Female	339 (22%)	Female	11 (5%)
Male	3,236 (86.5%)	Male	1,233 (78%)	Male	205 (95%)
Total	3,740	Total	1,572	Total	216

A Major Market: Los Angeles

From May 1974 until May 1977 women made gains at the stations. Los Angeles offers an example. In announcing, there was a decrease of 18 positions but an increase of 11 positions filled by women. For newscasting, 19 new positions were created, and women were in 44 more newscasting jobs. Four more women became sportscasters, although there were 23 more positions.

His most recent study found that women made up 23 percent of all TV news personnel in late 1977 compared to 20 percent in the spring of 1976. Radio news increased from 21 percent to 23 percent in a year and a half. And twice as many women were working in broadcast news in 1977 than in 1972. Moreover, those who hired women apparently appreciated their work, for those station managers were more likely to hire additional newswomen. The number of women working in broadcast news increased, but the number of stations employing newswomen did not change essentially from 1976 to 1977. Market size and region made little difference, although fewer small markets (those with under 50,000 population) hired women.

Usually one anchorwoman is on the air at stations in this country, regardless of station size. Women comprise 20 percent of anchors of TV news staffs. That shows greater acceptance of women than the networks had several years ago.

"I was told women's voices were not authoritative enough to do news," said Jessica Savitch.[8] "I don't know where they got that if they (CBS) had never tried it." Executives assumed that audiences would accept only male voices and faces reporting news on the air. In fact, in 1971 Reuven Frank, president of NBC News, was quoted, "I have the strong feeling that audiences are less prepared to accept news from a woman's voice than from a man's."[9] However, research has shown clearly that audiences do accept women whose ability is comparable to that of men on the air, both as anchors and as field reporters. News directors were studied. They thought their "viewers would prefer a man as an evening newscaster, but the most frequent response of all audience groups surveyed was that it made no difference to them whether the newscaster was a man or a woman. . . . Preferences for the male voice and a desire to retain what they were used to were the main reasons given by respondents who said they sometimes preferred a man to a woman for TV reporting. . . . Leaning toward a man was simply a habit."[10]

In 1975, the National Association of Broadcasters (NAB) funded a study which found no differences in audience preferences for male or female newscasters or in regard to effectiveness, believability, and acceptance.[11] Nevertheless, only one voice in six on radio belongs to a woman. Higher proportions of radio stations have retained their all-male sounds. Stone found that the larger the market, the more likely the station had a female newscaster. Seldom do they have more than one, however. For field reporting, only one woman was hired in most cases—regardless of market size.

Women on the air are more visible and less powerful than men in terms of control. Jo Moring, vice president, news, NBC radio in New York, advises "those with management aspirations not to be distracted by the glamour of announcers' positions but to go toward management." Current FCC figures show women in 16 percent of management and sales positions. [12]

Stone also found that women were heading commercial news operations at eight percent of radio stations; four years before, the number was four percent.[13] Half of these women were 21 to 25 years old. They tended to work in smaller markets.

More women are being hired for broadcast news, not only because of pressures from the FCC or women's liberation groups, but also because they have shown themselves equal in ability to men.

"In the other areas of our profession," said Alice Backes, "the other women's media committees and women's media groups can report that women are very slowly emerging as studio carpenters, film editors, directors, writers, producers." She cautioned that habits are hard to change: "Two women producers at Universal had to insist, when they were given office space, that they needed typing help and shouldn't have to be their own secretarial assistants." Backes terms this "lugubrious progress."

She deplores the lack of women in entertainment shows, asking, "Where are the women in game shows, except sewn into their briefies, helping point out what

8. Peter Ross Range, "I'm Not Going to Apologize for My Looks Any More," *TV Guide,* March 3, 1979, pp. 13–17.

9. "The New Breed," *Newsweek,* August 30, 1970, pp. 62, 63.

10. Vernon Stone, "Attitudes Toward Television Newswomen," *Journal of Broadcasting,* Winter 1973–74, pp. 49–62.

11. Susan Whittaker, "Male vs. Female Newscaster—A Study of the Relative Effectiveness, Believability, and Acceptance," unpublished research paper, University of Florida, Gainesville.

12. Carol Sommer, "In Search of—The Female Voice," *Radio/Active,* January 1979, pp. 16–17.

13. Vernon Stone, "Surveys Show Younger Women Becoming News Directors," *RTNDA Communicator,* October 1976, pp. 10–12.

the 'goodies' are that the carefully selected, breathless and screaming women from the audience are trying for. No women hosts or co-hosts appear on any of these tributes to materialism," Backes said.

Women tend to dominate comedies; they rarely star in serious drama. Exceptions are "action" shows where they play members of a police force or detectives. Research studies have documented that female roles have held at 25 to 30 percent of all TV characterizations. Surprisingly, this percentage has been constant for thirty years![14] In the past few seasons women on television dramas often were used to show off their bodies. Some actresses protested the special effects (lighting and camera angles) and costume requirements employed to reveal more of their bodies. Actresses in made-for-television movies felt sexually "exploited," and new hires in prime-time programs wiggled and jiggled across the screen. Many women's groups protested these shows, and some attempt was made to curb their frequency.[15] "Women . . . are desperately disheartened to be faced in 1978 with the disgraceful trash which is being transmitted in the guise that this is the American woman," said Kathleen Nolan, serving her second term as president of the Screen Actors Guild, in an article blasting television's portrayal of women. In the last ten years portrayal of women has not improved in television.[16]

Print Journalism

In the area of print journalism, particularly newspaper reporting and editing, specifics regarding the current status of women cannot be stated as definitively as with broadcasting. Radio and TV, on which the FCC keeps records, seem to be more closely monitored than privately held newspapers and magazines.

The status of women on newspapers remains at question. There is reason to believe that women working on papers have not achieved equality with men. The overwhelming majority of Pulitzer Prizes in reporting have gone to male journalists, and prominent editors and reporters have been mostly men. Women have been segregated in the "soft" news departments. "Hard" news was too "hard" for women, "soft" news too "soft" for men.

Traditionally, women on newspaper staffs have been assigned to the women's pages or to the food pages. They covered fashion shows or other social events or issues related to "society" or preparation of food and nutrition. A woman majoring in political science, minoring in journalism, who served as editor of her college newspaper, took a job with an urban daily in the Middle West upon graduating—writing about food and clipping recipes. A few years later she was promoted to education writer. That happened in the sixties. Fortunately such job placements are not as common in the seventies, and women on dailies writing about food now have home economics backgrounds or extensive knowledge in related fields.

Most society pages have been superseded by the "living" or "lifestyle" section, but since women's pages offered the only available slots to those who wanted newspaper work, a look at them could prove useful in assessing women's status in the press.

Researchers from the University of Missouri, home of the J.C. Penney-Missouri Newspaper Awards and workshops for women's pages, studied women's

14. Joseph Turow, "Advising and Ordering: Daytime, Prime Time," *Journal of Communication,* Spring 1974, pp. 138–44.

15. See the excellent two-part article in the *Washington Post* by Eileen Farley and William K. Knoedelseder, Jr., "Rub-a-Dub-Dub, Three Networks in a Tub," February 19, 1978, p. G–1; and "The Titillation of Sarah," February 19, 1978, p. G–3.

16. "SAG's Nolan Blasts TV Portrayal of Women," *Broadcasting* June 5, 1978, p. 55.

page editors on dailies and weeklies from around the country.[17] They learned that weeklies paid less than dailies; the higher the circulation, the better the salary in general; editors with more education received more money; and one's major or minor in college had no impact on one's salary.

Generally the men had some college or graduate school and thus were better educated than the women, although almost all respondents had taken college- or graduate-level courses. Men also tended to have more journalism experience than women. Women's salaries were significantly less than the men's; however, some men had been editors or publishers of small weeklies, experience the women lacked.

When women move to other places around a newspaper, do their by-lined stories carry the same weight and credibility with readers? (It's the issue of the authoritative-sounding voices again, translated into print.) For years women journalists used initials—particularly if they were writing sports or financial news. Those with first names like "Pat" or "Leslie" felt fortunate, because readers could not determine the sex of the writer.

A study from the University of North Carolina found that male readers were more "sensitive" to story by-lines than were women readers, and male readers were more "favorable" by and large to male by-lines. Women at the time were not very sensitive to by-lines. Researchers suggested that "as women more and more appear as by-line writers on all kinds of stories, doubtless reader judgments will gradually shift."[18]

Women who moved out of the "living" sections to cover hard news in the city room did not find fatter paychecks. For some, especially those with other means of support, usually husbands, accepting minimal pay became a way of life, their cross to bear for wanting to be in the marketplace. Those who needed to work were intimidated by fear of losing their jobs if they asked for more pay. In fairness, though, it must be said that many publications operate on marginal budgets and cannot afford to pay higher rates. However, rates should be the same for men and women.

Another form of discrimination, albeit more subtle, is the managerial practice of financing participation at conventions and workshops for male staff but not for women. In many cases women fund their own way, and, to add insult to injury, are docked pay for days away from work. Some managements substitute support in these endeavors for pay.[19]

Women are denied other benefits, too, such as stock options, deferred payments, travel privileges, and having club/association memberships and magazine subscriptions paid for by the company.

Discrimination can be seen with titles, also. Some women have titles but little pay. Others have inflated titles—director of—and then don't direct anyone but themselves.

"Unfortunately, a secretary who is called a manager of clerical services is still a secretary and probably still earns a secretary's salary," Christine Ogan of Indiana University told delegates to the 1978 annual convention of the Society

17. Won Chang, Joye Patterson, Robert Hosokawa, and Jack Dvorak, "Women's Page Editors: Self Perceived Status," paper presented at AEJ convention, San Diego, 1974.

18. Lynda Painter Cole, Donald Lewis Shaw, Roy L. Moore, and Richard R. Cole, "Reporters' Bylines: Does Sex Make a Difference?" paper presented to AEJ convention, 1975, Ottawa, Canada.

19. Lois Lauer Wolfe, "Competition Keen in Communications," *Press Women*, monthly publication of National Federation of Press Women, January 1975.

of Professional Journalists. "The titles are created, but they are devoid of accompanying decision-making power and high salary."

Employment of women on newspapers has shown slight but steady progress. From 1969 to 1975 the gain was only 2.4 percent, or 27,000 women in newsrooms; they represented 26 percent of the total. In 1977 women made up 33 percent of the work force in the newspaper business, according to figures from the American Newspaper Publishers Association (ANPA).

Press women often feel discrimination when assignments are made. Sometimes a woman is given a story when a male reporter isn't available, and editors have said they sometimes take sex into consideration when making assignments. For example, a story on a black mother's life was deemed more appropriate for a woman, while investigating Mafia tips on the Hoffa case was thought a man's domain.

When she was quoted in a women's paper at UCLA, Miriam Bjerre, network reporter for CBS television news, who is based in Los Angeles, summed up feelings of most women these days: "Sometimes I think being a woman is an advantage. I don't feel funny about admitting I'm ignorant about something. I'll say to somebody, 'I don't understand this, or I need some background on this and you know a lot about it—would you mind filling me in?' I don't have to put up a big macho front. I once heard [a male reporter] do a report on the air about how a reporter works—and bragging about all the tricks you can use to make somebody give you information without asking for it."

Bjerre began working at KNX radio and became the first female general reporter the all-news station had ever hired. She said: "When I first got to KNX . . . people didn't know whether to say 'anchorwoman,' 'anchorperson'—big deal, but it seemed very important then. Everyone was tiptoeing around trying not to be offensive or sexist. Everyone didn't want to be sexist. But if there's a story about raising kids or something like that and I can cover it better than a lot of the guys, I don't consider that a put-down. It's crazy to bend over backward and not use a person's resources. There were stories I was glad to cover, ones I was particularly interested in—breast cancer stories, rape, or wife-beating. There may have been some instances where it was easier for an interviewee to talk to me. I don't think I'm being typecast though. It's like pretending there aren't differences and we need to take advantage of what each person has to offer. I mean, I wouldn't want to do *only* these stories."

Management

Job aspirations of newspaperwomen are not high. Studies have found that most wanted to remain reporters; few have wanted to be news editors, managing editors, or editor and publisher.[20]

Nevertheless, recent studies indicate that more women are interested in and have opportunity for positions in newspaper management. Indiana University received funding from the Frank E. Gannett Newspaper Foundation for surveys

20. Patricia Ellen McCall, "The Current Status of Newspaperwomen in Wisconsin," paper presented to AEJ convention, San Diego, 1974, is one of these studies.

and a conference in 1977.[21] Mail and telephone sampling led to the following conclusions. Daily newspaper managements employ about one woman manager per newspaper, on the average. Women and men managers are equally qualified personally and professionally; there were few differences. Women receive substantially lower salaries than men, regardless of newspaper size or job area, but both men and women managers were equally satisfied with their jobs. In telephone interviews, women perceive differences in the treatment of men and women. Promotion criteria and the effort required to attain a position in management differ for men and women, the women said. Only about 2.4 percent of executives and managers of papers with daily circulations of greater than 40,000 are women, and that tiny percentage may be inflated because of titles minus corresponding responsibilities bestowed on women.[22, 23]

Each of 1,154 daily newspapers with less than 25,001 circulation, employs 1.1 women as managers; those with 25,001 to 50,000 circulation employ about .9 women managers per paper; those with 50,001 to 100,000 circulation employ about 1 woman manager per paper; and those with more than 100,000 circulation employ about .8 women managers per paper. By 1978, 300 more women held a managing position with newspapers, making an average of about 1.2 women per daily.

The Indiana team also concluded that the consistency of salary patterns across different circulation sizes and job areas of daily newspapers raises the possibility that these same salary inequities persist throughout much of the daily newspaper industry. "It is very difficult to determine whether this is so because many newspapers do not publish or release salaries of their managers" (or of others in their employ if they're not a guild paper). Salary differences may not be noticed by women because they are ignorant of their male colleagues' salaries and/or they believe they are doing well compared with other women.

A study of women in weekly paper management found that one-third of weekly editors are women and that women comprise over one-half of all weekly newspaper employees.[24] Women editors were less likely to hire and promote employees compared with men, and to own any part of the newspaper. Minimal differences existed in the areas of education and experience. However, once again, women editors were paid less than men but were satisfied with their jobs. Although women are under-represented in weekly newspaper management, opportunities for women on weeklies appear to be better than opportunities on dailies.

This indifference of women to their status and inferior salaries apparently is widespread and crosses all professions and workers. Women do not seem to be completely aware of job discrimination they endure. If they are aware, they don't know what to do about gaining parity with men.[25] Also, attitudes of inferior self-worth which women tend to hold are confirmed when men groom other men rather than women to replace them as they move up the management ladder.

21. Christine L. Ogan and Gretchen M. Letterman, "Report and Evaluation: Conference on Women in Newspaper Management," Indiana University School of Journalism, May 1977.

22. David H. Weaver, Christine L. Ogan, Charlene J. Brown, and Mary I. Benedict, "Women in Newspaper Management: A Status Report," Research Report No. 2, following Conference on Women in Newspaper Management, Indiana University School of Journalism, May 25–28, 1977.

23. Charlene J. Brown, Christine L. Ogan, and David H. Weaver, "Men and Women in Daily Newspaper Management: Their Characteristics and Advice to Future Managers," paper presented to AEJ convention, Seattle, 1978.

24. Susan Holly, "Women in Weekly Newspaper Management," paper presented to AEJ convention, Seattle, 1978.

25. "Why Aren't More Women Furious?" *Matrix,* Winter 1978–79, p. 10; see also, Manny Paraschos, "Survey Reflects Satisfaction," *Matrix,* pp. 10–11.

Another study investigated why women do not seem to advance farther and faster in media management.[26] It found that, in addition to the matter of who grooms whom, rules against nepotism and/or against allowing the spouse of a staff member to work for competing media usually militate against the wife's career; that men managers resist giving good assignments and promotions to women; and that marital status and personal circumstances influence employers when they dispense raises.

On the positive side, respondents agreed that time and money should be spent to groom a woman for a top management position; that employers should not inquire into women's marriage and family plans; that women want and will accept management responsibilities; and that family, job, and social life can be handled by a woman without putting her under too much stress to accept management responsibilities.

Respondents also felt that women should object to being asked automatically to take minutes in a group of equally educated or trained professionals when no secretary is present; that having a woman in middle to top management will not necessarily rob men of camaraderie they formerly enjoyed; that women are as comfortable as men with computer technology; and that a sense of teamwork can develop in a mixed group of men and women as well as in a group of men.

Men—even older men—tended to speak positively of the women with whom they worked, including women managers. Many admitted they changed their attitudes about women in newspapers as they worked with them.

Nepotism rules are very unpopular, and rules governing whether employees' spouses may work for competing media are almost equally unpopular.

Women do manage newspapers—and well! Marjorie Paxson, assistant managing editor, *The* (Idaho) *Statesman*; Christy Bulkeley, publisher, *Commercial-News*, Danville, Illinois; Carol Sutton, assistant to the editor and publisher, Louisville *Courier-Journal*; Jean Sharley Taylor, associate editor, *Los Angeles Times*; and Charlotte Curtis, associate editor, *New York Times*—these women did not inherit their positions, they broke the barriers against women in newspaper management.

Some women are not able to break through discrimination barriers. Women who feel discrimination in media jobs may file formal protests. They have learned they can protest effectively, and they can be compensated for lost wages. Group action seems to be more successful because of stiff legal fees, interminable delays, and difficulties in obtaining necessary-but-voluminous documentation. Battles fought through the Equal Employment Opportunity Commission (EEOC) take years to conclude, as does court action. Sometimes, while waiting for a judgment, women lose their jobs. Most, however, feel that the fight is worthwhile even so. Some of the best media have been found guilty of sex discrimination: *Newsday, Sacramento Bee, Washington Post, New Haven* (Conn.) *Register, St. Louis Post-Dispatch,* Baltimore *News American,* WREC-TV in Memphis, WTVT-TV in Tampa, *Detroit News,* among others.

26. Dru Riley Evarts, "Women in Media Management," unpublished paper presented at AEJ Theory and Methodology Division, regional meeting, Cleveland, Ohio, February 17, 1979.

In November 1977 an agreement between the Reader's Digest Association and a group of women employees, filed four years before, was settled with the Digest agreeing to an affirmative action plan. NBC lost a suit in August 1977, brought by sixteen former and current employees, and $2 million was awarded to those victims of sex discrimination. The settlement included provisions for more women in upper-level positions and in technical jobs, improving salaries and job assignments, and requiring a more open, documented personnel system.

In October 1978 *The New York Times* settled a suit out of court for $8 million. *The Times* agreed to fill 25 percent of senior news jobs with women. One consequence of *The Times* case was the hiring of Le Anne Schreiber, sports editor. Schreiber, who possessed extensive knowledge about sports and had taught English at Harvard, was quoted as saying that the women's action "made *The Times* more willing to consider me."[27]

Women at the wire services face problems. In 1973 EEOC charged discrimination at Associated Press. Only two of the 75 correspondents were female. There were no female bureau chiefs or general executives or foreign correspondents. UPI had one female executive among 66 males and six female bureau chiefs while there were 123 male chiefs. Not only was EEOC complaining about AP, but in September 1978, six AP staffers also filed suit, charging sex and race discrimination. The six women in the class action suit included Peggy Simpson, well known Washington, D.C. journalist.

"We are accusing AP of sex discrimination in hiring and promotion," said Virginia Tyson, with the AP Los Angeles office since October 1977. "They also have few blacks, and not one hispanic is on the AP editorial side." Tyson was hired as a "minority trainee" in 1974, with a bachelor's degree from Yale and a master's in journalism from Northwestern. "Assumptions are made here that you [woman] can't handle sports, and women get the worst schedules. They end up filing, or working on the overnight or in the broadcast division, reworking stories, which is dull," she said.[28]

Advertising

Although newswomen have had problems on the job, those in advertising have made extraordinary strides. Discrimination against women does exist, but some women own their own agencies. Some have sold their companies to larger, nationally known agencies.

Smart, ambitious, hard-working women can land the advertising jobs they want, eventually, although men usually will have an easier climb up the ladder. Jobs for women are in media, research, traffic, production, marketing, sales promotion, and public relations, as well as in the highly touted creative slots.

Traditionally, advertising has offered more job opportunities to women than has other journalistic work. In fact, advertising frequently meant a higher salary too. However, historically and traditionally, agencies employed women in the lower-paying job classifications, and women with superior qualifications received lower starting salaries than men. Their salary rate and rate of progress were lower than those for men as well.

27. "The New New York Times" *Newsweek,* November 20, 1978, p. 133.

28. Virginia Tyson, phone interview, March 1979.

The area still male-dominated is the account side, the positions of account executive or handler. Account executive positions remain closed to women as men use various excuses for not making changes: Clients don't want anything to be different; they're used to male executives. Industrial accounts are closed shops to women; women aren't supposed to get their hands dirty. Men are more appropriate for jobs involving travel; women shouldn't drive alone in a car at night. Handling accounts can be highly emotional; one must be able to get along with people, and women are more emotional. Evidence of sound reasoning?

The same kind of thinking can be seen with story assignments on newspapers, article assignments on magazines, client assignments in public relations. The walls of account management are beginning to come down.

"A woman with a master's degree in business administration will find the door wide open for her," said Joan Lipton, vice president, McCann-Erickson, New York.[29]

Women learn they are as good as men; they compete and are increasingly judged on their capabilities. Better educated young women are moving up. They tend to be very serious about a media career. Progressive managements recruit women, train them, promote them, and reward them with positions once exclusively male territory.

Another place customarily tabu for women is top management, supervising an agency or a branch of an agency. Mary Wells is an exception. A highly paid account executive with a top New York agency, she moved on to form her own— Wells, Rich and Green—which has current annual billings of $220 million, as listed in the February 1979 *Standard Directory of Advertising Agencies*. Mary Wells Lawrence (she married the head of Braniff International Airways, one of her clients) possesses enormous talent and great skills, but not all women on the corporate side do as well.

Jane Trahey, president of her own company, told those attending the Women In Communications, Inc. annual national meeting in Detroit in October 1978 that only fifteen women in the corporate structure in advertising earn $100,000 or more. "For thousands of men, that's a typical retirement income," she said. Women are getting $5,000 to $20,000 less than men in comparable jobs, she said.

Barbara Proctor agrees with Trahey. Head of Proctor and Gardner, Inc. advertising in Chicago, she grew up in a North Carolina shanty. She rode to school in a bus "too old for white kids to use." Now Proctor lives in a 22-room penthouse with her teenage son, Morgan. Her agency, of which she is sole owner, has billings of $6.2 million. Proctor says that in the top 20 agencies, only 12 women "have hacked their way to senior vice presidencies. Top women executives' average salaries of $40,000 compare poorly with male executives' $209,000. And that's before bonuses," she said. Proctor advises women to develop an "old-girl network," overcome fear of failure, define priorities, and maintain a sense of humor.

29. Patsy Miller, "Madison Avenue Advertising? It's Founded on Sound Marketing Principles," *Matrix,* Fall 1976, pp. 22–23.

Betty Lehan Harragan developed her priorities, but it took time. She worked eight-and-a-half years for J. Walter Thompson as a senior writer in the public relations department without being promoted to a supervisory position. She began a complaint against the agency in July 1971. The Equal Employment Opportunity Commission issued a determination in December 1976, in her favor. Now she is a management consultant "devoted to women's equal participation in the private enterprise system." She also teaches a course on corporate gamesmanship in New York City. In 1977 Warner Communications published her book *Games Mother Never Taught You: Corporate Gamesmanship for Women.* It should be required reading, especially for women.

As more opportunities become available, women will move into every single aspect of the business, from media buying to sales, to director of advertising. More entry-level positions are open to women now, making it easier for young women to enter the business. And more women are moving into middle management. Usually woman still have to work harder than men. "It's relative. They don't have an easy time, but breaking in and moving up are not as hard as years ago," said one media director.[30]

While women are being hired, trained, promoted, fired, or discriminated against, they are forming noncompetitive support systems, known as "new-girl networks" for women at all levels. For years career women have watched how men get ahead through the "old-boy network." Now women in media and in other fields can create the informal buddy system of college cronies and social ties to move up in their careers.

Several years ago it was common for women with media jobs to assume that there would be room for no more, for men ran things and would let in only a few tokens. Once those spaces were filled, the people in them fought for survival and were not, perhaps, passionate about promoting other women to enable them to get ahead, and instead were filled with feelings of self-protection.

Today networking is developing for women who want to succeed and for those who have "arrived" on the job. Women gather together to swap information, become acquainted, talk shop, see how they stack up among their peers, offer support and counsel to each other—all in an informal way. They need the example of being first, and they need female role models.

What about successful women? What's in it for them? They too need contacts to combat the isolation women at the top frequently experience. Also, they can increase their visibility, which helps to raise career goals of other women. Some groups have organized and compiled their own directories, listing women who make or influence decisions or work in areas affecting women in the field.

Networks tend to be city-based. There are groups in Washington, D.C., Dallas, Houston, Los Angeles, San Francisco, Chicago, Minneapolis-St. Paul, New York, and Boston.

Jane Wilson, writing in *New York* magazine, said the new-girl network can be effective in ending isolation and passivity among ambitious women. The network provides a sense of community as well as access to information. It enables

30. "Women Get Their Chance in Media," *Media Decisions,* August 1978, pp. 64 ff.

women to strengthen their motivations and replenish their own egos. It provides an incentive to move up, to evaluate themselves. "We need to stroke ourselves, to be told we're good," said one woman in the media.

Networks often represent working professionals in many different fields and are so diverse they cut across social, religious, ethnic, and political ties. Women get together for lunch, dinner, and wine and cheese gatherings. They exchange business cards. They identify themselves if they want to move up or if they are at the top.

Virginia Carter, vice president at Norman Lear's Tandem Productions in Los Angeles, waxed enthusiastic: "I'm most comfortable getting information in situations where I can trade—which means I go to women. With men it's usually a favor for which you're supposed to feel grateful. . . . Women must have trading networks of their own." Carter belongs to an informal network of women in the media and politics.[31]

As important as it is for women to become acquainted professionally and join groups, associations, organizations, and societies to promote and enhance their status, members of these groups never knew what members of other groups were doing. That changed for women in the media with the establishment of *Media Report to Women,* a monthly publication edited by Dr. Donna Allen in Washington, D.C. Allen, an economist, realized that women didn't know about each other's groups, studies, projects, challenges. Her publication serves to inform and inspire.

Founded in June 1972, *Media Report* appeared three times that year and three the next as a mimeographed nine-page newsletter. Its subtitle read, "Facts—Actions—Ideas—Philosophy." At the bottom of page 1, volume 1, number 1, was a notice of Women's Institute for Freedom of the Press, and its purpose: "According to the First Amendment, freedom of the press belongs to everyone, not just those who own the media. We must find ways for all Americans to have equal access to their fellow citizens—so people can get to know each other as they really are, not as interpreted by others, and so the public can hear and benefit from the contributions of all of us."

Volume 2, number 1 carried a new subtitle: "What Women Are Doing and Thinking About the Communications Media." Allen's efforts to reach women paid off. "I found I had 500 on the mailing list almost immediately. Then, in January 1974, we began to have it printed and offered it on a subscription basis," she said. The monthly periodical is self-supporting, and the Institute now publishes an annual *MRW Index/Directory.*

In 1977 the Institute also published its first full-length book, *Women in Media: A Documentary Source Book,* by Dr. Maurine Beasley and Sheila Silver, to provide primary source material not readily obtainable. Another work in progress to be entitled *The Source of Power: A Series of Books for Women,* a long-range study of the nation's communications system.

Allen believes communication holds the key to women's progress. "Communicators must keep in touch," she said. "When women had means of com-

31. *Newsweek,* December 4, 1978, p. 114.

munication they could do things . . . but they lost their means of communication in the fifties, when they were back in their homes after going out to work for the war effort."

She came to believe that building a communication system of their own was the key for women who want options. "I think women are treated the way they are portrayed in the media. If we want options, we must change the media," she said.

Her *Media Report* has proven helpful to researchers, students, and instructors, not only in journalism and mass communications, but also in women's studies.

Women members of journalism and mass communications faculties of colleges and universities formed their own committee within the Association for Education in Journalism, the national-plus-Canada society for academics. The committee concerns itself with the status of women in journalism education.

Since 1973 the committee has actively demonstrated its interests by presenting convention sessions about women and media, conducting salary surveys, reviewing attitudes of women faculty toward their own status, studying graduate and doctoral education patterns, looking at media sex-stereotyping practices, and so forth. In 1977 the committee began publishing "Status News," a quarterly newsletter.

Women in journalism education do not reach 30 percent of their faculties. When they do, they will have reached the ratio of faculty members in the thirties. Thus, it is important for the committee to promote a concern for affirmative action programs as well as for its overall goals to increase the visibility of women in journalism education and to encourage continued research on the role of women in the media.

Women in the media and in journalism education are discovering more about their status each year. They share a sense of community, a new enthusiasm for their professional work as they develop their careers, knowing that other women support and encourage their efforts.

Suggested Readings

*Caroline Bird. *Enterprising Women.* New York: W.W. Norton, 1976. Profiles women in business, including Mary Goddard and Sarah Josepha Hale and others in media.
———. *Everything a Woman Needs to Know to Get Paid What She's Worth.* New York: David McKay, 1973. A question-and-answer guide for detecting and preventing sex-related job problems.
Maurine Hoffman Beasley. *The First Women Washington Correspondents.* Washington, D.C.: George Washington University, Division of Experimental Programs, monograph no. 4, 1976. Profiles seven journalists: Swisshelm, Field, Ames, Briggs (Olivia), Lippincott (Grace Greenwood), Dodge (Gail Hamilton), Royall.
*Maurine Hoffman Beasley and Sheila Gibbons. *Women In Media: A Documentary Source Book.* Washington, D.C.: Women's Institute for Freedom of the Press, 1979. Background information providing an historical context for each of 31 selections. Extensive bibliography. Valuable resource.
Tamar Berkowitz and Jean Mangi, eds. *Who's Who and Where in Women's Studies.* New York: SUNY, The Feminist Press, 1975. Lists accredited programs, courses, teachers.

*Harold Bohne and Harry Van Ierssel. *Publishing: The Creative Business.* Toronto: University of Toronto Press, 1973. The business side, bookkeeping procedures, copyright protection, publishing agreements, and other forms.

*Bell Gale Chevigny. *The Woman and the Myth: Margaret Fuller's Life and Writings.* Old Westbury, N.Y.: The Feminist Press, 1977. Brings to life a complex woman.

*Victor B. Cline, ed. *Where Do You Draw the Line? An Exploration into Media Violence, Pornography and Censorship.* Provo, Utah: Brigham Young University Press, 1974. Freedom of speech, the law, pornography and erotica, violence in the media.

Laurily Keir Epstein. *Women in the Professions.* Lexington, Mass: D.C. Heath, 1975. Conference papers on status of women in higher education and the professions.

*Linda S. Fidell and John DeLamater. *Women in the Professions: What's All the Fuss About?* Beverly Hills, Calif.: Sage Publications, 1974. How differential treatment constitutes discrimination. Scholarly analysis; excellent documentation.

Ellen Frankfort. *The Voice, Life at the Village Voice.* New York: William Morrow, 1976. Describes the transformation of an underground newspaper into a highly successful paper reaching 200,000 daily.

*Jo Freeman. *The Politics of Women's Liberation.* New York: David McKay, 1975. Describes in detail the first national newsletter of the women's liberation movement, media coverage of movement, including sudden press blitz in 1970.

Norma R. Fryatt. *Sarah Josepha Hale.* New York: Hawthorn Books, 1975. For young people; all the activities of the editor of *Godey's Ladies Book.*

Cynthia Ellen Harrison. *Women's Movement Media, A Source Guide.* New York: Bowker, 1976. Indexes material not commonly available, including pamphlets, films.

*Molly Haskell. *From Reverence to Rape.* New York: Holt, Rinehart & Winston, 1974. Describes the portrayal of women in films through six decades.

*Ralph M. Jennings and Pamela Richard. *How to Protect Your Rights in Television and Radio.* New York: United Church of Christ, 1974. Describes broadcast regulation; explains broadcaster's responsibilities and relationship with public; discusses equal employment program and license renewal.

Josephine King and Mary Scott. *Is This Your Life? Images of Women in the Media.* London: Virago Ltd. in association with Quartet Books Ltd., 1977. Confined to the mass media myths about women.

Marion T. Marzolf. *Up From the Footnote.* New York: Hastings House, 1977. Chronicles progress and setbacks of women in journalism; well-written history with up-to-date information, too. Valuable source.

*Kathleen Burke McKee. *Women's Studies, A Guide to Reference Sources.* Storrs, Conn: University of Connecticut Library, 1977. Guides, library catalogs and collections, handbooks, directories, statistics, indexes, abstracts, bibliographies. Includes book reviews, dissertations, periodicals, and news indexes.

*Betty Medsger. *Women at Work, A Photographic Documentary.* New York: Sheed & Ward, 1975. Photographs of her United States odyssey, showing 170 different occupations.

*Casey Miller and Kate Swift. *Words and Women.* New York: Doubleday, 1977. Illustrates use of language referring to men and women, includes many from mass media.

*Judy E. Pickens, Patricia Walsh Rao, and Linda Cook Roberts. *Without Bias: A Guidebook for Nondiscriminatory Communication.* San Francisco, Calif.: International Association of Business Communicators, 1978. A 77-page manual on discrimination based on race, ethnic origin, sexist language, handicaps, visual media, face-to-face meetings.

*Marjorie Rosen. *Popcorn Venus: Women, Movies & The American Dream.* New York: Coward, McCann & Geoghegan, 1974. Traces the image of women in films, describing role models put on screen by male producers.

*Ethel Strainchamps. *Rooms with No View: A Woman's Guide to the Man's World of the Media.* New York: Harper & Row, 1974. Sixty-five women tell about their life in publishing and television.

Barrie Thorne and Nancy Henley, eds. *Language and Sex: Difference and Dominance.* Rowley Mass: Newbury House Publishers, 1975. Relates language and sex, includes a 100-page annotated bibliography on language, speech, and nonverbal communication.

*Available in paperback.

Latinos and the Media

Félix Gutiérrez

38

In September 1541 a tremendous earthquake and storm devastated Guatemala City in Central America. Not long after the disaster, an eight-page newssheet was printed and distributed in Mexico City describing the Guatemalan destruction.

This newspaper, written by Juan Rodríguez and printed by Juan Pablos, is apparently the first printed journalism in the Americas and even predates some early newssheets in Europe. Thus, the 1541 Mexican news report of the Guatemalan disaster is the first newspaper journalism on the American continents, coming more than a half-century before the 1609 German newssheets often cited as the first primitive newspapers.

The form used by Rodríguez and Pablos to tell the public about the Guatemalan earthquake was to become a popular journalistic medium in colonial Latin America. Called *hojas volantes* (bulletins), these pamphlets and broadside sheets were issued at irregular intervals when ships arrived with news from other ports. According to one historian, they carried lists of appointments, current events, and government orders but did not express opinions.

"These primitive newssheets were the prototypes of newspapers," wrote journalism historian Al Hester of the University of Georgia in a 1972 paper. "They treated significant happenings and made the 'news' of them widely available . . ."

But despite the work of Hester and Latin American scholars who researched early news reporting, the contributions of Latinos in inventing and developing print journalism have been all but ignored by United States journalism historians. However, these early contributions by Latinos demonstrate that news reporting and communication media are activities that Latinos have been doing for a long time.

As surprising as the historical firsts of Latino journalism may be, even more surprising to most people is the rapid current and projected growth of the Latino population in the United States. It is this trend that makes Latinos and the media that affect them an important topic of discussion.

Latinos are the nation's fastest growing population group, and it is projected to grow at an even faster rate in the future. The U.S. Census Bureau, which admits that it undercounts Latinos, put the U.S. Latino population at 12 million in 1978. Addition of 3.1 million Puerto Ricans and an estimated 6 to 8 million undocumented workers would easily push the figure above 20 million, about 9 percent of the U.S. total.

Félix Gutiérrez teaches journalism at the University of Southern California and is Executive Director of the California Chicano News Media Association. He is a frequent writer and speaker on the subject of Latinos and the media and prepared this article especially for this edition. He uses the term "Chicano" to signify people of Mexican descent living in the United States and the term "Latino" when referring to Spanish-speaking people in general.

Latinos in the United States

Because of a younger median age and larger family size, Latinos will some-day pass Blacks as the nation's largest minority group; the only question is how soon. Latinos may earn the dubious honor of being the nation's largest minority group early in the next century. However, when continued immigration and possible amnesty for undocumented workers are taken into account, some government officials predict that it could happen as early as 1990.

Long stereotyped as a regional group found in large numbers only in the Southwest, Latinos are actually dispersed throughout the country, with large concentrations in the Midwest, Northeast, and South. The states of New York, New Jersey, and Illinois each have more Latino residents than do Arizona, Colorado, or New Mexico. The U.S. city with the largest Latino population is not Los Angeles, San Antonio, or Miami, it is New York City.

Despite an image as rural farmworkers, 84 percent of all Latinos live in urban metropolitan areas (only 68 percent of all U.S. residents do). Latinos also have a lower percentage of their workforce employed in farm labor compared to the U.S. labor force overall. And, in spite of a common stereotype that Latinos do not learn English, census figures show 78 percent of all Latinos to be bilingual in Spanish and English.

But large numbers, dispersion throughout the country, urban residence, and bilingual ability have done little to improve the socioeconomic status of Latinos when compared with national averages. Latino median family income is 25 percent below the national average, and nearly one-fourth of all Latinos live in poverty. Other social indicators such as education, housing, health, employment, and political representation continue to show Latinos far below national norms.

Latinos can also be described as a hardworking people who take their family and community responsibilities seriously. However, many confront a system that was designed to work against them when they try to improve their lives. Communication media are among the many "systems" that Latinos confront in working to improve their lives in the United States. Although media are not usually considered a "bread and butter" issue, as are law enforcement, housing, health care, employment, and education, the issues involving media gained greater prominence among Latino activists in the 1970s.

This growing awareness of the importance of communication media has developed partly out of an understanding of the role played by media in shaping the collective consciousness of the public mind. It has also grown out of the need to develop communicators and communication media to serve Latino communities. Latino dealings with media systems have generally taken place on three levels. Each level represents a different media subsystem with which Latinos must deal with. These three subsystems can be broadly designated as: (1) Anglo media, (2) Spanish-language media, and (3) bilingual/bicultural media.

Anglo Media

Anglo media can be described as English-language communication media directed at the mass audience of the United States. Under this group would fall most television stations, daily newspapers, magazines, and motion pictures. These media are identified by the fact that their primary audience is essentially non-Latino. Therefore, their role in relation to the Latino communities is essentially attempting to explain or portray Latinos to a predominantly Anglo audience.

The national press called Chicanos (Latinos of Mexican descent) the "invisible minority" and "the minority nobody knows" when it suddenly "discovered" Chicanos in the late 1960s. However, much of the invisibility and ignorance was in the minds of the writers and editors. This is because consistent coverage of Chicanos and other Latinos in the national media was virtually nonexistent in the first seven decades of the twentieth century. A survey of magazine citations in the *Readers' Guide to Periodical Literature* from 1890 to 1970 reveals very few articles about Latinos in the United States. Articles that were listed often had a crisis or negative overtone. That is, they were written during periods when Mexican labor or immigration impacted national policy or when Latinos were involved in civil strife.

Local coverage apparently wasn't much better. One researcher noted that pictures of Chicana brides weren't even printed in El Paso newspapers until the 1950s; this in a town that was over half Chicano. Speaking to a 1969 media conference in San Antonio, veteran *Los Angeles Times* reporter Rubén Salazar said, "The Mexican American beat in the past was nonexistent. . . . Before the recent racial turmoil, Mexican Americans were something that vaguely were there but nothing which warranted comprehensive coverage—unless it concerned, in my opinion, such badly reported stories as the Pachuco race riots in Los Angeles in the early 1940s, or more recently, the Bracero program's effect on Mexican Americans."

Salazar also predicted that Anglo news media would not find the Chicano community easy to cover. "The media, having ignored the Mexican Americans for so long, but now willing to report them, seem impatient about the complexities of the story," Salazar continued. "It's as if the media, having finally discovered the Mexican American, is not amused that under that serape and sombrero is a complex Chicano instead of a potential Gringo."

Salazar's analysis was based on his long experience as a reporter, war correspondent, and bureau chief. It was also supported by the news media's bumbling efforts to "discover" the barrio during the late 1960s. Stories were often inaccurate and nearly always revealed more of the writers' own stereotypes than the characteristics of the people they tried to write about.

For instance, a *Time* magazine reporter riding through East Los Angeles in 1967 saw mostly "tawdry taco joints and rollicking cantinas," smelled "the reek of cheap wine [and] . . . the fumes of frying tortillas," and heard "the machine gun patter of slang Spanish." Such slanted reporting did little to promote intergroup understanding; rather, it reinforced the prejudices of many in the magazine's audience.

One reason for such biased and inaccurate reporting was that few Latinos worked as reporters and editors on Anglo publications during that period. Although many broadcasters and publications made affirmative efforts to hire

Latinos in the late 1960s and early 1970s, the numbers hired were far below fair representation of the population. The commitment often did not extend beyond hiring a few token staffers and sometimes did not continue to the promotion and upgrading of Latino employees.

A 1978 survey of minority employment on general circulation daily newspapers found that less than one percent of the editorial work force were Latinos, and that Latinos, like other racial minority groups, were underrepresented in management positions. Although broadcast employment was somewhat better, due in part to federal regulation of broadcasting, a 1977 U.S. Commission on Civil Rights study on minority employment and coverage was called "window dressing on the set" to illustrate the absence of minorities in policy-making positions.

By the end of the 1970s the amount of coverage of Latinos in Anglo media had increased. More examples of good reporting could be found. But many of the news stories still focused on Latinos as "problem people"—individuals causing or beset by problems. And stories often had a "zoo appeal," revealing the "strange" characteristics and cultural traditions of Latinos.

Continued immigration from Mexico spurred a barrage of reactionary and often inaccurate reports about people the media called illegal aliens. The Los Angeles *Herald-Examiner* ran a front page banner headline "State Threatened by Alien Horde" over a *New York Times* story on Mexican masses along the border that was untrue. A 1979 *U.S. News and World Report* cover story was headlined "Illegal Aliens: Invasion Out of Control?" A 1978 *Los Angeles Times* article contained an insensitive—and inaccurate—quote from an unnamed source that "urinating outdoors is a cultural thing in Mexico."

"We go after illegal aliens on a weekly basis," a *U.S. News and World Report* staffer told the *Washington Journalism Review* in 1978. One cause of the one-sided negative coverage was the types of sources reporters used in researching immigration stories. A fourteen-month analysis of California newspaper reporting of immigration in 1977 and 1978 revealed that reporters relied heavily on law enforcement and public officials in seeking information. Such sources tend to portray undocumented immigrants as police or public agency problems. Less than one percent of the stories even quoted or cited the undocumented themselves as sources.

Where an improvement in coverage was noted, it was often tied to the employment of Latino reporters or an enlightened management. Latino newspaper reporters such as the *Los Angeles Times's* Frank del Olmo, the New York *Daily News's* David Medina, and the *Miami News's* Helga Silva covered Latino stories with an insight few Anglo reporters could share.

But employment gains and reporting expertise did not always translate to upward mobility or professional recognition for Latino journalists. Some reporters complain that news editors do not allow them to develop investigative stories on Latino issues, preferring them to cover spot news. Some editors questioned the objectivity of Latino reporters, feeling that a Latino reporter covering a

Latino issue was biased. These editors failed to note that Anglo reporters cover Anglo issues every day without being accused of subjectivity.

But coverage and employment of Latinos in the news media constitute only one side of the issues Latinos confront in dealing with Anglo media. In dealing with Anglo entertainment media, another range of issues has emerged for Latinos.

Novelists, short story writers, movie makers, and television producers have long delighted in portraying Latinos in stereotyped roles revolving around the Latin lover, the bandit, the faithful servant, the mustachioed overweight slob, the mamacita, and the woman with dark eyes, a low cut blouse, and loose morals. These common stereotypes are nothing new. Neither is Latino reaction against them.

In 1911 *La Crónica,* a Spanish-language newspaper in Laredo, Texas, waged a hard-fought campaign against stereotyping of Mexicans and Native Americans in the cowboy movies then just emerging. The editor complained that Mexicans and Native Americans were almost always cast as "villains and cowards" and argued that Mexicans were the "most defamed in these sensational American films."

These negative stereotypes and other Latino caricatures continued in movies and television during the 20th century. Even when Mexicans and Chicanos are portrayed as lead characters, the role has often been stereotyped or distorted. Thus, Spencer Tracy's part in "Tortilla Flat," Wallace Beery's portrayal of Pancho Villa, Marlon Brando's lead in "Viva Zapata," and Valerie Harper's role in "Freebie and the Bean" reveal more of the actors' and actresses' preconceptions than the character of the people they are trying to portray.

Latino actors and actresses found themselves similarly typecast in stereotyped roles when they sought work in Hollywood, although there has been some improvement since 1970. Ricardo Montalban, who signed with MGM in the nineteen-forties, has written that he was condemned to "the bondage of 'Latin-lover' roles" early in his career. Rita Moreno, who won an Oscar for her part in "West Side Story" in the early 1960s, didn't make another movie for seven years because she refused to play roles as the "Latin spitfire," the only type-casting directors would offer her.

The coming of television in the 1950s added another weapon to the arsenal of the media barons. The most popular situation comedy of the period, "I Love Lucy," regularly made fun of Desi Arnaz's supposed inability to speak unaccented English and his lapses into fast-paced Spanish when Lucille Ball made him angry. Reruns of the program were still prime-time fare in many major metropolitan areas in the late 1970s. Other early stereotyped characters included Frank, the Chicano gardener on "Father Knows Best"; Pepino, the farmhand on "The Real McCoys"; Sergeant Garcia, the bumbling soldier on "Zorro"; and most of the secondary characters in "The Flying Nun."

The adult westerns of the late 1950s and early 1960s ushered in a recycling of the Latino villains and loose women from earlier periods. And comedians, such as Bill Dana's "José Jimenez," continued to poke fun at the way Latinos were supposed to think, talk, and live. The situation on television became so bad that the Mexican consul in Los Angeles officially protested to the NBC network in 1966.

The civil disorders of the late 1960s awakened much of Hollywood to the harmful social and psychological effects of stereotyped portrayals of Blacks. But the benefits of this new awareness did not result in accurate or dignified portrayals of Latinos. In a widely circulated 1969 article, a Chicano sociologist analyzed the racism behind portrayals of Latinos in advertising, including the corn chip stealing "Frito Bandito."

In 1970 two Chicano media activists issued a "Brown Position Paper" that charged the electronic media had made the Chicano "The White Man's New Nigger." "The greater openness of the media to the Black community spells a greater inaccessibility for the Chicano to the media," their report stated. "In providing access to the Black, the mass media believes itself to be free of prejudice or discrimination when, in effect, it is merely changing the emphasis from one group to another."

Latino media activist groups, such as the National Mexican American Anti-Defamation Committee, the National Chicano Media Council, Justicia, and Nosotros moved against advertising, television, and motion pictures on a national scale in the early 1970s. Their efforts were only partially rewarded. Television and movies increased the visibility of Latino characters in the 1970s, but these roles are often stereotyped by social class. Latinos portrayed as dignified, admirable characters are most often those with middle class credentials, such as teachers, police officers, social workers, or other professional positions. Lower class Latinos, particularly young people, are commonly portrayed as humorous characters or members of the underworld or as unable to deal with their own problems without assistance from Anglos.

The Anglo entertainment media continued to stereotype Latino characters through the 1970s. Particularly offensive to Latinos were the NBC television series "Chico and the Man," the Warner Brothers release "Boulevard Night," and the Universal film "Walk Proud." A number of television series treated Chicano youth gangs in episodes in which the Anglo hero of the series invariably rescued a salvageable Chicano youth from evil influences of his neighborhood peers at the last moment.

By the end of the 1970s Latinos were no longer the "invisible minority" in the Anglo media. But it was also clear that more media attention did not automatically equal better coverage and understanding. And, while there were more examples of balanced coverage and accurate portrayals than before, one-sided reporting and negative stereotypes still permeated much of the media's treatment of Latinos.

Although inaccurate and stereotyped coverage cheat the predominantly Anglo audience of such media from fully appreciating Latinos, it is doubtful that Latinos will ever attain full and accurate treatment from Anglo media. One reason is that Anglo media are primarily interested in attracting a non-Latino audience and apparently feel they can do so by offering shallow reporting and stereotypic portrayals.

Although Latinos are a secondary audience for Anglo media, they are the primary audience for the growing complement of Spanish-language print and broadcast media in the United States. The Spanish-language media have a long history in the United States, predating both the Black and Native American press by about two decades.

Spanish-language Media

The first U.S. Spanish-language newspaper, *El Misisipí,* was a bilingual four-page periodical begun in New Orleans in 1808. Other newspapers were started in New Mexico and Texas prior to the conquest of the territories by the United States in 1848. After the Yankee takeover of the Southwest, some Anglo newspaper publishers began printing a few pages of Spanish news, often to qualify for government printing subsidies for printing public notices in Spanish. Early Southwestern newspapers before and after the conquest include *La Gaceta de Texas* (1813), Santa Fe's *El Crepúsculo de la Libertad* (1834), Los Angeles' *La Estrella* (1851), and San Antonio's *El Bejareño* (1855).

These early Spanish-language newspapers regularly published jokes, short stories, poetry, and local commentary in addition to news coverage. News was generated out of local, national, and international news sources, with editors freely borrowing items from each other's newspapers. During the 1890s Spanish-language newspapers in New Mexico organized the Spanish American Associated Press to increase their viability as a force in the territory.

Since most early newspapers were dependent on a combination of government subsidies and advertising from Anglo merchants, they cannot be described as solely an activist press. However, it is possible to note periods and issues in which they spoke on behalf of their people against the Anglo power structure. Many of their issues are similar to those being raised by Latino activists today.

For instance, in 1855 *El Bejareño* called for bilingual education for Chicano children. In the 1870s Los Angeles's *La Crónica* argued that Chicanos living in the "Barrio Latino" paid their fair share of city taxes but didn't get an equal share of city services. In the 1880s *El Fronterizo* proposed a Chicano boycott of Tucson's Anglo merchants because some would not let Chicanos shop in their stores. In 1894 Santa Fe's *El Gato* printed an editorial on "The Capitalist and the Worker" that condemned local employers for extracting the labor of Chicano workers without paying decent wages.

A number of new Spanish-language newspapers were begun in the first two decades of the 20th century as civil strife in México and the promises of mine operators and growers brought a new wave of immigrants from México. Some of the newspapers, such as Ricardo Flores Magon's *Regeneración,* were organs for political movements in México. Others, such as San Antonio's *La Prensa,* were founded by former Mexican newspapermen who had moved to the United States.

A 1970 compilation identified nearly 200 Spanish-language newspapers that had been published in the five Southwestern states between 1848 and 1942. And, although a 1954 sociologist had predicted that the Spanish-language press would die within fifteen years, it continued to develop during the 1970s. In 1976 the *Miami Herald* began printing a separate edition in Spanish, and the number of U.S. Spanish-language dailies numbered nine in 1979.

But the biggest growth during the 1970s was experienced in Spanish-language broadcasting, both radio and television. Radio stations began programming in Spanish during the 1920s, often at odd hours of the early morning or weekends, when English-language listeners were scarce. After World War II more stations began programming in Spanish, and a growing number of Southwestern stations did so on a full-time basis. The 1978 *Broadcasting Yearbook* listed over 600 radio stations airing Spanish programs, about 100 of them on a full-time basis.

Almost all Spanish-language radio stations are commercial operations that turn a profit by cultivating their low-income and language-dependent audience as a consumer market for advertisers. Most stations are owned and managed by Anglos and staffed by Latinos from Latin America, not local Latinos. Station formats are heavily dependent on music, most of it imported from Latin America, with a sprinkling of news, public affairs, and other informational spots.

A newer entrant, but also rapidly growing, is U.S. Spanish-language television, which began in San Antonio. The 1978 *Broadcasting Yearbook* listed twenty television stations broadcasting in Spanish to U.S. audiences, some of them from the Mexican side of the border. There are Spanish-language full-time television stations in most major Southwestern metropolitan areas as well as Chicago, New York, and Miami.

The stations depend on imported programs produced and aired in Latin America. The largest U.S. network, Spanish International Network (SIN), is 75 percent owned by Mexico's Televisa television network and serves as an export market for the Mexican-produced programs.

Latino communities also have a full complement of record stores, movie theaters, and newsstands. But, like their broadcast counterparts, these media outlets are highly dependent on imports from Latin American countries. Just as Spanish-language broadcasters rely on records and programs from Latin America for their programming, barrio movie theaters generally show films produced across the border. Record stores are filled with tapes and records by artists from Latin America. Newsstands offer primarily magazines and newspapers published in Latin America.

Thus, the Latinos in the United States are largely a secondary audience for much of the Spanish-language media directed toward them. The language is the same, but there is a difference in the socioeconomic status of Latinos in Latin America (where we are the majority) compared to the United States (where we are a minority). Although some reinforcement of the identity with Latin America can have a positive effect, near total dependence on such media content can redirect the audience's attention away from the immediate reality in the United

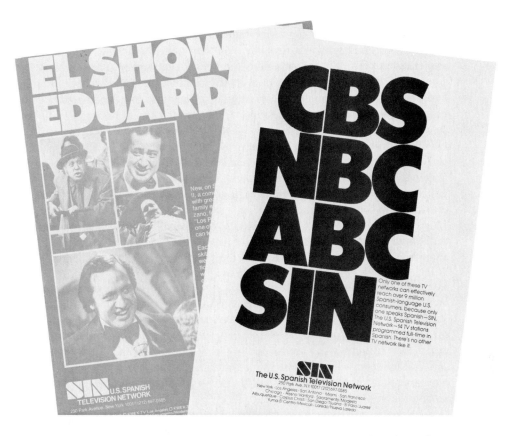

States. **The domination of media content** also serves to block local Latino talent from media exposure, limits information on local issues, and works against the building of a Latino identity based on life in the United States.

One group that has realized the potential influence of Spanish-language media in the United States has been the national and local advertisers who ride on the television and radio airwaves to reach Latino consumers. In the 1970s advertising publications began touting the "Spanish gold" that alert corporations could extract from the barrios. Attracted by what was called a "$30 billion consumer market," the advertisers invested more of their money in cultivating Latino consumers.

The Spanish-language broadcasters were quick to sell themselves as the most effective way to penetrate and persuade the Latino market. Some even played on the low socioeconomic status of their audience as a plus for advertisers. For instance, Spanish International Network told potential advertisers, "Latins are brand buyers because, for many, advertised brands represent a status symbol!" The same network showed that Latinos must spend more of their household budgets for groceries and that advertisers using Spanish-language television have sharply increased their sales.

In highlighting the exploitation of their audience and allowing advertisers to prey on it, Spanish-language broadcasters become part of the system of exploitation. Their growth is dependent on their ability to attract a large Latino audience with low cost programming and deliver that audience to advertisers as a consumer market ripe for exploitation. Since most stations also have minimal budgets for news and public affairs programs, they also fail to equip the Latino people with the information necessary to make substantive improvements in their condition.

In addition to the extractive nature of the commercial media, the pattern of Anglo control and heavy dependence on Latin American program sources makes the relations between Latinos and Spanish-language analogous to people in Third World countries. In these nations the people are also targets of media controlled by outsiders and delivering programs produced in other countries. Thus, Latinos share with other Third World people a basic contradiction in dealing with the media that considers them their main audience; the media are operated for the benefit of the dominating group and not the audience.

Bilingual / Bicultural Media

The third media subsystem affecting Latinos can be described as bilingual/ bicultural media. This level includes media that are directed at the Latino audience in English or a combination of Spanish and English. The first widespread use of this form came in the mid-1960s with the bilingual alternative media used by activists to arouse and organize Latinos around important issues.

These media are different from traditional forms in that their "profit" is measured in terms of dissemination of information and development of awareness among the audience, not in monetary terms.

Latino alternative media are most often operated as part of a community organization or a media collective, are staffed by community members who are often not media professionals, and provide information and analysis that is usually not presented in the established media. Their language, like the language of the people they are a part of, is usually a blend of Spanish and English, with frequent homegrown expressions in "barrio Spanish."

Latino alternative media include movement periodicals, alternative radio programming, guerrilla teatros (theatrical groups), film makers, videotape producers, and book publishers. Such media can play a useful role in providing needed information and interpretation on issues of importance to Latinos.

For instance, when a Los Angeles deputy sheriff killed journalist Rubén Salazar in 1970, *La Raza,* a local Chicano newspaper, furnished photographs of the events surrounding the shooting to local newspapers and the community. In the late 1960s El Teatro Campesino (The Farmworkers' Theater) toured the nation to raise awareness of the Chicano identity, the grape boycott, and other issues of importance to farmworkers. In the early 1970s Albuquerque's *El Grito del Norte* exposed mismanagement of a large foundation-funded project that was supposed to help low income rural residents but actually produced few benefits for them. San Francisco's *El Tecolote* worked with community groups

in the mid-1970s to persuade the Pacific Telephone and Telegraph Company to provide bilingual operator service for its many Spanish-speaking customers.

Chicano book publishers, such as Berkeley's Quinto Sol Publications and El Paso's Mictla Publications, produced several Chicano best sellers in the early 1970s. Commercial publishing houses often consider books by Latino authors either too political or too limited in appeal to warrant publication. Thus, when Denver's Rudolfo "Corky" Gonzales wrote his epic poem "I Am Joaquin" in the mid-1960s, he published it himself. The poem became instantly popular among Chicano activists, was later made into a film, and subsequently reprinted by Bantam Books.

Latino alternative newspapers, many of them based on college campuses, have made creative use of offset print technology in displaying stories, pictures, and graphics. Many feature full page pictures on the front page and elaborate borders. While some, like *El Popo* at California State University, Northridge, have been published continuously since the early 1970s, most have relatively short lives. A cause of this turnover is the lack of adequate financial backing and a constantly fluctuating staff. One publication that survived through the 1970s was San Francisco's *El Tecolote,* which began in 1970.

"We, of *El Tecolote,* see ourselves as an important political collective," reads a statement issued by the editorial staff. "*El Tecolote* is the major focus of our work. As writers we have a role to disseminate accurate information. We realize that the existing newspapers in the Mission, and the mass media in general, cannot be counted on to bring about any positive social, cultural and political awareness."

El Tecolote is operated collectively by the group, which is organized into subcommittees responsible for different aspects in operating the newspaper. The newspaper, which is circulated free, supports itself through limited advertising and contributions from supporters.

Other forms of Latino bilingual media include radio programs that mix community information with music, theatrical groups that blend political messages into their acts, and filmmakers who explore controversial topics commercial media usually avoid.

In the 1970s the bilingual format became more apparent in other, more traditional, media forms. El Teatro Campesino's organizers wrote and produced a bilingual hit play, "Zoot Suit," which exhausted several runs in Los Angeles and opened on New York's Broadway. In Santa Rosa, California, local Chicanos started a bilingual noncommercial radio station. Nationally syndicated educational television programs such as "Sesame Street," "Villa Alegre," and "Qué Pasa, USA?" used bilingual dialogue.

Other English-language media were developed to address Latinos along cultural, if not linguistic loyalties. *Nuestro,* an English-language magazine for Latinos, was started in 1977. Other ventures about the same time included *Somos,* an issue-oriented English-language magazine in Southern California, and *Lowrider,* a northern California magazine for Chicano car clubbers. These joined older English-language Latino magazines such as *Agenda* and *La Luz* in addressing Latinos along cultural lines.

The bilingual message was also found in traditional media. The Chicago *Sun-Times* printed a page of news in Spanish. Television stations from New York to California carried simulcasts of their news programs on Spanish-language radio stations so Latinos could hear the news in Spanish as they watched the television station. Some advertisements and public service announcements were aired bilingually, and a number of Spanish-language broadcasters programmed occasional English-language records and commercials.

As the United States approached the 1980s, the use of bilingual/bicultural media continued to increase. The prospects for such media appeared to be bright, given the increasingly bilingual abilities of the Latino audience. However, as the media became increasingly commercial, it was also clear that some of the idealistic motivation that spurred the development of bilingual/bicultural media in the mid-1960s had not been carried through by others who adopted the format for economic gain.

Given the current and projected growth of Latinos in the United States, it is **Conclusion** clear that Latinos will continue to have a growing impact on existing and developing media systems. What this impact will be is not yet clear. Much of the progress in Anglo media will depend on the upward mobility of Latinos already working in the profession and the fresh ideas of younger Latinos who enter that field. Spanish-language media, which have experienced tremendous growth in the 1960s and 1970s, will continue to develop if Latinos continue to prefer Spanish over English. However, there is a great need for development of local production and content for these media. Bilingual/bicultural media appear to have the greatest potential for growth, but there are serious problems of format and presentation to be overcome when using one language in a single medium.

For background information on the history of Latino journalism, see the "Spanish-language Media   *Bibliography*
Issue," *Journalism History,* Summer 1977. For demographic information on Latinos in the United
States, with special attention to media trends, see "Spanish-language Market Study," *Television/
Radio Age,* November 7, 1977; Joseph Aguayo, "Latinos: Los Que Importan Son Ustedes," *Sales
& Marketing Management,* July 11, 1977; and "So They All Speak Spanish," *Media Decisions,*
May 1977. For materials on the treatment of Latinos in Anglo media, see Francisco J. Lewels, *The
Uses of the Media by the Chicano Movement* (Praeger Publications, 1974); "Anti-Defamation Group
Fights Ads Using Spanish-Name Stereotypes," *Advertising Age,* September 30, 1968; José Limón,
"Stereotyping and Chicano Resistance: An Historical Dimension," *Aztlán,* Fall 1973; Thomas Mar-
tinez, "How Advertisers Promote Racism," *Civil Rights Digest,* Fall 1969; Alfredo López, "Latino
Journalists: Bringing New Fire to the Newsroom," *Nuestro,* March 1978; Félix Gutiérrez, "One
Critic's View: The News Is Not All Good," *Nuestro,* March 1978; and Georgia Jeffries, "The Low
Riders of Whittier Boulevard," *American Film,* February 1979. For information on Spanish-language
media, see previous historical and demographic references, plus Félix Gutiérrez and Jorge Reina
Schement, *Spanish-language Radio in the Southwestern United States,* Center for Mexican American Studies, University of Texas, 1979, and Daryl D. Enos and Ronald W. López, "Spanish-
language-Only TV," *Educational Broadcasting Review,* September/October 1973. For bilingual/
bicultural media, see above references and publications cited in the article.

The Persuasive Arts

Soap Gets in Your Eyes

Ron Rosenbaum

39

Eight years ago a 65-year-old adman with the improbable name Carroll Carroll had just retired from the J. Walter Thompson agency after 35 years in the ad business when Abel Green, editor of *Variety,* asked him what he planned to do with his future.

"Why don't you let me do reviews of TV commercials?" was Carroll Carroll's inspired suggestion.

"Try one," said Abel Green, a bit skeptically.

Carroll Carroll tried two. Abel Green liked them both. Carroll Carroll got his column. It's called "And Now A Word From . . ."; and it's the first and only regular review of TV commercials outside the advertising trade press.

I've always wondered why no one has followed in Carroll Carroll's footsteps. We live in a civilization that supports dozens of TV critics, scores of movie critics and hundreds of rock critics. Everyone knows that commercials are more complex and interesting than TV shows, more people see them than movies and they reveal far more about American culture than rock. Why then is Carroll Carroll alone in his important task?

Well, I've always had a minor ambition to review TV commercials, so this year I decided to see just what the work was like.

Maybe you think it would be easy street, reviewing TV commercials. Maybe you think there are plush screening rooms where the big national advertisers run preview showings of their fall campaigns for journalists. Maybe you think they provide you with transcripts and storyboards of each commercial for recollection in tranquillity. Maybe you think the leading frozen orange juice tastes more like fresh than Orange Plus.

Just look at the logistics of attempting even the most superficial review of the new season's commercials: Limiting oneself to just three hours of prime time and just three network outlets, that's still 9 hours a night, 63 hours a week, and—figuring 6 commercial minutes an hour, 2 spots a minute—it adds up to more than 750 commercial spots a week. Even though many of those 750 are repeated, so much calculation goes into the making of each second of a single 30-second spot that four or five attentive viewings are required before the craftier elements begin to become apparent. The job is overwhelming.

Most maddening is dragging one's way through hours and hours of pallid programming in search of a second glimpse of just one intriguing new commercial. Maybe someday someone will provide the commercial reviewers—and the commercial fan, for there are fans out there—with a kind of TV guide to com-

Ron Rosenbaum wrote this article for *New Times,* where it appeared in the fall of 1975. Copyright 1975 by New Times, Inc., reprinted by permission.

mercial scheduling. Maybe someday all steel-belted radials will be made like Firestones.

But for now I'm condemned to sit in front of my set with a cassette recorder and a notebook trying to find ways to fill the time between the breaks. I'll admit I must have missed more than a few: The only way to make sure you've seen every ad is to watch every minute of every show on TV, and the Geneva Convention has rules against things like that.

But I've seen enough and heard enough to pick up on some trends. After listening to 12 hours of pure commercials on tape, you begin to hear the spots talking to each other about certain common themes. In this first venture into commercial criticism, I'll forbear discussions of production, acting and directorial style and start by concentrating on the content of commercials that made their debut this season, specifically some strange new twists to some familiar old pitches.

Country Drug Taking

I knew a trend was in the making when Sominex sleeping tablets abandoned the mysterious "Uncle Ned" and other familial sleeping pill spokesmen. Now they've begun presenting cheery morning scenes in rural towns, complete with birds chirping on the soundtrack as several hearty, virtuous, hard-working plain ole country folk take time off from their country chores to confess that "even here," despite long hours of honest work in the fresh country air, people "occasionally" have trouble falling asleep and rely on pills to knock them out for the night. The new Excedrin P.M. spot features a healthy, young country wife, emerging from her old-fashioned country house amidst country-morning sunlight and bird chirps, walking her horse along a grassy creek bed, awake to all the wonder in nature because she went to sleep with the help of Excedrin P.M. And the new spot for Enderin, the non-aspirin pain reliever, presents a couple returning from a walk along a magnificent stretch of shoreline, awestruck by the grandeur of the ocean and by the ability of *just one* Enderin tablet to take care of a troubling headache.

Now, needless to say, the point of these pastoral pill-pushing pitches is not to convince country folk to take more drugs: There aren't enough country folk around to make it profitable. The point is to convince potential pill takers in cities and suburbs that they needn't feel *guilty* about taking pills, that even saintly country folk do it, that pill taking is an integral part of the natural way of life.

The Revolt Against the Natural

It's really a counterrevolution. In the past three years, "natural" and "country style" themes have spread like the plague through the commercial industry—let just one brand in a competitive category of products show a cow, and the others would shoot their next spots on dairy farms standing knee-deep in manure.

There's still an element of McCarthyism in the attacks on products accused of being infiltrated with un-natural (as in un-American) ingredients. Spokesmen for products such as Wise potato chips and Dannon yogurt go through "I have a little list" speeches in which they read, in outraged accusatory tones, the names of artificial ingredients on their rivals' labels.

But this year the natural revolution seems finally to have peaked—if only because there are few products left that haven't already been naturalized (in addition to country sleeping pills, we now have Country Dinner dog food). And this season a number of commercials have begun to manifest clear-cut anti-natural, anti-country style themes. One impetus for this trend may be that certain New York admen are thoroughly sick of the hick schtick and are beginning to exact revenge on country folk for the years they've had to spend writing cute country style ad copy. How else explain the unbridled ridicule of the country fellow in the Bic lighter commercial: An oafish hayseed offers to buy an attractive, urban-looking single woman a drink in a dimly lit bar. She lights her Bic lighter, illuminating his clownish, ill-fitting "country style" clothes and cretinous barn-yard leer. One look and she laughs scornfully in his face: "A flick of my Bic and I can see you're a hick."

And how about the merriment Madison Avenue has at the expense of the gulled rubes in the Golden Griddle syrup commercial. The spot shows a cross section of country people from "the heart of maple country" tasting two syrups. Time after time they choose Golden Griddle, a non-natural blend, over their own pure, natural maple syrup. And just to rub in the triumph of food processing artifice over nature, the commercial doesn't bother to claim that Golden Griddle tastes *like* real maple; instead they take a deliberately aggressive stance: "Golden Griddle has the taste that *beat* real maple."

And Total—a processed, vitamin-sprayed cereal—takes savage delight in its triumph over "the leading natural cereals" in the vitamin percentage numbers derby. (Total claims a 100 percent RDA score versus 6 percent for the leading brand X granolas.) Sowing salt in the wounds of the defeated wheat, the Total spot takes an airborne shot of a field of wheat, and, lo, the defeat is carved in acre-sized numerals on the face of the field—graffiti in the grain.

Things move fast in the ad world, and the counterrevolution against the natural revolution has given rise to a sophisticated third stage counter-counterrevolution. This year's Safeguard soap spot, for instance. A bit of background first. Some time ago Ivory soap jumped heavily on the Natural bandwagon and renamed itself Ivory "natural" soap, with spots featuring Ivory-natural people getting themselves clean and fresh without "harsh chemicals." This represented an assault on the whole premise of deodorant soaps, which had boasted for years about just how harsh their ingredients were on "odor-causing bacteria," those villainous microbes that turned natural sweat into problem perspiration. The Ivory commercials were clearly out to steal customers from the deodorant soaps.

More recently, deodorant soaps began to strike back. By far the boldest assault was last year's Lifebuoy commercial, which featured clean-cut people hopping up and down and crowing, "I smell clean." An admonitory slogan followed: "It's not enough to *be* clean. You have to *smell* clean."

The Original Skin Controversy

"Heavens! Buddy must have a girl!"

This gets us into some very tricky metaphysical questions of existence and essence: If there were people walking around who *were* clean but didn't *smell* clean, what *did* they smell like? Neutral? Natural? Unclean? What is the smell of clean anyway? What is the smell of skin? Does skin in its natural state smell good or bad? Did odor-causing bacteria exist in prelapsarian Eden? Could Adam have used an antiperspirant or did the malignant microbes only begin their iniquitous work after the Fall?

If this isn't complicated enough, this year Safeguard has added a new twist to this debate on the nature of Original Skin.

The scene: a kissing booth at a country fair. Two women, one married, one unmarried, are inside the booth. A man buys a kiss from the married woman and exclaims so feverishly over her "naturally clean-smelling skin" that the woman's husband has to intervene.

"What about me?" the unmarried woman in the kissing booth pipes up hopefully. "I use a deodorant soap."

Then the crusher. "*That's just it,*" the kiss-buying guy tells her. "You *smell* like a deodorant soap."

Stunned by this heartbreaker, the rejected woman in the kissing booth is probably unaware of the finely honed distinctions that are implicit in the rebuff.

It's not enough to be clean. You have to smell clean, says Lifebuoy. But, argues Safeguard, there are different *kinds* of clean. Lavatory disinfectant smells clean, but it doesn't smell good. Safeguard skin smells "*naturally* clean," which means it is clean, it smells clean and it smells natural. And natural smells good. But you can't smell natural with a "natural soap." You need a deodorant soap that doesn't smell like a deodorant soap to smell natural these days. The Safeguard commercial takes us from complexity back to simplicity—of a sort.

The next move in the skin smell dialectic is hard to predict. Now that there are "natural-scented" deodorant soaps on the market, perhaps the ultimate step will be the introduction of "natural-scented" perfume for people scared of smelling like a deodorant soap, worried that their own natural smell isn't good enough and so confused they've decided to forgo the risks of bathing altogether in favor of a cover-up perfume.

New Fears

It's been a good year for New Fears. Complex new fears, such as Fear of Smelling Like a Deodorant Soap. Old-fashioned new fears, such as Fear of Foot Odor. (A commercial for a product called Johnson's Odor-Eaters depicts an embarrassed father's foot odor driving him and his family out of their house.)

But the most characteristic fear of the year so far is Fear of Surprise. *Don't let life take you by surprise,* warns Metropolitan Life Insurance. *The best surprise is no surprise,* chimes the new Holiday Inn commercials. "It's the *unexpected* bills that really hurt," warns the doom-tinged voice of the Quaker State Motor Oil announcer.

Holiday Inn, which once promoted the adventure and delight of travel in its commercials, now focuses on nerve-wracking perils—collapsing beds, canceled reservations, unfamiliar food and other unpleasant surprises—which await travelers if they don't play it safe and lock themselves up in the predictability and security of a Holiday Inn.

Auto products such as Quaker State and STP once promoted themselves as lubricants to a life of challenge and daring, even risk. STP was the "racer's edge." Now they all push fear of breakdowns, fear of "internal corrosion" and sell themselves as play-it-safe insurance. It's more than just economic fears; it's a whole new defensive posture toward life-style.

Fear of Women

The woman is wearing a clinging cocktail gown, she's caressing the shaft of a pool cue with one hand while the other hand rests casually on a pool table littered with balls.

"Some men are intimidated by women these days," she smiles smugly. "Maybe because we're free to do much more. But some men aren't intimidated at all. They enjoy our freedom. Those are the men I like. . . . My men wear English Leather—or they wear nothing at all." Despite the infelicitous attempt at double entendre, the basic message is not sex but fear: The ad uses this caricature of a liberated woman to intimidate men into feeling they have to prove they're not intimidated by women.

And speaking of intimidation, the Wheaties commercial features a woman who beats the pants off her husband on the tennis court, then sits down at a courtside breakfast table and ridicules his slovenly eating habits while he cringes silently behind his newspaper. In a Jeep commercial a woman beats a man to the top of the hill in a king of the hill car race and laughs merrily at his humiliation.

The intimidated wretch is not just a new version of the old, stock henpecked husband. The women in these commercials beat men at their own games and mock them in defeat. One wonders if the real fear message built into all of these ads is that women's liberation inevitably means women's tyranny and male defeat.

There is a new breed of reformist women's commercials, but most of them are either of the "I like housework and motherhood, but I know there are other things in life, so I'm particularly grateful for the fast-working enzyme action of this pre-soak because it allows me to get the family's wash clean more quickly so that I can be an independent woman in my spare time," or they're about slim, determined independent women who have glamorous jobs and drink diet colas.

A couple of commercials have recently surfaced that show men engaged in what is traditionally considered "woman's work." But the one liberated woman commercial that truly breaks new ground this season is the Italian Swiss Colony wine ad. Right off the bat the woman in the ad announces that she's separated from her husband and that it's been good for her. "When my husband and I first separated," she says, "I didn't know how to do anything or think I'd ever learn, but I tried and proved I could." She offers as prime proof of her new-found self-sufficiency the ability to choose a wine all by herself with confidence in her choice.

The fact that she's so smug about the superiority of her choice—something called Italian Swiss Colony Chenin Blanc—makes me suspect that her ex-husband had kept her on a diet of Boone's Farm Strawberry up until the separation. But Italian Swiss Colony deserves credit for the forthrightness of its pitch.

Shaving Narcissism

An odd little twist in this season's shaving commercials. The two big concepts in shaving spots always used to be "smooth" and "close." The words were used to describe the shave, not the face. Now suddenly it's "love" and "super" and "perfect." And those words are used to refer to the *face,* not the shave.

"C'mere superface," purrs the Noxzema shave cream girls, lather at the ready. "You took your perfect face and gave it a perfect shave," exults the tuneful Trac II girl for Gillette.

"Send your face to Schick, let Schick love it," a girl singing group urges on behalf of that shaving company.

The visuals reflect this new preoccupation with the perfection and loveliness of men's faces. In shaving commercials of years gone by, once-grizzled men rubbed their newly shaven chins, women stroked their jaws. These days the archetypal post-shave shot shows a man gazing in his mirror, watching himself caress himself.

Is this a retreat from fearsome women into the self-sufficiency of infantile narcissism or adolescent autoeroticism? With such a perfect face and a perfect mirror image to love, who needs a third face to come between the two?

New and Improved

Few things are either [new or improved] this year. Retrenchment is all. Once the big rationale for advertising was its ability to educate consumers about valuable new products and improvements they would not know of otherwise. The only new product I noted was something called Egg Baskets, which seem to be pastry shells into which an egg can be cracked and baked if you are inclined to ruin your morning in that fashion.

And there's only one old-fashioned stop-the-presses announcement of a product improvement this year. "GREAT NEWS," says an excited voice. "New Ty-D-bol now has lemon fresh borax!"

Now this might seem anticlimactic to some, and the fact that it's the most exciting "new improvement" of the season may say something about the season. But you have to take into account that the Tidy Bowl announcement is delivered by a man in a glass-bottomed boat afloat in a toilet bowl, and that hasn't been done before.

The Official Cooking Oil of the U.S. Olympic Team

Something else to keep an eye on are the curious uses to which certain advertisers are putting the U.S. Olympic team. Consider the case of the perfect blower styler.

"Nothing demands perfection like athletic competition," begins a Sunbeam commercial over visuals of athletic competition and a blare of trumpets on the soundtrack. "Serious athletes expect it from themselves, expect it from the things around them." Perfection that is. So far so good.

Then, without transition, comes this portentous announcement: "The Sunbeam Professional Blower Styler. Selected for use by the United States Olympic team."

Wait a minute. Who selected it and how? Did the track and field coaches meet with the other team captains for a big blower styler try out? Or did Sunbeam send a truckload of blower stylers over to the Olympic Committee and get an official Olympic blower styler plug in return? Was there a cash contribution too? (The answer, according to a U.S. Olympic Committee spokesman, is that Sunbeam supplies blower stylers for the entire Olympic entourage and a $35,000 contribution, too.)

Then I noticed that Schlitz beer commercials feature the voice-over of a purported Olympic figure-skating hopeful as she describes the long, hard climb to Olympic glory. She never actually says she drinks Schlitz, but her "style" and "class" are attributes that the Schlitz announcer also imputes to his beer.

It seems to me that if the Olympic Committee is going to get into merchandising they ought to get into it in a much bigger way. Why not an Official Sleeping Pill of the U.S. Olympic team ("Yes, we athletes get real keyed up the night before a game . . ."). The Official Fish 'n Chips dinner of the U.S. Olympics. Perhaps even the Olympic torch bearer frying bread in Wesson Oil to prove that the oil doesn't soak through. The kind of thing you need for credibility.

Nathaniel Tweedy,
DRUGGIST,
At the GOLDEN-EAGLE in MARKET-STREET, near the COURT-HOUSE,
Has imported in the ANN and ELIZABETH, Capt. CHANCELLOR, from LONDON,
A large and univerfal Affort-ment of DRUGS and MEDICINES, which, as ufual, he will fell on the moft reafonable terms: among which are.——

Up-Front Post-Watergate Morality

First A&P led off the season confessing that it had let "Price" get ahead of "Pride," and then pardoned itself for that crime by pledging—it seemed—to raise prices. Now Parkay has leaped into the credibility contest with a totally original ploy. Perhaps remorse inspired Parkay, the shame of all those years when the talking Parkay margarine tub repeatedly and perjuriously told people who opened the refrigerator door that it was really butter.

None of that nonsense in this new commercial for liquid Parkay. The woman in the ad opens up by saying she works for the ad agency that peddles Parkay. She tells us she was skeptical about this liquid stuff when the Parkay people asked her to work on the pitch, but that she conscientiously tried a squeeze or two and found herself utterly knocked out by it. She raved about it so convincingly that the Parkay people asked her—a real advertising person—to be their TV spokesperson.

After all those years of trying to make the public think ads came from "real people" and not Madison Avenue, here's an ad exec to endorse the product. A brilliant turnabout. In a country where the President, the one man charged with the trust of the nation, turns out to be a liar and a cheat, why not promote the adman, traditionally considered most suspect and self-interested of all, as the only unimpeachable source of candor we can rely on?

Some people say the Golden Age of TV Commercials came to an end with the end of economic expansion and that thereafter nothing has approached the imagination, inventiveness, intelligence and cash expended on the finest of the late Sixties spots. And it's true that the TV commercial world this season is filled with signs of recession and regression: more dumb dishwasher demonstrations, contrived car comparisons, hideous "hidden camera" slices of life. But there's one genre that's entering a Golden Age all its own these days.

The Inspirationals

You know the ones. Generally they have a large, vibrant chorus filling the background with a strong upbeat tune. Half-hymn, half-marching song, they are the national anthems of their products. On the screen energetic people of all races, colors and creeds do energetic things such as jogging, marching and eating fried chicken while singing their anthem, or getting ready to burst into song. The United Airlines commercial is about a group of strangers riding an airport limo bursting into the "Mother Country" anthem. In other ads whole towns filled with jolly oldsters, rollicking youngsters and peppy people of all ages explode into tuneful, muscular joy on the screen.

The Inspirationals are all so infectiously entertaining it's hard to choose among them. McDonald's "Good morning, America!" breakfast commercials never fail to wake some sparks of innocent morning joy in me no matter how tired and wasted I am. The Beauty Rest "Good Day" anthem is almost as good. Colonel Sanders' "Real Goodness" anthem, STP, 7-Up, even, I'm ashamed to say, Coke's "Look Up America"—they all get to me. Some of them get to me too much. The Sanka anthem, for instance. I spent two miserable weeks this fall trying to get the Sanka anthem to stop repeating endlessly in the back of my mind. The tune's okay, but the lyric somehow doesn't live up to the soaring tones of the choir-like chorus. One feels a bit silly walking around town with a choir chanting in one's head: "WE'RE THE THIRD LARGEST COFFEE IN AMERICA."

Whence comes the revivalistic outburst in TV commercials this year? Is it a depression-induced Happy Days Are Here Again/Gold Diggers of '33 trend designed to get depressed consumers happy enough to spend what little they have? Is it a bicentennial rebirth of Whitmanesque celebratory optimism? A secular Great Awakening (most of them are anthems of the morning)?

Or is it something more calculated, like the pepped-up Muzak fed to workers in big factories just before closing time? Is there something even darker behind all this upbeat hysteria, a sense of some more final Closing Time closing in on America?

Perhaps those darker notes are there, but no matter how suspicious I get about them the new Inspirationals never fail to work their happy-making magic on me. That's what makes them so impressive, even scary. Inspirational technology has grown so sophisticated and powerful that TV commercial makers are capable of making one feel happy, *naturally* happy, without any sense of being manipulated into feeling happy. Something like the feeling you get from the deodorant soap that gets you naturally clean without making you worry that you smell like a deodorant soap.

Article 50 in this readings book, by Anne Branscomb and Maria Savage, is related to Ron Rosenbaum's concerns. It deals with broadcast reform groups and examines the subject of truth in advertising historically, beginning with patent medicine advertising in newspapers in the 19th century and the reform movements of the early 20th century. See the treatment and bibliographies in Edwin Emery and Michael Emery, *The Press and America,* 4th ed. (Prentice-Hall, 1978). A recent book is Stuart Ewen's *Captains of Consciousness: Advertising and the Social Roots of the Consumer Culture* (McGraw-Hill, 1976). Specifically rated to Rosenbaum's article is Dr. Ivan L. Preston's scholarly *The Great American Blowup: Puffery in Advertising and Selling* (University of Wisconsin Press, 1975). The Summer 1974 issue of *Ramparts* carried harsh attacks on the Advertising Council and the industry. Of course, the popular magazines continually carry articles on television commercials, FTC cases, and the activities of consumer group. See the guides to periodical literature.

A different advertising issue, but one that is very controversial today, is the matter of advertising to children. See William H. Melody, *Children's Television: The Economics of Exploitation* (Yale University Press, 1973) and Charles Winick et al., *Children's Television Commercials: A Content Analysis* (Praeger, 1973). Articles dealing with the same subject are Marilyn Elias, "How to Win Friends and Influence Kids on Television," *Human Behavior,* April 1974, which describes advertising research designed to find the best way to persuade children; Joan Barthel, "Boston Mothers Against Kidvid," *The New York Times Magazine,* January 5, 1975, pp. 14–15, which describes the development of Action for Children's Television (ACT); William H. Melody and Wendy Ehrlich, "Children's TV Commercials: The Vanishing Policy Option," *Journal of Communication,* Autumn 1974, pp. 113–125, which describes and attacks the FCC's handling of ACT's proposals to remove commercials from children's television; and Shel Feldman and Abraham Wolf, "What's Wrong With Children's Commercials?" *Journal of Advertising Research,* February 1974, pp. 39–43, which summarizes and categorizes criticism against children's advertising.

In the hotly contested and profitable area of children's food commercials, see *Advertising Age* for various articles, including "Government Looking for Shop to Test Nutrition Campaign," October 9, 1978. Two *Los Angeles Times* pieces were aimed at junk food: "A Captive Audience for Food Industry Pitchmen," June 16, 1978, and "Junk Food on TV: How Sweet It Isn't," March 21, 1978. Also see the *Journal of Nutrition Education.* Freedom of Information Center Reports 265 and 355—"Action for Children's Television" and "FTC vs. Advertisers"—provide background information. "The Federal Trade Commission Staff Report on TV Advertising to Children" is in *Advertising Age,* February 27, 1978. Industry protests have been recorded in a number of *Broadcasting* articles.

In addition to these background articles, see the indices to the *New York Times, Los Angeles Times,* and other newspapers for updated accounts. Also, check recent issues of *The Journal of Communication.* For detailed research, check *Journalism Abstracts,* published annually by the Association for Education in Journalism. It contains summaries of graduate research in mass communication. Each year a number of studies deal with the problem of advertising to children.

Bibliography

Dominant TV Has Vulnerable Underbelly

Alvin A. Achenbaum

40

Alvin A. Achenbaum is a principal in the New York marketing counseling firm of Canter, Achenbaum, Heekin. He was previously executive vice-president, and supervised media operations, among other duties, at both J. Walter Thompson Co. and Grey Advertising. Reprinted with permission from the September 25, 1978 issue of *Advertising Age.* Copyright by Crain Communications, Inc.

An objective and forthright appraisal of the advertising media function would reveal that national advertisers and their agencies have treated it in the most perfunctory manner during the last 15 years. This has happened largely because television has dominated the national media scene.

Nor does the fact that advertising agencies prepare elaborate media plans for their clients, that countless hours are spent discussing them, and that advertisers often fuss with their agencies over their recommendations invalidate this claim. The evidence is quite clear. When all is said and done, most national advertiser media dollars are spent on television irrespective of the media environment extant at the time.

Unfortunately, this domination by television has not been a total blessing. For one thing, it is importantly responsible for the obsession among national advertisers and their agencies that "creative" is the only thing that counts in the advertising process.

But perhaps what is most undesirable about this domination on the part of television is that it has allowed media prices to rise at an unprecedented rate in the last three years. Not only has the change in television rates exceeded the increase in the general price level, but the prices of the other national media have also jumped substantially during this period.

Yet, strange as it may seem, this situation and a confluence of other forces have created a new media reality, one whereby television's dominance could be threatened for the first time since it rose to prominence as a national medium. There are four reasons for television's latent vulnerability.

> This fall, a national television dollar will buy less than half of what it bought in 1975. The price of television has now reached a point where it makes little sense for some brands to use it. It is a wonder that so few brands have seen fit to move to other media. Perhaps all that some need is a good reason and a little nerve.

> For the first time in memory, if the Nielsen data are correct, both the number of homes tuning in to television and the hours spent watching television are declining. Moreover, a number of factors—the increase in working women and the decline in the birth rate, to mention only two—will undoubtedly reinforce these trends in the near-term future. It is wishful thinking to believe that these changes in viewing behavior are sampling aberrations.

> It is beginning to dawn on many advertising people that program content and instability and commercial clutter may well be debasing the television medium as an advertising vehicle. In addition, interference with network affairs by consumer groups and federal agencies is making it far more difficult and expensive to get and keep effective material on the air.

> And finally, in an effort to control costs and increase available commercial time, advertisers have supported the equivalent of a fourth network with the widespread use of syndicated programs. As a result, we are at the incipient stage of fragmenting the television audience. This could easily reduce the value of television as a mass medium much the way radio was hurt many years ago.

Paradoxically, despite what is occurring, television's vulnerability is largely being ignored by advertisers, agencies, and media alike. Although the advertisers and their agencies have complained bitterly about the networks' behavior, they have done very little about it but talk. The bald fact is that national advertisers are still spending as much on television as ever, other options to the contrary.

According to Bob Coen's estimates in *Advertising Age*, television got 53.9% of all national advertising expenditures in 1977. This was 0.7 of a percentage point less than in 1976 and 0.5 of a percentage point more than in 1975.

Moreover, Mr. Coen's most recent forecast indicates that television will account for approximately 54.2% of the national advertising dollars in 1978. So far, the flight to other media is all in the imagination.

Vulnerability Ignored

Under the circumstances, one can reasonably ask why national advertisers have continued to pour so much of their advertising money into television. In actuality, there are at least six strong forces inhibiting the movement away from television.

The first has to do with the media's current prosperity. The last two years—1976 and 1977—were exceptional ones for all national media. This year undoubtedly will also end on a very high note.

Media Prosperity

Bear in mind, too, that profit and loss statements are not based on abstractions such as "real income" but rather on actual or "current income." In the media business, inflation manifests itself not only on the cost side of the ledger, but also on the income side. Since the rise in media prices during the last three years exceeded the general price level, media profits have to be higher than usual.

Under the circumstances, it is understandable if the people who sell media space and time feel quite proud of their recent record and remain optimistic about the future. Success has a way of encouraging monotonic thinking.

Unfortunately, it also has a way of discouraging experimentation and change. Of all the businesses with which we have had experience, the media have been most loath to looking inward, of taking medicine. Now is no exception.

The fact that these three banner years were caused by economic forces beyond the control of any of the media and cannot be attributed to any brilliant or innovative selling approach on their part eludes them. Each medium has continued to sell itself essentially the same way it has for the past 20 years.

It is pretty clear that as long as that continues, television will dominate the media field. The arguments of 20 years ago have little relevance today.

The second inhibiting force also deals with success—that of the agencies. Not since the '50s, with the advent of television itself, have the advertising agencies— especially those serving the big television brands—experienced such marked prosperity. They, too, do particularly well during media inflation.

Agency Success

What has happened to them is quite simple. In coming out of the 1974–75 "stagflation," advertisers began to face relatively large profit prospects. They had raised prices in those two years in order to protect profits.

Then in 1976, when unit sales began to rise, total income, and hence profits, soared. Like most good managers, they preferred to invest many of their potential profit dollars in advertising rather than give them to Uncle Sam in taxes. Besides, a goodly number of these dollars were needed to keep up with the rapidly rising prices of the media.

Thus, the agencies found themselves in the enviable position of taking in many more dollars to turn out a disproportionately smaller number of media units. Needless to say, this is not a condition in which one tries very hard to change things around. Talk; yes, that is cheap. Action; no, because that is a horse of another color.

And who can fault them. They, too, are good business men.

The Golden Medium

The third force inhibiting change is the emotional bias toward television, a good deal of which is unwarranted but cannot be easily negated because much of it has been institutionalized.

Television is today's show business. It's entertainment, movie actresses, sports celebrities. It's the kind of excitement that not only turns on the creative man and makes him think he is a movie maker, but also entices the other people in the business. It is the big time; it is where the action is; it is where the advertising executive and agency man want to be at.

Television is also where the big money is. A network buy often involves $5,000,000 or $10,000,000 at one shot. It involves high-level, complex negotiation. It is a challenge, with winners and losers. Buying other media, on the other hand, is as exciting as writing a business letter. Guess which wins in that case.

But perhaps more important than all of this is that television has been the golden medium for at least 15 years. Almost everyone with decision-making responsibility in the agencies and at the advertisers grew up during its most fruitful days. Everyone who is anyone in the business has had experience with its fantastic ability to move merchandise economically.

It is, therefore, going to take a very persuasive story to move advertisers and agencies away from television—high cost, program instability, fragmentation and declining audiences notwithstanding. Rest assured, it won't be done with puffery or the conventional tools of the business. Something more substantive will be necessary.

Always a Way

The fourth force inhibiting change has to do with television's amazing flexibility. No matter what problem developed with television in the past, there was always a way around it.

If the prices were too high, you could reduce the time unit from 60 to 30 seconds; or you could flight instead of being on the air continuously; or, if worse came to worse, you could concentrate your expenditures in fewer markets. If time were lacking, there was always spot or syndication. The substitute for television was always television.

To this day, many believe another panacea will evolve to save the situation—perhaps a real fourth network, cable television or satellites. Among believers, hope always springs eternal.

In the meantime, many advertisers are again toying with piggybacks. If nothing else works, maybe the 15-second commercial will. In television, if there is a will, there is always a way.

A fifth inhibiting force is that the basic concept involved in the evaluation of media, that of reach and frequency, is essentially television oriented. The whole idea of reach and frequency from which gross rating points are derived was originally a television one. While an analogous concept is now used for the other media, it is often done as an afterthought.

Evaluation Bias

Moreover, the concept of gross rating points is conducive to thinking in terms of exposure tonnage. Television thrives on big numbers and television reach and frequency distributions serve them up.

On the other hand, the whole idea of frequently reaching the same audience with the same advertisement was originally anathema to the thinking of other media—and still is to some.

It was not that long ago that "duplication," for example, was a dirty word. There are some magazine people who to this day are inclined to give up audience numbers and return to circulation. Small wonder television has such weak competition.

The final inhibiting force has to do with the barrenness of media research. How the other media expect to compete against the emotion and experience associated with television without some solid evidence is beyond comprehension.

Barren Research

It may be hard to believe, but no intermedia research of significance has been conducted since the CBS "Apples and Oranges Study." That was done so long ago, it is hard to remember in what year it was done.

Ironically, that study was sponsored by the network in an effort to sell television against magazines when the latter was considered the dominant national medium. Although the study was severely criticized, it had a great deal of influence.

Now that the shoe is on the other foot, where is the magazine or magazine group which will take on the task of proving magazines' intrinsic advertising worth? All we get from the magazines is syndicated audience data which they themselves often don't accept.

Even so important a matter as advertising frequency has gotten short shrift. In a number of speeches, I cited six studies that touched on the subject. Not one was done by a medium. Only one—that done by Ogilvy & Mather—was a solid study, and even its results left much to be desired.

Since the frequency of exposure is critical to advertisers, why are the other media not studying it in depth? If ever the other media had an opportunity to get the ear of the advertiser on a major issue like this, it is now when television is exhibiting some vulnerability. Yet, nary a word is heard from them.

Media selection has essentially become a numbers game. If the other media are to have any sizable effect on television's stranglehold, it will have to be done with numbers and a relevant new concept for utilizing them.

Break TV Domination

The big issue, then, and the one I wish to raise here is whether those responsible for advertising are willing to reevaluate their views toward television, whether they are prepared to face up to the new media reality, latent as it may be? Are they to continue doing what they did in the past irrespective of television's current vulnerability? Are they going to let television continue to dominate the media scene?

It could well be that more can be achieved with advertising dollars today by putting greater emphasis on media rather than on copy. Considering how similar copy test scores are on established brands, one wonders why this hasn't been done before, why the obsession with creativity?

How, then, can television's dominance be ended so that all media will be given their proper consideration, so that existing media leverage opportunities can be intelligently exploited by advertisers? Four things are needed.

Recognize Situation

First and foremost, the other media must come to the recognition that the current situation is unique and will not persist, that the prosperity bubble for them will probably burst next year.

The very forces that created the last three years of prosperity are now in the process of reversing themselves. It is quite likely that the unit production of most advertisers will begin to recede next year; that is certainly what most reputable economists are predicting.

Since prices of goods and services are not expected to rise as rapidly as they did in the past, a profit squeeze is bound to ensue. Since national advertisers have almost never spent advertising dollars counter-cyclically, national advertising budgets will no doubt begin to shrink.

As long as the bias toward television remains—and as we saw, nothing has been done so far to dispel it—television will continue to take the cream off the top.

If this logic holds up, the other national media will experience a sharp downturn in unit sales. The chances are good—even with price increases—that they will be back to where they were in 1975. It is, therefore, incumbent upon them to plan now for this eventuality, to begin opening their minds and their pocketbooks for new ways to compete with television.

They must finally come to the realization that the agencies will not help them lick this problem. Nor will the advertisers. At best, the latter will only give them encouragement since almost all of them feel that it is the media's responsibility to sell themselves.

New Analytic Concepts

Secondly, the other media must come to the realization that the analytical concepts being used today are obsolete, that they are obscuring the situation. Instead, what is needed is a new "approach," one which accepts four very basic ideas about media in general:

Frequency of market target exposure is what media are all about. This may seem obvious but it is often ignored.

In selling, it is the sole purpose of the media function to expose prospective customers to the advertising often enough to have them consider the advertiser's product or service. Unless a message is seen or heard enough times, it has no value.

Needless to say, this exposure must be in an acceptable environment. But that is not the truly crucial matter.

"Actual exposures" and not "exposure opportunities" is the pertinent criterion in evaluating media. Unfortunately most media plans are based on exposure opportunities. This is particularly true for television because grp [gross rating points] analysis is usually based on television ratings, and ratings do not measure actual exposure. They measure sets in use.

Ratings do not account for the fact that many people who are tuned in to television do not always watch the commercial. There is ample evidence in the hands of every major agency—some of which has been published by Burke—that the program audience is different from the commercial audience, sometimes by as much as 35%. That is to say that a sizable number of people leave the room or are doing something else while the television set is on.

Moreover, ratings do not account at all for those who are not paying attention to the tube even when they are in the room, which would reduce the numbers still further. For grps to be valid, they must be adjusted downward for those who have not seen the commercial.

"Minimum" exposure and not "average exposure" is what is necessary to get people to act.

There is a growing body of evidence—flimsy to be sure—which indicates that the frequency of exposure has a differential effect on viewers—at least in television.

In general, this evidence suggests that the first few exposures of a television commercial are of little value; that individuals who see fewer than three are not significantly affected by the advertising; that little further benefit is obtained from advertising beyond 10 exposures over a given period of time, and that after 15 exposures, additional exposure may have a negative effect.

What this basically means is that until an advertiser has obtained some minimum of exposure for his commercials, he has wasted his advertising money.

This idea is the foundation upon which the concept of "effective exposure" is based and about which I have spoken on a number of occasions. By "effective exposure," I mean the actual exposure obtained from within the exposure frequency distribution where the advertising either has had some effect or is not redundant. In television, there is reason to believe it is the area between three and ten exposures during a four-week interval.

But no matter where it starts or ends, as long as each exposure is not equal, the concept of grps is invalid without some adjustment for the differential effect.

To make matters worse, no one knows whether the effect of exposure frequency varies by product category, time period, or anything else. There is certainly reason to think it varies by media.

Different media affect learning differently, and these differences do not necessarily operate in accordance with the conventional wisdom that an audio-visual medium is always better than an audio or visual medium alone.

For example, it is not inconceivable that someone who reads a full-page magazine advertisement could absorb more and perhaps be more affected by his first exposure to such an advertisement than he would be by his first exposure to a 30-second television commercial.

On the other hand, a person's third exposure to a magazine advertisement may have almost no effect when compared with the effect of his third exposure to a 30-second commercial. In other words, it is quite plausible that a reading medium is low-frequency-effective while an audio-visual medium is high-frequency-effective.

When you consider how little is learned in school via audio-visual techniques, you begin to realize how robust this idea is. It certainly deserves a great deal of advertiser attention in the future.

If these four ideas make sense, then their implications are large indeed. What it suggests is that other media may be a better option than television for small budget brands (those under $2,000,000), and that much can be gained by large budget brands (those over $10,000,000) using more than one medium.

Need Exposure Research

The third need for ending television's dominance is research in the area of exposure frequency. Frankly, it is rather appalling that the media have done so little research in this area even in these plush days. If not now when money is available, then when?

Certainly without some hard evidence, it will be very difficult to overcome both the emotional bias and previous experience media decision-makers have had with television.

What is needed is some solid research on how many exposures it really takes during a specific period of time to get a prospect to consider a brand. In addition, the other media should attempt to determine whether it takes fewer exposures of their media than of television to convey a message. From what little we know about communications, they should both prove positive.

With these two pieces of research in their armory, the other media should be in a relatively good position to pierce television's dominance.

Changes in the advertising industry are reflected rather clearly in the leading publications in the field, including *Advertising Age,* the major trade publication. For example, see "Marketing Trends in the 1980s," November 6, 1978. Criticisms are found in such diverse places as journalism reviews and academic journals. For example, the January/February 1979 issue of *Washington Journalism Review* carried Dom Bonafede's "We're the Good Rich Guys," an examination of "the current wave of corporate advertising" designed to gain credibility for the conglomerates. For statistics on advertising rates and advertising expenditures for various media, see *The Mass Media: Aspen Institute Guide to Communication Trends* (Praeger, 1978) edited by Christopher H. Sterling and Timothy R. Haight. For trends in broadcast advertising, also see journals in that field, such as *Broadcasting* and *Television/Radio Age.* Billing reports from the major markets, updates on the problem of comparative advertising, and the specifics on FCC and FTC cases can be found there. Also see Fairfax M. Cone, *With All Its Faults* (Little, Brown, 1969), which traces his forty-year career in advertising and ends with a discussion of advertising over cable television. Other research journals include: *Journal of Marketing,* issued by the American Marketing Association; *Journal of Advertising,* from the American Academy of Advertising; *Journal of Marketing Research,* the Advertising Research Foundation, which also produced "Evaluating Advertising: A Bibliography of the Communication Process."

Bibliography

A few of many recent books on the general advertising field include: Allen Hyman and M. Bruce Johnson, *Advertising and Free Speech* (Lexington Books, 1977); Frank W. Fox, *Madison Avenue Goes to War* (Brigham Young University Press, 1975); James E. Littlefield, *Readings in Advertising* (West, 1975); and David Ogilvy, *Blood, Brains and Beer: The Autobiography of David Ogilvy* (Atheneum, 1978).

The Corporate Image: PR to the Rescue
Business Week

41

For Frank R. Milliken, former chairman of Kennecott Copper Corp., the company's annual meeting last May was a personal nightmare. Already battling against Curtiss-Wright Corp.'s takeover attempt, he was now being denounced as an inept manager by stockholders angered by Kennecott's lackluster financial record and its acquisition of Carborundum Co. When the stormy, six-hour meeting ended, Milliken, who will retire this month, wearily lamented: "The problem is that we've done a lousy job of public relations. In hindsight, it was unfortunate that we kept this company under wraps."

Whether more aggressive PR could have camouflaged Kennecott's shabby earnings, improved Milliken's personal image, or dampened the controversy over the Carborundum deal is questionable. But Milliken's sudden enchantment with public relations is not an isolated case. Increasingly, other corporate leaders are becoming convinced that an organized and systematic program to win friends and influence people—that is, PR—is the remedy for the varied tribulations that beset their companies.

The corporate public relations business, which has had its ups and downs in the past few decades, is enjoying a new boom. Record sums are being spent

This long look at the corporate world of public relations appeared as a special report in *Business Week,* January 22, 1979. It is used with the permission of *Business Week.* Copyright 1979 by McGraw-Hill, Inc.

on a wide spectrum of activities that loosely fit under the umbrella of "public relations." Companies that slashed budgets during the 1974 recession are resurrecting their programs, many are increasing expenditures and expanding the scope of PR operations, and others are elevating the PR function to a loftier rung in their organizational hierarchies. On the agency side, most major firms are reporting new highs in fee income as they feed off the surge in corporate business.

The primary reason for the revival is that the corporation, more than ever, is operating in what David I. Margolis, president of Colt Industries Inc., calls a "pressure-cooker" environment. It is under siege from consumerists, environmentalists, women's liberation advocates, the civil rights movement, and other activist groups. Their demands are being steadily translated into an unprecedented wave of intervention by federal and state governments into the affairs of business. Even without government interference, the activists are forcing changes in corporate operating policies that range from a halt in loans to South Africa to curtailment of infant milk-formula sales in less developed countries.

The corporation also faces intensified competition in the marketplace, the growing threat of takeover by outsiders, and new challenges in employee relations. And all the while, the corporate community continues to be plagued by a negative public image. Only 22% of the general population has confidence in business leadership, down from 55% at the beginning of the decade, according to pollster Louis Harris. "A PR problem today does not simply mean loss of goodwill," says John J. Bell, senior vice-president for communications at the Bank of America. "It threatens a corporation's ability to achieve its business goals."

The Politicized Corporation

In response to the external pressures, the corporation is being forced to become a political animal as well as an economic machine. Says Loet A. Velmans, president of Hill & Knowlton, the nation's largest PR agency: "The corporation is being politicized and has assumed another dimension in our society that it did not have as recently as 10 years ago." As a result, the corporation has become more conscious of using communications in all its diverse forms as a tool to accomplish its objectives, and it is articulating its positions more clearly and urgently to government agencies, legislators, shareholders, employees, customers, financial institutions, and other critical audiences. Last year's boost in profits, of course, is providing more ample resources with which to do it.

"After limiting their thinking to engineering and financial variables for so long," says Professor Otto Lerbinger of Boston University's School of Public Communications, "business leaders now must get used to the human climate of political behavior, which is often the result of irrational acts."

Even companies that have traditionally maintained a low profile have developed a penchant for PR. Bechtel Corp., the privately held, multibillion-dollar construction colossus, is a typical example. The company has received a torrent of attention and criticism lately over delays and cost overruns on the Alyeska oil pipeline and San Francisco's BART subway projects, the Arab boycott, nuclear safety, and alleged connections with the Central Intelligence Agency.

"To cope with some of the knees in the groin"—as Vice-President Paul W. Cane puts it—Bechtel is countering with unprecedented measures. It runs institutional ads in the national media, makes its executives accessible to the press, participates in political action committees to support friendly political candidates, has expanded its PR staff, and has registered 8 of its 10 Washington representatives as lobbyists. Following publication last fall of the CIA allegations in *Mother Jones,* a San Francisco-based muckraking monthly, Bechtel put out a point-by-point rebuttal and demanded space in papers that had publicized the unfavorable article. Says Cane: "If this had happened five years ago, I doubt whether we would have done anything. But we're not a patsy any more." But such PR tactics can be effective only if the company that is engaged in public controversy possesses credibility. In such cases as Firestone Tire & Rubber Co. and its model 500 radials, Ford Motor Co. and its Pinto gas tanks, and Allied Chemical Co. and its Kepone pesticide, the companies failed to make full public disclosure of the product hazards involved. Their credibility was subsequently shattered, and they suffered public ordeals that no amount of PR brilliance could have alleviated.

PR's New Concerns

As the tempo of corporate PR activities rises, the very nature of the profession is changing profoundly. What was once scorned as press agentry and flackery and dismissed as a peripheral function of management is becoming a more consequential endeavor worthy of serious attention by senior management.

"PR used to be mainly how to get information into the media without having to pay for it," Edmund T. Pratt, Jr., chairman of Pfizer, Inc., says. "The aim was to get your name around and to get publicity for a new product and build a corporate reputation. We're now talking about much more sophisticated attempts to interact on issues of greater subtlety in quite different ways."

Pratt and many other top executives prefer to call what they are doing "public affairs" rather than "public relations." The concern with semantics reflects the pejorative associations with which PR is still afflicted. Ironically, a craft whose very purpose is to create and improve images has been unsuccessful in projecting its own. It still struggles to have its own professional legitimacy fully recognized and to live down the huckstering stereotype rooted in business folklore.

"I couldn't have used a glib PR guy who would have fed them a lot of bull," Data General Corp.'s President Edson D. de Castro recently said after meeting with his Massachusetts employees to assure them personally that their jobs were not in jeopardy because of plans to build a new plant in North Carolina.

Because PR's end product is normally intangible, practitioners of the craft are also hampered by the absence of satisfactory means to measure quantitatively the effectiveness of what they do. Despite the new boom, there are still those who are dubious of PR's methods and efficacy. And there are still top executives who believe simply that a healthy balance sheet and income statement represent the best PR. "When you see a lot of drum-beating, I tend to think a company

isn't as sound as it is trying to appear," says Gene M. Woodfin, chairman and CEO [chief executive officer] of Houston's Marathon Mfg. Co.

Pfizer, for one, has made a quantum jump from old-fashioned drum-beating to handling highly sensitive communications problems. Ever since the Kefauver investigations in the Senate, the drug industry has been flayed for everything from the safety to the prices of its products. Federal controls on new drug introductions have become increasingly complex and stringent, and state governments are now debating measures to regulate how drugs are priced and sold.

From PR to "Public Affairs"

To contend with the regulatory situation, Pfizer carefully monitors the deliberations of state legislatures, maintains contact with influential members, conducts seminars and dinners with leading academic figures to explain its viewpoints, and supports independent university research in such fields as chemical food additives. Pratt himself has joined the Business Roundtable to advocate tax reform and other legislative measures. He also campaigns for unrestricted world trade, advises New York City's Mayor Edward I. Koch on municipal economic problems, and "interacts" with U.N. officials on the question of multinational companies and with church and college groups on Pfizer's controversial operations in South Africa.

Call it "PR" or "public affairs," Pfizer and most other major corporations are making a carefully planned effort to communicate with multiple audiences, influence opinion, and create an environment more favorable to what they perceive to be their direct interests. They are taking PR far beyond the traditional functions of image-building and getting the company's name in the paper—or keeping it out.

"Fifteen or 20 years ago, you could be in this business with a mimeograph machine," says Harold Burson, chairman of Burson-Marsteller. "There was no real thought of why you wanted the client's name in the paper or what it would accomplish other than recognition and goodwill. Now you want to communicate such-and-such to such-and-such audience so you will be able to do thus-and-so better."

Corporate involvement in public issues is not exactly new. Business lobbying is as old as the nation itself. And George Westinghouse probably began what is now known as PR when he hired two men in 1889 to fight the advocates of direct-current electricity and to promote alternating current. What is new is a determination to identify budding political and social pressures before they get out of hand and to prepare a defensive corporate strategy in advance.

"PR can establish an early warning system to alert management to the things they're going to get nailed on," says Byoir's president, Robert J. Wood. PR men describe such efforts as "issue management" or "issue analysis," which have become the latest buzzwords in the business. Some PR practitioners are turned off by the terminology. Frank W. Wylie, a Chrysler Corp. PR executive and outgoing president of the Public Relations Society of America, derides the terms as "negative and probably self-defeating" because they suggest that highly sensitive political and social problems can be controlled by corporations through the fine-tuning of PR techniques.

"No Room for Neanderthals"

Nevertheless, all PR men would agree with Kalman B. Druck, chairman of the executive committee of Harshe-Rotman & Druck, when he tells clients that "every problem shouldn't have to be an unexpected pie in the face."

An important manifestation of the growing sophistication of PR practice is the increased personal involvement of chief executive officers. Pfizer's Pratt estimates that he spends up to 25% of his time on public affairs. Reginald H. Jones, chairman of General Electric Co., says he now devotes only about half his working hours to managing his company's operations and the rest to "externalities," speaking out on such issues as tax reform, capital formation, and inflation. "This will be true for all CEOs of major corporations," Jones predicts. "They will have to have extremely long antennae and be extremely sensitive to public opinion. They will have to become activists rather than adaptive. There will be no room for Neanderthals."

Says William M. Agee, chairman of Bendix Corp., who in the past year has made at least 15 speeches on topics ranging from Social Security and industrial innovation to the Bakke decision and pension funding: "Companies like ours are a public institution with several publics to account to, not just the shareholders. This requires a different type of informational approach. Part of my job is to be a public figure and to take positions on public issues, not just company activities."

Some executives believe that an articulate CEO who speaks out on issues transcending his company's own narrow interests strengthens its image as a credible, blue-chip competitor in the marketplace. Richard J. Jacob, chairman of Dayco Corp., a Dayton-based auto parts maker, for example, generates considerable publicity by speaking frequently on the burden of government regulation and the energy situation and by criticizing the overemphasis on dividend payment as a measure of corporate performance. (Despite increased profits, Dayco cut its cash dividend in 1975.) "He has provided us a vehicle to get the company and its products better known," a Dayco officer says. "So when a Dayco salesman arrives on the scene, he's not greeted as a Martian."

Mobil's Advocacy Campaign

But some PR counselors are discomforted by a CEO on the stump and advise their clients and companies to refrain from what they regard as simplistic, tub-thumping speeches to business groups on big government and free enterprise. "A lot of business people want to preach to the choir," says Richard A. Condon, West Coast director of public relations for TRW Inc. "That does no good whatsoever."

The most aggressive practitioner of issue advocacy is Mobil Corp. Last year it spent nearly a quarter of its $21 million PR budget to place ads in leading papers and magazines to argue for mass transit and a national energy policy, champion higher-quality TV fare, debunk congressional proposals to break up the oil companies, and to debate vigorously in print with the media whenever coverage of oil industry matters incurred the company's wrath.

Mobil's campaign has transformed Herbert Schmertz, a one-time labor relations lawyer who is the company's vice-president for public affairs, into a national PR celebrity. Most practitioners applaud his obvious zest for confrontation with his company's and industry's critics and envy his success in selling his ideas to Mobil's top management.

There are, however, some negative assessments. Hill & Knowlton's Velmans, whose agency numbers Atlantic Richfield Co. and Texaco Inc. among its clients, doubts that advocacy advertising accomplishes much. "What's the audience?" he asks. "Is Mobil speaking to the converted? I don't know who they're talking to." Craig Lewis, president of Earl Newsom & Co., whose small, blue-chip clientele includes Exxon Corp., says that Mobil's campaign "has gotten attention for the company but has not advanced the cause of the oil industry significantly. The tone of the ads has gotten too peevish." Some of this critical comment could be sour grapes, because Mobil has irritated the other oil majors with its maverick views on continuation of the highway trust fund and phased decontrol of crude oil prices.

Schmertz flippantly refers to Mobil's issue-advocacy program as "pamphleteering." He adds: "Our motivation is not to have people love us. It's more complex. We want to stimulate and participate in dialogue and want people to take us seriously intellectually."

Management Techniques

The emphasis on public issues and the growing participation of CEOs are only two important trends in PR that have been developing gradually and are now accelerating as the tempo of PR activity rises. Public relations men are striving to give an intellectual substance to what they do. They are moving away from the seat-of-the-pants approach that has characterized their activities in the past and are trying to adopt long-range planning and other apparatus of modern management. In the process, new conceptions are evolving as to what PR is, extending beyond the traditional functions of media, community, employee, and financial relations.

Says Boston University's Otto Lerbinger: "We now have a management-by-objectives mentality. MBO demands are being made of PR practitioners the same as with other staff and line officers. CEOs used to be satisfied with press clippings. Now they're saying, 'How is this helping?' " These demands have provoked a new interest in polls, surveys, and audits to measure opinion and attitudes quantitatively. The research is used for both the planning and subsequent feedback and evaluation phases of PR programs. But despite the extensive work performed in this field, some PR men remain skeptical about the techniques and even the value of trying to measure their performance in quantitative terms.

A broader view of PR's dimensions is illustrated at McGraw-Edison Co., the Chicago-based electrical products manufacturer. The company has increased its PR budget "several hundred percent" since 1973, when "the social pressures didn't exist," says John C. Tuffy, the company's director of communications. He views his expanded staff as the "watchdog" for corporate transgressions and boasts that it "heightened the awareness of corporate management" by inducing the company to abandon use of the chemical PCB in electrical capacitors and by encouraging the development of a safer substitute fluid.

On the Financial Front   In the financial PR field, the objectives have become more complex and stock-touting more subtle, largely because of the deregulation of brokerage commission rates 3½ years ago and the renewed wave of contested corporate takeovers. The end of fixed commissions on securities transactions forced many firms to merge and shut down, which shrank the ranks of securities analysts substantially. Says Gershon Kekst, a New York PR consultant: "The formula used to be to buy a directory of analysts and fly your client in to lunch with 25 of them en masse. But now you can't depend on being followed by analysts." The burden is now on the company to fill this void and to make its own direct impact on investment and lending institutions.

The upturn in unfriendly takeovers has given a higher priority to building a shareholder base loyal to management and has thrust many PR specialists more intimately into strategy-making in takeover battles. Hill & Knowlton, which defended Carrier Corp. against United Technologies Corp. and Kennecott against Curtiss-Wright, has moved into the proxy-solicitation business to strengthen its capabilities in tender offers and proxy fights. Meantime, the old-line proxy-solicitation firms of Georgeson & Co. and D.F. King & Co. are expanding their PR counseling.

Byoir, which also is becoming more deeply engaged in takeover strategy, has drafted a 23-point "takeover defense checklist" for its clients. Included is a recommendation to hire Georgeson or King—or both—in advance "to keep them out of the enemy's hands."

PR was an important factor in helping Marshall Field & Co. thwart the takeover attempt last year of California's Carter Hawley Hale Stores Inc. When the latter revealed its intent to make a tender offer, the local Chicago press was notably unsympathetic to Marshall Field's position, despite the retailer's historic links to the community and the large number of local shareholders. "It's unexplainable, but the local press is sometimes almost joyous about a takeover by outsiders," says Andrew P. Tothy, a vice-president and acquisition and merger specialist for the investment banking firm of Smith Barney, Harris Upham & Co. "Maybe it's the good old American tendency to kick the guys upstairs," he adds. "Nothing is more demoralizing to a company than to read that the home-town paper is rooting for the other side in a takeover." Only when it began to plead its case more vigorously and to argue the need to defend a local business from being taken over by "strangers" did Marshall Field belatedly win greater local support. Carter Hawley Hale eventually withdrew without even making a formal tender.

In the employee communications field, PR techniques are changing as management recognizes that it is dealing with a labor force that is more sophisticated and has greater personal expectations than an earlier generation. Another stimulus for change has been the rash of mergers that bring new employees into companies they know little or nothing about. As a result of such trends, house organs are becoming more journalistically professional, with an orientation more substantive than bowling scores. Audio-visual facilities are being introduced more widely, the tone of communications is changing ("Companies are getting away from trite messages that talk down to employees," says Byoir's Wood), and employees are being kept better informed on everything from fringe benefits to management's assessment of the business outlook.

Sperry Rand Corp.'s chairman, J. Paul Lyet, delivers an annual "state of the union" message via videotape to employees, similar to his annual report to shareholders. Lyet, who questions the effectiveness of issue advocacy to the general public, prefers to use employee publications to discuss how foreign trade restrictions, consumerism, inflation, and other public issues affect company jobs. Says he: "I'm not shooting at the world that way. I'd rather pay attention to our own knitting—our 88,000 employees. We should concentrate on our own house to make sure that the free-market system is understood and that misunderstandings about profits, for instance, are avoided."

The PR Man's Credibility

The new PR consciousness could be linked to the growing passion for corporate strategic planning. Electronic Memories & Magnetics Corp., a computer component maker in Encino, Calif., committed itself last year to a strategic plan for the first time. Now it is embarking on a full-scale PR program aimed to improve employee morale, help in management recruiting, and strengthen the company's image in the financial and computer communities. "[Until you can] answer the question of what EM&M is and where it's going, you don't want to talk with outside people," says Thomas S. Benson, vice-president for development.

The Top 10 PR Agencies

	1978 fee income (millions of dollars)	Employees
Hill & Knowlton	$22.6	672
Burson-Marsteller	22.2	670
Carl Byoir & Associates	12.5	408
Ruder & Finn	7.8	240
Harshe-Rotman & Druck	4.8	165
Daniel J. Edelman	4.7	164
Manning, Selvage & Lee	4.7	111
Doremus	4.3	130
Ketchum, MacLeod & Grove	3.6	116
J. Walter Thompson PR Dept.	NA	203

NA = Not available
Data: O'Dwyer's Directory of Public Relations Firms

Despite the boom in PR activity, PR practitioners remain troubled about their own status. Indeed, the PRSA has set up a task force to improve the profession's image. William A. Durbin, chairman of Hill & Knowlton, may claim that "the PR function is about to cross the threshold from a primarily communications function to a management function participating systematically in the formulation of policy and the decision-making process itself." But many PR men are not impressed by such exalted talk and suffer from what amounts to a professional inferiority complex.

One reason is that executives who are not communications professionals are, in the words of Byoir's Chairman George Hammond, "moving onto our turf." It has long been commonplace for lawyers, financial specialists, economists, and operating executives to hold down the high-level PR jobs in companies. In the Bell System, the job has been regarded as a necessary way station in a promising executive's career path. In other corporations, it has simply been an organizational dumping ground for middle- and even top-management people awaiting retirement. Now, however, the noncommunications executives are taking over because CEOs are saying, in effect, that PR has become too important to be left in the hands of old-line PR men.

"Coming from the operating side, I had more credibility than a PR man," says Antonio Navarro, W.R. Grace & Co.'s vice-president in charge of PR, a chemical engineer who once ran the company's sugar operations in Peru. Kerryn King, senior vice-president of public affairs at Texaco and the PRSA's new president, explains why: "Many people still equate the field with media relations, product publicity, and promotion. Public affairs goes beyond that. The problem is that there are not enough PR men with the skills to deal with their peer groups on the executive and management levels. If you can't talk the language of the peer group, you're not accepted by the management."

A Test of Value

To obtain "peer group acceptance" by management, PR men are obsessed with the need for professional self-improvement. Jack O'Dwyer, who publishes a weekly newsletter for the PR business, reports that at least 40 educational seminars for public relations practitioners were conducted in New York during the last four months of 1978. He estimates that it would have cost $9,245 to attend them all.

There is considerable cause for the hypersensitivity of PR men, because corporations question whether they are getting their money's worth for the increasing millions of dollars being spent on PR. A recent survey of 50 top corporate officers by Towers, Perrin, Forster & Crosby Inc., management consultants, showed that only half were satisfied with the results of their corporate communications programs. About 60% of CEOs responding to a questionnaire by public affairs consultant W. Howard Chase declared that they had no confidence in their public relations officers.

The big test of the corporate perception of PR will come if the economy slumps later this year, as many economists are predicting. In past recessions, expenditures on public relations were among the first items cut. Many PR men fret that this is likely to happen again. But some CEOs sound as if they would take a different tack if the economy were to turn down now.

For example, at Interpace Corp., a New Jersey-based building materials producer, William R. Hartman, the president, contends that he would not reduce the PR budget, which has grown fivefold over the past three years. During this period, the number of Interpace stockholders grew by 30% (after virtually no change in a decade), institutional holdings increased five times, and the stock price nearly doubled in a depressed market. An 80% boost in profits obviously helped, but Hartman is convinced that without an aggressive financial PR campaign, the improved results would not have had the same impact. Says he, sounding almost like a PR man himself: "A program like ours has to be looked at as a long-term, sustaining kind. You can't do it for a couple of years, then cut the heart out of it, then feel you can start again where you left off."

Sperry Rand's Lyet says that "cutting PR—or R&D—would be false economy, P&L window dressing." Pratt of Pfizer calls PR "a key element of proper management of the future, which would be one of the last things to be cut."

Such comments may be sheer hyperbole. But they may also indicate that CEOs now recognize public relations as a tool for problem-solving as well as attention-getting. PR, they seem to be saying, does not have to be old-time flackery and drum-beating; that if it is conducted in a dignified and intelligent fashion, it can help the corporation function more effectively in a crisis-ridden environment.

The PR Presence in Washington

As companies cope with pressures for greater government control of business, Washington has become a more vital arena for corporate public relations activity. About 500 major corporations have set up offices there with PR functions, some 1,700 trade associations are now headquartered in the capital, and the local PR agencies are burgeoning in both size and number.

The upsurge in Washington PR is also tied to the city's increasing dominance as the nation's No. 1 news center. In 1968 *Hudson's Washington Directory of News Media* listed 1,322 "news outlets"—newspapers, wire services, magazines, syndicates, broadcasters, and newsletters. The 1979 edition has twice as many.

In the year just ended, business lobbyists and other corporate PR practitioners had a field day in the nation's capital. Such outfits as the Business Roundtable, the National Association of Manufacturers, the U.S. Chamber of Commerce, and leading trade associations, aided by their hired guns in the PR agencies, managed to win big despite the huge Democratic majorities on Capitol Hill. Among the major triumphs were the defeats of the labor reform bill, a new consumer advocacy proposal, the common situs picketing bill, and hospital cost containment, and a successful campaign to roll back the capital gains tax.

These victories were in part attributable to the fact that more and more corporate chief executives are being persuaded that it pays to get more and better information and advice on what is happening in Washington. Irving S. Shapiro, Du Pont Co.'s chairman, says that "people realize you have to deal with the government and suggest alternatives. . . . And these new CEOs are making a difference." He contends that "the old skills are not enough," and that from here on out, the outstanding chief executive has to be able to "talk to the Administration . . . work the Hill, etc. . . . I spend a lot of my time down here in Washington, probably more than my Washington office would like. But it's necessary."

The corporate PR office in Washington, meanwhile, is assuming far more significant functions than before. Says a New York executive: "It's no longer a matter of having an old retainer padding around the halls in the Capitol picking up press releases."

Increasingly, corporate PR men and the public relations agencies are tracking congressional hearings, covering deliberations by the regulatory agencies, setting up testimony by corporate spokesmen, analyzing bills and policy issues, and keeping tabs on general matters of concern. To be sure, such functions have long been the stock-in-trade of many corporate Washington representatives. What has changed is that there are far more people—including PR practitioners—doing it for far more clients or employers.

Until recently, says PR counselor Tom Mathews, who helped John Gardner start Common Cause, "business believed you had to conduct public affairs in secret, like a commercial campaign. The single most important discovery they've made is that public battles can't be settled in private any more."

Bibliography

The student should note that there is much overlap in the techniques of corporate public relations and corporate advertising. See the bibliography for the Achenbaum article, no. 40, in this section. The business pages of leading newspapers, in addition to *Business Week*, occasionally carry articles which look at the activities of a particular firm. Of note are accounts in the *Wall Street Journal*. Also check the guides to popular magazines, including *U.S. News and World Report*. The student interested in a public relations career is advised to regularly check such journals as *Public Relations Journal*, *Public Relations Review*, and *Public Relations Quarterly* and to join the student chapter of Public Relations Society of America (PRSA). Of importance are the annual bibliography of the Foundation for Public Relations Research and Education and *PR News*, a newsletter. A leading text in this field is *Effective Public Relations*, by Scott M. Cutlip and Allen H. Center (Prentice-Hall, 1978).

We Are Advocates!

Joseph P. McLaughlin

42

For several decades the goal of achieving for public relations the status of a profession, accepted as such by government, the academic community, business and opinion leaders, other professional societies and associations, and laymen generally has been an elusive one.

There is not even agreement among public relations practitioners and public relations educators as to what needs to be done in order to raise what now is regarded essentially as an art or trade to professional status.

This despite the fact that public relations practitioners constantly use the term professional in talking loosely about other practitioners and their qualifications.

The passage of time alone will not bring this goal closer, as optimists among us continue to hope. But much can be accomplished, we believe, if the practitioner can be persuaded to regard himself as what he truly is—*an advocate*—and to act in accordance with that self-image.

Among the more frequently mentioned ingredients that many in the field contend are essential to the "mix" that spells professionalism are: (a) a code of ethics with procedures and machinery for disciplining those who violate its provisions; (b) an agreed-upon "body of knowledge" which undergirds public relations theory and practice; and (c) a system of examinations to determine the basic knowledge of those entering the public relations field coupled with certification of their qualifications and character by a panel of their peers. Some also believe that a system of governmental licensing should be added.

Largely through the efforts of the Public Relations Society of America and its various sections, particularly the Counselor's Section, two of these ingredients already are in being, though perhaps not fully developed. PRSA has a code of ethics binding on all of its almost 7000 members with provisions for enforcement and penalizing of transgressors. Through its Accreditation Program, PRSA also requires all who seek active membership to pass an examination and to satisfy a panel of already-accredited members as to their qualifications and character. The desirability of requiring government licensing of public relations practitioners is under study.

But the problem of what constitutes an accepted "body of knowledge" and how it is to be developed remains largely unresolved and may continue to defy solution for some time.

It is the purpose of this article to set forth the proposition that there is still another ingredient necessary for achievement of professional status—an attain-

Joseph P. McLaughlin was president of the Beacon Agency, Inc., Philadelphia, and an accredited member of PRSA. He is the author of a number of articles in *Public Relations Quarterly*. This article appeared during the summer of 1972. Reprinted by permission of *Public Relations Quarterly*.

able one—that is little talked about but is at least as important as the others mentioned and, in the opinion of the writer, may be a prerequisite for solving the knotty problem of developing a body of knowledge concerning which there can be general agreement. That ingredient is independence.

It can be achieved only if the individual practitioner and the societies and associations to which he belongs can sharpen their perception of the public relations man's fundamental role in a society dominated by public opinion, which in turn is molded largely by the mass media of communication. This role is shaped by the fact—indisputable, the writer thinks—that public opinion can impose sanctions that are sometimes more severe than legal ones.

The PR man should be an advocate in the same sense that lawyers are advocates. It may be that he also should be granted legally the privilege of confidentiality insofar as conversations with clients [are] concerned, but that is a separate question.

We may speak of the PR man's role as an interpreter to his client or clients of society and events; an evaluator of the meaning and consequences of social and economic change; a prognosticator of future troubles; a prudent and imaginative preparer of programs designed to deal with problems before they descend in full force upon his employer; a transmission belt to carry the client's messages to various publics and to convey back to the client the reactions of those publics to his programs and activities. He undoubtedly, at various times, depending upon the scope of his responsibilities, is all of these. But primarily he is an advocate.

A fascinating chain of events that began in the fall of 1971 in Philadelphia, in which the writer was deeply involved, provided him an insight into the implications of the PR man's role as an advocate. Out of it grew a conviction as to how important recognizing this role is to the achievement of professional status.

Early in October of 1971, Philip Bucci, a highly respected PR counselor with several decades of experience—an accredited member of PRSA and a member of its Counselor's Section—agreed to accept as a client a man who had been publicly described by the Pennsylvania State Crime Commission and other law enforcement officials as a leader in organized crime in Pennsylvania.

The man, Peter Maggio, owner of a South Philadelphia cheese plant, became the subject of controversy and newspaper headlines when he submitted what he thought was a routine request for a zoning change that would permit him to close a small street, unused by the public, so that he could expand his business. He asked the City Councilman representing the district in which the plant was located, William J. Cottrell, to introduce the necessary ordinance.

Cottrell did so, and the bill, after the usual hearing at which no opposition was voiced, was reported to the floor of the Council. District Attorney Arlen Specter then sent two assistant district attorneys to see Cottrell to inform him of the State Crime Commission characterization of Maggio, and at the same time a story was leaked to the Philadelphia newspapers. Cottrell immediately backed away from the bill, which was sent back to committee, presumably to die.

Mutual friends brought Maggio, who was smarting under the unfavorable publicity, and Bucci together. Maggio asked Bucci to help him. Before agreeing to do so, Bucci, in accord with his usual practice, researched the accusations to the best of his ability. He read all of the newspaper clippings and visited the South Philadelphia neighborhood to talk with district police officers and Maggio's neighbors and customers.

He also read all of the available literature on the Mafia and the reports of the U.S. Senate (McClelland) Committee, which had investigated organized crime.

He also wrote to the late J. Edgar Hoover, then Director of the Federal Bureau of Investigation, whom he knew, and asked whether there was anything in FBI files to substantiate the accusation. Hoover sent him a letter stating that there was no derogatory information on Maggio in the files. Bucci's first impulse was to make this letter public, but, on mature consideration, he decided to give it instead to City Council President Paul D'Ortona. By this time he was convinced that Maggio was the victim of character assassination and that he was entitled to public relations help in having his name cleared and in obtaining the necessary Councilmanic approval for his expansion plans.

Before accepting Maggio as a client—and aware of the possibility of censure by the public and colleagues—he discussed the advisability of doing so with several public relations practitioners who also were close friends, including the writer. We finally advised him to accept and also pledged that, should he encounter adverse criticism, we would come to his defense.

Bucci's first action on behalf of Maggio was to set up an interview with the *Philadelphia Evening* and *Sunday Bulletin,* which was published over several columns with photographs of Maggio and his wife, a talented amateur artist, in the editions of Sunday, September 12, 1971. In the interview, Mr. Maggio denied any connection whatsoever with the Mafia and said he doubted the existence of such an organization. He said he was harassed by governmental officials because he is the brother-in-law of Angelo Bruno, described by the FBI as a national leader of organized crime in the U.S. At the time Bucci was hired, Mr. Bruno was in prison in New Jersey following his refusal to answer questions at a hearing before a New Jersey commission investigating crime.

Two days later, the *Bulletin* carried a column-length story on page nine about Bucci and his representation of Maggio under the head "Maggio Hires PR Man For a New 'Image.' " It was factual and generally favorable to Bucci, detailing his representation of blue chip clients in the past, which included U.S. Senator Hugh Scott (R., Pa.), Superior Court Judge John B. Hannum (now a Federal Circuit Court Judge), the American Legion, Fraternal Order of Police, and sports personalities like heavyweight boxing champion Joe Frazier. The article also noted that among Bucci's references was one from Hoover and one from former Pennsylvania Governor Raymond P. Shafer.

Meanwhile, armed with Hoover's letter, Council President D'Ortona wrote to Specter and demanded that he state publicly whether he had any evidence connecting Maggio with the Mafia. Specter wrote back a few days later stating that he had no such evidence.

The zoning bill then was revived in City Council and, at Cottrell's urging, passed unanimously. However, former Mayor James H.J. Tate did not sign it before leaving office. Cottrell was defeated for re-election to Council, but his successor, Natale F. Carbello, re-introduced the bill. It was passed by Council and signed into law by Tate's successor, Mayor Frank L. Rizzo.

The signing was a personal victory for Bucci. Without his courageous public relations advocacy—at considerable risk to his own image—in Maggio's behalf, City Hall observers say that the zoning change would have been dead and Maggio would have suffered not only financial loss, but also his reputation would have been irrevocably damaged. As evidence of the sanctions that can be inflicted by public opinion, the Maggio firm showed a loss in excess of $100,000 in 1971, the first such loss in 55 years of business. Because of the unfavorable publicity, also, many of his customers had ceased doing business with him.

However, even before Maggio was cleared, Bucci and the writer agreed that a fundamental principle relating to the practice of public relations was involved, namely the right of a reputable public relations practitioner to represent any client without having attributed to him "the reputation, character or beliefs of the client." Even though Bucci believed, and publicly stated, that he was convinced that Maggio had no connection with the Mafia and had been maligned (as later developments were to demonstrate), we both agreed that the principle was important enough to have it endorsed by a professional public relations association made up of a jury of our peers.

We chose the Philadelphia Public Relations Association as the appropriate vehicle. This association, although it is unaffiliated with any state or national organization, is the largest group of public relations practitioners in the Philadelphia area (more than 225 members) and enjoys considerable prestige, particularly with the news media.

At the writer's request, a meeting of the directors of the Philadelphia Public Relations Association was held at the Poor Richard Club on October 6, 1971 at which, after considerable, sometimes sharp, discussion, the following statement was approved. It is reproduced here in full.

"A Public Relations practitioner, like an attorney, primarily is an advocate.

"An attorney seeks to represent his client in the most favorable light, consistent with the rules of evidence, his duty as an officer of the Court and the canons of ethics of the organized Bar in the various tribunals in the field of Jurisprudence. Through advice and consultation the lawyer endeavors also to help his client avoid situations which will involve him in litigation or criminal proceedings.

"A Public Relations practitioner seeks to represent his client in the most favorable light consistent with the facts and the ethical codes of professional Public Relations organizations, in the Court of Public Opinion.

"Except for the possible deprivation of his life or freedom, a client can be damaged as severely in the Court of Public Opinion as in a Court of Law.

"Many local and state bar associations have adopted resolutions which assert, in essence, that a lawyer may represent any client without having attributed to him the reputation, character and beliefs of the client. If, by virtue of such representation of an unpopular client, a lawyer incurs hostility, resentment or adverse criticism, the organized bar has committed itself to come to his defense.

"The Philadelphia Public Relations Association claims the same privilege for the Public Relations practitioner, operating in the Court of Public Opinion.

"It asserts that a Public Relations practitioner has the right to represent any client without having attributed to him the reputation, character or beliefs of the client.

"It asserts, also, the corollary right of any person who could benefit from such services, to representation by a competent Public Relations practitioner of good character and reputation."

The statement in its original version read "present his client in the most favorable light"—not "represent"—but got changed in the final, somewhat confusing, moments of this meeting.

The action formed the basis of a news article the following day in the *Philadelphia Inquirer*. The vote of the directors was 24–0 in favor of the statement. A small committee of the directors subsequently was appointed by Charles Ellis, president of the Philadelphia Public Relations Association, to draft a change in the association's by-laws to incorporate into that document the principle outlined in the statement. The directors, incidentally, also approved a resolution expressing their confidence in and admiration for Bucci.

Meanwhile, the writer wrote to Paul M. Werth, a Columbus, Ohio, public relations practitioner who at the time was chairman of the Counselor's section of PRSA, advising him both of the intention to have the matter considered by the Philadelphia Public Relations Association and of its subsequent unanimous approval of the statement. In reply, Mr. Werth described the situation as "very interesting" and said he would bring it to the attention of the Executive Committee of the Counselor's section. Copies of the letters of Mr. Werth and the newspaper clippings also were sent to Dr. Robert O. Carlson, president of the Public Relations Society of America.

What are the broad implications of this chain of events for the practice of public relations in the United States?

As far as the counselors are concerned, we think it is obvious that, if they are to be recognized as members of a profession, they must come out from behind the shadow of the client. They must not be considered merely a part of the client's retinue, lumped together with those who write speeches, arrange schedules, or merely carry valises. They must be "in charge" of the case, just as a lawyer, because of his superior training, knowledge, and experience, is in charge of his client's case. To their credit, some counselors already operate in this manner.

Even those who are corporate or association or foundation public relations directors or staff members, we believe, must come to look upon themselves as advocates. They have the same problem as lawyers who serve as house counsel for corporations—who have a single client. But if they look upon themselves primarily as advocates, some of the doubts and confusions that have troubled them may be removed. For instance, many corporate PR men have been at a loss as to how to resolve the inner doubts and the conflict produced by charges of magazine writers that it is the job of public relations always to present the client in the most favorable possible light—to ignore the bad and publicize only the good and beneficial. In short, always to tell half truths instead of the whole truth. If the PR man frankly accepts his role as that of advocate, these doubts and conflicts largely will disappear. No one expects a lawyer to present, even to a jury deciding the question of freedom, or life itself, information damaging to his client. As an officer of the court, the lawyer is bound not to tell untruths or to deny the truth if it is brought out under questioning of opposing counsel. As a man of conscience, bound by the code of ethics of professional associations like the Public Relations Society of America, the corporate PR Director or staff member is bound not to tell untruths to the media or any of his client's publics and to answer truthfully the questions of the representatives of the media.

Our job as advocate is to present our client in the best possible light. It is an honorable role, and we should not feel defensive about it.

Bibliography

Another article dealing with the difficulty of defining and establishing standards in the field of public relations is Neil A. Lavick's "Public Relations Council: An Alternative to Licensing?" which appeared in *Public Relations Quarterly,* Spring 1975. Related articles appear in *Public Relations Journal.* Various items from the Public Relations Society of America (PRSA) also might be helpful. For further research, bibliographies are: Robert L. Bishop, compiler, *Public Relations: A Comprehensive Bibliography: Articles and Books on Public Relations, Communication Theory, Public Opinion, and Propaganda, 1964–1972* (A.G. Leigh-James, 1974); and Scott M. Cutlip, compiler, *A Public Relations Bibliography,* 2d ed., (University of Wisconsin Press, 1965). The Bishop volume up-dates Cutlip's compilation. Also useful for students who wish to dig deeply is Raymond Simon, compiler, *Bibliography of Masters' Theses and Doctoral Dissertations Dealing with Public Relations Subjects 1960–1970* (Foundation for Public Relations Research and Education) with supplement for 1971–72 by Marie E. Mastin, undated.

43 Media Use of Polls
Dom Bonafede

Dom Bonafede is the White House correspondent for the *National Journal.* This article, which originally appeared in the September-October 1978 issue of the *Washington Journalism Review,* is used with that journal's permission.

Seated in a small, glass-partitioned office on the periphery of the *Washington Post's* coliseum-sized newsroom, Barry Sussman is musing on the nature of individual polling operations by a growing number of newspapers and broadcasting organizations. Formerly city editor and a key supervisory figure in the

Post's Watergate coverage, Sussman currently serves as the paper's polling specialist, having made the transition willingly and successfully but not without suffering occasional withdrawal symptoms.

That, however, is an occupational hazard among newspaper pollsters who move back and forth between traditional journalism with its frenetic pursuit of instant news and the even-paced, quasi-academic world of public opinion research, all the while seeking to provide a rational explanation of the former by the scientific and analytical techniques of the latter.

"If we can find out what people are thinking in basic, simple terms on clear-cut issues and no longer have to be captives of politicians and others who spout off, it is a device, when done right—which is not easy—that allows us to make broad, sweeping generalizations with confidence, something that an individual reporter has one hell of a time doing," Sussman comments.

He recalled that in last year's Virginia gubernatorial election, the *Post* polled voters as they left the election area and consequently was able to report in a first-day story that Republican John Dalton's victory was based mainly on public sentiment against his Democrat opponent, Henry Howell.

"We were able to say that because at least one out of two Dalton voters we polled said they were voting more because they disliked Henry Howell than they liked John Dalton," Sussman said. "You might be able to guess at that but you could never say it conclusively the way we could without taking a poll of that kind."

Over the last several years, more and more newspapers have accepted public opinion polling as a legitimate news-gathering function. There is a certain irony in this since the first recorded newspaper poll was conducted in 1824 by the *Harrisburg Pennsylvanian* in Wilmington, Del., regarding voter preference in the presidential election, subsequently won by John Quincy Adams. For the most part, however, newspaper surveys have been restricted to marketing studies. And although polling is roughly viewed as "an extension of journalism," it was the professional pollsters who lifted the craft to its current eminent status, notably George Gallup and Hadley Cantril, who conducted surveys for President Franklin D. Roosevelt, and later, Lou Harris and others.

Then in 1967, Phil Meyer, of the Knight newspapers, surveyed the underlying causes of the Detroit riots by applying social science techniques. Meyer's findings deflated the generally accepted conceptions which were believed to have provoked the rioting. They indicated that participants were not confined to one sector of the population, that there was more involvement by native blacks than by migrant blacks.

"Previously, we would have gone to the sociologists to determine the causes of the riot, but things happened so fast that in this case the sociologists came to us," Meyer said.

A few newspapers such as the *Minneapolis Tribune* and *Des Moines Register* had been doing their own surveys before that, but Meyer's findings underscored the potentiality of the scientific approach to news analysis. Since then, many other newspapers and the television networks have joined the parade in establishing their own public opinion research operations. This has given rise to a small, loosely knit fraternity of newspaper pollsters.

Some, like Sussman, concentrate exclusively on polling studies, while others double as reporters and conduct surveys on a part-time basis, although invariably they are assisted by outside experts.

At least all of those who have gained recognition for their work have had special instruction as given, for instance, at the University of Michigan's Survey Research Center and the Northwestern University Medill School of Journalism. Among them: Joel Shurkin, the *Philadelphia Inquirer*; Mike Smith, *Chicago Tribune*; Bernie Bookbinder, *Newsday*; and John McCormick, Dubuque (Iowa) *Telegraph-Herald*.

Essentially, media polls are another instrument to probe beneath the surface of events and explore public attitudes. The findings help diagnose behavioral patterns and possibly provide a hedge against the unexpected. At their best, they add an element of precision to what is too often a haphazard approach by the press in gathering and interpreting information.

No newspaper or commercial pollster subscribes to the notion of the infallibility of public opinion surveys. They recognize the opportunities for technical flaws, such as improperly worded questions or inadequate sampling, and errors of judgment in interpreting accumulated data. As Sussman observed, "Polling is part science and part a matter of judgment."

Not surprisingly, private pollsters contend that media polls vary in degree of quality from one extreme to another. "Some are very good but many others are not so good," remarked Tom Reinken, a Gallup Poll editor. "The quality varies so much, it is unbelievable," commented Washington pollster Peter Hart.

"It runs the gamut," said David Neft, of the Lou Harris organization. "The part I deplore is where newspapers do it but don't have the proper personnel to analyze and draw proper conclusions."

Neft cited a *New York Daily News* poll of last June in which residents of metropolitan New York were asked if they would go to Atlantic City to participate in legalized gambling there. Of those questioned, 35% replied yes, 63% no, and 2% were undecided. Based on the figures, the newspaper published a story carrying a lead saying that nearly two-thirds of the metropolitan area residents do not expect to go to Atlantic City to gamble at the newly legalized casinos— leaving the inference that one-third might go.

"If the casino operators thought they could attract one-third of all New Yorkers, they would break open the champagne and celebrate," Neft said. "That was a terribly naive interpretation."

The perils of unsophisticated polling were further illustrated in a *Miami News* survey centering on a proposed referendum to repeal a mass transit authorization. In its regular editions, the paper printed coupons in which readers were asked to indicate their preference and mail them in. It was soon discovered, however, that numerous coupons had been duplicated on a copy machine by a subcontractor with a vested interest in the outcome of the issue.

Nonetheless, private pollsters—whose own infallibility is hardly guaranteed and are themselves occasionally criticized by their counterparts in the media, particularly by Sussman and Meyer—generally agree that among media public opinion operations which maintain high professional standards and attract a national audience are those run by *New York Times*-CBS, *Washington Post,* Knight-Ridder, and AP–NBC.

Above all, it should be stressed that the contrast between the old man-in-the-street polls ("Are you planning to go to the beach or the mountains this summer?") and today's scientific surveys is comparable to the difference between a Model-T and a Jaguar XJS. (There is some question as to just how scientific polling is, but as Sussman points out, practitioners must follow rigid scientific procedures, on which they must base their conclusions eliminating as much as possible any subjective biases.)

There is no set format within the media as to the manner in which polling studies are conducted. Meyer notes that there are basically three courses of action open to newspapers: they can hire outside pollsters, train reporters and operate their own field operations, or they can develop any number of variations.

As a case in point, the *Post* hires outside commercial firms, called "suppliers," to do its polling. Also, Sussman works closely with an academic specialist, Gary Orren, of Harvard. Similarly, *Newsday* uses the services of sociologist Stephen Cole, of the State University at Stony Brook, and the *Los Angeles Times,* which has been stepping up its public opinion research operations, retains William Schneider, of Harvard, as a consultant. Usually, the academics assist in the preparation of the questionnaires, help select demographic targets, and draft analyses from the findings.

Some newspapers rely to a large extent on commercial pollsters. The *Boston Globe* and *Newsday* each employ Irwin ("Tubby") Harrison, of the Research Analysis Corp., Boston, Mass., to do their test sampling. In May, Harrison did a statewide poll for the *Globe* which implied that Sen. Edward Brooke (R-Mass.) was politically vulnerable even before the furor over his divorce and related statements concerning his finances.

The survey showed that the majority of those queried thought the Senator was too much of a dilettante, that he owned an inordinately large amount of property considering his principal source of income was his Senate salary, and that he was not doing as much for Massachusetts as they thought he should be doing.

Yet, in a classic case, demonstrating how polls can quickly become outdated, Harrison said that the massive publicity later showered on Brooke could conceivably produce a backlash to his advantage, thereby making the poll obsolete.

There are also variations on variations, such as the combined operations of the *New York Times* and CBS. AP and NBC have a similar deal. A few years ago, the Gannett chain even purchased the Lou Harris organization and added it to its media empire.

As part of a special arrangement, since 1974 *Newsday* and Gannett have teamed up to conduct political polls in New York State, with Harrison's Boston firm doing the field work. Gannett pays for the upstate interviewing, *Newsday* for that done on Long Island, and they split the cost for New York City. Afterwards, they simultaneously receive from Harrison an identical report, which includes the accumulated data and his analyses. Each is then at liberty to draft a separate interpretation, but it can be released only at an agreed upon date.

Polling techniques also vary somewhat among newspapers. But mainly, they prefer telephone interviewing since it is more economical than person-to-person contact, it is faster, and the margin for error is believed to be only slightly higher.

"I haven't done any door-to-door polling and I don't intend to," Sussman said. "There is an argument that goes on among people who are deeply into polling methodology as to whether telephoning is as good as door-to-door interviewing. What they seem to come up with is that you get more people undecided when you ask questions over the telephone but not a great many more. And that you can't do the kind of lengthy polls that you can do if you get into somebody's home.

"You can poll for an hour in somebody's house; you probably can't poll that long on the phone. I try to keep my interviews no longer than 15 minutes on the phone. But other than that, phone technique is very much faster; the results are essentially the same, and if we can't do as deep and probing a poll, we can still do something that is quite useful."

Both the *Post* and *New York Times*-CBS employ George Fine Research, Inc., a New York firm, for its telephone surveys on national issues. Mike Fine, president, said that a "rule of thumb" regarding costs was $10 per interview. However, he reported, the price may vary depending on the importance of the story, the characteristics of the issue being measured, and the precision sought by the customer. Normally, for a case study involving 1,500 respondents, the price comes to about $18,000, including the printing and tabulation of the data.

In comparison, door-to-door interviews for a study involving the same number of respondents would cost between $30,000 and $40,000, according to Albert H. Cantril, president of the National Council on Public Polls (NCPP) in Washington.

For local issues, the *Post* hires a Washington supplier with a large corps of telephone interviewers at its disposal. Said Sussman, "We bring them into the *Post,* where they use a large classified sales room; it has about a hundred desks with telephones, so it is an ideal place for calls to be made at a time it is not being occupied and it works out very nicely."

Sussman also conducts surveys by mail, particularly when it involves a special interest group. Last summer, for example, he surveyed members of the legal community concerning courtroom coverage by radio and television. Of 750 questionnaires sent out, 55 per cent were returned, the vast majority of which favored radio-TV coverage.

Some newspapers, including *Newsday* and the *Philadelphia Inquirer,* have used reporters, interns, and students for personal interviews. During the 1976 bicentennial year, for instance, the *Inquirer* sent out a large group of journalism students from Temple and the University of Pennsylvania to ask a set of questions designed to determine why the anticipated tourist influx had failed to materialize.

"We wanted to know where the tourists were," said Shurkin, a science writer. "Advertisers had increased their budgets, and it was expected it would be impossible to get a hotel room. But from our findings, it was learned that tourists were using Philadelphia simply as a one-day stopover between New York and Washington and were gone by nightfall.

"Philadelphia was either in the way or on the way. Surveys showed there was attendance only where the attraction was free, like Independence Hall or the Liberty Bell, but if it cost money, there was no impact at all. We got the same response at Valley Forge. As a result, advertisement was cut back or switched to New York. Our findings were so accurate that we were able to predict attendance within 1–2% at certain places."

Bookbinder, senior editor for special projects at *Newsday,* which publishes a polling feature every Sunday, reported that the articles are based on material gathered by 20 to 25 telephone interviewers hired through an employment agency. They work two nights each month using a random digit dialing system with the objective of obtaining a total of 500 to 600 interviews. "We poll mostly on social questions," Bookbinder said. "Everything from, 'Do you believe in God?' to 'What's your favorite room in the house?' "

He recalled that in 1973 the newspaper took on a major study project to compile a demographic profile of Long Island's suburban population. Using mostly reporters and interns, about 350 interviews, involving 180 questions each, were held over a two-month period. As a result of the survey, the newspaper ran more than 30 articles.

Among its findings: the decision to move outside the metropolitan core is shaped more by the "pull" of the suburbs (the yearning to own a home, have more space, and provide a suitable environment for children) than the "push" of the city; newcomers to the suburbs are likely to be politically conservative before they make the move, debunking the notion that they become conservative after moving there; although suburban housewives almost always said they were happy in their new surroundings, it was difficult to determine if they were being entirely objective in view of the major commitment they had made to move to the suburbs.

As part of the series, *Newsday* identified 10 suburban stereotypes—such as a middle income black family living in a white neighborhood, a cosmopolitan couple who worked in New York and commuted, a low income family living in slum conditions and a family with established roots on Long Island—and arranged to have a reporter stay in each of their homes for three days. The purpose was to learn first hand how they really lived. "We were dealing with answers people were willing to give us and limited by their candor and honesty," commented Bookbinder.

"In one case, our reporter (Lynn Rossellini) living with the black family had repeatedly been told by the husband how great it was to be living in the suburbs. Then just before Lynn was ready to leave, she had a conversation alone with the wife, who told her, 'He's full of shit,' and admitted they were miserable living in a white neighborhood. That made me wonder about the authenticity of what we base our reporting on."

Unlike *Newsday,* the *Chicago Tribune* conducts a survey "only when we have something to survey," in the words of Mike Smith, editor of the paper's Sport's Week section and supervisor of its public opinion studies. He reported the paper has initiated only about a dozen polling projects in the last four years, focusing mainly on public attitudes and perceptions. "We don't do single-issue polls such as a popularity poll between two candidates," he said. "They are too powerful for using a single-dimensional approach. Numbers are not as important as perceptions."

In one poll, the *Tribune* questioned Catholics on liberal innovations by the church. It found that many Catholics were uncomfortable with the new liturgy, disapproved of having Mass said in English, and disliked John Cardinal Cody, whom they mischievously referred to as "New Orleans Cody."

In another survey, the paper sought to determine if there were any attitudinal differences between blacks and whites on significant issues. Its findings indicated that, indeed, there existed remarkable differences: blacks did not think there had been much progress in civil rights, while whites thought there had been a great deal of progress; the major concerns of blacks were job security and their personal economic situations, for whites it was inflation and the national economy.

Interestingly, only black interviewers were used for the survey, which was conducted by telephone. "There is a better response level if the interviewer is black," Smith remarked. "They are able to establish a rapport (with other blacks) and instill confidence in the respondent."

Oftentimes, newspapers and news magazines will commission special surveys from commercial pollsters. In a typical example, the July 24 issue of *Newsweek* included the results of a poll which Gallup had taken expressly for the magazine on the question of U.S.-Soviet relations.

Probably the easiest and least expensive way for newspapers to get into the polling business is to buy syndicated studies from the more popularly known research organizations, such as Gallup and Harris. Gallup reportedly syndicates its findings to about 140 press clients.

Newspapers may also negotiate for access to computerized data on a time-sharing basis. Shurkin reported that the *Philadelphia Inquirer* has arranged with NBC to plug into the network's computer facilities at Cherry Hill, N.J. on election night this November to receive voting data on the New Jersey political contests.

Besides the normal perversities indigenous to polling, some editors and reporters view them as alien forces in their midst; the undeviating formality of the scientific process is anathema to those accustomed to more flexible and individualistic ways of gathering information and drawing conclusions. Despite the folklore about freewheeling newsmen, most are traditionally resistant to change.

Whatever the reasons, many newsmen, including some of the most respected, have little faith in polls. Commenting on this, Sussman said: "Reporters, like any group, are divided in the way they look at polls. Some of them don't like polls at all; they don't trust poll findings. Larry Stern, our national editor, is not one who loves polls. Some reporters use polling data very well.

"After all, if a poll is done well, there is probably no better way to find out what people are thinking. The problem is a lot of reporters distrust polls because they don't understand the methods all that perfectly. They don't think you can pigeonhole people into little yes-no or agree-disagree answers and say, 'Now I'm going to describe to you the feelings of the electorate of the United States.' And there is a lot to say for that kind of viewpoint."

At the *Philadelphia Inquirer,* editor Gene Roberts and other members of the paper's editorial management are reported to take a dim view of polls, especially those involving political issues and candidates. Shurkin said the feeling is that the *Inquirer* is a fairly activist paper locally and that it might inject itself as a factor if it conducted a political poll. That, however, is considered a specious argument by some staff members.

Meyer observed, "It is easier now to get reporters interested in polls than it was five or ten years ago. Young reporters are quick to pick up on it."

The enthusiastic advocacy of one editor is credited with the involvement of the Dubuque *Telegraph-Herald,* an Iowa paper with 40,000 circulation, in polling studies. John McCormick, general assignment reporter, recalled that in the spring of 1974, the paper's managing editor, Jim Geladas, "came into the newsroom with several copies of Meyer's book (*Precision Journalism*) and tossed them on the desks of reporters and suggested we take a look at it."

Since then, the paper has conducted several noteworthy surveys, refuting the argument that only the big, elitist news organizations can afford polls. In one study, McCormick and the paper's police reporter analyzed 2,400 traffic accidents committed in the Dubuque area over a complete year in an attempt to obtain a demographic pattern of offenses and drivers involved. The information was coded and fed into a computer.

"As a result," McCormick said, "we were able to say, here are the places, times, and situations where accidents are most likely to occur." The study further showed that there were fewer automobile accidents while it was snowing than afterwards when drivers thought the streets were safe.

The paper also did a study of physicians' attitudes and another which took a look at juvenile crimes over the past 40 years. "The juvenile crime study may have offended traditional liberal thought, but it suggested that juveniles who are not coddled, so to speak, who are brought into court and forced to confront a judge, for example, and thus are scared, are less likely to be repeat offenders," McCormick reported.

Another reporter on the paper has been assigned to compare the handling of drunk driving cases in two different cities.

Newspaper problems with polls, however, are not solely confined to the reluctance of some staff members to accept their findings. Editors and reporters may be unskilled in handling them or not informed enough to correctly interpret their meaning.

Illustrative of this, Sussman tells of a *Post* poll intended to assess the attitude of Washington football fans toward George Allen, then the coach of the Redskins. Although a winning coach, Allen had a propensity for creating controversy and was not wholly loved by local sportswriters, who resented his imperial manners.

As Sussman recalled the incident, "We ended up with a finding of something like 80% of the people who said they followed the Redskins and approved of George Allen as a coach; 75% of the people said they wanted George Allen to stay on as coach—a tremendously high number. The sportswriter who wrote that story started off by saying one of the greatest surprises in the poll was the support for George Allen. Well, of course, it was a surprise to sportswriters but not to the fans. I took it out immediately."

Sussman said that many prominent *Post* reporters, such as Bill Greider, David Broder, and Morton Mintz (who proposed the lawyers' poll), have a "keen and critical interest" in public opinion surveys. "But," he acknowledged, "it is quite correct there are any number of people around here who either don't know anything about polls, don't want to know anything about polls, or do know something about polls and don't trust them and want to stay as far away from them as they can. And I imagine that will continue."

Normally, it is believed that newspapers do best with polls on local issues, those with which they are familiar and their readers are most concerned. Yet some, like the *Post* and the *New York Times*, which are close to being national newspapers, often take on national issues.

Early in his career as a pollster, Sussman, along with three specialists from Harvard, polled Congress to determine if the new members of the class of 1974 were as different from their predecessors as generally believed. Their findings showed that the new members were different in some respects—they didn't care much for the CIA, for example—but "they were more alike than unlike."

"For example," Sussman said, "in terms of where they got their campaign money, these people were tremendously well financed. Mind you, none of them had been a member of Congress before, getting all kinds of labor and business money, at least to the extent that veteran members of Congress were.

"It shows you how alert the people who make campaign contributions are; they were not taking any chances, they were backing these new members or possible new members. And it shows you how these people were not as anti-politics as you might have expected. Almost all of them were getting a lot of this money."

One of the rare studies on the use of polls by newspapers was done last year by Albert Cantril and Jay T. Harris, an associate director at the Medill School of Journalism.

Analyzing 270 newspaper articles on polls from 30 metropolitan newspapers published during the 1976 presidential campaign, they found:

> There was a preoccupation with polls that assessed relative candidate strength. Sixty-one percent of the reports focused on matches between rival candidates, while 20% dealt with the attributes of candidates, and only 8% on the principal issues.

> Forty-six percent of the survey reports were based on telephone interviews.

> In less than a third of the stories was the wording of the questions included (as recommended by the NCPP) in whole or in part.

Perhaps the most encouraging aspect of the trend towards greater use of polls by newspapers is that even those newsmen who believe in them and work with them retain the same level of skepticism towards them as they do towards information gained through regular reporting techniques.

"There's a lot of validity to them but there's also a lot of black magic," Shurkin remarked.

"Numbers should be a starting point," said McCormick, "not a finishing point; they just point you in a direction."

With the midterm elections coming up, with intensive efforts being made to measure the depth of the so-called tax revolt, with Jimmy Carter still a question mark, polls will be increasingly tapped to help find the answers. Newspapers will want to know if voters, tired of high taxes and government inefficiency, are going to send Washington a message by supporting Republicans. And what effect is the continuing distrust of government having on the national psyche?

As the questions become more complicated, as the issues become more perplexing, the polls gain in usage. But no one, including their staunchest advocates, contends that they are a curative capable of healing our intellectual voids. Or that they will ever replace personal journalism. Yet, it is apparent they have found a place in the newsroom.

Bibliography

The use of the mass media and polling techniques in political campaigns has long been a concern in the United States. The advent of television and far more sophisticated polling techniques have exacerbated the problem. An article by Burns W. Roper helps explain the function of polls: "Misleading Measurements," *Society*, September/October 1976. A popular text dealing with the gathering and analyzing of public opinion is Bernard Hennessy's *Public Opinion* (Duxbury Press, 1975). A classic work is Walter Lippmann's *Public Opinion* (Harcourt Brace, 1922). For current articles, see *Public Opinion Quarterly, Journalism Quarterly,* and the *Journal of Communication.*

For additional background information, the following are suggested. An excellent bibliography of books and articles dealing with this subject is Lynda Lee Kaid, et al., *Political Campaign Communication: A Bibliography and Guide to the Literature* (Scarecrow Press, 1974). The literature in this field is extensive. Students can find useful information in the following books, which are listed in chronological order of publication: Gene Wyckoff, *The Image Candidates: American Politics in the Age of Television* (Macmillan, 1968); Joe McGinnis, *The Selling of the President, 1968* (Trident Press, 1969); Kurt Lang and Gladys Engel Lang, *Politics and Television* (Quadrangle, 1968);

Edward W. Chester, *Radio, Television and American Politics* (Sheed & Ward, 1969); Harold Mendelsohn and Irving Crespi, *Polls, TV and the New Politics* (Chandler, 1970); Sig Mickelson, *The Electric Mirror: Politics in the Age of Television* (Dodd, Mead, 1972); Robert E. Gilbert, *Television and Presidential Politics* (Christopher Publishing, 1972); Newton N. Minow, et al., *Presidential Television* (Basic Books, 1973); Kevin P. Phillips, *Mediacracy: American Parties and Politics in the Communications Age* (Doubleday, 1975); Thomas E. Patterson and Robert D. McClure, *The Unseeing Eye* (G. P. Putnam's Sons, 1976). Of particular interest to the student interested in the use of polls during campaigns is Ray E. Hiebert et al., eds., *The Political Image Merchants: Strategies for the Seventies* (Acropolis Books, 1975), the result of a conference held for political campaign managers, journalists, and social scientists. This up-date version of an earlier edition has useful, if uneven, contributions on the how and why of campaigns in the 1970s. See also *Political Broadcast Catechism,* 8th ed. (National Association of Broadcasters, March 1976), for questions and answers on broadcaster responsibilities for political broadcasts.

44 Presidential Nominations and the Media
The American Assembly

Preamble

At the close of their discussions the participants in The American Assembly on *Presidential Nominations and the Media,* at Seven Springs Center, Mount Kisco, New York, May 11–13, 1978, reviewed as a group the following statement. The statement represents general agreement; however, no one was asked to sign it. Furthermore, it should not be assumed that every participant subscribes to every recommendation. The document is used with the permission of The American Assembly.

The presidential nominating process begins long before the national conventions name their choices. Crucial decisions start even before the first caucuses and primaries, in obscure and relatively unexamined definitions of who the serious contenders are, what their chances might be, what sorts of Presidents they might make. For most of the electorate, these early processes are nearly invisible. For a relatively small and scattered set of active and attentive decision-makers, they are matters of intense professional concern. Linking the deliberations of these contrasting categories is a—perhaps *the*—critical task of democratic politics.

Recently we have seen a rapid and radical shift in the composition of the key figures in this linkage process. Democratizing reforms have produced a proliferation of presidential primaries and helped hasten the decline in the influence of political party leaders, particularly in their traditional roles as screeners of candidates and mobilizers of voter support. Into the resultant vacuum, the mass media of communication have been progressively drawn in the role of conscious deliberator and perhaps arbiter. Candidates for the Presidency have rapidly adapted to this shift, recognizing that there stands between them and their hoped-for voters a newly significant intermediary: the media themselves, who, like it or not, must direct the national attention to a reasonably recognizable selection of candidates, issues, and probabilities.

We see the track record of presidential nominations since World War II as mixed and uncertain—in need of careful scrutiny with a view to improvement. But awareness of the problems is no trustworthy guide to the solutions. Indeed, the political reforms of recent years have had unanticipated consequences which give us pause in prescribing new structural changes. Chary of contributing even more uncertainty to the inevitable flux of historical development, we confine our recommendations to but one reconstruction of the nominating process. Our sense is that much of what needs doing can be done within the system as it is.

The number of dates upon which presidential primaries can be conducted should be substantially reduced, and the intervals between primary dates should be lengthened beyond the current, typical one-week lapse.

Recommendations

The effect of limiting the number of primary dates would be, we think, to broaden the representativeness of early choices; the media would thus be pressed to extend their coverage beyond any one state and to present the public with a wider array of voter reactions and candidate performances. The complex reality of the early emerging situation would be more accurately conveyed, in contrast to the present overly simplistic concentration on a single state constituency.

Changes in the Process

This restructuring of the primary system might diminish concentration on the horserace aspect of the process—an exaggerated stress on the calculation of odds at the expense of attention to matters of greater long-range significance, such as the assessment of policy positions and presidential qualities.

At the same time, providing a sequence of primaries punctuated by intervals for deliberation would enable the press and public to digest one result before confronting the next set of choices, in a cumulative learning process. If the earliest results were in some important sense unrepresentative of an emerging popular consensus, later calculations could make the necessary corrections.

Journalism has a responsibility, heightened by its escalating influence, to persist in exploring new and better ways to inform the widest possible audience about the candidates. In many ways, the journalists' task is to respond to the candidates' actions and words. However, much news is generated through deliberate decisions by journalists and their organizations as to what topics deserve coverage. Currently we find the need particularly pressing for highlighting the candidates' issue stands, describing and analyzing the candidates' records, and discovering and communicating the personality characteristics which may affect the candidates' suitability for the Presidency.

Changes in
Journalistic Practices

Among the approaches that seem especially promising are these:

Focusing more reports on comparisons of the candidates' positions on a single issue or set of issues, as distinguished from reports which simply describe the issue stands of a single candidate without the comparative dimension.

Using journalists with specialized knowledge in specific subject matter areas to examine the candidates' issue stances.

Rotating reporters among the candidates' campaigns (including that of an incumbent President seeking renomination) to furnish a fresh perspective and to guard against reporters acquiring vested interest in "their" candidate's success.

Encouraging careful reporting and interpretation of the ways the candidates are presenting themselves through campaign advertising and through national and local news media.

Concentrating more journalistic resources on explorations of the candidates' political and personal histories—allowing for the possibilities that human beings do change, but recognizing the probabilities of continuity.

Comparing systematically the candidates' present pronouncements with their previous statements and practices.

Strongly encouraging those journalists familiar with the candidates and their campaigns to find ways to express—with all due care and caution—their own judgments and observations about the candidates.

Describing and assessing the persons chosen by candidates to staff their major campaign posts, with particular attention to the ideological configurations they may represent.

Cooperating enthusiastically with efforts to facilitate comparisons among candidates through such formats as debates and hearings, arranged by party, media, or interest group organizations.

Finally, we address the problem of timing. The tendency at present is for the media to devote space and time to close examination of candidate qualifications early in the nominating season—when, however, few voters are motivated to pay attention to these reports. Later, when increasing numbers are increasingly interested, the media, having already presented much of this information, subordinate it to more current and often less significant topics. We urge the journalistic profession to take a new look at this problem, to devise ways to deliver to the electorate the information the people need *when they need it*. For example, national media that have already done extensive analyses of candidates must try to find means to reiterate this information later in the campaign. And as the campaign moves from state to state, local media should take advantage of heightened campaign interest to publish and broadcast more of this type of material.

Candidates and the media should remain watchful, lest either coopt or manipulate the other to the detriment of the voting public. But vigilance alone will not suffice. The quest for novelty should not be allowed to detract from the overwhelming need for substantial and consistently developed political information. Candidates and journalists must be prepared to find new strategies to meet and channel—rationally and interestingly—the rush of political experience.

Conclusion

A thorough description of how the press corps covers presidential politics is found in Timothy Crouse's *The Boys on the Bus* (Random House, 1973). See *Columbia Journalism Review* for articles related to the 1976 and 1980 campaign maneuvers. Background books include Nathan Blumberg's *One Party Press?* (University of Nebraska Press, 1954); C. Richard Hofstetter, *Bias in the News: Network Television Coverage of the 1972 Election Campaign* (Ohio State University Press, 1976); William L. Rivers and Wilbur Schramm, *Responsibility in Mass Communication* (Harper & Row, 1969); Theodore H. White's series of books beginning with *The Making of the President—1960* (Atheneum, 1960, 1964, 1968, 1972) and Jules Witcover's *Marathon: The Pursuit of the Presidency, 1972–76* (Viking Press, 1977).

Also see "The Broadcast Media and the Political Process," *Broadcasting,* January 3, 1977; "Reporting the 1976 Campaign," *Columbia Journalism Review,* January/February 1977; "What Makes the Apple Machine Run?" [*more*], July/August, 1976; and the index to *Journalism Quarterly,* a research journal that has carried many articles on campaign coverage.

Bibliography

International Communications

Multinational Media

William H. Read

45

As the Canadian Parliament reconvened (in January 1975), a strange and perplexing, although not unique, immigration case confronted Prime Minister Trudeau's Cabinet. A very prominent American's offspring, who went north a few decades back and won fame and fortune, faced deportation. The ministers were pressed to decide whether to have their parliamentary majority yank this popular and successful American's visa. His foes, a vocal band of nationalists, had waged a bitter campaign, while millions of friends remained loyal although somewhat placid.

Who was this controversial American? Well, it happens to be son-of-*Time*, or, as the news magazine calls itself above the 49th parallel, *Time Canada*. And its "visa" has been a special tax law, vital to its extraordinary success as evidenced by 3 million Canadian readers.

This is not a unique case, for *Time Canada* is but one of many wares which America's mass media mercantilists have peddled abroad so successfully that they, like multinational corporations, are significant and controversial transnational forces.

Not only are images of the United States presented around the world by globetrotting American magazines, news agencies, movies, and TV shows, but foreigners rely also on these media to be windows on third countries. What a Berliner knows about political developments in Japan may well come to him via a U.S. news agency; thus Germany's window on the world is partly through New York, headquarters of the Associated Press and United Press International. Indeed, foreigners even rely on U.S. media to mirror their own societies. The family of nations, particularly non-Communist members, have been bonded in recent times by a "made-in-America" mass media central nervous system.

Consider, for example, that besides the global reach of the giant American news agencies (AP and UPI), *The New York Times* news service is transmitted daily to 136 of the world's major newspapers, and *The Washington Post-Los Angeles Times* joint news service is purchased by about 60 other foreign newspapers. This means that in Hong Kong, for instance, it is possible to read China-watching stories written there by *New York Times* correspondents whose copy, after being edited in New York, is cabled back to *The South China Morning Post* and *The Hong Kong Standard*.

Or consider that American television companies earned $130 million in 1973 from foreign sales of programs (mainly entertainment shows). Who abroad watched "All in the Family" and "Gunsmoke"? It's easier to say who didn't:

William H. Read is a Research Fellow at the Harvard University Center for International Affairs. Reprinted with permission from *Foreign Policy, XVIII,* Spring 1975. Copyright by National Affairs, Inc.

Chinese, Mongolians, North Koreans, North Vietnamese, and Albanians. One of the major TV programming distributors with a six-language catalogue boasts, "our audience is everywhere," by which is meant it sells in more than 100 countries doing business from offices in Toronto, São Paulo, Zug (Switzerland), Rome, Beirut, Madrid, London, Tokyo, Sydney, and Seoul.

That distributor, Viacom International, Inc., while not nearly so large as Exxon or ITT, is no less a multinational corporation than either. In fact, TV program distributors are the inheritors of an early multinational enterprise—the American film industry. The development pattern of the movie business—national saturation followed by exporting and internationalization—is a course print and electronic media unwittingly may be following. The foreign policy implications of internationalization—a process by which an organization becomes *controlled* by parties of more than one nationality—are probably the same for the mass media as for a manufacturing firm. Such an organization is expected to be less inclined to faithfully support Washington's policies. The days when Henry Luce spoke of "our policy," reflecting the outlook of both *Time* and the Department of State, have faded not only with Luce's passing, but also as it acquired a 1.3 million international circulation.

Whether the mass media support government policies (as *Time* did, for example, by selecting General Westmoreland as "man of the year") or oppose them (as *The New York Times* did by publishing the "Pentagon Papers") is essentially an internal matter. But there are foreign public opinion implications. The more direct foreign policy considerations stem from the unhappiness of other governments, which feel their countries are victimized by powerful American media mercantilists. The issue can be described in terms of free flow of information versus what may be called the right of information privacy. For years, this was mainly an East-West dispute with the Communist jamming of our short-wave broadcasts as the focal point. Then a North-South dimension emerged. And now, in the case of direct satellite broadcasting (DBS), it's everybody against us, with the United States opposed to any restrictions on DBS, while all others prefer some controls.

The controversy over the transnational outpouring of information from the United States, of which DBS is only the tip of the iceberg, can no longer be analyzed in Cold War terms, as not much useful mileage can be gained by driving that ideological vehicle today. Furthermore, some of our best friends are crying the loudest. A good example is Canada. In one battle, a popular Canadian author, Richard Rohmer, attacked *Time* for "shoving the American point of view at all its readers in Canada" (where the magazine's circulation figures, as a percentage of population, are higher than in the United States). Rohmer had a specific complaint about *Time Canada*. One of his books was then first on *The Toronto Star's* best-seller list, but was not included among *Time Canada's* list of best-selling books (in the United States). There is also controversy in broadcasting, where the Canadian Broadcasting Corporation has established "Canadian content" goals which limit foreign (read American) imports.

About a year ago, a symposium on the international flow of TV programs was held at the University of Tampere, Finland. During the meeting, the attitude of those critical of what has been termed "information (or cultural) imperialism" was summarized by Finnish President Urho Kekkonen. He said that he had "read a calculation that two-thirds of the communications disseminated throughout the world originate in one way or another in the United States." He felt that this constituted an unacceptable, one-way, unbalanced flow that did not possess the depth and range which the principles of freedom of speech require.

Such a harsh conclusion seems prematurely unjustified, given the paucity of data so far collected about transnational media. But the concern is genuine. What is the cultural impact of our news agencies, magazines, and television programs abroad? How do they affect public opinion in other countries? What does this mean for foreign policies? These important questions have not yet been given adequate examination.

The Information Elite

Some preliminary work by researchers of the U.S. Information Agency concludes that a so-called "international information elite" is growing. This group, an Agency document says, is "linked by many factors transcending national, cultural, or regional differences. These factors have mainly to do with increasing similarities in their education, in their exposure to contemporary ideas, and *through increasing use of international media.*" (The emphasis is mine.)

A typical member of the international information elite could be described as "a 37-year-old non-American, who has attended either a university or technical school, probably is now a business executive earning $13,386 a year, which enables him to own a car, buy life insurance, and occasionally travel to foreign countries." That happens to be a composite profile of a person who either subscribes to *Time* or buys a copy at a newsstand each week outside the U.S.

Not so many years ago when this country was deeply engaged in ideological warfare, the international spread of our mass media would have been a welcome development. It still can be, and should be. For our ability to influence foreign events rests partly on "presence," and the international dissemination of our mass media is a highly visible sign of U.S. overseas involvement and is, on balance, a credible American representative. But this has not been, nor will it be, a trouble-free development.

TV-Watching Abroad

Anyone who has traveled abroad knows that American TV programs are as popular abroad as Coca-Cola. Foreign sales in virtually every country of the world account for nearly a fifth of the producers' revenue. The biggest buyers in dollar terms are Canada, Japan, Australia, and the United Kingdom. But in terms of broadcast hours—it is estimated that between 100,000 and 200,000 hours of programming are exported annually from the United States—the distribution is approximately equal in Latin America, Asia, and Europe.

The United States has a dominant position in the international TV program marketplace; a domination achieved in the now classic operating methods of many multinational enterprises. Television, a highly technical field, developed rapidly in the United States and saturated the domestic market in a few years. Initial random sales of popular programs to stations abroad sparked interest and created overseas markets before there was significant competition.

A boom in overseas sales during the last decade appears to have peaked, partly due to growing foreign competition. Still, American firms have a lion's share of the profitable international TV market. The following table, taken from [a 1973] study, illuminates two striking facts about world television commerce:

1. There is considerable empirical evidence supporting the charge that the flow of information is essentially one-way. There were only three stations [of the sample] which imported as little as 1 per cent of their programs: the American commercial stations (which certainly must be the world's most prolific television broadcasters), the Japanese educational station, and the Chinese station in Shanghai. Small and less-developed countries, on the other hand, often imported a majority of their programs.

2. The flow of TV programs is far from unrestricted, although only a few countries—such as Canada and Britain—actually have established quotas. Other apparently potent limiting factors are political considerations and cultural barriers: witness the comparatively low percentage of programs imported by France—9 per cent, the Soviet Union—5 per cent, China—1 per cent, Japan's commercial station—10 per cent. Even when percentages are higher, these factors

Television Programming 1970–1971

Country/Television Station	% Imported	% Domestic
Canada/CBC*	34	66
Canada/RC*	46	54
United States/16 commercial*	1	99
United States/18 noncommercial*	2	98
Argentina/Canal 9	10	90
Argentina/Canal 11	30	70
Chile*	55	45
Colombia	34	66
Dominican Republic/Canal 3/9	50	50
Guatemala*	84	16
Mexico/Telesistema	39	61
Uruguay*	62	38
West Germany/ARD	23	77
West Germany/ZDF	30	70
Finland	40	60
France	9	91
Iceland	67	33
Ireland	54	46
Italy	13	87
Netherlands	23	77
Norway	39	61
Portugal	35	65
Sweden	33	67
Switzerland/Deutsch*	24	76
United Kingdom/BBC	12	88
United Kingdom/TV*	13	87
Bulgaria	45	55
German Democratic Republic	32	68
Hungary	40	60
Poland	17	83
Rumania	27	73
Soviet Union/Cent. 1st*	5	95
Soviet Union/Estonia	12	88
Yugoslavia/Beograd	18	82
Australia	57	43
People's Republic of China/Shanghai*	1	99
Republic of China/Enterprise	22	78
Hong Kong/RTV & HK-TVB (English)*	40	60
Hong Kong/RTV & HK-TVB Guiness*	31	69
Japan/NHK General	4	96
Japan/NHK Educational	1	99
Japan/Commercial Stations	10	90

This data is based on sample week(s); all other figures are based on the full year 1970–1971. Repeats are included.

Television Programming 1970–1971 (contd.) Country/Television Station	% Imported	% Domestic
Republic of Korea/Tong-yang	31	69
Malaysia	71	29
New Zealand*	75	25
Pakistan	35	65
Philippines/ABC, CBV	29	71
Singapore*	78	22
Thailand/Army TV*	18	82
Dubai	72	28
Iraq	52	48
Israel	55	45
Kuwait	56	44
Lebanon/Telibor	40	60
Saudi Arabia/Riyadh TV*	31	69
Saudi Arabia/Aramco TV*	100	0
United Arab Republic	41	59
Yemen*	57	43
Ghana*	27	73
Uganda*	19	81
Zambia*	64	36

*This data is based on sample week(s); all other figures are based on the full year 1970–1971. Repeats are included.

still can come into play. For example, during the Allende administration in Chile, where 55 per cent of TV programs were imported, an episode of "Mission Impossible," which dramatized the fall of a Castro-like regime, was cancelled. And in Saudi Arabia, where 31 per cent of programs shown were imported, the initial selections were "Wild Kingdom" and "Victory at Sea," neither of which showed unveiled women.

An unanticipated sensitive area encountered by some American television merchants, and one which, as most domestic station owners know, can be very profitable, was the area of operations. American expertise and capital flowed abundantly to TV stations around the world during the early and mid-1960s. NBC, for example, had financial interests in TV stations in Australia, Venezuela, Mexico, Jamaica, Barbados, and Hong Kong and management and technical assistance contracts in Saudi Arabia, South Vietnam, West Germany, Wales, Mexico, Lebanon, Sweden, Peru, the Philippines, Argentina, Yugoslavia, Jamaica, Kenya, Nigeria, and Sierra Leone. In recent years, however, NBC's international business dwindled, partly because, an NBC official says, "foreign television systems became more and more self-sustaining."

Moreover, some seemingly promising ventures, such as Time-Life's broadcasting activities in Latin America, came a cropper for deeper reasons. "To make money you've got to control an operation and no government is going to let outsiders control its television," says Barry Zorthian, former head of the now defunct Time-Life Broadcasting, which once was deeply involved in Venezuela, Argentina, and Brazil.

Today the question increasingly being faced by U.S. program exporters is whether foreign stations, most of which are government-operated, will continue to import large quantities of American shows. It may be premature, but it is not unreasonable to conjecture that the U.S. television production industry will internationalize as did its Hollywood film-making predecessors. There have already been some coproductions of television programs in foreign countries which bypass quotas and assure access to at least one important foreign market. Last summer, for instance, U.S. public television screened "The Impeachment of Andrew Johnson," a coproduction between Washington's National Center for Television and the British Broadcasting Corporation.

If the TV industry takes this route, two results may be anticipated: (1) the television production industry should become less controversial and, at the same time, (2) cross-national cooperation will mean diminution of any participating nation's ability to control the cultural and social content of its TV programming. The explanation is simple—joint ventures undercut cries of imperialism, and they also require production of programs suitable for ("salable to" is perhaps more apt) at least two countries.

The Print Media

The transnational dissemination of American print media, unlike TV, is not comparatively new nor does it reach the vast foreign audiences that television does. Its expansion into the world market has occurred under various circumstances.

Reader's Digest, with a foreign readership of 100 million, in 13 language editions, brought out its first foreign language edition—Spanish—in 1940 in an attempt by its patriotic publisher, DeWitt Wallace, to counter Axis influence in Latin America. Thirty-three years later *Newsweek* launched what it proclaimed to be "the world's first *truly* international newsweekly" intended to inform "corporate decision-makers and government leaders around the world."

With less ballyhoo, American news agencies grew to the point that UPI has subscribers in 113 foreign countries and territories and says that its dispatches are translated into 48 languages. News agency logos have been joined abroad by those of the U.S. supplemental news services and the unique *International Herald Tribune* (in which *The New York Times* and *The Washington Post* are part owners), which is available at newsstands in over 70 countries. When the Bamboo curtain lifted a bit, AP and UPI quickly signed exchange agreements with Hsinhua, the Chinese news agency. Our print media have not cornered the international market, of course. But the fact is that Agence France Presse and *The Economist* are not really dangerous competitors for UPI and *Time*.

How News Travels in a High-Speed World

In today's worldwide AP communications network a straight line often is not the quickest route between two points.

To make the point, take a major news story breaking in Kuala Lumpur, Malaysia. It involves a top Japanese personality which makes it paramount news in Tokyo. It's also a big story in the United States and the rest of the world.

As the jetliner flies, it's 3,000 northward miles from Kuala Lumpur to Tokyo, where AP subscribers publish around-the-clock editions that run to 10 million copies a day. It's nearly 10,000 miles eastward to New York.

Correspondent Hari Subramanian writes the story and it moves from Kuala Lumpur via teleprinter. Before the operator finishes transmitting the 200-word urgent, it is being received in Tokyo—and by AP members around the world.

Here's how the story is routed:

Kuala Lumpur has an AP circuit that carries the story southeast to Singapore. There it is automatically relayed northward via undersea cable to Hong Kong. Autorelay moves it again by undersea cable southeast to Manila, then eastward to a cablehead in San Francisco and overland relay to New York. Circuit delay—elapsed time—one second. At New York it is available to the AP A wire and for overseas relay to Europe.

A New York computer turns the story around, sends it back via land lines and microwave to the earth-satellite relay station at Marysville, Calif.

From there it is bounced off an Intelsat IV satellite parked above the Equator 22,300 miles above the Gilbert Islands in the South Pacific. The downward bounce from the Intelsat IV carries the story into Tokyo — seconds from the time it was transmitted from Kuala Lumpur.

The story has traveled halfway 'round the world eastbound, and back again westbound, bounced from tropical Malaysia to wintry New York to the Equator and again to chilly Tokyo.

There's a comparable program for Wirephoto, which today has the capacity to transmit a top-priority picture from almost anywhere and deliver it within 12 minutes to just about every major newspaper in the world — via the Wirephoto networks in the U.S. and overseas and interchange arrangements with such national services as Russia's Tass and China's Hsinhua.

Suppose there's a bulletin picture from Frankfurt, Germany: It moves over AP land and microwave lines to the European network into London. Automatic relays direct it to New York via cable or satellite and to the Middle East, Australia, and the Asian subcontinent nations of India, Pakistan, and Bangladesh by cable and radiophoto circuits.

New York relays the picture automatically via satellite to Tokyo, via radiophoto and cable to Latin America.

Meantime the AP's photo computer is receiving the London signal, modifying it to the U.S.A. standard, and transmitting to the Wirephoto network.

All in a matter of minutes. The picture is completed in Miami, Chicago, Los Angeles, and Tokyo at almost the same minute it's finished at Frankfurt—or London, Copenhagen, Johannesburg, Sydney. Laserphoto reception puts it on editors' desks immediately.

Why the roundabout routing? Eugene A. Juerling, AP's coordinator of world-wide communications, says that studies show a longer route often is faster and more efficient than a direct line.

Moving into the main lines of world communications means that the most advanced equipment is available. That means improved speed, higher accuracy, and very often lower rates. In this age of high-speed communications, distance becomes a relatively minor factor, particularly when measured with reliability.

Routing through areas of high-density traffic is a key part of AP operations for the largest communications network of any news agency in the world. The AP network today collects news from every corner of the world and distributes news to more than 3,500 member and subscriber newspapers and broadcasters in 125 nations.

Historically, the main line of AP world communications has been New York to London. At this point in the technological progress of that service, there are 33 separate news wire channels and two photo channels for two-way service. Primary New York-London routing is by leased cable, with optional satellite lines available at the flick of switches in the New York Communications Department, now headed by Chief of Communications Dominick LiCausi.

Much of the news interchange with Europe, the Middle East, and Africa moves through London's computers. Strategic bureaus in Europe, among them Frankfurt, Paris, and Stockholm, are computerized. A number of others will be converted this year.

All major bureaus in Latin America file news directly into the New York computer complex. The AP report in English and Spanish comes back to them in many modern transmission systems.

A sidelight: CRT consoles at the New York World Service Desk are multilingual, as are the staffers who man them. The same CRT on which a story is written in English is regularly used by editors who translate the story into Spanish for relay south of the border.

Satellite circuits connect New York to Santiago, Lima, Buenos Aires, and Rio de Janeiro. Cables link New York to San Juan, Caracas, Bogota, and Santo Domingo. Land lines and microwave systems exchange news among New York, Mexico City, Costa Rica, El Salvador, Panama, and the other nations of Central America.

The whole worldwide AP communications system has been striding in seven-league boots for three decades. And the pace is accelerating.

[Ed. note: United Press International's international satellite system is similar. See the *AP Log* and *UPI Reporter* for a continuous update of these and domestic computerized operations.]

Like TV, U.S. print media frequently are controversial, although foreign leaders tend to view the putative dangers of print more in political than cultural terms. Virtually every week either *Time* or *Newsweek* (or both) is censored, banned, or confiscated by a government somewhere. News agencies are usually more immune, because their copy passes first through the hands of local editors.

All this is taken as a fact of life in international business by the print merchants, most of whom are deeply committed to (i.e., financially dependent

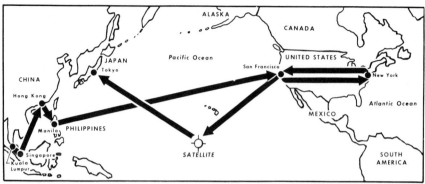

THE LONG WAY IS THE BEST WAY— This map by Walter Harasek, Wirephoto's
chief artist, traces the news story route from Kuala Lumpur to Tokyo — via New York.

upon) continued successful foreign operations. To insure success, these communicators have adapted their organizations to not merely exporting an American product, but to tailoring their information wares for foreign consumption.

There are differing opinions, however, on the extent to which editorial content should be modified and the way in which it should be marketed to foreign
audiences. *Time,* influenced by the success of its Canadian edition, convinced
that a strong American identity remains crucial, and mindful that it must offer
something more than its many national imitators, is thinking regional. *Time*
launched a European edition in March 1973 modeled on its Canadian format,
adding a short, usually four- to six-page section of European news to an otherwise
U.S. magazine. *Time Asia* may follow. *Newsweek,* with a global strategy in
mind, began publishing an international edition. Its editorial content is about 50
per cent different from its U.S. edition.

Before American publishers began adapting editorial content for non-American readers, they already had adopted geographic advertising editions, enabling
advertisers to reach audiences in specified areas such as the Atlantic region,
Common Market countries, or the British Isles.

Even though these and other adaptive processes have occurred, there is still
the question of socio-political influence. That question can be debated from either
a push or a pull viewpoint. Is *Time Europe* helping to lead the continent to
greater cohesion or merely following a trend? Is *Newsweek International* cham-
pioning global interdependence or just reflecting it? Either way, both have made
commitments, and these commitments, it should be emphasized, have an American perspective.

A Question
of Influence

American mass media certainly have a dominant position in the international
marketplace, but seldom do they overwhelm a single national market. (Notable
exceptions are *Time* and *Reader's Digest* in Canada, where these two American
publications account for more than 50 per cent of all magazine advertising in

the country.)[1] Declassified U.S. Information Agency media habit surveys reveal that U.S. mass media products are usually part of an informational mix, and the U.S. position varies from country to country.

There are, however, some commonly discernible influences. Standards are set by the American mass media, as evidenced, for example, by the numerous imitations of the *Time* and *Life* formats or the duplication of scheduling of television programs. Also, much information gets disseminated simply because of the economics of mass distribution. (I recall, for example, that newspapers in Southeast Asia printed the same news agency accounts of the Vietnam war as did the U.S. press, instead of more relevant stories about social, political, and economic issues in their neighboring country.)

This exposure to U.S. values has prompted consideration as to whether there is a causal relationship between U.S. mass media and certain desired or undesired (depending on your viewpoint) attitudes and actions in foreign countries. Opinions vary. U.S. diplomats argue that our media generate an aura of credibility and stability for the United States—net pluses in the conduct of foreign policy. Foreign leaders, especially those average politicians who seek to divine the national will and then champion its causes, can get caught between competing demands. On the one hand, there may be apprehensions about cultural and informational encroachments, perhaps prompted by and/or coupled with protectionist demands by indigenous mass media producers. On the other hand, there may be popular appetites for consuming U.S. exports, the supposed benefits of favorable international publicity, or sought-after local investment. Finally, there are a few social scientists (most have ignored international media) who share Professor Herbert I. Schiller's worry about the possible emergence of "knowledge conglomerates."

How did such U.S. influence come about? In reality, the pervasiveness of American electronic and print media abroad grows not out of some conceptual design, but out of the same interacting phenomenon that enabled the widespread growth of our multinational corporations. The media reaped the benefits of our large capitalist system, the development of technology at home, the post-war economic and political positions of the United States, and the increasingly international use of English. Its penetration of foreign markets, however, goes beyond economic impact. It is a profound challenge to cultural integrity as well.

John Kenneth Galbraith, the Canadian-born Harvard economist, has said that while his former countrymen "talk about economic autonomy," they might well be advised to be "much more concerned about maintaining the cultural integrity of the broadcasting system and with making sure that Canada has an active, independent theatre, book publishing industry, newspapers, magazines, and schools of poets and painters." These, in Galbraith's opinion, "are the things that count." Few intellectuals would disagree, but popular appetites remain hungry for American magazines, TV dramas, and the rest. The middleman is the official who sits in Ottawa while the masses happily watch "All in the

1. *Time* and *Reader's Digest* have shared a unique status in Canada. They were specifically exempted from a tax law making advertising in foreign magazines nondeductible. In other words, a Canadian company advertising in *Time* deducted the cost from its taxable income but could not do so for ads placed in *Newsweek*. Ed.

Family," and while a small elite group screams that he should pull the plug on the value-loaded American world of Archie Bunker.

Nations which have been politically and economically dependent on the United States have, perhaps unwittingly, become culturally dependent too. And we know even less about the impact of multinational mass media than we do about multinational businesses.

Putting aside the closed-door stance of Communist countries, what might be a reasonable policy on this issue of foreign governments to follow? I suppose the ideal goal would be to attempt a balance which would preserve native culture while remaining open to the Americanized world culture. Such a two-tiered approach may be put to the test shortly, as new technology, such as satellites, has offered American mass media mercantilists new means to turn their present international communications flow into a torrent. Hours of as yet inconclusive United Nations debate have taken place about direct broadcasting by satellite.

Will the answer be found calmly in the open international marketplace? Or, if there is an outcry, will it be muted, even stilled, by reciting the U.N. Declaration on Human Rights' freedom of information passage? Perhaps. But not for much longer, I suspect. And if I'm right, then we may soon be facing an international cultural crisis just as we have had to face an international economic crisis. "Cultural protectionism" may be on its way.

Bibliography

This listing supplements both the Read and Schiller articles, nos. 45 and 46. An excellent overview of the development of national and international systems of broadcasting is Walter B. Emery's study of the same name, sub-titled *Their History, Operation and Control* (Michigan State University Press, 1969). Another book that provides a certain kind of overview, primarily directed toward issues, is Heinz-Dietrich Fischer and John C. Merrill, eds., *International and Intercultural Communication* (Hastings House, 1976). Supplementary sources are: Andrew R. Horowitz, "The Global Bonanza of American TV," *More*, May 1975, pp. 6–8; Tapio Varis, "Global Traffic in Television," *Journal of Communication*, Winter 1974, part of a special issue on international communication, or see the larger report from which his article is drawn: Kaarle Nordenstreng and Tapio Varis, *Television Traffic—A One-Way Street? A Survey and Analysis of the International Flow of Television Programme Material*, Paper No. 70, in the Reports and Papers on Mass Communication Series (Unesco, 1974); and Alan Wells, *Picture-Tube Imperialism: The Impact of U.S. Television on Latin America* (Orbis Books, 1972). For a closely related problem on the use and control of satellite communication, see especially Olof Hultén, "The Intelsat System: Some Notes on Television Utilization of Satellite Technology," *Gazette*, 1973, pp. 29–37, and the special issue of *Society*, September/October 1975, on "Communications vs. Powers," especially the article by Ithiel de Sola Pool, "Direct-Broadcast Satellites and Cultural Integrity," pp. 47–56. An article dealing with the political development of Intelsat is Steven A. Levy, "INTELSAT: Technology, Politics and the Transformation of a Regime," *International Organization*, Summer 1975, pp. 656–680.

Recent studies include Jeremy Teinstall, *The Media Are American* (Columbia University Press, 1977), and Glen Fisher, *American Communication in a Global Society* (Ablex Publishing Corp., 1979). For a contrary view, see Kaarl Nordenstreng and Herbert I. Schiller, eds., *National Sovereignty and International Communication* (Ablex Publishing Corp., 1979).

The Electronic Invaders

Herbert I. Schiller

46

For twenty-five years, the "free flow of information" between nations has been a widely sought objective of the United States, generally supported in the international community. Enunciated and promoted by the United Nations Educational, Scientific, and Cultural Organization (UNESCO), with more than a little U.S. prodding, there was general, if not unanimous, agreement that an unimpeded communications traffic was a good thing and that people everywhere benefited when it occurred. If the concept was not always respected in practice, at least it was never frontally attacked as a principle.

A dramatic reversal of this outlook is now underway. It is becoming apparent to many nations that the free flow of information, much like free trade in an earlier time, strengthens the strong and submerges the weak. In the case of information, the powerful communicator states overwhelm the less developed countries with their information and cultural messages.

Though information that moves internationally flows through many channels—movies, books, periodicals, television programs, radio broadcasts, tourists, merchandise exports, cultural exchanges—the medium which has brought the issue into focus is the new technology of communications satellites, broadcasting from space. Communications satellites which will soon bring television programs *directly* into individual living rooms across the globe (an informed guess puts direct satellite broadcasting less than ten years away) is forcing a long hard look at just what imagery already is flowing across national boundaries through more conventional means.

Currently, television is either imported on film or tape and used locally; moves across contiguous national frontiers (most Canadians, for example, can and do watch U.S. programs from stations across the border); or is picked up from communications satellites by ground receiving stations, under *national* control, and distributed to local audiences through national networks. Broadcasting directly into home receivers from sky-borne satellites which respect no national frontiers will be accomplished with more powerful satellites and modified receivers, both of which are already technologically feasible but not yet operable.

Two decades of exposure to U.S. television exports ("I Spy," "Mission Impossible," "Laugh In") make the possibility of direct, unmediated television transmission from the United States to *any* home in *any* nation a cause for traumatic anxiety in international communications-cultural circles.

Herbert I. Schiller is professor of communications at the University of California, San Diego. His books are *Communication and Cultural Domination* (International Arts and Science Press, 1976), *Mass Communications and American Empire* (Kelley, 1969), and *The Mind Managers* (Beacon Press, 1973). This article is reprinted with permission from *The Progressive,* August 1973. Copyright 1973 by the Progressive Publishing Co.

After all, television is a global phenomenon. In 1970 more than 250 million television sets were in use around the world in 130 countries. The United States had 84 million, Western Europe had 75 million, the Soviet Union 30 million, and Japan 23 million. China had only 200,000 sets, Indonesia had 90,000 and India a mere 20,000. Yet other developing nations had considerable numbers of receivers. Brazil, for example, had 6.5 million sets; Argentina, 3.5 million; Venezuela, 720,000; the Philippines, 400,000; South Korea, 418,000; Nigeria, 75,000; and Egypt, 475,000.

The President of the United Nations General Assembly, Poland's Stanislaw Trepczynski, expressed anxiety over unrestricted transmissions at the opening of the 27th General Assembly [1972]: "In an age of unprecedented development of information media, of tremendous flow of ideas and of artistic achievements, concern for preserving the characteristics peculiar to the different cultures becomes a serious problem for mankind."

UNESCO itself, the acknowledged guardian if not parent of the free flow of information concept, has had some second thoughts recently about its hitherto favored principle. In October, 1972, it adopted a declaration of "Guiding Principles on the Use of Satellite Broadcasting for the Free Flow of Information." Article IX of the draft read: ". . . it is necessary that States, taking into account the principle of freedom of information, *reach or promote prior agreements* concerning direct satellite broadcasting to the population of countries other than the country of origin of transmission." (Emphasis added.)

The U.N. General Assembly passed a similar resolution in November by a vote of 102 to 1—the United States was the single dissenting voice.

A sample of national views, expressed in the United Nations' Political Committee before the vote, is illuminating for what it reveals about the widespread feelings and fears over cultural matters of which we hear or see little in our own mass media. For example, the French delegate asserted that "each state has the right to protect its culture." The delegate from Colombia expressed fear of "an ideological occupation of the world by the superpowers and their advertising mentality." Zaire's delegate said his country had been subject to subversion by private radios and was therefore aware of the possible danger of direct television broadcasting by satellites. His country, he added, wanted to be able to have control over information from outside. The Minister for Home Affairs of India said direct television broadcasting could be used to generate mistrust and conflict or for undesirable or harmful propaganda, and such use "would certainly constitute interference in the internal affairs of States." The delegate from Chile said that if new space techniques were not subjected to international rules, Latin America would be subjected to the political, economic, and cultural contagion of the large imperialist monopolies of North America. He added that the people of Latin America were rebelling against imperialism which was trying to impose on them a culture contrary to their well-being.

Aware of the extent and depth of these national sentiments, in both UNESCO and the U.N. General Assembly, that cut across ideological lines, the official U.S. position has tried to deflect the argument into a discussion of technological feasibility. Former Ambassador George Bush in the United Nations and chief U.S. delegate William Jones in UNESCO minimized the dangers of cultural invasion and insisted that direct broadcasting was many years away and therefore no cause for immediate concern or organizational effort to regulate it.

Ironically but predictably, the U.S. diplomatic effort, formulated to sidestep an issue which unites most of the world against America as the foremost source of global communications pollution, incurred the wrath of the media moguls in the United States. Unwilling to accept a tactical retreat, insistent on their right to dominate world information flows, and indifferent to the needs and opinions of weaker states no matter how numerous, the no-nonsense American media managers reacted sharply.

Frank Stanton, then CBS president, member of the Presidentially appointed U.S. Advisory Commission on Information, and longtime chairman of the Radio Free Europe organization, wrote a lengthy article, "Will They Stop Our Satellites?" published in *The New York Times* October 22, 1972. In it he claimed that "the rights of Americans to speak to whomever they please, when they please, are [being] bartered away." His chief objection to the UNESCO draft of Guiding Principles on the Use of Satellite Broadcasting is that censorship is being imposed by provisions which permit each nation to reach prior agreement with transmitting nations concerning the character of the broadcasts.

Stanton finds the right of nations to control the character of the messages transmitted into their territories both dangerous and a gross violation of the U.S. Constitution's provision for freedom of speech: "The rights which form the framework of our Constitution, the principles asserted in the Universal Declaration of Human Rights, the basic principle of the free movement of ideas, are thus ignored."

Stanton apparently believes that the U.S. Constitution, fine document that it is, should be the binding law for the international community, whether it wishes it or not. Yet as long ago as 1946 the Hutchins Commission on Freedom of the Press rejected the easy assumption that the espousal of free speech in the U.S. Constitution was the basis for insisting on an unrestricted international free flow of communication.

"The surest antidote for ignorance and deceit," the Commission noted, "is widest possible exchange of objectively realistic information—*true* information, not merely *more* information; *true* information, not merely, as those who would have us simply write the First Amendment into international law seem to suggest, the *unhindered flow* of information! There is evidence that a mere quantitative increase in the flow of words and images across national borders may replace ignorance with prejudice and distortion rather than with understanding." (Emphasis in text.)

Moreover, is the freedom of speech that the U.S. Constitution guarantees to the individual applicable to multi-national communications corporations, of which Stanton is so powerful an advocate? Are CBS, ABC, and RCA "individuals" in the sense that most people understand the term? And, if a nation does not have the right to regulate and control the information flowing into and past its borders, who does? CBS? ITT? Stanton?

Stanton's view assumes an identity between the profit-making interests of a handful of giant communications conglomerates and the informational needs of the American people. The error is compounded when the same corporate interests are placed above the needs of all nations for cultural sovereignty. The great majority of Americans have absolutely no capability, financial or techno-logical, of speaking "to whomever they please, when they please," outside their own country (or inside, for that matter). The voices and images which are now, and will be, transmitted overseas are those produced by our familiar communi-cations combines, scarcely grassroots organizations.

Stanton, in the best prose of the Cold War decades, argues that "leaders of too many countries have a deadly fear of information which could lead their people to topple the regimes in power." Possibly. More likely, many leaders have a "deadly fear" of the cultural effects of the programming the major U.S. commercial networks would be pumping into their countrymen's television sets. Some leaders are aware that many Americans are troubled with the character of the material that floods their homes. They know that there is an increasing number of parents who are outraged with the daily television shows that assault their children's minds (and from which, incidentally, CBS in 1970 derived $16.5 million in profits).

Perhaps those who are concerned with national cultural development in other countries do not want to wait the twenty-five years it took before Americans began to question the effects of exposure of their children and themselves to cartoons, commercials, and the likes of "Dragnet," "Mod Squad," "I Spy," and other well known commercial offerings.

Arthur Goodfriend, a former State Department consultant, recently wrote in *The Annals,* "In an era of electronic communication . . . what is imperialism? Is it simply a policy of territorial extension? Or does it embrace the invasion of human minds?"

Should the international community be criticized for also asking this ques-tion? International regulation of direct satellite broadcasting is not an example of censorship that strikes at "the fundamental principle of free speech." It is a necessary measure to enable all societies to have a role in determining their cultural destinies.

Stanton and his friends—*The New York Times* supported his position editorially and complained about "censorship of the global air waves"—have it wrong. Liberty is not threatened. CBS profits could be. Freedom of thought is not challenged. RCA's markets may be.

The UNESCO declaration of "Guiding Principles" and the U.N. General Assembly's resolution regulating space broadcasting will not eliminate the cul-tural domination by a few that already exists in the world. They do signify, however, that the brief era of American global/cultural hegemony, established under the seemingly innocuous principle of "the free flow of information," is coming to an end.

There will be difficulties in the transitional period ahead. Some arbitrary national actions are inevitable. But the worldwide homogenization of culture is too high a price to pay for the maintenance of an arrangement which produces benefits for only a tiny cluster of U.S. communications conglomerates.

Bibliography

The bibliography that follows the Read article, no. 45, also is useful here. For a further exposition of Schiller's views, see his latest book *Communication and Cultural Domination* (International Arts and Sciences Press, 1976) and his article "Freedom From the 'Free Flow,' " *Journal of Communication,* Winter 1974, pp, 110–117. Also concerned about the effects of American television upon other cultures is Carroll V. Newsom, "Communication Satellites: A New Hazard for World Culture," *Educational Broadcasting Review,* April 1973, pp. 77–85. The best single source of information on national and international mass communication is *World Communications: A 200-Country Survey of Press, Radio, Television and Film* (Unesco Press, 1975). This publication provides relevant facts and figures from around the world as well as special chapters on problem areas, such as communication via satellites and training facilities in mass media. A number of publications from the Aspen Institute Program on Communications and Society deal with international media problems. These include: *Regulation of Direct Broadcasting from Satellites* by Benno Signitzer (Praeger, 1976), *International Commercial Satellite Communications* by Marcellus S. Snow (Praeger, 1975), and *Economic Policy Problems in Satellite Communications* (Praeger, 1977) by Snow and Joseph N. Pelton.

The rising controversy over the handling of Third World news led to a statement by UNESCO on the control of information. That crisis of late 1978 will be followed by more arguments. Background information on that important development in international communications includes a set of articles in *Journal of Communication,* Autumn 1978. Stanley Meisler, a foreign correspondent for the *Los Angeles Times,* wrote "Covering the Third World (Or Trying To)" for the *Columbia Journalism Review,* November/December 1978. See *Columbia Journalism Review* for other international communication pieces, such as "Dateline Moscow: Censorship of Our TV News," September-October 1975; "Kissinger and the Press," May-June 1974; and "Chile: Why We Missed the Story," March-April 1976. The *UPI Reporter* and *AP Log* also have carried information on the coverage of foreign news and the use of new satellite equipment. John Hohenberg's two books provide details on the history of foreign reporting. They are *Foreign Correspondence* (Columbia University Press, 1964) and *Free Press, Free People* (Columbia University Press, 1971). Robert W. Desmond's 1977 book *The Information Process* (University of Iowa Press, 1978) traces foreign reporting to the 20th century. Theodore H. White's *In Search of History* (Harper & Row, 1978) is one of the best accounts of the life of a foreign correspondent.

Multiplying Media Debates

When the last edition of this book was being prepared, in 1976, there was a great preoccupation in the United States with the power of The Media. In the aftermath of Watergate and Vietnam—and during the Carter-Ford election campaign—average persons and pundits alike were wondering about the performance, politics, ethical standards, and financial interests of media persons and organizations. At the same time, thoughtful media representatives were concerned over new efforts by government officials on all levels to curb "news leaks."

Not much has changed. The general level of public understanding about The Media remains quite low, despite the attention given news coverage, television commercials, new movies, best-selling books, and the world of public relations and advertising.

One thing should be kept in focus during these debates about media performance and responsibility. There are in this nation many persons who do not respect the First Amendment. This became clear during the Nixon years when high government officials attempted to manipulate the public against the press and used illegal means to intimidate those who were reporting events crucial to the survival of this country.

The Congress has continued to debate legislation designed to codify, revise, and reform federal criminal law which contained sections putting greater controls on the flow of information from the government to the public. Formerly called Senate Bill 1, the legislation was passed by the Senate as S 1437 and was being considered by the House as HR 6869. Thomas I. Emerson, professor emeritus of the Yale law school, felt the bill retained "a large number of provisions which individually or in totality are gravely detrimental to the American system of individual rights." Congress is still considering the legislation as we go to press.

At the same time the Carter administration took steps toward enacting classification regulations which alarmed journalists and others who felt the government used its rubber stamps with enough authority. One noted author, David Wise, claimed the United States was approaching an "official secrets act" similar to those of other nations. That too remained to be seen.

If those who wish to pass repressive laws against reporters get their way (whether on the national, state, or local level), the erosion of freedoms will include those of speech, assembly, and political action. The key to all of these is the press freedom guarantee. So while it is admirable that all forms of media action are analyzed by media critics, citizens groups, and even in some cases government agencies (Federal Communications Commission, Federal Trade Commission), it is First Amendment language which makes healthy criticism possible.

Following the resignation of President Nixon, the news media gained in general popularity. While there was a deep sense of dissatisfaction across the land, caused mainly by a disheartening economic crisis, many persons seemed to at least tolerate the "bad news" which came from the television screen or headline. During the Ford and Carter years the national mood continued to be vague and it appeared possible that another Spiro Agnew could turn the people against "the messengers" if deep political splits developed such as those caused by Vietnam and Nixon's policies.

While the credibility of newspersons gained slightly because of Watergate and other scandals, other areas in the media world were opened to heavy criticism. Television networks battled critics over the issues of commercials, hiring practices, and specialized programming such as documentaries.

Of course, some media persons damaged their own credibility and that of the profession by shoddy performances. Too many newspapers continued to push ads at the expense of extra news. Television stations aimed violence-laden news and R-rated entertainment at their vulnerable audiences. Advertising, public relations, and magazine journalists did their share of the damage. In the midst of all of this many men and women carried out their journalism jobs with high integrity and impressive skill.

In the world of television there continued to be concern about the merits of the Fairness Doctrine—and in fact, of the right of government to control the airwaves at all. Public television was still searching for its identity. There was a leveling off of criticism of "happy talk" local news personalities—a product of the early 1970s—but deep puzzlement and worry over the increasing use of valuable airtime for relatively meaningless features and regular slots for nonnews personalities. Many persons gained an appreciation of the immediacy of radio and the professionalism of some radio news operations, including the popular "all-news" stations and quality FM stations.

Concerns about values being disseminated by all forms of media caused a spate of discussions about sex and violence. Some of these debates concerned the alleged sophistication of the general audience and how commonly used words could be put into print or onto the air without embarrassment. Of note was the "7 Dirty Words" case where the Federal Communications Commission ruled certain words, aired by a New York Pacifica station from a George Carlin recording, could not be broadcast in the future. Other debates were about the number of murders (11,000 or 18,000?) an average child would witness on television and in the movie theatre before age 18. Still others dealt with the theory that sex should be discussed more—in a healthy way—and that the real obscenities are unlawful acts, such as those portrayed on violent television police shows and often committed by the actor policemen themselves. Some were worried that the censors in society would continue to allow great amounts of violent material to be displayed—attempting to impose their moral standards mainly in the area of sexually explicit books and movies—and would stop political comments which they deemed "unpatriotic" or "harmful to the public."

While all of this was going on, there was concern that the ethical standards of many media persons—news, entertainment, public relations, advertising, management—were no higher than those of persons in other areas. Out of this comes the realization that while the media institutions sometimes set standards and dictate taste, for the most part they cater to popular demand and reflect current standards and attitudes.

This means the private citizen must constantly demand superior performance of those who bring us the news or make those commercials, while simultaneously

"Where do you guys think you are . . . America?"

protecting the basic rights of those media persons. By logic that includes not only the Walter Cronkites and the editors of the well known newspapers, but also the editors of the local underground newspaper, the off-beat radio station announcer, and those who sometimes irritate us with their overplay of news, creation of disgusting movies, or publication of cheap magazines or books.

The laws of sedition, libel, and obscenity offer protection against dangerous or grossly offensive media acts, while the avalanche of media criticism found in print and on the air today seems to insure constant discussion of media behavior which some would like to improve.

Government and the Media

Our Fragile First Amendment

Michael Emery

47

American journalists were being thrown into jail before the Bill of Rights was 10 years old, despite the First Amendment's underscoring of the concept of press freedom and the "people's right to know."

Since those early days of the republic, events have demonstrated that the First Amendment guarantee of freedom of the press is a fragile thing, its potency largely dependent upon the administration in power, the makeup of the courts, and the support of the people.

This delicate balance was reflected in Richard Nixon's battles with the Senate committee investigating Watergate and later with Judge John J. Sirica and Special Prosecutor Leon Jaworski, before an astonished and confused public.

That was followed by a rash of "gag orders" by judges, arguments over the need for a national shield law to protect reporters' sources, and great anxiety over the ominous nature of Senate Bill 1, called by leading reporters a repressive bill against the flow of information. The future of the First Amendment was not clear, and it probably never will be perfectly protected.

Nearly 200 years ago similar uncertainty and controversy marked the birth of the Bill of Rights.

The 55 founding fathers who drew up the Constitution in 1787 seemed more concerned with the mechanics of setting up a new government than in protecting the people against repression by that government.

James Madison's journal of the secret proceedings, published 53 years later, showed only one reference to press freedom—a motion by delegates from Massachusetts and South Carolina "that the liberty of the press should be inviolably observed."

But most delegates agreed with the argument that "it is unnecessary. The power of Congress does not extend to the press." The motion died, seven states to four.

So it went with proposals to insure other freedoms. Delegates argued that there was no need to mention rights which either were assumed to exist automatically or were under the jurisdiction of state constitutions (religion, assembly, trial by jury, speech, press).

Thus the framers of the Constitution finished their remarkable document that summer in Philadelphia with no Bill of Rights.

State conventions, however, as they met to ratify the Constitution, called for restrictive amendments to prevent misconstrual or abuse of power.

Michael Emery, coeditor of this book, is a member of the journalism faculty at California State University-Northridge. He also is coauthor of the fourth edition of *The Press and America* (Prentice-Hall, 1978) and coeditor of *America's Front Page News, 1690–1970*. This updated overview of press freedom battles originally was prepared for the *Los Angeles Times.*

The first time a printer affirmed the right to publish without prior authority of a government official was in 1721 when James Franklin published his *New-England Courant*, a copy of which is shown here with brother Ben's pseudonym "Silence Dogood" appearing on the right side.

THE   [Nᵒ 58
New-England Courant.

From MONDAY September 3. to MONDAY September 10. 1722.

Quod est in corde sobrii, est in ore ebrii.

To the Author of the New-England Courant.

SIR,   [No XII.

T is no unprofitable tho' unpleasant Pursuit, diligently to inspect and consider the Manners & Conversation of Men, who, insensible of the greatest Enjoyments of humane Life, abandon themselves to Vice from a false Notion of *Pleasure* and *good Fellowship*. A true and natural Representation of any Enormity, is often the best Argument against it and Means of removing it, when the most severe Reprehensions alone, are found ineffectual.

I WOULD in this Letter improve the little Observation I have made on the Vice of *Drunkenness*, the better to reclaim the *good Fellows* who usually pay the Devotions of the Evening to *Bacchus*.

I DOUBT not but *moderate Drinking* has been improv'd for the Diffusion of Knowledge among the ingenious Part of Mankind, who want the Talent of a ready Utterance, in order to discover the Conceptions of their Minds in an entertaining and intelligible Manner. 'Tis true, drinking does not *improve our Faculties*, but it enables us to *use* them; and therefore I conclude, that much Study and Experience, and a little Liquor, are of absolute Necessity for some Tempers, in order to make them accomplish'd Orators. *Dic. Ponder* discovers an excellent Judgment when he is inspir'd with a Glass or two of *Claret*, but he passes for a Fool among those of small Observation, who never saw him the better for Drink. And here it will not be improper to observe, That the moderate Use of Liquor, and a well plac'd and well regulated Anger, often produce this same Effect; and some who cannot ordinarily talk but in broken Sentences and false Grammar, do in the Heat of Passion express themselves with as much Eloquence as Warmth. Hence it is that my own Sex are generally the most eloquent, because the most passionate. " It has been said in the Praise of some Men, " (says an ingenious Author,) that they could talk " whole Hours together upon any thing ; but it " must be owned to the Honour of the other Sex, " that there are many among them who can talk " whole Hours together upon Nothing. I have " known a Woman branch out into a long extempo- " re Dissertation on the Edging of a Petticoat, and " chide her Servant for breaking a China Cup, in all " the Figures of Rhetorick. "

BUT after all it must be consider'd, that no Pleasure can give Satisfaction or prove advantageous to a reasonable Mind, which is not attended with the Restraints of Reason. Enjoyment is not to be found by Excess in any sensual Gratification; but on the contrary, the immoderate Cravings of the Voluptuary, are always succeeded with Loathing and a palled Appetite. What Pleasure can the Drunkard have in the Reflection, that, while in his Cups, he retain'd only the Shape of a Man, and acted the Part of a Beast; or that from reasonable Discourse a few Minutes before, he descended to Impertinence and Nonsense ?

I CANNOT pretend to account for the different Effects of Liquor on Persons of different Dispositions, who are guilty of Excess in the Use of it. 'Tis strange to see Men of a regular Conversation become rakish and profane when intoxicated with Drink, and yet more surprizing to observe, that some who appear to be the most profligate Wretches when sober, become mighty religious in their Cups, and will then, and at no other Time address their Maker, but when they are destitute of Reason, and actually affronting him. Some shrink in the Wetting, and others swell to such an unusual Bulk in their Imaginations, that they can in an Instant understand all Arts and Sciences, by the liberal Education of a little vivifying *Punch*, or a sufficient Quantity of other exhilerating Liquor.

AND as the Effects of Liquor are various, so are the Characters given to its Devourers. It argues some Shame in the Drunkards themselves, in that they have invented numberless Words and Phrases to cover their Folly, whose proper Significations are harmless, or have no Signification at all. They are seldom known to be *drunk*, tho they are very often *boozey*, *cogey*, *tipsey*, *fox'd*, *merry*, *mellow*, *fuddl'd*, *groatable*, *Confoundedly cut*, *See two Moons*, are *Among the Philistines*, *In a very good Humour*, *See the Sun*, or, *The Sun has shone upon them* ; they *Clip the King's English*, are *Almost froze*, *Feavourish*, *In their Altitudes*, *Pretty well enter'd*, &c. In short, every Day produces some new Word or Phrase which might be added to the Vocabulary of the *Tiplers* : But I have chose to mention these few, because if at any Time a Man of Sobriety and Temperance happens to *cut himself confoundedly*, or is *almost froze*, or *feavourish*, or accidentally *sees the Sun*, &c. he may escape the Imputation of being *drunk*, when his Misfortune comes to be related.

I am SIR,
Your Humble Servant,

SILENCE DOGOOD.

FOREIGN AFFAIRS.

Berlin, May 8. Twelve Prussian Batallions are sent to Mecklenburg, but for what Reason is not known. 'Tis said, the Emperor, suspecting the Designs of the Czar, will secure all the Domains of the Duke of Mecklenburg. His Prussian Majesty, to promote the intended Union of the Reformed and Lutherans in his Dominions, has charged the Ministers of those two Communions, not to make the least mention in the Pulpits of the religious Differences about some abstruser Points, particularly the Doctrine of Predestination, and to forbear all contumelious Expressions against one another.

Hamburg, May 8. The Imperial Court has order'd the Circles of Lower Saxony, to keep in Readineſs

4

Sharpening the debate was the growing struggle between Federalists, like Alexander Hamilton, who favored strong centralized government, and anti-Federalists, like Thomas Jefferson, who believed the new nation should be a union of states, each keeping strong local control.

Proposals to amend the Constitution were part of a scheme by states-rights advocates to weaken and discredit it, the Federalists asserted.

Nevertheless, drawing upon Virginia's Declaration of Rights, among other sources, 12 amendments were proposed, and 10 eventually were submitted to the states for ratification as the Bill of Rights.

The press freedom clause went through various forms, some of which would have applied to the states, or to all branches of government, not just Congress. As eventually worked out by Madison and others in a House-Senate conference committee and submitted to the states in 1789, the First Amendment provided:

"Congress shall make no law respecting an establishment of religion, or prohibiting the free exercise thereof; or abridging the freedom of speech, or of the press, or the right of the people peaceably to assemble, and to petition the government for a redress of grievance."

The strength of the press guarantee was soon to be tested, when Congress, controlled by the Federalists, suddenly drew the issue of national power vs. individual rights by passing the Alien and Sedition Acts during the estrangement with France in 1798.

The sedition law made it a federal offense to "write, utter or publish . . . any false, scandalous or malicious writing . . . against the government of the United States, or either house of Congress . . . or the president" or to stir up opposition to any lawful act of Congress or of the president.

Opponents of the restrictive laws, led by Madison and Jefferson, relied on the inherent power of the states to defend the rights of the individual, while also dramatizing the government's political persecution to gain public support.

The sedition law died in 1801, not to be revived until World War I. But its repressions—11 federal sedition trials including eight involving newspapers, plus prosecutions at the state level—awakened many persons to the freedom issues involved.

Theorists already had before them the 1793 book on liberty and press freedoms by Robert Hall, an Englishman, which had drawn the distinction between sentiment and opinion on one hand, and conduct or behavior on the other. Only overt acts should be considered sedition, he wrote.

The Alien and Sedition Acts were only one of the many crises for the American press. Mob action, wartime censorship, court orders and government secrecy continued to hamper newsmen.

Mob action swirled around abolitionist editors in the 1830s as dissension grew over slavery. In 1837, Elijah Lovejoy, editor of the *St. Louis Observer*, was killed when he refused to renounce his right to condemn slavery.

In 1835 a Southern-dominated Congress passed a gag law which prohibited abolitionist literature from entering Southern states. By 1859 it was a crime in some states to subscribe to a newspaper opposed to slavery.

During the Civil War, Secretary of War Edwin Stanton caused telegraphed news reports to be checked first by his office, then sometimes delayed or stopped.

Government and press clashed in 1908 when President Theodore Roosevelt, angered by allegations that an American syndicate had corruptly gained millions of dollars during building of the Panama Canal, sued Joseph Pulitzer's *New York World* and the *Indianapolis News* for criminal libel. The government lost both cases when the courts denied federal jurisdiction.

But far worse was to come in the Espionage and Sedition Acts in the closing years of World War I. There were 900 convictions in 1917–18, amid widespread abuses of personal freedoms by government and the courts. Congress also allowed the government to ban from the mails about 100 newspapers, mainly unpopular radical and pro-German papers, reviving memories of the abuses under the Alien and Sedition Acts of 1798.

Fear of communism also has brought heavy pressures on the press.

In the so-called "Red Scare" of 1919–20, brought on by the Bolshevik takeover in Russia and the Industrial Workers of the World (IWW) movement in America, Atty. Gen. A. Mitchell Palmer instigated the arrests of socialists, labor union advocates and alleged radicals by the thousands.

Sen. Joseph R. McCarthy of Wisconsin touched off another "Red Scare" in the early 1950s, capitalizing on fears stemming from the success of Communists in China and America's confrontation with Communist forces in Korea. Newsmen who punctured McCarthy's allegations of Communists in the State Department were accused of being "soft" on communism, or "pink."

The Vietnam war brought similar pressures on journalists to accept the administration's view of the conflict.

These culminated in the Pentagon Papers case of 1971, in which for the first time in history the government got the courts to impose prior restraint—to stop four newspapers from publishing articles on the Pentagon Papers. The restraining order later was lifted.

Moves against television reporters have been at least as strong.

CBS President Frank Stanton was threatened with contempt of Congress because he refused to release unbroadcast materials and notes used in making the devastating documentary "The Selling of the Pentagon," stimulating a struggle over whether these "outtakes" of unbroadcast film can be demanded by investigators.

Apprehension among broadcast journalists was heightened by the Nixon administration proposal that renewal of local station licenses hinge upon the local manager's handling of network news, which he does not initiate.

These moves were accompanied by vigorous attacks from former Vice President Agnew on the fairness of the press and finally from President Nixon himself—notably in a televised news conference on Oct. 26, 1973—as the Watergate scandal swept away the final bits of the President's credibility.

Within hours of the President's charges that he had been a victim of "outrageous, vicious, distorted reporting," his aide, Patrick Buchanan, was pressing for legislative and legal action to "break up the power" of the three major television networks. Singled out as a target for bitter criticism was CBS news correspondent Walter Cronkite, the acknowledged dean of broadcasters.

Taking note of moves and threats against the media, the International Press Institute of Geneva in its 1973 report warned that the Nixon administration was bent on "chipping away at press freedom through the courts and by the threat of court action."

The Supreme Court upheld the right of newspapers to publish government documents detailing how the U.S. got into the Vietnam War, after a classic battle between lawyers for the papers and the government.

CBS's Morley Safer reported this story of Marines burning huts in 1965 and was subjected to intense pressure because he tried to show the brutal nature of some U.S. actions.

But the words "Congress shall make no law . . . abridging the freedom . . . of the press" do not cover all threats to press freedom, even if the courts give them their strongest interpretation.

And the current Supreme Court, despite earlier encouraging interpretations of press law, in the late 1970s permitted searches of newsrooms and continued to narrow the definition of a "public figure" in libel cases.

Historically, the press's record has been mixed.

On the one hand, it has lived up to its highest ideals with the powerful antislavery editorials of Horace Greeley in the last century and support of integration in this century; with exposure of corruption in business and government; with denunciations of abuses of immigrants, poor housing, exploitation of children and women, and discrimination at all levels; and with facts and opinions on foreign ventures ranging from the War of 1812 to the bombing of Hanoi.

On the other hand, the press has had many failings over the years. Much of the press was slow to push for progress in race relations, education, and health and ecology matters. Handling of technical subjects has not always been adequate. Most papers were unable or unwilling to recognize the significance of Watergate and the secret Laotian and Cambodian bombings.

It should not go unnoticed that many newspaper and broadcast executives who advocate strong press freedom laws are the same persons who work hand-in-glove with government and law enforcement officials. Treating their papers and stations mainly as business operations, they often support the candidacies of narrow-minded, partisan politicians who end up being negative influences in society.

The need for a continued fight against legislative and judicial tyranny is obvious. The *Los Angeles Times* lamented in late 1975: "For the first time in the history of the country, the courts, the chief defender of the Constitution and in utter distain of that Constitution, have claimed the power of wide censorship over the American people, a censorship that strikes at the heart of democratic government."

The paper, commenting on a decision by Justice Harry A. Blackmun which temporarily upheld a controversial Nebraska "gag order," left this argument for its readers: "The courts, no less than legislatures and executives, are accountable to the people, and must function in the spotlight of public exposure and scrutiny."

This concern over judicial abuses heightened following more disclosures of CIA and FBI crimes against persons and property and widespread corporate corruption—shocking, disgusting stories which demonstrated the absolute need for fearless reporting and the leaking to newspersons of documents which reveal misuse of power and money. The First Amendment guarantees such journalism and must not be blue-penciled by the timid or the vindictive.

The Stamp Act—1976

Bibliography

The colorful story of American press freedom battles is contained in Edwin Emery and Michael Emery, *The Press and America,* 4th ed. (Prentice-Hall, 1978), an interpretative history of newspapers and broadcasting. Two excellent surveys are Leonard W. Levy, ed., *Freedom of the Press from Zenger to Jefferson,* and Harold L. Nelson, ed., *Freedom of the Press from Hamilton to the Warren Court* (Bobbs-Merrill, 1966). The Reporters Committee for Freedom of the Press (Room 1112, 1750 Pennsylvania Avenue, N.W., Washington, D.C. 20006), the Society of Professional Journalists, Sigma Delta Chi (35 E. Wacker Drive, Chicago, Ill. 60601), and the Freedom of Information Center (University of Missouri) issue frequent reports on cases and yearly analyses, all of which are available upon request. Journalism reviews also should be checked when studying press freedom incidents, along with the editorial pages of leading papers and the commentaries/editorials of broadcast stations. Other background sources: William L. Rivers, *The Adversaries: Politics and the Press* (Beacon Press, 1970); Walter B. Emery, *Broadcasting and Government: Responsibilities and Regulation* (Michigan State, 1971); Donald M. Gillmor and Jerome A. Barron, *Mass Communication Law: Cases and Comment* (West, 1978); Harold L. Nelson and Dwight L. Teeter, Jr., *Law of Mass Communications* (Foundation Press, 1978); Marc A. Franklin, *Cases and Materials on Mass Media Law* (Foundation Press, 1977); William E. Francois, *Mass Media Law and Regulation* (Grid, 1975); Donald R. Pember, *Mass Media Law* (Wm. C. Brown, 1977); Kenneth S. Devol, *Mass Media and The Supreme Court: The Legacy of the Warren Court* (Hastings House, 1971, revised 1976); William A. Hachten, *The Supreme Court on Freedom of the Press* (Iowa State University Press, 1968). Also see the bibliographies in the Legal Restraints section of this book, articles 17–21.

Still widely discussed are the Hutchins Commission findings of 1947. The Autumn 1976 *Nieman Reports* carried an abstract of the report of that Commission on Freedom of the Press. Also basic is *Four Theories of the Press* (University of Illinois Press, 1956) by Fred S. Siebert, Theodore Peterson, and Wilbur Schramm. A new book is John Hohenberg, *A Crisis for the American Press* (1978), a description of the constant state of tension between the news media and governmental/judicial agencies. Of note also are two sources that describe conditions within media institutions which often pose dangers to the flow of information as great as those presented by the government. They are Hillier Krieghbaum, *Pressures on the Press* (Crowell, 1972), and Donald McDonald, "The Media's Conflict of Interest," *Center Magazine*, November/December 1976.

48 The New Secrecy
David Wise

David Wise lectures in political science at the University of California, Santa Barbara, and was an associate of the Center for the Study of Democratic Institutions. He was Washington bureau chief of the *New York Herald Tribune* before its demise and authored *The Politics of Lying* (Vintage Books, 1973). His latest book is *The American Police State* (Random House, 1976). This article appeared in *Inquiry* magazine October 16, 1978 and is used with Mr. Wise's permission.

On June 29, 1978, readers of the *New York Times* were assured in a page one story that President Carter was about to effect a "sweeping liberalization" of the government's system of classifying documents. The headline read: PRESIDENT TO ISSUE ORDER TO LIBERALIZE RULE ON SECRET DATA.

The story below went on to say that Carter would "shortly" issue an executive order designed to demonstrate "the President's commitment to open government." The *New York Times*, the article said, had obtained a copy of the document. The dispatch carried the byline of Martin Tolchin of the newspaper's Washington Bureau.

The story was a public relations triumph for the White House, but hardly a recognizable description of the secrecy order that Carter issued later that very day. While an improvement on the draconian version circulated in draft form by the administration last fall, the Carter order—like the Nixon order it replaces and all previous presidential secrecy decrees—permits the government, if it wishes, to classify a document *forever*. If read carefully, the fine print contains more than enough ambiguities, loopholes, and exceptions to allow continued government secrecy as usual.

The *Times* had a one-day beat on its laudatory preview of Carter's order, but almost no one appears to have noticed the exquisite irony involved: a presidential order designed to protect secrets and prevent leaks to the press had itself been leaked.

The executive order was dated June 28, but it was not released by the President, along with a covering statement, until June 29, by which time the *Times* was already on the streets. Asked whether the White House had leaked the document to the *Times*, Rick Neustadt, the National Security Council aide who was the order's chief architect, replied: "It's possible. I don't do the PR around here." Had he leaked it? Neustadt declined to answer directly. "Jody

[Powell] calls the shots," he said. Neustadt added that "there were a number of copies floating around," since the draft had been "discussed with people on the Hill and a few outside experts, and five subcommittees on the Hill saw final drafts." He also said that a newsletter had run a story about the order a week before the *Times* piece.

Be that as it may, the President's order to prevent leaks had been leaked, and in a manner that artfully diffused much of the unfavorable publicity generated by the draft version circulated last year. "The selling of the order," one White House official conceded, "was as important as the drafting."

But in Washington, leaking, as with other forms of infidelity, is still subject to a double standard. Only a few days later, Carter summoned key leaders of the House and Senate to a closed meeting at the White House to complain that leaks of classified information from Capitol Hill were drying up intelligence sources and damaging America's security. Sitting in on the meeting were the President's national security heavies, including Admiral Stansfield Turner, director of the Central Intelligence Agency; Zbigniew Brzezinski, the President's national security adviser; Secretary of State Cyrus R. Vance; and Defense Secretary Harold Brown.

Senator Barry Goldwater, the Arizona Republican, one of those called in to the Oval Office, said afterward that the President's concern resulted from "leaks that have appeared in the *New York Times* and the *Washington Post* over a long period of time." But other than mentioning the Pentagon Papers, which leaked to the press seven years ago, Goldwater provided no examples.

Nor did Jody Powell. "I don't know of any specific story," he told reporters. "You're talking about an accumulation of events. . . ." Powell became annoyed when the reporters suggested that, without examples, Carter's complaint of congressional leaks lacked credibility. "I really don't give a damn whether you believe it or not," he snapped.

Powell repeated that the President's concern was prompted by "a number of situations in which classified information was improperly released." He admitted that some of these disclosures had come from the executive branch. And from the White House?

"When we decide to make a leak," Powell replied, "we make sure it does not jeopardize national security."

John Shattuck, Washington director of the American Civil Liberties Union, expressed disappointment over the Carter order, although he said it was a "mild improvement" over Nixon's version. But Shattuck argued that any improvement in the executive order is outweighed by "the administration's effort to create an official secrets act through the enforcement of a secrecy contract against Frank Snepp, and the use of the Federal theft statute to prosecute espionage cases."

Snepp, the former CIA officer who wrote *Decent Interval*, a critical account of the agency's role in Vietnam, was ordered by a federal court on July 7 to surrender his "ill gotten gains" from the book. The decision was a victory for the CIA and the Carter administration, which had clearly decided to challenge Snepp in order to discourage other former agents from writing their memoirs. Snepp had declined to clear his book in advance with the CIA, as required by a secrecy agreement he had signed in 1968. The Justice Department brought suit against him even though the government admitted that the book contained no classified information and gave away no secrets.

The Carter administration could scarcely have found a better hanging judge for the case than Oren R. Lewis, a 75-year-old Eisenhower appointee who angrily lectured Snepp from the bench ("I think it was a willful, deliberate breach of contract . . . he did it for money") and who at one point remarked that the evidence "won't make any difference." It didn't. Lewis decided the case himself, without a jury, and his ruling, after he had spent two days interrupting and criticizing Snepp and his defense lawyers, was predictable.

The Snepp trial received considerable publicity, as did the government's successful prosecution of another Vietnam-related case against Ronald Humphrey, the former USIA official, and David Truong. Both Humphrey and Truong were convicted in May of spying for Vietnam, and later sentenced to long prison terms. Less widely noticed was the fact that in addition to the espionage charges, both men were convicted of theft of government property under Section 641 of the federal criminal code.

The same charge of theft was brought by the government against Daniel Ellsberg in the Pentagon Papers case, but the issue never came to court because, it will be recalled, Judge William Matthew Byrne, Jr., dismissed the case when Nixon administration's improper actions were revealed. These included the plumbers' break-in at the office of Ellsberg's psychiatrist, and an offer of the job of FBI director to Judge Byrne—proffered by John Ehrlichman at San Clemente—while the Ellsberg trial was in progress.

In the Humphrey-Truong case, however, the government's theft-of-documents gambit worked, and the implications for government control over information are frightening.

The defendants were charged with willfully converting information belonging to the U.S. government to their own use. Judge Albert V. Bryan, Jr., instructed the jury that this could include "information copied from and the contents of records or copies made of records. The information may be government property apart from the documents or sheets of paper themselves."

Thus the court agreed with the government's theory that it owns ideas and information, not merely the documents on which they are recorded. Nor, under this approach, does government information have to be classified in order for it to be "stolen." *Any* government information—from the size of last year's alfalfa crop to the number of postage stamps printed last week—could, if leaked, result in a criminal prosecution. This rationale is at the heart of the British Official Secrets Act, which prohibits the unauthorized disclosure or possession of any government information, regardless of whether it involves national security.

According to Morton H. Halperin, director of the Center for National Security Studies, the government's successful use of Section 641 means that "a newspaperman who receives information from a government official who leaks it to him could be prosecuted." Both Halperin and the ACLU's Shattuck believe the new executive order must be read against the background of the Snepp case and the use of the theft statutes in the espionage case. "The basic issue," said Shattuck, "is that they are trying to create an official secrets act by various means."

Carter's Executive Order 12065 is but the latest in a series of presidential directives classifying government information. It is a direct descendant of the first such order, issued by President Truman in 1951. Until then, there was no formal system of classifying government information in civilian departments.

Carter's order does improve on Nixon's in several respects: Some documents—Carter promised it would be "most" documents—are to be declassified in six years. Under Nixon, documents classified "Confidential" could be declassified in six years, "Secret" in eight years, and "Top Secret" in 10. Secrecy labels may now be applied only to documents which, if released, "could reasonably be expected" to cause some stated degree of damage to national security; information must now fall into certain categories in order to be classified (a provision that is not entirely comforting since the last category is called, simply, "other categories"); and for the first time, information must be declassified if the need for secrecy is "outweighed by the public interest in disclosure of the information," a balancing test that Halperin, in particular, fought successfully to include in the order.

Despite these changes, the Carter order continues to permit thousands of government officials to stamp "Top Secret," "Secret," and "Confidential" labels on literally millions of government documents every year—4.5 million in 1976, according to a House subcommittee.

And despite the hosannas of the *New York Times*, buried in the order is a Catch-22 provision that has the effect of allowing government officials to classify a document indefinitely. The order provides that documents must be declassified in "no more than six years"—except that officials with authority to stamp documents "Top Secret" "may classify information for more than six years." This power shall be used "sparingly" a term nowhere defined. (If "sparingly" means that, say, only one out of four documents may be classified beyond six years, that would still permit 1.1 million documents to be given long-term classifications each year, using 1976 figures.)

When documents are stamped secret beyond six years, the order provides three options for declassification: either a declassification date, or an event that would make classification unnecessary, "or a date for review" must be set "no more than twenty years" after the document is classified (30 years in the case of information provided by foreign governments). It is this third option, the provision for "review" in 20 years, that provides the opening in the tent for the camel's nose of secrecy.

Obviously, a classified document marked "for review in twenty years" will not in every case be declassified at the end of that time. The bureaucrat "reviewing" the document may decide to declassify it, but he may just as easily decide to continue the classification. Thus, marking a document for "review" might be interpreted as a form of indefinite classification. Jerry Berman, legislative counsel to the Washington ACLU office, who has studied the order closely, termed the review provision "ambiguous."

"Review was a battleground," one administration official who worked on the secrecy order declared. "It was clear you had to have a third option. But what happens if the twenty year review date passes and no one reviews the document. Does the document remain classified?"

Rick Neustadt said he thought that in such a case the document would be declassified, but he could point to no language in the order that said so. "After twenty years a document marked for review is legally not classified," he said. "But it is still in the filing cabinet, so it isn't released, either."

Suppose a document *is* reviewed in 20 years. Under another section of the Carter order, authorized officials "may extend classification beyond twenty years," but must set a date no more than 10 years later "for the next review. . . . Subsequent reviews for declassification shall be set at no more than ten year intervals." In other words, a document may be classified for 20 years, then kept secret indefinitely, with its secrecy renewed every 10 years.

In many cases it might not even be necessary to bother with the 10-year extensions. The order sets up a new Information Security Oversight Office whose director has power to extend the time between periodic reviews "for specific categories of documents or information."

According to Rick Neustadt, this provision was included "particularly for cryptographic information. We know that some material pertaining to cryptology is going to have to be classified indefinitely. I can't go into details on that because it's classified."

Neustadt agreed that under the Carter order, as under previous presidential orders, the government could keep a document classified forever. "That's always been true for a narrow set of documents, such as ones naming foreign agents. Cryptography would be another example."

The executive order states that only higher-level officials can classify documents for more than 20 years, and that "this authority may not be delegated." In reality, the language will not prevent lower-level aides from exercising authority in their bosses' names. "It doesn't mean the Secretary of State will review every document," Neustadt explained. "Let's face it. It means the extended classification has to be done on his authority. As a practical matter, what happens is that a staff assistant goes through a whole batch of documents, decides which ones should stay classified, and takes them in to the Secretary of State for his approval."

One of the unquestioned virtues of the Carter secrets order is that for the first time classifiers are required to mark which paragraphs or portions of a document are secret and which are not. (The provision was included over the objections of the Energy Research and Development Administration, which controls classified documents dealing with nuclear weapons.) In the past, entire documents could be classified because one word or sentence might be secret. There is an interesting qualification buried in the order, however, which states that the new director of Information Security Oversight may waive this requirement in certain cases.

"They are talking about information classified by machines," the ACLU's Jerry Berman explained. "You know that machines classify documents now. Some machines are computer-programmed to look at a document and stamp it 'Top Secret.' But the machines have a hard time marking paragraphs."

Behind almost every sentence of the secrets order there were bureaucratic battles, often with Neustadt and his NSC staff assistants arrayed against the classifying hardliners of the CIA and the Pentagon. For example, Nixon's order permitted the "Confidential" label to be stamped on a document if its disclosure could "cause damage to the national security." The NSC aides drafting Carter's order wanted to qualify the word "damage" with an adjective. In the draft circulated last year, the words used were "significant damage." The Pentagon objected to "significant" as too strong. In the final version signed by the President the phrase appears as "identifiable damage."

Carter glided over this watering-down in the statement he issued on signing the new order. "The standard for classification has been tightened," he said. "No document is to be classified unless its release reasonably could be expected to cause identifiable damage to the national security. Insignificant damage is not a basis for classification."

Carter added: "The government classifies too much information, classifies it too highly and for too long. These practices violate the public's right to know. . . . The new order will increase openness in Government. . . ."

But the Carter rhetoric conflicts with the reality of official secrecy. It was one thing for a former Georgia governor to campaign as an outsider, promising to open up government to the people. It is another thing to govern. Like presidents before him, Carter, once in the White House, discovered that secrecy is one of the tools of power. Frustrated by leaks, he has not, apparently, set up his own plumbers in the White House basement. Instead, he has substituted public relations for meaningful reform of the classification system, unleashed his attorney general and the power of the federal government against a book, and successfully established the legal concept that the government owns words and ideas—which is more than Richard Nixon's Justice Department was able to prove in the Ellsberg prosecution.

And, although the outlines are shadowy, there are indications that, behind the scenes, the administration has vigorously been pursuing leaks of information to the press. At least four articles in the *New York Times*, as well as stories carried by the Associated Press and the *Washington Star*, have reportedly been the subject of Justice Department or FBI investigations.

The administration gumshoes are believed to have pressed particularly hard to uncover the sources of a story by Seymour M. Hersh about CIA covert operations. The article, published on an inside page of the *Times* on June 1, described details of operations in the Middle East and Africa and suggested that Congress may not be exercising as much control over such operations as had been thought. Hersh disclosed that the CIA was delivering radio and communications equipment to President Anwar el-Sadat of Egypt and to the government of the Sudan, and had organized an anti-Cuban propaganda campaign during the fighting between Ethiopia and Eritrean insurgents. One knowledgeable observer in Washington suggested that the administration might have taken even more drastic action to track down the leakers but feared that this would only draw wider public attention to Hersh's story.

In short, the atmosphere and the prosecrecy actions in the capital speak louder than the rhetoric of dedication to open government. The "euphoria of secrecy," C. P. Snow suggested, "goes to the head."

And nowhere is this truer than in the nation's capital. It was, consequently, something of a surprise when William T. Bagley, the chairman of the Commodity Futures Trading Commission, recently ordered the agency's eight "Confidential" rubber stamps brought to his office to be destroyed. "I know of no other way to deter indiscriminate use of a confidential stamp other than to destroy any and all of them," he said. Too often, he added, the secrecy label is used "to keep the public out of the business of government."

I asked Bagley what had inspired him to take this extraordinary step. "I've lived for fifty years without a secrecy stamp and I don't need one now," he replied. "I don't see any reason whatsoever to have an executive order and a bureaucracy of secrecy. If you have something that must be secret, you just don't divulge it—you don't have to stamp it. What happened was that some people in our office—I guess it's endemic to Washington—just went out and bought these damn stamps. Next thing I knew, documents were coming to my desk marked 'Confidential.' It's absurd. I gathered up the eight stamps and literally threw them into the Potomac."

Bagley's attitude is commendable, and his actions, for a government bureaucrat, almost incredible. Someone should warn him, however, that he is swimming upstream against a swift current. He has no future in Carter's Washington.

Bibliography

Another of David Wise's articles, "Toward an Official Secrets Act," *Inquiry,* February 20, 1978, should be read along with this selection. His article "The President and the Press" (a section from *The Politics of Lying*), in the third edition of this reader, offered background for current discussions about the abuse of executive power and attempts to intimidate newspersons. Testimony at Congressional hearings in 1975 indicated that the privacy of newspersons was invaded by government officials, through the FBI, as far back as 1940, and that the electronic surveillances increased in the early 1960s. A thorough analysis of the Nixon administration's battles with the networks—which relates directly to the Wise article—is found in *The New Yorker* of March 17, 1975, written by Thomas Whiteside. CBS News Correspondent Dan Rather's book *The Palace Guard* (with Gary Paul Gates, Harper & Row, 1974) offers a close look at the Nixon White House and attitudes held toward the news media by high officials. When updating this information and studying the present administration, students might check the *Columbia Journalism Review* and the *Alfred I. Dupont-Columbia University Survey of Broadcast Journalism*, an annual summary of various developments in broadcasting which includes government attempts to hinder the flow of information.

Another article in the third edition of this book includes facts on how the executive branch misused the Fairness Doctrine: "What's Fair on the Air?" by Fred W. Friendly, from his book *The Good Guys, The Bad Guys and The First Amendment* (Random House, 1976).

Regarding the Pentagon Papers case of 1971 and the struggle of reporters to cover the Vietnam fighting, some basic sources are: Sanford J. Ungar, *The Papers and the Papers* (Dutton, 1972); David Halberstam, *The Making of a Quagmire* (Random House, 1965); and Dale Minor, *Information War* (Hawthorn, 1970). Three highly acclaimed books on the total Vietnam picture are David Halberstam, *The Best and the Brightest* (Random House, 1972); Frances FitzGerald, *Fire in the Lake* (Little, Brown, 1972); and Bernard Fall, *Two Vietnams: A Political and Military Analysis* (Praeger, 1967). In the broadcasting field there is Michael Arlen, *Living Room War* (Viking, 1969). A critical view of press performance is found in Peter Braestrup's monumental two-volume study *Big Story: How the American Press and Television Reported and Interpreted the Crisis of Tet 1968 in Viet Nam and Washington* (Westview Press, 1978).

In addition to the Dan Rather book listed above, other Watergate-related books are: Carl Bernstein and Robert Woodward, *All the President's Men* (Simon & Schuster, 1974); "Watergate: Chronology of a Crisis," issued by *Congressional Quarterly* (1975); Jimmy Breslin, *How the Good Guys Finally Won* (Viking, 1975); and William E. Porter, *Assault on the Media* (University of Michigan Press, 1976). In the broadcasting field, William Small, *To Kill a Messenger* (Hastings House, 1970) chronicled attempts to intimidate the networks.

Why a Second-Class First Amendment for Broadcasting?

49

Eric Sevareid

As the basic communications law of the land is being reviewed by Congress, this speech by Eric Sevareid makes thoughtful reading. Commending the respected broadcaster's views to his Congressional colleagues, Rep. Lionel Van Deerlin, Chairman of the House Subcommittee on Communications, noted that the onrush of technological change has left the Communications Act of 1934 "in many ways inadequate to the probable needs of the next two decades, let alone the 21st century."

I was not present at the creation of electronic journalism, but almost. What CBS' first real managing editor, Paul White, called the fine, careless rapture of the early radio days is gone. The miracles of communication have become commonplace. The gaudy process is now more routinized, institutionalized. But much better, I do believe; more responsible, better educated, as well as more efficient. This has been the first truly new form of journalism ever, and I have no regrets at having been part of the agony and the ecstasy almost from the start.

We began with no form sheet, no precedents, no comforting tradition like that of the printed press, no proved techniques, no standards. We had to invent them as we went along; like politicians and children, we were educated at the public's expense.

Eric Sevareid retired as national correspondent of CBS News in November, 1977 after 38 years with the network. These remarks, used with permission, were made to the convention of the National Association of Broadcasters in Washington, D.C. March 28, 1977. Among his many writings are *Not So Wild a Dream* (Knopf, 1946) and *This is Eric Sevareid* (McGraw-Hill, 1964).

And broadcasting as an industry began in its own special way. Most newspapers were started by men who wanted an outlet for their views, usually political. Most broadcasting stations were started by men who wanted an advertising medium, a business. They found themselves, in time, co-trustees of the First Amendment, a positive challenge to some, a discomfiture to others. But that goes with the job, with the right and the privilege. Station or network owners and managers unwilling to fight for full constitutional freedoms ought not be in the business.

I am not a spokesman for broadcasting as an industry. I have never paid much attention to its technical, managerial, or financial problems. My bosses don't tell me what to say on the air, and I don't tell them—not often, anyway—how to run the network's business. I don't know, quite, whether I'm in the news end of the broadcasting business or in the broadcasting end of the news business.

But I do represent news, the hasty, often improvised and unstructured, often agonizing attempt to give the world a little glimpse of itself every day. It is not a profession in any strict sense, not exactly a business or a trade. It is a calling. We have to try to live at the growing points of human society, at the cutting edges of history. Wits and resourcefulness play a bigger role than learning or intellectual disciplines. We are pinch hitters every other inning. All one can hope for is a respectable batting average. What saves us is that the news business, broadcast or print, is a self-correcting institution.

Public officials, private cause groups, many lawyers, and quantifying sociologists who work by slide rule may not approve, but the fact is that the theory of the free press never was that the full truth of anything would be revealed in any one account or commentary. The theory is that with free reporting and free discussion, the truth will *emerge*. It is a process, and must be followed, day by day, by readers and listeners as well as by writers and speakers.

There is, of course, the Sevareid Solution. I have offered it before; there were no takers. That is, news every other day. No newspapers or news broadcasts, except to warn of nuclear attack or bubonic plague, on Monday, Wednesday, Fridays. We would do a better job; the public's nerve ends would be rested. I could go fishing more often. Short of that, we are obliged to wing it. Our condition is no different from that described a hundred years ago by James Russell Lowell:

> In a world of daily, nay, almost hourly journalism, every clever man, every man who thinks himself clever or whom anyone else thinks clever, is called upon to deliver his judgement, point-blank and at the word of command, upon every conceivable subject of human thought.

But *that's the way it is*, as a colleague of mine would say. I have been at this calling some 38 years now and I am perfectly sure that the grave, built-in fault of the press is not really bias. It is *haste*, and, particularly in broadcasting, the severe compression of the material required.

A central point about the free press is not that it be fair, though it must try to be; not that it be accurate, though it must try to be that. But that it be *free*.

I don't even want it to be too respectable. I would rather it be at least a little bit irresponsible than over-cautious and timid. It is the press that makes the community weather and sounds the notes of the day. Slide rules can provide only poor measurement of its performance.

This city of Washington is the greatest single center of world news since ancient Rome. I incline to the notion that it contains, at present, too many of two kinds of people: lawyers and press people. The lawyers complicate and paralyze everything. The press chews everything to bits, or tries to; every reputation, new idea, policy line, before they have much chance to mature.

Whenever lawyers and journalists come together, sometimes even when they are on the same side of an issue, they tend to reach a separating point. The lawyers are obliged to keep their eyes on the rules of the game; the journalists must keep their eyes on the game.

I have tried to do that over many years of reading and hearing the arguments about broadcasting and the First Amendment. The notions that occurred to my unscientific, un-legal mind early on are still my notions, for whatever they are worth.

They seem to be mostly negatives.

I have never understood the basic, legally governing concept of "the people's airways." So far as I know there is only the atmosphere and space. There can be no airway in any practical sense, until somebody accumulates the capital, know-how, and enterprise to put a signal into the atmosphere and space. I have never understood why government should be empowered to affect the content of the signals any more than it should affect the content of the newspapers carried in the newspaper truck on the people's streets. I thought the traffic laws, in both cases, were enough.

I have never understood the concept of "the people's right to know"; they have the right to find out, but that depends upon the publishers' right to publish. Publishers, print or electronic, have no constitutional right to be read or to be listened to. That, they have to earn, as the people have to earn knowledge.

I could never understand why so basic a right as the First Amendment could be diluted or abridged simply because of technological change in the dissemination and reception of information and ideas. Particularly when the new technologies are becoming, almost everywhere, the most pervasive technologies. Though not necessarily the most persuasive.

I could never understand the court's argument that the Fairness Doctrine for broadcasting enhances the First Amendment. The First Amendment is a prohibition. How do you enhance a negative? No means No.

I have never understood the reasoning of those critics who seem to be saying that broadcasting will enjoy full rights under the First Amendment, when it is worthy of them. Who could be the timekeeper? In any case, constitutional rights do not have to be earned; we were all born with them.

I can understand those who say that three big commercial networks plus public broadcasting and smaller groupings are not enough, though I suspect they would say the same were there four. Four, or even five, would be all right with me and, I think, all right with most broadcast journalists, assuming they would be economically viable; and if they could provide the marvelously superior and different kinds of program fare that is supposed to be out there, somewhere, then everybody would be happy indeed.

Because there are only three, we are told their content must be monitored, guided by government at various points. Their alleged power is too concentrated, we're told. Suppose there were only three daily newspapers which everyone read. No doubt there would be official and officious types who would feel the need to lay hands upon them. But the great majority of people, I suspect, would insist that their very scarcity made even more imperative their absolute freedom from the power of government, if this is to remain a free society, as the First Amendment commands.

I have never quite grasped the worry about the power of the press. It has influence, surely, and influence is a kind of power—but diffuse, hard to measure. The press, after all, speaks with a thousand voices, in constant dissonance. It has no power to arrest you, draft you, tax you, or even make you fill out a form, except a subscription form if you're agreeable. It is the power of government, especially the federal government, and more particularly its executive arm, that has increased in my time. Many politicians have come to power in many countries and put press people in jail. I can't think of any place where the reverse has occurred.

The censorious instinct is always present and it shifts its operating base from time to time. The federal government, under Nixon, tried prior restraint, which not even the Alien and Sedition Acts permitted. The federal government went through a spasm of subpoenas against news people but has since tried to restrain itself. Courts have increased their gag rules on journalists, and both prosecuting and defending attorneys increasingly try to compel journalists' disclosure, sometimes just to make their own work easier.

I can think of innumerable cases where the press has led authority to situations of crime and corruption. I can't think of any case where sins of commission or omission by the press have resulted in gross injustice, at least in the sense of innocent people going to jail. History and experience have their claims, too; on the whole, the freer relationship had worked well.

Now we have entered a period where the censorious instinct concentrates on another nebulous concept called the right to privacy. To quote one leading communications lawyer:

> In five short years the Supreme Court has taken a number of confused steps backwards, leaving journalists, broadcasters and publishers at the mercy of unclear laws, inconsistent judges and subjective juries. As a result no one can say

for sure what the law of libel is in this country, who constitutes a public figure, when malice must be proved, what standards of negligence will be applied to reporters making valiant efforts to untangle judicial cats' cradles, what incredibly expensive and time-consuming legal proceedings might threaten.

One result of all this nervous confusion is clear—it will increase another nefarious form of censorship—self-censorship.

Thomas Jefferson said that for his time the biggest threat of oppression would come from the legislature, but that the time would arrive when it would come from the executive. I don't believe he thought of the judiciary, which has had far too much responsibility thrown upon it and has asserted far too much in the compulsory arrangements of our daily lives.

Most judges are un-elected. That, said Mr. Agnew, some eight years ago, is the trouble with those presumptuous characters the network reporters and commentators. Literal election, of course, would mean that the majority would hear only commentary and see news reports agreeable to it. That is not quite the idea of the free press. But in a sense we are the most elected people around. Every time a listener turns his dial to the right number, he elects me; every time he turns it to the wrong number, he un-elects me.

Still, this is not good enough. Many years ago some psychologist said the Achilles heel of television would prove to be the fact that people can't talk back to the little box. They can, but not enough. Here the networks are found wanting, more than most local stations. I have argued this for years, at some risk perhaps of arguing myself out of a job or into a diminished job. It has not been a policy problem, but a problem of program rigidities. I want to see network air time opened up a good deal more to listeners' rebuttal and to differing persuasions. That would be one advantage inherent in expanding the network evening news programs to an hour. There must be ways to do it, not, certainly, under legal compulsion, but by the free decision of broadcasting's managers.

It has been, in considerable part because of this imbalance between speaker and listener—as well as because my own temperament is what it is—that I have tried, all these years, to use this privileged position with restraint. I have been much criticized for my approach, especially by the zealots of so-called "advocacy journalism." I have my evangelical moments at times, but on the whole I have tried to illuminate more than to advocate, to teach more than to preach.

I have tried to remain objective, always aware, however, that objectivity and neutrality are not the same thing. Objectivity is a *way* of thinking *about* an issue, not the summation of the thought.

Such an approach will not often excite the multitude or bring rave reviews. But it has seemed to me the best way, for all the seasons, for the long haul. And my haul has been a long one.

Broadcasting steadily evolves and changes. For the better, in my opinion. It must do so, on its own, with the help of private citizens and their groups, with the help of the printed press, tainted with self interest though it often is—not with the help of government and its powers.

The wonder of television is not that it is as bad as it is, but that it is as good as it is. It will get still better, in news and in entertainment, if we have enough confidence in ourselves. We must not just *react*, particularly to the printed press. We have to keep in mind that we are the only business—or the only one I can think of anyway—that has its chief competitor as its chief critic. That set of dice is permanently loaded against us.

It is a long time since the night when I was sitting at a United Press desk in Paris and a fellow named Ed Murrow called me from London and asked me to throw in my lot with him.

He said, in effect, that I would never be pressured to produce scoops, or drama (though those things transpired), never expected to inflate the news beyond its honest dimensions. He said, "I have an idea people might like that."

So, in my unimaginative way, I did so and do so now. I conclude that by and large people *have* liked it.

If they hadn't, it would not have taken the Stanton retirement rule at CBS to envelop me in the blessing of silence, come the year's end.

I don't much fear it. Trout fishermen have an affinity for quiet places.

Bibliography

Some broadcasters believe the Fairness Doctrine is unconstitutional; others want it repealed because they don't want to be bothered with the demands of community groups desiring more access. Other persons, although believing that the rules don't work as intended, fight repeal because they fear that the corporate power of the networks will only increase over the years. The debate is endless. Fred W. Friendly's book *The Good Guys, The Bad Guys and The First Amendment* (Random House, 1976) gives the necessary background for the controversy. See other articles in this book dealing with the problems of access. Also valuable are Harry S. Ashmore, *Fear in the Air: Broadcasting and the First Amendment—the Anatomy of a Constitutional Crisis* (Norton, 1973), and *The Center Magazine*, May/June, 1973. The legal citation for the Supreme Court decision which upheld the Fairness Doctrine is *Red Lion Broadcasting Co.* vs. *FCC*, 395 U.S. 367, 89 S. Ct., 1794 (1969).

Edwin Diamond, "The First Amendment Dilemma," *TV Guide* (October 29, 1977) poses the question: "Freedom of expression is a guaranteed right, but then what should be done about the demands for fair and clean television?" As this book was being prepared, Congress was preparing to debate a proposed rewrite of basic broadcasting regulations. Representatives for every consumer group and broadcasting organization were getting their arguments ready. Students are advised to keep track of these developments in the popular press and *Broadcasting* magazine. Another development was that the Carnegie Commission on the Future of Public Broadcasting concluded in January 1979 that public broadcasting funds for radio and television should be more than doubled to $1.6 billion a year by 1985 and that commercial broadcasters should pay part of this funding. The report was entitled "A Public Trust."

The Broadcast Reform Movement: At the Crossroads

50

Anne W. Branscomb
Maria Savage

Genuine broadcast reform is most likely to be achieved through established organizations with credibility and political clout.

The first U.S. national association concerned with the "public interest" in broadcasting—now known as the National Association for Better Broadcasting (NABB)—was formed in 1949; the second, the American Council for Better Broadcasts (ACBB), dates from 1953. Yet, during the first decade of media reform and beyond, groups could do little more than tabulate and disseminate consumer reactions to broadcast programming, because the Federal Communications Commission (FCC) refused to admit representatives of the public as "parties in interest" in administrative licensing proceedings. Finally, in 1966, as a result of litigation pursued doggedly for two years by the Office of Communication of the United Church of Christ (UCC) *(United Church of Christ* vs *WLBT)* (359 F. 2d 994, 1005 [D.C. Circuit 1966]), the Court of Appeals issued a decision requiring the FCC to permit citizens to participate in Commission proceedings. The attention and relative success generated by this decision encouraged the formation of additional broadcast reform groups. Several organizations such as Action for Children's Television (ACT), the Gray Panther Media Task Force (GP), the Media Committee of the National Organization for Women (NOW), the Chinese for Affirmative Action (CAA), and the National Black Media Coalition (NBMC) are the direct result of concern for groups underserved or excluded by television.

Several of these groups initiated legal proceedings before the FCC to deny the license renewal applications of broadcasters they deemed deficient in serving the public interest. Several hundred petitions were filed from 1969 to 1972; although only a few were set for hearing—some of them still in process—just the initiation of these procedures required expert legal representation. A combination of *pro bono* public interest lawyers and several public interest law firms sprang up to meet this need, among them the still-active Citizens Communications Center (CCC), a general purpose law firm whose services many media reform organizations have used, as clients or at least for advisory purposes.

Other groups, of which the Committee on Open Media (COM) is a prime example, sought reform through increased access to the broadcast media for under-represented groups. Although the legal actions during this period which sought access as a major motive—either through counter advertising on television under the Fairness Doctrine or as a mandated right to paid time under the First

Anne W. Branscomb is Chairman of the Board and Maria Savage is a Research Analyst at Kalba Bowen Associates, Inc., communications consultants. The authors wish to acknowledge the support of the National Citizens Committee for Broadcasting, the Veatch Program, and the Rockefeller Family Fund in conducting the research reported herein. The full report from which this article has been taken is available from Kalba Bowen Associates, Inc., 12 Arrow Street, Cambridge, MA 02188. The article appeared in the Autumn 1978 issue of *Journal of Communication* and is used with permission.

Amendment—did well at the Court of Appeals level, they ultimately fared badly because the Supreme Court was unwilling to enforce paid access without the support of a responsible administrative agency. The FCC also declined to enforce the counter advertising policy for advocacy advertising because it saw a threat to the economic base of what had been characterized as "free" television.

The efforts of COM were joined by those of other organizations such as Accuracy in Media (AIM), who sought to use the Fairness Doctrine to obtain greater balance in TV and radio public affairs programming. AIM filed several actions with the FCC concerning alleged inaccuracies on commercial TV news reporting and urged the Commission to enforce objectivity and balance in public broadcasting.

Not to be forgotten during this period was the effort to produce a television channel to serve as a quality alternative to the three commercial networks. Out of the anticipated need for a national organization to lobby for the passage of what became the Public Broadcasting Act of 1967 and to support public broadcasting generally came the National Citizen's Committee for Broadcasting (NCCB), supported by a consortium of five foundations.

With the exception of a few church-related groups and the national associations developed in the early fifties, a majority of the broadcast reform groups which sprang up in the late sixties reflect the needs felt by minorities to be heard by a larger audience.

The purpose of this study was to compare the goals, resources, activities, and operating procedures of a sample of these media reform groups and to assess how the changing environment for reform will affect them in the future.

Findings are based on telephone and personal interviews with 13 reform groups which are concerned primarily with the broadcast media, a review of the literature, and a long-standing familiarity with public interest policy. The following groups, most of whom have been mentioned above, were interviewed: Accuracy in Media (AIM), Action for Children's Television (ACT), American Council for Better Broadcasts (ACBB), Chinese for Affirmative Action (CAA), Citizens Communications Center (CCC), Committee for Open Media (COM), Gray Panther Media Watch (GP), Inter-religious Committee for Corporate Responsibility (ICCR), National Association for Better Broadcasting (NABB), National Black Media Coalition (NBMC), National Citizens Committee for Broadcasting (NCCB), National Organization for Women Media Committee (NOW), and the Office of Communication of the United Church of Christ (UCC).

In almost every case, the group has been established and sustained through the leadership of a strong individual. The contributions of these leaders ranged from substantial financial assistance to long hours of free labor. In most cases, their desire to gain access, broadly defined, to broadcast media for their particular constituency has shaped the focus and actions of the group. While several groups attempt to represent a broad range of interests, it appears difficult to sustain a consistent "general purpose" broadcast reform effort.

Centralized leadership located in one individual has led further to a membership which, despite intentions to represent a geographically spread constituency, is primarily locally based. For example, the ACBB and its only state affiliate, the Wisconsin Association for Better Broadcasts (WABB), are both located in Madison and WABB generates much of its parent's activities; the COM relies on the faculty and students of San Jose State University and has conducted many of its reform efforts in conjunction with local broadcast reform groups in the San Francisco Bay area; and NCCB has relied primarily on its own staff and the leaders of other national broadcast reform groups in Washington and New York.

In most cases, the broadcast reform groups we interviewed have deliberately chosen not to establish formal ties with local affiliates which would broaden their membership base because they either cannot afford or do not want to provide specific services to individual organizations. Moreover, these "national" groups do not want to oversee or be responsible for the activities of local groups, preferring to let each group develop its own indigenous strategy. Perhaps the only exceptions are the NBMC, which is striving to establish an effective affiliate network in the top 20 broadcast markets, and the NOW Media Committee, which operates through local NOW affiliates around the country.

Using budget and funding sources, the groups divide into two categories: small groups with budgets of under $100,000 and large groups with budgets of $300,000 or more.

Seven of the groups we interviewed fall into the small group category (ACBB, COM, GP, NABB, NBMC, NCCB, NOW), and of these, only one (NCCB) has a budget over $20,000.[1] Their funding sources include a parent organization, membership fees averaging $10, individual donations, and personal funds. Much of their support comes in the form of the personal involvement of unpaid staff, sporadic volunteer help, legal interns, and occasional lecture and/ or film fees. None of the small groups can afford to spend any appreciable time in fund-raising; subsequently, it is no surprise that none has substantial foundation, government, or corporate support. When questioned as to what an ideal budget would be, most of these groups suggested that $50,000 per year would allow them to hire some professional staff for fund-raising and membership broadening activities.

The five large groups (AIM, ACT, CCC, ICCR, UCC) we interviewed all (with the exception of AIM) have large foundation funding (Ford, Markle, Carnegie, Rockefeller Family, etc.). Additional funding comes from diverse sources including parent organizations, membership fees, corporate donations, contributions from local foundations, and occasional fees for services. The $300,000 budget mark seems to be the break-even point for institutional security

1. The total budget of CAA is over $100,000 but only a portion of this money goes toward their media activities.

and none of the large groups questioned feel they need more than $500,000 yearly to sustain the full gamut of their activities (although one aspired to a million). Neither small nor large budget groups receive government assistance (except an NEA grant to ACT in 1975).

With the exception of the Gray Panther Media Watch and the National Organization for Women Media Committee, which have a 501(c)(4) status allowing them to lobby, all the organizations we interviewed maintain a nonprofit (501(c)(3)) corporate status.[2] Most of them have Boards of Directors ranging from 9 to 36 members but only three have Public Advisory Committees. Large-budget groups retain legal assistance on their own while small-budget groups rely on advice from board members or seek the assistance of the CCC.

Although the groups' goals and judgments of the success or failure of broadcast reform reflect their own particular perspectives, many of their areas of concern, strategies, and arenas of operation overlap.

Almost all of the groups are concerned about program quality, format, and stereotyping; hand-in-hand with this concern frequently goes an emphasis on viewer education. While several groups confine their concerns to these two areas, others are also interested in access-oriented issues—equal employment opportunities, access to airtime, diversified ownership, and the enforcement of broadcast regulations. Only UCC is able to involve itself in a broad spectrum of activities including program production, viewer education, and professional training, although ACT is close to reaching this plateau of full service.

The tactics and strategies of the groups reflect their concerns. Those interested in programming improvements use monitoring, evaluation, and criticism techniques, pressure on the broadcast and advertising industries, and awards to those broadcasters and advertisers who demonstrate concern. These groups advocate public participation, both in monitoring and in viewer education activities, which range from teacher-training seminars and credit courses to conferences and seminars. Several of these groups also issue periodic newsletters. Many, including both those interested in program changes and those concerned with access issues, participate in legal activities ranging from license renewal challenges to rule-makings. Finally, almost all the groups we interviewed have given testimony in Congressional hearings. Perhaps the only strategies not pursued by the majority of groups were actual production of programs or public service announcements, time-consuming and costly conferences, and formal research.

2. The Gray Panthers, as a parent organization, does have a tax exempt status, and NOW has a 501(c)(3) subsidiary, the NOW Legal Defense Fund, which was instrumental in negotiating airtime for PSAs concerning sexual stereotyping.

Even more overlap occurs among these groups in the arenas in which they operate. Indeed, with only one or two exceptions, the groups are in constant contact with the Federal Trade Commission, FCC, courts, Congress, corporations, the Corporation for Public Broadcasting (CPB), and the public.

To date, the interrelationships among groups remain largely informal, consisting of information exchange through personal contacts, membership of staff on several boards, or participation in conferences and workshops. Although such contact is irregular, it is not insignificant. Occasionally, groups such as the Gray Panthers or NOW have participated in the monitoring activities of ACT or NCCB. Perhaps the greatest interactions have occurred between the smaller groups and both CCC, which has provided legal support, and UCC, which has provided start-up advice.

By coincidence, many of the groups found themselves represented in 1969 on the Advisory Committee of National Organizations (ACNO) of the CPB, and this further stimulated cooperation. Indeed, the abolition of ACNO in late 1977 has denied media reform groups a forum in which to meet until some regular conference or coalition is organized to fill this need. Although the two conferences organized by the Aspen Institute in 1976 and NCCB in 1977 were assumed to be the forerunners of an annual event, no one has come forward to convene a 1978 gathering. Two conferences in 1978, the CPB-funded conference of the Public Interest Satellite Consortium and the fifth annual Telecommunication Policy Research Conference, did bring some of the leaders together again, but neither was directed towards the special needs of media reform.

Perhaps the greatest problem each one of these groups faces is financial. Small groups find their transition from an *ad hoc* group of individuals to an established organization thwarted by lack of funding. This obviously places them in a chicken-egg situation in which they are unable to hire and retain professional personnel who might strengthen their financial bases through fund and membership drives. On the other hand, although large groups have achieved organizational status and adequate financial backing, they must nevertheless devote substantial time and effort to maintaining and often increasing their funding levels. To cut back on their activities or the glossiness of their publications would give funders, legislators, etc., excuses to cut back support or ignore them.

What can it be said that these media reform groups have accomplished?

Although the achievements of the media reform groups are almost impossible to track and frequently too subjective to quantify, we have noted several developments over the past 10 years for which the media reform movement can surely take partial credit. These are:

Establishment of the right of the public to participate in administrative proceedings at the FCC.

More vigorous enforcement of the Fairness Doctrine as watchdog groups and individuals exert their rights to hear conflicting views on issues of public importance.

Modification of the equal time requirements of the Communications Act to facilitate direct confrontation of presidential candidates Ford and Carter.

Opening up the processes of administrative agencies with "sunshine laws" and the invitation by the FCC of consumer groups to air their concerns in informal meetings.

Defeat of broadcasters' efforts to obtain five-year licenses and to avoid the danger of comparative hearings at renewal time.

Breaking up of media concentration and greater diversification of ownership; there have been numerous transfers of broadcast properties while proposed FCC rules were pending and in litigation, although the Supreme Court in *FCC* vs *NCCB* (Docket no. 76-1471) affirmed the FCC's grandfathering of existing cross-owned media in large markets.

Increased minority employment from 9 percent in 1971 to 14 percent in 1976 and increased female employment from 22 percent in 1971 to 28 percent in 1978 (Annual Employment Statistics prepared by OCC, released February 17, 1978).

Some progress in programs and policies related to minority station ownership, particularly in opening up supportive Federal policies.

More female and minority faces on the media, particularly in major markets, among newscasters; substantial change in the use of ethnic and regional accents in commercials and in programming.

Improved network operating standards for news and public affairs, greater willingness to air corrections of errors, and increased responsiveness to letters of complaint about news distortion and error.

Many interactive radio talk shows showing a substantial increase in the access of a wide range of individuals and groups to public affairs programming.

Free speech messages in a number of markets including the San Francisco Bay area, Pittsburgh, Twin Cities, Los Angeles, Denver, New Orleans, and the District of Columbia.

Innovations in news coverage such as interactive, in-depth reporting, or use of the simultaneous feedback format.

An expanded 90-minute local news format in some of the major markets.

In children's television since 1967, the establishment of a consortium of public agencies and private foundations; fewer commercials on children's programs; and a mounting awareness of and concern over the effect of television on children.

Withdrawal of ads by corporate advertisers concerned about the impact of violent episodes on viewers.

New entries of a cultural nature into the television diet.

The opening up of a national television debate on environmental problems, on nutrition and obesity, on many taboo subjects such as abortion and homosexuality, and on health habits as evidenced by the popularity of jogging, biking, health foods, etc.

Corporations' sponsorship of quality dramatic productions about current social issues.

Experimentation with the mini-series or docudrama format.

A number of new programs which are directed to the special concerns and interests of women viewers.

Inclusion of women along with minorities in annual employment reports of broadcasters to the FCC.

Inclusion of the word "age" into the National Association of Broadcasters TV Code Special Program Standards (section 4, standard 7).

What can be expected for media reform groups in the future?

There is every indication that the legislative forum is likely to re-emerge as a primary focus for future media reform. Congress is in a more receptive mood for media reform than it has been since the early sixties. The House Subcommittee on Communications has been actively seeking input from industry and media reform groups into a revision of the Communications Act of 1934. However, although many of the reform groups have testified before the Van Deerlin Committee, only the UCC has recently undertaken a systematic analysis of underlying principles and proposed substantive changes to the legislation. A citizens license renewal bill was put forward in 1976 through the concerned effort of a cooperating group of broadcasting reform groups coordinated by UCC, CCC, and the National Citizens Communications Lobby, an independent but affiliated NCCB activity. Yet, few of the groups are well staffed enough to participate in the legislative process in a manner which could begin to counterbalance the very large presence and pressure which industry is able to bring to bear on legislation. Indeed, the recalcitrance of broadcasters has been a major deterrent to action in this area, and a strong constituency for change will be necessary if any genuine change is to be enacted into law.

Clearly, the 1977 NCCB Conference, entitled "Communications Policy: The Public Agenda," was conceived as an effort to mobilize resources toward the legislative process. It was also an effort to broaden the vista for reform beyond broadcasting to other areas of concern including common carrier and cable television. Participants split on the issue of whether to recommend more specific regulation or encourage greater deregulation. Nevertheless, informal liasions between disparate components of the media reform movement have resulted, and dialogue continues even though the conference produced no clear focus or mandate for the future.

The ten years of broadcast reform from 1966 to 1976 were characterized by cracking open a closed legal system; the next ten years will present a substantially different environment. This environment results in part because of rapid systematic changes in our communications system which will increase the availability of channels of expression. Increased channels will diminish both the practical restricts of television channels and, at the same time, the legal justification for broadcast regulation. For example:

1. The national public broadcasting system is a viable fourth channel in most of the country, reaching about 65 percent of its potential audience.
2. A substantial part of the country is now cabled (30 percent), with some 13 million cable subscribers (18 percent), and 1.3 million pay TV subscribers.
3. Satellite technology is opening new opportunities for individual networks or programs, not only to cable systems such as Time/Life's Home Box Office, but also to independent and unaffiliated broadcasters. Many special purpose networks are developing, such as UPI, Newstime, Spanish International Network, the religious broadcasters (the Christian Broadcasting Network and PTL [People that Love or Praise the Lord]) and sports services (Ted Turner's WTCG-TV, Atlanta, and the Hughes Sports Network). There are 14 networks soon to be using satellite dishes for delivery of programming services.
4. The Public Service Satellite Consortium with the help of NASA is attempting to provide expertise to public service institutions that wish to use satellite interconnection, and the CPB has already put into place the first pieces of a satellite network for the Public Broadcasting System (PBS) stations. National Public Radio (NPR) will follow in 1980.
5. There are a number of *ad hoc* networks, such as the one Mobil Oil Corporation has put together for its recent programs "Between the Wars" and "Ten who Dared." Mobil selectively negotiates participation with stations within the particular market which it wants to reach.
6. Finally, the impending growth of video cassette (and/or video disc) recorders into the home may open up opportunities for the production of special audience programming never economically feasible before.

Although the extent to which such increased opportunities will decentralize or centralize programming is not quite fully understood, it is clear that the opening up of alternative delivery systems will result in an increased ability to reach discrete audiences either regionally or nationally and a greater emphasis on mobilizing financial and human resources to create new vehicles for programming. Unfortunately, very few of the media reform groups are organized to take advantage of these new opportunities.

Another development having an effect on media reform is the diminishing and/or changing supply of volunteers for public interest activity. Volunteers are not as readily available for *ad hoc* protest as they were in the mid-sixties. This is partially the result of success in achieving some of the reforms sought. For example, with greater participation of women in the work force, groups such as NOW and ACBB, which have depended upon educated but unemployed females for their human resources, are finding themselves understaffed. In addition, as the population of the United States continues to age, and retirees live longer and in greater health than previously, we may anticipate that the concerns of the elderly will receive higher and higher priority on the agenda of media reformers. Thus, the pool of available volunteers may be drawn more heavily from this group. This shift portends a media reform movement which is likely to reflect the political complexion of elderly activists as the reform movement in the sixties reflected the frustrations of students and minority activists.

Often reformers seek solutions through direct confrontations with the media, by applying direct pressure through citizen lobbies and through shareholder actions.

For example, activities to influence corporate advertisers on violent programs have been clearly a shared effort. NCCB, drawing on research conducted by Gerbner and others, procured the services of a professional monitoring firm with funds made available by the American Medical Association (AMA) to survey those corporations providing financial support to the most violent and least violent programs,[3] and published the results. Taking this information to its members, the Parents Teachers Association (PTA) mobilized 6,500,000 members in nationwide hearings and awareness sessions to protest to local broadcasters the carriage of offensive programs. The networks give credit for the shift away from violence-prone programs to sexploitation to the PTA (NBC Evening News telecast, May 2, 1978).

Relying on the same evidence, the National Council of Churches organized ICCR, which mobilized participating church groups owning stock in the corporations with highest attributed violence-prone programs to seek stockholder resolutions condemning sponsorship of excessive violence on television. Seven capitulated without a fight; only one carried the stockholders' resolution to the SEC, which refused carriage on the proxy material. Clearly, 6.5 million members of the PTA and 42 million members of the National Council of Churches, with millions of dollars worth of corporate control, carry clout in our society. Although it may not be more effective than legal avenues of redress, this approach is certainly more direct and less expensive. It shares responsibility for decision-making with more than nine robed men, and it requires the cooperation of a variety of individuals and organizations who do not normally work in unison.

Out of these experiences, one can derive the major components of an effort to reform program content which would not rely upon government edict for its direction: (a) credible research; (b) translation of the credible research for public consumption; (c) wide public dissemination of the research; (d) expressed concern by organized groups with established credentials and sizable membership; (e) responsive media executives; and (f) wide distribution of production skills and resources through all segments of society.

3. Upon request, ACBB will also supply a list of 150 sponsors of network television and radio, but without the program evaluations.

*Genuine reform of program content, which is the bottom line for many
reformers, is a very complicated process in our pluralistic society.*

It entails not only the ability to curtail outrageously discriminatory practices
through the regulatory process, but also the ability to muster a broad-based
public constituency that is willing to actively express its concern. It also includes
the ability to participate actively in the production of alternative messages. To
date, at least two organizations have been established specifically to produce
public service messages (PSAs), Public Advertising Council and Public Media
Center, and both NOW and ACT have been successful in obtaining time for
PSAs on the impact of television on women and children.

Furthermore, as the leaders of the reform movement who met at the Aspen
Institute in 1976 to discuss their goals and objectives discovered, consensus
concerning content is impossible. Only consensus concerning methodology and
procedures is feasible. Moreover, it is immediately apparent that most media
reformers are not content eunuchs promoting the free marketplace of ideas as
a goal—each wants a free marketplace in which his or her wares can be mer-
chandised to a sophisticated consuming public, which, being discerning, will
naturally agree with the proponent's conclusions. Furthermore, while the reform
groups which are affiliated with an established institution seem strong enough
to weather the storms of adversity, most of the *ad hoc* groups must ride the tides
of popularity which bring in both volunteers and money.

We believe the major thrusts in broadcast reform will be in arenas outside
the federal administrative agencies and the courts. These areas would appear to
be shareholder pressure on corporate decision-making, mobilization of public
opinion to influence Congress, the development of rating systems which measure
targeted audience responses to particular program content, increased research on
the effect of program content on particular audience segments, and the development of production skills which will translate into a more varied and balanced
representation of American society on the television scene.

The landscape of reform is likely to remain a kaleidoscope of distinct groups,
each dedicated to its own mirror image of reality—working together when their
goals converge and operating independently on issues where they diverge. The
building of a large constituency for reform not only depends upon such diversity,
but the politics of special interests dictates that the reform movement's success
may depend upon what one reformer called "the myth of the marching millions."

But it is not too far off the mark to say that genuine reform will come when
the myth becomes the reality, and that is likely to be achieved by a massive
direct appeal using the medium itself or through established organizations with
credibility and political clout.

See the bibliography for the Sevareid article, no. 49, and the bibliographies for the articles on advertising, nos. 39-44. Also see Jerry Mander, *Four Arguments for the Elimination of Television* (Morrow, 1978), "Media Watch," the newsletter of the National Citizens Committee for Broadcasting, headed by Nicholas Johnson, Ralph Nader, and other consumer activists. That group also published *access*, a journal of media reform. Check "Freedom of Information Reports" (it is indexed) for a number of summaries of legal disputes.

Bibliography

The Problems of Television News

The Selection of Reality

Edward Jay Epstein

51

Each weekday evening, the three major television networks—the American Broadcasting Company, the Columbia Broadcasting System, and the National Broadcasting Company—feed filmed news stories over lines leased from the American Telephone & Telegraph Co. to the more than six hundred local stations affiliated with them, which, in turn, broadcast the stories over the public airwaves to a nationwide audience. The CBS Evening News, which is broadcast by two hundred local stations, reaches some nineteen million viewers; the NBC Nightly News, broadcast by two hundred and nine stations, some eighteen million viewers; and the ABC Evening News, broadcast by a hundred and ninety-one stations, some fourteen million. News stories from these programs are recorded on videotape by most affiliates and used again, usually in truncated form, on local news programs late in the evening. Except for the news on the few unaffiliated stations and on the noncommercial stations, virtually all the filmed reports of national and world news seen on television are the product of the three network news organizations.

The process by which news is gathered, edited, and presented to the public is more or less similar at the three networks. A limited number of subjects— usually somewhere between twenty and thirty—are selected each day as possible film stories by news executives, producers, anchor men, and assignment editors, who base their choices principally on wire-service and newspaper reports. Camera crews are dispatched to capture these events on 16-mm. color film. The filming is supervised by either a field producer or a correspondent—or, in some cases, the cameraman himself. The film is then shipped to the network's headquarters in New York or to one of its major news bureaus—in Chicago, Los Angeles, or Washington—or, if time is an important consideration, processed and edited at the nearest available facilities and transmitted electronically to New York.* Through editing and rearranging of the filmed scenes, a small fraction of the exposed film—usually less than ten per cent—is reconstructed into a story whose form is to some extent predetermined. Reuven Frank, until two months ago the president of NBC News, has written:

> Every news story should, without any sacrifice of probity or responsibility, display the attributes of fiction, of drama. It should have structure and conflict, problem and denouement, rising action and falling action, a beginning, a middle and an end.

Edward J. Epstein, a political scientist, is the media critic who earned his credentials with the much discussed book *News From Nowhere: Television and the News.* His *Between Fact and Fiction: The Problem of Journalism* is a collection of ten of his essays. This article is from *News From Nowhere,* copyright © 1973 by Edward Jay Epstein. Reprinted by permission of Random House, Inc.

*Electronic newsgathering (ENG) may reduce the time but will not change the process. Ed.

David Brinkley (*top*, talking to student editors) worked with Chet Huntley for fourteen years on NBC. Following Huntley's retirement, Brinkley served as a "roaming commentator" and later joined John Chancellor (*middle left*) in the anchor position. Edwin Newman (*bottom left*) continued as a leading correspondent.

A popular alternative to the nightly network newscasts is The MacNeil/Lehrer Report (*right*), co-produced by WNET/13 in New York and WETA/26 in Washington. The show, which began in 1972, is distributed nationally by the Public Broadcasting Service.

After the addition of a sound track, recorded at the event, the story is explained and pulled together by a narration, written by the correspondent who covered the event or by a writer in the network news offices. Finally, the story is integrated into the news program by the anchor man.

Network news organizations select not only the events that will be shown as national and world news on television but the way in which those events will be depicted. This necessarily involves choosing symbols that will have general meaning for a national audience. "The picture is not a fact but a symbol," Reuven Frank once wrote. "The real child and its real crying become symbols of all children." In the same way, a particular black may be used to symbolize the aspirations of his race, a particular student may be used to symbolize the claims of his generation, and a particular policeman may be used to symbolize the concept of authority. Whether the black chosen is a Black Panther or an integrationist, whether the student is a militant activist or a Young Republican, whether the policeman is engaged in a brutal or a benevolent act obviously affects the impression of the event received by the audience. When the same symbols are consistently used on television to depict the behavior and aspirations of groups, they become stable images—what Walter Lippmann, in his classic study *Public Opinion* has called a "repertory of stereotypes." These images obviously have great power; public-opinion polls show that television is the most believed source of news for most of the population. The [former] director of CBS News in Washington, William Small, has written about television news:

> When television covered its "first war" in Vietnam, it showed a terrible truth of war in a manner new to mass audiences. A case can be made, and certainly should be examined, that this was cardinal to the disillusionment of Americans with this war, the cynicism of many young people toward America, and the destruction of Lyndon Johnson's tenure of office. . . . When television examined a different kind of revolution, it was singularly effective in helping bring about the Black revolution.

And it would be difficult to dispute the claim of Reuven Frank that "there are events which exist in the American mind and recollection primarily because they were reported on regular television news programs."

How were those events selected to be shown on television, and who or what determined the way in which they were depicted? Vice-President Spiro Agnew believes the answer is that network news is shaped "by a handful of men responsible only to their corporate employers," who have broad "powers of choice" and "wield a free hand in selecting, presenting, and interpreting the great issues in our nation." Television executives and newsmen, on the other hand, often argue that television news is shaped not by men but by events—that news is news. Both of these analyses overlook the economic realities of network television, the effects of government regulation on broadcasting, and the organizational requirements of the network news operations, whose established routines and procedures tend to impose certain forms on television news stories.

David Brinkley, in an NBC News special entitled "From Here to the Seventies," reiterated a description of television news that is frequently offered by television newsmen:

What television did in the sixties was to show the American people to the American people. . . . It did show the people places and things they had not seen before. Some they liked, and some they did not. It was not that television produced or created any of it.

In this view, television news does no more than mirror reality. Thus, Leonard Goldenson, the chairman of the board of ABC, testified before the National Commission on the Causes and Prevention of Violence that complaints of news distortion were brought about by the fact that "Americans are reluctant to accept the images reflected by the mirror we have held up to our society." Robert D. Kasmire, a vice-president of NBC, told the commission, "There is no doubt that television is, to a large degree, a mirror of our society. It is also a mirror of public attitudes and preferences." The president of NBC, Julian Goodman, told the commission, "In short, the medium is blamed for the message." Dr. Frank Stanton, vice-chairman and former president of CBS, testifying before a House committee, said, "What the media do is to hold a mirror up to society and try to report it as faithfully as possible." Elmer Lower, the president of ABC News, has described television news as "the television mirror that reflects . . . across oceans and mountains," and added, "Let us open the doors of the parliaments everywhere to the electronic mirrors." The imagery has been picked up by critics of television, too. Jack Gould, formerly of the *Times*, wrote of television's coverage of racial riots, "Congress, one would hope, would not conduct an examination of a mirror because of the disquieting images that it beholds."

The mirror analogy has considerable descriptive power, but it also leads to a number of serious misconceptions about the medium. The notion of a "mirror of society" implies that everything of significance that happens will be reflected on television news. Network news organizations, however, far from being ubiquitous and all-seeing, are limited newsgathering operations, which depend on camera crews based in only a few major cities for most of their national stories. Some network executives have advanced the idea that network news is the product of coverage by hundreds of affiliated stations, but the affiliates' contribution to the network news programs actually is very small. Most network news stories are assigned in advance to network news crews and correspondents, and in many cases whether or not an event is covered depends on where it occurs and the availability of network crews.

The mirror analogy also suggests immediacy: events are reflected instantaneously, as in a mirror. This notion of immediate reporting is reinforced by the way people in television news depict the process to the public. News executives sometimes say that, given the immediacy of television, the network organization has little opportunity to intervene in news decisions. Reuven Frank once declared,

At ABC, Barbara Walters was noted for her interviews, and Max Robinson (*top*), Frank Reynolds (*right*), and Peter Jennings (*bottom*) were the mainstays of the evening news show.

on a television program about television, "News coverage generally happens too fast for anything like that to take place." But does it? Though it is true that elements of certain events, such as space exploration and political conventions, are broadcast live, virtually all of the regular newscasts, except for the commentator's "lead-ins" and "tags" to the news stories, are prerecorded on videotape or else on film, which must be transported, processed, edited, and projected before it can be seen. Some film stories are delayed from one day to two weeks because of certain organizational needs and policies. Reuven Frank more or less outlined these policies on "prepared," or delayed, news in a memorandum he wrote when he was executive producer of NBC's Nightly News program. "Except for those rare days when other material becomes available," he wrote, "the gap will be filled by planned and prepared film stories, and we are assuming the availability of two each night." These "longer pieces," he continued, were to be "planned, executed over a longer period of time than spot news, usable and relevant any time within, say, two weeks rather than that day, receptive to the more sophisticated techniques of production and editing, but journalism withal." The reason for delaying filmed stories, a network vice-president has explained, is that "it gives the producer more control over his program." First, it gives the producer control of the budget, since shipping the film by plane, though it might mean a delay of a day or two, is considerably less expensive than transmitting the film electronically by satellite or AT&T lines. Second, and perhaps more important, it gives the producer control over the content of the individual stories, since it affords him an opportunity to screen the film and, if necessary, reedit it. Eliminating the delay, the same vice-president suggested, could have the effect of reducing network news to a mere "chronicler of events" and forcing it "out of the business of making meaningful comment." Moreover, the delay provides a reserve of stories that can be used to give the program "variety" and "pacing."

In filming delayed stories, newsmen are expected to eliminate any elements of the unexpected, so as not to destroy the illusion of immediacy. This becomes especially important when it is likely that the unusual developments will be reported in other media and thus date the story. A case in point is an NBC News story about the inauguration of a high-speed train service between Montreal and Toronto. While the NBC crew was filming the turbotrain during its inaugural run to Toronto, it collided with—and "sliced in half," as one newspaper put it—a meat trailer-truck, and then suffered a complete mechanical breakdown on the return trip. Persistent "performance flaws" and subsequent breakdowns eventually led to a temporary suspension of the service. None of these accidents and aberrations were included in the filmed story broadcast two weeks later on the NBC evening news. David Brinkley, keeping to the original story, written before the event, introduced the film by saying, "The only high-speed train now running in North America has just begun in Canada." Four and a half minutes of shots of the streamlined train followed, and the narration suggested that this foreshadowed the future of transportation, since Canada's "new turbo just might shake [American] lethargy" in developing such trains. (The announcement of the suspension of the service, almost two weeks later, was not carried on the program.) This practice of "preparing" stories also has affected the coverage of more serious subjects—for instance, many of the filmed stories about the Vietnam war were delayed for several days. It was possible to transmit war films to the United States in one day by using the satellite relay, but the cost was considerable at the height of the war—more than three thousand dollars for a ten-minute transmission, as opposed to twenty or thirty dollars for shipping the same film by plane. And, with the exception of momentous battles, such as the Tet offensive, virtually all of the network film was sent by plane. To avoid the possibility of having the delayed footage dated by newspaper accounts, network correspondents were instructed to report on the routine and continuous aspects of the war rather than unexpected developments, according to a former NBC Saigon bureau manager.

The mirror analogy, in addition, obscures the component of "will"—of initiative in producing feature stories and of decisions made in advance to cover or not to cover certain types of events. A mirror makes no decisions; it simply reflects what takes place in front of it. . . .

The search for news requires a reliable flow of information not only about events in the immediate past but about those scheduled for the near future. Advance information, though necessary to any news operation, is of critical importance to the networks. For, unlike newspapers, and radio stations, which can put a news story together within minutes by means of telephone interviews or wire-service dispatches, a television network usually needs hours, if not days, of "lead time" to shoot, process, and edit a film story of even a minute's duration. The types of news stories best suited for television coverage are those specially planned, or induced, for the convenience of the news media—press conferences, briefings, interviews, and the like—which the historian Daniel J. Boorstin has called "pseudo-events," and which by definition are scheduled well in advance and are certain to be, if only in a self-fulfilling sense, "newsworthy." There are also other news events, such as congressional hearings, trials, and speeches, that, although they may not be induced for the sole purpose of creating news, can still be predicted far in advance. The networks have various procedures for gathering, screening, and evaluating information about future events, and these procedures to some degree systematically *influence* their coverage of news.

Most network news stories, rather than resulting from the initiative of reporters in the field, are located and assigned by an assignment editor in New York (or an editor under his supervision in Washington, Chicago, or Los Angeles). The assignment desk provides material not only for the evening news program but for documentaries, morning and afternoon programs, and a syndicated service for local stations. Instead of maintaining—as newspapers do—regular "beats," where reporters have contact with the same set of newsmakers over an extended period of time, network news organizations rely on ad-hoc coverage. In this system, correspondents are shunted from one story to another—on the basis of availability, logistical convenience, and producers' preferences—

The late Edward R. Murrow (*bottom left*) was one of America's most distinguished journalists. His "See It Now" documentary series and "Person to Person" interview show were popular in the 1950s. Murrow, who earned his reputation as a radio reporter and commentator in the late 1930s and 1940s, brought his style to television—one of deep seriousness and high integrity—and left an everlasting impression on the television news business.

In stark contrast to the television of Murrow's day is this fancy studio at KNBC, Los Angeles (*top*), where two hours of local news are produced nightly.

Keeping up with American habits was Charles Kuralt (*bottom right*), who was "On the Road" for CBS. Kuralt traveled the nation's backroads and delighted viewers with his findings.

The mainstay of the CBS News team was Walter Cronkite (*top*), considered the ''dean'' of television newscasters. Cronkite broadcast a daily commentary on CBS Radio in addition to his many television responsibilities.

Harry Reasoner (*middle left*) was added to the team in 1979. Originally a CBS reporter, he was anchor man of the ''ABC Evening News'' for eight years before returning to CBS. Reasoner was a veteran of election night broadcasts, offering his observations in a dry, humorous style.

Lesley Stahl (*middle right*), was one of many talented women to enter the broadcast news field. A veteran political reporter, she became White House Correspondent.

The CBS News show ''60 Minutes'' became the first news show in television history to make the ''top ten'' in the ratings. The documentary team of Dan Rather, Morley Safer, and Mike Wallace (*below*) offered a diversity which attracted faithful fans.

after the assignment editor has selected the events to be covered. A correspondent may easily be assigned to three subjects in three different cities in a single week, each assignment lasting only as long as it takes to film the story. To be sure, there are a number of conventional beats in Washington, such as the White House, but these are the exception rather than the rule. Most of the correspondents are "generalists," expected to cover all subjects with equal facility. And even in fields for which networks do employ specialist correspondents, such as sports or space exploration, better-known correspondents who are not experts in those fields may be called on to report major stories. The generalist is expected not to be a Jack-of-all-trades but simply to be capable of applying rules of fair inquiry to any subject. One reason network executives tend to prefer generalists is that they are less likely to "become involved in a story to the point of advocacy," as one network vice-president has put it. It is feared that specialists, through their intimate knowledge of a situation, would be prone to champion what they believed was the correct side of a controversy. But perhaps the chief reason that generalists are preferred to specialists is that, being able to cover whatever story develops, they lend themselves to an efficient use of manpower. The use of ad-hoc coverage leads to the constant appearances "on camera" of a relatively small number of correspondents. One network assignment editor has suggested that it is "more for reasons of audience identification than economy" that a few correspondents are relied on for most of the stories. The result, he continued, is a "star system" in which producers request that certain leading correspondents cover major stories, whatever the subject might be. Another consequence of having small, generalist reporting staffs is that the networks are able to do relatively little investigative reporting. . . .

What is seen on network news is not, except in rare instances, the event itself, unfolding live before the camera, or even a filmed record of the event in its entirety, but a story about the event which has been constructed on film from selected fragments of it. Presenting news events exactly as they occur does not meet the requirements of network news. For one thing, the camera often is not in a position to capture events while they are happening. Some news events are completely unexpected and occur before a camera crew can be dispatched to the scene. Others cannot be filmed either because of unfavorable weather or lighting conditions (especially if artificial lighting is unavailable or restricted) or because news crews are not permitted access to them. And when institutions, such as political conventions, do permit television to record their form proceedings, the significant decisions may still take place outside the purview of the camera. But even if coverage presents no insurmountable problems, it is not sufficient in most cases simply to record events in their natural sequence, with all the digressions, confusions, and inconsistencies that are an inescapable part of any reality, for a network news story is required to have a definite order, time span, and logic.

In producing most news stories, the first necessity is generating sufficient film about an event, so that the editor and the writer can be assured of finding the material they need for the final story. Perhaps the most commonly used device for producing this flow of film is the interview. The interview serves several important purposes for television news. First, it enables a news crew to obtain film footage about an event that it did not attend or was not permitted to film. By finding and interviewing people who either participated in the event or have at least an apparent connection with it, the correspondent can recreate it through their eyes.

Second, the interview assures that the subject will be filmed under favorable circumstances—an important technical consideration. In a memorandum to his news staff, Reuven Frank once gave this advice about interviewing:

> By definition, an interview is at least somewhat controllable. It must be arranged; it must be agreed to. . . . Try not to interview in harsh sunlight. Try not to interview in so noisy a setting that words cannot be heard. Let subjects be lit. If lights bother your subject, talk to him, discuss the weather, gentle him, involve his interest and his emotions so that he forgets or ignores the lights. It takes longer, but speed is poor justification for a piece of scrapped film.

To make the subjects appear even more dignified and articulate, it is the customary practice to repeat the same question a number of times, allowing the respondent to "sharpen his answer," as one correspondent has put it. At times, the person interviewed is permitted to compose his own questions for the interviewer or, at least, to rephrase them. Rehearsals are also quite common.

Third, interviews provide an easy means of presenting an abstract or difficult-to-film concept in human terms, as Reuven Frank has explained:

> The best interviews are of people reacting—or people expounding. . . . No important story is without them. They can be recorded and transmitted tastefully . . . nuclear disarmament, unemployment, flood, automation, name me a recent major story without its human involvement.

Although the networks have instituted strict policies against misleading "reenactments" and "staging," film footage is sometimes generated by having someone demonstrate or enact aspects of a story for the camera. Bruce Cohn, a producer for ABC news at the time, explained the practice last year to the House Special Subcommittee on Investigations during hearings on "news staging." Describing the difference between hard news and feature stories, Cohn said, "Generally speaking, a feature story is only brought to the public's attention because the journalist who conceived of doing such a report thinks it would be of interest or of importance. Therefore, a feature story must be 'set up' by a journalist if it is to be transformed into usable information. There is no reason why this 'setting up' cannot be done in an honest and responsible manner . . . people involved in feature stories are often asked to demonstrate how they do something . . . in fact, by its very nature, a feature story may be nothing but what the subcommittee negatively refers to as 'staging. . . .' "

Since network television is in the business of attracting and maintaining large audiences, the news operation, which is, after all, part of the networks' programming schedule, is also expected to maintain, if not attract, as large an audience as possible. But a network news program, unlike other news media, apparently can't depend entirely on its content to attract and maintain an audience. To a great extent, the size of its audience is determined by three outside factors. The first is affiliate acceptance. If a program is not carried, or "cleared," by the affiliates, then it simply is not available to the public. (ABC has significantly increased the audience for its evening news program since 1969 by increasing the number of stations that clear it from a hundred and twenty to a hundred and ninety-one.) The second is scheduling. A program that is broadcast at 7 P.M., say, stands a good chance of drawing a larger audience than it would at six-thirty, since more people are usually watching television at the later hour. (The television audience increases all day and reaches a peak at about 9 P.M.) The third factor is what is called "audience flow." Network executives and advertisers believe that a significant portion of the audience for any program is inherited, as they put it, from the preceding program. According to the theory of audience flow, an audience is like a river that continues in the same direction until it is somehow diverted. "The viewing habits of a large portion of the audience—at least, the audience that Nielsen measures—are governed more by the laws of inertia than by free choice," a network vice-president responsible for audience studies has remarked. "Unless they have a very definite reason to switch, like a ballgame, they continue to watch the programs on the channel they are tuned in to."

Many network executives believe that network news is even more dependent on audience flow than are entertainment programs, or even local newscasts featuring reports on local sports and weather conditions. Richard Salant, the president of CBS News, has said that "you'll find a general correlation between the ratings of the network news broadcast and the local news broadcast—and probably the local news is the decisive thing." But what of the selective viewer, who changes channels for network news? Network executives, relying on both audience studies and personal intuition, assume, first, that there is not a significant number of such viewers and, second, that most of them choose particular news programs on the basis of the personalities of the commentators rather than the extent of the news coverage. Acting on these assumptions about audience behavior, the networks attempt to improve the ratings of their news shows by hiring "star" commentators and by investing in the programs that precede the network news. For example, in a memo to the president of NBC several years ago, a vice-president responsible for audience analysis made this suggestion for increasing the ratings in Los Angeles of the network's evening news program:

> It seems to me the only surefire way to increase our audience at 3:30 P.M. (and actually win the time period) is with Mike Douglas [a syndicated talk show, which NBC would have had to buy from Group W Productions, a subsidiary of the Westinghouse Broadcasting Company]. At 5–6 P.M. our news then should get at least what KABC is getting (let's say a 7 rating).
>
> Coming out of this increased lead-in—and a *news* lead-in, at that—I believe that [the evening news] at 6 P.M. will get a couple of rating points more. . . .

Similarly, a network can invest in the local news programs that precede or follow the network news on the five stations it owns. NBC concluded from a detailed study that it commissioned of the Chicago audience that local news programs, unlike network news, which builds its audience through coverage of special events, can increase their ratings through improved coverage of weather, sports, and local events. The study recommended, for example, that the network-owned station in Chicago hire a more popular local weather-caster, since "almost as many viewers look forward to seeing the weather as the news itself." The networks also assist the affiliated stations with their local news programs by providing a news syndication service. This supplies subscribing stations with sports and news stories through a half-hour feed, from which the stations can record stories for use on their own news programs.

Implicit in this approach to seeking higher ratings for network news programs is the idea that it doesn't make economic sense to spend large amounts on improving the editorial product. Hiring additional camera crews, reporters, and researchers presumably would not increase a news program's audience, and it definitely would be expensive. For instance, not only does each camera crew cost about a hundred thousand dollars a year to maintain, in equipment, salaries, and overtime, but it generates a prodigious amount of film—about twenty times as much as is used in the final stories—which has to be transported, processed, and edited. NBC accountants use a rule-of-thumb gauge of more than twenty dollars in service cost for every foot of film in the final story, which comes to more than seven hundred and twenty dollars a minute. And it is the number of camera crews a network maintains that defines, in some ways, the scope of its newsgathering operation. "The news you present is actually the news you cover," a network news vice-president has said, "The question is: How wide do you fling your net?"

In 1968, when I had access to staff meetings and assignment sheets at the three networks, NBC covered the nation each day with an average of ten camera crews, in New York, Chicago, Los Angeles, Washington, and Cleveland, plus two staff crews in Texas [L.B.J. was President] and one staff cameraman (who could assemble camera crews) in Boston. (In comparison, CBS's local news operation in Los Angeles, according to its news director, uses nine camera crews to cover the news of that one city.) Today, NBC says it has fifty domestic camera crews, but this figure includes sports, special events, and documentary crews, as well as local crews at the network's five stations. CBS says it has twenty full-time network news crews, in New York, Chicago, Los Angeles, Atlanta, and Washington, and ABC says it has sixteen, in New York, Chicago, Los Angeles, Washington, Atlanta, and Miami. Each of the networks also has camera crews in nine cities overseas. To be sure, when there is a momentous news event, the networks can quickly mobilize additional crews—those regularly assigned to news documentaries, sports, and local news at network stations, or those of affiliated stations—but the net that is cast for national news on a day-to-day basis is essentially defined by the crews that are routinely available for network assignment, and their number is set by the economic logic of network television.

Another element in the economics of network news is the fact that it costs a good deal more to transmit stories from some places than it does from other places. The lines that connect the networks with their affiliates across the country can normally be used to transmit programs in only one direction—from the network's headquarters in New York to the affiliates. Therefore, to transmit news reports electronically from any "remote" location—that is, anywhere except network facilities in a few cities—to the network for rebroadcast, a news program must order special "long lines" between the two points from the American Telephone & Telegraph Co. The charges for the "long line" are now fifty-five cents a mile for up to an hour's use and seven hundred and fifty dollars for a "loop," which is the package of electronic equipment that connects the transmission point (usually an affiliated station) with the telephone company's "long lines." It is even more expensive to order stories sent electronically by means of the satellite-relay system—eighteen hundred and fifty dollars for the first ten minutes of a story from London to New York and about twenty-four hundred dollars for the first ten minutes of a story from Tokyo to New York—and these costs are charged against the program's budget. The weekly budget for the NBC Nightly News is in excess of two hundred thousand dollars, and that of the CBS Evening News is almost a hundred thousand dollars, but more than half of each is committed in advance for the salaries and expenses of the producers, editors, writers, and other members of the "unit" and for the studio and other overhead costs that are automatically charged against the program's budget. (Differences in the billing of these charges account for most of the difference in the budgets of the NBC and CBS programs.) At CBS, about forty-nine thousand dollars a week, or eight thousand dollars a program, is left for "remotes." Since a news program needs from six to eight film stories a night, and some satellite charges can be as high as three thousand dollars apiece, the budget, in effect, limits the number of "remote" stories that can be transmitted in an average week.

Because of differences in transmission costs, producers have a strong incentive to take news stories from some areas rather than others, especially when their budgets are strained. The fact that networks base most of their camera crews and correspondents in New York, Washington, Chicago, and Los Angeles reinforces the advantage of using news stories from these areas, since they involve less overtime and travel expense. It is not surprising, then, that so many of the film stories shown on the national news programs originate in these areas. Although the geographical distribution of film stories varies greatly from day to day, over any sustained period it is skewed in the direction of these few large cities. It is economically more efficient to consign news of small-town America and of remote cities to timeless features such as Charles Kuralt's "On the Road" segments of the CBS Evening News. This suggests that if network news programs tend to focus on problems of a few large urban centers, it is less because, as former Vice-President Agnew argued, an "enclosed fraternity" of "commentators and producers live and work in the geographical and intellectual confines of Washington, D.C. or New York City . . . [and] draw their political and social views from the same sources" than because the networks' basic economic structure compels producers, willy-nilly, to select a large share of their filmed stories from a few locations.

The Fairness Doctrine requires broadcasters to provide a reasonable opportunity for the presentation of "contrasting viewpoints on controversial issues of public importance" in the course of their news and public-affairs programming. Unlike the "equal time" provisions of Section 315 of the Communications Act—which applies only to candidates running for a public office and requires that if a station grants time to one candidate it must grant equal time to other candidates, except on news programs—the Fairness Doctrine does not require that opposing arguments be given an equal number of minutes, be presented on the same program, or be presented within any specific period. It is left up to the licensee to decide what constitutes a "controversial issue of public importance," a "fair" reply, and a "reasonable time" in which the reply should be made. Moreover, broadcasters are apparently not expected to be equally "fair" on all issues of public importance; for example the Commission states in its "Fairness Primer" that it is not "the Commission's intention to make time available to Communists or to the Communist view-points."

Although no television station has ever lost its license because of a violation of the Fairness Doctrine, the doctrine has affected the form and content of network news in a number of ways. Most notably, the Fairness Doctrine puts an obligation on affiliates to "balance" any network program that advances only one side of an issue by themselves providing, in the course of their own programming, the other side, and the affiliates, rather than risk having to fulfill such an obligation, which could be both costly and bothersome, insist, virtually as a condition of taking network news, that the networks incorporate the obligatory "contrasting viewpoints" in their own news reports. The networks, in turn, make it a policy to present opposing views on any issue that could conceivably be construed as controversial.

This pro-and-con reporting is perfectly consistent with the usual notion of objectivity, if objectivity is defined, as it is by many correspondents, as "telling both sides of a story." It can, however, seriously conflict with the value that journalists place on what is now called investigative reporting, or simply any reporting the purpose of which is "getting to the bottom" of an issue, or "finding the truth," as correspondents often put it. A correspondent is required to present "contrasting points of view" even if he finds the views of one side to be valid and those of the other side to be false and misleading (in the Fairness Doctrine, truth is no defense), and therefore any attempt to resolve a controversial issue and "find the truth" is likely to be self-defeating. . . .

A frequent criticism of television news is that it is superficial—that it affords only scant coverage of news events, lacks depth or sufficient analysis of events, and engages in only a minimum of investigative reporting. The assumption of such criticism is that television newsmen lack journalistic credentials, that producers and executives are lax or indifferent toward their responsibilities, and that changing or educating the broadcasters would improve the news product. But the level of journalism in network news is more or less fixed by the time, money, and manpower that can be allocated to it, and these are determined by the structure of network television. Any substantial improvement in the level of network journalism, such as expanding coverage of events to a truly nationwide scale, would therefore require a structural change in network television that would effectively reorder its economic and political incentives rather than merely a change of personnel.

Another common criticism is, again, that network news is politically biased in favor of liberal or left-wing causes and leaders, because a small clique of newsmen in New York and Washington shape the news to fit their own political beliefs. In this critique, network news is presumed to be highly politicized by the men who select and report it, and the remedy most often suggested is to employ conservative newsmen to balance the liberal viewpoints. Since, for economic reasons, much of the domestic news on the network programs does in fact come from a few big cities, and since in recent years many of the efforts to change the distribution of political values and services have been concentrated in the big cities, the networks perhaps have reported a disproportionately large share of these activities. The requirement that network news be "nationalized" further adds to the impression that the networks are advancing radical causes, for in elevating local disputes to national proportions, newscasters appear to be granting them uncalled-for-importance.

Left-wing critics complain that network news neglects the inherent contradictions in the American system. Their critique runs as follows: Network news focuses not on substantive problems but on symbolic protests. By overstating the importance of protest actions, television news invites the audience to judge the conduct of the protesters rather than the content of the problem. This creates false issues. Popular support is generated against causes that on television appear to rely on violent protests while underlying economic and social problems are systematically masked or ignored. Broadcasters can be expected to help perpetuate "the system" because they are an important part of it. Thus one critic writes, "The media owners will do anything to maintain these myths. . . . They will do anything to keep the public from realizing that the Establishment dominates society through its direct and indirect control of the nation's communication system." In fact, however, the tendency to depict symbolic protests rather than substantive problems is closely related to the problem of audience maintenance. Protests can be universally comprehended, it is presumed, if they are presented in purely symbolic terms: one group standing for one cause challenging another group and cause. The sort of detail that would be necessary to clarify economic and social issues is not easily translated into visual terms, whereas the sort of dramatic images that can be found in violent protests have an immediate impact on an audience. Newsmen therefore avoid liberal or radical arguments, not because they are politically committed to supporting "the system," but because such arguments do not satisfy the requisites of network news.

Finally, in what might best be called the social-science critique, network news is faulted for presenting a picture of society that does not accurately correspond to the empirical data. Spokesmen selected by television to represent groups in society tend to be statistically atypical of the groups for which they are supposedly speaking; for example, militant students may have appeared to be in the majority on college campuses in American during the nineteen-sixties because of the frequency with which they were selected to represent student views, when in fact data collected by social scientists showed that they constituted a small minority. It is generally argued that such discrepancies stem from a lack of readily usable data rather than any intent on the part of journalists to misrepresent situations. The implication in this critique is that if network news organizations had the techniques of social scientists, or employed social scientists as consultants, they would produce a more realistic version of the claims and aspirations of different segments of society. However, the selection of spokesmen to appear on television is determined less by a lack of data than by the organizational needs of network news. In order to hold the attention of viewers to whom the subject of the controversy may be of no interest, television newsmen select spokesmen who are articulate, easily identifiable, and dramatic, and the "average" person in a group cannot be depended on to manifest these qualities. Moreover, the nationalization of news requires that spokesmen represent the major themes in society rather than what is statistically typical. Given the organizational need to illustrate news stories with spokesmen who are both dramatic and thematic, network news cannot be expected to present a picture that conforms to the views of social scientists, no matter how much data or how many technical skills the social scientists might supply.

As long as the requisites remain essentially the same, network news can be expected to define American society by the problems of a few urban areas rather than of the entire nation, by action rather than ideas, by dramatic protests rather than substantive contradictions, by "newsmakers" rather than economic and social structures, by atypical rather than typical views, and by synthetic national themes rather than disparate local events.

Bibliography

There are dozens of books and articles important to this subject. First, see other articles in this book. For additional views, consult Paul H. Weaver, "Is Television News Biased?" *The Public Interest* (Winter 1972); Edith Efron, *The News Twisters* (Nash, 1971); William Small, *To Kill a Messenger: Television News and the Real World* (Hastings House, 1970); Fred Friendly, *Due to Circumstances Beyond Our Control* (Random House, 1967); Daniel St. Albin Greene, "Making a Television News Show," *Seminar Quarterly* (March 1970); and Spiro T. Agnew, November 13, 1969 speech to Iowa Republicans. Useful background information can be found in: Ben Bagdikian, *The Information Machine* (Harper & Row, 1971); the Columbia University annual *Survey of Broadcast Journalism*; Robert McNeil, *The People and the News* (Pacific Books, 1968). Also see regularly: *Journal of Broadcasting, Television Quarterly,* and other periodicals. In his 1975 work *Television: The Most Popular Art*, Horace Newcomb compares the drama and ritual found in entertainment programs to the action in television news and offers some thought-provoking comments.

52 Local News: Knuckling Down to Basics
Broadcasting

When Pope Paul VI died, CBS, ABC, and NBC covered the events from Rome. So did CBS-owned WCBS-TV New York, KNXT(TV) Los Angeles, and WBBM-TV Chicago. So too did Westinghouse Broadcasting. And, reports news consultant Al Primo, so did most of the 15 stations he works for. That's just for openers. A sizable portion of the world's press covering the Vatican in the last few weeks has been local television units, many competing with others from their own markets for stories that were intended exclusively for their home-town audiences.

It is indicative of the state of local television journalism today that so many would fly way around the world to score a beat on a television story that five years ago would have been entrusted exclusively to the networks. The competition among local outlets is fierce and getting fiercer. News budgets and staffs are growing, and not just because of the ever-increasing prices paid for premium news personalities. Stations are installing new equipment, increasing their staffs and, as in the Rome story, spending freely for remotes.

In the fast-motion history of local television, this kind of news competition is old news—although it was only a dozen years ago that many large-market television news operations consisted of a single anchorman, a news ticker and a handful of anonymous reporters. The token expense associated with news in those days has mushroomed, it's estimated, into a $1 million annual budget at many stations in the top 30 markets, and $2 million-plus in the top 15 markets. Those in the cat bird seat of the business think $8 million–$10 million is not an unreasonable estimate of how much is being spent on news by stations in New York and Chicago. And the longest news program in the country—a two-and-a-half hour early-evening program at KNXT—is said to cost $15 million–$16 million, although CBS won't confirm that guess.

In few instances are stations losing money on those kinds of outlays. In the case of affiliates, most of the program and commercial day is commanded by the networks, and the early and late-evening news blocks are among the few large-audience time periods local stations can claim as their own. And the stations have made them lucrative. That they make 40%–60% of their revenues from advertising on their local news shows has become an industrywide assumption.

So it is not surprising that local stations consider primacy in the news ratings their first priority. Ed Bewley, a former news consultant with Frank Magid Associates, now head of his own Dallas-based consulting shop, observes: "Everybody has tasted the wine. They have seen that if you spend more money for the

This treatment of techniques used in handling local television news appeared as a special report in *Broadcasting*, August 28, 1978. It is used with the permission of *Broadcasting*.

news, it would come back to them two- or three-fold." Can the news expenditures be expected to plateau soon? No, says Richard Mallary, director of news operations for Cox Broadcasting. "We haven't reached the top end in spending yet. The profits are that great."

A business where stakes are so high and the difference between success and failure so small as two or three rating points has, like other intensely competitive businesses, produced its share of trends. And it is still, says one less charitable observer, "a business that abounds in gimmicks."

The rise of local TV news can even be traced along parallel lines with some of those fashions. There was "happy talk," an attempt at many stations some five years ago to infuse the news presentation with some of the more informal and friendly atmosphere of entertainment shows by having anchorpeople casually converse, even clown, between news items. "Happy talk" in its most bizarre form—as in the true case of the anchorman who was pelted on-camera with a rubber chicken—has disappeared, news experts say, although the informality lingers.

The "war of the sets" is also said to have waned somewhat after most stations spent thousands of dollars to design the most attractive setting—anchor desks, carpeting, paneling, weather maps, ceiling lights—in which to present the news. Nearly all stations have matched one another for graphics, too, making use of chroma keys, character generators, and staff artists.

The use of news personalities—anchorpeople, sports, and weather people—is a trend that was at the heart of TV news's great awakening. As stations learned that viewers tuned in to see their favorite news celebrity, the trade in anchorpeople especially became frenetic, with the biggest prizes—big city markets and high salaries—going to the anchors with the best combination of personality and good looks.

In the early days, anchorpeople were mentioned by TV's critics in the same disdainful breath as "happy talk." Today they continue to be the center of attention in trade talk, largely because of the meteoric rise and fall in fortunes of some and because of their salaries, which range from $25,000 to more than $250,000.

Those salaries, though more in line with entertainers than news professionals, are often defended as the best investments local stations can make. Mr. Bewley says that audience research consistently shows that the anchorperson is the number-one reason most people watch local news. "Talent boils down to being the number-one distinction between stations," he says.

Still, the news experts detect a slight change in the winds in the anchor trend. "I'm not sure that classic good looks are important any more," says Mr. Bewley. "They're more qualified journalistically than 10 years ago," he says.

It is doubtful, nevertheless, that stations will stop looking at potential anchorpeople for their cosmetic appeal. No less a defender of journalistic quality than Pat Polillo, vice president of TV news operations, Westinghouse Broad-

As television journalism matures, it is becoming more adept at bringing viewers the news when it happens from where it happens. To expand live coverage of its ADI, KRON-TV San Francisco developed a sophisticated microwave system (adapted from military applications) to connect its five bureaus and city hall office with the station (see map). The three microwave dishes and fleet of mobile vans enable the station to handle three feeds simultaneously from distances of more than 100 miles from the studio.

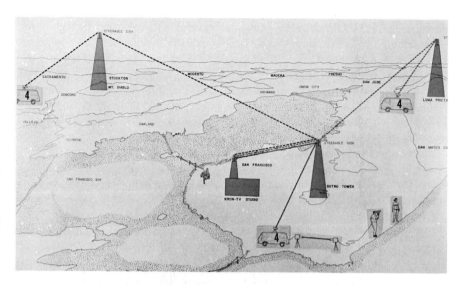

Viewers of WXYZ-TV Detroit watch a little technical slight of hand as anchor Bill Bonds gets ready to turn things over to reporter Rob Kress covering a January blizzard—a combination of technical wizardry and an emphasis on hard news common now, but infrequent just five years ago.

casting, acknowledges that "if you can get a pretty news anchor who is at the same time bright and can do the job, I'm for that."

One of the most expensive trends in recent years has been electronic news gathering, whose first adherents voiced the hope that its tremendous initial costs might one day be offset by savings in film and film processing. Such has not been the case, however, reports Peter Hoffman of one of the older consulting firms around, McHugh & Hoffman. "I don't know of anybody yet who saved money by going from one camera to another," he says. ENG has already run through one generation of technology, and the second—tougher, smaller, and even more expensive than the first—is being snapped up. Those stations that converted completely to ENG with first-generation hardware, says Mr. Hoffman, "got stuck."

Despite its escalating cost, ENG is destined to become the prevalent mode for collecting the news, the observers say—for two reasons. One is that as it becomes more portable, it will be more convenient than film, and with its live capability, simply better. The other is competition. Says Mr. Polillo: "If two stations are coming live out of an event and you aren't there, you're basically finished as a source of news. . . . You could lose your entire standing in a community without it."

These trends—the personalities, graphics, sets, live scenes—have blended to form the type of news presentation that local TV does best. It is in its stride when covering police stories, disaster stories, human drama and controversy, stories with lots of pictures and action.

But most of the stations in a market, having adopted the same fashions, have found roughly equal ground now. They can't get an edge over the competition with ENG, or a designer set, because usually everybody already has it, says Mr. Polillo. And it is possible, he and others think, that the technological frontier has been pushed to its limit.

They see a new trend creeping up—the one they should have embarked on at the start, the critics would say. And that is simply trying to do a better job of covering news, including political and investigative stories that are difficult to illustrate.

Efforts in this direction are being greeted as bold experiments in some areas. Hard news is, for example, the avowed purpose of KNXT, which recently instituted its two-and-a-half-hour evening format and increased its news staff by 50 (for a total of 145) to start a run out of deep third place in the Los Angeles market. Van Gordon Sauter, who was transferred from his post as vice president for program practices at the network to head that station's operations, is not enamored of local TV journalism. As for criticisms about vacuous anchorpeople, happy talk, and shallow coverage: "Most of them are justified," he says. "Too much TV news pays scant attention to journalism content."

KNXT, he says, has decided that its "market entry point" is to be the production of straight news "with more spontaneity and serendipity" than that of the competitors. Since putting the longer news show on the air in June, however, the ratings have hardly budged. The station is still a "deep-third" in the market, Mr. Sauter says. But he adds that he doesn't expect much change in the market until the middle of next year. If it doesn't work, he adds, it will bode poorly for local TV news.

Mr. Polillo, meanwhile, has one of his stations, WBZ-TV Boston, heavily committed to investigative reporting—with gratifying results. Begun as an experiment last fall, WBZ-TV put in action a seven-person investigative unit, the "I-team" Mr. Polillo calls it, to do one "heavy piece" a month. In practice it has done much better, including a single 39-minute piece on conflict of interest and influence peddling in the Massachusetts legislature that he says resulted in a new ethics bill being introduced there. The group, which is autonomous in the newsroom from all but the news director, has done stories on contracts, housing, and business and in addition has fed news tips to the newsroom that have resulted in another 40 stories by the regular news staff—a happy side benefit that had not been anticipated.

The experience tells Mr. Polillo "that stories that people thought couldn't be done on TV can be done. . . . It knocks down the last excuse for not doing serious investigative work." As a result, Westinghouse has authorized similar investigative units for stations in Philadelphia (KYW-TV) and San Francisco (KPIX).

Cox's Mr. Mallary tells of similar pro-news efforts at Cox stations. WSB-TV Atlanta, he says, is readying a "Segment 3" format similar to the one now on NBC nightly news for longer treatment of stories that might usually be handled in bits and pieces. The thrust there, he says, is to concentrate on the "why of a story, and on what it means to you," a generally more difficult task for TV news than newspapers to perform. The station has also put in place a desk assistant to handle hour-by-hour assignments, to free the news director to develop ideas. Experience has shown, he says, that original stories don't get done because no one has time to think them up.

Mr. Mallary is another alumnus of Magid Associates, which used to be accused of counseling stations to keep stories down to a minute and a half or less. But the mood has changed, Mr. Mallary says, so that "now a good news director can say, 'I don't care if a talking head is four minutes long—as long as he is saying something.' "

Mr. Primo concurs that local TV outlets are aiming for better quality in reporting. Some stations, he says, are doing more than just shooting pictures of a fire. They're finding out how it got started, interviewing the people who lived inside, and further, are finding out how the damage to the structure will affect the surrounding community.

But the trend results from more than just a heightened sensitivity to the rules of good journalism, Mr. Primo says. It's because of competition. "There's more of a commitment to finding out why, because the guy across the street is doing that."

The commentators acknowledge that the advances are largely centered in the biggest cities. The trickle-down process into the large and medium markets is still more a hope than a reality. Comments Mr. Polillo, there is still "the propensity for duplicating the past . . . I see people who take over an operation in trouble, and the first thing they do is hit the cosmetics."

Mr. Polillo is a proponent of the school that says that cosmetics are not enough any more, largely because of the local news audience. If there is one point he and the others mentioned here can agree on, it is that the local TV audience has changed. It's more fickle than it was five years ago; viewers won't tune in the same news program night after night just out of loyalty, says Mr. Primo. "They recognize when a station is doing a good news job, and they are demanding a more professional execution." A flashy new look alone won't beef up the ratings any longer. "What we've learned is that you can't fool all of the people all the time," he says.

Mr. Hoffman says his firm's research shows that local TV news viewers are more "introspective" than a few years ago. They want the news to be placed in a perspective they can understand and one that is meaningful to their own lives. This introspection, he says, defines the new front that has to be attacked in the TV news war.

Mr. Polillo agrees. As a practical matter, he says, the only way a station in a close market race can run away with the ratings now "is with original reports." But beyond that, better news is almost a moral obligation to him. Local audiences, tuning in an average of three to five nights a week to the news, have demonstrated their trust in the local stations to tell them what is important in the community and the world.

"It's time for local TV news to redeem itself," he says.

Bibliography

There are many critics of local television news and the heavy use of news consultants by local stations. Ron Power's book *The Newscasters* (St. Martin's, 1977) poked into this show-biz world of broadcast news. *Broadcasting* has carried a number of pieces. For example, "Experts Debate Skin Tests in News," December 20, 1976, and "TV Happy Talk, Tabloidism in San Francisco Target of '60 Minutes' " March 11, 1974. *TV Guide* also covers the local news controversies. On the national level, *Cosmopolitan* told of "Good Morning America: ABC's A.M. Success Story" in its September, 1978 issue. In its January/February 1978 issue, *Columbia Journalism Review* ran a piece by Chris Welles wondering, "Do Most People Depend on TV for News?" The piece disputed a Roper survey showing that most persons obtained most of their news from television. Also see *Journalism Quarterly*, Summer 1975, "TV Journalism v. Show Biz." The following segment from *Broadcasting*, the last article in this book, reports many fine achievements of various local broadcast news units around the country.

53 The Live One: Spot Coverage Is TV's Biggest Advantage

Broadcasting

ENG use increases every year and in 1978–79 an extensive commitment to the technology was shown by KRON-TV San Francisco. With 83% of the station's area of dominant influence outside the city, the station developed a network of five bureaus: Santa Clara county, Alameda county, San Mateo county, Contra Costa county, and the state capital, Sacramento, more than 90 miles away. These are in addition to a full-time urban affairs office in city hall.

To implement the concept, the chief engineer, Larry Pozzi, adapted technology used in the military and erected three steerable microwave dishes. In conjunction with a fleet of ENG vans, the station has fed live broadcasts from as far as 125 miles away. Also, with the system KRON-TV can handle three microwave feeds at once. In one newscast it was able to air seven remotes.

The microwave switchers and digital video effects system cost the station close to $1 million. The vans were outfitted at $20,000 each and six RCA TK-76 cameras ran $240,000.

Another station using the bureau approach is WNAC-TV Boston. Three regional offices—north, west, and south—were set up with the reporter/bureau chiefs reporting nightly during the newscast. The station has also installed "hot lines" to provide community leaders direct access to the bureau chiefs.

New Jersey has been the focus of an increased number of WPVI-TV Philadelphia news stories. Last fall the station began operating a microwave link between the station and Trenton, New Jersey's capital, about 40 miles away. The system uses an antenna mounted on a hotel across the street from the capitol building. A signal can be beamed to that antenna from a wide area around Trenton, then to WPVI-TV's ENG antenna in Philadelphia, and finally to the station.

Among the live stories aired over this facility were: the inauguration of New Jersey Governor Brendon Byrne for his second term, coverage of February's crippling snow storm in Trenton, and coverage of the N.J. state legislature as it decided such matters as the legalization of casino gambling and an extension of state income tax. Also live, through land lines, not microwave, were the station's stories on the opening of the casinos in Atlantic City in May.

Two KPRC-TV Houston reporters, Jack Cato and Phil Archer, were seriously injured while investigating a riot in the city's Moody Park last May. While filming the incident, the mob attacked the reporters. Both men were beaten and stabbed and their equipment, but not their film, was destroyed.

This article accompanied the preceding one in the August 28, 1978 issue of *Broadcasting*. It is reprinted with the permission of *Broadcasting*.

Pounding the pavement. WNAC-TV Boston produced numerous specials leading up to the famous Boston Marathon. And on race day it was there from start to finish, and in between.

By late evening, KPRC-TV was ready with several reports on the disturbance. There was a live report from the police command post near the park. Mr. Cato told his story from the emergency room of the hospital, and the salvaged film was aired.

The following night, KPRC-TV put on a half-hour special covering the riot and its aftereffects on the community. The special included a live interview with both reporters from their hospital beds.

In Laurel, Miss., WDAM-TV's viewers witnessed a real-life "dragnet" episode when reporters followed a high speed convoy of law enforcement officers to a remote location in Percy county, Miss. for a series of late night raids. All on film, the raids were the climax of an investigation into corruption in the county that led to the arrests and federal indictment for racketeering of the Perry county sheriff and the state indictment of a prominent businessman for the attempted bribery of the district attorney.

In January when Columbus, Ohio was hit hardest, WCMH-TV there set up broadcast headquarters in the National Guard Armory where anchor Leon Bibb stayed with a cameraman for four days, going live when needed. The weather was so severe that when the station's ENG van arrived at the Armory, the van's doors were frozen. It took blow torches to thaw things out so the broadcasts could get under way.

WCMH-TV also devised a 30-minute energy quiz to give information on how to best utilize energy around the home.

WXIA-TV Atlanta made news last year with its hiring of former Director of the Office of Management and Budget Bert Lance as a commentator.

Its ENG equipment was put to the test last October when a jet was hijacked from Grand Island, Neb. and flown to Atlanta. WXIA-TV was on hand at the airport for the landing and stayed with the story, providing uninterrupted cov-

Above and beyond. While responding to a police call of a riot at a city park and filming the action (top), KPRC-TV Houston reporters Jack Cato (l) and Phil Archer were beaten and stabbed by members of the mob.

erage for 10½ hours. Two live cameras were on both sides of the plane with five reporters assigned. A third live camera was atop the control tower. In all, the station had 40 people involved in the coverage which lasted until the passengers were released and the hijacker killed himself. The station estimated its coverage cost more than $35,000 in lost revenue and thousands more in overtime pay and use of equipment.

On February 6 and 7, a snowstorm dumped 54 inches of snow on Rhode Island. When the severity of the storm became apparent, WJAR-TV Providence, R.I. set up a live newscam and its microwave facilities in Civil Defense headquarters in the statehouse. Throughout the storm, Jack Kavanaugh worked closely with Governor J. Joseph Garrahy, disseminating storm-related information and becoming a link between government officials and the people. When the state's Emergency Broadcast System was activated on Feb. 9, the live microwave hook-up of WJAR-TV served as a pool for the other stations as the governor spoke to the people on the status of the emergency.

The blizzard which immobilized Central Indiana last January did not keep the WRTV Indianapolis news team from their jobs. In anticipation of the storm, key staffers were housed in a nearby motel, and a handful of others braved the hazardous conditions to make it to the station.

Among those staffers was the meterologist, who remained at the station day and night providing bulletins to supplement regular coverage.

A helicopter was rented to enable crews to report the situation in remote areas of the state where conditions were even worse. The microwave van was also employed for live updates from the blizzard-swept streets. The news team also took one of the first trips with the National Guard on a mercy mission.

WKYC-TV Cleveland, Ohio gave special spot coverage to the severe winter weather. In January, the station sent four film crews and three reporters to cover a blizzard which brought a large part of the state to a stand still. A live unit was sent to the transmitter in case power was lost at the stations. A conference call between three reporters in key areas around the state was set up with a map pinpointing their locations. All school closings and cancellations were reported. Later in the season, when the snow and ice started melting, the station covered flooding in areas where rivers overflowed. Co-anchor Doug Adair reported from a flooded area and conducted a live interview with the mayor of an inundated suburb.

In other spot coverage, co-anchor Amanda Arnold, two film crews, two ENG crews, and three reporters were sent to Brunswick, where striking teachers were being released from a week in jail.

While the station was presenting its live coverage of Cleveland's police strike in July, a settlement was reached. With Mr. Adair at city hall and with six crews (three ENG, three film) and four reporters, WKYC-TV presented stories on lootings and robberies and the city's attempt to get the national guard. The news team then went live to the Justice Center, where the court ordered a compromise, the police decided to return to work, and the mayor held a news conference.

Plane facts. When a hijacker forced a jet to land at the Atlanta airport, WXIA-TV had its minicam there for the duration.

Official word. WJAR-TV Providence, R.I. reporter Jack Kavanaugh (r) interviews the state's governor, J. Joseph Garrahy (l), and Congressman Edward Beard after they returned from a helicopter inspection of the storm-struck state last winter.

Light traffic. This shot of uncrowded downtown Indianapolis was part of WRTV's blizzard coverage.

February saw the worst blizzard in 30 years hit New York. WCBS-TV covered the city with specials, weather advisories, expanded newscasts, and cut-ins every hour and crawls every hour. Reports were also filed by helicopter and from the outlying suburbs.

While blizzards were not a worry in some parts of the country, the weather provided WFLA-TV Tampa with an important spot news story. In May a tornado touched down in Pinellas county at lunch time, demolishing an elementary school. The station aired live reports throughout the afternoon citing food and shelter areas and meeting points for parents and children as well as reports on the injured.

In Phoenix, driving rains caused serious flooding in March. KTVK-TV stationed reporters in the hardest hit flood areas for on-the-spot coverage. During this crisis, Arizona Governor Wesley Brolin died of a heart attack, and the news team broadcast live bulletins and an hour-long newscast on developments.

A flood story was one of the year's biggest for WOWT Omaha. The Platte River in Nebraska overflowed its banks in March, forcing the evacuation of about 4,000 persons and causing an estimated $240 million in damage. The station aired bulletins and advisories throughout two days, and the evening news was expanded to an hour and devoted mostly to the flood.

Another WOWT live effort involved efforts of farmers to get 100% parity prices for their products that resulted in a farm strike. Chief newscaster Gary Kerr anchored a live remote on the story from the Omaha stockyards and introduced stories by other station reporters on various aspects of the strike.

KXAS-TV Fort Worth made heavy use of its ENG gear with some stories that came from places not in its coverage area. In January, as the Dallas Cowboys and the Denver Broncos prepared to meet in Super Bowl XII, the station sent two sports reporters, a minicam photographers, and a technician to New Orleans. During the course of the week they sent back both live and taped reports for each days 5 P.M. and 10 P.M. news. The day before the game a second minicam was dispatched for game highlights as well as live reaction from the Cowboys' headquarters hotel at the victory party.

Even further away was the story on Braniff Airway's attempt to open service between the Dallas-Fort Worth airport and London and the ensuing rate squabble. KXAS-TV sent back a live satellite report from London and a taped one on the first flight of the new service and the welcoming ceremonies. The live report was prepared with the help of an NBC producer and editing station and was fed into the station's noon newscast.

Early in the morning of July 29, a train car began leaking hydrogen chloride, a toxic gas that endangered the lives of thousands of residents on the northwest side of Jacksonville, Fla. Shortly thereafter, WJXT Jacksonville was on the scene providing live bulletins on the situation. At 10 A.M. the station aired its first special program, including reports from the scene, interviews with the people in charge of the evacuation, a weather report on wind conditions in the area, and a studio interview with a chemist on the dangers of the gas. These reports were

In the middle. Chris Borgen, WCBS-TV New York correspondent (l, rear) became part of a news story when he successfully negotiated for the release of a hostage being held at knife point by prison escapee Anthony Ricco (light coat). Later Mr. Borgen described the situation with an artist's sketch to fellow correspondent John Tesh.

updated several times during the day and, at 11:30 P.M., a news special recapped the day's events. Five reporters, five photographers, three producers, and two engineers worked in the field to provide the extensive coverage. Five minicams on the scene were linked to the station by a van equipped with a microwave transmitter.

KSTP-TV Minneapolis-St. Paul spent more money than it ever had on a story to cover a murder trial involving a man accused of killing his wealthy mother-in-law and her night nurse. Because a change of venue moved the trial 120 miles from Duluth to Brainerd, Minn., cars, planes and, on one occasion, a helicopter were needed to provide daily coverage of the trial, which lasted two-and-a-half months. Coverage was expanded with film of locations and people mentioned in testimony, artwork from the courtroom, and re-enactments of some of the testimony. The station assigned four persons to work exclusively on the story.

The collapse of an earthen dam 100 miles north of Atlanta provided WAGA-TV's news department with a challenge. But it managed to broadcast from the scene using a helicopter and leapfrogging microwave units to feed tape.

A major story for WMTV Madison, Wis. began 70 miles away in a Waukesha, Wis. courtroom. There a man grabbed a deputy's gun, shot and killed him and another deputy, and escaped with a woman hostage in her car. The car was finally stopped in a Madison intersection and its tires shot out by police. For the next five hours WMTV diverted most of its news resources to the intersection and the story. A minicam crew, stationed just 100 feet from the scene, and microwave van provided live bulletins. Two film crews, one stationed on the ground, the other on a roof top, also recorded the action, while reporters at the scene gathered information. Other reporters at the station received reports by telephone and two-way radio and kept in telephone contact with authorities. The incident ended after a brief shootout. Within minutes, the station reported that the gunman was under arrest and the hostage safe, though both had been slightly wounded.

When an alleged bank robber, Thomas Michael Hannon, hijacked a Frontier Airlines jet in Nebraska and demanded that it be flown, with crew and passengers,

Saying goodbye. KMSP-TV
Minneapolis captured these
scenes at the funeral of
Senator Hubert Humphrey.

to Atlanta, WSB-TV Atlanta was live on the scene to cover the events as they unfolded.

Live minicam crews were sent to Hartsfield International Airport, where the plane landed, and to the control tower as well. A third crew was dispatched to the Fulton county jail where George David Stewart, Hannon's alleged partner in crime and who's release was among the demands, was being held.

The news team was on live when the plane touched down, and spot coverage continued throughout the day. When the drama came to a close—the hostages were released and the hijacker fatally shot himself—WSB-TV was on live.

WIIC-TV Pittsburgh interrupted its regular prime time programming for some live Memorial Day fireworks, the demolition of the city's Brady Street Bridge. The explosion was the climax of a story that began a week earlier when a man who was working on the bridge was pinned between collapsing girders. WIIC-TV covered the efforts to free the man, which culminated when doctors amputated his leg. The accident caused fears that the bridge was shifting and might collapse into the adjacent replacement bridge, already open to traffic. After inspection, a decision was made to blow up the bridge instead of disassembling it. On May 29 two WIIC-TV ENG crews were on hand all day for the placing of the charges and the 8:40 P.M. spectacle. An instant replay followed the live coverage, and the story was reported in detail on the station's 11 P.M. news. The station's coverage was also seen the following morning on NBC's "The Today Show."

Although Hubert Humphrey's death was felt throughout the country, it was one of the biggest stories in his home state of Minnesota. And in Minneapolis, KMSP-TV provided constant coverage of the events following the senator's death as well as reviewing his life.

The morning after Mr. Humphrey died, KMSP-TV went live for nearly one hour from the airport as the coffin and family were flown to Washington. Later that evening they broadcast an hour-long obituary produced by reporter Steve Doyle, who had served as an intern on the senator's staff. He had also made a three-year study of Mr. Humphrey, interviewing him at his home in Waverly, Minn., and traveling to South Dakota, Mr. Humphrey's birthplace, to talk with former teachers and friends. The station also covered the burial and dedicated an entire evening news broadcast to the life and death of the senator.

As a service to the 200,000 Catholics in its market, WISC-TV Madison, Wis. broadcast live the ordination of Auxiliary Bishop George Wirz on March 9 at St. Raphaels Cathedral in Madison. A 10-man staff of reporters and technicians used two stationary cameras and one minicam to cover the two-and-a-half hour ceremony.

With "Jaws 2" once again bringing sharks to the public eye, WTNH-TV New Haven, Conn. had a real shark story last June when a great white shark was harpooned off Montauk, Long Island. After getting a call from ABC in New York and making sure the shark story was not a hoax, General Manager Pete Orne (also a pilot) flew a reporter and cameraman to search for the fish and the

State story. KYW-TV
Philadelphia went to the
Pennsylvania capital to
cover the state budget
deadlock with reporters
Dick Sheeran (r) and
Harrisburg correspondent
Sandy Starobin.

boat trying to land it. The captain of the boat was interviewed via ship-to-shore radio, and a boat was chartered to get some shots of the struggle. Back at the station an interview was conducted with an icthyologist from Yale. After more than 12 hours, the shark, which was estimated at 25 feet long and between 3,500–4,000 pounds, broke loose and got away.

KDKA-TV Pittsburgh and KYW-TV Philadelphia, both owned by Westinghouse Broadcasting Company, pooled their resources on two occasions to provide comprehensive statewide coverage of stories of statewide interest. The first occasion was precipitated by the Pennsylvania state legislature's failure to agree on a new budget. When money began running out, state employes stopped receiving paychecks, state services began shutting down, and a crisis ensued. On August 16, 1977, the stations, along with reporters in the state capital of Harrisburg, were linked together for a live simulcast. While anchormen at KDKA-TV reported the impact of the crisis in western Pennsylvania, a KYW-TV anchor reported repercussions in the eastern half of the state. The reporters in Harrisburg, one from each station, reported on activities at the state house and the reactions of Governor Milton Shapp.

The simulcast setup was repeated this spring for another story of statewide interest in Pennsylvania—the May 17 primary election. Through the cooperation of the two stations, viewers were given live coverage from the headquarters of all the major candidates.

The last act. WAPA-TV San Juan, P.R. got some of the most dramatic and most requested footage of the year as it caught the fatal fall of aerialist Karl Wallenda.

WAPA-TV San Juan, Puerto Rico captured on video tape one of the most dramatic moments in spot news, the fatal fall of aerialist Karl Wallenda from a high wire during a performance in San Juan. The tape was rebroadcast worldwide.

Another WAPA-TV story that received national attention in the United States was the takeover of the Chilean consulate and the kidnapping of the Chilean consul in San Juan by two supporters of Puerto Rican independence. As part of its coverage, the station did a live telephone interview with the consul and with one of his two captors. The station later broadcast a statement by the governor of Puerto Rico, who rejected one of the kidnappers' demands, that July 4 festivities be suspended.

WTAE-TV Pittsburgh's news department has made a commitment to go anywhere for a story. The station covered the collapse of the water tower in Willow Grove, W.Va., 100 miles from Pittsburgh. In July 1978 its cameras went to Johnstown, Pa. for a half-hour special on the community's recovery from the flood of 1977.

When a man suspected of as many as 17 murders in the Pittsburgh area was arrested in St. Augustine, Fla., WTAE-TV dispatched reporter Debra Fox to the scene. She spent three days there as law enforcement officials questioned the suspect, and she reported discussions regarding trials and extradition proceedings.

A stroke patient at the University of Maryland hospital in Baltimore seized two nurses in his room, threatened them with a pipe, and barricaded the door. He then told police he wanted to talk to someone from WJZ-TV Baltimore.

The station sent Frank Luber. Mr. Luber talked with the man throughout the morning and finally made a deal—if Mr. Luber would broadcast the message that the hospital was trying to kill him, the man would release his hostages and give up. WJZ-TV instructed Mr. Luber to comply. The station's programming was interrupted and, in a live report, Mr. Luber described the stiuation and delivered the man's message. The door immediately opened and the man and his hostages came out.

Two major stories developed for KSBY-TV San Luis Obispo, Calif., over the last year—demonstrations against a nuclear power plant and disastrous floods that followed two years of drought in central California. The station mobilized its entire news staff to cover the demonstrations against the Diablo nuclear power plant and presented a report on the protests that included film of protestors climbing over fences onto plant property and interviews with other protestors sitting in a road waiting to be arrested.

Heavy rains fell in the first three months of 1978, causing extensive flooding. Part of the station's coverage centered on families in Atascadero who lost part of their backyards when a river bank collapsed, threatening their homes for several hours. Coverage also included stories of bridge and road washouts that left several families stranded.

When former Maryland Governor Marvin Mandel and his five co-defendants were found guilty on various counts of mail fraud and racketeering, WJLA-TV Washington responded with a live phone report at the time (11:06 A.M.) and 15 minutes of coverage on the noon news. The coverage continued through the day and was capped with a special half-hour perspective show, "The Mandel Verdict."

WJLA-TV also created "instant news specials" on big stories airing at 7:30–8 P.M. on the day each story broke. Included were: the Bakke decision, the Bullets NBA championship, the death of Hubert Humphrey, and George Allen's leaving the Redskins.

WCCO-TV Minneapolis's coverage of one of its biggest stories—the death of Senator Hubert Humphrey—began with a live report from the Humphrey home in Waverly, Minn. Then followed some 10 hours of local live programming with reports on the departure of the body to Washington, a two-hour tribute to the senator the night after his death (including live reports from Washington, coverage of the return of the body, and five hours of continuing live coverage on the day of the funeral).

Thirty-six people were killed last December when a grain elevator exploded in Westwego, La., across the Mississippi River from New Orleans. Within 20 minutes WWL-TV New Orleans had a crew on the scene. A second ENG truck arrived 30 minutes later, and seven film crews were dispatched for the station's hours of coverage.

Heavy rains last year caused an earthen dam at Toccoa Falls, Ga., to collapse, killing 39 people. WSPA-TV Spartanburg, S.C. was on the scene with several news crews providing live reports and film footage. At the same time, heavy rains were flooding the western part of North Carolina, and members of the station's sports department were sent to cover the story. By the 11 P.M. news, the station was able to air a special 45-minute newscast covering both areas of flooding and interviews with Georgia's governor and First Lady Rosalynn Carter.

The rains came. When a dam broke, killing 39 people in Toccoa Falls, Ga., WSPA-TV Spartanburg, S.C. reporter Paul Brown covered the story.

Day in court. As part of a year-long experiment, cameras were allowed in Florida courts. Here WPLG Miami is covering the proceedings.

Proposition 13 and the June primary elections were the big news for KCRA-TV Sacramento, Calif. The station's election night coverage extended from Sacramento to Los Angeles. Two reporters at different Los Angeles remotes fed reports back to the station. In addition, a live unit and a tape unit were shuttled to various campaign headquarters in Sacramento, and there were regular live feeds from Stockton, Calif.

In addition, KCRA-TV also connected its character generator to the computer run by the secretary of state to provide instant display of the returns as they came in.

A gun battle with police turned a quiet Saturday into a fast news day for WWLP Springfield, Mass. Cameraman Mark Langevin responded to a police call and found them exchanging shots with a man held up in a house. The man killed one man and wounded a 12-year-old girl before police cornered him. Mr. Langevin recorded the battle until the barrage of tear gas drove the man out and he was captured.

Last year included an interesting experiment for TV stations in Florida—they were granted temporary permission to film in the courts. The most famous result of the experiment was the Ronny Zamora trial. But that was not all that was done. As WPLG Miami said, "local television stations have covered literally hundreds of court cases." WPLG used the camera in the courts for a five-part series by consumer reporter Molly Turner which showed how such courts as traffic, small claims, probate, and divorce work.

Another station to cover courts was WTVT Tampa, Fla., which was on hand at a trial of a man charged with kidnapping and raping a Cleveland, Ohio school teacher and taking her to Florida. The station switched live to the courtroom for the verdict which found the defendant guilty on all counts.

KOTV Tulsa, Okla., received permission from the state supreme court to telecast the four-week preliminary hearing of an accused murderer via closed circuit to a 500-seat auditorium "to extend the courtroom." The action was considered a victory for broadcasting in that a camera was allowed in the courtroom and the presiding judge seemed pleased with the result. A group of news organizations has petitioned the court to allow courtroom coverage routinely, and a commission has been named to consider it.

In a state where cameras are not allowed in the courtroom, stations must find other ways to provide coverage. An unusual situation arose when KUTV Salt Lake City covered a trial in Los Angeles of a man accused of conspiring to murder a man who defected from a polygamy cult in Utah. The chief prosecution witness had given a sworn deposition but died before he was able to appear on the witness stand. The court agreed to permit a stand-in to read the deposition. KUTV then decided to reconstruct the scene by hiring people to stand in for the judge, the prosecution, and defense attorneys as well as the deceased witness. Clearly labeled dramatizations were presented on five successive nights.

In Cleveland, WEWS received permission to make what it believes was the first broadcast of a murder trial in Ohio. A courtroom in Akron had been equipped with small TV cameras several years ago to aid the judge in maintaining security. He agreed to let WEWS patch into the system, and five other Ohio stations shared the WEWS feed at one time or another during the trial. A committee of newsmen, judges, and attorneys is now working out details of camera coverage of all Ohio courts.

One of the top news stories for KTVY Oklahoma City happened this summer when two escaped convicts shot and killed three Oklahoma highway patrol troopers. A team of KTVY news people were covering the search for the convicts when the word came over police radios that they had shot their way through a roadblock and were holed up in a small town, surrounded by officers. When the KTVY crew arrived on the scene they got graphic film of a trooper wounded in the shootout and the aftermath of the story. The highway patrol and other law enforcement agencies have since requested copies of the footage to use as a special training film.

WISH-TV Indianapolis went to the aid of the National Weather Service and the public as well when a storm front knocked out power and radar in the area. The station pre-empted regular evening programming to broadcast its color "rainbow radar" so that NWS meterologists could track the tornadoes on their television sets. The station's late newscast, usually 30 minutes, was extended to 55 minutes and included live reports from the scene of the most extensive tornado damage.

Just 40 minutes after the Springfield, Mo., police walked off their jobs last June, KYTV had seven reporters and three ENG cameramen on the scene with a live report. The news team stayed with the story, providing extended, live evening reports until the strike ended two days later.

WFAA-TV Dallas made a total switch to ENG this year, enabling it to go live from almost anywhere. Last spring, for instance, live reports from London were broadcast, using satellite relay.

The new equipment was particularly useful in covering Hurricane Anita last year. Crews were dispatched to various parts of the state where it was believed the storm would hit and reports were fed back live via microwave.

The range of WLKY-TV Louisville, Ky.'s live coverage is demonstrated by two of the past year's stories. The first involved a firemens strike with the station using two microwave vans and providing coverage until sign-off many days during the week.

The second was coverage of the Kentucky Derby Festival's Great Steamboat Race. The race between the two ships is 12 miles. The station had five reporters covering it with live cameras at four positions, including one aboard one of the boats.

Spot news was the story for KEVN-TV Rapid City, S.D. A rock slide at the Big Thunder Gold Mine, a tourist attraction, injured seven people. When the station's ENG unit arrived on the scene it was discovered that the terrain made microwave transmission impossible, so the tape was driven back to the station, where it was rushed on the air in time for the early evening newscast along with new information supplied by the reporter and photographer who were still at the scene. And less than a week later, another tourist attraction exploded and burned, and the same technique was used.

WCSC-TV Charleston, S.C. beefed up its commitment to live journalism and news in general with its largest-ever budget of $250,000. Among the live broadcasts were coverage of visits by Prince Charles, President Carter, the Rev. Jesse Jackson, Senator Strom Thurmond, and Miss U.S.A.

A busy year. Reporting was in abundance at WJKW-TV Cleveland with (top, l to r): reporter Neil Zurcher braving the elements to report on last winter's blizzard; an interview with Cleveland's police chief after his firing; an investigative report by Jim Finerty on airport security; Bill McKay covering the city's Democratic mayoral convention. Bottom, l to r: Britain's Prince Charles's visit to the city; a documentary on a program to help the families of terminally ill children; coverage of a Florida trial of a man accused of kidnapping and raping a Cleveland woman, and a gas main explosion in nearby Euclid, Ohio.

A blizzard hit Detroit in January and WXYZ-TV responded by sending four ENG units to areas hardest hit. At the storm's peak, the station aired three continuous hours of blizzard coverage with live reports from reporters sending stories back to the station via two microwave dishes.

Going out to get the stories is the philosophy at WCPO-TV Cincinnati. One 11 P.M. report included live film or taped reports from the following places: Tampa, Fla.; Lawrenceville, Ga.; Columbus, Ohio; Peebles, Ohio; Warsaw, Ky.; Aurora, Ind.; and Hamilton, Ohio.

Appendix
Current Statistics on Mass Media in the United States, 1979

Statistics on media in the United States are readily available in many categories, such as the number of television or radio sets, the amount of time spent watching television, the number of newspapers, and so forth. Most of this information has been produced by commercial sources which gather data to sell to the various media and to advertisers and advertising agencies. Some data are also gathered by associations, such as the Newspaper Advertising Bureau of the American Newspaper Publishers Association (ANPA), the Magazine Publishers Association (MPA), and the National Association of Broadcasters (NAB). It is important to know this about the sources, and also to know that even when the data are reported with reasonable accuracy, the surveys may not have asked the kinds of questions we should be looking at; and when the data themselves are suspect, it may be because of data-gathering errors or biased research. Both inadequacies are the result of cutting corners to save money. Even government research, except that done during census years or for special studies, relies heavily on commercial sources. These points should be kept in mind when examining the data presented in the following pages. However, the information is the best and most current we have been able to obtain.

Television

Sets

Approximately 98 percent of the 76,240,000 households in the U.S. have television receivers, according to Nielsen's annual September update. That means 74,500,000 households with television (which becomes the basic figure by which ratings can be interpreted). Of this total, approximately 81 percent have at least one color television receiver; the remaining 19 percent have only black and white sets. Forty-eight percent of the television households (36,040,000 households) have two or more sets.

Stations

As of January 31, 1979, according to the FCC, there were 992 stations in the U.S., of which 73 percent, or 732, were commercial and the remaining 27 percent, or 260, were public. These stations were located so that 96 percent of the country's television homes can receive four or more stations, according to Nielsen, 66 percent can receive seven or more stations, and 38 percent can receive ten or more stations. In 1964, for comparison, 78 percent of the television homes could receive four or more stations, 26 percent could receive seven or more stations, and only 4 percent could receive ten or more stations.

UHF Facilities	Television stations are either VHF (Very High Frequency) or UHF (Ultra High Frequency). VHF stations operate in the 2–13 channel range; UHF stations operate in the 14–83 channel range. Because UHF was late in developing in the U.S., there have always been fewer UHF stations as well as fewer sets capable of receiving the signals. As of January 31, 1979, there were 374 UHF stations in the U.S. This is 37 percent of all television stations. The totals are as follows: commercial stations, 516 VHF, 216 UHF; public stations, 102 VHF, 158 UHF. As of fall 1978, according to an Arbitron Television Census, there were 69,331,600 UHF television households. This was 94 percent of all television homes.
Revenues	In 1978, the last year for which official FCC figures are available, the television industry had total revenues of $6.9 billion, with $1.6 billion profits. Total revenues were up 17.3 percent over 1977; income (before taxes) was up 17.5 percent.
Audiences for Television	Americans spend a great amount of time watching television—an estimated average of 6 hours, 13 minutes a day per television household. Average viewing in February 1978 was *7 hours a day,* while in July 1978 it was slightly over 5 hours, 30 minutes. Average daily viewing has been above the 6-hour figure since the 1970–71 season. For a comparison, during the 1965–66 season, according to Nielsen, average viewing was 5 hours, 30 minutes daily. Nielsen has shown that Sunday night is the most popular viewing night of the week. An estimated 99 million people watch television during prime time on Sunday evenings. Friday is the lowest audience, with approximately 84 million watching television during prime time. The average nightly audience during the week is approximately 90 million people. The Nielsen estimates were made during November 1978; the figures would vary according to the time of the year.
Cable Television Sets	Cable television grew approximately 10 percent during 1978. At the end of the year there were approximately 13.4 million television household subscribers to cable, or 18 percent of all television households. (Others estimate the penetration at 20 percent.) A May 1978 Nielsen all-market study showed that the penetration of cable into television households was highest in the less urban markets. Cable has penetrated only 8 percent in the largest counties in the U.S.; approximately 54 percent of all cable television households are in the C and D counties (which have the least population). This reflects the fact that cable television has from the first been a service to those people who have not had excellent television reception or have not been able to receive a large number of television stations.
Systems	There are over 4,000 cable television systems in the country. Most of them are small systems without large audiences or large resources. Others are giants with great penetration into their areas. One of the latter is Mission Cable in San Diego. Mission Cable is the largest system in the country, with more than 230,000 households wired. This is 34 percent of all San Diego television households.

Cable television systems receive their income from subscribers to the system; from pay television (where a fee is charged for a specific program or for access to a special channel providing first-run movies and sporting events); from advertising over local programming channels; and from special services, such as fire alarm and burglar alarm. Total income, including subscription and installation charges, is reported at over $1.2 billion. Income from advertising in 1978, according to a survey conducted by the National Cable Television Association (NCTA), was 300 percent above advertising income in 1976. This remarkable increase is tempered, however, by the knowledge that advertising income in 1978 was only $8.5 million. Advertising on cable is inserted into locally originated programming. At present, 81 percent of the systems originate local programming. This varies from a camera scanning instruments that show time, temperature, and tide (or skiing conditions) to local coverage of sports and elections. Of all systems that originate programs, 41 percent claimed they accepted advertising. According to the NCTA survey, only one in ten stations received as much as 10 percent of its income from advertising. Pay cable income, according to the FCC, increased 85 percent, to $85.8 million in 1977.

Surveys conducted over the past few years have revealed that viewers who subscribe to cable television watch approximately 11 percent more television than nonsubscribers. Penetration of the number of television households affects viewing. Twenty-four DMAs (Designated Market Areas) have over 50 percent of their television households hooked up to cable. However, these DMAs constitute only 2,745,000 households, or less than 4 percent of all television households. Most locally originated programs attract few viewers. A few exceptions seem to occur with pay television programming, according to a Video Probe Index survey in November 1977. During prime time on Saturday and Sunday, the system in Mobile, Alabama "had a 19.3 rating and a 27 share in those homes that had pay cable." Normally a 19.3 *rating* reflects the percentage of the *total number of television households* in the market that were tuned to the station; the 27 *share* reflects the percentage of households *watching television* during that viewing period that were tuned to that station. Here the figures *seem to mean* that of all households which subscribe to pay cable, 19.3 percent were watching the system; the 27 share seems to mean that of all cable television homes which subscribe to the pay system and which were watching television during that period, 27 percent were watching the cable system. One can see why it is important to read ratings carefully, since in this case the figures do not seem to mean what they normally mean.

Motion Pictures

The motion picture industry for the fifth year in a row set new income records, with $2.65 billion in 1978. This was 12 percent above 1977. Even with inflated ticket prices, the industry had a rise in real income.

Focusing on total income is a little deceptive, if one is concerned about the impact of the film industry in 1979. Attendance, which is a more accurate gauge, also

Revenues

Audiences

Income

Audience

has increased, but the total number is far below what it once was in the U.S. In 1978, according to Jack Valenti, president of the Motion Picture Association of America (MPAA), average weekly attendance at the movies was 22,460,000, the highest attendance since 1961, when the weekly average was 23,540,000. Even this figure does not provide us with a good idea of how the industry is doing today, so far as reaching people is concerned. If we divide the number of households in the U.S. by the weekly attendance, we arrive at an average weekly attendance per household. In 1978 that figure was 0.30. In 1948, just before television became a national medium, an estimated 90 million people attended the movies weekly, an average of 2.22 persons per household. The highest figure in the history of the movies occurred in 1930, when an estimated 90 million people attended weekly, but because there were far fewer households then, that averaged 3.0 persons per household.

Films

Total "product" from the industry has created problems during the past decade. There were approximately 80 motion pictures started in 1976; 92 in 1977, and only 80 again in 1978. This drop in production creates massive financial problems for the exhibitors of those films. There just are not enough films for the market, or so they argue. According to one report, of all films rated by the MPAA during 1976 and 1977, 70 percent were made by independent producers. Few of these films attracted large audiences for those independent producers generated only 15 to 20 percent of the film rental market. Based upon another survey, which was conducted of films with rentals of $1 million, the situation was even worse: "The top eight film producers have 92 percent of the market."

Advertising

Total Expenditures

Media in the United States rely heavily upon advertising for support. In a growing economy, advertising continued to exhibit strength. In 1978 an estimated $43.74 billion was expended in advertising, a 14.6 percent increase over 1977. This increase was greater than the growth of the economy itself.

Distribution Among Media

The chart on the following page reflects the allocation of total advertising to the mass media over the past fifteen years. When distribution of advertising revenues is separated into local versus national, the media change position on the scale. For instance, newspapers, which have remained relatively constant in their percentage of total advertising since 1963, continue to hold a large lead in local advertising. In 1978, 24.9 percent of all advertising was local advertising placed in newspapers. Television had only 5.4 percent from local sources; radio had 5.0 percent. In national advertising, however, television played an extremely important role. National (network and spot) advertising on television constitutes 14.8 percent of all advertising. For newspapers, the figure is a meager 4.1 percent; radio, 1.8 percent. In 1978, according to preliminary figures issued by *Advertising Age,* advertising distribution among the media was as follows:

Medium	Total (in Millions)	Percentage of Total
Newspapers	$12,690	29.0
Television	8,850	20.2
Direct mail	6,030	13.8
Radio	2,955	6.8
Magazines	2,595	5.9
Business publications	1,420	3.3
Outdoor	464	1.1
Farm publications	105	0.2
Miscellaneous	8,630	19.7
Total	$43,740	100.0

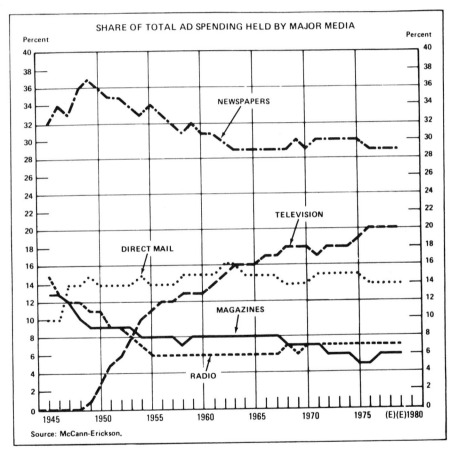

SHARE OF TOTAL AD SPENDING HELD BY MAJOR MEDIA

Source: McCann-Erickson.

Chart prepared by Kidder, Peabody & Co. Reprinted with permission from *mac, Western Advertising News,* April 23, 1979, special edition on "The Power of the Press." *mac* is an acronym for Media Agencies Clients.

Advertising Expenditures Year-to-Year Change

| Year | GNP | Advertising in All Media | Advertising As a Percent of GNP | Newspapers | | | | Television | | | | Mag-azines Total |
				Total News-paper	Retail	Clas-sified	National	Total Televi-sion	Net-work	Spot	Local	
1979(E)	9.8%	10.5%	2.09%	11.0%	11.5%	10.0%	8.0%	11.0%	11.0%	10.0%	12.0%	10.0%
1978(E)	11.5	14.7	2.08	14.4	12.8	20.8	8.0	16.3	13.0	18.0	20.0	20.0
1977	11.0	12.9	2.02	12.3	10.0	17.5	11.7	13.3	21.1	2.3	13.9	20.8
1976	11.2	19.5	1.98	17.4	14.0	21.8	23.0	27.7	23.9	32.7	28.2	22.1
1975	8.2	5.6	1.85	5.5	8.9	0.4	2.3	8.4	7.5	8.4	10.1	(2.6)
1974	8.1	6.4	1.89	5.3	7.5	0.3	7.5	8.8	9.0	8.7	8.7	3.9
1973	11.6	7.8	1.92	8.4	7.1	15.4	0.7	9.0	9.1	4.5	15.1	0.6
1972	10.1	12.3	1.99	13.1	11.1	18.4	11.3	15.8	13.2	15.1	21.7	5.1
1971	8.2	6.1	1.95	8.7	8.2	8.2	11.2	(1.7)	(3.9)	(7.2)	13.1	6.0

Sources: Department of Commerce. Newspaper Advertising Bureau. Television Bureau of Advertising. McCann-Erickson.
(E) Kidder. Peabody & Co. Incorporated estimates.
( ) Parentheses denote decline.

Table reprinted with permission from *mac, Western Advertising News*, April 23,1979, special edition on "The Power of the Press."

Advertising Agencies

Gross income and gross billings for advertising agencies continued strong in 1978. According to *Advertising Age,* 629 agencies earned $3.46 billion in gross income from $23.3 billion in gross billings. Gross income was 20 percent above 1977 (which was $2.86 billion). It should be noted that the *Advertising Age* figures for 1977 were calculated from reports by 583 agencies, 46 *fewer* than in 1978. This may have affected the difference in the figures.

For the first time in history, four American agencies billed over $1 billion in world billings in a year. They were as follows (in millions):

	1978	1977
J. Walter Thompson Co.	$1,476.5	$1,258.9
McCann-Erickson	1,404.5	1,083.5
Young & Rubicam	1,359.5	1,133.4
Ogilvy & Mather Int'l.	1,003.7	872.2

Despite this showing, the world agency with the largest billings is not American. It is the Japanese agency Dentsu Inc. In 1978, with worldwide billings of $2.210 billion, it was far ahead of second-place J. Walter Thompson. Dentsu did equally well with world gross income, placing first with $321.4 million gross income to second-place J. Walter Thompson's $221.5 million. Those agencies which were ranked by *Advertising Age* on the basis of U.S. income were (in millions):

	1978	*1977*
Young & Rubicam	$118.0	$101.1
J. Walter Thompson Co.	106.6	92.8
Leo Burnett Co.	89.0	84.3
BBDO International	80.1	66.9
Foote, Cone & Belding	75.7	59.0

Complete data on advertising agencies and agency totals can be found in the annual report appearing in March each year in *Advertising Age*.

Radio

Facilities and Income

As of January 1979, 4,549 AM stations, 3,104 FM stations, and 985 FM educational stations were in operation. According to FCC figures for 1978, the latest official data available, the commercial radio industry reported gross income of $2.63 billion, up 15.9 percent over 1977; profits were $311.1 million, up 26.4 percent. The radio networks grossed $89.8 million; profits were $15.3 million. In 1977 the radio networks netted $25.3 million. In 1976 they *lost* $5 million.

There are four national networks. One of them (ABC) has four national services; MBS has two. The networks and the number of affiliates are:

CBS	275 stations
MBS	863
NBC	274
ABC	
Contemporary	388
Entertainment	474
FM	195
Information	497

FM Radio

In 1978, according to FCC data, FM stations (independents and those reporting separately from co-owned AMs) had revenues of $570.5 million; pretax profits of $73.6 million. This was the third year in a row that the service as a whole had made a profit. One of the reasons for the success of FM radio was the penetration of FM receivers into the U.S. market. Approximately 98 million FM sets were sold in 1976–1978. The Electronic Industries Association (EIA) estimated that 205 million FM radios were in use in 1977. Set penetration was about 95 percent of U.S. households. One problem still facing FM station owners, however, is that only an estimated 41.7 percent of car-owning adults have at least one FM-equipped car. This means that during the important Drive-Time, radio is largely AM.

Newspapers

Audience

Every day except Sunday nearly 62 million copies of newspapers are circulated throughout the United States. There are 1,756 daily newspapers (360 morning papers, 1,430 evening papers, and 20 "all-day" papers which are counted as both morning and evening but only once in the final total). The total weekly circulation is more than 40 million. The newspaper audience continues to grow. U.S. Sunday papers increased in number from 668 to a record 696, and in circulation from just under 52.4 million to nearly 54 million. The number of weeklies jumped from 7,466 to 7,673. And the circulation of dailies increased by about 500,000 copies a day.

The great bulk of daily newspapers, nearly 1,500 in fact, serve smaller communities and have circulations of under 50,000. Only 269 dailies, or 15.3 percent, boast circulations of more than 50,000. The breakdown is: 140 in the 50,000–100,000 group, 92 in the 100,000–250,000 group, and 37 in the over 250,000 group. It can be easily seen that most daily and weekly newspapers are active in the nation's middle-sized and smaller communities.

Leaders

The paper with the largest daily circulation is the *New York Daily News,* with a total of about 1.65 million. Following are the *Los Angeles Times,* with about 1 million, and the *New York Times,* which has dropped below 800,000. Others include the *Chicago Tribune,* roughly 750,000; the *Detroit Free Press* and *Detroit News,* both at about 620,000; the *New York Post,* 615,000; and the *Chicago Sun-Times,* about 580,000. The *Washington Post* claims about 540,000 and the *Philadelphia Bulletin* about the same. The four regionally printed editions of the *Wall Street Journal* total about 1,600,000.

On Sundays the *New York Daily News* prints about 2,650,000 copies, about twice as many as each paper in the next group—the *New York Times, Los Angeles Times,* and *Chicago Tribune.*

Advertising

Revenues from advertising are at the record high of $12.7 billion. This is a 29 percent share of all advertising spending and greater than television and radio combined. Of these dollars, $10.8 billion comes from local advertising. The grand total represents a 14 percent increase from 1977 figures. About 62 percent of a daily newspaper's total space is used for advertising, and on Sunday the figure rises to about 67 percent. In 1946 a Sunday paper ran about 53 percent advertising.

Endorsements

Most newspapers endorse Republicans for political office. A look at editorial page support of presidential candidates since 1940 shows that of Democratic Party candidates, only Lyndon Johnson in 1964 received more endorsements than the Republican candidate. Some facts: Franklin D. Roosevelt received support from 22.7 percent of dailies in 1940 and 22 percent in 1944; Harry Truman got 15.3 percent; Adlai Stevenson 14.5 percent and 15.1 percent; John Kennedy 16.4 percent; Johnson 42.3 percent; Hubert Humphrey 14 percent; George McGovern only 5.3 percent; and Jimmy Carter 12.1 percent. About 25 percent of dailies do not endorse, accounting for 15 percent of the daily circulation. Republicans have received from 71.4 percent of the endorsements (Nixon in 1972) to 35.1 percent (Goldwater in 1964). This accounts for an average of more than 70 percent of the total circulation. Democrats have broken the 20 percent mark in circulation only three times, FDR with 25.2 percent in 1940, Johnson with 61.5 percent in 1964, and Carter with 22.8 percent in 1976.

More than 60 percent of daily newspapers are using the Video Display Terminal (VDT) system for writing-editing-production or are making plans to switch to that computerized method. About 475 papers still use the letterpress method to set type, but 97 percent of all dailies use photocomposition methods of page production. Three-fourths of these papers are printed by the offset method, while most of the others use the direct plate process. About 3 percent use other methods. The *Wall Street Journal* uses satellites to beam stories to regional printing plants, and other papers are following suit. Reporters with portable computers can send stories back to their newsrooms in much the same way live-action television cameras are used. The possibilities for the future of newspaper technology are limited only by the economic differences between publishers and unions.

Technology

Delivering the bulk of the news—an estimated 80 percent—to newspapers and broadcast stations are the men and women who work for the world's two largest press associations, United Press International and Associated Press. The latest advances in communications technology are used. Laser beams send photographs, VDTs allow faster editing and distribution, computerized storage and retrieval systems help guarantee comprehensive coverage, and satellites carry the stories to the thousands of subscribers around the world.

Press Associations

Not many of the daily newspapers can afford to have reporters in Washington, major U.S. cities, and overseas, so they rely on the press associations (the "wire services") to bring them the news. The biggest U.S. dailies, however, use both their own stories and wire news.

While many print-oriented journalism students desire to be reporters or editors with a newspaper, it should be noted that many "big league" reporters and editors began their careers with one of the press associations or one of the supplemental "city news services" found in major cities.

Founded in 1907 as the United Press by press lord E.W. Scripps, this organization became known as United Press International in 1958 when it merged with the old International News Service (1909) of William Randolph Hearst. UPI serves its "clients" as a business serves its customers: the newspapers and broadcast stations buy news on a contract basis. The world headquarters in New York is linked by telephone, cable, microwave relays, wireless, and satellites to thousands of persons in UPI "bureaus" from North Dakota to the tip of Asia.

United Press International

Like its longtime rival the Associated Press, UPI provides a full range of services: print and broadcast news, news photos, audio and television reports, cable television news reports, features, stock market, weather, and sports news.

About 20 percent of U.S. dailies use both wire services. The Associated Press claims that about 47 percent of newspapers subscribe to it solely, while UPI has about 27 percent. The rest, 6 percent, use no service. UPI claims that it has more U.S. broadcast subscribers, 3,680 to 3,462 (1977 figures). Overseas figures are disputed by both organizations. The key to understanding the press associations is to appreciate the fierce competition between them to land stories in newspapers or to get them on the air first.

Associated Press

The AP, which stems from cooperative news-gathering practices used by New York dailies in the 1840s, took its modern form in 1900 after a series of bitter fights between rival association leaders. The AP theoretically works like a cooperative: the "members" help develop the news package and then share with each other through the services of the AP. Actually, the system works pretty much like UPI, with publishers and broadcast executives purchasing news. But AP "members" have votes in how the organization works while UPI "clients" do not. The best vote any "member" or "client" has, of course, is to tell a particular organization it is switching to the other unless service improves. That happens frequently.

Both AP and UPI pride themselves on developing new packages or services for subscribers: special features; in-depth treatment of complicated issues like energy; new foreign bureaus; additional satellites; faster news printers; expanded audio and television services; and so forth. All of these achievements can be read about in the weekly *AP Log* and *UPI Reporter* (both issued by the New York headquarters and probably available in your journalism library) or in the annual reports to the clients/members.

Important in this worldwide system are "stringers," persons hired to report local happenings for a few dollars per story. Both services use "stringers" extensively. In addition, AP "members" are supposed to share their stories or tips with local AP bureaus, while UPI "clients" are under no such obligation. AP member newspapers often "carbon" their stories, which then are re-written for the wire. Both services do a lot of rewriting of previously published material while providing a comprehensive daily news file.

Public Relations

About 1600 public relations counseling firms in the United States employ many thousands of persons trained in writing, editing, graphics, film, interviewing, photography, and other journalistic skills. They also are trained in marketing, public opinion surveying, and other statistical techniques. In addition to these "PR" people who serve as counselors, tens of thousands of others work for the nation's corporations, trade and professional organizations, and state, regional, and local organizations or institutions. PR firms range in size from the large ones with regional headquarters to one-person offices.

The largest corporations spend millions of dollars annually to enhance their images and to engage in "two-way" communication with their public (employees, stockholders, customers, and general public). To fulfill their goals, all use mainly the techniques of publicity writing and advertising (the purchase of time or space to promote a product, person, or idea).

Much of the improvement in the public relations profession has come about through the Public Relations Society of America, an organization with more than 7,000 members.

Thousands of periodicals are being published in the U.S. in the "magazine" category. Perhaps 600 fall loosely in the "general interest" grouping. There are 2,500 business and trade journals, about 1,300 religious publications of different types, another 700 agricultural periodicals, and an estimated 9,000 industrial-corporate publications.

Of those magazines in the general interest category, the highest circulations belong to *TV Guide* and *Reader's Digest,* each with about 18–20 million. In the news field, *Time* is the circulation leader with about 4.5 million; *Newsweek* has about 3 million, and *U.S. News and World Report* about 2 million. The circulations of *Ebony* and *Jet,* black magazines, are about 1.2 million and 600,000, respectively.

A good number of the circulation leaders are women's magazines, such as *Redbook, Ladies' Home Journal, Good Housekeeping, McCall's, Woman's Day, Family Circle, Better Homes and Gardens. Ms.* is the leader of magazines in the "feminist" category, and other women's magazines try to aim at specialized interests like sports.

Credits

Index

54324282